Bioethics, Law, and Human Life Issues

Catholic Social Thought

Series Editor: Ryan J. Barilleaux

This series focuses on Catholic social thought and its application to current social, political, economic, and cultural issues. The titles in this series are written and edited by members of the Society of Catholic Social Scientists. They survey and analyze Catholic approaches to politics, sociology, law, economics, history, and other disciplines. Within these broad themes, authors explore the Church's role and influence in contemporary society.

The Society of Catholic Social Scientists was formed in 1992 to rejuvenate a distinctively Catholic scholarship in the social sciences.

1. *The Public Order and the Sacred Order,* by Stephen M. Krason, 2009.

2. *Bioethics, Law, and Human Life Issues,* by D. Brian Scarnecchia, 2010.

Bioethics, Law, and Human Life Issues

A Catholic Perspective on Marriage, Family, Contraception, Abortion, Reproductive Technology, and Death and Dying

D. Brian Scarnecchia

THE SCARECROW PRESS, INC.
Lanham • Toronto • Plymouth, UK
2010

Nihil Obstat:
Alan Schreck, Ph.D.
Censor Librorum

Imprimatur:
Bishop R. Daniel Conlon, Ph.D, J.C.D.
Bishop of Steubenville
February 1, 2010

Published by Scarecrow Press, Inc.
A wholly owned subsidary of The Rowman & Littlefield Publishing Group, Inc.
4501 Forbes Boulevard, Suite 200, Lanham, Maryland 20706
http://www.scarecrowpress.com

Estover Road, Plymouth PL6 7PY, United Kingdom

British Library Cataloguing in Publication Information Available

Library of Congress Cataloging-in-Publication Data

Scarnecchia, D. Brian, 1954–
  Bioethics, law, and human life issues : a Catholic perspective on marriage, family, contraception, abortion, reproductive technology, and death and dying / D. Brian Scarnecchia.
    p. cm. — (Catholic social thought)
  Includes bibliographical references and index.
  ISBN 978-0-8108-7422-0 (cloth : alk. paper)
  ISBN 978-0-8108-7423-7 (electronic)
  1. Bioethics—Religious aspects—Catholic Church. 2. Catholic Church—Doctrines. I. Title.
  R725.56.S26 2010
  174.2—dc22   2009052266

♾™ The paper used in this publication meets the minimum requirements of American National Standard for Information Sciences—Permanence of Paper for Printed Library Materials, ANSI/NISO Z39.48-1992.

Printed in the United States of America

This book is dedicated to all those who labor thanklessly on behalf of the most vulnerable members of our human society.

Contents

World (*Familiaris Consortio*) (1981).

FR   John Paul II, *On the Relationship between Faith and Reason* (*Fides et Ratio*) (1998).

GS   Vatican Council II, *Pastoral Constitution on the Church in the Modern World* (*Gaudium et Spes*) (1965).

HV   Paul VI, *On Human Life* (*Humanae Vitae*) (1968).

LF   John Paul II, *Letter to Families* (*Gratissimam Sane*) (1994).

LG   Vatican Council II, *Dogmatic Constitution on the Church* (*Lumen Gentium*) (1964).

MM   John XXIII, *On Christianity and Social Progress* (*Mater et Magistra*) (1961).

PH   Sacred Congregation for the Doctrine of the Faith, *Declaration on Certain Questions Concerning Sexual Ethics* (*Persona Humana*) (1975).

PCHP   Congregation for the Doctrine of the Faith, *On the Pastoral Care of Homosexual Persons* (1986).

SC   Vatican Council II, *The Constitution on the Sacred Liturgy* (*Sacrosanctum Concilium*) (1963).

SD   John Paul II, *On the Christian Meaning of Human Suffering* (*Salvifici Doloris*) (1984).

ST   St. Thomas Aquinas, *Summa Theologica*.

VS   John Paul II, The Splendor of Truth, *Veritatis Splendor* (1993).

Abbreviations

ATF   John Paul II, *To Defend the Faith (Ad Tuendam Fidem)* (1998).

CA   John Paul II, *Centesimus Annus* (1991).

CCC   *The Catechism of the Catholic Church* (1994).

CHCW   Pontifical Council for Pastoral Assistance, *Charter for Health Care Workers* (1994).

CIC   The Code of Canon Law, *Codex Iuris Canonici* (1983).

DH   Vatican Council II, *Declaration on Religious Liberty (Dignitatis Humanae)* (1965).

DP   Congregation for the Doctrine of the Faith, *On Certain Bioethical Questions (Dignitas Personae)* (2008).

DPA   Congregation for the Doctrine of the Faith, *Declaration on Procured Abortion* (1974).

DV   Sacred Congregation for the Doctrine of the Faith, *The Gift of Life (Donum Vitae)* (1987).

ERD   United States Conference of Catholic Bishops, *Ethical and Religious Directives for Catholic Health Care Services, 4th ed.* (2001).

EV   John Paul II, *The Gospel of Life (Evangelium Vitae)* (1995).

FC   John Paul II, *On the Role of the Christian Family in the Modern*

Acknowledgments

First of all, thanks be to God and to the many students who inspired me over the years to teach and to write. Next I wish to acknowledge those who helped me with my research for this book—Atty. Kellie Fiedorek, James Devine, Amy Pedagno, and Mr. John Hinkle, my faculty assistant—all from Ave Maria School of Law, as well as Laura Hanley from Franciscan University of Steubenville. I wish to thank in a special way my daughter and son-in-law, Maria and Atty. Joshua Montagnini, for their helpful suggestions and indispensible efforts editing this book while looking after their first newborn child, Greta, studying for the bar exam, and moving across country to start a new job. Finally, I am forever grateful to my wife of twenty-five years, Vickie, for her love, prayers and sacrifices without which I would never have been able to begin or to complete this book.

Introduction

Many of the defining issues of our time, abortion, euthanasia, contraception, human cloning, and homosexual lifestyle, are all defended by one word—"choice." This isn't the first time slogans have won revolutions. In 1917, Lenin and Trotsky sealed the doom of Imperial Russia with the slogan, "Peace, Bread and Land!" Two centuries ago, the word "Liberty" ushered in successful revolutions in the American colonies and in France. The slogan "The Right to Choose" has led the cultural revolutionaries of our day into the White House, Hollywood, the Ivy League, Madison Avenue, and Wall Street. Like the Roman Emperor Constantine of old, under their banner, "The Right to Choose," Post-Modern revolutionaries have conquered.

Shakespeare asked, "What's in a word?" Certainly the reality a word signifies remains the same by any other name, but the impression conjured in the minds of the beholder can be radically altered as happened when the white tuna company ran the following ad: "White Tuna: Guaranteed not to turn pink in the can." The court ruled that even though the advertisement was true on its face it falsified and libeled its competitor's canned pink tuna.

The slogan—"the Right to Choose"— may be true on its face but it, too, falsifies and libels the nature of liberty. The words "liberty" and "choice" bespeak freedom and stir powerful emotions and because of this, we often fail to make careful distinctions. We may be led to believe as The Who sang in the chorus of the rock opera, "Tommy," that any and all "freedom tastes of reality."

Certainly some choices, some expressions of freedom, expand our experience of reality. Who can deny the exhilaration of rapid movement? Why else do children run rather than walk? Why do some people race cars, parachute, skate board, ski, take up flying? Because it is exhilarating and makes them feel free and more alive. Why do other people take time to practice karate, gymnastics, figure skating, or learn a new language or the fine arts? Because they know that "practice makes perfect" and with mastery comes freedom and the experience of being more alive.

But what about those people who choose to use street drugs, go on a killing spree or commit rape? Don't they feel an adrenalin rush and exhilaration, too? Aren't they freer and more alive in their crimes than in the drudgery of their daily routine?

Ronald Reagan, in his successful bid for president of the United States, was asked in a televised debate if he was in favor of a woman's right to choose. He replied that it "all depends on *what* she chooses." As we all know from sad experience, some personal decisions arise out of and compound one's inner frustration. The so-called freedom experienced in rage or addictive sexual behavior is not the equivalent of the freedom born of self-mastery. Not all choices bring us closer to reality. Not every freedom unfolds our personality. Some choices paralyze us and thereby slander freedom. Only choosing right, in the sense of deliberating well and not knowingly choosing evil, makes us freer and more alive.

We must take seriously the claim—"It was for liberty that Christ set us free."[1] In the light of Christian moral principles we are able to intelligently direct our free will. With the self-mastery that comes to us through virtue, transformed and elevated by Christ's grace, we become "partakers of the divine nature"[2] we come to know divine freedom—"I came that they may have life and have it to the full."[3]

The light of right reason and the light of Christ must illumine one's right to choose. A drug addict is not free. We need virtue to choose. It's absurd to define freedom as the ability to become a slave. That is why the Founders of the American Republic fashioned a Constitution that made it impossible for us to make ourselves indentured servants: "On a purely political definition of freedom, we may concede that a people is free to institute slavery or to adopt a totalitarian form of government, but in so doing they damage or destroy their own freedom."[4] Just as the goal of political freedom is not to extinguish itself in slavery but to fulfill the duties of citizenship, so the goal of all human freedom is not to extinguish itself in unreasonable conduct but to fulfill the basic goods and duties of human nature: "Acting is morally good when the choices of freedom are *in conformity with man's true good* the supreme good in whom man finds his full and perfect happiness."[5]

The writings of St. Thomas Aquinas and Pope John Paul II provide, in Part One, basic moral principles from the perspective of a Catholic philosophy of the human person. These Christian moral principles are applied in Part Two to current issues in bioethics informed by the social teaching of the Catholic Church. The light to choose in conformity with the true good of human nature reveals it is always wrong to grasp at conjugal pleasure while taking steps to block procreation through contraception, no matter how good one's motive or dire one's circumstances. This same light also exposes that it is wrong to directly target the pre-natal child for destruction through procured abortion. However, a medical intervention that unintentionally causes a pre-natal child to expire while attempting to save the life of the mother may be morally justified. Reproductive technology conforms to the true good of the human person if it assists but does not replace the conjugal act in its performance or in attaining its end once performed. Interventions at the end of life conform to the true good of human nature if they entail medical care that is proportionate or ordinary insofar as it does not produce more burdens than benefits for the patient. An objective disorder such as same sex attraction cannot fulfill human nature because it does not express the innate complementary of the sexes in a gift of self open to procreation. Therefore, civil society must not allow the institution of marriage to be diminished through legal recognition of so called same-sex marriage.

Acceptance of contraception, abortion, in vitro fertilization, co-habitation, divorce and euthanasia all show a common rejection of suffering, of being foiled, in one way or another, in a person's pursuit of pleasure needless of the true good of human nature. All of these practices exhibit an objectification of others and oneself. This denigration and objectification of the human body lays the anthropological foundations for a "culture of death."[6] The Church's social teaching on all these human life issues makes sense only if we understand that human suffering united to Christ enables one to "make up what is lacking in the sufferings of Christ for the sake of his body the Church."[7] Christ's redemption, though it was accomplished once and for all on Calvary, remains continually open to all the love expressed in human suffering.[8] The Church's social teaching helps us to carry our crosses and become co-redeemers with Christ and in this way its kindly light illumines the path to the Beatific Vision, our ultimate good. At the very least it is hoped that this study of bioethics, law and human life issues will help the reader think more clearly and take action to bring about a culture of peace and a truly human civilization.

Notes

1. Gal. 5:1; see also VS, no. 86.
2. CCC, no. 460.
3. John 10:10.
4. Avery Dulles, "The Truth about Freedom: A Theme From John Paul II," *Veritatis Splendor and the Renewal of Moral Theology* (Princeton, N.J.: Scepter Pub., 1999), 139.
5. VS, no. 72.
6. John Paul II, *Letter to Families*, no. 19 (1994); Michael Schooyans, *The Totalitarian Trend of Liberalism*, (St. Louis, MO: Central Bureau, 1997), 152.
7. Col. 1:24.
8. SD, no. 24.

Part I:
Christian Moral Principles

Chapter 1
Rational Anthropology and the Difference between Persons and Animals

Introduction

The human person made in the image of God expresses himself through the faculties of his soul, reason and will, and through his emotions which arise from his body and form a bridge between his body and soul.[1] Grace builds on human nature. It heals, perfects and elevates our humanity and transforms us at that mysterious core of our being, our relationship with God.

This chapter explores the interaction of body and soul and our relational identity. This relational mystery is at the heart of human dignity which each of us shares because we are all from, for and in the image of God.[2] It is at the same time the ground of our common human dignity and the source of the absolute uniqueness of each human person. Pope Benedict reminds us science cannot speak to man "in his own mystery"—who he is, where he comes from or where he is going.[3] The dignity of the human person rests not so much on human genetics or even human nature expressed through emotions and the faculties of the soul, reason and free will. Personhood is the ultimate basis of human dignity but it is not a legal construct, like corporate personality (something the law bestows or takes away), rather, it is an innate relational reality as it is in an analogous manner for the three Divine Persons of the Blessed Trinity: "The divine image is present in every man. It shines forth in the communion of persons, in the likeness of the union of the divine persons among themselves."[4] The deepest truth about ourselves is who we are in the eyes of God: "We *are* a relationship with God. Before all else, we belong to God, and that belonging is our very identity."[5] This anthropology and moral principles that flow from it are discussed in Part I and ground the moral analysis of human life issues that follows.

Reason and Skepticism

Immanuel Kant argued in *The Critique of Pure Reason* that man can only know
the categories of thoughts in his mind, not objective reality, or that which he
called "things-in-themselves." He described man as living in a virtual mental
reality triggered by "things-in-themselves" (objective reality) which created
sense impressions which his mind then classified according to inherent *a priori*
mental categories.

> Kant's "Copernican revolution" does not imply the view that reality can be re-
> duced to the human mind and its ideas. He is not suggesting that the human
> mind creates things, as far as their existence is concerned, by thinking them. . . .
> It means, rather, that the mind imposes, as it were, on the ultimate material of
> experience its own forms of cognition, determined by the structure of human
> sensibility and understanding, and that things cannot be known except through
> the medium of these forms.[6]

Errors in speculative philosophy traceable to Kant have led to errors in ethics
and contributed to moral relativism and to errors in biblical studies. The debate
as to whether the mind has direct knowledge of reality or only knowledge of its
mental categories goes on to this day. The significance of this debate cannot be
underestimated. For if Kant and his disciples are correct, we cannot have objective proof for the existence of God, the immortality of the human soul, or a universal natural law of moral behavior.

However, from Divine Revelation we know that the human mind can attain
certain knowledge of God from the things He has made.[7] Therefore, it would
appear that Kant's theory of knowledge (epistemology) is in error:

> The Bible, and the New Testament in particular, contains texts and statements
> which have a genuinely ontological content. The inspired authors intended to
> formulate true statements, capable, that is, of expressing objective reality. It
> cannot be said that the Catholic tradition erred when it took certain texts of St.
> John and St. Paul to be statements about the very being of Christ. In seeking to
> understand and explain these statements, theology needs, therefore, the contri-
> bution of a philosophy which does not disavow the possibility of a knowledge
> which is objectively true, even if not perfect.[8]

While St. Thomas Aquinas (1224–1274) did not consider the issues in epistemology raised five hundred years later by Immanuel Kant (1724–1804), he did
show that we can know the essence of things and learn objective truth from
sense experience. This occurs through what he called the "process of abstraction."[9] Aquinas accepted the Aristotelian premise that all material reality is
composed of prime matter and form. The form is the principle of organization

which shapes and animates matter. Prime matter is simply pure potency.[10] Only man, of all bodily creatures, has a non-material (spiritual) rational soul.

Aquinas argued that man's soul can be proven to be non-material from the fact that it can entertain non-material ideas or thoughts. For instance, we know there are laws of physics which govern the phenomena which our senses present us. These physical laws of nature are reducible to mathematical formula. However, numbers are immaterial, non-material or spiritual. Hence, there must be something about us that corresponds to these spiritual realities. Put simply, if we were not on the same frequency, we could not pick up non-material spiritual reality. Functions follows being, and effects cannot be greater than their cause. Therefore, because the human mind grasps and contains immaterial/spiritual reality, our soul must be immaterial/spiritual.[11]

Man is, therefore, a composite being of spirit (an immaterial reality) and body, and therefore, "a certain struggle of tendencies between 'spirit' and 'flesh' results."[12] By contrast, an animal's soul is material and not rational.

Aquinas taught that all rational knowledge comes to man through his bodily senses. He did not believe, as did Plato and St. Augustine, that we have innate ideas or aver to mental "forms" to which we compare sense data. Rather, man distills, if you will, universal ideas from the sense objects themselves in a mental process called "abstraction" or "abstracting the universal from the particular."[13]

First, man's five senses (sight, hearing, smell, taste and touch) make contact with reality. For example, the human eye, through the medium of light, receives the optical sense impressions of physical things in the retina of the eye and this sensation is conveyed through the optic nerve to the brain.

Then, these sense impressions act upon man's imagination creating an imaginative image or *phantasm* of the object in his brain. For example, an image of a tree appears when we close our eyes after looking at a tree or when we dream of a tree. There is a neurological memory of such phantasms in the human brain. All animals experience sense impressions and retain an unconscious memory of them.

What occurs next, however, is uniquely human and involves a faculty of man's rational soul, the *active intellect*, which abstracts the *universal* from the *particular* features of the phantasm. The universal (also called a form) is the intelligible essence or the "whatness" of the thing. The universal is what is common in all members of a species of genus. Abstraction de-materializes the unique features of a particular member of a species. For example, all the particular features in the phantasm of "this tree"—its height, girth, color, branches, etc.—are shed in the light of the active intellect, which then reflects the de-materialized universal of "Treeness" onto what Aquinas termed as the *passive intellect*.

Finally, the passive intellect then reacts to the universal in a "mental word," i.e., a concept, idea. This is the moment of understanding, when the so-called "light bulb" first goes on. In the life of Helen Keller, the girl who went blind and deaf shortly after birth, this moment of understanding occurred when she was an adolescent. While having her hands washed by her teacher at a well, she grasped the relationship between a letter, a "W" traced on her palm, and the water flowing over her hand. She suddenly knew she knew and heard herself think a mental word for the first time. Until then, she had used signals stored in neurological pathways to blindly signal in order to satisfy her desires. But she had done so unconsciously like an animal or a baby that coos or cries to get its way without knowing it is signaling. That day at the well, Helen came to the long-delayed "age of reason." From that day on, she began to abstract the universal from the particular and ceased to merely signal like a dumb/witless animal.

Interior words are formed when the active intellect abstracts universals from imaginative phantasms and projects the abstracted universal onto the passive intellect. For example, if a person was knocked off a horse while riding through a forest and woke up laying on the forest floor, he would see a blur of colors and shapes that he might slowly recognize as leaves, branches, and trees as his mind began again to abstract the universal essence from the mass of strange sense data.

Because the human person is a compound substance of body and soul, his mind needs phantasms in order to think. A distortion of images in one's brain due to lack of development of brain structure in a fetus, inebriation, brain injury, or mental illness hinders the intellect in the process of abstraction so that it remains silent or abstracts universals from phantasms that do not correspond to true sense impressions.[14]

Having formed items of intellectual knowledge, the mind next compares various interior words through *subject judgments* or *predicate judgments*. This comparison involves use of the first principle of the speculative intellect, the principle of non-contradiction[15] which is an innate orientation of the mind that recognizes that something cannot *be* and *not be* at the same time. This is not so much an innate idea as an ordering that simply makes thinking possible. For example, the passive intellect either affirms or denies that one thing is or is not of the same kind as another thing. A subject judgment would consider, for instance, whether this plant is or is not a tree while a predicate judgment would consider whether this plant has or does not have bark, a feature which distinguishes all trees.

Third, discursive reasoning, logic, occurs when the passive intellect compares diverse subject and predicate judgments. In a syllogism, one uses the principle of non-contradiction to compare two known facts to discover implicit new information in conclusion.

Free Will and Happiness

Because man can reason, he is able to direct himself and act for an end to achieve some purpose. Aquinas distinguishes between "human acts" which are conscious, free, and acted upon "with a deliberate will," and unconscious "acts of a man" committed involuntarily without reflection, such as yawning.[16]

The human will is free to seek good: "whatever man desires, he desires it under the aspect of good."[17] A corollary of this is the human person never chooses evil in itself, *per se*. When a person chooses something that is objectively evil, he chooses it as subjectively good in some respect: "Even in his sinful acts a man is seeking good, that is, satisfaction, although he is perversely seeking it in the wrong place."[18]

This orientation of man's free will to choose good demonstrates the essential relation between man's practical intellect[19] and his free will. The first principle of natural law within the practical intellect is to "seek good and shun evil."[20] First, reason shows whether some course of action is good, i.e., capable of providing some good, some satisfaction.[21] Then the human person, through his will, is free to choose or reject it in favor of some other good.[22] The end is the first in the order of intention, but the last in the order of execution.[23]

The will is blind and requires the intellect to present objects under some aspect of good to it in order for it to choose one of them as "ultimate" and act.[24] Unless there is an ultimate end, no lesser ends or means will be executed. Man's ultimate end is that which contains all goodness, and its possession is his perfect joy. Therefore, for any choice or act of the will to be objectively good, it must lead one to their final end, perfect happiness:

> God created man a rational being, conferring on him the dignity of a person who can initiate and control his own actions. God willed that man should be "left in the hand of his own counsel", so that he might of his own accord seek his Creator and freely attain his full and blessed perfection by cleaving to him.[25]

St. Augustine said in his *Confessions* that our hearts are restless until they rest in God.[26] St. Thomas demonstrates this truth by first considering all other possibilities and proving that true joy cannot be found in the possession of any earthly object as an ultimate end. Wealth and bodily pleasure, he says, cannot satisfy the human heart because, like drinking salt water, the more one sips, the thirstier one becomes. What happens to a person who sets his heart on becoming a millionaire? As soon as he gets a million dollars, he is envious of the person with two million. What happens to the hedonist who becomes enthralled with bodily pleasure? He finds that his desire for pleasure exceeds his satisfaction and he keeps coming back for more. In short, seeking wealth and bodily pleasure as ultimate ends is enervating and leads to boredom.[27]

Honor and fame suffer from a different defect—they are fickle. Many people who are true heroes are ignored or soon forgotten. Others who are fools or cheats often become famous. The problem is that fame and honor do not reside in the person but in those who choose to bestow or withhold it. However, for perfect happiness to be perfect, it must consist in an interior quality and be a permanent possession.[28]

However, the search for perfect happiness is not in vain. Christ has promised us the Beatitudes:

[The Beatitudes] invite us to purify our hearts of bad instincts and to seek the love of God above all else. It teaches us that true happiness is not found in riches or well-being, in human fame or power, or in any human achievement—however beneficial it may be—such as science, technology, and art, or indeed in any creature, but in God alone, the source of every good and of all love.[29]

Emotions

The *emotions* or *passions* of the sensitive appetite belong to the order of bodily faculties.[30] Emotions are a "movement of the sense appetite (emotional power), which follows from the apprehension of the senses, and is accompanied by a bodily transmutation."[31] For example, a cat sees a dog and it experiences the passion of fear which transmutes its body to fight or flee. In another case, a man sees a woman bathing and he experiences desire (sexual) which transmutes his body to enable him to "have relations with her" and she conceives a child.[32]

The term "passion" belongs to the Christian patrimony. Feelings or passions are emotions or movements of the sensitive appetite that incline us to act or not to act in regard to something felt or imagined to be good or evil.[33]

It is important to recall that both man and animals have sense appetites and emotions which originate in the body. However, because man is a composite being of body and soul, his emotions, which originate in his body, affect his whole person, his mind and will. The human person, then, is the subject of the passions. In this sense, the human soul can be spoken of as the subject of the passions because emotions so readily impact upon the powers (faculties) of the soul. Emotions "form the passageway and ensure the connection between the life of the senses and the life of the mind."[34] In sum, human passions or emotions arise from the body, cause a transmutation in the body to make it apt to respond to the stimuli, and at the same time, they impact upon the faculties of the soul; i.e., reason and free will.[35]

Emotions are amoral, neither morally good nor evil in themselves —"they are morally qualified only to the extent that they effectively engage reason and will."[36] King David accidentally saw a young woman bathing and suddenly experienced sensual desire. At this point, he had committed no sin. But he did not guard his senses and flee from the temptation. Instead, he gazed at her lustfully—committing adultery with her in his heart, which he then acted upon by summoning her to his palace.

On the other hand, emotions may also aid a person to choose goals in conformity with his true final end and to act on those decisions, as when we are moved by the emotions of sadness, desire and hope wrapped up in pity to perform acts of charity. To the extent the human will accepts or rejects their influence, emotions have a moral dimension. Emotions may enhance or diminish one's moral culpability.[37] Even criminal law recognizes this. For example, wives who murder good and kind husbands for insurance money are given no mitigation of sentence, while battered wives often receive lesser sentences when found guilty of the same charge. "Passions are morally good when they contribute to a good action, evil in the opposite case."[38] Christian charity is not simply an act of the will moved by grace willing the true good of another. A good graced deed performed with strong emotion adds to the perfection of the act since it more perfectly expresses the action of the whole man.[39] "Moral perfection consists in man being moved to the good not by his will alone, but also by his sensitive appetite, as in the words of the psalm: 'My heart and flesh sing for joy to the living God.'"[40]

However, the spiritual life is often brought to new heights in times of persecution and emotional dryness. Even then, man's sensitive appetite can well up and move him to act uprightly as did the crucified Christ when he heard the good thief's confession and beheld his faithful disciple and his sorrowful mother—he was touched.

> Emotivity includes sensations, feelings, and emotions. Emotivity runs between and links corporality and spirituality. It cannot be reduced to the reactivity of the body although it is conditioned by it. It is a psychical event rather than a reaction. Emotivity is responsible for man's sensitivity to values and provides the will with a "special kind of raw material" in its spontaneous attraction to values. The will itself is an intellectual response to values. A deep emotional response wells up in the person in response to truth, goodness, and beauty.[41]

Our emotional life or sensitive appetite has two fundamental orientations: 1) towards good and away from evil simply or in general and 2) toward good and away from evil under the aspect of difficulty. The Scholastics referred to the former as the concupiscible appetite and the latter as the irascible appetite. Our emotional life, then, is composed of two complementary sets of emotions. Diagram 1, at the end of this chapter, shows each emotion of the concupiscible and irascible appetites and their object of desire. For example, when an evil object is present, the concupiscible appetite reacts to it with an emotion of hate which makes a person experience disgust. The irascible appetite also responds simultaneously toward the evil object with the emotion of anger which increases a person's blood pressure, readying him to flee or fight the present evil object.

The Relational Nature of Persons

The word "person" was derived from the Latin word for a Roman actor's mask, "persona", during the great Trinitarian controversy with the Arians in the fourth and fifth centuries:

> The word person seems to be taken from those persons who represented men in comedies and tragedies. For person comes from sounding through (personando), since a greater volume of sound is produced through the cavity in the mask. These "persons" or masks the Greeks called [them] . . . were placed on the face and covered the features before the eyes.[42]

> The urgency of confuting heretics made it necessary to find new words [persona/mask] to express the ancient faith about God. Nor is such a kind of novelty to be shunned; since it is by no means profane, for it does not lead us astray from the sense of Scripture.[43]

The Council Fathers of the early Church adapted the word for an actor's mask, "Person" and used it to denote what is most perfect in all nature—that is, a "subsistent individual of a rational nature."[44] When applied to God, this definition must not be thought to suggest that the Divine Persons of the Trinity use discursive thought, but rather, that they have an intelligent nature.[45] Person became a term of art used to describe the relation and distinction (all that was not common to their divinity) between the Father, the Son, and the Holy Spirit in God.

Person, when used to describe God signifies relation.[46] The Father, Son and Holy Spirit are distinct from each other as Persons, not as God.[47] A person or "hypostasis is a really distinct divine relation, in which subsists one and the same undivided divine nature or 'ouses.'"[48] This distinction of relationship does not imply a cleavage of the divine essence.[49] "The divine persons do not share the one divinity among themselves but each of them is God whole and entire."[50] Person also signifies what is distinct and not shared in common.[51] In God what is distinct and distinguishes the divine Persons are their relations of origin, i.e., the Father is the source, not cause, of the Son whom he begets eternally, who together with the Father, eternally spirate (breathe forth) the Holy Spirit.[52]

Divine Persons are essentially relational; that is, the words "from", "with", and "of" (as in "from the Father", "with the Father", "Word of", "Spirit of", or "origin of") define the very identity of the divine Persons. We cannot understand the Divine Persons without reference to their relations to each other: the Father is the origin of the Son; the Son is not the origin of the Father; the Holy Spirit proceeds from the Father and the Son.[53]

Each Divine Person is essentially a gift, a complete self offering to the other Divine Persons. St. John tells us that God is Love, which may be described as a self-gift of one divine Person to the other Divine Persons "for God is love. God's love was revealed in our midst in this way: he sent his only Son to the world that we might have life through him."[54]

The distinction of persons in the Trinity and their essential relationality make love the essence of God and thus, makes love the foundation of the universe. If somehow God was not a Trinity of person-in-relation for the divine Others, then love would be impossible. Love as self-gift is impossible if no persons or only one person exists. It is nonsense to speak of being a self-gift to one's self.

All creation reflects the perfections of God. Rational creatures, angels and man, reflect God's image and qualities most perfectly. Angelic and human persons are essentially distinct (undivided and non-absorbable) intellectual or rational substances.[55] They receive their nature and existence from God.[56] Relationality has an accidental existence in rational creatures, angels and men; that is, it adheres in their soul as an inclination which they must perform and practice in order for them to attain their own perfection as persons.[57]

Because the human person is "an individual substance of a rational nature", he can give himself to others without fear of "smudging" his identity, losing himself, or being absorbed by another. John Paul II understands that distinctness or incommunicability is essential for love, understood as a rational self-gift to others, to exist:

> The definition of Boethius determines above all the "metaphysical site", or in other words, the dimension of being in which the personal subjectivity of man is realized, creating, so to speak, the right conditions for building upon this "site" on the ground of experience.[58]

Human nature is the locus of personal activity, but the human person is not synonymous with human nature; there is a distinction between a person and his human nature:

> With respect to the idea of a distinction between person and human nature, there simply is in the mind of the Church such a distinction; for otherwise how could there have been a divine person (the Word of God) who first did not have human nature and then took it on? Another way to see this with respect to Christ is to note that He is one person but has two natures; this means that there is a distinction between person and human nature. . . . Now, to say that "all human beings are persons" is true, but to interpret that utterance to mean that there is nothing more to personhood than humanity, or to mean an identity of personhood with humanity is an error.[59]

The distinctness or incommunicability of man's self, especially when man actualizes his potential through self-control, is the foundation of the self-fulfillment he realizes in giving himself, even to the point of laying down his life for others. The passage most quoted by John Paul II from Vatican Council II is *Gaudium et Spes* no. 24. His use of this passage throws a new light on the nature of man and the meaning of human existence:

> With the introduction of the notion of person in the Pastoral Constitution of the Church in the Modern World, no. 24, as "achieving self by the gift of self," the notion of person as "gift", and hence as revelation, has universally and constantly been offered as the core concept in all papal pronouncements and magisterial offerings [since Vatican II and especially in the pontificate of John Paul II].[60]

The core concept and truth about God and man is that the divine Persons of the Trinity and each human person redeemed in Christ are called to be "one," not in a monist absorption of personality, but in a communion of love between distinct persons (individual rational substances) who give themselves and receive the other in truth and freedom:

> Furthermore, the Lord Jesus, when praying to the Father "that they may all be one . . . even as we are one," has opened up new horizons closed to human reason by implying that there is a certain parallel between the union existing among the divine persons and the union of the sons of God in truth and love.[61]

Because man is rational he has free will. But what is the purpose of freedom? Are we free so as to become slaves of sin? John Paul II recognizes that man is, in some mysterious way, inclined to betray true freedom and prefer "ephemeral goods." But he tells us the real value of freedom lies not in its annihilation, by enslaving oneself to sin, but in "inalienable self possession and openness to all that exists, in passing beyond self to knowledge and love of the other. *Freedom then is rooted in the truth about man, and it is ultimately directed toward communion*" with God and others.[62] The communal identity of Israel as the people of God made clear that the human person is a relational being: "[B]iblical man discovered that he could understand himself only as 'being in relation'—with himself, with people, with the world and with God."[63]

True freedom, then, is directed toward communion that leads ultimately to perfect happiness. John Paul begins *Veritatis Splendor* with a meditation on the dialogue between Christ and the Rich Young Man. Jesus is asked, "Master, what good must I do to have eternal life?" Jesus replies by enjoining him to first observe the Commandments concerning love of God and neighbor, and then, if he would be "perfect" to sell all that he owned, give to the poor, and come follow Him. This answer shows us that morality is not so much about "dos and don'ts" or "rules to be followed but about the full meaning of life" and what can truly satisfy the yearnings of the human heart.[64] What truly satisfies the cravings of the human heart is communion, realized through the exercise of reason and free will in a gift of self that places one in right relationships that fulfill one's innate relationality: "Man becomes the image of God not so much in the moment of solitude as in the moment of communion."[65]

"Animal Rights" Denies Man's Relational Nature

Because God made man in his image, his whole being is designed to signify spiritual realities. Man's soul and his body reflect the image of God; the soul exhibits this in its faculties of intellect and free will, and the body demonstrates this in its nuptial capacity to make present a gift of self and a gift of new life. However, the image of God in human nature is falsified when we grasp at the qualities of an order of being other than our own.

Both occultism and animal rights falsify human nature in this way. Occultists grasp at a higher order of being attempting to imitate angels in their power of communication and movement. This attempt at transcendence through so-called 'psychic powers' really implodes man's relational capacity and exacerbates pride and concupiscence as the occultist tries to manipulate persons and future events.

Animal rights eugenicists, on the other hand, grasp at a lower order of being, attempting to imitate animals in their unconscious expression of hedonist sensuality and utilitarian survival of the fittest. This attempt at immanence with nature also paralyzes man's relational capacity and inflames selfishness and concupiscence as animal rights eugenicists take, use, and control human beings as they would any other species of animal.

By grasping at an order of being above or below human nature, by aping angels or aping apes, both occultists and animal rights eugenicists lose purity of heart, and through their idolatry and propaganda, legitimize the treatment of persons as objects which advances a culture of death.

There is a difference of *kind*, not merely of *degree* between man and animals. Animals are not just less intelligent than we. They are simply non-rational, dumb and witless. Animals have the same five external senses and, like human persons, they experience emotions and images of sense impressions in their brains. However, their senses, emotions and images are not integrated under the control of reason and free will as in man. Diagram 2 at the end of this chapter illustrates each of the salient differences between man and animals.

There is a strict one-way analogy between man and God. Man is like God, but God is not like man. Similarly, there is a quasi-one-way analogy between man and animals: man's bodily physiology is similar to animals, but man's soul is not similar to that of animals. Moreover, because man's body is informed by his rational soul, his experience of pain and sexual passion is altogether different from that of animals:

> Now deep reflection on the concise text of the first and second chapters of Genesis permits us to establish with certainty and conviction that right from the beginning a very clear and univocal boundary is laid down in the Bible between the world of animals (*animalia*) and the man created in the image and likeness of God . . . .
>
> In fact, the particular characteristics of man compared with the whole world of living beings (*animalia*) is such that man, understood from the viewpoint of species, cannot even basically qualify as an animal, but a rational animal.[66]

Man must look *up*, not *down*, to learn how to behave. We must look up to the other orders of being that possess themselves as persons, angels and the three Divine Persons in the Blessed Trinity, to understand how to behave as persons. Man is *in* but not *of* the kingdom of *animalia*. Therefore, to look down at the animal kingdom and extrapolate rules of moral behavior for man and human society from what we observe animals doing or to transfer what is appropriate in the treatment of animals to our treatment of human persons is tragic. Moreover, it is self-evident from our observation of the world that man and animals are distinguishable; one has the light of intelligence in her eyes, the other is dumb and witless.

> The simplest truth about man is that he is a very strange being; almost in the sense of being a stranger on the earth. In all sobriety, he has much more of the external appearance of one bringing alien habits from another land than of a mere growth of this one. He has an unfair advantage and an unfair disadvantage, he cannot sleep in his own skin; he cannot trust his own instinct. He is at once a creator moving miraculous hands and fingers and a kind of cripple. . . . It is not natural to see man as a natural product [of evolution]. It is not common sense to call man a common object of the country or seashore. It is not seeing straight to see him as an animal. It is not sane.[67]

Peter Singer, philosopher and noted animal rights activist, fails to acknowledge an essential difference between animals and persons. He claims that those who, like John Paul II, see such a difference are simply bigots and guilty of "speciesism," that is, "a form of prejudice no less objectionable than prejudice about a person's race or sex."[68]

For many, animal rights may seem like a harmless boon to animals, a benign sentimentality. One may be tempted to simply dismiss this issue—who cares if Rover gets another bone? On the contrary, we really do have a bone to pick with the ideology of animal rights. Quite simply, if animals are equal to man, then man is equal to animals. If this is true, then what is morally permissible in the treatment of animals is also morally permissible in the treatment of human beings. This is exactly what Singer recommends: "It is only our misplaced respect for the doctrine of the sanctity of human life that prevents us from seeing that what is obviously wrong to do to a horse [one that is lame and incurable] is equally wrong to do to a defective infant."[69]

A culture of death is nothing more than the systematic application of the principles of good animal husbandry to the human herd. Good animal husbandry selectively breeds for desirable traits and breeds out less desirable ones. When applied to the human herd this is the pseudo-science of eugenics. Why shouldn't we attempt to breed better people just as we do animals? If it is good game management to selectively cull animal herd so as to maintain the proper balance between the animal populations and the carrying capacity of the eco-system, why not apply the same criterion to human populations. This is what environmentalism and population control policies seek to achieve through so-called sexual and reproductive rights of contraception, sterilization, and abortion. After all, don't we spay and neuter our pets and livestock? Why not do the same with poor and degenerate people? We use animals for scientific experiments; why not human embryos who appear less developed anatomically than animals? Why not harvest the organs and tissue from human fetuses for the same reason? We hardly notice if animals copulate or masturbate so long as they don't overpopulate. So what's wrong with pan-sexual gender mainstreaming for a global culture?

Each of the major tenets of the culture of death—contraception, abortion, sterilization, euthanasia, in vitro fertilization, cloning, fetal experimentation, sexual liberation, gay rights, and population control—is morally permissible with animals. Singer applies this ethic of animal husbandry/animal rights to the issue of abortion. He concludes that women who abort their children are more morally upright than women who unthinkingly eat fish, because he presumes animals and human beings possess equal dignity and women who abort their children give greater thought to their decision than women who eat fish.[70]

Singer argues that because both man and animals can suffer, both have equal dignity and must be treated equally.[71] However, Singer confuses physiological pain with suffering in its uniquely human and moral dimension. Although animals react to pain, they are not self-conscious, nor are they potentially self-conscious, a trait unique to human beings endowed with a rational nature. The passions of animals do not serve as a bridge between the life of the body and the life of the spirit as with human beings.

Human suffering is essentially different from the pain experienced by animals. Both man and animals cry out in pain if they are attacked or wounded. Both may whimper if they are confined. But a person suffers most intensely when she asks "why" and there seems to be no answer to explain her suffering. When we submit to a dentist's drill or to field surgery without anesthesia the pain may be nearly unbearable and we are frightened but we are at peace and submit ourselves to these tortures because we can see a good reason to do so. However, should these same persons experience pain from a minor but senseless accident, they may experience rage or despair not being able to discern any purpose in their suffering.

But even seemingly senseless injuries caused by negligence or random violence have significance in the mysterious plan of God, hidden from the ages. That salvific plan was revealed in the fullness of time in Jesus Christ when God became man and experienced human suffering to redeem the world so that we might become sons and daughters of God through his grace.[72] Therefore, all human suffering, especially the most senseless and hence, most acute, when united to Christ's suffering and death, becomes redemptive: "I make up in my own body the sufferings that are lacking in the suffering of Christ for the sake of his body the Church."[73]

Human suffering has salvific significance if it is offered and united to Christ's infinite sacrifice. The person who suffers united with Christ extends redemption, through time and space, in a manner analogous to the sacraments of the Church. Those who suffer united to Christ become a eucharistic monstrance, if you will, that carries Christ crucified down the corridors of time to the ends of the earth:

> The cross is the unique sacrifice of Christ, the "one mediator between God and man." But because in his incarnate divine person he has in some way united himself to every man, "the possibility of being made partners, in a way known to God, in the paschal mystery" is offered to all men. He calls his disciples to

"take up (their) cross and follow (him)," for "Christ also suffered for (us), leaving (us) an example so that (we) should follow in his steps." In fact Jesus desires to associate with his redeeming sacrifice those who were to be its first beneficiaries. This is achieved supremely in the case of his mother, who was associated more intimately than any other person in the mystery of his redemptive suffering.[74]

What about sexual feeling? Many people speak about a "sexual instinct" in man "transferring onto the level of human reality what is proper to the world of living beings, of animals." But this "naturalistic category" is completely inadequate to describe the attraction between a man and a woman.[75]

The reason we blush and laugh while animals do not is because they are incapable of possessing themselves as a subject and are incapable of knowing the discrepancy between *what is* and *what should be*. When we note that difference, as for instance when someone trips, we may laugh at seeing someone out of control. If I trip, I may blush because I realize other people are looking at me as an object of humor and not a subject worthy of honor.

> Alone among the animals, he is shaken with the beautiful madness called laughter; as if he had caught sight of some secret in the very shape of the universe hidden from the universe itself. Alone among the animals he feels the need of averting his thoughts from the root realities of his own bodily being; of hiding them as in the presence of some higher possibility which creates the mystery of shame. Whether we praise these things as natural to man or abuse then as artificial in nature, they remain in the same sense unique.[76]

We experience shame when we are appropriated (taken) as an object. A lustful look embarrasses the person who is ogled; she already feels appropriated, taken hold of, and used as an object for another's satisfaction. An ogler also feels shame. In glaring, he feels dominated and "thingified" by an object that holds him bound. Both the ogled and the ogler experience being taken over either by another or by their own concupiscence: "The function of shame is to exclude . . . an attitude to the person incompatible with its essential, supra-utilitarian nature. . . . [T]he spontaneous need to conceal mere sexual values [is] . . . the natural way to the discovery of the person as such."[77]

Animals go into heat without blushing. But man must retain possession of himself even in giving himself in conjugal affection. On the other hand, the "concupiscent man," the man who looks lustfully at a woman[78] blushes seeing himself in heat and out of control, on fire with concupiscence.[79] In this sense, failing in self-mastery, man can be said to create a sexual instinct in himself; one that he gives birth to by forming a habit of lust which becomes second nature to him.

The beauty of animals tends to blur our perception of these spiritual realities and essential distinctions between animals and persons. We confuse human thinking with animal instincts and human language with unconscious animal signaling. We can't help but personify animals with human ideation and feeling, that what animals feel when they go into heat is identical to the feelings of men and women, and that the sufferings of men and women are no different from those of animals.

In all these ways, animal rights has put a cuddly face on eugenics. Beware of Bambi! If the human race is merely another herd of animals, then the earth, like a big zoo, requires a few benign managers. Singer may not be a Nazi as his critics claim, but his ideology *is* compatible with a new totalitarianism that seeks to spay the Developing World for the sustained hegemony of the elite of the First World. Singer exploits our feelings of wonder and awe before the mysteries of nature, our delight in the beauty of animal, and our affection for our pets in order to introduce "confusion between good and evil."[80]

In the *Catechism* we read that our dominion over animals is not absolute.[81] When we are cruel to animals, we sin against God and abuse our human dignity, but we do not violate their "rights."[82] Animals do not have rights. Persons created in the image and likeness of God have a duty to make a self-gift of themselves to others and so enjoy a corresponding inalienable right not to be deterred in the performance of those duties. Human beings possess those rights from the first moment of their existence when they are created in the image of the Divine Persons in God.[83] All the same, even if animals do not have rights, we must be kind to them like St. Francis of Assisi,[84] but we should not be sentimental: "one should not direct to them the affection due only to persons."[85] We may appropriate animals for our food and clothing and use them for humane scientific experimentation since it contributes to caring for or saving human lives.[86] It is unworthy of man to waste money on animals that should go "to the relief of human misery."[87]

It would seem that much of Singer's efforts are directed toward what is unworthy—an idolatrous inflation of the prerogatives of animals, and those who claim to speak for them, at the expense of the poor and the relief of human misery. Singer's insistence upon man's equality with animals closes the horizon on man's transcendence and advances a culture of death. In this sense animal rights leads to spiritual despair.

The Good News is that the "Son of God became man so that we might become God."[88] "The only Begotten Son of God, wanting to make us share in his divinity, assumed our nature, so that he, made man, might make men gods."[89] Because man is called to beatitude with God, no one may treat him like an animal. Those who would blind us to our spiritual transcendence further our enslavement. We are not a herd of animals, "a field of appropriation," reducible to mere creatures of the state. God made us in his image and we are destined for Paradise not *Animal Farm*.

Diagram 1.1
Emotions*

Concupiscible Appetite

(movement toward Good in general)		(movement away from Evil in general)	
Emotion	**Object**	**Emotion**	**Object**
Love	for the good *in general*	Hate	for evil *in general*
Desire	for the good *if absent*	Aversion	for evil *if absent*
Joy	for the good *if present*	Sadness	for evil *if present*

Irascible Appetite

(movement—difficult to obtain Good)		(movement—difficult to avoid Evil)	
Emotion	**Object**	**Emotion**	**Object**
Hope	for *attainable absent* good	Courage	for *conquerable absent* evil
Despair	for *unattainable absent* good	Fear	for *unconquerable absent* evil
Anger	for evil *present*		

* See S.T. I-II, qq. 22–48; For a psychological explanation of neurosis utilizing Aquinas's analysis of emotions see Baars, W. Conrad M.D., *Born Only Once: The Miracle of Affirmation* (Chicago MI: Franciscan Herald Press, 1975); and Anna A. Terruwe, M.D. and Conrad Baars, M.D., *Loving and Curing the Neurotic*, (New Rochelle, NY, Arlington House Pub., 1972).

Diagram 1.2
A Comparison of Persons and Animals

Similarities—The Human Body Is Similar to That of the Higher Animals

Human Persons (material body)	**Animals** (material body)
5 Senses	5 Senses
Reflex Action	Reflex Action
No Instincts *per se*	Instincts
Disposition	Disposition
Emotions	Emotions
Imagination (interior imaginations)	Imagination (interior images)
Memory (of interior images)	Memory (of interior images)
Learned Conditioning	Learned Conditioning
Unconscious Signaling	Unconscious Signaling

Differences—The Human Person Bears the "Image of God"

Man (spiritual soul)	**Animals** (material soul)
Faculties of the soul	None
Reason and Language	None
Intellectual Memory	None
Free Will	None
A Relational Being	An Instinctual Being
Knows Laughter and Shame	None

Differences—a Human Person Becomes Divine

Man has potential for Divine Life by participation in grace	**Animals** have no potential for Divine Life

Note

1. Gen. 1:27; CCC, no. 355.
2. See CCC, no. 1934.
3. Peter J. Colosi "Are Zygotes People? The Personhood of Embryos: Framing the Question," Eighteenth Annual University Faculty for Life Conference, Marquette University (May 30–June 1, 2008); citing an address of Pope Benedict XVI to participants in an inter-academic conference on "The Changing Identity of the Individual," organized by the *Académie des Sciences* of Paris and by the Pontifical Academy of Sciences, given Monday, January 28, 2008. The text can be found at http://www.vatican.va/holy_father/benedict_xvi/speeches/2008/january/documents/hf_ben-xvi_spe_20080128_convegno-individuo_en.html (accessed November 14, 2008).
4. CCC, no. 1702.
5. Peter J. Cameron, "The Lord's Prayer," *Magnificat*, Vol. 11, No. 8, (Ft. Collins, CO: Magnificat USA, 2009), 2.
6. Fredrick Copleston, *A History of Philosophy, Vol. 6, Modern Philosophy Part II* (Garden City, NY: Doubleday, 1964), 20–21.
7. Rom. 1:20, Wisd. of Sol. 13:5.
8. FR, no. 82; see also FR, nos. 5, 22, 55, 56, 94.
9. Fredrick Copleston, *A History of Philosophy, Vol. 1, Modern Philosophy Part II* (Garden City, NY: Doubleday, 1962), 108.
10. ST I, q. 65, a. 1, reply obj. 3; q. 66, a. 1.
11. See Charles Rice, *50 Questions on the Natural Law*, rev. ed. (San Francisco, Ignatius Press 1999), 143–46.
12. CCC, no. 2516.
13. ST I, qq. 84–86. See also ST I, q. 94 a. 2.
14. ST I, q. 84, a. 7.
15. See FR, no. 4.
16. ST I-II, q. 1, a. 1.
17. ST I-II, a. 8, a. 1.
18. Paul J. Glenn, *A Tour of the Summa* (Rockford, IL: Tan Books, 1960) 99–100; ST I-II q. 13, a. 6.
19. ST I-II, q. 3, a. 5.
20. ST I-II, q. 94, a. 2.
21. ST I-II, q. 9, a. 1.
22. ST I-II, q. 10, a. 2.
23. ST I-II, q. 1, a. 1, rep, obj. 1.
24. ST I-II, q. 83, a. 3, rep. obj. 3.
25. CCC, no. 1730; citing GS, no.17. See also Sir. 15:14; ST I-II, q. 1, aa. 4–8.
26. St. Augustine, *Confessions*, I, no.1 (Minge, Patrologiae Latinae Cursus Completus, 32:661).
27. ST I-II, qq. 1, 5, 6.
28. ST I-II, qq. 2, 3.
29. CCC, no. 1723.
30. ST I-II, q. 22, a. 3.
31. ST I-II, q. 22, a. 1.
32. 2 Sam. 11.
33. CCC, no. 1763.
34. CCC, no. 1764.

35. ST I-II, q. 22, a. 3; q. 23, a. 1.

36. CCC, no. 1767.

37. ST I-II, q. 24, a. 1.

38. CCC, no. 1768.

39. ST I-II, q. 24, a. 3.

40. CCC, no. 1770, citing Psalm 84:2

41. Mary Shivanandan, *Crossing the Threshold of Love: A New Vision of Marriage* (Catholic Univ. Press, 1999), 64–65; summarizing John Paul II, *The Acting Person*, ed. A. Tymieniecka trans. Andrzej Potochi, *Analecta Husserliana* 10 (1979): 221–27.

42. ST I, q. 29, a. 1, obj. 2; citing Boethius, *De Duab. Nat.*

43. ST I, q. 29, a. 3, rep. obj.1.

44. ST I, q. 29, a. 3.

45. ST I, q. 29, a. 3, rep. obj. 4.

46. ST I, q. 29, a. 4; CCC, no. 255.

47. ST I, q. 30, a. 3

48. ST I, q. 30, a. 4; CCC, no. 254.

49. ST I, q. 31, a. 2.

50. CCC, no. 253.

51. ST I, q. 29, a. 4.

52. ST I, q. 33, a. 1; q. 36, aa. 2–3.

53. ST I, q. 40, a. 3; q. 36, a. 2.

54. 1 John 4:8–9. Cf. 1 John 4:16.

55. ST I, q. 29, a. 4.

56. ST I, q. 44, a. 1.

57. ST I, q. 28, a. 2.

58. Rice, *50 Questions*, 258; citing Cardinal Karol Wojtyla, *Subjectivity and the Irreducible in Man, in The Human Being in Action*, Ann-Teresa Tymieniecka, ed., (1978), 107.

59. Peter J. Colosi, "Personhood, the Soul, and Non-Conscious Human Beings: Some Critical Reflections on Recent Forms of Argumentation within the Pro-life Movement," *Life and Learning XVII*, Joseph Koterski, ed. (Bronx, NY: University Faculty for Life, 2007), 294.

60. Robert A. Connor, "The Person as Resonating Existential," *66 American Catholic Philosophical Quarterly* 39, 42 (1992); cited by Rice, *50 Questions*, 218.

61. GS, no. 24; quoting John 17:21–22.

62. VS, no. 86.

63. FR, no. 21.

64. VS, no. 7; Matt. 19:16.

65. John Paul II, *Theology of the Body Human Love in the Divine Plan* (Boston: Daughters of St. Paul, 1997) (General Audiences, November 14, 1979).

66. John Paul II, *Theology of the Body: Human Love in the Divine Plan* (General Audience of April 28, 1982), 282–83.

67. G. K. Chesterton, *The Everlasting Man* (Garden City, NY: Image Books, 1925) 36–37.

68. Deborah Danielski, "Paradise by way of 'Animal Farm,'" *Our Sunday Visitor*, 29 November 1998, 8.

69. Michael Burleigh, "History Today", Oct. 1994, Vol. 44, Issue 10, 6.

70. Danielski, "Paradise by Way of 'Animal Farm," 8.

71. Peter Singer, Applied Ethics (Bethesda, MD: Oxford University Press, 1986) 222.

72. Eph. 1:9.

73. Col. 1:24.

74. CCC, no. 618; see also SD, part 5.

75. John Paul II, Theology of the Body, (General Audience of April 28, 1982), 282.

76. Chesterton, Everlasting Man, 37.

77. Mary Shivanandan, Crossing the Threshold of Love: A New Vision of Marriage (Washington, DC: Catholic University Press, 1999), 43 n.17; quoting John Paul II, Love and Responsibility, trans. H.T. Willetts (San Francisco: Ignatius Press, 1993), 178–79.

78. Matt. 5:28.

79. John Paul II, Theology of the Body (General Audience of August 27, 1980), 142.

80. EV, no. 24.

81. CCC, no. 2415.

82. CCC, no. 2418.

83. Rice, 50 Questions, 74–79.

84. CCC, no. 2416.

85. CCC, no. 2416.

86. CCC, no. 2417.

87. CHCW, no. 79.

88. CCC, no. 460; citing St. Athanasius, De Inc., 54, 3: PG 25, 192 B.

89. CCC, no. 460; citing St. Thomas Aquinas, Opusc. 57:1–4; see also CCC, no. 1999.

Chapter 2
Human Freedom and Conscience

Freedom and Truth

In this chapter we explore the relationship between human freedom, truth and law as presented in *Veritatis Splendor* by Pope John Paul II and in the writings of St. Thomas Aquinas. The political slogan "the right to choose" is exercised well only if through the exercise of free will guided by right reason we make choices in conformity with the innate truth of our moral being. John Paul II explains: "Our freedom is therefore freedom for truth, for the good, for love, for happiness. [Then] it is in touch with reality."[1] Some expressions of human freedom lead to frustration, others to fulfillment. Choices that lead to frustration betray freedom because those choices fail to unfold one according to the truth about the human person.[2] For this reason, freedom cannot be an absolute value. Rather, just as a man must walk in the light if he is not to stumble and fall, so do we need the light of truth to choose:

> Rational reflection and daily experience demonstrate the weakness which marks man's freedom. That freedom is real but limited: its absolute and unconditional origin is not in itself, but in the life within which it is situated and which represents for it, at one and the same time, both a limitation and a possibility . . . . Reason and experience not only confirm the weakness of human freedom, they also confirm its tragic aspects. Man comes to realize that this freedom is in some mysterious way inclined to betray [its] openness to Truth and the Good . . . .[3]

When we deliberately choose unreasonable goals, we conform ourselves to those ends. If we do what is reasonable we become virtuous and good, if we repeatedly do what is unreasonable and sinful, we become vicious:

> Human acts are moral acts because they express and determine the goodness or

evil of the individual who performs them. They do not produce a change merely in the state of affairs outside of man but, to the extent that they are deliberate choices, they give moral definition to the very person who performs them, determining his *profound spiritual traits*.[4]

The basic duties of human nature, the essential goods of human flourishing, are self-evident to reason. We are to do good and avoid evil, transmit and nurture human life, refine and develop the material world, cultivate social life, know the truth and live in accord with it, i.e., practice good, and contemplate beauty.[5] To act against these innate and transcendental values is unreasonable conduct, an objective evil. It leaves us out of touch with reality, bound up, not free:

> To have become free is to have been able to overcome or avoid those distractions and obstacles which frustrate or inhibit the development of a capacity for judgment by standards whose rational authority we are able to recognize for ourselves and for action in accord with such judgment. To have failed to become free is to have rendered oneself subject to frustration or inhibition in respect or such development. And the exercise of choice as such may contribute as easily and as often to failure as to success in becoming free. What we all have to learn is how to make right choices.[6]

We read in *Veritatis Splendor* that "freedom of conscience is never freedom 'from' the truth but always and only freedom 'in' the truth."[7] God's eternal law, his providential plan for the universe, is the objective norm of morality.[8] Conscience is the proximate norm of morality, God's herald, who guides us in making right choices.[9] But we can set ourselves against God's herald, and attempt to gag it and create for ourselves an idol, that is, a false and absolute conscience of our own making. Christ came to topple idols and dispel the illusions that blind and bind us. He came to un-gag our true interior voice, and set us free from a false conscience that shackles freedom:

> What is more, within his errors and negative decisions, man glimpses the source of a deep rebellion, which leads him to reject the Truth and the Good in order to set himself up as an absolute principle unto himself: "You will be like God."[10] Consequently, freedom itself needs to be set free. It is Christ who sets it free: he "has set us free for freedom."[11]

Human freedom is oriented toward self-possession through virtuous self-mastery and openness to others[12] and, so, is only "acquired in *love*, that is, in the *gift of self*."[13] True freedom is opposed to individualism because freedom is meant to put us in right relations with others, not in isolation or opposition to them. If we fail to love—to give and receive the gift of self—so as to fulfill the basic duties of human nature, then we tend to use our freedom in ways that contradict our interior freedom and is destructive towards others:

God gives everyone freedom, a freedom which possesses an *inherently relational dimension* . . . but when freedom is made absolute in an individualistic way, it is emptied of its original content, and its very meaning and dignity are contradicted. . . . [It] negates and destroys itself, and becomes a factor leading to the destruction of others, when it no longer recognizes and *respects its essential link with the truth*.[14]

Like an artist who knows the laws of form, contrast and proportion, but violates them intentionally in an attempt to make war on civilization, so the laws of human flourishing must be respected lest we destroy ourselves and all that is beautiful in life. Picasso (d. 1973) revolutionized painting. He used art to wage war on the basic values associated with human flourishing. He said, "I want to give it [art] a form which has some connection with the visible world even if it is only to wage war on that world." [15] Picasso sought to inspire wanton and destructive expressions of human freedom in both art and in culture at large:

In both his [degenerate] sexual behavior and his art. . . . Picasso was mounting what he saw as a frontal assault on the traditions of the West. In the final analysis, the formalists were right. There was a connection between Western art and Christian morals. Realism [in art] could not thrive in a climate that denied the transcendent values of the human person. . . . Picasso's mutilation of the female body bespeak the modern version of human sacrifice; they presage simultaneously in a visual way the concentration camp, the abortion clinic, and the pornographic film, and may well have helped pave the way for all three. Picasso's war on representation was a war on the tradition that begot it as well, a tradition that saw the human being as possessing infinite value. . . . It was an attempt to throw off the value that the person had acquired as a result of the thousands of years of Western civilization.[16]

The transcendental dignity of the human person that modern artists have tried so hard to distort is brought back into focus in the writing of John Paul II. In his *Letter to Families* (1994), we read that the mystery of the Incarnation extols the capacity of human nature to reveal divinity. Just as the Church fought the iconoclast heresy in the eighth century A.D, so today she resists the degradation of the human form in pornography and in what has just been described as degenerate art:

All this [the beauty of fairest love] is confirmed by the mystery of the incarnation, a mystery which has been the source of a new beauty in the history of humanity and has inspired countless masterpieces of act. . . . [T]he Christian era began . . . to portray in art the God who became man, Mary his Mother, St. Joseph, the saints of the old and new covenant and the entire created world redeemed by Christ. . . . It can be said that this new artistic canon, attentive to the deepest dimensions of man and his future, originates in the mystery of Christ's incarnation. . . . This is why the Church is so concerned with the direction taken by the means of social communication . . . of the dangers arising from the manipulation of truth. Indeed what truth can there be in films, shows and radio and television programs dominated by pornography and violence? Do these really serve the truth about man?[17]

In *Veritatis Splendor*, John Paul II shows that Christ restores the essential link between human freedom and the truth of human nature, its purpose and fulfillment. First, Jesus Christ reveals man to himself; that is, he shows us human nature fully actualized in himself. [18] After providing us with his own life as an example of human freedom in action, he then transforms us in his grace so that we have the capacity to be free to follow his example and fulfill the moral law in the power of the Holy Spirit: to interiorize the law, to receive the law and to live it as the motivating force of true personal freedom: 'the perfect law, the law of liberty.'[19]

Of course, we can close our hearts to Christ's love and reject his grace-given freedom to live and love like God. But if we dare to make of ourselves a gift for others in imitation of Christ, we must look to Christ crucified and take up our cross daily: "Contemplation of Jesus Crucified is thus the highroad which the Church must tread every day if she wishes to understand the full meaning of freedom: the gift of self in service to God and one's brethren. Communion with the Crucified and Risen Lord is the never-ending source from which the Church draws unceasingly in order to live in freedom, to give of herself and to serve."[20]

Human freedom, therefore, is not an end in itself. Unrestrained freedom in morals, as in art, destroys the medium and the man. Freedom must be oriented toward self-possession and openness to others and therein, we discover ourselves.[21] We must possess ourselves through virtue so as to be able to give the gift of our self to others. We must serve others if we would be as free as God, the Master Artist and Servant of the servants.

In the award winning film *Life is Beautiful* by Roberto Benigni, the wise manager of the Grand Hotel, Zio (uncle) Elisio, explains to his nephew Guido the difference between being a servant and serving. He makes a comparison to the sunflower whose flowery head looks like the sun and turns through the day so as to always point towards the sun. Then, teaching his nephew how to bow (but not too low), he said: "But if you see some that are bowed down, it means they are dead. You're serving. You are not a servant. Serving is a supreme art. . . . God serves men, but he's not a servant to men." So, to be truly free, we must imitate God who came to teach us this supreme art: "the Son of Man who came 'not to be served but to serve, and to give his life as a ransom for many."[22]

Freedom and Law

"Law is an ordinance of reason, made and promulgated for the common good by one who has authority over a society."[23] Law is a light to the mind that enables us to choose in conformity with the truth inscribed in our being. However, law does not of itself give us the power to follow it or to live well. It is grace, a new divine principle of life that transforms and divinizes the soul[24] that enables us to live well and follow the path marked out for us by true law so as to achieve our salvation. "According to Christian tradition, the Law is holy, spiritual and good, yet still imperfect. Like a tutor, it shows what must be done, but does not of itself give the strength, the grace of the Spirit to follow it."[25]

Law may be affirmative, negative or both in what it commands or enjoins. For example, "honor your parents" is an affirmative law whereas "thou shall not kill" is a negative precept. "Thou shall not steal" includes both a negative injunction (not to take what belongs to another) and an affirmative command (to pay one's just debts).

Law is referred to as "positive" when it is promulgated (made known and effective) through human words. Hence, both human law and divine revelation are positive in this sense; the former made known through the publication of the civil government, and later through the words of the prophet.

"Legal Positivism" is a theory of law that claims any law duly enacted, promulgated and enforced by a law giver rightfully in office is good law and obliges in conscience the citizens to obey it. So, for example, because laws enforcing racial segregation were duly promulgated by those lawfully elected or appointed to office in the United States and India until the second half of the twentieth century, one subject to those laws was duty-bound to obey them, and acts of civil disobedience protesting them deserved criminal punishment. Thus, Mahatma Gandhi and Martin Luther King, Jr. were both put in jail under this theory. Positivism denies the existence of a universal moral law and can provide no intellectual defense to the legalization of slavery, apartheid, abortion (voluntary or forced). There can be no inalienable rights under the premises of legal positivism.[26] Natural Law jurisprudence as understood by the Church is a theory of law based on reason and revelation,[27] and asserts that human laws are only legitimate if they give expression to a higher law inherent in human nature naturally known to all persons who attain the use of reason. Any human law that fails to give expression to this innate higher moral law inscribed in human nature is no law at all but an act of tyranny that does not bind in conscience, because it does not respect the truth of human nature.[28]

The trouble with natural law theory, however, is that because of original sin, reasonable minds differ as to its precepts. "The precepts of the natural law are not perceived by everyone clearly and immediately. In the present situation sinful man needs grace and revelation so moral truths may be known 'by everyone with facility, with firm certainty and with no admixture of error.'"[29] Because there is no agreement as to who understands the precepts of the natural law correctly, it is nearly impossible to refer to a higher law in the process of adjudication. Judge Robert Bork said a judge's reference to a higher law usually turns out to be nothing more than the judge giving vent to his "viscera," i.e, predispositions, prejudices and value preferences.[30]

For this reason Christ established the Catholic Church as the infallible interpreter of the whole moral law including the precepts of the Natural Law so that the whole human family, Christian and non-Christian, could benefit from a correct understanding of the basic rules for human flourishing.

Let no one of the faithful deny that the Magisterium of the Church is competent to interpret the natural moral law. For it is indisputable—as Our Predecessors have often declared—that when Jesus Christ imparted His divine authority to Peter and the other apostles and sent them to all nations to teach His Commandments, He established those very men as authentic guardians and interpreters of the whole moral law, that is, not only of the Gospel, but also of natural law. For natural law declares the will of God; faithful compliance with the natural law is necessary for eternal salvation.[31]

The human race has benefitted from the Church despite the fact that only one billion of the earth's present six billion inhabitants are Catholic. It has occurred due to the influence of the Church over the development of world community imbued with a fundamental respect of the innate worth of the human person reflected and passed on in the cultural, scientific, and judicial traditions of Western civilization. This is the reason the Catholic Church intervenes in the affairs of nations, because of its Great Commission from Christ to make disciples of all nations (Mt. 28:19-20) which consists of two parts: to convert the whole world and baptize as many as possible and, secondly, to preach the Gospel and allow it to be a leaven and force for good in the many cultures of the world: "While working to *convert* all nations, Christianity wished also to *unite* them, and to introduce into their relations principles of justice and peace, of law and mutual duties."[32]

The Four Kinds of Law

Catholic tradition recognizes four basic categories of law that give structure to human freedom: eternal law, divine law, natural law and human law. To view human law in isolation from the others impoverishes one's respect for the rule of law, that what legitimizes law is not the will or power of the lawmaker but its own ability to unfold the human person. Law does not spring from the barrel of a gun, but from the mind and heart of every man and woman.

Eternal Law

"Eternal law is the plan of government in the Chief Governor."[33] It is a type of Divine Wisdom (God's Providence) moving all things to their due end.[34] Irrational creatures obey God's providence or blueprint for the universe guided by the forces of nature or their instincts. Rational creatures must obey God and the Eternal Law voluntarily or suffer God's displeasure. However, even if they disobey God's plan, it is still fulfilled when they are compelled to obey his just punishments, in this life or the next. All true law "finds its first and ultimate truth in the eternal law"[35] and its fullness in Christ who bestows the grace to live justly and thereby be justified by faith in Christ.[36]

Natural Law

The light of understanding infused in us by God, whereby we understand what must be done and what must be avoided, is referred to as the natural law.[37] The natural law is the image of God's eternal law impressed in our minds, and like a signet ring leaves its image in hot wax so does the eternal law leave its image deep in the recesses of the human heart or conscience.[38] It is man's rational participation in God's eternal law:

> It follows that the natural law is itself the eternal law, implanted in beings endowed with reason, and inclining them toward their right action and end; it is none other than the eternal reason of the Creator and Ruler of the universe.[39]

> But God provides for man differently from the way in which he provides for beings which are not persons. He cares for man not "from without," through the laws of physical nature, but "from within," through reason, which by its natural knowledge of God's eternal law, is consequently able to show man the right direction to take in his free actions. . . .[40] The *natural law* enters here as the human expression of God's eternal law.[41]

Natural law is inherent in human nature and becomes naturally known or promulgated when one attains the "age of reason." Hence it is natural to us. It is a part of our human nature. It is objective, universal, one and the same for all mankind.[42] In itself it is changeless, but it must be faithfully applied to changing circumstances, times and places.[43] It cannot be effaced from human nature and imposes upon all men "common principles."[44] St. Paul tells us that this interior moral law is known naturally by all men. The Gentiles who do not have the Mosaic Law have a law by which they are judged "writ on the fleshy tablets of their hearts."[45]

> The natural law is immutable and permanent throughout the variations of history; it subsists under the flux of ideas and customs and supports their progress. The rules that express it remain substantially valid. Even when it is rejected in its very principles, it cannot be destroyed or removed from the heart of man. It always rises again in the life of individuals and societies. . . .[46]

Human reason has the role of learning and applying the natural law to the circumstances of daily life. Human freedom depends on the mind's grasp of the natural law to provide the light by which to choose freely. This higher law is the light to choose and set our feet running, to recognize the form, shape, mass and proportionality that enable us to create beauty in stone, wood and colored oil. Human nature is not fulfilled in the contemplation or creation of what is ugly, lurid and bent. To go against the moral law in the name of freedom and the "right to choose" and to eat the forbidden fruit, attempting to define good and evil without reference to the innate truth within us, "far from furthering freedom, sooner or later restricts it,"[47] which is the death of true freedom:

> The rightful autonomy of the practical reason [conscience] means that man possesses in himself his own law, received from the Creator. Nevertheless, the autonomy of reason cannot mean that a denial of the participation of the practical reason in the wisdom of the divine Creator and Lawgiver, or were it to suggest a freedom which creates moral norms, on the basis of historical contingencies or the diversity of societies and cultures, this sort of alleged autonomy would contradict the Church's teaching on the truth about man. It would be the death of true freedom: "But of the tree of knowledge of good and evil you shall not eat, for in the day that you eat of it you shall die."[48]

The natural law is the voice of God sounding deep within our conscience "do good and avoid evil." This innate sense of justice is the raw ore of the metal of the mind which we are called to refine: "Deep within his conscience man discovers a law which he has not laid upon himself but which he must obey. Its voice, ever calling him to love and to do what is good and avoid evil, sounds in his heart at the right moment. . . . For man has in his heart a law inscribed by God."[49]

The first principle of the natural law is a basic orientation of the human mind to seek good and avoid evil called *synderesis*. This orientation gravitates like a magnet, if you will, to certain transcendental values or the basic inclinations of human nature placed in human nature by its Creator. As soon as a child matures to the age of reason, his practical intellect begins to operate with an orientation, a ballast or balance, or what may be called a *"principle of obedience vis-à-vis the objective norm."*[50] In the depths of his heart man has a rational ballast, if you will, that rights him, straightens him, and gives him a moral equilibrium. He finds that he has an innate moral compass that points toward good and away from evil. Reason draws upon the first principle of the practical reason, a habit of mind, synderesis, (that principle of obedience or moral compass that directs us to do good and to avoid evil) to form an act – a judgment of conscience.[51]

> First moral principles, or will-principles (that is, laws of conduct), are drawn from the direct awareness that there is such a thing as right and good, such a thing as wrong and evil, such a thing as obligation or duty. And thus, first moral principles are "Do good," "Avoid evil." And, since the knowledge of good is not wholly abstract, it involves certain manifest objective instances of what is good and what is bad. This fundamental moral equipment of a human being, achieved as a person emerges from infancy to an age of responsible conduct, is called synderesis. Now, first principles, intellectual or moral, are habits, that is, enduring qualities, of intellect and will. Knowledge of first truths (that is, intellectual principles) is an intellectual habit; so is synderesis in so far as it is knowledge; synderesis in so far as it is a habitual guide and influence upon the will is a moral habit.[52]

This principle of obedience, synderesis, behaves like a compass that always points to good and away from evil and acknowledges certain inherent values which govern man's most basic relationships.[53] For man to unfold himself and display the dignity proper to a human person, he must honor and cultivate these six basic inclinations that guide him in forming right relations with the world, himself, and others, and so ultimately with his final end:

> In order to perfect himself in his specific order, the person must [1] do good and avoid evil, [2] be concerned for the transmission of life, [3] refine and develop the riches of the material world, [4] cultivate social life, [5] practice good [know truth and live accordingly], and [6] contemplate beauty.[54]

The secondary precepts or principles of the natural law, confirmed and revealed for us by God in the Ten Commandments, follow from an application of the first principle of the natural law to the six basic inclinations of human nature. Like the colors of light, the range of genuine human values are a given although each person is free to apply them in varying degrees or hues on the canvas of our lives:

> The natural law states the first and essential precepts which govern the moral life. It hinges upon the desire for God and submission to him, who is the source and judge of all that is good, as well as upon the sense that the other is one's equal. Its principal precepts are expressed in the Decalogue. This is called "natural," not in reference to the nature of rational beings, but because reason which decrees it properly belongs to human nature.[55]

All who attain the use of reason know the voice of conscience, wherein the natural law sounds in the depths of their hearts. Unless one has been corrupted by scandal (bad example), everyone feels the compelling force of the Ten Commandments if they choose to reject them. A warning is heard and a sense of disquiet settles on us when we break these moral laws. Like venturing out too far on a frozen pond and hearing a crack, an alarm is sounded when we break one of the Commandments.

However other moral decisions having to do with what is implicit in the Ten Commandments are not so easily grasped. Fallen humanity, subject to the effects of Original Sin, has no clear comprehension of the remote conclusions of the natural law. For example, everyone has a natural moral intuition that it is wrong to steal, which is a violation of a secondary precept of the natural law, the seventh commandment. But that we should return lost property is not so clear because it is a remote conclusion of the natural law implicit in the seventh commandment. Haven't we all sung lustily, "finders keepers, loser weepers" when we found ourselves a finder of lost property? Because of this "darkening of the mind and weakening of the will" (the effects of Original Sin) we need Divine Revelation to grasp readily and easily the full implications of the natural law.[56]

Divine Law

Revelation, including the Old and New Testaments, is a form of positive law known as the Divine Law. The primitive precepts of the Divine Law include striving to serve God as He revealed Himself to Adam, Noah, Abraham and the patriarchs. The Mosaic Law includes the ceremonial and judicial precepts as well as the precepts of the natural law. The binding force of the primitive and Mosaic law passed away with the coming of Christ except those aspects contained in them which are part of the natural law.[57]

The Law of Christ is principally Grace, i.e., the indwelling of the Holy Spirit in our soul and the transformation or divinization of our nature. By participation in grace we become a son or daughter of God and acquire a new divine power of will expressed in the virtue of Charity.[58] Secondarily, the Law of Christ is a new teaching, the chief precept of which is to accept the teachings of Christ and live the beatitudes, a life transfigured in grace:

> The New Law is the grace of the Holy Spirit given to the faithful through faith in Christ. It works through Charity; it uses the Sermon on the Mount to teach us what must be done and makes use of the sacraments to give us the grace to do it. [59]

Human Law

There are two kinds of human law, ecclesiastical or canon law and civil law or that law which governs civil or secular society. Ecclesiastical law is an expression of the authority given by Christ to St. Peter to provide order to the Church, the body of Christ here on earth. In some circumstances it may bind all baptized persons; in others, it extends only to Catholics. With regards to non-baptized individuals the Church has authority, a right given to her by Christ, to preach the Gospel to all nations and to interpret for them the truths of faith and morals and to receive them into the Church by baptism irrespective of civil laws:

> Like their Master, the apostles too recognized legitimate civil authority: "Let every person be subject to the governing authorities . . . he who resists the authorities resists what God has appointed."[60]

> At the same time they were not afraid to speak out against public authority when it opposed God's holy will: "We must obey God rather than men."[61]

The two poles that mark the path a Christian must walk in his allegiance to the State are Rom 13:12 ("Let every person be subject to the governing authorities") and Acts 5:29 ("We must obey God rather than men"). The former command binds him to obey just human laws and authentic civil authority. Acts 5 demands that a Christian not obey unjust human laws and to engage in acts of civil disobedience, if need be, rather than deny the truths of the faith or cooperate with those who deny and violate her moral teachings in grave matters. The Church has the right to punish those who violate her laws. Today it is confined to spiritual penalties. A person is excused from observing certain Church laws, such as going to Mass on Sunday, when he is physically or morally unable to observe it due to grave inconveniences to him or to another. For example, a Catholic might be excused from going to Mass if he thought he was under surveillance and might reveal the whereabouts of an illegal underground Church.

Civil authorities have the right to pass civil law because they are God's representatives.[62] However, any human law that does not comport with the natural law is not law at all but an act of tyranny that does not bind in conscience.[63] In some cases one may never obey them. For example, if laws are passed that require physicians to formally cooperate in the act of abortion by either performing an abortion or referring the patient to a physician who will perform an abortion, a physician should suffer the loss of his medical license rather than formally cooperate with such unjust human laws. In other cases one may cooperate materially and obey unjust human laws if greater evil would result from disobeying them. For example, one may pay unjust taxes, which are excessive to most citizens or discriminatory towards some persons who, for instance, would have to pay twice to educate their children according to their sincerely held religious beliefs, first in taxes to the public school system and then in tuition to a faith based school. Due to the disruption of vital services that might occur or the harsh treatment one would suffer for refusing to pay unjust taxes, one should bear with these injustices unless the burdens outweigh the benefits of obeying such unjust laws.[64]

Today, tyranny is thought to exist when the executive, legislative and judicial branches of government reside in one person or office regardless of the nature of the laws passed. This is a procedural notion of tyranny that rests on the theory of legal positivism. A correct understanding of tyranny is substantive rather than procedural: a government is tyrannical if it promulgates laws contrary to the natural law regardless of the form of government.

Pope John Paul II reminds us that when fundamental rights, defined by the natural law, are subject to a vote or the decision of a court, democracy is transformed into a "tyrant state" which still maintains the "appearance of strictest respect for legality" but is, however, the "tragic caricature of legality" and the "democratic ideal is betrayed in its very foundations."[65]

Human law ought not attempt to suppress every vice lest the cure (a severe police state) be worse than the illness. Some sins are best treated in the private forum through sacramental confession rather than through the enactment of positive law.[66] Natural law serves as a model and guide for good human laws that promote the common good, family life, and the suppression of the grossest vices. It serves as an intellectual shield against tyrannical human laws. Without reference to the natural law the concept of inalienable rights disappears; rights not subject to negotiation and amendment have no foundation unless they are grounded upon moral absolutes.[67]

Law is a light to the mind that requires grace and virtue to order free will and guide human freedom along the paths of human flourishing. Unjust human law may provide order, but never peace. Law unsupported by the virtue of justice results in structures of sin and a culture of death where, perhaps, all the trains run on time but, as history has shown, they go straight to concentration camps!

Conscience

Which culture in the world, past or present, has ever honored a man who has betrayed those who were good to him? A traitor is universally despised. Where on earth are hypocrites or cowards respected? On the other hand, which civilization has not held in esteem the virtues of hospitality and loyalty? Who can violate these universal moral norms with impunity? Who can erase these reflections of the natural law simply by saying it is so: "Woe to those who call evil good and good evil, who put darkness for light and light for darkness, who put bitter for sweet and sweet for bitter."[68]

The three witches in Shakespeare's tragic play, *Macbeth*, attempt to conform reality to their desires by their magic spell: "Fair is foul, and foul is fair." But no incantation can make foul to be fair as Macbeth and his temptress, Lady Macbeth, discover. They plot and kill their cousin, the king, while he is a guest sleeping in their home. To steel herself for this unnatural murder which breaks this multi-ply cord of relationship and duty, Lady Macbeth asks the spirits to "unmake" her:

> Come you spirits
> That tend on mortal thoughts, unsex me here,
> And fill me, from crown to the toe, top-full
> Of direst cruelty! Make thick my blood,
> Stop up th' access and passage to remorse,
> That no compunctious visitings of nature
> Shake my fell purpose.[69]

Immediately after Macbeth murdered the King, he recounts to his wife his act of murder and his strange inability to say "Amen" to the prayers of the King's drugged and drowsy guards. As he snuck down the stairs after murdering the King in his bed chamber he overheard the King's guards muttering in their stupor a familiar prayer to which he attempted to reply "Amen" but the word stuck in his throat. His wife upbraids and warns him not to dwell on what he has done or his inner turmoil: "These deeds must not be thought/ After these ways; so, it will make us mad."[70] She further admonishes her blood-stained husband not "to think/ So brainsickly of things. Go get some water,/ And wash this filthy witness from your hand."[71]

Later in the play, however, it is Lady Macbeth who walks about her castle at night "brainsickly," and unable to wash her hands of "this filthy witness":

> Enter LADY [MACBETH] with a taper.
> Lo you here she comes! This is her very guise, and,
> upon my life, fast asleep! Observe her; stand close . . . .

DOCTOR
You see, her eyes are open.
GENTLEWOMAN
It is an accustom action with her,
To seem thus washing her hands: I have known her
Continue in this a quarter of an hour.
LADY MACBETH
Yet here's a spot.
DOCTOR
Hark! She speaks. I will set down what
Comes from her, to satisfy my remembrance the more
Strongly.
LADY MACBETH
. . . Out, damned spot! Out, I say!
LADY MACBETH
Here's the smell of the blood still,
All the perfumes of Arabia will not sweeten this little
Hand. Oh, oh, oh![72]

All who have done evil and stained their hands with a "damned spot" know how hard it is to be rid of "this filthy witness," conscience. Even without Christian revelation or the benefit of God's grace, one can still hear the voice of God in their thoughts, in the intuitive grasp of the natural law "writ upon the fleshy tablet of their hearts."[73] Scripture describes conscience as the "heart" of a person. The heart is a place of encounter with God.[74] King David, like Macbeth, also sinned by cutting the multi-ply cord of relationship and obligation. He killed one of his own loyal soldiers, Uriah the Hittite, so that he could marry Uriah's wife, Bathsheba, after he had committed adultery with her.[75] But unlike Macbeth, David repented of his sins and prayed for a conscience that would no longer reprove him: "A clean heart create for me oh, God, and a steadfast spirit renew within me."[76] It is from one's heart that one learns how to act and how to govern others. King Solomon prayed for such wisdom: "Give your servant, therefore, an understanding heart to judge your people and to distinguish right from wrong."[77]

In the New Testament, Jesus spoke of the heart as the place of inner deliberation and decision: "Wicked designs come from the deep recesses of the heart; acts of fornication, theft, murder..."[78] He warned us to be prudent about the goals we pursue in life and be sure that they are oriented toward eternal life: "Wherever your treasure lies, there your heart will be."[79] Many people followed Jesus for the wrong reason and he rebuked them: "how accurately Isaiah prophesied about you hypocrites when he wrote, 'This people pay me lip service but their hearts are far from me.'"[80] Judas was so set against Jesus and his mission that as he left the Last Supper, "Satan entered his heart."[81] In his agony in the garden, Jesus experienced the emotions of fear and distress and cried out: "My heart is filled with sorrow to the point of death."[82] However, even though Mary's heart was pierced with a sword[83] her faith did not waver as she watched her dying son. Rather, she treasured her son's passion as she did his nativity and "reflected on them in her heart."[84]

Although we associate our hearts with our feelings, conscience is not essential-ly a feeling even though it may provoke strong emotions. Conscience is not a sepa-rate faculty of the human soul. Rather, conscience is a judgment of the faculty of reason. It is a judgment of the practical reason perfected by the virtue of prudence which assesses past acts and tells us what to do or to avoid.[85] It "is a judgment of reason whereby the human person recognizes the moral quality of a concrete act that he is going to perform, is in the process of performing, or has already com-pleted."[86]

Conscience has three functions, assumes three different roles and speaks with three voices: as a Judge who prohibits or commands; as a Counselor who counsels; and as a Witness who permits future acts, and praises or blames past acts. Moreo-ver, a man's conscience speaks to him with an authority greater than the man him-self. How is that? St. Paul warns us that we have an interior witness to God's law residing within—conscience accuses or excuses us in an interior dialog with our very "self" and with God. Therefore, St. Bonaventure calls conscience God's he-rald:

> According to St. Paul, conscience in a certain sense confronts man with the law, and thus becomes a "witness" for man; a witness of his own faithfulness or un-faithfulness with regard to the law, of his essential moral rectitude or iniquity. . . . The importance of this interior dialog of man with himself can never be adequately appreciated. But it is also a dialog of man with God, the author of the law, the primordial image and end of Man. St. Bonaventure teaches that "conscience is like God's herald and messenger; it does not command things on its own authority, but commands them as coming from God's authority, like a herald when he proclaims the edict of the king. This is why conscience has binding force."[87]

The objective norm of morality is the Eternal Law. The Eternal Law is God's plan, his providence, his unchanging eternal ideas for the governance of the universe and the behavior of angels and man.[88] With respect to the objective norm of moral be-havior, the Eternal law, man's conscience may be true or false, that is, in conformity or at variance with it. A person with a false conscience holds an opinion contrary to God's idea for human behavior, i.e. the Eternal Law. He may or may not be guilty of sin depending on whether or not he is invincibly ignorant. Was he diligent? Did he take reasonable steps to know the truth? If so, being invincibly ignorant, he would not be guilty of sin even though he performed an objectively evil act.

The proximate norm of morality is conscience. A person "must always obey the certain judgment of conscience. If he were deliberately to act against it, he would condemn himself."[89] An invincibly ignorant false conscience still binds or obliges one to follow it. To act contrary to it would be sinful. St. Thomas says that, "abso-lutely speaking, every will at variance with reason [conscience], whether right or erring, is always evil."[90] One "must always obey the certain judgments of his con-science. If one were to act against it, he would condemn himself. Yet it can happen that moral conscience remains in ignorance and makes erroneous judgments about acts to be performed or already committed."[91]

If a person were to deliberately will his own ignorance or was negligent in seeking knowledge of what he could and should have known, then he would be guilty of sin, and his ignorance would not excuse him:

> If then reason or conscience err with an error that is voluntary, either directly, or through negligence, so that one errs about what one ought to know; then such an error of reason or conscience does not excuse the will, that abides by that erring reason or conscience, from being evil.[92]

> As the Council puts it, "not infrequently conscience can be mistaken as a result of invincible ignorance, although it does not on that account forfeit its dignity; but this cannot be said when a man shows little concern for seeking what is true and good, and conscience gradually becomes almost blind from being accustomed to sin." In these brief words the Council sums up the doctrine which the Church down the centuries has developed with regard to the erroneous conscience.[93]

God's providence, his Eternal Law, directs all creation to its end. The physical elements, plants and animals behave with purpose and design, not because they possess innate intelligence but, like an arrow, because of the intelligence of the Archer who designed them, sighted them, and sent them flying toward their mark.[94]

On the other hand, angels and human beings are self-directed in their course of action. Like a pilot we must direct our life to its final destiny. To fly to our mark, perfect happiness with God, we must follow the map and signals provided by an informed conscience. In this way man is his own "parent" who is called to give birth to himself through his moral acts:

> It is precisely through his acts that man attains perfection as man, as one who is called to seek his Creator of his own accord and freely to arrive at full and blessed perfection and cleave to him. Human acts are moral acts because they . . . do not produce a change merely in the state of affairs outside of man but, to the extent that they are deliberate choices, they give moral definition to the very person who performs then, determining his *profound spiritual traits*. This was perceptively noted by Saint Gregory of Nyssa . . . "Now, human life is always subject to change; it needs to be born ever anew . . . but here birth does not come about by a foreign intervention, as is the case with bodily beings . . . ; it is the result of a free choice. Thus *we are* in a certain way our own parents, creating ourselves as we will, by our decisions."[95]

Even though an invincibly ignorant erroneous conscience excuses a person from sin, one suffers harm all the same. Therefore, in charity, we have a relative moral obligation to correct the erring as well as to rebuke the sinner.[96] Today, many Catholic couples use contraceptives after having been advised by a priest that it is up to them as a couple to decide if using contraception, under their circumstances, was good or bad. Often, the couple had consulted another expert and was given the same bad advice. Ignorant or not, contracepted conjugal relations wound spousal relationships. Contracepted conjugal acts cannot unite a couple; rather, they drive them apart because they are essentially an act of withholding; an act of self gratification, not self gift. Increased use of contraception has led to a rise in divorce rate in the United States.[97]

One has a lifelong duty to inform their conscience and conform it to the objective norm of moral behavior, the Eternal Law, if one wishes to enjoy true freedom and possess peace of heart: "The education of conscience is a lifelong task . . . [it] guarantees freedom and engenders peace of heart."[98]

An Absolute Conscience

It was the imprint of the Eternal law in her reason, the natural law and its basic inclinations, that Lady Macbeth tried to "unmake." Some people in their pursuit of ephemeral goods, power or pleasure, not only violate the natural law, but try to break and unmake this indelible imprint and teach others to do the same. Macbeth broke the natural law when he murdered his cousin, the king but he never really believed that he had done right; he knew he had committed murder in order to satisfy his ambition and become king. His wife, on the other hand, refused to admit that she was a murderess. Instead she went mad trying to unmake her nature and justify her vicious deed:

> It is quite human for a sinner to acknowledge his weakness and to ask mercy for his failings; what is unacceptable is the attitude of one who makes his own weakness the criterion of the truth about the good, so that he can feel self-justified, even without the need to have recourse to God and his mercy. An attitude of this sort corrupts the morality of society as a whole, since it encourages doubt about the objectivity of the moral law in general and a rejection of the absoluteness of moral prohibitions regarding specific human acts, and it ends up by confusing all judgments about values.[99]

Because we are creatures, we receive our human nature as a given that we must honor and understand, and not as some natural resource that we can manipulate according to our unfettered desires. We are incapable of re-creating ourselves in the sense of giving birth to a new human nature, one that no longer recognizes the principle of obedience and moral balance placed in our minds by the Eternal law. We are incapable of re-programming our conscience, the moral hard drive of human nature, if you will, and overwriting what is "foul" and making it "fair." Pope John Paul II taught conscience in this sense is not absolute:

> Certain currents of modern thought have gone so far as to exalt freedom to such an extent that it becomes an absolute, which would then be the source of values. The individual conscience is accorded the status of a supreme tribunal of moral judgment which hands down categorical and infallible decisions about good and evil.

. . . As is immediately evident, the crisis of truth is not unconnected with this development. Once the idea of a universal truth about good, knowledgeable by human reason, is lost, inevitably the notion of conscience also changes. . . . [T]here is a tendency to grant to the individual conscience the prerogative of independently determining the criteria of good and evil and then acting accordingly. . . . Taken to its extreme consequences, this individualism leads to a denial of the very idea of human nature.[100]

In the moral life one can conform their thoughts and desires to objective moral truth, or attempt to conform moral truth to one's desires. Christ contrasted these two attitudes in the parable describing the self-satisfied and self-justifying prayers of the Pharisee and the humble prayer and repentant conscience of the tax collector. Pope John Paul II warned that our age is becoming Pharisaical:

The Pharisee, on the other hand, is self-justified, finding some excuse for each of his failings. Here we encounter two different attitudes of the moral conscience of man in every age. The tax collector represents a "repentant" conscience, fully aware of the frailty of its own nature and seeing in its own failings, whatever their subjective justifications, a confirmation of its need for redemption. The Pharisee represents a 'self-satisfied' conscience, under the illusion that it is able to observe the law without the help to grace and convinced that it does not need mercy.[101]

All people must take great care not to allow themselves to be tainted by the attitude of the Pharisee, which would seek to eliminate awareness of one's own limits and of one's own sin. In our day this attitude is expressed particularly in the attempt to adapt the moral norm to one's own capacities and personal interests, and even in the rejection of the very idea of a norm.[102]

Human nature and the natural moral law cannot be changed or redefined by one's absolute conscience nor can it be amended by the Church,[103] much less by theologians,[104] nor by the behavioral sciences,[105] cultural factors,[106] or by the democratic process.[107] Jesus Christ "whose image is reflected in the nature and dignity of the human person" is the Truth and objective norm of conscience.[108]

Notes

1. Servais-Théodore Pinckaers "An Encyclical for the Future: Veritatis Splendor," eds. J. A. DiNoia and Romanus Cessario, *Veritatis Splendor and the Renewal of Moral Theology* (Princeton: Scepter Pub., 1999), 38; commenting on VS, no. 34.

2. VS, no. 72.

3. VS, no. 86.

4. VS, no. 7.

5. ST I-II, q. 94, a. 2; cited in VS, no. 51.

6. Alasdair MacIntyre, "How Can We Learn What *Veritatis Splendor* Has to Teach?" *Veritatis Splendor and the Renewal of Moral Theology* (Princeton: Scepter Pub., 1999), 83.

7. VS, no. 64.

8. ST I-II, q. 93, a. 1–2; VS, no. 43.

9. ST I-II, q. 19, a. 5; VS, no. 60.

10. Gen. 3:5.

11. Gal. 5:1; VS, no. 86.

12. VS, no. 86.

13. VS, no. 87.

14. EV, no. 19.

15. E. Michael Jones, *Degenerate Moderns: Modernity As Rationalized Sexual Misbehavior* (San Francisco: Ignatius Press, 1993), 150; citing Françoise Gilot, *Life with Picasso* (New York, NY: McGraw-Hill, 1964), 270.

16. Jones, *Degenerate Moderns*, 142–43.

17. LF, no. 20.

18. GS, no. 22.

19. VS, no. 83; citing James 1:25.

20. VS, no. 87.

21. GS, no. 24.

22. VS, no. 87; quoting Matt. 20:28.

23. ST I-II, q. 90, a. 4; CCC, no. 1951.

24. CCC, no. 460.

25. CCC, no. 1963; Rom. 7:12, 14, 16; Gal. 3:24.

26. See Charles Rice, *50 Questions on the Natural Law*, rev. ed. (San Francisco: Ignatius Press, 1999), 90–93.

27. Rom. 2:15.

28. ST I-II q. 96, a. 4.

29. CCC, citing Pius XII, *Humani Generis*: DS 3876, *Dei Filius* 2: DS 3005.

30. Robert H. Bork, "Neutral Principles and Some First Amendment Problems," *Indiana Law Journal* 47, no. 1 (fall 1971): 30.

31. HV, no. 4.

32. Robert Araujo and John Lucal, *Papal Diplomacy and the Quest for Peace*, 3–4 n.6, quoting John K. Cartwright, "Contributions of the Papacy to International Peace," *Catholic Historic Review* 8 (1928): 157, 159; quoting Gilot, *Life with Picasso*, 270 (emphasis in original).

33. ST I-II, q. 93, a. 3.

34. CCC, no. 1950–51; VS, no. 43.

35. CCC, no. 1951.

36. CCC, no. 1952; Rom. 10:4.

37. CCC, no. 1955; VS, no. 40.

38. VS, no. 51, citing St. Augustine, *De Trinitate*, XIV, 15, 21, CCL 50/A, 451.

39. VS, no. 44, citing *Libertas Praestantissimum* (20 June 1888): Leonis XIII P.M. acta, VIII, Romae 1889, 219.

40. ST I-II, q. 90, a. 4, rep. obj. 190, a. 4, rep. obj.1.

41. VS, no. 43.

42. CCC, no. 1956.

43. CCC, no. 1957.

44. CCC, no. 1957; ST I-II, q. 94.

45. Rom. 2:15.

46. CCC, no. 1958.

47. Peter Bristow, *The Moral Dignity of Man* (Dublin: Four Courts Press, 1997), 189.

48. VS, no.40; citing Gen. 2:16.

49. CCC, no. 1776; quoting GS, no. 6.

50. VS, no. 60.

51. ST I, q. 79, aa. 12–13, ST I-II, q. 57, aa. 4–6.

52. Paul J. Glenn, *Tour of the Summa* (Rockford, IL: Tan Books, 1998), 66–67. See also ST I, q. 79, a. 12

53. ST I-II, q. 94, a. 1–2.

54. VS, no. 51; quoting ST I-II, q. 94, a. 2.

55. CCC, no. 1955.

56. CCC, no. 1960.

57. ST I-II, q. 103, a. 3.

58. VS, no. 45.

59. CCC, no. 1966, CCC, no. 1983, ST I-II, q. 106, aa. 1–2.

60. Rom. 13:12.

61. DH, no. 12; citing Acts 5:29.

62. John 19:11, Rom. 13:1.

63. ST I-II, q. 96, a. 4.

64. Rice, *50 Questions*, 83–90.

65. EV, no. 4, 11, 68. Democracy is a form of government that seeks to secure justice for all. However, majority rule and judicial review, procedural mechanisms intended to preserve justice for all, can be abused so as to deny fundamental justice (life, liberty, or property) to a class of human beings in civil society (such as pre-natal children). When this happens the democratic ideal of justice for all is betrayed by the very mechanism meant to secure it.

66. ST I-II, q. 96, a. 3.

67. Rice, *50 Questions,* 83–90.

68. Isa. 5:20; VS, no. 93.

69. *Macbeth*, 1.4.40-46 in *The Complete Signet Classic Shakespeare*, ed. Sylvan Barnet (New York, NY: Harcourt Brace Jovanovich, 1972), 1237.

70. *Macbeth*, 2.2.33–34.

71. *Macbeth*, 2.2.45–46.

72. *Macbeth*, 5.3.21–54.

73. Rom. 2:15.

74. 1 John 3:18–20.

75. 2 Sam. 11:12.

76. Ps. 51:12.

77. 1 Kings 3:9.

78. Mark 7:21.

79. Luke 12:34.

80. Mark 7:6.

81. John 14:27.

82. Mark 14:34.

83. Luke 2:35.

84. Luke 2:19; Luke 10:27; Matt. 22:37; Mark 12:30; Heb. 4:12; Heb. 8:10.

85. VS, no. 59; VS, no. 40; ST I-II, q. 57, a. 4; ST II-II, q. 47, aa. 1–4.

86. CCC, no. 1778.

87. VS, no. 57–58.

88. ST I-II, q. 93, a. 1; VS, no. 43.

89. CCC, no. 1790.

90. ST I-II, q. 19, a. 5.

91. CCC, no. 1790.

92. ST I-II, q. 19, a. 6.

93. VS, no. 62; quoting GS, no. 16; CCC, no. 1791.

94. ST I, q. 2, a. 3.

95. VS, no. 71; citing Gregory of Nyssa, *De Vita Moysis*, II, 2–3:
PG, 44, 327–28.

96. CCC, nos. 2447, 1829.

97. See Mercedes Wilson, *Love and Family: Raising a Traditional Family in a Secular World*, (Ignatius Press, 1996), 260–62; citing Janet E. Smith, *Humanae Vitae: A Generation Later*, (Washington, DC: Catholic Univ. Press, 1991), 127; citing Robert T. Michael, "Why Did the U.S. Divorce Rate Double within a Decade?" Research in Population 6 (Greenwich, CT: JAI Press, 1988), 361–99.

98. CCC, no. 1784. See also CCC, nos. 1783, 1793.

99. VS, no. 104.

100. VS, no. 32.

101. VS, no. 104; referring to Luke 18:9–14. See also Jones, *Degenerate Moderns*,
11.

102. VS, no. 105

103. VS, no. 95.

104. VS, no. 116.

105. VS, no. 112.

106. VS, no. 55.

107. VS, no. 113.

108. VS, no. 95.

Chapter 3
The Three Moral Determinants and Doubts of Conscience

The Three Sources of Morality

How does one live well? Jesus told the rich young man, who asked what he must do to inherit eternal life, to imitate God, who alone is good: "Only the act in conformity with the good can be a path that leads to life."[1] We have free will but we are obligated to behave reasonably,[2] that is, in line with truth: "The rational ordering of the human act to the good in its truth and the voluntary pursuit of that good, known by reason, constitutes morality."[3]

In the concrete particular situations that confront us daily, how do we make reasonable choices? What principles guide a person in his or her deliberations, decisions and deeds? There are three moral determinants (also known as the three sources of morality) that affect the moral quality of every human act and render each human act either good or evil: the object chosen (the moral deed); the end in view or the intention (the motive); and the circumstances of the action (how, when, where, and who performs the moral deed including the foreseeable consequences of the deed).[4]

The very idea of inalienable human rights depends upon a correct understanding of the three moral determinants. Properly understood, the sources of morality establish the existence of moral absolutes inherent in human nature which prohibit certain actions (moral deeds) always and without exception. If we say there are no absolute moral norms, no intrinsically evil acts governing private morality, then there can be no inalienable human rights which govern political life. If we have no inalienable human rights which the state must recognize, then democracy is betrayed, and we have no intellectual defense against state sponsored terrorism or totalitarianism. If we say that "anything goes" in terms of our personal morality, then how can we object when a terrorist or a dictator says that anything goes? If the end justifies the means with regard to sexual morality, the same relativistic logic governs political affairs.[5]

It's as simple as that: "Just as individuals forfeit their own freedom when they try to liberate themselves from moral norms, so society surrenders its freedom if it fails to respect the personal dignity of its members." [6]

The Moral Object

The moral object, the deed itself, is the primary moral determinant. "The morality of the human act depends primarily and fundamentally on the 'object' rationally chosen by the deliberate will."[7] As a knowing subject, when I act deliberately, I evaluate what I am about to do before doing it. Even natural bodily actions, mere acts of man, take on a moral quality when attended to with a deliberate will. For example, I may kick or jerk in my sleep unconsciously. This is a mere unintentional act of man. On the other hand, if I am playing soccer, when I kick the ball, I intend to kick the ball in such manner that my teammates or I score a goal. This act of kicking a ball with skill in a soccer game in order to make a goal is a deliberate act rationally chosen. To the extent that playing soccer well is ordered to building up the basic human good of "cultivating social life," it is a good moral object: "The rational ordering of the human act to the good in its truth and the voluntary pursuit of that good, known by reason, constitutes morality." [8] The moral object I chose was a well-placed kick, one "rationally chosen by a deliberate will," ordered to one of the basic duties of human nature:

> The object chosen is a good toward which the will deliberately directs itself. It is the matter of a human act. The object chosen morally specifies the act of the will, insofar as reason recognizes and judges it to be or not to be in conformity with the true good. [9]

One might object and say that kicking a ball well is hardly a moral action, that the whole action is merely a physical act, not a moral act. But anyone who has ever attended a soccer game knows better. If a soccer player "rationally chose with a deliberate will" to not take good shots when opportunity presented itself, the fans would "boo" his or her bad performance. Similarly, if a boxer failed to throw hard punches in a prize fight and just stood there, allowing himself to be pummeled, the fans would understand that his action of throwing a few weak punches amounted to the moral object of deliberately "throwing" the fight (losing intentionally):

> The [moral] object is not merely the act considered in its physical make-up. It is the act viewed in its moral nature; i.e., the act considered in its relationship to the moral law. Of it the question is asked: Does it conform, or is it contrary to the standard of right conduct? In theft, for example, the physical act of taking money from another is not the [moral] object. The object is the unjust taking of property belonging to another. It is the taking of another's money considered in the light of the moral law. [10]

It is important to note that a human act, a choice of the will, to strive towards a moral object, may remain completely interior. It is nonetheless a completed human act that perfects or corrupts the human will as when one commits adultery in their heart: "You have heard the commandment, 'You shall not commit adultery.' What I say to you is: anyone who looks lustfully at a woman has already committed adultery with her in his thoughts."[11]

> Wicked designs come from the deep recesses of the heart: acts of fornication, theft, murder, adulterous conduct, greed, maliciousness, deceit, sensuality, envy, blasphemy, arrogance, an obtuse spirit. All these evils come from within and render a man impure.[12]

There are three categories of moral objects: intrinsically good, intrinsically evil, or hypothetically neutral/indifferent: objective or intrinsically good acts, such as alms-giving;[13] objective or intrinsically evil acts, such as lying, calumny, theft;[14] and indifferent or morally neutral acts such as talking, reading and walking. However, hypothetically neutral acts are always morally specified either good or evil when acted out by one's motive and circumstances.[15] There is also a distinction between an "act of man" or an unintentional act, as when a person blinks, and a "human act," that is, one done with intelligence and free will, as when a person winks.[16] All human acts involve an intelligent choice of some good, some object. Often a person chooses certain goods as steps to achieving some further end. Although this further end may be the last thing to be accomplished in the order of execution, it comes first in the order of intention.[17] As we shall see when considering the principle of double effect below, one may never do what is intrinsically evil that good come of it, although one may do what is morally neutral even when one foresees bad effects may accompany the good one does.

The Motive

Why a soccer player deliberately refused to kick the ball into the goal or *why* the prize fighter deliberately threw the fight (because they were bribed or lost heart after being jilted by their fiancée), concerns another essential component of every human act, that is, the motive also known as the end, goal or intention of the agent.

> In contrast to the object, the intention resides in the acting subject. . . . The intention is a movement of the will toward the end: it is concerned with the goal of the activity. It aims at the good anticipated from the action undertaken.[18]

A person is first moved to act by some motive or end. It may be to satisfy an emotional tug or pull, a desire or fear. It could also be a goal suggested by reason, such as the proposition that a good way to get ahead in the world is to get a liberal arts college education. Other people may be motivated to go to college not so much to get ahead as for the love of learning a subject that they have never had time to study before, as when a retired physician goes back to college to study history or theology. So the same act (in this case, going to college) may be informed by several different motives or intentions.[19] But this final end, although it came first as the motivation that got one going, will be the last thing to be achieved.[20] Before a college degree can be obtained, each course must be passed, which is achieved by completing assignments within each course. So one's primary objective can inform and guide many other actions as the means to a further end:

> The end is the first goal of the intention and indicates the purpose pursued in the action. . . . Intention is not limited to directing individual actions, but can guide several actions toward one and the same purpose; it can orient one's whole life toward its ultimate end. One and the same action can also be inspired by several intentions, such as performing a service in order to obtain a favor or to boast about it.[21]

One way to complete course assignments is to put time in, study hard, and achieve good grades on the tests and papers. Another method is to goof off, waste time, party all night, and then cheat on the tests and turn in plagiarized papers. Both the student who studies hard and the plagiarizer could have the same motive and ultimate end or intention, that of getting ahead in the world. But the moral objects they chose as the means or proximate ends to their ulterior/remote goal are quite different:

> The "object" is the "proximate" or "immediate" end of an act of willing because it is what one chooses to do here and now. There is also a further or ulterior end of most human actions, the end for whose sake one chooses to do this here and now.[22]

> The object of a human act is that which the one acting sets out to do, as distinguished from his ultimate purpose in doing it; it is that which the action of its very nature tends to produce. For example, the object of a suicide's act is the blowing out of his brains; his purpose is to escape evils which he is unwilling to bear.[23]

The moral object may be referred to as the *finis operis* (the end of the object) and the motive of the agent as the *finis operantis* (the end of the subject). For instance, a clock maker uses material, plastic and metal (its material cause) to build an instrument to tell time (its formal cause). This would be the *finis operis* or built in intentionality of a clock. Why he does so (the *finis operantis*) may be to wake himself or others from sleep or it may be he wishes to use this clock as a paper weight and so he does not wind it up (final cause).

By analogy, all human acts especially the human acts expressed in a person's body, are governed by these twin intentionalities, one built-in, the other either in conformity with the built-in intentionality or foisted on it. Hence, carnal intercourse is specified morally by whether it can express the basic duties of human persons who act in this way, i.e., its total self-giving expressed in openness to life and the inner communion of spouses. These basic duties and goods can only be realized if a man and woman are exclusively committed to each other for life in marriage and behave lovingly towards each other as subjects not objects in their conjugal act.[24]

The intentions of fornicators might be good but their withholding of a final and complete commitment to each other falsifies the built-in, incarnate, moral meaning of this human act meant to express total commitment. The *final* intention of a temporary liaison is incompatible with the *formal* intention of total union built into the moral object of sexual intercourse which can only be actualized through a permanent union of man and woman in marriage open to the possibility of new life:

> Hence the matter of an act may be such that it is not congenial to the form of an agent's purpose, just as clubbing with a baseball bat is not congenial to the form of the purpose of expressing friendly comradery. The *finis operantis* receives this matter from the *finis operis*, and is limited thereby. Likewise, moral theology is not moral alchemy, and human intention cannot make inherently distelic acts to be naturally perfective.[25]

The Circumstances

The situations or settings of human acts make each one absolutely unique and unrepeatable. For instance, never again will this person ever say or do this thing at this precise moment in history: "For each specific action, circumstances serve as the individuating principle that account for its concrete singularity." [26] If the moral object addresses the question "what" and the intention or motive explains the reason "why," the circumstances fill out the rest of the questions, that is, the "who" (status), "when" (time), "where" (place), "how" (manner) and the consequences (effects):

> For a circumstance is described as something outside the substance of the act, and yet in a way touching it. Now this happens in three ways: first, inasmuch as it touches the act itself; secondly, inasmuch as it touches the cause of the act; thirdly, inasmuch as it touches the effect.[27]

Those circumstances which touch the act itself affect the moral object directly and are amalgamated into the object modifying or changing the human act itself. For example, the place an act is committed can change the moral object of theft into an act of sacrilege, as when a thief without permission removes property from a church.[28] Also, the status of the persons may change the moral complexion of an act. For example, performing an act of intercourse determines whether it is a morally good deed or a sinful act of fornication depending on whether the man and woman are married to each other or not. "A circumstance is sometimes taken as the essential difference of the object as compared to reason; and then it can specify a moral act. And it must need be so whenever a circumstance transforms an action from good to evil."[29]

Generally however, circumstances, as accidental moral qualifiers, do not make an act good or evil in itself independently of the will of the actor striving towards a moral object:

[T]here are no pure types of actions which enjoy full existence outside of an agent who performs them. Concretely, then, human action means individual action. Though each human act transpires only within a given set of historical conditions, these contingencies, no matter how pressing or dramatic they may be, never adequately reveal the full moral meaning of action. Instead, they modify the shape of an action in a way which is analogous to how accidental modifications vary the substantial being of a nature.[30]

Circumstances that do not condition the moral object do not determine the *kind* but only the *degree* or *intensity* of concrete human acts. The setting or circumstances in which one performs a human act, choosing a moral object with a particular motive, will either lessen or enhance one's good or evil deed. It should be mentioned that motive is really a kind of circumstance.[31] But because it inevitably conditions the moral object, it is given special consideration as described above.

Rules for Applying the Three Moral Determinants

The fundamental rule applying the three moral determinants to moral dilemmas can be illustrated by the story of the little old lady who invited her pastor over for his favorite dessert, chocolate brownies. To bake her brownies, she used only the finest imported chocolate, fresh chopped nuts, whole goat milk, pure cane sugar, and a handful of cat manure. When her pastor visited her, she served him the brownies. He gagged on the brownies and demanded an explanation. She recited her list of ingredients, saying her brownies were just like his homilies: "99 percent good with just a handful of heresy thrown in."

The fundamental rule of the three moral determinants is this: if a human act isn't *all* good in its moral object, motive and circumstance, it's simply no good. The morality of the human act, like a chain, is as weak as its weakest link. St. Thomas explained that "evil results from each particular defect, but good from the whole and entire cause."[32]

A car just returned from a mechanic, with a few loose nuts rolling around in it and rattling all the time, may run alright but is miserable to drive. A medical operation in which a surgeon leaves a glove inside his patient's abdomen is considered malpractice, even if no other harm is done. And who would be pleased if, when going out to eat at an expensive restaurant, their favorite dish is served to them cold by a curt waiter? In all these examples, people got *almost* what they expected. But in each case they got less than they deserved because of a "particular defect" in the moral object, motive, or circumstance:

A *morally good* act requires the goodness of the object, of the end, and of the circumstances together. An evil end corrupts the action, even if the object is good in itself. . . . *The object of the choice* can by itself vitiate an act in its entirety. . . . The *circumstances* . . . contribute to increasing or diminishing the moral goodness or evil of human acts.[33]

The following moral principles help us to evaluate which human actions conform to our true good.

First Principle

Intrinsically evil moral objects (acts) never become good acts even if they are done with a good motive and/or under good circumstances, including the likelihood of good consequences, effects or outcome: "Consequently, circumstances or intentions can never transform an act intrinsically evil by virtue of its object into an act 'subjectively' good or defensible as a choice."[34] One may never do evil that good may come of it.[35] In other words, the end does not justify the means. Good motives and hoped-for good consequences do not justify committing intrinsically evil intermediary steps to reach this hoped-for goal.

> A good intention (for example, that of helping one's neighbor) does not make behavior that is intrinsically disordered, such as lying and calumny, good or just. The end does not justify the means. Thus the condemnation of an innocent person cannot be justified as a legitimate means of saving the nation.[36]

> In teaching the existence of intrinsically evil acts, the Church accepts the teaching of Sacred Scripture. The Apostle Paul emphatically states: "Do not be deceived: neither the immoral, nor idolaters, nor sexual perverts, not thieves, not the greedy, nor drunkards, nor revilers, nor robbers will inherit the kingdom of God."[37]

> Reason attests that there are objects of the human act which are by their nature "incapable of being ordered" to God because they radically contradict the good of the person made in his image. These are the acts which, in the Church's moral tradition, have been termed "intrinsically evil" (*intrinsece malum*); they are such always and *per se*, in other words, on account of their very object, and quite apart from the ulterior intentions or the one acting and the circumstances . . . . The Second Vatican Council itself . . . gives a number of examples of such acts: "Whatever is hostile to life itself, such as any kind of homicide, genocide, abortion, euthanasia and voluntary suicide. . . . Intrinsically evil acts [also include] contraceptive practices whereby the conjugal act is intentionally rendered infertile."[38]

This is the most disputed principle in ethics today—that there are intrinsically evil acts. The legal justification of abortion, embryo destructive research and assisted suicide all attempt to finesse doing evil that good come of it by arguing there is either no evil in disposing of or experimenting on a blob of tissue (not a human being) or that sometimes you just "have to do, what you have to do" and you are justified in doing evil that good come of it because there are no intrinsically evil actions.

Second Principle

Intrinsically evil acts may become less evil or worse, or of a different kind through motive or circumstance. Circumstances change either the *degree* of evil, as by aggravating or diminishing it, or change the *kind* of evil, as by altering its species or essential character.[39] Intrinsically evil acts may be less evil or more evil due to motive and circumstance, but can never become good because of circumstance. If a crime is committed by a sane person, a verdict of guilty is rendered regardless of his personal motive or the surrounding circumstance. However, the punishment may well vary according to that particular criminal's motive and circumstances. Stealing from a holy place changes the species of the moral object from theft into a sacrilege.[40] However, whether one is stealing a "large or small quantity" does not change the *kind* of the sin. Nevertheless it can aggravate or diminish the *degree* of sin, changing it from a mortal sin to a venial sin, petty theft to grand theft, or vice versa.[41]

Third Principle

Intrinsically good moral objects may become better through motive or circumstance in degree or kind. A good moral object chosen with the best of intention under adverse circumstances is made even better: "If anyone suffers for being a Christian, however, he ought not to be ashamed. He should rather glorify God in virtue of that name."[42] But intense charity of the will often times does not have the physical means to express itself in exterior acts, as in the case of the widow's mite: "I want you to observe that this poor widow contributed more than all the others who donated to the treasury. They gave from their surplus, but she gave from her want, all that she had to live on."[43] The intensity of the will in doing good or in doing evil determines the degree of virtue in the act.[44]

Fourth Principle

Intrinsically good moral objects may become completely evil or less good through a bad motive, and less good if performed under bad circumstances. To give a kiss as a moral object is an objective sign of friendship, an intrinsic sign of a gift of self and affection. It can, however, be turned into an evil moral object by an evil motive that conditions the significance of the embrace: "The betrayer had arranged a signal for them saying, 'the man I shall embrace is the one; arrest him and lead him away, taking every precaution.'"[45] Jesus did not let his betrayer go unchallenged: "Judas, would you betray the Son of Man with a kiss?"[46]

> The act of the will cannot be said to be good, if an evil intention is the cause of the willing. For when a man wills to give alms for the sake of vainglory, he wills that which is good in itself, under the species of evil; and therefore, as willed by him, it is evil. Wherefore his will is evil.[47]

As we know, the path to hell is paved with good intentions. "[T]he quantity of goodness in the interior or exterior act does not depend on the quantity of the good intended. . . . And hence it is that a man does not merit as much as he intends to merit: because the quantity of merit is measured by the intensity of the act.[48] For instance, St. Peter's good intention to die rather than betray Christ did not make him a saint when, in a few hours time he denied Christ three times.[49] Rather it was his set purpose and witness to Christ many years later in Rome when he was crucified upside down that proved the goodness and intensity of his will. Likewise the good intention of getting up on time when the alarm goes off is often undone when one rolls over and shuts it off to fall back to sleep.

It seems ironic at first glance, but we are as evil as we intend, but not necessarily as good as we intend. Judas was as evil as his interior intention when he cooperated in the betrayal of Christ with an outward sign of affection. St. Peter, on the other hand, was not as good as he intended when he boastfully claimed he would die for Christ only to flee and abandon Christ in the garden and then later lie that he even knew the man.

Fifth Principle

Circumstances make hypothetical indifferent acts (neutral moral objects in the abstract) good or evil in real life. Every human act is either good or bad, if not intrinsically, then through motive or the other circumstances. In the abstract, talking is neither intrinsically evil nor intrinsically good. However, Christ taught that in daily life, talking is not a neutral deed: "I assure you, on judgment day people will be held accountable for every idle word they speak."[50]

> [St.] Gregory says in a homily: "An idle word is one that lacks either the usefulness of rectitude or the motive of just necessity or pious utility.". . . Therefore every word is either good or bad. For the same reason every other action is either good or bad. Therefore no individual action is indifferent.
>
> *I answer that*, It sometimes happens that an action is indifferent in its species, but considered in the individual it is good or evil. . . . And every individual action must needs have some circumstance that makes it good or bad, at least in respect of the intention of the end.[51]

In the same way no conscious and competent person has ever engaged in an act of intercourse as a neutral act. Rather, they have either performed a virtuous act of conjugal love or a sinful act of fornication or adultery. Besides the above mentioned rules applying the three moral determinants to the concrete decisions of daily life, there are other moral principles that provide the light to choose.

Positive and Negative Moral Precepts

The negative precepts of the moral law, those that are intrinsically evil, bind in conscience all the time, that is, one may never consciously and directly choose to violate them under any circumstance. However, acts which are objectively and intrinsically good in themselves do not bind in conscience under all circumstances. Why is that? Just as an objectively good act must be chosen with a good motive and under favorable circumstances to be a truly good human act, so under less favorable circumstances, an objectively good act may be omitted in order to prevent greater harm.

The scripture and tradition presents us with a list of seven intrinsically good corporal and spiritual works of mercy: corporal alms include feeding the hungry, giving drink to the thirsty, clothing the naked, visiting the sick, sheltering the homeless, ransoming/visiting the captive, and burying the dead; spiritual alms include praying for others, instructing the erring, counseling the doubtful, comforting the sorrowing, reproving sinners, pardoning those who injure you, and bearing with the burdensome, as well as bearing the burdens of others.[52] But St. Thomas Aquinas points out that these acts of virtue, these intrinsically good deeds, must still conform to the estimate of prudence, i.e., be chosen as the right means to the right end, and the rule of charity, i.e., loving other as one's self, in order to be truly virtuous:

> On the other hand, *the positive precepts* are about acts of virtue to be performed, whose perfection requires due ordering of all the circumstances. An example of this can be seen in the gospel precept of fraternal correction. Positive precepts oblige *semper sed non pro simper*—always, but according to the circumstances.[53]

The love of God and neighbor as expressed in the positive precepts of the moral law is aspirational because, although all are called to be generous, generosity permits of degrees according to circumstances. On the other hand, love of God and neighbor as expressed in the negative precepts of the moral law is normative because, due to the innate dignity of each person, there is a minimum exercise of virtue below which one may not descend. Moreover, the external expression of virtue may be stymied, but no external force can move the will of a person to sin if he or she is prepared to die in defense of virtue:

> [T]he commandment of love of God and neighbor does not have in its dynamic any higher limit, but it does have a lower limit beneath which the commandment is broken. Furthermore, what must be done in any given situation depends on the circumstances, not all of which can be foreseen; on the other hand, there are kinds of behavior which can never, in any situation, be proper reasons – a response which is in conformity with the dignity of the person. Finally, it is always possible that man, as the result of coercion or other circumstances, can be hindered from doing certain good actions; but he can never be hindered from not doing certain actions, especially if he is prepared to die rather than to do evil.[54]

Impediments to Free Will

The impediments to free will are violence, fear, concupiscence, and ignorance. These conditions make human acts less voluntary or completely involuntary.[55] Violence is physical force that compels a person to permit what he does not will to do. Acts done from violence are involuntary when a person is physically overcome and is prevented from doing an act, or forced to passively suffer an act against his will.

When one is forced against their will to endure evil (as in the case of rape) so as to avoid a greater evil (death or serious bodily harm), one has no moral obligation to continue to resist and may endure the sexual assault passively. In this case, the violence is said to be *morally perfect*. On the other hand, if one resisted the sexual assault until one was unconscious through drugs or a blow to the head, the violence would be said to be *physically perfect*.[56] In both cases, one would not be culpable for sinning against purity or cooperating, formally or materially, in the sin of another (see the Principle of Cooperation below). "If one sees that any resistance would be wholly ineffective, there is no obligation to resist. The reason is that one is not obligated to do what is useless."[57]

However, if one fails to resist the violence of an evil act and cooperates when more resistance would be possible and effective, that person chooses to sin. But his culpability may be lessened by the duress/fear he experiences. Cardinal Mindszenty of Hungary resisted Communist torture heroically but was broken for a time and signed a false confession. Only God knows whether he suffered morally perfect violence in December of 1949 in the infamous secret police headquarters at 60 Andrassy Street in Budapest. But the following description would seem to indicate that he did:

> [Cardinal Mindszenty] was stripped of his cassock and dressed in a clown suit. He was beaten repeatedly, deprived of sleep, and drugged. One night he was forced to run naked about a room chased by a man with a club in one hand and a knife in the other. "I'll kill you!" the man snarled to Mindszenty. "By morning I'll tear you to pieces and throw the remains of your corpse to the dogs or into the canal. We are the master here now. . . . If you don't confess I'll have your mother brought here tomorrow morning. You'll stand naked before her. She'll probably have a stroke. Rightly so, she deserves it, since she brought you into the world. And you will be responsible for her death."[58]

Fear is an aversion to threatened future evil. Fear may be light or grave either objectively so or relatively so with respect to a particular person. If it is so grave as to deprive a person of the use of their reason that person is not subjectively culpable should he or she commit an objectively evil act. Fear which does not deprive a person of the use of reason does not excuse one from sin although it may lessen one's culpability. Grave fear could excuse one from observing a positive law (for example, Sunday observance of Mass if one believed they would be put in jail), but not from doing what is intrinsically wrong (for example, denying the faith). Fear may be grounds for an annulment of a sacramental marriage: "marriage is invalid if it is entered into due to force or grave fear inflicted from outside of the person, even when inflicted unintentionally, which is of such a type that a person is compelled to choose matrimony in order to be free from it."[59]

Concupiscence (passion) is a disorderly desire for emotional or bodily pleasure. It is not sinful but inclines one to sin:

> Etymologically, "concupiscence" can refer to any intense form of human desire. Christian theology has given it a particular meaning: the movement of the sensitive appetite contrary to the operation of the human reason. The apostle St. Paul identifies it with the rebellion of the "flesh" against the "spirit." Concupiscence stems from the disobedience of the first sin. It unsettles man's moral faculties and, without being in itself an offense, inclines man to commit sins.[60]

Any passion not directly willed that deprives one temporarily of the use of reason and free will may remove culpability for sin.[61] Habit or addiction may deprive one of the use of reason in a particular area of one's life. However, if one knowingly and freely entered into a sinful addictive practice, one is morally responsible for objectively evil acts involuntarily committed later under compulsion from the addiction unless one takes steps to break the habit. If a person does nothing to break the sinful addictive habit, such as praying and taking steps to avoid the near occasion of sin, then he is culpable for his habitual (addictive) sins.

To illustrate this moral principle, let us briefly consider the Church's teaching on sins of impurity. The Church teaches that masturbation may become compulsive, which may diminish or remove culpability but this should not be presumed:

> On the subject of masturbation . . . [p]sychology helps one to see how the immaturity of adolescence (which can sometimes persist after that age), psychological imbalance or habit can influence behavior, diminishing the deliberate character of the act and bringing about a situation whereby subjectively there may not always be serious fault. But, in general, the absence of serious responsibility must not be presumed: this would be to misunderstand people's moral capacity. . . . In particular, one will have to examine whether the individual is using the necessary means, both natural and supernatural, which Christian asceticism from its long experience recommends for overcoming the passions and progressing in virtue.[62]

Temptations to impurity are not sins if one does not consent to them with their will. One cannot simply command impure thoughts to go away with an act of the will. Rather, one must resist disordered desires until they subside: "No one can demand of himself either that he should experience no sensual reactions at all, or that they should immediately yield just because the will does not consent, or even because it declare itself definitely 'against.'"[63]

Ignorance is a lack of knowledge in a person who should possess such knowledge. One is not subjectively culpable for committing objectively evil deeds if one is invincibly ignorant of the evil nature of the act before and during its commission. Invincible ignorance occurs when one acts with due diligence to inform oneself on matters one is obligated to understand and, through no negligence of one's own, still fails to know the truth and act correctly.

On the other hand, one may be subjectively culpable of committing an objectively evil deed if one is vincibly ignorant. One is vincibly ignorant if one acts negligently in searching for truth on matters one is obligated to understand, in resolving a doubt of conscience or, worse yet, if one deliberately wills their ignorance (crass ignorance).[64]

Violence, fear, and concupiscence affect the will, whereas ignorance affects the practical intellect. The four impediments to free will make it more difficult to decide correctly and act uprightly. But to the victor, he who resists and removes these impediments, goes the crown, and he is rewarded with purity of heart:

> "Pure in heart" refers to those who have attuned their intellect and wills to the demands of God's holiness, chiefly in three areas: charity, chastity or sexual rectitude, love of truth and orthodoxy of faith. There is a connection between purity of heart, of body, and of faith.[65]

Doubts of Conscience

If someone has attempted to know the truth concerning the decision he faces, if he has consulted experts, read learned books on the subject and prayed about the matter, and because of the well-researched but bad advice, he still chooses a course of action contrary to the Eternal Law, he is not culpable of sin. As noted above, such a person is *invincibly ignorant*.[66] However, if he is negligent in seeking the truth, then his *vincible* ignorance is no excuse and he is guilty of sin if he freely chooses to do what is intrinsically evil negligently or wantonly: "This is the case when a man 'takes little trouble to find out what is true and good, or when conscience is by degrees almost blinded through the habit of committing sin.'[67] In such cases, the person is culpable for the evil he commits.[68]

If a person knows that he does not know, if his conscience is doubtful regarding the right course of action, he must resolve his doubt before acting in important matters. To do otherwise would amount to showing contempt for whether what he chose was right or wrong or whether he was sinning or not. For instance, a man would be charged with manslaughter if he took a shot gun and fired into a bush during hunting season, not knowing whether or not it was hunter or a deer. One must resolve such "positive practical doubt" before acting in serious matters. One's doubt is positive if there are solid reasons for and against doing or not doing some weighty action. It is a practical doubt if it concerns an action to be performed imminently as opposed to a hypothetical act:

> By practical doubt is meant a doubt about the moral goodness or badness of an in-

dividual action, here and now, in these particular circumstances. To act in such a doubt is tantamount to accepting evil, since one would be seeking an object, whether the object be morally good or morally evil.[69]

Positive practical doubts may occur with regard to issues of law or issues of fact. Issues of law concern whether a particular law exists or what the scope of a law is. Issues of fact address whether the act one is about to perform is the kind of act forbidden or allowed by law.[70] If a lawyer were representing a defendant in a criminal trial who deliberately shot into a bush not knowing whether it was a deer or his hunting partner concealed there, he would probably urge his client to enter into a plea bargain with the prosecutor. Otherwise, such a confession of wanton and willful disregard for human life (a depraved heart) would nearly assure his client's conviction for voluntary manslaughter.

It would seem that this basic moral wisdom of criminal law, however, is lost on the members of the United States Supreme Court. The Court confessed ignorance as to whether the child within her mother's womb was a person. They concluded, therefore, that they need not resolve this doubt before they allow a physician to kill whatever or whoever is growing in the womb:

> We need not resolve the difficult question of when life begins. When those trained in the respective disciplines of medicine, philosophy and theology are unable to arrive at any consensus, the judiciary, at this point in the development of man's knowledge, is not in a position to speculate as to the answer.[71]

Normally, when one is faced with a weighty decision and has a positive practical doubt of conscience, one may not act but must resolve the doubt through study, questioning experts, and careful reflection. However, in situations where such consultation and resolution of doubt is impossible, one is entitled to rely on certain presumptions or "reflex principles." In the law of contracts one enjoys the presumption that any ambiguity in a contract shall be resolved against the interests of the one who drafted the contract. In domestic relations law, there is a presumption that any child born during a marriage is legitimate and was begotten by his or her mother's husband. These are rebuttable presumptions, but until better evidence to the contrary is presented, they form a sound and predictable basis for resolving doubts.

A Vietnam War veteran told the story of how he followed the rules of engagement (a presumption or reflex principle) that led to his own personal tragedy. The rules of engagement for those on sentry duty were to demand a password before admitting a U.S. infantry patrol back into camp at night. If no password or the wrong password were given, the sentries were to presume it was the enemy and open fire on them. Late one night, after one of their patrols had gone out, he and the other sentries heard an exchange of small-arms fire. Shortly thereafter they could hear and dimly see a number of soldiers running toward their lines. The sentries called out for the password but none was given. They hesitated for a brief moment as the running soldiers neared their lines and then they opened fire. In fact, it was their own patrol fleeing the enemy. He shot his best friend through the eye and killed him. The man who told this tragic story was justified in relying on the rules of engagement. He committed no sin. He did not need to go to confession for the sin of murder, but he did have to go to psychological counseling later. If one commits an objectively evil act, even without moral culpability, one still bears the cost in mind and heart.[72]

Another important reflex principle is that of "probablism." One may resolve a dilemma of conscience not otherwise resolved by study or consultation or any other reflex principle in favor of liberty if there is "a solidly probable opinion" favoring doing it, even if there are more probable opinions against doing it. Usually a solidly probable opinion amounts to the learned opinion of one or many experts schooled in ethics or moral theology. However, a Catholic may follow only the opinions of those moral theologians faithful to the Magisterium of the Catholic Church, not dissenting experts that provide false solutions:

> "A solidly probable opinion". . . is had if one trained at least somewhat in moral theology can defend the opinion with good arguments (intrinsic probability) or if a number of authentic moral theologians propose the opinion as probable (intrinsic probability). By "authentic moral theologians" is meant someone skilled in moral theology and who adheres to the teachings of the Church. It should be evident that the arguments of dissident theologians, teaching contrary to the teaching authority of the Church, cannot engender *a solid probability* in favor of their dissident opinions.[73]

Diagram 3.1
The Three Moral Determinants and Principles of Moral Decision Making

I. The 3 Moral Determinants

1   Moral Object—The object chosen, the action or deed itself—committed mentally or externally with a "built-in morality;" The end, goal or purpose of the act itself, the *finis operis*; "what" a person wills to do, taking into account the moral values that define it.
2   Motive—The Agent's intention; the end, the goal or purpose of the agent, the *finis operantis;* "why" the agent wills.
3   Circumstance—The place, time, person's status, manner, consequences of an act of the will. The where, when, who, how and the results of a person's actions.

II. Classification of the Moral Deed

1   Objectively or intrinsically good acts
2   Objectively or intrinsically evil acts
3   Hypothetically indifferent or morally neutral acts

III. Further Implications—6 Principles for Analyzing Moral Behavior

1   Objectively evil (intrinsically evil) acts never become good acts through motive and/or circumstance.
2   Objectively evil acts may be less evil (but never good) due to circumstances.
3   Objectively good acts may become better through motive or circumstance.
4   Objectively good acts may become evil through motive and circumstance.
5   Objectively good or evil acts receive additional moral specificity through circumstances. Circumstances either (a) aggravate the evil or enhance the good (change of degree); or (b) they may change the species of the moral action (change of kind).
6   Indifferent acts become good or evil in any given concrete situation through motive and/or circumstance.

Diagram 3.2
Dilemmas of Conscience—Moral Doubt

I doubt if this will help. But if you doubt your understanding of doubt, no doubt, you may find this *positive* and *practical,* not *negative* nor *speculative.* In fact, you may come to know the *Law of Doubt*!

Doubt of Law—doubts as to the existence and/or scope of the law.

Doubt of Fact—doubts as to the performance of some act (fact) relating to the fulfillment of a law.

Positive Doubt—when there are solid reasons, pro and con, for following a law and for liberty. The degree of evidence is substantial on both sides.

Negative Doubt—when there is little or no evidence for one side (law or liberty). Ordinarily, a negative doubt is to be disregarded.

Practical Doubt—is concerned with the morality of an act if performed by me.

Speculative Doubt—is concerned with the morality of an act in itself, hypothetically.

Principle Rule of Doubts of Conscience—One *may not act* with positive practical doubt. For me to act with weighty reasons for and against the licitness of an act indicates that I don't really care if I am about to offend God. One must first resolve the doubt—seek advice, consult a text, or employ a Reflex Principle if direct certainty is unavailable and a decision can't be postponed.

Reflex Principles—are general rules of construction and presumptions, such as "a doubtful law does not bind," "the possessor is to be favored," "any ambiguity in a contract shall be construed against the drafter," etc. They provide indirect certainty in acting for or against law or liberty. One does not sin formally if he chooses what is objectively wrong under these conditions. The speculative doubt remains, but the practical doubt is resolved in favor of liberty. But if one commits an objective evil for which one is not culpable, one still suffers the physical and psychological consequences often times.

Notes

1. VS, no. 71; commenting on Matt. 19:17.
2. ST I-II, q. 9, a. 1.
3. VS, no. 72. See also VS, no. 71.
4. CCC, no. 1750.
5. VS, no. 96–97.
6. Avery Dulles, "The Truth About Freedom: A Theme from John Paul II," in *Veritatis Splendor and the Renewal of Moral Theology: Studies by Ten Outstanding Scholars*, ed. J. A. DiNoia, O.P. (Chicago: Midwest Theological Forum, 1999), 139.
7. VS, no. 78; referring to ST I-II, q. 18, a. 2. See also VS, no. 79.
8. VS, no. 72.
9. CCC, no. 1751.
10. Edwin Healy, *Moral Guidance: A Textbook in Principles of Conduct for Colleges and Universities* (Chicago: Loyola Univ. Press, 1942), 7.
11. Matt. 5:27–28.
12. Matt. 7:21–23. See also Matt. 15:21–28.
13. CCC, no. 1753; VS, no. 52; ST I-II q. 19, a. 7, reps. obj. 2, 3; ST II-II, q. 33, a. 2.
14. CCC, no. 1761; VS, no. 79–82; GS, no. 27; ST I-II, q. 20, a. 2.
15. ST I-II, q. 18, aa. 8–9.
16. ST I-II, q. 1, a. 1, ad. 1.
17. ST I-II, q. 1, a. 1, ad. 1. See also ST I-II, q. 18, a. 7, rep. obj. 2.
18. CCC, no. 1751.
19. ST I-II, q. 18, a. 7.
20. ST I-II, q. 18, a. 7, rep. obj. 2.
21. CCC, no. 1752. See also ST I-II, q. 18, a. 6, rep. obj. 3.
22. William May, *Catholic Bioethics and the Gift of Human Life* (Huntington, IN: Our Sunday Visitor Pub., 2000), 51.
23. Healy, *Moral Guidance*, 7.
24. Thomas J. O'Donnell, *Medicine and Catholic Morality*, 3d ed. (New York, NY: Alba House, 1997), 24–25.
25. Romanus Cessario, *Introduction to Moral Theology* (Washington, DC: Catholic University of America Press, 2001), 177.
26. Cessario, *Introduction to Moral Theology*, 179.
27. ST I-II, q. 7, a. 3. See also VS, no. 77.
28. ST I-II, q. 18, a. 10.
29. ST I-II, q. 18, a. 5, rep. obj. 4.
30. Cessario, *Introduction to Moral Theology*, 179.
31. ST I-II, q. 7, a. 4.
32. ST I-II, q. 19, a. 7, rep. obj. 3. See also q. 19, a. 6, rep. obj. 3.
33. CCC, nos. 1754, 1755.
34. VS, no. 81.
35. Rom. 3:8.
36. CCC, no. 1753. See also John 11:50.
37. VS, no. 81; quoting 1 Cor. 6:9–10.
38. VS, no. 80; citing GS, no. 27; HV, no. 14.
39. VS, no. 81.

40. ST I-II, q. 18, a. 10.

41. ST I-II, q. 18, a. 11.

42. 1 Pet. 4:16.

43. Mark 12:43–44.

44. ST I-II, q. 20, a. 4.

45. Mark 14:44.

46. Luke 22:48.

47. ST I-II, q. 19, a. 7, rep.obj.2.

48. ST I-II, q. 19, a. 8.

49. Mark 14:29, 71.

50. Matt. 12:36.

51. ST I-II, q. 18, a. 9.

52. ST II-II, q. 32, a. 2; CCC, no. 2447.

53. Servais Pinchears, "An Encyclical for the Future: Veritatis Splendor," *Veritatis Splendor and the Renewal of Moral Theology*, 54. See also ST II-II, q. 33, a. 2.

54. VS, no. 52.

55. ST I-II, q. 6, a. 1–8.

56. Edward Hayes, et al., *Catholicism and Ethics: A Medical/Moral Handbook* (Norwood, MA: C.R. Publications, 1997), 33–34.

57. Healy, *Moral Guidance*, 16.

58. Warren Carroll, *The Rise and Fall of the Communist Revolution* (Front Royal, VA: Christendom Press, 1995), 371; citing Jozef Cardinal Mindszenty, *Memoirs* (New York, NY: Macmillan, 1974), 112.

59. CIC, no. 1103.

60. CCC, no. 2515.

61. CCC, no. 1735.

62. Congregation for the Doctrine of Faith, *Declaration On Certain Questions Concerning Sexual Ethics* (1975), no. 9.

63. John Paul II, *Love and Responsibility*, trans. H.T. Willetts (San Francisco: Ignatius Press, 1993), 162.

64. ST I-II, q. 6, a. 8.

65. CCC, no. 2518.

66. CCC, no. 1787.

67. GS, no. 16.

68. CCC, no. 1791.

69. O'Donnell, *Medicine and Christian Morality*, 13–14.

70. Hayes, *Catholicism and Ethics*, 29.

71. *Roe v. Wade*, 410 U.S. 159, 93 S.Ct. 705, 730 (1973).

72. Personal anecdote told to the author by his secretary's husband at St. Matthew's Parish in Akron, Ohio on or about 1986.

73. O'Donnell, *Medicine and Christian Morality*, 16–17. See also VS, no. 75.

Chapter 4
The Principle of Double Effect and Consequentialism

The Principle of Double Effect

The Church's absolute rejection of the idea of doing evil that good may come of it is given full expression in the principle of double effect. Another way of saying this is—the ends never justify the means.[1] For instance, the Fifth Commandment allows no exception—"Thou shall not kill," period. However, there are times when it would seem one is justified in killing other human beings, as in the case of self-defense or the defense of an innocent third party or in the defense of one's country against an unjust aggressor. The moral object of self-defense is not killing *per se*, but to defend oneself against an unjust aggressor. The moral object of self-defense has two consequences—defense is directly intended; killing, even if it is foreseen as possible or even likely, is not directly intended and should be avoided if at all possible. It is always evil to *directly* intend to kill another human being with a deliberate will:

> The fifth commandment forbids *direct and intentional killing* as gravely sinful.[2]

> Divine Law and Natural reason, therefore, exclude all right to the direct killing of an innocent man.[3]

> Human life is sacred because from its beginning it involves "the creative action of God," and it remains forever in a special relationship with the Creator, who is its sole end. God alone is the Lord of life from its beginning until its end: no one can, in any circumstance, claim for himself the right to destroy directly an innocent human being.[4]

The Church teaches that killing in order to defend one's life, to protect one's nation when at war with an unjust aggressor, or for society to protect itself through capital punishment ("when it would not be possible otherwise to defend society"[5]) is not murder in violation of the Fifth Commandment:

> [T]he Church has acknowledged as well-founded the right and duty for legitimate public authority to punish malefactors by means of penalties commensurate with the gravity of the crime, not excluding, in cases of extreme gravity, the death penalty. For analogous reasons those holding authority have the right to repel by armed force aggressors against the community in their charge.[6]

The principle of double effect permits sufficient force to be used to deter an unjust aggressor. If more force than is required is used to end the aggression the moral object ceases to be one of self-defense and turns into one of unjust aggression in return, as Aquinas observed:

> Therefore neither is a man guilty of murder if he kill another in defense of his own life.
>   *I answer that*, Nothing hinders one act from having two effects, only one of which is intended, while the other is beside the intention. Now moral acts take their species according to what is intended, and not according to what is beside the intention, since this is accidental. . . . Accordingly that act of self-defense may have two effects, one is the saving of one's life, the other is the slaying of the aggressor. Therefore this act, since one's intention is to save one's own life, is not unlawful, seeing that it is natural to everything to keep itself in *being*, as far as possible. And yet, though proceeding from a good intention, an act may be rendered unlawful, if it be out of proportion to the end. Wherefore if a man, in self-defense, uses more than necessary violence, it will be unlawful: whereas if he repel force with moderation his defense will be lawful.[7]

The fifth commandment does not forbid the legitimate right of lethal force in the defense of the basic goods of human nature which include our duty to preserve our lives (as well as an aggressor's) and to cultivate the good of human society:

> There are, in fact, situations in which values proposed by God's Law seem to involve a genuine paradox. This happens for example in the case of *legitimate defense*, in which the right to protect one's own life and the duty not to harm someone else's life are difficult to reconcile in practice. Certainly, the intrinsic value of life and the duty to live oneself no less than others are the basis of *a true right to self-defense*.[8]

As we can see, there are times when one human act may have two effects—one good, the other evil. Provided the moral object directly chosen (the *finis operis*) is good and the motive for choosing it (the *finis operantis*) is good, the actor is not morally culpable for any foreseen but unintended and unavoidable concomitant evil effects, provided the primary good end directly chosen is at least as serious or grave as the secondary unintentional evil outcome he foresees will also occur. The principle of double effect can be broken down into the four elements given below.

A Good Moral Object

The moral object chosen by the acting person cannot be intrinsically evil. The moral object must be intrinsically good or hypothetically neutral (before being specified morally by motive and circumstance). The moral object chosen that is the proximate cause of two effects, one good, the other evil, may not be evil in itself:

> The action itself must be good, or at least indifferent. If the action itself is evil, evidently it is forbidden. This second condition is verified if the contemplated action is not included in either class of actions that are evil in themselves (e.g., blasphemy and stealing).[9]

A Good Motive

The actor's motive, the ulterior purpose for which he strives, must be to bring about only the good effect. The foreseen evil effect which is also caused by his choice of a good moral object is only tolerated or permitted. Therefore, the acting person must do everything reasonable to avoid or mitigate the foreseen but unintended evil effects: "The agent's intention is good. That is, he in no way intends the bad effect; he does not act because he wants to achieve the bad effect."[10]

The Causal Priority of Good Consequences

The good effect must come before the evil effect. The actor's motive, to strive only for the good effect, is established and confirmed only if the good effect is initiated (in the order of causality) before or simultaneously with the evil effect, even if the evil effect may come to fruition first (in chronological order). Otherwise one would be doing evil that good come of it: "The first effect must be good or at least equal first with the evil effect (this prevents a good effect resulting from an evil one)."[11]

The Proportionality of Good and Evil Consequences

The good effect must be proportionate to the evil effect; it must be as grave as the evil effect otherwise one is not justified in producing more harm than good. The good effect directly intended by the actor's choice of a good/neutral moral object must be at least as great as the other effect is evil:

> The good effect must be sufficiently beneficial to compensate for the permitting of the bad effect. . . . Thus, a greater good is *per se* required to compensate for the permitting of a morally bad effect (the sin of another) than for the permitting of a physically bad effect; a greater good is required when the bad effect is sure to fol-

low than when it will only probably follow: a greater reason is required only when the bad effect is injurious to the common good than when it is harmful only to an individual.[12]

A Critique of Revisionist Moral Theology: *Veritatis Splendor* (1993)

Pope John Paul II in *Veritatis Splendor* [13] criticized certain "teleological ethical theories," namely: fundamental option, consequentialism and proportionalism. He said we must reject these theories because, in one way or another, they teach that one may do evil (not that they call it evil) that good may come of it.[14] He characterized these ethical theories as "false solutions, linked in particular to an inadequate understanding of the object of moral action."[15]

Fundamental Option

The following story illustrates the harm that can be inflicted on society by errors in moral theology. There was a man who had studied in the seminary in the late 1960s but he had never been ordained and was happily married with three children and was a volunteer catechist in a parish. Striking a serious pose before his wife he said with a wink, "You know, you get one free adultery." He waited just long enough for dramatic effect and then explained that this was what he was taught in the seminary some years ago. "That's right," he said, "our professor in moral theology said you can't commit a mortal sin in one act. We were taught that one act of weakness could not break one's fundamental option for God and so it would not be a serious sin. That's why you get to commit one act of adultery without committing a serious sin." His wife played along with him by lightly tapping his head with a frying pan, saying, "Well, I don't know about God, but it would break your fundamental option for me!"[16]

Even though the notion of fundamental option may be abused, there is a sense in which it expresses a profound truth about how the life of a Christian must show an overarching orientation to Christ. Daily we must follow Christ.[17] Daily we must forgive our enemies and pray to be spared from evil.[18]

> There is no doubt that Christian moral teaching, even in its Biblical roots, acknowledges the specific importance of a fundamental choice which qualifies the moral life and engages freedom on a radical level before God.[19]

The problem comes when one's general commitment and faith in Christ is put to the test in the concrete particular activities of everyday life. John Paul II in *Veritatis Splendor* reaffirmed the reality of *mortal sin*: one may fall away from Christ not just through an outright loss of faith but in any human act contrary to the Commandments involving grave matter.

> The separation of fundamental option from deliberate choices of particular kinds of behavior, disordered in themselves or in their circumstances, which would engage that option, thus involves a denial of Catholic doctrine on *mortal sin*: "With the whole tradition of the Church, we call mortal sin the act by which man freely and consciously rejects God, his law, the covenant of love that God offers, preferring to turn in on himself or to some created and finite reality, something contrary to the divine will. . . . This can occur in a direct and formal way, in the sins of idolatry, apostasy and atheism; or in an equivalent way, as in every act of disobedience to God's commandments in a grave matter."[20]

Fundamental option theory exaggerates a valid point—that the human will always chooses some good, and in this life, all created things are only partial goods; hence the will is free to choose them as partial goods or reject them as devoid of other partial goods.[21] However, it is not true that the choice of a partial good does not specify the moral object just because it fails to completely captivate the will as only God can in the Beatific Vision.[22] It is not true that the choice of adultery fails to specify the moral object as evil just because it fails to completely satisfy the will of the adulterer. The wife, in the story about how we are all entitled to one free adultery, understood that her husband's choice of adultery would change his fundamental option for her and fundamentally alter her relationship with him. It is foolish to believe that the Sixth Commandment or genuine human love would welcome even one act of adultery or recognizes it as good for any reason:

> These tendencies are therefore contrary to the teaching of Scripture itself, which sees the fundamental option as a genuine choice of freedom and links that choice profoundly to particular acts. By his fundamental choice, man is capable of giving his life direction and of progressing, with the help of grace, towards his end, following God's call. But this capacity is actually exercised in the particular choices of specific actions, through which man deliberately conforms himself to God's will, wisdom and law. It thus needs to be stated that the *so-called fundamental option* [for God] . . . *is revoked when man engages his freedom in conscious decisions to the contrary, with regard to morally grave matter.*[23]

Proportionalism and Consequentialism

Corporations often require long term planning. Typically, a feasibility study is completed before any major project is undertaken. As part of the feasibility study, a cost/profit or benefit/burden analysis is projected. Even Christ recommended weighing the cost of being his disciples. He said, if one were to decide to build a tower without calculating the cost, or if a King were to march against an enemy without calculating the relative size of his army versus that of his rival's, he would be foolish.[24] Certainly the foreseeable consequences of an action must be taken into consideration by a prudent person. Foresight and circumspection, quasi-integral parts of prudence, when developed, help guide a person to choose the right means to the right end.[25]

The erroneous moral systems of consequentialism and proportionalism take a benefit/burden analysis and exaggerate it, applying it to every human act. Every human act is weighed and measured strictly in terms of motives and consequences. Like corrupt business executives, in these moral systems each person is free to choose anything that maximizes his profit because so long as it maximizes his profit, it cannot be called bad for him or his business:

> This new system of judging actions . . . turns morality into a kind of technique. Its rational methods are much like those used in industry for evaluating projects by calculating profit and loss to efficiency and utility. . . . This is confirmed by the choice of examples which proportionalist writers use, borrowed as a rule from medical, industrial, economic, or social techniques. Actions, for example, are often described as "productive" or "counterproductive."[26]

Consequentialism exaggerates the partial virtue of prudence, foresight. It looks principally to the future and "weighs foreseeable consequences." Proportionalism exaggerates another partial virtue of prudence, circumspection, and considers "various values" in terms of how they maximize the greater good or reduce the evil in the present situation.[27]

Both of these "false solutions" miss the mark of the virtue of prudence because they focus only on the right end while forgetting about the right means to that end, which is the very definition of the virtue of prudence. Therefore, it is not surprising that both of these errors misconstrue the principle of double effect:

> The various construals of the Principle of Double Effect represent so many ways in which moral theologians grappled with the case of effects which were caused, but not intended. And it seems significant that the history of twentieth-century proportionalism as a school of moral argumentation began with an attempt once again to puzzle out the Principle of Double Effect.[28]

Proportionalists get two out of four of the elements of the principle of double effect right, motives and consequences, elements two and four given above. They are happy to weigh the benefits of the good effects versus the burdens of the bad effects and they agree that the bad effects should only be permitted, not willed in themselves. However, they fail to hold that the good effect must come prior to the bad effect chronologically, materially, or causally, i.e., element three mentioned above. Rather, they "morph" this element, if you will, and transfer it from the temporal/causal order to an order of intentionality so that if the will tends to the good effect with greater intensity because more good than bad effects are foreseen as likely to occur, then the good effect has priority intentionally even if the bad effect may come first chronologically and bring about the good effect causally.

> The root idea of the system [proportionalism/consequentialism] was to apply the

principles of double effect to all moral actions, thus giving this principle a general impact in moral teaching, but revising it in such a way as to order the effects to the end sought. In the classical teaching, the good effect had to precede the bad effect in the temporal, material, or causal order so as to avoid contradicting a principle taken from St. Paul: "it is not licit to do evil that good may come of it" cf. Rom. 3:8. . . . In line with the new concept, priority among effects will be established according to the requirements of a proportionate reason for acting, and more precisely with the help of a comparison of the good and evil effects in view of the end sought. If the good effects outweigh the evil effects, they are given priority by the will and the action becomes lawful, correct, and good.[29]

Finally, revisionist moral theologians subtly deny the first and most important element of the principle of double effect—that the human act that produces two effects, one good, the other evil, must be intrinsically good or neutral and never intrinsically evil. They do not claim one *may* do what is intrinsically evil. What they claim is that no one *can* do what is intrinsically evil because no human act is ever intrinsically evil. Rather, all human acts are neutral (physical or ontic—mere acts of man) until one's motive and all the effects have been evaluated, and the bad consequences subtracted from the good consequences and a tally, a proportion, of moral worth decided upon. Only then does one arrive at a moral object which, if it tallies up evil, one may not choose that good come of it.

Revisionist moral theologians are thus able to have their cake and eat it too. Their moral ideology mystifies an agenda. It flaunts absolute moral norms while at the same time denying that it has done so.

> The trick is . . . this theory is not only erroneous, but moreover dangerously confusing moral reasoning. Proportionalism is a methodology by which one in fact always can *with good conscience* act according to the principle "let us do evil so that good come about," because the methodology gives one the conviction that, provided good comes foreseeable about, what you did was not evil at all, but just the morally right thing, so that the ominous principle does not apply in your case. Whoever nevertheless reproaches you for trying to justify, on the grounds of "good reason," what in reality is morally evil, will be "misrepresenting" your position.[30]

The universal recognition of villainy and heroism give the lie to the errors of consequentialism/proportionalism. Every civilization recognizes good and bad behavior and lionizes those who give their all for a cause, a person they love, for their God and demonize those who break faith and betray those who have been loyal to them as the following section shows.

Assassins and Martyrs Give Witness to Moral Absolutes

Although the killing of a tyrant may be justified according to a criteria similar to that of a just war, the assassination of political leaders for purely political con-

venience is universally condemned. However, assassination for political convenience is implicitly justified by consequentialism/proportionalism. For instance, in
order to win the Vietnam War, it appears the United States government helped to
topple the South Vietnam government of Ngo Dinh Diem in 1963. It appears that
certain United States State Department officials hoped to increase the likelihood of
winning the war by replacing a loyal ally, South Vietnam President Diem, a Catholic, with a Buddhist military junta. Ironically, the coup served only to further desta-
bilize the government and lose the war. When Ngo Dinh Diem and his brother, Ngo
Dinh Nhu, were betrayed they took refuge in a Catholic church in Saigon on November 2, 1963. After attending morning Mass and receiving Holy Communion
they were taken prisoner by disloyal South Vietnam military officers. Instead of the
safe passage they had been promised, as soon as the military officers had them
handcuffed in the street, they blew their brains out. The coup was apparently
planned by the United States, and Diem's murder was foreseen and condoned in a
communiqué from Assistant Secretary of State, Roger Hilsman: "If the family is
taken alive, the Nhus should be banished to France or any other country willing to
receive them. Diem should be treated as the generals wish."[31]

But this relativist reasoning didn't wash with everyone. One journalist who was
privy to the decision to oust and assassinate Diem telephoned Assistant Secretary of
State Roger Hilsman at 2:00 a.m. and got him out of bed to say, "Congratulations,
Roger! How does it feel to have blood on your hands?"[32] Trying to predict the future is risky. Doing evil to maximize future good is often tragic.

Martin Rhonheimer recounts another example of consequentialist logic, that of
Paul Touvier, a French Nazi collaborator, who was recently brought to trial in Israel
and charged with killing seven innocent Jews back in 1944. Mr. Touvier admitted
he performed the killings but offered in his defense that he did so only because he
knew that if he did not kill those seven, the Nazis had threatened to kill one hundred
Jews. He argued in his defense that what he had done was not evil but good—he
had saved the lives of ninety-three Jews.

The moral object for Paul Touvier was first expanded to include all foreseeable
consequences and amalgamated into a mere physical (morally neutral) act of killing.
What he chose was good because it, the neutral act of killing, was specified good by
his good intention and by the fact he foresaw that more good consequences than bad
would follow.

> Touvier came to the conclusion: If I do not kill the seven, then one hundred (these
> seven probably included) will be killed. Therefore, in killing the seven (which *as
> such* is beyond good and evil), I can save ninety-three Jews. Thus Touvier rea-
> soned: The morally relevant 'object' of my action—that is, *what I am really
> doing*—has to be called meritorious or at least responsible and justified as life-
> saving.[33]

But not every so-called physical act freely chosen (as a human act) is compatible
with just any intention. We simply do not have the power to define moral reality.

We can no more suspend the laws of gravity than we can suspend the built in moral reality of human acts. To consciously blow the brains out of an innocent person is incompatible with the basic goods of human nature always and everywhere which is why Mr. Touvier was convicted for his crimes of murder and not given a medal of honor for saving lives.

> Thus Paul Touvier had no power to decide what would be his basic intention in killing seven innocent people. To describe his action properly, one must include the purpose or the intention, "wanting them to be dead"; (even if he would *regret* it; that is only a motivational side feature, but not the every intention of his acting). Touvier clearly *wanted* the seven to be killed; he chose their deaths for the sake of some greater benefit.[34]

At the end of his reflection on the problems at the very foundations of moral theology Pope John Paul II turns in *Veritatis Splendor* to the example of those who surely died in vain if there are no moral absolutes. The examples of these heroes serve as the most convincing refutation of erroneous moral systems. The story of one such hero was told to me by her niece, a former student of mine.[35] Trudy described her aunt, a professed sister of the Adorers of the Blood of Christ, as her "favorite person" while she was growing up. Her aunt's name was, Sister Jo El Colmer. She was a missionary in Africa, but returned regularly to visit her family in Ohio and took time to patiently listen to Trudy and help her deal with her teenage growing pains. Her aunt's loving example kept Trudy going to church and prevented her from becoming too wild, as she said, during her high school years.

She recalled the day that her family first received word that Sister Jo El was missing. There was a civil war in Liberia in 1992 where her aunt was serving at an orphanage for Liberian girls. She said at first her family was hopeful that her aunt would turn up alright. In the past, Sister Jo El had hid out during previous civil upheavals and returned to the mission when peace was restored. On this occasion, however, the days without word stretched on as her family prayed for her safety. Finally the family received word that Sister Jo El Colmer had been killed. Trudy said that the really hard thing to take was the fact that her aunt's body would not be returned and was still laying unburied in the street where she had been gunned down.

Insurgent terrorists had come into the village as Sister Jo El ran out to protect her frightened orphans who had strayed out into the street. The marauding gang of terrorists began to spray the children with automatic small-arms fire. Sister Jo El was cut down along with the orphans she died trying to save out for love of Christ. Four other sisters from her order were also murdered during the insurrection rather than break faith with Christ and the virtues associated with the practice of their Christian faith. The young girls at Sr. Jo El's orphanage were then all abused and destroyed by the insurgents. Months later Sister Colmer's body was returned to her family for burial. But Sr. Jo El's story did not end in blood, dust and decay. Instead she was raised up onto the high altar of the Basilica of Saint Peter in Rome. In

1997, Pope John Paul II canonized Sister Jo El and the other four sisters who were martyred for their love of Christ in defense of the sanctity of innocent human life. The following prayer is on the reverse side of a holy card honoring the Five Martyrs of Charity of Liberia:

> Creator God, you fashioned the universe and all that it contains. You made us in your image: You sent your Son to show us your way of love. Jesus treated all as sister and brother. Jesus suffered, died and rose from the dead to show us that all-embracing love cannot be overcome by death.
>
> And now the example of the Five Martyrs of Charity of Liberia reminds us again that Christian lives may not be lived in isolation.
>
> In solidarity with our sisters and brothers in Liberia, we unite our voices to the cry of their sacrifice as we pray for peace and the rebuilding of their war-torn country.
>
> May we live our prayer by stretching our hearts to make room for all who suffer and by being your peacemakers in the midst of violence and oppression. We are confident that you will hear us.
>
> Saint Jo El Colmer, pray for us.

John Paul II points out in *Veritatis Splendor* that the blood of the martyrs disproves the false solutions of revisionist moral theologians more eloquently than papal teaching. Martyrs died rather than do evil that good come of it. Those who offered their lives for Christ do not weigh the consequences of their sacrifice so much as they regarded the cost of his sacrifice for them—to set them free for liberty. This is especially true of she whom the Holy Spirit prophesied would have her own heart pierced so that the secret thoughts of many would be laid bare.[36] Mary, Queen of Martyrs protects us from beguiling doctrines: "She understands sinful man and loves him with a Mother's love. . . . Nor does she permit sinful man to be deceived by those who claim to love him by justifying his sin, for she knows that the sacrifice of Christ her son would thus be emptied of its power. No absolution offered by beguiling doctrines . . . can make man truly happy: only the Cross and the glory of the Risen Christ can grant peace to his conscience and salvation to his life."[37]

Notes

1. F.J. Fitzpatrick, *Ethics in Nursing Practice: Basic Principles and Their Application* (London: Linacre Center, 1988), 133.
2. CCC, no. 2268.
3. DPA, no. 14.
4. CCC, no. 2258; citing DV, no. 41. See also EV, no. 53.
5. EV, nos. 27, 56.
6. CCC, no. 2266.
7. S.T. II-II, q. 64, a. 7.
8. EV, no.55; citing CCC, no. 2265.

9. Edwin Healy, *Moral Guidance: A Textbook in Principles of Conduct for Colleges and Universities* (Chicago: Loyola Univ. Press, 1942), 20.

10. Fitzpatrick, *Ethics in Nursing Practice*, 125.

11. Peter E. Bristow, *The Moral Dignity of Man: An Exposition of Catholic Moral Doctrine With Particular Reference to Family and Medical Ethics in the Light of Contemporary Development* (Dublin: Four Courts Press, 1997), 52.

12. Francis J. Connell, *Outlines of Moral Theology* (Milwaukee, WI: Bruce Publishing Co., 1953), 23.

13. VS, no. 64–83.

14. Rom. 3:8.

15. VS, no. 75. See also VS, nos. 79, 82.

16. This incident happened while I was having dinner with one of my catechists and his wife in Akron, Ohio on or about 1987.

17. Matt 19:21.

18. Matt 6:9–15; Luke 11:2–4; see also Deut. 6:40.

19. VS, no. 6.

20. VS, no. 70; citing Post-Synodal Apostolic Exhortation *Reconciliatio et Paenitentia* (2 December 1984), 17: AAS 77 (1985), 222.

21. S.T. I-II, q. 13, a. 6.

22. VS, no. 65.

23. VS, no. 67.

24. Luke 14:29–33.

25. S.T. II-II, q. 49, aa. 6–7.

26. Servais-Théodore Pinckaers, "An Encyclical for the Future: Veritatis Splendor," eds. J. A. DiNoia and Romanus Cessario, *Veritatis Splendor and the Renewal of Moral Theology* (Princeton: Scepter Pub., 1999), 53.

27. VS, no. 75.

28. Romanus Cessario, *Introduction to Moral Theology* (Washington, DC: Catholic Univ. Press, 2001), 107.

29. Pinckaers, "An Encyclical for the Future," 51.

30. Martin Rhonheimer, "Intentional Actions and the Meaning of Object: A Reply to Richard McCormick," eds. J. A. DiNoia and Romanus Cessario, *Veritatis Splendor and the Renewal of Moral Theology* (Princeton: Scepter Pub., 1999), 264–65.

31. Warren H. Carroll, *Rise and Fall of the Communist Revolution* (Front Royal, Va.: Christendom Press, 2004), 527; citing Ellen J. Hammer, *Death in November* (New York, NY: E.P. Dutton, 1965), 225.

32. Carroll, *Rise and Fall*, 527; citing Marguerite Higgins, *Our Vietnam Nightmare* (New York, NY: Harper & Row, 1965), 225.

33. Rhonheimer, "Intentional Actions," 250.

34. Rhonheimer, "Intentional Actions," 256.

35. Trudy was an undergraduate student in a Christian Moral Principles class I taught at Franciscan University of Steubenville in the late 1990's. She told the story of her aunt, Sr. Jo El Colmer, in a brief reflection paper she wrote as a class assignment. Members of her order confirmed the story and sent me a holy card honoring the heroic witness of the Five Martyrs of Charity of Liberia.

36. Luke 2:35.

37. VS, no. 120.

Chapter 5
Cooperation and Scandal

Cooperation

Cooperation is the participation of more than one person in the same good or evil act. Although this topic is usually considered under the aspect of aiding and abetting someone in the performance of evil, it applies equally to good deeds: "We can co-operate with others in the performance of good deeds, and when we do this, we share in the merit."[1] The *Catechism of the Catholic Church* refers to cooperation in the sins of others as a personal act whereby one participates directly and voluntarily in the evil acts of others by ordering, advising, praising, or approving them; by not disclosing or not hindering them when one has an obligation to do so; or by protecting evil doers.[2] Cooperation in the evil act of another occurs in two ways—formally or materially.

Formal Cooperation

To will interiorly, in one's mind and heart, that evil comes to pass is already a completed evil act, a sin. Christ said that he who lusts after a woman has already committed adultery with her in his heart.[3] Formal cooperation occurs when one's interior evil will is set in motion externally through an act ordered to the furtherance of the evil act of the principle wrongdoer in such a way that they strive jointly to bring about the same completed evil deed. Therefore, a formal cooperator is always as guilty as the principal wrongdoer.

In criminal law both parties in a drag car race would be charged with voluntary manslaughter, even if only one of them accidentally runs over and kills a pedestrian during their illegal race. The same criteria apply to two individuals who hold up a bank, one participating as the escape car driver, the other as the gun man. If the gun man shoots and kills the bank guard, both he and the escape car driver will be charged with murder. The get-away-driver is a formal cooperator in the scheme to commit armed robbery, who assumed and condoned all the foreseeable risks including that an innocent person may be killed in the bank robbery. In a civil lawsuit, if a subcontractor, a plumber for instance, is negligent and installs an upstairs bathroom shower which leaks and causes the downstairs ceiling to collapse, both he and the general contractor, who is responsible for the overall supervision of the job, are held jointly and severally liable for the damages, i.e., the property owner may elect to sue one or the other, or both for the total cost of repair, or to allocate the total cost between them.

> To actually intend the evil purpose is formal cooperation, no matter how small one's share in the actual physical execution [of the evil]. Advising, counseling, promoting, or condoning an evil action, even when sometimes merely by being silent when one has a duty to speak up or express an opinion, is formal cooperation because such actions signify agreement with evil.[4]

One can cooperate formally in the sin of another in two ways: by freely choosing the same evil moral object (same *finis operis*) as the principal wrongdoer so as to assist him to achieve the same evil goal (same *finis operantis*); or by freely choosing a different moral object than that of the principal wrongdoer (different *finis operis*) but one that is nonetheless ordered towards furthering the same goal as that of the principal wrongdoer (same *finis operantis*). For example, a law school admission counselor who recruits prospective students and the law professors who later teach those same students have the same *finis operis*; they both actively cooperate in the same enterprise, the legal education of law school students. Likewise, one may counsel and encourage a young woman to get an abortion. In this case the counselor and the abortionist perform the same moral object. On the other hand, a parent may wish that their son or daughter follow in their footsteps and become a lawyer. So the parent hands their son or daughter their mail with a brochure for law school on the top of the stack of mail hoping that their child will read it and be influenced to apply to law school. The *finis operis* of the parent and the law professor are different, one hands their son or daughter a stack of mail, the other teaches law, but their *finis operantis* (motive) is the same, i.e., both hope to further the education of a future lawyer. Similarly, a parent may wish to subtly influence their daughter to get an abortion by handing their daughter the mail with a teen magazine on top featuring a story about how their daughter's favorite singer had an abortion in order to further her successful career. Although the act of handing someone their mail (*the finis operis*) is neutral it may be calculated to produce an effect. Such calculation (*finis operantis*) makes one a formal cooperator in the good or evil deed they seek to bring about.

Material Cooperation

Material cooperation occurs when one does not choose the same evil moral object as that of the wrongdoer, but rather chooses a good moral object foreseeing, however, that one's external or material cooperation will be used by the wrongdoer in the furtherance of his evil plan. A material cooperator may or may not be guilty of the sin of the wrongdoer, depending upon the circumstances which influenced him. As a general rule, charity requires that one must not perform even a good or neutral deed that one foresees another person will use to aid them to commit an evil act. Love of neighbor forbids one from knowingly hurting another person even indirectly through the performance of good or neutral deeds unless one is threatened by a proportionate harm according to that same measure given to us by Christ—"to love one's neighbor *as oneself.*"

> If, then, one were entirely free to pick and choose whether or not to cooperate in someone else's evil act—if there were no compelling reason for cooperating in it despite its evil character—one would be obligated not to cooperate. The onus of proof, in other words, always rests with the person who cooperates. It is up to him to show that certain conditions obtaining in this particular case justify him in cooperating. In the absence of compelling reasons for cooperation, material cooperation in evil is morally wrong.[5]

Immediate, proximate, remote and necessary cooperation are terms which describe the degree of influence, control or discretion one has over the initiation, course or outcome of the evil act of another.

An immediate material cooperator helps to perform the evil act in unison with the wrongdoer. The *finis operis* (moral object) of the principal and the cooperator is the same and the *finis operantis* (motive) is almost always the same. Therefore, immediate material cooperation usually translates into formal cooperation.[6] In the case of the gun man and the get-away driver to a bank robbery "it is vacuous to say that a person in his right senses performs a criminal action without intending, in his will, to do so."[7]

There are occasions, however, when an immediate material cooperator does not become a formal cooperator as, for instance, when a bank robber hands stolen money to some hapless bystander and orders him at gun point to carry the money out of the bank. The moral object of the innocent immediate material cooperator who acts together with the bank robber has changed. Granted, it is still a "taking" but it is no longer an "unjust taking" against the will of the private property owner(s).

The bystander enlisted at gun point to carry the money out of the bank does not choose the moral object of theft. Private property under these circumstances reverts to its more basic character in the sense of having a universal destination: "The principle of the universal destination of goods is an affirmation both of God's full and perennial lordship over every reality and of the requirement that the goods of creation remain ever destined to the development of the whole person and of all humanity."[8] The plenteous blessings of the earth belong to everyone equally until someone by mixing their labor with these goods reduces them to their private property to better secure his own survival and flourishing.[9] However, a property owner exercises a relative, not an absolute right, over his private property. If it is ever unreasonable to withhold private property from another by reason of the other's extreme necessity (as for instance when a starving person needs another's surplus food), then to "take" that property is not theft, because it is reasonable and cannot be against the right reason and good will of its owner(s).[10]

In the case of an immediate material cooperator in a bank robbery who cooperates at gun point, the status of the money changes from private to universal, but its status as private property does not change for the bank robber. The bystander commandeered to assist a bank robber is an immediate material cooperator but not a formal cooperator and is innocent of the sin of theft since the moral object of his taking is not the removal of private property against the will of its owner, which is the case with the principal wrongdoer.

The principle of double effect when applied to the hapless bystander to a bank robbery exonerates him of complicity in the crime. The moral object, the *finis operis*, of the bystander is a hypothetically neutral act—a taking of property—that is morally specified by his *finis operantis* as a lawful taking of property, given his extreme necessity. He foresees that this good deed will produce two effects, that of saving his life and the concurrent evil effect of furthering the robber in his sin. But he directly intends only the good effect and for proportionate reasons, merely tolerates the evil effect. So neither the moral object nor the intention of the bystander and the robber agree. Only their external physical actions are in agreement as together they remove the money from the bank. Their moral deeds are specified differently, the bank robber performs an act of theft, while the bystander engages in a just taking of money that is not contrary to the intention of the reasonable depositors at the bank due to his extreme necessity.

In mediate material cooperation both the *finis operis* (the moral object) and the *finis operantis* (motive) of the cooperator differ from that of the principal wrongdoer. In this case, a person performs an act lawful in itself which under the circumstance, he foresees, but does not intend, will be used by the wrongdoer for an evil purpose. The morality of mediate material cooperation depends on the proportion between the gravity of the immoral act of the principal and the proximity, necessity and compensating good results of the lawful deed to be gained by the cooperator. Therefore, the greater the influence one's actions have, due to proximity or necessity, upon the probability or severity of the evil action, the greater must be the justifying reason:

> The morality of mediate material cooperation is to be sought in the principle of double effect, with special attention to the proportion between the cooperation (how proximate or remote, how necessary or unnecessary, to the crime of another), and the gravity of the crime in connection with which another will make use of it.[11]

Remote material cooperation describes the situation where one's action has little influence on the outcome of the evil effect. In this case, one is permitted to perform a lawful deed that remotely supports the foreseen but unintended evil action of another. For example, clerks and mere employees who must follow the detailed instructions of their employers, who have little or no discretion in the terms of their employment, are remote cooperators when they "ring up" sales, point out items for sale, or fill orders authorized by their supervisors.

A grave reason is required to justify one's material cooperation if it is proximate in the preparation or execution of the evil act of another. Here, the cooperator still performs what is hypothetically a good or at least indifferent (not an intrinsically evil) act. The cooperator's moral object (*finis operis*) is at least neutral in the abstract. The principle of double effect must supply the final moral specificity to this act, establishing the uprightness of the cooperator's intention (*finis operantis*) by weighing the due proportion between the good and evil effects that follow concurrently from the performance of a good or indifferent moral object. Independent contractors, skilled tradesmen and professionals are less remote/more proximate in their cooperation with the wrongdoing of others. Whereas editors, chief executive officers and administrators, managers or partners are either formal or proximate cooperators in the evil deeds of their business and its associates:

> A Catholic would never be allowed to edit or publish a book against the faith, for this would be proximate material cooperation, or perhaps even formal cooperation. But printers, typesetters, etc., in a firm that prints such literature occasionally would be acting lawfully, as long as they can get no other equally good job.[12]

Usually no reason will suffice to justify one's material cooperation if one's personal services are both proximate and uniquely necessary in the preparation or execution of the evil act of another as when an anesthesiologist assists an abortion. Here, the anesthesiologist performs what is hypothetically a good or at least indifferent (not an intrinsically evil) act. The cooperator's moral object (*finis operis*) is at least neutral in the abstract. Again, the principle of double effect must supply the final moral specificity of this act, establishing the uprightness of the cooperator's intention (*finis operantis*) by weighing the due proportion between the good and evil effects that follow concurrently from the performance of the good or indifferent moral object. Regardless, "[i]f the refusal of the anesthetist to cooperate would prevent the abortion, it is difficult to see how he could agree to do so under any circumstances."[13]

Cooperation Outlined

Remote	Mediate	Proximate	Necessary or Immediate
Less serious reasons required		More serious reasons required	
Less inconvenience		Greater inconvenience	
Less control, more replaceable		More control, more necessary	

Scandal

Cooperation in the evil doings of others or the appearance of such often provides an occasion of sin by giving bad example or scandal. The sin of scandal[14] occurs when a person either performs a public bad deed or the appearance of a bad deed without sufficient justification. It is always sinful to intentionally try to tempt another person to sin by one's own bad example. It is also sinful to give a bad example even if one does not wish others to follow it. Scandal is seriously sinful if one foresees others will follow one's own bad example even if one's sin were only venial. The Catechism defines scandal as follows:

> Scandal is an attitude or behavior which leads another to do evil. The person who gives scandal becomes his neighbor's tempter. . . . Scandal is a grave offense if by deed or omission another is deliberately led into a grave offense. Scandal takes on a particular gravity by reason of the authority of those who cause it or the weakness of those who are scandalized.[15]

One may cause scandal and yet not be guilty of the sin of scandal if one performs a good or indifferent act which under the circumstance appears evil to others for a proportionately good reason. Under the principle of double effect a person may perform a good or indifferent act which will have two effects: first, the good directly intended, and second, the appearance of an impropriety which he foresees may lead some to imitate his seemingly bad example. Provided one has a proportionate reason for acting, he may do the good deed even if it has the appearance of an impropriety. For instance, a priest may go into a house of prostitution to administer the last rites to a dying person even though someone is likely to draw the wrong conclusion regarding his intentions in entering the house of ill repute. If possible, the priest would be required to clarify his motives to those persons he knows may have been scandalized.

A politician might be guilty of the sin of scandal if, for instance, he voted in favor of a bill that allows abortion under some circumstances but tended to reduce the overall number of abortions. He may vote for such a bill provided he does not give scandal to others by clearly explaining his reasons for doing so (to reduce the total number of abortions with the passage of a bill that was the best he could hope to pass under the circumstances) and his "absolute personal opposition to procured abortion" (even in cases of rape, incest or to save the life of the mother).[16]

On the other hand, Catholic politicians who vote in favor of abortion in order to curry favor with pro-abortion voters or benefactors and try at the same time to win the support of pro-life voters by saying they are "personally opposed to abortion" but must not impose their beliefs on others are mostly likely formal cooperators in abortion and are guilty of the sin of scandal. They create "structures of sin"[17] that lead others to sin:

> Therefore, they are guilty of scandal who established laws or social structures leading to the decline of morals and the corruption of religious practices, or to "social conditions that, intentionally or not, make Christian conduct and obedience to the Commandments difficult and practically impossible." This is true of business leaders who make rules encouraging fraud, teachers who provoke the children to anger, or manipulators of public opinion who turn it away from moral values.[18]

In order to prevent scandal the Church permits a priest to refuse Holy Communion to public figures "who obstinately persist in manifest grave sin." This applies to Catholic politicians who consistently vote in favor of abortion or same-sex marriage yet come to Mass to receive the Eucharist. The Church prohibits persons in a state of mortal sin from receiving Communion, except on the rare occasion when it is impossible for them to go to Confession before hand and they have a grave reason for receiving the Eucharist.[19] The Church refuses to give Holy Communion to pro-abortion Catholic politicians not to humiliate them but to stir them to repentance and to prevent scandal lest other parishioners wrongly conclude the Church is unconcerned with "establishing laws or social structures leading to the decline of morals."[20]

Notes

1. Francis J. Connell, *Outlines of Moral Theology* (Milwaukee, WI: Bruce Publishing Co., 1953), 92.

2. CCC, no. 1868.

3. Matt. 5:28.

4. F.J. Fitzpatrick, *Ethics in Nursing Practice: Basic Principles and Their Application* (London: Linacre Center, 1988), 130; citing Benedict Ashley and Kevin O'Rourke, *Health Care Ethics: A Theological Analysis* (St. Louis, MO: Catholic Health Association of the United States, 1981), 191.

5. Fitzpatrick, *Ethics in Nursing Practice*, 130.

6. Thomas J. O'Donnell, *Medicine and Catholic Morality*, 3d ed. (New York, NY: Alba House, 1997), 35.

7. O'Donnell, *Medicine and Christian Morality*, 35-36.

8. Pontifical Council for Justice and Peace, *The Compendium of the Social Doctrine of the Church* (Libreria Editrice Vaticana, 2004), no. 177.

9. *Compendium of the Social Doctrine of the Church*, no. 176.

10. *Compendium of the Social Doctrine of the Church*, no. 177.

11. O'Donnell, *Medicine and Christian Morality*, 37.

12. Connell, *Outlines of Moral Theology*, 94.

13. O'Donnell, *Medicine and Christian Morality*, 38.

14. CCC, nos. 2284–87

15. CCC, nos. 2284–85.

16. EV, no. 73.

17. CCC, no. 1869

18. CCC, no. 2286.

19. CCC, no. 1457. See also CIC, no. 916.

20. CCC, no. 2286.

Chapter 6
Virtues—Natural and Supernatural

Introduction

The natural virtues and vices are both habits. No one is born vicious or virtuous. Rather, it is the role of habits to condition the use of a person's faculties and appetites. Aquinas defined a habit as "a quality difficult to change whereby a power potential to several things is disposed to one line of action easily and readily at will."[1] Habits are not the same as the faculties and appetites of a person; rather, habits are impressed upon persons and dispose the faculty or appetite to act readily in a constant manner through constant repetition and training.[2] All habits, good or bad, render us ready to behave in some way quickly and easily. Once acquired, habits are a quality difficult to change that dispose the subject to behave readily and with ease for good or ill with respect to their true good and that of others. In other words, once acquired a habit becomes "second nature" and, just as it gives any creature pleasure to behave according to their nature, we too enjoy doing what we have trained ourselves to do well.[3]

Habits affect us at all levels. There are habits of the physical order, the intellectual order and the moral order.[4] For the sake of comparison and review, emotions change quickly and easily, habits do not; emotions are natural endowments, but habits are conditioned behavior; emotions are amoral, habits are morally specified—good or bad.

Natural Virtues

Virtue in Latin means strength or valor. Natural virtues are good habits that perfect the faculties of reason and free will, as well as the concupiscible and irascible appetites that a person may acquire without the aid of grace but which grace builds upon through the infused and theological virtues.[5]

The natural virtues that perfect the operation of reason are called intellectual virtues, whereas those that perfect the operation of the will and emotions are called cardinal virtues. Both the intellectual and the cardinal virtues are natural virtues in the sense that the human person, without the aid of grace, can acquire them through human effort and frequent repetition. In themselves, the natural virtues are not salvific, their practice does not merit salvation. However, grace builds upon nature. Once a person receives from Christ supernatural life through faith, baptism, and the power of the Holy Spirit, the natural virtues are elevated and reoriented toward eternal life by the theological and supernatural virtues and the Gifts of the Holy Spirit. "Human virtues acquired by education, by deliberate acts and by a perseverance ever-renewed in repeated efforts are purified and elevated by divine grace."[6]

Intellectual Virtues

Human reason in its orientation to know truth and "what is" from "what is not" is often referred to as the speculative intellect. The first principle of the speculative intellect is the principle of non-contradiction—something cannot be and not be at the same time. The three intellectual virtues that perfect the speculative intellect are wisdom, understanding and science. The speculative intellect seeks to know what is true. The intellectual virtues help us to know truth and to think well. Wisdom contemplates the ultimate meaning of life, truth, happiness and the first principles of being. Understanding considers the first principles of the various disciplines or sciences and contemplates self-evident truths. Science considers the implications of the first principles of the sciences and that which is proven by evidence and logic.[7]

On the other hand, when human reason considers "how to" make or behave it is referred to as the practical intellect. The practical intellect pursues what is true not for its own sake so much as for its usefulness, to either behave well, or to make things well. The first principle of the practical intellect is "do good, avoid evil." This principle informs and guides our thinking process regarding how to do or how to behave. The virtue of art perfects the practical intellect in its striving to make things well; this includes the fine arts and crafts, everything from gardening and carpentry to law and medicine. The virtue of prudence perfects the practical intellect to choose to do good and to avoid evil, that is, to live well. As such it is classified as one of the four cardinal virtues and not an intellectual virtue. The intellectual virtues of wisdom, understanding, knowledge and art help us to think clearly or make things well, but they do not direct our will to choose good over evil which is the task of the cardinal virtues.

The Four Cardinal Virtues

The four cardinal virtues of Prudence, Justice, Courage and Temperance are virtues that perfect human acts. They are called "moral virtues" because they concern choosing and acting in the light of knowledge. The cardinal virtues make their possessor good. Persons who exercise these virtues behave morally.

"Cardinal" in Latin means "hinge." Cardinal virtues are the pivotal virtues from which the lesser virtues (integral, subjective and potential) and the greater virtues (theological, infused and Gifts of the Holy Spirit) hang. The cardinal virtues are acquired with human effort and practice, that is, with the performance of similar acts of the same virtuous deed. Once acquired, these virtues are hard to change and direct and perfect one's actions smoothly toward naturally good deeds. Cardinal virtues help us to survive and succeed in attaining the good things of this life such as health, success, natural happiness and fulfillment. Cardinal virtues perfect the acts of the will.[8]

However, it is also correct to say that prudence is not just in the will but in the practical intellect and that courage is in the irascible appetite, and temperance is in the concupiscible appetite. Why this apparent discrepancy? Prudence perfects the practical intellect regarding how to live or act rightly. Prudence guides the judgment of conscience.[9] Its functions are deliberation, judgment and command. Therefore, prudence directs the will and recommends or commands a course of action to the will. But it is up to the will to enforce this command or reject it. Because prudence "is so intimately bound up with will-action that all moral virtues require its direction . . . [it] is commonly listed with the moral virtues."[10]

Aquinas teaches that the irascible and concupiscible appetites are the subject of the virtues of courage and temperance, respectively.[11] Animals do not possess moral virtues. Nonetheless, we can see that animals can be trained to overcome fear and desire by the will of their trainer. Similarly, men (with reason and will power) train their emotions to resist the tugs and pulls of passion and the "slings and arrows" of danger:

> [W]hence the Philosopher [Aristotle] says that the reason rules the irascible and concupiscible powers by a political command such as that by which free men are ruled, who have in some respects a will of their own. And for this reason also must there be some virtues in the irascible and concupiscible powers, by which these powers are well disposed to act.[12]

However, this potency for conditioning that resides in the irascible and concupiscible appetites of man must be developed by his will. These qualities of the irascible and concupiscible appetites only come to perfection in man under the direction of his will, as a moral virtue. Therefore, we can speak of the irascible and concupiscible appetites as the subjects of the virtues of courage and temperance while at the same time we can speak of these virtues as moral qualities of the human will.

Prudence

Each cardinal virtue treats a difficult area of man's life bringing order, harmony and control to the operation of one of the faculties of one's soul or his sensitive appetite. The cardinal virtue of prudence[13] treats that aspect of one's rational life concerning command—commanding the right thing, at the right time, for the right reason. Prudence is right reason applied to human conduct.[14] Prudence perfects the practical intellect, enabling one to choose the right means to the right in ordering one's behavior and living well. It is the measure of the other moral virtues, guarding them from excess or deficiency.[15] It informs, suffuses, and links all the virtues.[16] Prudence shows the will the best path to take and commands the will to choose accordingly.[17] The natural virtue of prudence, often referred to a "common sense," is not necessarily common or a natural endowment but can be developed naturally,[18] without the aid of grace, through teaching and experience.

Prudence is the virtue that disposes practical reason to discern our true good in every circumstance and to choose the right means of achieving it: 'the prudent man looks where he is going.' 'Keep sane and sober for your prayers.' Prudence is 'right reason in action,' writes St. Thomas Aquinas.[19] It is not to be confused with timidity or fear, nor with duplicity or dissimulation. It is called *auriga virtutum* (the charioteer of the virtues), for it guides the other virtues by setting their rule and measure. It is prudence that immediately guides the judgment of conscience. The prudent man determines and directs his conduct in accordance with this judgment. With the help of this virtue we apply moral principles to particular cases without error and overcome doubts about the good to achieve and the evil to avoid.[20]

> The three functions of prudence serve to perfect deliberation (evaluating the possible means to a goal), judgment (deciding on the best means to a goal) and command (ordering the will to execute the best means to the goal). The potential parts of prudence include those virtues connected with prudence that do not rise to the level of a complete virtue by themselves such as *eubulia* of sound judgment or an ability to deliberate properly with regard to details; *synesis* or good judgment in the ordinary things of life; and *gnome* or exceptional judgment with regards to exceptional circumstances.[21]

The sins against prudence include imprudence, or a lack of good judgment including precipitousness or lack of deliberation; thoughtlessness or a wanton disregard of sound judgment; and inconstancy or lack of perseverance in commanding the right means to the right end and negligence or lack of due care in meeting or performing one's daily duties.[22]

Justice

The cardinal virtue of justice[23] perfects that most difficult area of one's life concerning giving to each person their due and showing respect for the rights of others.[24] Regardless of the unequal distribution of "talents"[25] we must always regard others as our equal, never as objects to be used for our pleasure or convenience because we are all radically equal as creatures before our Creator—all of us are equally from, for, and in the image of God.[26] Justice perfects the faculty of the will by providing it with a rectitude to honor the rights of others readily and with ease.[27]

In practice, justice consists of the constant and firm will to give what is due to God and neighbor. Justice towards God is called the 'virtue of religion.' Justice toward men disposes one to respect the rights of others and to establish in human relationships the harmony that promotes equity with regard to persons and to the common good. The just man, often mentioned in the Sacred Scriptures, is distinguished by habitual right thinking and the uprightness of his conduct toward his neighbor. 'You shall not be partial to the poor or defer to the great, but in righteousness shall you judge your neighbor.' "Masters, treat your slaves justly and fairly, knowing that you also have a Master in heaven."[28]

Justice is concerned with relationships between persons. These relationships may be considered from the perspective of legal or general justice, that is, what the individual owes the community, and particular justice or what the community owes the individual is owed to the individual persons by either the community (i.e., distributive justice), or by other individuals (i.e., commutative justice).[29]

General justice, also known as legal or social justice, regulates what the members owe the group and what each person must contribute toward the common good. To the extent that human laws reflect the natural law, they are ordered to man's final end. So one ought to obey the just laws of one's country and serve one's country in times of need. Laws requiring individuals to pay just taxes must be obeyed. Similarly, laws that outlaw fornication and contraception because they protect family stability, prevent fatherless delinquents and willfully childless couples that fail to contribute to the next generation, give expression to general or social justice.

Particular justice is composed of distributive and commutative. Distributive justice regulates what an individual receives from the group which may vary from individual to individual.[30] Invidious discrimination offends distributive justice by treating differently individuals similarly situated but for some benign characteristic, such as race, color, sex, or religion. On the other hand to not discriminate between individuals not similarly situated, such as children and adults, also violates the virtue of distributive justice.[31] Because the souls of all men are created directly by God, and are in his image, and because each person is invited to eternal beatitude, civil society must recognize in each person the same transcendental dignity and accord to each the same basic rights under distributive justice from the first moment of their existence until natural death.[32] The talents that God has not distributed equally among his children are not grounds for denying the weakest the most basic guarantees of life and its blessings, but rather those with more talents should share what they have received with those who need them so that they, the talented, may also learn generosity and kindness.[33]

Whereas distributive justice considers what society owes individuals proportionately in various circumstances, commutative justice regards individuals as equals.

Commutative justice regulates the exchanges that occur between individuals. Commutative justice considers contract obligations as well as the restitution due someone who has suffered personal offenses. Besides restoring or making an individual whole, commutative justice also seeks to make satisfaction or compensation for personal injury. In civil litigation, awards for pain and suffering or punitive damages for wanton and willful negligence attempt to provide satisfaction beyond mere restitution.

The virtue of justice also concerns the Common Good,[34] Solidarity,[35] and Subsidiarity.[36] These principles of social justice ensure a sound basis for domestic and international relations based on friendship. For instance, solidarity addresses the requirements of commutative justice between individuals since it is "manifested in the first place by the distribution of goods and remuneration for work."[37] Unjust labor conditions or hoarding wealth by employers are also sins against solidarity and commutative justice:

> Socio-economic problems can be resolved only with the help of all forms of solidarity: solidarity of the poor among themselves, between rich and poor, of workers among themselves, between employers and employees in a business, solidarity among nations and peoples. International solidarity is a requirement of the moral order; world peace depends upon this.[38]

Some sins against the virtue of justice include murder,[39] theft,[40] false testimony,[41] reviling, backbiting and talebearing,[42] usury,[43] superstition,[44] idolatry,[45] and magic.[46]

Fortitude

The cardinal virtue of fortitude, or courage,[47] treats that most difficult area of one's life when one must confront danger, especially the risk of death in, the performance of one's duty and doing good, staying the course, and seeing the job through.[48] Fortitude perfects the irascible appetite, those energy emotions which impel one to seek the good and avoid evil and moderate and channel the emotion of anger.[49]

> Fortitude is the moral virtue that ensures firmness in difficulties and constancy in the pursuit of the good. It strengthens the resolve to resist temptations and to overcome obstacles in the moral life. The virtue of fortitude enables one to conquer fear, even fear of death, and to face trials and persecutions. It disposes one even to renounce and sacrifice his life in defense of a just cause.[50]

The parts of fortitude or virtues associated with the virtue of fortitude are magnanimity which inclines one to perform great deeds,[51] and magnificence or a lofty undertaking in the sense of making something good and noble, confidence or firm hope in a noble undertaking, patience or prolonged endurance and perseverance or a fixed persistence.[52]

Vices opposed to fortitude include timidity or cowardliness, the inordinate fear which leads one to avoid what virtue requires.[53] Insensibility to fear is a false fortitude that fears no dangers rather than admitting there are dangers to be feared and, yet, faces those dangers.[54] Foolhardiness or audacity is a rushing into dangers, an overly bold reckless action in conflict with right reason.[55] Presumption is opposed to the virtue of magnanimity, which dares great deeds that lie within one's power to attain. Presumption vainly dares to attain what is beyond one's reach.[56] Faint-heartedness or pusillanimity is refusal to face up to a difficult situation one could overcome, like the servant who buried his one talent.[57] Meanness or Littleness is opposed to magnificence insofar as it aspires to only little things when better things should be attempted, or inclines one to be too tightfisted or cheap to attempt a noble endeavor.[58]

Temperance

Temperance perfects that most difficult area of one's life that deals with the control of the concupiscible appetite and control of the desire for bodily pleasure.[59] It moderates our desire for pleasures of sense such as those derived from food, drink (intoxicants), and sex, and moderates the sorrow or distress caused by the lack of such goods.[60] Temperance directs and perfects the concupiscible appetite.[61] The pleasures associated with food, drink, and sex are intended by our Creator to ensure that we do not neglect the duties necessary to sustain one's own life and that of the human race. Temperance orders our enjoyment of these pleasures to the needs of life.

> Temperance is the moral virtue that moderates the attraction of pleasures and pro-
> vides balance in the use of created goods. It ensures the will's mastery over in-
> stincts and keeps desires within the limits of what is honorable. The temperate per-
> son directs the sensitive appetites toward what is good and maintains a healthy
> discretion: "Do not follow your inclination and strength, walking according to the
> desires of your heart." Temperance is often praised in the Old Testament: "Do not
> follow your base desires, but restrain your appetites." In the New Testament it is
> called "moderation" or "sobriety." We ought "to live sober, upright, and godly
> lives in this world."[62]

The subjective parts or species of temperance are abstinence, sobriety, chastity and purity while the potential parts of temperance include continence, humility, meekness and modesty.[63]

Abstinence is that virtue which moderates one's desire for the pleasures associated with food and beverages so that one refrains from these in some degree or entirely.[64] Gluttony is opposed to the virtue of abstinence. It consists of excess in eating or drinking either with regard to the quality, delicacy or expense of food, the importance one attaches to fine dining, or the quantity of food one consumes.[65]

Sobriety (which means "measure") is that virtue which moderates the use of intoxicants.[66] Sobriety is opposed by the vice of drunkenness which is a mortal sin if one knowingly, willingly, and without just cause drinks to the point of depriving oneself of the use of reason.[67]

Chastity, once acquired, renders one able to avoid temptation to lust readily and with ease. Continence is the virtue which enables one to resist sexual desires, to fight against the sexual temptation which still strongly attracts one.[68]

The vice of lust consists in indulging in unlawful sexual pleasures.[69] The only licit enjoyment of sexual pleasure is in chaste marital relations.[70] The species of lust includes fornication, adultery, incest, seduction, rape, and unnatural vice, i.e., all acts from which conception cannot inherently follow such as masturbation, sodomy, bestiality[71] and contraception. "The lustful man intends not human generation but venereal pleasures. It is possible to have this without those acts from which human generation follows: and it is that which is sought in the unnatural vice."[72]

The vice of impurity or immodesty consists in acts which are not in themselves lustful but are calculated to arouse lust and lead to unchaste relations. If one is immodest so as to deliberately arouse lust, their actions are mortally sinful. If, on the other hand one is attempting to arouse curiosity, then they sin venially. If one has no intention to arouse either lust or curiosity by one's immodest act it is not sinful (such as a medical exam).[73]

Immodesty in dress occurs when one dresses in costly, dazzling, or gaudy apparel. Excessive pleasure in dressing is vainglorious, while slovenliness in dress also offends against modesty.[74] Women must be conscious that men are tempted to lust by a woman's immodest attire, whereas it is less likely that women are tempted by a man's immodest attire.[75]

Clemency regulates anger in one in a position to punish an inferior, whereas meekness controls the impulses of anger in oneself.[76] Modesty regulates both interior attitudes (such as studiousness) and external behavior, movement and attire.[77] Humility is a species of modesty which consists in appraising (seeing) oneself and others as God does, no more or no less. It curbs the inordinate desire to display one's excellence, that is, to flaunt.[78] Studiousness opposes the vice of curiosity (pursuit of vain or useless knowledge) or negligence and steadies the mind to acquire knowledge that is appropriate for one's state in life. Eutrapelia is moderation in recreation, and is a form of modesty which regulates one's outer decorum so that it is well-ordered, fitting, and beautiful.[79] Eutrapelia provides times of bodily repose and relaxation which often occurs in games which create "the habit of a pleasant and cheerful turn of mind" which is the very meaning of eutrapelia. This virtue is opposed by a habit of playing games or recreating in ways which are indecent or injurious, by an addiction to games, or by playing games under inappropriate circumstances.[80]

The natural virtues dispose one to follow the natural law and to be open to God's grace. However, in themselves they are not salvific. One does not get to heaven by simply being more prudent, just, courageous or temperate than the next person. As we shall see more fully in the next chapter, without God's grace reorienting the natural virtues so that divinized we can live like Christ, we are nothing: "If I . . . have not charity," says the Apostle, "I am nothing." Whatever my privilege, service, or even virtue, "if I . . . have not charity, I gain nothing."[81]

Notes

1. ST II-II, q. 49, a. 1.
2. ST II-II, q. 51, a. 3.
3. ST II-II, q. 51, a. 2.
4. ST II-II, q. 54, a. 3.
5. ST II-II, qq. 55–70.
6. CCC, no. 1810.
7. ST I-II, qq. 57–58.
8. ST I-II, qq. 57–61.
9. CCC, no. 1806.
10. Paul J. Glenn, *A Tour of the Summa*, (Rockford, IL: Tan Pub. 1960), 144; ST I- II, q. 61, a. 1.
11. ST I-II, q. 56, a. 4.
12. ST I-II, q. 56, a. 4, rep. obj. 3.
13. CCC, no. 1805–6; ST II-II qq. 47–56.
14. ST II-II, q. 47, a. 2.
15. ST II-II, q. 47, a. 7.
16. ST II-II, q. 47, a. 14.
17. ST II-II, q. 47, a. 8.
18. ST II-II, q. 47, a. 15.
19. CCC, no. 1806; citing ST II-II, q. 47, a. 2.
20 CCC, no. 1806.
21 ST II-II, q. 51, aa. 1–4.
22. ST II-II, q. 53, aa. 1–6; q. 54, aa.1–3.
23. CCC, nos. 1805, 2411; ST II-II, qq. 57–80.
24. ST II-II, q. 58, a. 1.
25. CCC, no. 1937.
26. CCC, no. 1934.
27. ST II-II, q. 58, a. 4.
28. Col 4:1 cited in CCC, no. 1807.
29. ST II-II, q. 58, aa.5, 6, 11.
30. ST II-II, a. 61, a. 6.
31. Francis J. Connell, *Outlines of Moral Theology* (Milwaukee, WI: Bruce Publishing Co., 1953), 104.
32. CCC, no. 1934.

33. CCC, no. 1936.

34. CCC, nos. 2420–25; Pontifical Council for Justice and Peace, *The Compendium of the Social Doctrine of the Church* (Libreria Editrice Vaticana, 2004), nos. 160, 164–65.

35. CCC, nos. 1939-42; *Compendium of the Social Doctrine of the Church*, nos. 351, 475, 529, 580.

36. CCC, nos. 1883–85, 2209; *Compendium of the Social Doctrine of the Church*, nos. 160, 185–88.

37. CCC, no. 1940.

38. CCC, no. 1941.

39. ST II-II, q. 64.

40. ST II-II, q. 66.

41. ST II-II, qq. 69–71.

42. ST II-II, qq. 72–74.

43. ST II-II, q. 78.

44. ST II-II, q. 93.

45. ST II-II, q. 94.

46. ST II-II, q. 96.

47. CCC, nos. 1805, 1808, 1831; ST II-II, qq. 123–40.

48. ST II-II, q. 123, aa. 4, 6.

49. ST II-II, q. 123, a. 11.

50. CCC, no. 1808.

51. ST II-II, q. 129.

52. ST II-II, q. 128, a. 1.

53. ST II-II, q. 125, a. 1.

54. ST II-II, q. 126.

55. ST II-II, q. 127.

56. ST II-II, q. 130.

57. See Matt. 25:24–29; ST II-II, q. 133.

58. ST II-II, q. 135.

59. CCC, nos. 1805, 1809; ST II-II, qq. 141–70.

60. ST II-II, q. 141, a. 3.

61. See Chapter One.

62 CCC, no. 1809.

63. ST II-II, q. 143, a. 1.

64. ST II-II, q. 146, a. 1.

65. ST II-II, q. 148, a. 4.

66. ST II-II, q. 149, a. 1.

67. ST II-II, q. 150, a. 1.

68. ST II-II, q. 155, aa. 1–2.

69. ST II-II, q. 153, a. 1.

70. ST II-II, q. 153, a. 2.

71. ST II-II, q. 154, aa. 1, 12.

72. ST II-II, q. 154, a. 11, rep. obj. 3.

73. Connell, *Outlines of Moral Theology*, 172–73.

74. ST II-II, q. 169, a. 1.

75. ST II-II, q. 169, a. 2.

76. ST II-II, q. 157, a. 1.
77. ST II-II, q. 160, a. 2.
78. ST II-II, q. 161.
79. ST II-II, q. 168, a. 1.
80. ST II-II, q. 168, aa. 1–2.
81. CCC, 1827; citing 1 Cor. 3:14.

Chapter 7
Sin and Grace

Sin and God's Forgiveness

Sin is like a slip on the ice: it entails a loss of balance and a fall, an experience of being out of control, then pain and finally trying to pick yourself up again. A slip on the ice is a physical evil. To deliberately trip someone to hurt them is a moral evil, a sin. Both are privations of necessary goods.[1] The *Catechism of the Catholic Church* defines sin as whatever is contrary to the Eternal Law or God's design for rational creatures.[2] Mortal sin is a "privation of sanctifying grace."[3] Grave sin "makes us incapable of eternal life, the privation of which is called the 'eternal punishment of sin."[4] Original Sin is described as "a deprivation of original holiness and justice."[5] Our first parents "transmitted to their descendants human nature wounded by their own first sin and hence deprived of original holiness and justice; this deprivation is called 'original sin.'"[6] All subsequent actual sin partake of a similar "disobedience toward God and lack of trust in his goodness."[7]

The evil of sin is unmasked in relation to God's call for each of us to live in union with him as a "divinized" son or daughter.[8] The true identity of sin is recognized in "humanity's rejection of God and opposition to him;" it is "an abuse of the freedom that God gives to created persons" to enslave oneself and reject the unimaginable relationship he wishes to bestow on us through Jesus Christ, in the power of the Holy Spirit.[9] In the first two chapters of Genesis, sin is described as a loss of trust, a break of friendship, a revolt, and a rebellion of man against God. The prophets of the Old Testament describe this break of man from God as comparable to the sexual infidelity of an unchaste wife.[10] Christ reestablishes this bond between himself and his people, the New Israel, his bride, the Church which union is comparable to the conjugal union of husband and wife.[11]

Moreover, in Christ the sufferings a person endures due to physical or moral evil are salvific when united to Christ and take on a redemptive quality.[12] We must never forget it is not so much we who suffer as Christ who suffers in us.[13] Pope

John Paul II writes, "In bringing about Redemption through suffering, Christ has also raised human suffering to the level of the Redemption. Thus each man, in his sufferings can also become a sharer in the redemptive suffering of Christ."[14]

Original Sin

Through no fault of his own, a "crack baby" inherits his mother's dependency and craving for cocaine and suffers withdrawal if deprived of it, as well as other long-term effects. The mother passes on her addicted state to her offspring and because of this the child's nature is wounded, and he may suffer the effects of this condition his whole life. The human nature we received after the Fall of our first parents is analogous to that of a cocaine dependent child; we inherit her unhappy cravings and disorders:

> [W]e know by Revelation that Adam had received original holiness and justice not for himself alone, but for all human nature. By yielding to the Tempter, Adam and Eve committed a *personal sin*, but this sin affected the human nature that they would then transmit *in a fallen state*. It is a sin which will be transmitted by propagation to all mankind, that is, by the transmission of a human nature deprived of original holiness and justice. And that is why original sin is called "sin" only in an analogical sense: it is a sin "contracted" and not "committed"—a state and not an act.[15]

> Adam and Eve transmitted to their descendants human nature wounded by their own first sin and hence deprived of original holiness and justice; this deprivation is called "original sin."[16]

> As a result of original sin, human nature is weakened in its powers; subject to ignorance, suffering and the domination of death; and inclined to sin (this inclination is called "concupiscence").[17]

Some people scoff at the notion of an Original Sin that was committed by the progenitors of the human race. First they contend that mankind did not have just two first parents but, rather, whole herds of "missing links" in the chain of evolution gradually made the transition to man, some in Africa, some in Asia. Whether or not man's physical body evolved from lower forms of biological life, Revelation tells us each person's spiritual soul is infused directly from God. There was no parceling out of so much rational soul to this proto-human ape and so much more to her descendants. Our first two parents had a complete human soul directly infused by God, and their parents, if they had any, did not have any part of a human soul. Pope Pius XII condemned "polygenism":

> For the faithful cannot embrace that opinion which maintains either that after Adam there existed on this earth true men who did not take their origin through

natural generation from him as from the first parent of all, or that Adam represents a certain number of first parents.[18]

The second reason some people deride the doctrine of Original Sin is because it seems to them as unsophisticated; eating an apple hardly seems a proper explanation for the origin of evil. The Church, of course, does not hold to a literal reading of the Book of Genesis. For instance, St. Thomas Aquinas taught that the "days" used to describe the phases of God's creation of the world should not be read as a literal twenty-four hours.[19] To criticize the Church for teaching a literal reading of the Fall of Adam and Eve is to erect a "straw man."

On the other hand, to say the first two chapters of Genesis are a fable or morality play with no connection to the events and persons mentioned in the narrative is equally untrue. The description of the Garden of Eden in Genesis is comparable to the realism of an icon, and ridiculing it because it does not appear life-like is a sad misunderstanding of its significance: "The account of the fall in Genesis 3 uses figurative language, but affirms a primeval event, a deed that took place at the beginning of the history of man."[20]

Before one criticizes the doctrine of original sin for sounding simplistic, one should first consider the other alternative explanations for the origin of evil. Perhaps we post-moderns are content with the explanation of evil "it just happens!" In other words, there is no explanation, no reason why bad things befall good people. Some prefer the idea that evil (and good) are illusions or polar opposites that eventually reconcile and vanish. Some are tempted to think that the universe was created by either an all-powerful god who isn't all good because he created evil, or is not all-powerful because he couldn't prevent evil.

Every explanation of the problem of evil may appear simplistic. However, like an icon, the figures and events portrayed in the Garden of Eden present the cosmic drama in archetypal genera:

> The "tree of the knowledge of good and evil" symbolically evokes the insurmountable limits that man, being a creature, must freely recognize and respect in truth. Man is dependent on his Creator and subject to the laws of creation and to the moral norms that govern the use of freedom.[21]

> Man, tempted by the devil, let his trust in his Creator die in his heart and abusing his freedom, disobeyed God's command. This is what man's first sin consisted of. All subsequent sin would be disobedience towards God and lack of trust in his goodness.[22]

God is all-powerful, but even he can't create absurdities—free creatures without the ability to abuse their freedom. In the first place, evil entered the world because of the envy of the Devil. Secondarily it is attributable to the free choice of our first parents who listened to Satan and not to God.

Adam and Eve chose to be rid of God and his commands. God granted them their wish: he left them to their own resources. God continued to hold them in existence but he withdrew his friendship and grace of "original justice"—a three part grace of harmony of (1) mind, body, and emotions whereby their emotions were docile to the commands of reason, (2) the harmony of man and woman, and (3) their harmony with nature.[23]

The "happy fault" of the rebellion of Adam and Eve against their Creator is that God didn't really leave us, but immediately after the Fall promised us a Savior to crush the head of Satan and restore to us what our first parents had lost. God offered us a second chance to accept his friendship through faith in His son, Jesus Christ. By faith in Jesus Christ *we obtain more than was lost* by our first parents. Their "happy fault" has won for us an even greater friendship through the grace won for us by Jesus Christ, God Incarnate:

> St. Leo the Great responds, "Christ's inexpressible grace gave us blessings better than those the demon's envy had taken away." And St. Thomas Aquinas wrote, "There is nothing to prevent human nature's being raised up to something greater, even after sin; God permits evil in order to draw forth some greater good. Thus St. Paul says, 'Where sin increased, grace abounded all the more'; and the Exultet sings, 'O happy fault, which gained for us so great a Redeemer!'"[24]

Those who dismiss the Fall and humanity's Original Sin are flirting with danger. Without an understanding of our wounded nature many presume the human person is naturally perfectible and they are tempted to do whatever it takes to eliminate human imperfection through drastic measure so as to usher in a new paradise. Many evils have been justified as means to the end of achieving paradise now, such as the elimination of private property, genetic engineering, eugenic sterilizations, and state control of populations and children. The Church recognizes that "Ignorance of the fact that man has a wounded nature inclined to evil gives rise to serious errors in the areas of education, politics, social action, and morals."[25] Divine Revelation confirms our intuition—that even with the best of hereditary endowment and the best of education and nurture we are still attracted to evil: "without the knowledge revelation gives of God we cannot recognize sin clearly and are tempted to explain it as merely a developmental flaw, a psychological weakness, a mistake, or the necessary consequences of an inadequate social structure."[26] The doctrine of original sin is an antidote to vanity and prevents us from making an idol of ourselves—wanting to "'be like God, but without God.'"[27]

Actual Sin

Actual sin is any utterance, deed, or desire contrary to the eternal law.[28] Sacred Scripture teaches there are some sins which are so contrary to the eternal law as to be deadly and destroy the life of grace whereas other sins, although they wound the life of grace, do not destroy it. "Anyone who sees his brother sinning, if the sin is not deadly, should petition God, and thus life will be given to the sinner. This is only for those whose sin is not deadly. There is such a thing as a deadly sin. . . . [A]ll wrongdoing is sin, but not all sin is deadly."[29]

The Church, relying on scripture and tradition, refers to this division of actual sins as mortal[30] and venial.[31] To commit a mortal sin one must do what is gravely wrong, that is, explicitly or implicitly contrary to the Ten Commandments,[32] with full knowledge and deliberate consent of their will.[33] Mortal sin is a "privation of sanctifying grace."[34] One commits a venial sin if what one does is not grave, or if what one does is grave one does it without full consent or knowledge.[35]

Actual sins develop a proclivity to sin by engendering a bad habit, a vice, which makes repetition of the same sin easier and more natural.[36] Personal sin has an accumulative effect and can lead not only to the formation of vice, but to societal structures of sin which lead their victims to become victimizers who do evil in turn to others.[37] For instance, in cultures where bribery is expected, one is first victimized and quickly learns to give and take bribes in turn.

Finally, unrepentant mortal sin leads the sinner to Hell—a place of no return and final separation from God and the blessed in Heaven.[38] For we have the radical freedom to make choices that last forever.[39] The inability of the damned to repent after death, however, is not due to "a defect in the infinite divine mercy" but to the power of our will to choose right or wrong.[40] One can damn themselves by committing one unrepentant mortal sin.[41] Some actual sins are referred to as "capital sins" because they tend to engender other sins and vices. They are pride, avarice, envy, wrath, lust, gluttony, and sloth.[42]

The Effects of Sin

Every serious sin produces four effects: insult to God; theological guilt in the sinner; chaos in the universe; and chaos in the "self" of the sinner. Mortal sins must be confessed to a priest:

> All mortal sins of which penitents after diligent self-examination are conscious must be recounted by them in confession, even if they are most secret and have been committed against the last two precepts of the Decalogue; for these sins sometimes wound the soul more grievously and are more dangerous than those which are committed openly.[43]

These four effects of serious sin are remedied in the sacrament of Penance. The insult to God and theological guilt are removed when the priest absolves the penitent. The disharmony the sinner introduced into himself and into the world by his sin is counteracted by the penance given the penitent which, united to the infinite merits of the passion and death of Jesus Christ, is able to reach out in time and space to draw good out of evil.

The first effect of serious sin, insult to God, is forgiven when the priest absolves the penitent, since "Sin is before all else an offense against God, a rupture of communion with him."[44] The spiritual effects of the sacrament of penance are "reconciliation with God by which the penitent recovers grace."[45]

The second effect of serious sin is theological guilt, that is, the fact of being guilty before God whether or not one actually feels guilty. It also is removed when the priest absolves the penitent: "Reconciliation with God is . . . the purpose of this sacrament. . . . [It] brings about a true 'spiritual resurrection,' restoration of the dignity and blessings of the life of the children of God, of which the most precious is friendship with God."[46] Another spiritual effect of the sacrament of penance is "remission of the eternal punishment incurred by mortal sins."[47]

The chaos the sinner introduced into himself, the third effect, is remediated through the penance given to the penitent by the priest: "The forgiven penitent is reconciled with himself in his inmost being, where he regains his inner-most truth."[48] The sacrament of penance brings "peace and serenity of conscience, and spiritual consolation"[49] and "reestablishes habits befitting a disciple of Christ."[50] Also, the inordinate attachment to creaturely satisfactions is lessened by the sacrament of penance: "[E]very sin, even venial, entails an unhealthy attachment to creatures, which must be purified either here on earth, or after death in the state called Purgatory. This purification frees one from what is called the 'temporal punishment' of sin."[51]

Finally, the chaos the sinner introduced into the universe through his or her sin, the fourth effect, is treated in a mysterious way through the penance given to the penitent by the priest. The forgiven penitent "is reconciled with his brethren whom he has in some way offended and wounded. He is reconciled with the Church. He is reconciled with all creation."[52] "The confessor proposes the performances of certain acts of 'satisfaction' or 'penance' to be performed by the penitent in order to repair the harm caused by sin."[53] A basic understanding of the human nature, the natural virtues and sin provides a foundation for comprehending the mystery of grace.

Grace and Divinization

In the days past it was often heard that someone was or was not in the King's good *graces*. Today we still speak of being in or having fallen out of *favor* with another. Grace means favor with God.[54] Grace bespeaks the "free and undeserved help" of God.[55] Grace refers to God's help beyond his creating us out of nothing and sustaining us in existence each moment lest we fall back into nothingness. Grace is God's "undeserved help" merited and bestowed upon us through the passion and death of Jesus Christ[56] transforming us from the mere human beings into divine beings by his adoption, that is a participation and transformation in grace . The Eastern Fathers of the Church referred to our participation and transformation in grace as "divinization":

Created in a state of holiness, man was destined to be fully "divinized" by God in glory. Seduced by the devil, he wanted to "be like God," without God, before God, and not in accordance with God.[57]

The Word became flesh to make us "partakers of the divine nature": "For this is why the Word became man, and the Son of God became the Son of man: so that man, by entering into communion with the Word and thus receiving divine sonship, might become a son of God." "For the Son of God became man so that we might become God." "The only-begotten Son of God, wanting to make us shares in his divinity, assumed our nature, so that he, made man, might make men gods."[58]

By the participation of the spirit, we become communicants in the divine nature. . . . For this reason, those in whom the spirit dwells are divinized.[59]

The grace of Christ is the gratuitous gift that God makes to us of his own life, infused by the Holy Spirit into our soul to heal it of sin and to sanctify it. It is the *sanctifying* or *deifying graces* received in Baptism. It is in us the source of the work of sanctification.[60]

Grace is a twofold reality: first, it is God's undeserved gift of Himself to us through the Redemption won for us by the passion and death of Jesus Christ; second, it is the effect that close intimacy with God, the indwelling of the Holy Spirit, has upon human nature. God's gift of Himself, to a soul in grace is referred to as "Uncreated Grace." The transformation produced in human nature as a result of the indwelling of the Blessed Trinity is called "created grace."

The process of transformation or divinization in grace begins when God comes to dwell within a soul through faith and baptism. Recall in the Old Testament, when a mortal man sees or speaks with God intimately, face to face, he must die: "But my face you cannot see, for no man sees me and still lives."[61] In the New Testament we learn that through faith in Christ the person who sees and hears God dies only to rise again "deified" as a new creation.[62] "This we know; our old self was crucified with him so that the sinful body might be destroyed and we might be slaves to sin no longer. . . . If we have died with Christ, we believe that we are also to live with him."[63] The man who sees God in grace dies only to be reborn as "God" by participation in grace, as Saints Athanasius and Thomas Aquinas tell us.[64] So, in grace we are transformed—we die to the flesh and are reborn in the spirit and our human nature undergoes a transformation, that is, we are "divinized" or "deified":

That divine power of his has freely bestowed on us everything necessary for a life of genuine piety. . . . By virtue of them [his glory and divine power] he has bestowed on us the great and precious things he promised, so that through these you who have fled a world corrupted by lust might become sharers of the divine nature.[65]

But what does it mean to "become sharers of the divine nature"? Does it mean we will exercise God's infinite power over the laws of nature and perform miracles? Does it mean we will enjoy the gifts of impassibility (an inability to suffer hurt) and infused knowledge lost after the Fall? Does it mean we will be given the gifts of bilocation, levitation, or mystical ecstasy manifest in the lives of some of the saints? The answer is, generally, no. Then what exactly *does* it mean to share in God's divine nature?

To understand what it means, we must first ask, what is the essence of God? Philosophers explain that God's essence is his existence: God *is*—He who exists. This is one interpretation of the name given to Moses from the burning bush, "I am, who am."[66] However, St. John the Beloved Disciple explained that the inner nature of God is love.[67] Therefore, to be divinized is to be taken up and to participate in the procession of divine love of the Father, Son and Holy Spirit.

This divine love is especially manifest when, sustained by grace, we suffer all things for love of God and turn the other cheek and forgive, in imitation of Christ.[68] This sounds simple. Anyone can say it. Anyone can claim their human efforts, their spiritual exercises, meditative techniques, etc. produce in their soul the quality of unconditional love. But saying it, describing it or understanding the concept does not give the capacity to *do* it. To say "yes" to this new way of living is a daily contest even for Christians and it is impossible to turn the other cheek to affronts without the aid of God's grace. This simple command is the test of our union with Christ and transformation in grace:

> We, for our part, love because he first loved us. If anyone says, "My love is fixed on God," yet hates his brother, he is a liar. One who has no love for the brother he has seen cannot love the God he has not seen. The commandment we have from him is this: whoever loves God must also love his brother.[69]

The New Law of Christ is principally grace which divinizes a person's soul and elevates their will through the infused theological virtue of charity, divine love, enabling one to live the beatitudes.[70] God's supernatural help, his grace, healing us, transforming us and elevating us to a divine level of activity does not, however, destroy our free will; grace does not make it impossible to say "no" to the promptings of the Holy Spirit:

> When God touches man's heart through the illumination of the Holy Spirit, man himself is not inactive while receiving that inspiration, since he could reject it; and yet, without God's grace, he cannot by his own free will move himself toward justice in God's sight.[71]

In sum, Christ merited through his passion atonement for the sins of all mankind.[72] The Redemption Christ won is applied to us in Baptism, through which we are justified[73] by the Holy Spirit and grace.[74] The Holy Spirit first brings about conversion as illustrated in the parable of the Prodigal Son,[75] then the remission of sins, and then an on-going sanctification and renewal of man.[76] Justification also entails the receipt of the gift of the theological virtues of faith, hope and charity[77] and the sanctification of man's whole being.[78] This grace received in Baptism is sanctifying or "deifying grace."[79] Sanctifying grace is a habitual gift enabling the soul to live with God and act by his divine love; whereas actual graces are those constant ways God intervenes in each of our lives, exterior (good influences—persons, places, or things) and interior promptings (inclinations to prayer, angelic illuminations, inspirations to works of mercy), which incite us to ongoing deeper conversion.[80] But grace demands a free response, as "God immediately touches and directly moves the heart of man. He places in man a longing for truth and goodness that only he can satisfy."[81]

Transformation in Grace

To what may we compare the transformation of human nature in grace? The theological virtues of faith, hope and charity[82] and the supernatural virtues given with sanctifying grace elevate the natural virtues, but they "remain under the direction of our own ingenuity and resources."[83] The seven gifts of the Holy Spirit are identified by the same names as the infused supernatural virtues—wisdom, knowledge, understanding, counsel, piety, fortitude, and fear of the Lord.[84] The gifts of the Holy Spirit make us docile, teachable, and open to the inspirations of the Holy Spirit "readily obeying divine inspirations."[85] St. Thomas Aquinas taught the unique moral dynamism of Christians is largely a result of the gifts of the Holy Spirit.

A seventeenth century Dominican, John of St. Thomas, contrasted the graced acts facilitated by the gifts of the Holy Spirit with those performed through the natural or infused virtues. Through connatural knowledge the soul in grace impelled by the gifts of the Holy Spirit tastes the goodness of God and hungers for more moved by an appetite other than his own:

> This interior illumination, this experiential taste of divine things and of other mysteries of the faith, excite our affections so that they tend to the object of virtue by a higher mode than these very same ordinary virtues do themselves. . . . As a result, the gifts effect a different kind of moral action. . . . [I]ndeed we are led to a divine and supernatural end by a mode which differs from the rule formed by our own efforts and labors (even in the case of infused virtue), that is, one formed and founded upon the rule of the Holy Spirit.[86]

John of St. Thomas then compares the graced good deeds done under the inspiration of the gifts of the Holy Spirit to a ship propelled by wind in its sails, as opposed to the graced good acts performed through the theological and infused virtues which he compares to oars: "In a similar way, the work of oarsmen moves a ship differently than the wind does, even though the waves waft it toward the same port," he says.[87] Through His seven-fold gifts the Holy Spirit inspires us like a cheer leader or a theatrical aide who helps actors emote their part, or like "a prompter on a theatrical set, [Who] can inspire a virtuous action in accord with a measure that surpasses that of human reason."[88]

The early Church Fathers compared the transformation in grace, the diviniza- tion of a Christian to a bar of iron placed in a white hot furnace. Imagine a dark cold room into which one enters with a bar of iron just removed from a fiery fur- nace. What do you notice? First the room is suddenly lit up with light emanating from the bar of iron. Next you would feel the warmth flowing from the iron bar. However light and heat are not naturally properties of iron; they are properties of fire. But after being immersed in fire, the bar of iron exhibits the properties of fire—it gives off light and heat. Moreover, the dross, the impurities in the iron are sloughed off. The iron bar is purified or healed and elevated to a new level of exis- tence by participation in the fire, yet it does not cease to be iron, its ferrous material is preserved not consumed, but like a wick in a candle it supports a new fiery na- ture.

St. Augustine tells us that grace like a white hot fire is the cause of a Chris- tian's new way of life and transfuses the dull and heavy iron of human nature and our good works with a fiery halo of Christ's holiness:

> Indeed we also work, but we are only collaborating with God who works, for his mercy has gone before us. It has gone before us so that we may be healed, and fol- lows us so that once healed, we may be given life; it goes before us so that we may be called, and follows us so that we may be glorified; it goes before us so that we may live devoutly, and follows us so that we may always live with God: for with- out him we can do nothing.[89]

> Human virtues acquired by education, by deliberate acts and by a perseverance ev- er-renewed in repeated efforts are purified and elevated by divine grace.[90]

An even more fitting analogy for how grace transforms human nature is the effects of human love and friendship. Consider how friends inevitably pick up each other's characteristics. This is especially noticeable in young lovers. They begin to dress alike and use the same expressions. Also, after a long married life together a hus- band or wife know each other so well that they can usually complete each others' sentences.

In the novel *Don Quixote* by Miguel de Cervantes, we read about the transfor- mative power of love. Dulcinea, a young bar maid and loose woman, is greeted by the knight errant, Don Quixote, as "my lady." This salutation causes the local male patrons of the bar to scoff and laugh at her and the fool who obviously doesn't know that her reputation is certainly not that of a lady. This scene is reminiscent of the incident described in all four Gospels of the young woman who washed Christ's feet with her tears and dried them with her hair while the guests at the banquet murmured to themselves "he obviously doesn't know what manner of woman is kissing his feet."[91] Don Quixote, in order to defend the wounded honor of Dulcinea, challenges the men at the bar to a duel. At first, even Dulcinea laughs at Don Quix- ote's seemingly foolish defense of her lost honor. But by the end of the novel she has been transformed by his friendship and love, and has reformed. She is no longer a loose woman, but the "lady" that only his eyes could see in her when they first met.

In similar fashion, Christ's love for us not only forgives and overlooks our faults but it reaches out and, if we allow it through an act of faith, heals, transforms, and elevates us, changing us from sinners to saints. However, since the Reformation we are tempted to believe, with Martin Luther and John Calvin, in a mere forensic or legal notion of justification in grace. The Reformers erroneously taught the human will was totally corrupted by Original Sin and even after a person's conversion and baptism it remained corrupt and incapable of graced good works. On the contrary, Vatican Council II assures us that, like Mary, the faithful participate in Christ's savings works which show forth his power to save sinners:

> No creature could ever be counted along with the Incarnate word and Redeemer; but just as the priesthood of Christ is shared in various ways both by his ministers and the faithful, and as the one goodness of God is radiated in different ways among his creatures, so also the unique mediation of the Redeemer does not exclude but rather gives rise to a manifold cooperation which is but a sharing in this one source.[92]

If Christ enables us to cooperate with him in performing graced good works then we are held accountable for whether we cooperate generously. If we do not say "no" to the grace Christ offers, he will offer us more and more opportunities to grow in grace. On the other hand, if we say "no" to his grace, if we bury our talents, we will be punished as Christ taught in the parable of the sower,[93] in the parable of the Good Samaritan,[94] in the parable of the fig tree[95] and the parable of the Talents.[96]

Even in grace no one has a right in strict justice to merit their own salvation or that of others based on equality because we are not divine by nature.[97] However, by divine adoption—a free and undeserved gift—we acquire a new divine nature through incorporation into the Body of Christ. Our merit before God for the graced good works we do as Christ's disciples consists in saying yes by the power of his grace to all he wishes to do through us by the power of his grace. If we allow the Holy Spirit to act in our lives, if we do not hinder Him, we may merit an eternal reward in this relative sense:

> The merit of man before God in the Christian life arises from the fact that God has freely chosen to associate man with the work of his grace. The fatherly action of God is first on his own initiative, and then follows man's free acting through his collaboration, so that the merit of good works is to be attributed in the first place to the grace of God, then to the faithful.[98]

> Moved by the Holy Spirit and by charity, we can merit for ourselves and for others the graces needed for our sanctification, for the increase of grace and charity, and for the attainment of eternal life. Even temporal goods like health and friendship can be merited in accordance with God's wisdom. These graces and goods are the

object of Christian prayer. Prayer attends to the grace we need for meritorious actions.[99]

The following personal example may help to explain the difference between meriting in strict justice versus that of gratuitous justice.[100] We had several horses and goats on our farm. Now, because I enjoy my youngest daughter's company, I made this deal with her one day as I prepared to water the horses. I said to her: "Rosarie, if you help me carry the heavy five-gallon water buckets to the horse stalls, I'll give you an ice cream cone when we're done. Now, if you get distracted, let go, and run off to chase butterflies, I'll let go, too. But if you just keep your hand on the handle of the water bucket, so will I; so follow me."

Now what would you think if, after we were finished carrying water to all the horses, I sat down with Rosarie and explained the reality of the situation and said: "Rosarie, you know when we were carrying those buckets of water to the horse stalls, it was really me who carried the whole weight of those full and heavy buckets, right? Why, your little arms couldn't even budge them. All you did was hold on to the bucket and walk along next to me. Quite simply, I did all the work. Therefore, you are not really entitled to an ice cream cone." She then looked up crying and stuttering, "Why you, you, lawyer! You promised!"

In strict justice, I was right—I did all the work. But justice would be denied if I failed to reward her since I conditioned my outpouring of strength (such as it is) on whether or not she let go of the handle of the water bucket; on whether or not she said "no" to my lead and ran off. She followed my instructions and cooperated. She gave it her all and kept me company. Together, her work plus my work got the job done. Therefore she truly, albeit gratuitously, merited an ice cream cone.

Jesus himself gave us a similar analogy when he described the duties of a Christian in terms of being yoked with him: "Take my yoke upon your shoulders and learn from me, for I am gentle and humble of heart. Your souls will find rest, for my yoke is easy and my burden is light."[101] In another passage Jesus tells says "take up your cross and follow after me."[102] We are tempted to think of this yoke Christ lays on our back as a solitary cross that we must drag around. Rather, it is a double yoke for a *pair* of oxen, a double yoke laid upon both the shoulders of Christ and our own. The one ox cannot pull without the cooperation of the other. But if we take up our cross daily and follow Christ he carries the entire weight and this enables "us to collaborate in the salvation of others and in the growth of the Body of Christ, the Church."[103]

In this sense, although not formally defined as yet, the Church does not hesitate to call Mary "Co-Redemptrix," i.e., she collaborated with Christ to achieve our redemption. The word "co" in Latin means "with"; it does not mean "co-equal." The truth is that without Christ we are nothing, but with him we can do even greater deeds than he while he walked the dusty roads of Galilee and Judea. "I solemnly assure you, the man who has faith in me will do the works I do, and greater far than these. Why? Because I go to the Father, and whatever you ask in my name I will do."[104]

Therefore, the Church teaches that Mary, totally dependent upon her Son, especially through the sufferings they shared in His Passion and death, merited favor and grace for the whole human race. In a similar fashion St. Paul tells us that he, too, "makes up for the sufferings that are lacking in the sufferings of Christ for the sake of the Church."[105] The mission of each Christian is to be an imitator of Christ. This is possible only if we, with expectant faith, extend in time and space the saving work of Jesus Christ. He has no hands or feet but ours, but with his Spirit filling us, like wind in the sail, we can carry his love throughout the whole world and help him to transform a culture of death into a civilization of love.

Notes

1. SD, no. 7. See also SD, nos. 5, 6.
2. CCC, no. 1849; cf. ST I-II, q. 71, a. 6.
3. CCC, no. 1861.
4. CCC, no. 1472.
5. CCC, no. 405.
6. CCC, no. 417.
7. CCC, no. 397.
8. CCC, nos. 398, 1988.
9. CCC, nos. 386, 387.
10. See Hos. 1–3; Isa. 62; Jer. 2:1–2, 3:1–4.
11. Eph. 5:26–32. See also Rev. 21:2–3.
12. See Col. 1:24.
13. See Luke 9:23; 2 Cor. 1:5; Gal. 2:19–20.
14. SD, no. 19.
15. CCC, no. 404.
16. CCC, no. 417.
17. CCC, no. 418.
18. Pope Pius XII, *Humani Generis* (1950), no. 37.
19. ST I, q. 74, aa. 1–3.
20. CCC, no. 390.
21. CCC, no. 39.
22. CCC, no. 397.
23. CCC, nos. 399, 400.
24. CCC, no. 412
25. CCC, no. 407; citing CA, no. 25.
26. CCC, no. 387.
27. CCC, no. 398.
28. CCC, no. 1849.
29. 1 John 5:16–17, 19:11; Jer. 7:26; Lam. 4:6. See also CCC, no. 1854.
30. Eph. 5:5–7; Gal. 5:19–21.
31. James 3:2; 1 John 1:8; Eccl. 7:21; VS, no. 69.
32. CCC, no. 1858.
33. CCC, no. 1857. See also VS, no. 70.

34. CCC, no. 1861.

35. CCC, no. 1862.

36. CCC, no. 1865.

37. CCC, no. 1869.

38. CCC, no. 1861. See also CCC, no. 1033.

39. CCC, no. 1861.

40. CCC, no. 393.

41. VS, no. 70.

42. CCC, no. 1866.

43. CCC, no. 1456; citing Council of Trent (1551: DS 1680 (ND 1626)). Cf. Exod. 20:17; Matt. 5:28.

44. CCC, no. 440.

45. CCC, no. 1496.

46. CCC, no. 1468.

47. CCC, no. 1496.

48. CCC, no. 1469.

49. CCC, no. 1496

50. CCC, no. 1494.

51. CCC, no. 1472.

52. CCC, no. 1469.

53. CCC, no. 1494.

54. ST I-II, q. 110, a.1.

55. CCC, no. 1996.

56. CCC, no. 1992.

57. CCC, no. 398; citing St. Maximus the Confessor, Ambigua: PG 91, 1156C. See also Gen 3:5.

58. CCC, no. 460.

59. CCC, no. 1988, citing St. Athanasius, Ep. Serap. 1, 24: PG 26, 585 and 588.

60. CCC,. no. 1999; see also Jn. 4:14, 7:38–39.

61. Exod. 33:20; see also Exod. 20:19; Judg. 13:22; Isa. 6:5.

62. CCC, no. 1999.

63. Rom. 6:6–8.

64. CCC, no. 460.

65. 2 Pet. 1:3–4.

66. ST I, q. 2, a. 1.

67. 1 John 4:8–16.

68. Luke 6:29; Matt. 5:39.

69. 1 John 4:19–21.

70. CCC, no. 1966.

71. CCC, no. 1993 citing the Council of Trent (1547): DS 1525.

72. CCC, no. 1992.

73. CCC, no. 1992

74. CCC, no. 1987.

75. Luke 15:11–32.

76. CCC, no. 1989.

77. CCC, no. 1991.

78. CCC, no.1995.

79. CCC, no. 1997.

80. CCC, no. 2000.

81. CCC, no. 2002.

82. 1 Cor. 13:13; CCC, nos. 1812–29.

83. Romanus Cessario, *The Virtues, or the Examined Life* (New York, NY: Continuum, 2002), 16.

84. See Isa. 11:2–3; CCC, no. 1830–31.

85. CCC, no. 1831.

86. Cessario, *The Virtues*, 16, citing John of St. Thomas, *Disputatio* XVIII, a. 2, n. 29.

87. Cessario, *The Virtues*, 16, citing John of St. Thomas, *Disputatio* XVIII, a. 2, n. 29.

88. Cessario, *The Virtues*, 16, citing John of St. Thomas, *Disputatio* XVIII, a. 2, n. 29.

89. CCC, no. 2001; citing St. Augustine, *De natura et gratia*, 31 PL 44, 264.

90. CCC, no. 1810.

91. See Luke 7:36–50; Matt. 26:6–13; Mark 14:3–9; John 12:1–8.

92. LG, no. 62.

93. Luke 8:4–16.

94. Luke 10:25–37.

95. Luke 13: 6–9.

96. Luke 19:11–27.

97. CCC, no. 2007.

98. CCC, no. 2008.

99. CCC, no. 2010.

100. See CCC, no. 2009.

101. Matt. 11:29–30.

102. Luke 9:23, 14:27; Matt. 10:38, 16:24; Mark 8:34.

103. CCC, no. 2003.

104. John 14:12–13.

105. Col. 1:24.

Chapter 8
Revelation

Christian moral principles are partially derived from reason. Through reason we can know objective reality outside our mind and an objective natural law of moral behavior written deep within our mind and heart. Because we can reason, our will is free to seek happiness in the pursuit and attainment of good. Moreover, we see that everyone desires perfect happiness. Consequently, something or Someone must exist that will satisfy this deepest longing or else we are absurd creatures.

The second source of Christian moral principles is divine revelation; "Indeed, Sacred Scripture remains the living and fruitful source of the Church's moral doctrine."[1] Revelation provides assurance, through God's direct testimony, that we are not absurd creatures longing for something which does not exist.[2] Rather, God has revealed he created man for himself, and that "from his conception, [man] is destined for eternal beatitude."[3]

Reason can know with certainty that God exists and is the Creator, Designer, and Sustainer of all contingent being. However, because the human person "is the only creature on earth that God has willed for its own sake," God desires that we come to know, love, and serve him in this life for who He is in Himself.[4] We cannot gain this kind of intimate knowledge of God through reason alone. Therefore, since we cannot ascend to intimate knowledge of God though reason, God descended and revealed Himself to us:

> There exists a two-fold order of knowledge, distinct not only as regards their source, but also as regards their object. With regards to their source, because we know in one by natural reason, in the other by divine faith. With regard to the object, because besides those things which natural reason can attain, there are proposed for our belief mysteries hidden in God which, unless they are divinely revealed, cannot be known.[5]

Revelation—God's Mode of Operation

God revealed himself to man employing those qualities of human nature which most bear His image. He used *words* and *acts* to reveal himself and his mysterious plan hidden from the ages.[6] God revealed himself in salvation history beginning with our first parents, but especially to the children of Abraham, our father in faith. God revealed his saving plan for Israel, and the authority of the Word of God (the Logos) over his chosen people in the words he inspired conveyed without error by the patriarchs, prophets, priests, and kings of Israel:

> God inspired the human authors of the sacred books. "To compose the sacred books, God choose certain men who, all the while he employed them in this task, made full use of their own faculties and powers so that, though he acted in them and by them, it was as true authors that they consigned to writing whatever he wanted written, and no more."[7]

God also revealed his power over cosmic and human history in theophanies, mighty deeds of supernatural power, such as he displayed in the exodus of Israel from Egypt:

> Theophanies (manifestations of God) light up the way of the promise, from the patriarchs to Moses and from Joshua to the visions that inaugurated the missions of the great prophets. Christian tradition has always recognized that God's word allowed himself to be seen and heard in these theophanies, in which the cloud of the Holy Spirit both revealed him and concealed him in its shadow.[8]

Both the words he inspired and the mighty works he performed cast light on each other and gradually revealed the inner life of God:

> Revelation is realized by deeds and words, which are intrinsically bound up with each other. As a result, the works performed by God in the history of salvation show forth and bear out the doctrine and realities signified by the words; the words, for their part, proclaim the works, and bring to light the mystery they contain.[9]

The Complete Revelation of God in Jesus Christ

God's self-disclosure reached perfection in the Incarnation of the Second Person of the Blessed Trinity. The Logos, the Word of God, emptied himself and descended into time, and was conceived beneath the Immaculate Heart of Mary, who became the Mother of God. St. John tells us that "The Word became flesh and dwelt amongst us, and we have seen his glory; the glory of an only Son coming from the Father, filled with enduring Love."[10] Mary is then the "definitive theophany" predicted by Isaiah, a living "burning bush"—"filled with the Holy Spirit", she makes the Word visible in the humanity of his flesh."[11]

Jesus Christ is the full and complete revelation of God.[12] His words are God's words[13] and his works are the Father's.[14] Jesus completes the process of divine revelation begun through the patriarchs, prophets, priests, and kings of Israel. He employs the same mode of operation as they, using divinely inspired words to reveal the secrets of God and works of power and miracles to corroborate his authority.

Jesus is the sacred sign, the sacrament that reveals and embodies as fully as possible in human form the face of God. However, after three years of constant communication with Christ even the Apostle Phillip did not understand this. He begged Jesus at the Last Supper to grant him one last favor—"show us the Father and that will be enough for us." Jesus may have hung his head in disappointment as he said: "[A]fter I have been with you all this time, you still do not know me? Whoever has seen me has seen the Father. How can you say, 'show us the Father'?" Then Jesus pointed to his words and works as proof of his equality with the Father: "The words I speak are not spoken of myself; it is the Father who lives in me accomplishing his works. Believe me that I am in the Father and the Father is in me, or else, believe because of the works I do."[15] Previously he had answered in similar fashion the question posed by the disciples of John the Baptist after the Baptist was taken into prison. They asked Jesus if he was indeed God's Messiah. In reply Jesus pointed to the irrefutable corroborating evidence of his deeds:

> Are you "He who is to come" or do we look for another? In reply, Jesus said . . . "Go back and report to John what you hear and see: the blind recover their sight, cripples walk, lepers are cured, the deaf hear, dead men are raised to life, and the poor have the good news preached to them."[16]

Jesus' answer to his Apostle and his Precursor show that even God could not improve upon the living portrait of Himself which he gave us in the person of Jesus Christ, true God and true man, in his person expressed in his divine words and grace-filled deeds:

> [Jesus completed revelation] by the total fact of his presence and self-manifestation, by words and works, signs and miracles, but above all, by his death and glorious resurrection from the dead, and finally by sending the Spirit of truth.[17]

> God has revealed himself and given himself to man. This he does by revealing the mystery, his plan of loving goodness, formed from all eternity in Christ, for the benefit of all men.[18]

Jesus' Words and Works Continued in the Church

After his resurrection from the dead Jesus first forgave his apostles and then elicited from them an act of faith.[19] An act of faith in Christ is not a logical demonstration. It is not susceptible to laboratory experimentation. To crave for sensory manifestations of God is superstitious. Superstition "can even affect the worship we offer the true God"[20] as when we only look to the externals of religious practice without the interior dispositions that they demand. The interior disposition demanded is an act of faith. St. Thomas defined faith as "an act of the intellect assenting to the divine truth by command of the will moved by God though Grace."[21]

Believing is also a human act. Whether someone is telling the truth can be subject to rigorous scrutiny, to rules of evidence, and to the cross-examination of witnesses as in a criminal trial. At the end of a trial, the jury is asked to decide who they believe. They are asked to render a verdict, make an act of faith, based on the credibility of the witnesses and their testimony. We may arrive at truth in such ways.[22]

The two men on the road to Emmaus failed to recognize Jesus by his words alone, even though their hearts burned listening to him as they traveled along. It was only after he gave further testimony of his identity, by his deeds, in the breaking of bread, that they recognized him. After he disappeared, they reproved themselves for not having believed the testimony their burning hearts had given them of the mysterious stranger's divine authority.[23] St. John explains that if we are willing to accept human testimony as a basis for crucial decisions, we should be willing to listen to the witness of our own heart when it convicts us. For our hearts bear witness to the testimony God himself gives on behalf of his own Son:

> Do we not accept human testimony? The testimony of God is much greater: it is the testimony God has given on his own Son's behalf. Whoever believes in the Son of God possesses that testimony within his heart.[24]

After Jesus forgave his Apostles, he then commanded them to preach the Gospel to all nations until the end of time.[25] They went out to all nations and preached what they had seen and heard Jesus say and do. They themselves were a continuation of the saving message and powerful works of Jesus. In their words, men heard the Good News. By their touch, miracles were performed and the Holy Spirit was bestowed.[26] Their successors (bishops) continued to extend the saving words and works of Jesus through time and space down through centuries throughout all the earth:

> [Divine revelation was transmitted in its entirety] by the apostles who handed on, by the spoken word of their preaching, by the example they gave, by the institutions they established, what they themselves had received—whether from the lips of Christ, from his way of life and his works, or whether they had learned it through the prompting of the Holy Spirit.
>
> In order that the full and living Gospel might always be preserved in the Church, the apostles left bishops as their successors. . . . Thus, the apostolic preaching . . . was to be preserved in a continuous line of succession until the

end of time.[27]

Jesus' Words Continued in Scripture and Tradition

The Gospel of the Lord Jesus was passed on in two ways, orally and in written form.[28] The apostles warned their successor bishops to maintain the Apostolic Tradition they received whether by word of mouth or letter: "Therefore, brothers, stand firm. Hold fast to the traditions you received from us, either by our word or by letter."[29] The Apostolic Tradition was also committed to writing[30] as St. Luke testifies:

Many have undertaken to compile a narrative of the events which have been fulfilled in our midst, precisely as those events were transmitted to us by the original eye witnesses and ministers of the word. I too have carefully traced the whole sequence of events from the beginning, and have decided to set it in writing for you.[31]

The Second Vatican Council explained that the Church's living memory of Jesus Christ is contained in Tradition and Scripture which are "like a mirror" in which the Church contemplates God.[32] Tradition and Scripture are like "two streams" that flow from the same source and form one river. Both Tradition and Scripture make up a single deposit of the Faith. Scripture is not greater than Tradition; rather, both must be equally honored:

Sacred Tradition and sacred Scripture, then, are bound closely together, and communicate one with the other. For both of them, flowing out from the same divine well-spring, come together in some fashion to form one thing, and move towards the same goal. Sacred Scripture is the speech of God. . . . And Tradition transmits in its entirety the Word of God. . . . Thus it comes about that the Church does not draw her certainty about all revealed truths from the holy Scriptures alone. Hence, both Scripture and Tradition must be accepted and honored with equal feelings of devotion and reverence.[33]

Jesus' Works Continued in the Seven Sacraments and the Liturgical Acts of the Church

The Church founded by Christ extends his saving work to all places throughout all time through the seven Sacraments, the Mass, and the other liturgical acts. Before he left them, Jesus enjoined his Apostles to perform these sacred actions on his behalf: "This is my body to be given for you. Do this in remembrance of me."[34] The Apostles were given a command to perpetuate and extend through time and space the mysteries they had experienced that night in which they were consecrated priests at the Lord's Last Supper:

[God] also willed that the work of salvation which they [the apostles] preached should be set in train through the sacrifice and sacraments, around which the entire liturgical life revolves.[35]

It is really Christ who acts through his ministers extending his presence sacramentally:

> To accomplish so great a work, Christ is always present in his Church, especially in her liturgical celebrations. He is present in the Sacrifice of the Mass not only in the person of his ministers . . . but especially in the eucharistic species. By his power he is present in the sacraments so that when anybody baptizes, it is really Christ himself who baptizes.From this it follows that every liturgical celebration, because it is an action of Christ the Priest and of his Body, which is the Church, is a sacred action surpassing all other.[36]

The Interpretation of Divine Revelation

To understand divine revelation properly, all of it must be considered, both words and works—Tradition, Scripture, Sacraments, and Liturgy—by one competent to interpret it, i.e., the Magisterium or teaching authority of the Catholic Church.

Although the deposit of the faith was completed with the death of the last Apostle,[37] it must be conveyed in its first freshness ever again in new historical and cultural situations. However, it can only impart its original splendor of truth if it follows "the line of interpretation given to it by the great Tradition of the Church's teaching and life, as witnessed by the Fathers, the lives of the Saints, the Church's Liturgy and the teaching of the Magisterium."[38] As St. Paul himself warned, the work of God has been transmitted by the Apostles both orally and by letter.[39] Therefore, to consider Scripture apart from oral Tradition is unscriptural.[40] Likewise, to reflect upon the words of Christ without the mirror of Christ's saving works is also unsound.

> [N]o less attention must be devoted to the content and unity of the whole of Scripture, taking into account the Tradition of the entire Church and the analogy of faith, if we are to derive the true meaning of the sacred texts.[41]

But who is competent to properly understand the relation of the words of Christ, written and oral, to the works of Christ, the seven sacraments and liturgy contained in his church? Who may legitimately interpret the true meaning of divine revelation? The meaning of Revelation is reached through a process of discernment as described below.

The Sense of the Faithful

Every Christian is called upon to deepen his faith. Theology is simply faith in search of understanding. Each Christian, because he is a temple of the Holy Spirit[42], has a certain connatural understanding of God and the things of God. Connatural knowledge means that things with the same nature like and dislike the same things. Because God and the Christian have the same Spirit, they love the same things. As we grow in holiness, our knowledge of God's mysteries increases:

> There is an organic connection between our spiritual life and the dogmas. Dogmas are lights along the path of faith; they illuminate it and make it secure. Conversely, if our life is upright, our intellect and heart will be open to welcome the light shed by the dogmas of faith.[43]

The way the Holy Spirit gradually melts and molds our hearts to love the things he loves and hate what he hates is comparable to human love. Did you ever notice that when young people fall in love, they tend to imitate each other? They take on similar gestures and expressions and may even dress alike. After a life-time of marriage, they know and love each other so well that they unconsciously complete each other's sentences, and have even grown to physically resemble each other. If someone were to suggest to a woman that her teetotaler husband was falling down drunk the other night, she would probably laugh and say—"Oh wouldn't that be a sight! But it can't be. I know him too well. You've mistaken him for someone else." In similar fashion God's spirit dwelling in us gives us the ability to appraise things as He does:

> There is, to be sure, a certain wisdom which we express among the spiritually mature . . . what we utter is God's wisdom: a mysterious, hidden wisdom. . . . The Spirit scrutinizes all matters, even the deep things of God. Who, for example, knows a man's innermost self but the man's own spirit within him? Similarly, no one knows what lies at the depth of God but the Spirit of God. The Spirit we have received is not the world's spirit but God's Spirit, helping us to recognize the gifts he has given us . . . thus interpreting spiritual things in spiritual terms . . . [and] can appraise everything, though he himself can be appraised by no one.[44]

Collectively, the connatural knowledge that individual Christians have of God, through the indwelling of the Holy Spirit, is referred to as the "sense of the faithful" (sensus fidei):

> The whole body of the faithful . . . cannot err in matters of belief. This characteristic is shown in the supernatural appreciation of faith (*sensus fidei*) on the part of the whole people, when "from the bishops to the last of the faithful," they manifest a universal consent in matters of faith and morals.[45]

Only those Christians in a state of grace can contribute to the sense of the faithful. The sense of the faithful adds to the development of doctrine in the Church. Because divine charity fills the souls of the true and holy believers with God's own sentiments, they find heresy disquieting and truth peaceful. This wisdom from on high is a gift of the Holy Spirit:

> The Tradition that comes from the apostles makes progress in the Church, with the help of the Holy Spirit. There is a growth in insight into the realities and words that are being passed on. This comes about in various ways. It comes through the contemplation and study of believers who ponder these things in their hearts. It comes from the intimate sense of spiritual realities which they experience.[46]

> Aquinas was keen to show the primacy of the wisdom which is the gift of the Holy Spirit and which opens the way to a knowledge of divine realities. . . . This wisdom comes to know by way of connaturality; it presupposes faith and eventually formulates its right judgment on the basis of the truth of faith itself: "The wisdom named among the gifts of the Holy Spirit is distinct from the wisdom found among the intellectual virtues. This second wisdom is acquired through study, but the first 'comes from on high', as St. James puts it."[47]

Tradition and the Fathers of the Church

The Fathers of the Church are a unique witness to the teachings of the Apostles. These learned and saintly church leaders lived from the first to the eighth century. One can go so far as to say that if the roots of a proposed dogma cannot be found in the writings of the Fathers of the Church, it is not a part of Apostolic Tradition:

> The sayings of the Holy Fathers are a witness to the life-giving presence of the Tradition, showing how its riches are poured out in the practice and life of the Church, in her belief and her prayer.[48]

The Fathers did not always agree in the way they approached a theological issue, nor necessarily in their conclusions. But their general consensus on an issue is considered a touchstone of the correct interpretation of divine revelation. Moreover, the Fathers of the Church shaped the issues and often the actual formulations of Christian dogma in the seven Ecumenical Councils of the ancient Church. At that time, before the schism of the Orthodox Church, both the Latin and Greek speaking Churches were in communion. Together they defeated a series of heresies which denied either Christ's divinity or his humanity.

Arius, a fourth-century Christian heretic, argued from tradition and scripture that Jesus was created before time by God who then became a Father. This false teaching denied the Incarnation and Redemption. Arius claimed that "God has not always been Father, there was a moment when he was alone, and was not yet Father; later he became so. The Son is not from eternity; he came from nothing."[49]

Later Nestorius, Patriarch of Constantinople during the mid-fifth century, denied that God the Son ever became incarnate. He taught that the Father adopted the man, Jesus, while in his Mother's womb, and that there was perfect moral union of will and sentiments between the human person, Jesus, and God the Son, a divine Person, but not a true Incarnation. Nestorius argued that the child born of Mary was merely a human person who was called Christ by virtue of his office as Messiah. He said it is proper to call Mary *Christotokos* or "Christ-bearer," but not *Theotokos*, or "God-bearer." Nestorius gave the following explanation:

> They ask whether Mary may be called God-bearer. But has God, then a mother? . . . Mary did not bear God. . . . [T]he creature did not bear the Creator, but the man who is the instrument of the Godhead. . . . He who was formed in the womb of Mary was not God Himself, but God assumed him.[50]

To summarize, Arius taught that Jesus was comparable to a super angel, while Nestorius taught that Jesus was comparable to a super saint. The former denied he was true God, the latter denied that there was ever a true incarnation of God. The Fathers, supported by the sense of the faithful, rejected these heresies and declared to Arius in Creeds we still repeat today that the Son of God in his relation to the Father is "light from light, true God from true God." The Ecumenical Council of Ephesus in 431 condemned Nestorius and held that Mary was indeed that unique creature made by God, who in turn bore God in her womb:

> Receiving the news with joyous shouts of "Mother of God! Mother of God!" they formed torchlight processions to escort the bishops to their residences. Soon after, [St.] Cyril described Mary to the people of Ephesus as "the Mother of God, the holy ornament of all the universe, the unquenchable lamp, the crown of virginity, the scepter, the container of the uncontainable, mother and virgin."[51]

The Church's Teaching Office

Just as human reason can err with regards to truth in the natural order, so personal Christian reflection can err regarding divine truth. How many people give friends directions to their home only to receive a call saying that their friends lost their way. They then have to go and find their lost friends and guide them to their home. Christ did not merely leave us written directions or a map by which to find our way to heaven, he also left us an infallible guide. The teaching office of the Catholic Church or Magisterium is the infallible interpreter of the words and works of Christ continued in the Church's Tradition and Scripture, Sacraments and Liturgy. It cannot add or subtract to this deposit of the faith, but must guard it and faithfully explain it for the salvation of souls. The teaching office of the Church consists of the Pope or the bishops in union with the Pope when they teach with authority on matters of faith and morals:

> But the task of giving an authentic interpretation of the Word of God, whether in its written form or in the form of Tradition, has been entrusted to the living teaching office of the Church alone. . . . Yet this Magisterium is not superior to the Word of God, but is its servant. It teaches only what has been handed on to it.[52]

The relationship of Scripture, Tradition, and Magisterium is comparable to a tripod that is solid when each leg supports the others but fails when any of the three are removed:

> It is clear, therefore, that, in the supremely wise arrangement of God, sacred Tradition, sacred Scripture, and the Magisterium of the Church are so connected and associated that one of them cannot stand without the others. Working together, each in its own way under the action of the one Holy Spirit, they all contribute effectively to the salvation of souls.[53]

Scripture, therefore, is not the Church's sole point of reference. The "supreme rule of her faith derives from the unity which the Spirit has created between Sacred Tradition, Sacred Scripture, and the Magisterium of the Church in a reciprocity which means that none of the three can survive without the others."[54]

Infallibility

The Magisterium of the Church has the competence to explain and reconcile conflicting interpretations in the deposit of faith. Christ willed that his Apostles choose worthy successors to follow after them and that their line continue until Christ comes again.[55] St. Peter was appointed by Christ to "feed [his] sheep."[56] The successors of the Apostles would continue to receive the ministrations of a servant who would be their head for the sake of unity and harmony:

> Jesus Christ the eternal pastor, set up the holy Church by entrusting the apostles with their mission as he himself had been sent by the Father (cf. John 20:21). He willed that their successors, the bishops namely, should be the shepherds in his Church until the end of the world. In order that the episcopate itself however, might be one and undivided, he put Peter at the head of the other apostles, and in him he set up a lasting and visible source and foundation of the unity both of faith and communion.[57]

The Pope is an infallible interpreter of divine revelation when he "proclaims in an absolute decision a doctrine pertaining to faith or morals":

> For in such a case the Roman Pontiff does not utter a pronouncement as a private person, but rather does he expound and defend the teaching of the Catholic

faith as the supreme teacher of the universal Church, in whom the Church's chrism of infallibility is present in a singular way.[58]

Taken individually, the Bishops of the Church do not enjoy the gift or charism of infallibility. However, when they teach in union with the Pope as one on a matter of faith or morals and agree that a particular teaching is to be held definitively and absolutely, then they can proclaim infallibly the doctrine of Christ.[59]

Even when the Pope does not teach in such manner as to proclaim infallible doctrine "Ex Cathedra," that is, "from the chair," or through an ecumenical council he convokes, attends or ratifies,[60] the faithful are still bound to offer to his authentic teaching authority their loyal submission of mind and will.[61]

It is important to note that the venue of infallible teaching concerns not just dogmatic statements on matters of systematic theology, such as the nature of the Trinity, Christ, and His Church, but also includes the whole moral law, including the natural law and the social order:

> To the Church belongs the right always and everywhere to announce moral principles, including those pertaining to the social order, and to make judgments on any human affairs to the extent that they are required by the fundamental rights of the human person or the salvation of souls.[62]

Some scholars have argued that the dogmas of the Church are not absolute but relative statements applicable to a given time and culture. They rest their opinion on the epistemological theories criticized previously which posit that human thought cannot know objective truth from reason. They believe that just as reason cannot know things-in-themselves, so faith cannot know the facts of salvation history in themselves. The events of salvation history, they argue, are not presented to us in scripture. What is presented is the faith of the scripture writer and the special interests of his believing community. The New Testament simply presents the categories of faith of the writer, not Christ himself.[63] This philosophical presumption often animates a historical/literary critical methodology. It has led many biblical scholars to conclude that not only were the books of the Old Testament traditionally believed to have been authored by Moses and those of the New Testament ascribed to eyewitnesses of the life of Christ in fact written by others with no first-hand knowledge of the facts, but that any reference to miracle or predictive prophecy is a myth to be demythologized.[64]

Such an ideologically driven use of historical critical methodology in scripture exegesis is not unrelated to what some refer to as a crisis of faith which has tended to exacerbate the crisis of morality at the heart of the culture of death. Pope John Paul II assures us that human language can express immutable truth known from reason and revelation:

> Human language may be conditioned by history and constricted in other ways, but the human being can still express truths which surpass the phenomenon of language. Truth can never be confined to time and culture; in history it is known, but is also reaches beyond history.[65]

As for the meaning of dogmatic formulas, this remains ever true and constant in the Church, even when it is expressed with greater clarity or more developed. The faithful, therefore, must shun the opinion, first, that dogmatic formulas (or some category of them) cannot signify the truth in a determined way, but can only offer changeable approximations to it, which to a certain extent distort or alter it.[66]

The mystery hidden from the ages,[67] the mission of the Son of God has *soteriological* significance. The "logic of salvation" expressed in divine revelation, as understood in the Church, teaches that the Father sent his Son in the fullness of time, "born of a virgin."[68] Jesus Christ, a divine Person with both a human and divine nature, is true God and true man. Therefore, he could suffer and die to take away the many sins of the world, which were infinite in offense due to the dignity of the infinite divine Persons offended. Because he was man, Christ could suffer, and because he was true God, his sufferings had infinite atonement value – more than enough to make up for all the many sins of the world, which no finite human person, nor all men together, could do:

> It is love "to the end" that confers on Christ's sacrifice its value as redemption and reparation, as atonement and satisfaction. . . . No man, not even the holiest, was ever able to take on himself the sins of all men and offer himself as a sacrifice for all. The existence in Christ of the divine person of the Son, who at once surpasses and embraces all human persons and constitutes himself as Head of all mankind, makes possible his redemptive sacrifice for all.[69]

His living voice is still heard and his grace-filled touch is still felt as his body, the Church, extends these in time and space through Sacred Tradition and Sacred Scripture, the Seven Sacraments and her liturgical acts. The teaching office of the Church, its Magisterium, together with the assistance of the theologians and the faithful, meditates upon the deposit of faith entrusted to her. When this reflection is mature, the Magisterium may define infallibly dogmas of faith and morals. Later developments of doctrine do not add or subtract but only further elucidate the mysteries of faith which were present from the beginning. The process of Divine Revelation and the development of doctrine is guided by the inspiration of the Holy Spirit.

Many Protestant denominations accept the Church's doctrines on the Blessed Trinity and Christ as formulated by the early Church in the Nicene-Constantinopolitan Creed which used words not found in the Bible to explain that "there are three divine Persons in One God" and that there are "two natures in Christ", one human, one divine. Together with the Church, they believe that the Holy Spirit inspired the Evangelists to faithfully record the words of Christ without error. They believe with the Church that the Holy Spirit inspires Ministers of the Word to proclaim the Good News. However, they deny that Sacred Tradition, Sacraments, and Mass, and other liturgical acts are a continuation of Jesus' saving words and works. They reject the role of the Magisterium to authentically guide the development of doctrine. Instead, they believe that the Holy Spirit inspires each individual Christian so that each Christian can correctly interpret the meaning of sacred Scripture.

Key Magisterial Document:
To Defend the Faith (Ad Tuendam Fidem) (1998)

Although it is not often mentioned, the Church still condemns heresy. Today we hear of "cafeteria Catholicism" or God's "Ten Suggestions" instead of his Ten Commandments. St. Thomas defined heresy in similar terms—as obstinately picking and choosing what articles of the Faith one will believe, rather than believing as the Church believes:

> Now it is manifest that he who adheres to the teaching of the Church, as to an infallible rule, assents to whatever the Church teaches; otherwise, if, of the things taught by the Church, he holds what he chooses to hold, and rejects what he chooses to reject, he no longer adheres to the teachings of the Church as to an infallible rule, but to his own will. Hence, it is evident that a heretic who obstinately disbelieves one article of faith, is not prepared to follow the teaching of the Church in all things; but if he is not obstinate, he is no longer in heresy but only in error. Therefore it is clear that such a heretic with regard to one article has no faith in the other articles, but only a kind of opinion in accord with his own will.[70]

On May 18, 1998, John Paul II issued *To Defend the Faith* (Ad Tuendam Fidem, hereinafter referred to as ATF) in order that the Catholic faith may be safeguarded against errors arising from those who study theology and to provide in Canon Law just penalties for those who persist in teaching "heresy" or "rash and dangerous" ideas.

The instruction notes that the duty to profess the faith of the Church is imposed in particular upon those who assume offices ordered to the study and exposition of the truths of faith and morals or those who govern the Church.[71] The profession of faith required is the Nicene-Constantinopolitan Creed together with three propositions or clauses added in 1989 by the Congregation of the Doctrine of the Faith, "Profession of Faith and Oath of Fidelity in Assuming an Office to be Exercised in the Name of the Church".

The First Proposition requires that an "assent of theological faith" be given by the faithful to everything contained in God's word, in Scripture or Tradition, as divinely revealed by the ordinary Magisterium of the Catholic Church or in solemn judgment. Those who persistently refuse to do so fall under the "censure of heresy." Cardinal Ratzinger explained that this category of divinely revealed truths includes the Creed, Christological dogmas, Marian dogmas, Sacraments and their conferral of grace, the Real Presence of Christ in the Eucharist, the Sacrifice of the Mass, the Church founded by Christ, Papal infallibility, Original Sin, the immortality of the human soul, the judgment of the dead, the divine inspiration of Scripture, and the immorality of the direct and voluntary killing of innocent human life.

The Second Proposition refers to all that is proposed by the Church definitively with regards to matters concerning faith and morals even if they have not yet been proposed by the Magisterium of the Church as "formally revealed."[72] The faithful are required to give "firm and definitive assent to these truths." This gives witness to one's faith in the Holy Spirit's assistance to the Church's Magisterium. Those who reject these truths reject truths of the Catholic doctrine and are no longer in full communion with the Church. Cardinal Ratzinger gave as examples of this category of doctrinal truth the following: expressions of papal infallibility prior to its solemn definition at Vatican Council I. This was always a true doctrine from the beginning that was subsequently held to be definitive doctrine. The priesthood being limited to men is one example. The immorality of prostitution and fornication are also included. The legitimacy of papal elections, ecumenical councils, canonization of saints, and the invalidity of Anglican orders also fall into this category. Then Cardinal Ratzinger explained such doctrines are infallible by reason of ordinary and universal magisterium in both explicit and implicit formulations:

> Such a doctrine [second proposition] can be confirmed or reaffirmed by the Roman Pontiff, even without recourse to a solemn definition, by declaring explicitly that it belongs to the teaching of the ordinary and universal magisterium as a truth that is divinely revealed (1st paragraph) or as a truth of Catholic doctrine (2nd paragraph). Consequently, when there has not been a judgment on a doctrine in the solemn form of a definition, but this doctrine, belonging to the inheritance of the *depositum fidei*, is taught by the ordinary and universal magisterium, which necessarily includes the pope, such a doctrine is to be understood as having been set forth infallibly. The declaration of confirmation or reaffirmation by the Roman pontiff in this case is not a new dogmatic definition, but a formal attestation of a truth already possessed and infallibly transmitted by the church.[73]

> It should be noted that the infallible teaching of the ordinary and universal magisterium is not only set forth with an explicit declaration of a doctrine to be believed or held definitively, but is also expressed by a doctrine implicitly contained in a practice or the Church's faith, derived from the revelation or, in any case, necessary for eternal salvation and attested to by the uninterrupted tradition: such an infallible teaching is thus objectively set forth by the whole episcopal body, understood in a diachronic and not necessarily merely synchronic sense. Furthermore, the intention of the ordinary and universal magisterium to set forth a doctrine as definitive is not generally linked to technical formulations of particular solemnity; it is enough that this be clear from the tenor of the words used and from their context.[74]

The Third Proposition includes those teachings of the Pope or bishops in union with him when they exercise authentic Magisterium even if they proclaim those teachings in an act that is not definitive. The faithful are required to give a religious assent of will and intellect to such non-definitive expressions of the Ordinary Magisterium of the Church regarding faith and morals. To teach contrary would be the "rash" and "dangerous" expression of "erroneous ideas" and would subject one to canonical penalties.[75]

To summarize then, in the "Commentary of Profession of Faith's Concluding Paragraphs" issued together with *Ad Tuendam Fidem*, Cardinal Ratzinger said that Church doctrines are either *infallible* (unreformable/unchangeable) or *fallible* (reformable/changeable). Infallible dogmas are promulgated in either *"defining"* or *"non-defining"* acts. Defining acts are issued in a precise verbal formula by an Ecumenical Council or *Ex Cathedra* by the Pope. Non-defining acts are found in the constant and clear teachings on faith and morals expressed by the Ordinary Magisterium or the Pope repeating the infallible teachings of the Ordinary Magisterium.

In conclusion, Catholics are bound in conscience to obey the Church's teachings on faith and morals when these are taught with authority by the Magisterium. Moreover, the teachings of the Church that pertain to human life issues such as those examined in the second part of this book also contain infallible teaching and must be obeyed under pain of serious sin. Even those who are not members of the Catholic Church are expected to heed the moral teaching of the Church on human life issues because they are based on reason and the natural law as understood by the Magisterium, the arbiter of the whole moral law, including the natural law.[76]

Notes

1. VS, no. 28. Cf. GS no. 22.
2. 1 John 5:9–12; FR no. 9.
3. CCC, no. 1703.
4. GS, no. 24; Luke 17:33.
5. FR, no. 9; CCC no. 50; citing Vatican Council I, *Dei Fillius*, IV: DS 3015.
6. Eph. 1:8, 3:4–6.
7. CCC, no. 106; DV, no. 11.
8. CCC, no. 707.
9. DV, no. 2. See also CCC, no. 53.
10. John 1:14.
11. CCC, no. 724; cf. Isa. 8:10–14.
12. 2 Cor. 1:20, 3:16, 4:6.
13. John 1:14.
14. John 5:36, 17:4.
15. John 14:8–11.
16. Matt. 11:2–6.
17. DV, no. 4.
18. CCC, no. 50.
19. John 20:19–20; 27–29; 21:15–17.
20. CCC, no. 2111.

21. CCC, no. 155; citing ST II-II, q. 2, a. 9.

22. CCC, no. 154.

23. Luke 24:13–35.

24. 1 John 5:9–10.

25. Matt. 28:19–20; Mark 16:15; Acts 1:8.

26. Acts 3:4–10.

27. DV, no. 7, 8. See also 1 Tim. 1:3; 3:1–17; 4:6–16; 6:3–4; 2 Tim. 3:14–17; 4:1–5; Tit. 1:6–16; 2:1, 2:15; 3:8.

28. CCC, no. 76.

29. 2 Thess. 2:15.

30. DV, no. 7.

31. Luke 1:1–4.

32. DV, no. 7.

33. DV, no. 9.

34. Luke 22:19–20.

35. SC, no. 6.

36. SC, no. 7.

37. CCC, no. 84, citing DV, no. 10, sec. 1.

38. VS, no. 27.

39. 2 Thess. 2:15; 3:6.

40. Scott and Kimberly Hahn, *Rome Sweet Home: Our Journey to Catholicism* (San Francisco: Ignatius Press, 1993), 74.

41. DV, no. 13.

42. 1 Cor. 6:19.

43. CCC, no. 89. See also John 8:31–32.

44. 1 Cor. 2:6–16.

45. LG, no. 12, as cited in CCC, no. 92 and in VS, no. 109.

46. DV, no. 8.

47. FR, no. 44; also see VS, no. 64.

48. CCC, no. 78; citing DV, no. 8.

49. Warren H. Carroll, *The Building of Christendom*, vol. 2 of *A History of Christendom* (Front Royal, VA: Christendom College Press, 1987), 10.

50. Carroll, *The Building of Christendom*, 92; quoting Carl Joseph von Hefele, *History of the Councils, 1894–96*, vol. 3, trans. William R. Clark, 2d ed. rev. (Edinburgh: T. & T. Clark, 1894–96), 12–13.

51. Carroll, *The Building of Christendom*, 94; quoting von Hefele, *Councils* vol. 3, 46–52.

52. DV, no. 9.

53. DV, no. 10. See also CCC, no. 95.

54. FR, no. 55; citing Vatican Council I, *Dei Filius*, IV: DS 3018, nos. 10, 21.

55. LG, no. 21.

56. John 21:16.

57. LG, no. 18.

58. LG, no. 25.

59. LG, no. 25.

60. LG, no. 22.

61. LG, no. 25.

62. CIC, 747, sec. 2; cf. HV, no. 4.

63. See generally Anthony C. Thiselton, *The Two Horizons: New Testament Herme-*

neutics and Philosophical Description with Special Reference to Heidegger, Bultman, Gadamer and Wittgenstein (Grand Rapids, MI: W.B. Eerdmans Pub. Co., 1979).

64. See Warren H. Carroll, *The Founding of Christendom*, vol. 1 of *A History of Christendom* (Front Royal, VA: Christendom College Press, 1985), 59–80, 287–98.

65. FR, no. 95.

66. FR, fn.113; citing CDF, Declaration in Defense of the Catholic Doctrine on the Church (*Mysterium Ecclesiae*) (24 June 1973), 5: AAS 65 (1973), 403.

67. Eph. 1:9–10, 3:6.

68. Gal. 4:40.

69. CCC, no. 616; cf. CCC, nos. 590, 600, 601.

70. ST II-II, q. 5, a. 3.

71. ATF, no. 1.

72. ATF, no. 2.

73. ATF, Commentary no. 9.

74. ATF, fn.17 of the Commentary.

75. ATF, no. 3; See LG, no. 25.

76. HV, no. 4.

Part II:
Bioethics in Light of
Christian Moral Principles

Chapter 9
Reproductive Technologies

Introduction

The immensity of outer space presented to us by an orbiting radio telescope showing colliding galaxies each containing billions of suns makes our little earth fade into insignificance. The millions of light years it has taken for the light of these galaxies to reach us makes our puny life span seem less than leaves of grass that sprout in the morning and wither by noon. The power released in exploding red giants, or imploding black holes, whose gravitational vortex sucks out the light of stars, tempts us to imagine that the foundation of the universe is some vast cosmic energy of which human consciousness is but another manifestation. The *awe*someness of outer space is *aw*ful if this is the context in which we must appraise the meaning of our lives. Against this material backdrop governed, we are told, by blind chance, human life, we are tempted to believe, seems utterly meaningless. If our lives and self-consciousness came to be by chance through the exigencies of impersonal cosmic and nuclear energy, there is absolutely nothing special about human life, and so-called human dignity is but self-praise and human rights a mere convention.

Truly, the stars seen at night put human life into perspective. Materially, we are nothing in comparison with the universe: none of us individually, or all of us collectively, are even noticeable. However if personhood is the foundation of reality, if it is bigger, stronger, and more magnificent than impersonal energies, then we are absolutely singular. If an Omnipotent, all-wise and loving divine Person created, sustains and guides the universe then we, weak though we may be, are unique in the material universe. If human beings alone in all the vast reaches of space bear his personal image, then the whole physical universe fades into insignificance in comparison with the grandeur of one human child. The stars in the heavens have led some into atheism and despair,[1] but for others they have revealed the power and providence of God and provided evidence of human dignity and inalienable human rights:

> When I behold the heavens, the work of your fingers,
>   the moon and the stars which you set in place—
> What is man that you should be mindful of him,
>   or the son of man that you should care for him?
> Yet, you have made him little less than the angels,
>   and crowned him with glory and honor.[2]

More fearsome than the collision of galaxies in space is the moral collision of world views today reflected in our national and international debate over artificial reproduction of human life:

> This human embryo lying in a Pctri dish was created a little lower than the angels and is destined to be crowned in glory and honor. To destroy it, to experiment upon it, to use it for the benefit of others is to violate its dignity and the dignity of those who would so use it.[3]

Nothing less is at stake than whether human procreation will remain deeply personal (a sacred act) or become commoditized (profaned)[4] through an impersonal production and a technological rape (a sacrilege):

> I insist that we are faced with having to decide nothing less than whether human procreation is going to remain human, whether children are going to be made rather than begotten, whether it is a good thing, humanly speaking, to say yes in principle to the road that leads (at best) to the dehumanized rationality of *Brave New World.*[5]

Plants and animals may be used, killed and eaten because they are not even potentially self-conscious persons. Made by God they reflect some of God's perfection but they are not made in the image of the three divine Persons of the Blessed Trinity. Therefore, they may be used by us in reasonable ways that do not cause human misery by depriving those in need[6] and does not demean us by causing animals to suffer needlessly.[7] We may reproduce plants and animals to suit our designs through technological interventions including artificial insemination, surrogacy, in-vitro fertilization, sterilization, abortion and cloning.[8]

Although we have a physical body similar to animals, we, unlike them, have a composite nature composed of a body and rational soul. Therefore, we must resist the temptation to look *down* and model human sexual behavior on the instinctive mating of animals, or the reproductive technologies permissible in the manipulation of these impersonal creatures. On the contrary, we must look *up* to God, to divine Persons, to understand the unique dignity of human procreation[9]:

> Human procreation is a similitude of the procession between the Father and the Son, which is its prototype. . . .
>   God's relationship with his creatures is creative. He is the ultimate cause of all things that are created. But in creating human beings in his own image, he creates them so that they themselves can be procreative and thus imitate his

Triune Life. Therefore, the relationship of parent-to-child, on a human, biological level, must mirror the divine in honoring its intimacy, equality, and consan-
guinity.[10]

If divine personhood is the ultimate foundation of reality, then *right relationships* put into place by moral and supernatural virtues define the moral universe
as surely as cosmic and nuclear energy defines the physical universe. This explains why the reproduction of impersonal things composed of purely physical
energies does not and cannot possibly occur in a profoundly personal relationship. On the contrary, the coming into being of a new person must occur in a
relational act of procreation—a deeply personal act between spouses and the
three divine Persons. The human body, unlike that of plants and animals, is a
quasi-sacred sign (analogous to a sacrament) which conveys the reality it sym-
bolizes. The bodies of spouses made one flesh in intercourse become a meeting
place of interpersonal activity, human and divine—the gift of self is given between spouses and God also gives a gift of Himself—an increase of his divine
life, i.e., grace, and sometimes creates the soul of a new person in an act of procreation. In an act of conjugal union the bodies of the spouses symbolize a complete openness and vulnerability to each other and to God's creative touch.[11]

Intimate personal relationships are necessary at moments of profound human vulnerability. The thought of dying alone in a sterile but impersonal institution is dreadful, and so by analogy we should dread the thought of an impERSON-
al, sterile, unloving and inhuman conception. Our vulnerability at the moment of
death is exceeded only by the moment we were conceived. For whatever reason,
an impersonal forced conception is never forgotten, even though it occurred to
one not yet self conscious. Although the essential human dignity of a child conceived in rape is undiminished, the shame given in the moment of this child's
conception is carried to the grave. Animals cannot know shame—the recognition of what *is* compared to what *should be*. They cannot be embarrassed by the
knowledge that they were conceived in rape or through the forced and unloving
manipulations of artificial insemination. But a child can. She can be teased. She
can cry. She can hate. And, with God's grace, she can forgive.

Social planners dismiss such considerations as sentimental. The replace-
ment of human acts concerning "civilization issues" (such as sexual intercourse)
with technological tools oriented toward a more efficient "planned society" is
the defining feature of modern culture.[12] Belief in technology is *the* core cultural
value of the first world; not belief in machines *per se,* but "the machine insofar
as it promises an activity superior to the human act."[13]

The promise of reproductive technologies is already reshaping our culture.
For instance, by providing the means of making inherently infertile couples
seemingly fecund, it is changing public opinion and family law legitimizing
homosexual marriages[14]:

It is not merely coincidental that cultural and legal approbation of the homosexual family followed after the contraceptive pill [which separated sex from

procreation], and after the development of the in-vitro technologies which re-
produced human life independent of any particular social form.[15]

A nation whose public policy is directed towards the reduction of fertility at
home and abroad through contraception, abortion and sterilization is not really
concerned with remedying the infertility of childless couples through sponsoring
research in reproductive technologies. All rhetoric about individual liberty aside,
the real beneficiaries of reproductive technology are not infertile couples but a
technologically elite sect: social engineers, medical professionals together with
accommodating bioethicists, and jurists who aim at a society better planned by
them.[16] As C.S. Lewis noted, man's conquest of Nature through "technique,"
i.e., technology, only serves to strengthen the hand of inhumane rulers, the
"Conditioners," and so "turns out to be a power exercised by some men over
other men with Nature as its instrument."[17]

As the Human Genome Project nears completion and the prospect of human
cloning looms on the horizon, slavery (the breeding, buying, selling and destruction of human persons for the benefit of a powerful few) has begun to regain
social acceptance. Genetic and reproductive companies are a growth industry:
they already market better babies produced through donor gametes and *in-vitro*
technologies.[18] Reminiscent of the *Dred Scott* decision that held black slaves
were not persons within the meaning of the Constitution of the United States,
legal opinion supports an implied contract theory that human embryos left frozen but unpaid-for are the property of the reproductive clinic.[19] The lure of a
perfect baby for infertile couples is a ruse that contributes to a totalitarian control of human population:

> The "perfect baby," of course, is the project not of the infertility doctors, but of
> the eugenic scientists and their supporters. For them, the paramount right is not
> the so-called right to reproduce, but what biologist Bentley Glass called, a quar-
> ter of a century ago, "the right of every child to be born with a sound physical
> and mental constitution, based on a sound genotype . . . the inalienable right to
> a sound heritage." But to secure that right and to achieve the requisite quality
> control over new human life, human conception and gestation will need to be
> brought fully into the bright light of the laboratory, beneath which the child-to-
> be can be fertilized, pruned, weeded, watched, inspected, prodded, pinched, ca-
> joled, injected, tested, rated, graded, approved, stamped, wrapped, sealed, and
> delivered. There is no other way to produce the perfect baby.[20]

Without Christian hope and a belief in the redemptive value of human suffering
united to Christ, childless couples will be tempted to look for an escape from
infertility by any means. For them, IVF promises a "take-home-baby." For the
"Conditioners," each "take-home-baby" technologically produced helps perfect
the technique necessary for a society planned to perfection by, and for, them. To
them we are buffoons—the laughable "Keepers of the Holy Embryos."[21] No
matter how cogent the arguments in defense of the sacredness of human life and
procreation are, increasingly these words will fall on deaf ears in a culture waste

land indifferent to Christ:

> Is it realistic to think that we will win over the majority of Americans on this point based on reasoned arguments alone? Without hope, will not the prolife position always seem unrealistic and impractical as applied to difficult cases? More importantly, are arguments any substitute for Christian hope in the lives of the women who are faced with making these choices?[22]

As we review the Church's teaching on reproductive technologies we must never forget it is only in Christ, true God and *true man,* that we discover what it is to be truly human. The natural law is indelibly etched on the heart and soul of every man and woman. Even without the aid of Revelation this primordial law provides the general principles of morality as found in the Decalogue. That is why few apologists defend abortion for what it is—the murder of an innocent human being. The prohibition against murder is a clear injunction that sounds deep in every person's conscience that only a coarse and depraved upbringing can block-out for a time. Therefore, abortion must be rhetorically finessed: those who perpetrate abortion must say there is no one killed; that just a "blob of tissue" is removed. But contraception and reproductive technologies, on the other hand, concern remote conclusions of the natural law dealing with more subtle violations of the natural law such as the loss of human dignity, the falsification of a gift of self in feigned intercourse, and the profanation of procreation. Without the Church's guidance few will have the light to choose truth, and without Christian hope even fewer will have the strength provided by grace to choose right. Jaded and desperate, their moral imagination impaired and their conscience confused by propaganda, few infertile couples will recognize the spiritual pain they experience in being treated as customers of consumer goods, i.e., commoditized throwaway children: "The end product is a human being, produced without conjugal sex, without emotion, and, for that matter, without parents in the usual sense. The scenario is that which was conceived by science fiction novels of a few generations ago, novel such as Aldous Huxley's *Brave New World.* Only, now it is no longer science fiction. It is routine!"[23]

Let us keep perspective. Our job is not so much to *win* arguments, as to pray, give good example, and lay out sound reasons for our hope in the inviolate sacredness of human life and procreation. Our primary goal must remain focused on a new evangelization, renewing all things and refocusing our culture's worship of technology and fascination with death to reverence for Christ and his Gospel of life:

> There is no gospel of life except the integral gospel that Jesus preached. There is no culture of life other than the culture that is formed by the redemptive work of God in Christ and built up by those who carry on his mission. And the culture of life will always be challenged by the culture of death until Jesus comes again and hands over to the Father a kingdom of truth and life, of holiness and grace, of justice, love, and peace.[24]

The Key Magisterial Documents:
Donum Vitae (1987) and *Dignitas Personae* (2008)

Donum Vitae

Promulgated February 22, 1987 by the Sacred Congregation for the Doctrine of the Faith, *Instruction on Respect for Human Life in Its Origin and on the Dignity of Procreation* (*Donum Vitae*)[25] was the Church's first word on contemporary reproductive technologies. However, because of the many new technologies to emerge since then, the Congregation for the Doctrine of the Faith released *Dignitas Personae* (The Dignity of the Person) in September of 2008. Therefore, both of these documents will be carefully considered below.

    Donum Vitae first recalls that human life is a gift of inestimable value from God the Creator and Father; a gift entrusted to man and for which he is responsible. Science and biotechnology now make it possible for man to either assist or to dominate the process of procreation; they may contribute to genuine progress in the service of mankind or they may tempt him to "go beyond the limits of a reasonable dominion over nature."[26]

    The Church is not an expert in experimental sciences, but is an "expert in humanity" and the dignity of the human person. Therefore, she has the duty to expound criteria of moral judgment regarding the applications of scientific research, especially to the beginnings of human life. There are four specific moral criteria that must be respected: 1) "respect, defense and promotion of man;" 2) "his 'primary and fundamental right' to life;" 3) "his dignity as a person who is endowed with a spiritual soul and with moral responsibility;" and 4) man's "call[ing] to beatific communion with God." [27] It is in contemplating the "mystery of the incarnate word" that the Church comes to understand the "mystery of man," and in this light that she invites him to discover the truth of his own being and puts forth the divine law to accomplish his liberation.[28]

    Scientific research is an exercise of the dominion God gave man over the earth.[29] However, an advance in scientific or technological knowledge is not the measure of true human progress. Scientific research and its application are not morally neutral, nor are efficiency, usefulness to others, or conformity to prevailing ideologies, valid criteria to guide science:

> Thus, science and technology require for their own intrinsic meaning an unconditional respect for the fundamental criteria of the moral law: That is to say, they must be at the service of the human person, of his inalienable rights and his true and integral good according to the design and will of God. . . . Science without conscience can only lead to man's ruin.[30]

Any valid moral criteria must rest upon a proper idea of the nature of the human person in his bodily dimension. Man's nature is a substantial union of a spiritual soul and a corporeal body. Man's body is not like that of animals; "rather it is a constitutive part of the person who manifests and expresses himself through it." Natural law is not a set of norms drawn from the biological level, but conforms to a rational order whereby man must govern his life and make use of his own body. As a consequence, "[a]n intervention on the human body affects not only the tissues, the organs and their functions, but also involves the person himself on different levels," as John Paul II has said, "in the body and through the body, one touches the person himself in his concrete reality."[31]

Because man and woman share in the mystery of God's "personal communion and in his work as Creator and Father," marriage possesses "specific goods and values in its union and in procreation" that makes them unlike lower forms of life. These goods and values are of a "personal order" and determine the limits of licit artificial intervention in procreation. (It is not the artificial aspect that is suspect in these interventions, but whether they comport with the dignity of the human person that is critical.)[32]

There are two fundamental values that serve as references in evaluating various techniques of artificial procreation: 1) "the life of the human being called into existence" and 2) "the special nature of the transmission of human life in marriage." The physical life of a human being is not his supreme good, called as he is to eternal life, yet it is the foundation of all other values of the person. The inviolability of the physical life of an innocent human being (from conception to death) is a "sign and requirement of the very inviolability of the person" created by God. The transmission of human life, unlike that of other life forms, has a special character based on the special nature of the human person which requires a "personal and conscious act" and is subject to the laws of God. "He is not therefore permitted to use certain ways and means which are allowable in the propagation of plant and animal life."[33] Even if technology has made it possible to procreate apart from sexual relations through in-vitro fertilization, still, "what is technically possible is not, for that very reason, morally admissible."[34]

From both right reason and revelation we can see the human person is God's special creation, who of all creatures on earth is "wished for himself" by God, his sole end, whose soul is created directly by God, and whose whole life is, therefore, sacred. Beware! No one can "destroy directly an innocent human being," and spouses may actualize the gift of human life only in "marriage through the specific and exclusive acts of husband and wife, in accordance with the laws inscribed in their persons and in their union."[35]

Part I. Respect for Human Embryos

1. To what respect is the human embryo entitled, taking into account his nature and identity? *"The human being must be respected—as a person—from the very first instant of his existence."*[36]

The aims of artificial fertilization range from diagnostic to therapeutic; from scientific to commercial. The legitimacy of the varying aims depends upon the nature and specific identity, the "status," of the human embryo. Drawing upon Vatican Council II and the *Declaration on Procured Abortion,* and on the findings of human biological science, reason may discern "a person present at the moment of this first appearance of a human life" and how could this "human individual not be a human person?" The Magisterium has not committed herself to whether or not a spiritual soul is present from the moment two gametes fuse, but it has always condemned any kind of direct abortion:

> Thus, the fruit of human generation from the first moment of its existence, that is to say, from the moment the zygote has formed, demands the unconditional respect that is morally due to the human being in his bodily and spiritual totality . . . and therefore from that same moment his rights as a person must be recognized, among which in the first place is the inviolable right of every innocent human being to life.[37]

Therefore, human embryo must be "tended and cared for, to the extent possible, in the same way as any other human being as far as medical assistance is concerned."[38]

2. Is prenatal diagnosis morally licit? "*If prenatal diagnosis respects the life and integrity of the embryo and the human fetus and is directed toward its safeguarding or healing as an individual, then the answer is affirmative.*"[39]

Procedures that make possible advanced knowledge of the condition of the human embryo still in its mother's womb are permissible with parental consent, provided they are therapeutic. Such procedures are licit, "if the methods employed safeguard the life and integrity of the embryo and the mother, without subjecting them to disproportionate risks. But this diagnosis is gravely opposed to the moral law when it is done with the thought of possibly inducing an abortion depending upon the results."[40]

A pregnant woman would commit a "gravely illicit act" if she requested prenatal diagnosis with the intention of having an abortion should abnormality be detected, as would those who counseled or performed prenatal diagnosis for this purpose. Worse yet, if authorities or health organizations passed a law or required such procedures, they would violate the "unborn child's right to life" and the "rights and duties of spouses."[41]

3. Are therapeutic procedures carried out on the human embryo licit? "*As with all medical interventions on patients, one must uphold as licit procedures carried out on the human embryo which respect the life and integrity of the embryo and do not involve disproportionate risks for it, but are directed toward its healing, the improvement of its condition of health or its individual survival.*"[42]

Therapeutic medical interventions may be carried out on human embryos, provided informed parental consent is obtained and, as John Paul II has said, "it is directed to the true promotion of the personal well-being of the individual without doing harm to his integrity or worsening his conditions of life."[43]

4. How is one to morally evaluate research and experimentation on human embryos and fetuses? "*Medical research must refrain from operations on live*

embryos, unless there is a moral certainty of not causing harm to the life or integrity of the unborn child and the mother, and on condition that the parents have given their free and informed consent to the procedure."[44]

Any research, even mere observation, that posed a risk to the human embryo's physical integrity or life, by the methods used or their effects, is illicit. Any experimentation on living human embryos, "whether they are viable or not, either inside or outside the mother's womb," is illicit. Parents cannot grant informed consent to dispose of the physical integrity or life of their unborn children.

> To use human embryos or fetuses as the object or instrument of experimentation constitutes a crime against their dignity as human beings having a right to the same respect that is due to the child already born and to every human person. . . . The practice of keeping alive human embryos in-vivo [within the womb] or in-vitro [outside the womb] for experimental or commercial purposes is totally opposed to human dignity.[45]

Experimental drugs or procedures may be used in a last attempt to save the life of a human embryo in the absence of other reliable treatments. Corpses of human embryos or fetuses must be respected the same as other human beings, even if they have been aborted, and not subjected to commercial trafficking. They must not be subject to mutilation or dissection if their death is not verified or consent is not given by their parents; complicity in a direct abortion or the risk of scandal must also be avoided.[46]

5. How is one to evaluate morally the use for research purposes of embryos obtained by fertilization "in-vitro?" "*It is immoral to produce human embryos destined to be exploited as disposable 'biological material.'*"[47]

In the process of in-vitro fertilization "not all embryos are transferred into the woman's womb; some are destroyed. Just as the Church condemns induced abortion, she also forbids acts against the life of these human beings." It is particularly grave to destroy human embryos obtained from in-vitro fertilization solely for research. Observations or experimentation which place disproportionate risks upon the life or integrity of the human embryo obtained in-vitro are also illicit. No one has the right to use other human beings as instruments for the advantage of others.

> It is therefore not in conformity with the moral law deliberately to expose to death human embryos obtained "in-vitro." In consequence of the fact that they have been produced in-vitro, *those embryos which are not transferred into the body of the mother and are called "spare" are exposed to an absurd fate, with no possibility of their being offered safe means of survival which can be licitly pursued.*[48]

6. What judgment should be made on other procedures of manipulating embryos connected with the techniques of human reproduction? Attempts to fertilize human and animal gametes, gestate human embryos in an animal uterus or

construct an artificial womb are *"contrary to the human dignity proper to the embryo, and at the same time they are contrary to the right of every person to be conceived and to be born within marriage and from marriage. Also, attempts or hypothesis for obtaining a human being without any connection with sexuality through 'twin fission,' cloning or parthenogenesis are to be considered contrary to the moral law, since they are in opposition to the dignity both of human pro-creation and of the conjugal union."*[49]

Freezing human embryos (cryopreservation), even in an attempt to preserve their life, is an offense against their dignity, depriving them of maternal gesta-tion and shelter, and exposing them to further harm. Chromosomal manipula-tions geared toward sex selection or "other predetermined qualities," which are neither therapeutic nor beneficial to the embryo, are also contrary to the human dignity and integrity of the embryo. Supposed improvements in the gene pool beneficial for the future of humanity cannot and could never legitimize such genetic manipulations: "Every person must be respected for himself: In this con-sists the dignity and right of every human being from his or her beginning."[50]

Part II. Interventions Upon Human Procreation

Artificial fertilization is a technical procedure directed toward obtaining a human conception other than through the sexual union of a man and woman. *Donum Vitae* considers in-vitro fertilization (IVF) (the fertilization of an ovum in a petri dish) and artificial insemination (the transfer into a woman's genital tract of previously collected sperm). The culling of spare human embryos living in a Petri dish or after implantation in a woman's uterus is routine in IVF proce-dure. However, this destruction of human embryos is a direct abortion. An "abortion mentality" has made IVF possible, and this mentality "leads, whether one wants it or not, to man's domination over the life and death of his fellow human beings and can lead to a system of radical eugenics."[51]

A.) Heterologous Artificial Fertilization (techniques used to obtain a human conception artificially by the use of gametes coming from at least one donor other than the spouses who are joined in marriage).

1. Why must human procreation take place in, and only in, marriage?[52] *"Every human being is always to be accepted as a gift and blessing of God. However, from the moral point of view, a truly responsible procreation vis-à-vis the unborn child must be the fruit of marriage."*[53]

Human procreation "must be the fruit and the sign of the mutual self-giving of the spouses, of their love and of their fidelity. *The fidelity of the spouses in the unity of marriage involves reciprocal respect of their right to become a fa-ther and a mother only through each other. . . .* The child has the right to be conceived, carried in the womb, brought into the world and brought up within marriage," because only in right relation to his parents can a child discover his identity and achieve his full development. Society's stability requires "that children come into the world within a family and that the family be firmly based on marriage." An indissoluble marriage is "the only setting worthy of truly responsible procreation."[54]

2. Does heterologous artificial fertilization conform to the dignity of the couple and to the truth of marriage? "*Heterologous artificial fertilization is contrary to the unity of marriage, to the dignity of the spouses, to the vocation proper to parents, and to the child's right to be conceived and brought into the world in marriage and from marriage.*"[55]

The unity and fidelity spouses pledge to each other in marriage demands their children be conceived only in marriage:

> The bond existing between husband and wife accords the spouses, in an objective and inalienable manner, the exclusive right to become father and mother solely through each other. Recourse to the gametes of a third person in order to have sperm or ovum available constitutes a violation of the reciprocal commitment of spouses and a grave lack of regard to that essential property of marriage which is its unity.[56]

Heterologous IVF or artificial insemination, besides offending the unity of marriage, violates the rights of the child by depriving him of his relationship with his parental origin and so hinders his self-identity. It ruptures genetic and gestational parenthood and lessens a progenitor's responsibility for raising the child. Consequently,

> [F]ertilization of a married woman with the sperm of a donor different from her husband and fertilization with the husband's sperm of an ovum not coming from his wife are morally illicit. Furthermore, the artificial fertilization of a woman who is unmarried or a widow, whoever the donor may be, cannot be morally justified.[57]

Good motives and circumstances, such as the desire to remedy a couple's infertility, cannot render heterologous IVF conformable to the "inalienable properties of marriage" or the rights of a child.[58]

3. Is "surrogate" motherhood morally licit? A surrogate mother is either: a) "[t]he woman who carries in pregnancy an embryo implanted in her uterus and who is genetically a stranger to the embryo because it has been obtained through the union of the gametes of 'donors;'" or b) "[t]he woman who carries in pregnancy an embryo to whose procreation she has contributed the donation of her own ovum, fertilized through insemination with the sperm of a man other than her husband." In either case, "[s]he carries the pregnancy with a pledge to surrender the baby once it is born to the party who commissioned or made the agreement for the pregnancy."[59]

Surrogate motherhood is not licit for the same reasons as heterologous artificial fertilization is not. It fails "to meet the obligations of maternal love, of conjugal fidelity and of responsible motherhood; it offends the dignity and the right of the child to be conceived, carried in the womb, brought into the world and brought up by his own parents" and divides the "physical, psychological and moral elements" which constitute a family.[60]

B) *Homologous Artificial Fertilization* (in-vitro fertilization and embryo transfer or artificial insemination between husband and wife).[61]

4. What connection is required from the moral point of view between procreation and the conjugal act? *The moral relevance of the link between the meanings of the conjugal act and between the goods of marriage, as well as the unity of the human being and the dignity of his origin [directly from God], demand that the procreation of a human person be brought about as the fruit of the conjugal act specific to the love between spouses."*[62]

a) There is a link between the goods of marriage and the meanings of the conjugal act. An "inseparable connection" exists "between the two meanings of the conjugal act"—its unitive meaning and the procreative meaning. By safeguarding both these essential aspects, the conjugal act preserves the full sense of "true mutual love" and its "ordination to parenthood." Contraception breaks this link by depriving the conjugal act of its openness to procreation. Homologous artificial procreation breaks this link by "seeking a procreation which is not the fruit of a specific act of conjugal union." Both effect "an analogous separation" of the goods and meanings of marriage. Procreation "*is deprived of its proper perfection when it is not desired as the fruit of the conjugal act, that is to say, of the specific act of the spouses' union.*"[63]

b) The link between the two aspects of the conjugal act and the goods of marriage is based on unity of body and spiritual soul in the human being. Spouses express their personal love in the "language of the body" which involves spousal and parental meanings—"their self-gift" and "openness to the gift of life"—an act which is inseparably corporal and spiritual. Procreation is linked to the biological and spiritual union of the parents, made one by the bond of marriage. The *in-vitro* fertilization outside the bodies of a couple is deprived of the values "expressed in the language of the body and in the union of human persons."[64]

c) "Only respect for the link between the meanings of the conjugal act and respect for the unity of the human being make possible procreation in conformity with the dignity of the person." Otherwise a child is treated as unequal "in personal dignity to those who give him life"—not a gift formed from the gift of self of his parents, not "the fruit of that mutual giving," but a mere "product," an "object of scientific technology."[65]

5. Is homologous "in-vitro" fertilization morally licit? An infertile couple may have praiseworthy motives and generous sentiments in seeking homologous *in-vitro* fertilization, but the procedure itself is the deciding moral factor, not "the totality of conjugal life of which it becomes part of from the conjugal acts which may precede or follow it." Even if masturbation in order to obtain the husband's sperm and the abortion of spare embryos were avoided, in itself, in-vitro fertilization and embryo transfer are neither achieved nor willed "as the

expression and fruit of a specific act of the conjugal union," and so the act of procreation is "objectively deprived of its proper perfection"—the fruit of a conjugal act in which the spouses cooperate with God.[66]

Certainly, homologous IVF is "not marked by all the negativity found in extra-conjugal procreation; the family and marriage continue to constitute the setting for the birth and upbringing of the children." However it remains "in itself" illicit—*"opposed to the dignity of procreation and of the conjugal union."* Regardless of the illicitness of in-vitro fertilization, every IVF baby is to be cherished since "every child which comes into the world must in any case be accepted as a living gift of the divine Goodness and must be brought up with love."[67]

6. How is homologous artificial insemination to be evaluated from the moral point of view? *"Homologous artificial insemination within marriage cannot be admitted except for those cases in which the technical means is not a substitute for the conjugal act but serves to facilitate and to help so that the act attains its natural purpose."*[68]

The conjugal act is an expression of the mutual gift by which husband and wife become "one flesh." To the extent technical means help them to give themselves to become "one flesh" they *may* be licit: "Thus moral conscience does not necessarily proscribe the use of certain artificial means destined solely either to the facilitating of the natural act or to ensuring that the natural act normally performed achieves its proper end. If, on the other hand, the procedure were to replace the conjugal act, it is morally illicit." [69]

Masturbation, usually associated with homologous artificial insemination, is a further sign of the disassociation of the two meanings of the conjugal act. "Even when it is done for the purpose of procreation the act [masturbation] remains deprived of its unitive meaning," and fails to conform to the demands of the moral order.[70]

7. What moral criterion can be proposed with regard to medical intervention in human procreation? *"The moral criteria for medical intervention in procreation are deduced from the dignity of human persons, of their sexuality and of their origin. . . . A medical intervention respects the dignity of persons when it seeks to assist the conjugal act either in order to facilitate its performance or in order to enable it to achieve its objective once it has been normally performed."*[71]

The medical act must remain at the service of the conjugal act and not appropriate to itself, "the procreative function," and thus violate the "inalienable rights of the spouses and of the child to be born." The "humanization of medicine" requires respect for the dignity of the human person in the act and moment in which spouses transmit new life to a new person. Catholic doctors, nurses, scientists, and hospital administrators must bear exemplary witness to the dignity of procreation and the human embryo by following these norms.[72]

8. The suffering caused by infertility in marriage: Sterility is a difficult trial. Spouses in this situation are "called to find in it an opportunity for sharing in a particular way in the Lord's cross, the source of spiritual fruitfulness." They

must recall that even when deprived of fecundity "conjugal life does not for this reason lose its value." In fact, it is an opportunity for other "important services": adoption, educational work, assistance to other families, the poor or handicapped children. Scientific research should continue to seek to remedy infertility "so that sterile couples will be able to procreate in full respect for their own personal dignity and that of the child to be born."[73]

We must recall that marriage and the desire for a child do not confer upon spouses the "right to have a child, but only the right to perform those natural acts which are per se ordered to procreation." A "right to a child" reveals an attitude that treats a child as "an object of ownership." On the contrary, a child is *"a gift, 'the supreme gift' and the most gratuitous gift of marriage, and is the living testimony of the mutual giving of his parents."* A child has the right to be conceived in a specific act of conjugal love by his parents and thereby "respected as a person from the moment of his conception."[74]

Part III. Moral and Civil Law: The Values and Moral Obligations that Civil Legislation Must Respect and Sanction

Political authorities need to intervene in the field of biotechnology because such techniques could lead to dire consequences for society. Biotechnologists have no right to "govern humanity" in the name of scientific progress and alleged "improvements" in humanity. Such eugenics would legitimize discrimination and serious offenses against the fundamental rights of the human person.[75]

Civil law has the task of ensuring the common good through the recognition of "fundamental rights," the "promotion of peace," and promotion of "public morality." Fundamental human rights do not depend on concessions from individuals, parents, society or the state; but rather, they "pertain to human nature and are inherent in the person by virtue of the creative act from which the person took his or her origin." These fundamental rights include in a special way the right of every human being to "life and physical integrity from conception until death," and the "rights of the family and of marriage" and the "child's right to be conceived, brought into the world and brought up by his parents."[76]

The "very foundation of a state based on law are undermined" when the "suppression of innocents" and the most vulnerable are not recognized. Therefore civil law must not expose human embryos to the grave risks associated with artificial procreation, which "would widen the breach [between civil law and moral law] already opened by the legalization of abortion." Rather, civil law must enact penal sanctions for deliberate violations of the child's rights to not be subject to non-therapeutic scientific experimentations, mutilation or destruction "with the excuse that they are superfluous or incapable of developing normally." Civil law must not take away rights inherent in the relationship of spouses by legalizing the "the donation of gametes" between persons not legitimately married. Civil law must also prohibit "embryo banks, post-mortem insemination and 'surrogate motherhood.'" The civil laws of many states legitimize certain immoral practices, while at the same time fail to guarantee morality in conformity with natural law. This must be remedied by all men of good will operating within their professional field who exercise their civil rights, and through "conscientious objection" and "a movement of passive resistance to the legitimization of practices contrary to human life and dignity."[77]

Conclusion

The Church invites those responsible for the formation of consciences and of public opinion (scientists, medical professionals, jurists, and politicians) to defend human dignity and oppose the spread of immoral biotechnology. She invites in particular theologians and moralists to study more deeply, and make available the teachings of the Church in "the light of a valid anthropology in the matter of sexuality and marriage in the context of the necessary interdisciplinary approach." Everyone is called to behave like the Good Samaritan and recognize a neighbor in "the littlest among the children of men,"[78] recalling Christ's words "What you do to one of the least of my brethren, you do unto me."[79]

Dignitas Personae

Instruction *Dignitas Personae* on Certain Bioethical Questions, the long awaited follow-up to *Donum Vitae*, was signed on September 8, 2008 and released December 12, 2008. In the twenty-year interval many "new problems regarding procreation" had arisen that *Donum Vitae* failed to specifically address. In certain cases bioethicists faithful to the Church had been divided in their conclusions as they sought to apply the principles laid out in *Donum Vitae* to the new and sometimes dark paths forced open by biotechnology. Human cloning, designer babies, human-animal hybrids, vaccines obtained unethically, preimplantation drugs, germ line therapy, frozen embryo experimentation and adoption and a "eugenic mentality" threaten "an unjust domination of man over man." *Dignitas Personae* is a prophetic call for science to be true to the integrity and orientation of human reason that "participates in the creative power of God and is called to transform creation" for the good of "the human person in his entirety."[80]

Introduction

1. The fundamental principle of bioethics expresses a great "yes" to human life: "The dignity of a person must be recognized in every human being from conception to natural death." The principles and moral evaluations of *Donum Vitae* remain completely valid, however, new biomedical technologies have raised further questions that require answers.[81]

2. This study benefited from the analysis of the Pontifical Academy for Life and consultation with numerous scientific experts in light of a Christian anthropology and moral evaluation presented in the Encyclicals *Veritatis Splendor* and

Evangelium Vitae of Pope John Paul II. It is noted that some scientists and philosophers see the goal of medical science aimed at the cure of disease and the relief of suffering, whereas many others view biomedical technology from a eugenic perspective.

3. The Church's moral evaluations regarding biomedical research draws on faith and reason and sets forth an integral vision of the human person and his vocation incorporating various cultural and religious traditions that demonstrate a great reverence for life. The Church supports the view that science performs an "invaluable service to the integral good of the life and dignity of every human being." The Church desires that many Christians will dedicate themselves to biomedicine and bear witness to their faith and make available to the poor the results of their research.[82]

Dignitas Personae is addressed to the Catholic faithful and to all who seek the truth. It has three parts, which: 1) concern important anthropological, theological and ethical principles; 2) address new problems regarding procreation; and 3) examine new procedures that manipulate human embryos and the human genetic patrimony.

Part I: Anthropological, Theological and Ethical Aspects of Human Life and Procreation

4. The developments in medical science are positive when they "serve to overcome or correct pathologies and succeed in re-establishing the normal functioning of human procreation." However, "they are negative and cannot be utilized when they involve the destruction of human beings or when they employ means which contradict the dignity of the person or when they are used for purposes contrary to the integral good of man."[83]

The fundamental ethical criterion of biomedicine is that "the body of a human being, from the very first stages of its existence, can never be reduced merely to a group of cells." As *Donum Vitae* stated, the human zygote from the first moment of its existence demands the same unconditional respect that is morally due to any human being and his rights as a person must be recognized from the moment of conception, including in the first place the right to life.[84]

5. The foregoing ethical principle, which is in conformity with reason and the natural law, should serve as the basis for civil law in this area.[85] The conclusions of science give a valuable indication of a personal human presence at the first appearance of human life. The reality of the human being for the entire span of his or her life, does not allow a gradation in moral value before or after birth. The human embryo has the dignity proper to a person.

6. Procreation that shows responsibility for the child to be born must be the fruit of marriage. Marriage is providentially instituted by God to fulfill his plan for human beings, that in the reciprocal gift of self they give to each other they procreate and bring forth new life. Their reciprocity is an expression of natural law:

Natural law, which is at the root of the recognition of true equality between persons and peoples, deserves to be recognized as the source that inspires the relationship between the spouses in their begetting new children. The transmission of life is inscribed in nature and its laws stand as an unwritten norm to which all must refer.[86]

7. The Incarnation of Christ reveals the full dignity of the human body: "Christ did not disdain human bodiliness, but instead fully disclosed its meaning and value: 'In reality, it is only in the mystery of the incarnate Word that the mystery of man truly becomes clear.'"[87] In becoming one with us, Christ raises us to being one with God, "sharers in the divine nature."[88] This does not diminish or conflict with the dignity of our humanity but "elevates it into a wider horizon of life which is proper to God." Therefore, there is no contradiction between affirming the dignity of human life and affirming its sacredness in God.[89]

8. In fact, considering both his human dignity and his divine calling in Christ, man has unassailable value. Simply by existing, every human being must be fully respected. Therefore, biological, psychological, educational or health-related criteria discrimination must be rejected. God made man in his image and loves him because man reflects the face of Christ. This means human life is always a good, always a manifestation of God regardless of a particular person's intelligence, beauty, health, youth, integrity, and so on.

9. The two dimensions of the human person, natural and supernatural, allow us to better understand how procreation is a reflection of God's own Trinitarian love. Christian marriage is based on the natural complementarity of man and woman and a personal willingness to share their entire life-project, the fruit and sign of a profoundly human need. In Christ, God takes up this human need and purifies and elevates it through the sacrament of matrimony, an image of the unity which makes the Church the Mystical body of Christ.

10. The Church's ethical judgment on some recent developments of medical research do not trespass into an area reserved to medical science, but call everyone to be responsible for their actions in reference to the "unconditional respect owed to every human being at every moment of his or her existence, and the defense of the specific character of the personal act which transmits life." It is the mission of the Magisterium of the Church to form consciences in "the principles of the moral order which spring from human nature itself." [90]

Part II: New Problems Concerning Procreation

11. In light of the preceding ethical and anthropological principles consideration of new problems concerning procreation arising after *Donum Vitae* may be undertaken.

Techniques for assisting fertility

12. Infertility techniques must respect three fundamental goods: a) the right

to life and to physical integrity of every human being from conception to natural death; b) the unity of marriage, and the right within marriage to become a father or mother only together with the other spouse; and c) the specifically human values of sexuality which require "that the procreation of a human person be brought about as the fruit of the conjugal act specific to the love between spouses."[91]

Therefore, all techniques of heterologous and homologous artificial fertilization which substitute for the conjugal act must be excluded, whereas those techniques which "aid the conjugal act and its fertility are permitted." Even in the case of homologous artificial insemination within marriage, it is illicit "except in those cases in which the technical means is not a substitute for the conjugal act, but serves to facilitate and to help so that the act attains its natural purpose."[92]

13. Techniques that remove obstacles to natural fertilization, such as hormonal treatments for infertility, surgery for endometriosis, unblocking or repairing fallopian tubes are licit because the physician's action does not directly interfere with or replace the conjugal act itself. Adoption needs to be facilitated by appropriate legislation so that many children who lack a home may find one with infertile couples. Research into sterility prevention should also be encouraged.

In vitro fertilization and the deliberate destruction of embryos

14. Experience shows that "all techniques of *in vitro* fertilization proceed as if the human embryo were simply a mass of cells to be used, selected and discarded." One third of the women who avail of artificial procreation succeed in giving birth. But many more embryos are produced than those who are eventually born through artificial procreation. The process simply fails to respect the right to life of each individual embryo.[93]

15. Some say the risk to the embryo in artificial procreation is comparable to that in natural procreation. Although not all the loss of embryos in the in vitro process is attributable to a will to abandon them, in many cases it is foreseen and willed. Defective embryos conceived through IVF are routinely discarded. Even worse, fertile couples are starting to use IVF to design the genetic features of their offspring. In many countries it is routine practice to stimulate ovulation to obtain a large number of oocytes for fertilization with the intention of transferring only a few into the woman's uterus in the hope that at least one will implant. "In this way, the practice of multiple embryo transfer implies a purely utilitarian treatment of embryos." So, instead of serving life these techniques open the door to new threats to life.[94]

16. Human procreation is a personal act of husband and wife which strengthens the respect owed to the child to be conceived, whereas, the blithe acceptance of innumerable abortions in the IVF process show that this process weakens the respect due to every person. "The desire for a child cannot justify the 'production' of offspring, just as the desire not to have a child cannot justify the

abandonment or destruction of a child once he or she has been conceived." The logic of purely subjective desires and economic pressure seem to be the only guide to some biomedical researchers.[95]

Intracytoplasmic sperm injection (ICSI)

17. Intracytoplasmic sperm injection (ICSI) is technique used to overcome male infertility by "the injection into the oocyte of a single sperm, selected earlier, or by the injection of immature germ cells taken from the man."[96] ICSI is illicit because "it causes a complete separation between procreation and the conjugal act." Fertilization occurs outside the body of the couple through intervention of third parties: "Such fertilization is neither in fact achieved nor positively willed as the expression and fruit of a specific act of the conjugal union."[97]

Freezing embryos

18. To avoid having to take oocytes again and again from a woman's body, technicians in a single intervention take multiple oocytes and then cryo-preserve many of them for later use if necessary. Sometimes all the embryos are frozen because the hormonal stimulation used to obtain the oocytes affects the physiology of the woman's body in such a way that it is better to wait until it returns to normal before attempting embryo transfer back into her body. Cryopreservation disrespects the dignity of human embryos by exposing them to serious risks of death or physical harm, depriving them of maternal gestation, at least temporarily, and leaving them vulnerable to further manipulation.[98] Thousands upon thousands of unused embryos are "orphans" in the sense their parents do not ask for them.

Frozen embryo adoption

19. What is to be done with the large number of frozen embryos already in existence? Obviously proposals to use them for research or the treatment of disease are unacceptable. They are not mere biological material or analogous to cadavers. So, may frozen embryos be adopted or rescued? There seems to be no licit way for benevolent genetic strangers to intervene on their behalf:

> The proposal that these embryos could be put at the disposal of infertile couples as a treatment for infertility is not ethically acceptable for the same reasons which make artificial heterologous procreation illicit as well as any form of surrogate motherhood; this practice would also lead to other problems of a medical, psychological and legal nature.
>
> It has also been proposed, solely in order to allow human beings to be born who are otherwise condemned to destruction, that there could be a form of "prenatal adoption." This proposal, praiseworthy with regard to the intention of respecting and defending human life, presents however various problems not dissimilar to those mentioned above.

All things considered, it needs to be recognized that the thousands of abandoned embryos represent a situation of injustice which in fact cannot be resolved. Therefore John Paul II made an "appeal to the consciences of the world's scientific authorities and in particular to doctors, that the production of human embryos be halted, taking into account that there seems to be no morally licit solution regarding the human destiny of the thousands and thousands of "frozen" embryos which are and remain the subjects of essential rights and should therefore be protected by law as human persons."[99]

The freezing of oocytes

20. The technique of freezing oocytes not penetrated by a sperm has been developed in order to avoid the serious ethical problems posed by freezing embryos. However, "the cryopreservation of oocytes for the purpose of being used in artificial procreation is to be considered morally unacceptable."[100]

The reduction of embryos

21. The term "reduction of embryos" refers to a selective abortion technique following IVF and multiple embryo transfer to ensure that at least one of them implants and continues to develop. The extra embryos that have implanted are reduced in number, aborted, so that the mother is not subject to multiple pregnancies. This technique "constitutes a grave moral disorder." The principle of double effect or the lesser of two evils do not apply in this case: "It is never permitted to do something which is intrinsically illicit, not even in view of a good result: the end does not justify the means."[101]

Preimplantation diagnosis

22. Preimplantation diagnosis [PID] occurs when embryos procreated artificially through IVF undergo genetic diagnosis before being transferred into a woman's womb so that only "embryos free from defects or having the desired sex or other particular qualities are transferred." PID is connected with IVF, which is always intrinsically evil, and is "directed toward the qualitative selection and consequent destruction of embryos, which constitutes an act of abortion." PID expresses a eugenic mentality directed toward the abortion of human embryos deemed unfit to be born because they do not fall "within the parameters of 'normality' and physical well-being, thus opening the way to legitimizing infanticide and euthanasia as well."[102]

Treating the human embryo as laboratory material lessens human dignity and leads to discrimination. Just as in the past unjust discrimination was visited upon human beings for no other reason than their race, skin color or nationality, so "today there is a no less serious and unjust form of discrimination which leads to the non-recognition of the ethical and legal status of human beings suffering from serious diseases or disabilities."[103]

New forms of interception and contra gestation

23. Contraceptives interfere with the union of egg and sperm. Interceptives, such as the IUD or so-called morning after pill, interfere with the implantation of the embryo in the uterine wall while contra gestatives, including RU-486, synthetic prostaglandins or Methotrexate (MTX), cause the elimination of an embryo implanted within the uterine wall.

It is disingenuous to claim one is re-establishing menstruation through the use of a contra gestative when what clearly takes place "is the abortion of an embryo which has just implanted." The sin of abortion includes interception and contra gestation and "when there is certainty that an abortion has resulted, there are serious penalties in canon law."[104]

Part III: New Treatments which Involve the Manipulation of the Embryo or the Human Genetic Patrimony

24. Research on adult stem cells has produced effective results in the areas of regenerative medicine and genetically based diseases, while research on embryonic stem cells has not. Nonetheless, some maintain that possible medical advances may occur from research on embryonic stem cells. Attentive moral discernment is required when it comes to gene therapy, cloning, and the use of stem cells.

Gene therapy

25. Gene therapy is genetic engineering of human beings for therapeutic purposes. This can occur on two levels: *Somatic cell gene therapy* seeks to eliminate or reduce genetic defects on non-reproductive cells, aimed at certain individual cells and limited to a single person. *Germ line cell therapy*, on the other hand, seeks to correct genetic defects in reproductive cells so as to transmit the therapeutic effects to the offspring of the individual. Somatic or germ line cell therapy can target a fetus before birth or after birth or a child or an adult.

26. "Procedures used on somatic cells for strictly therapeutic purposes are in principle morally licit" as when they "seek to restore the normal genetic configuration of the patient or to counter damage caused by genetic anomalies or those related to other pathologies" provided the patient will not be exposed to health risks disproportionate to the gravity of the pathology to be cured. On the other hand, "germ line cell therapy in all its forms is morally illicit" because such genetic modifications will be transmitted to potential offspring and pose risks not fully controllable in future progeny.[105]

27. Using genetic manipulation for non-therapeutic purposes with the aim of improving the gene pool would promote a "eugenic mentality" leading to an "indirect social stigma with regard to people who lack certain qualities, while privileging qualities that happen to be appreciated by a certain culture or society;

such qualities do not constitute what is specifically human." In the end this mentality would harm the common good "by favoring the will of some over the
freedom of others" and establishing "an unjust domination of man over man."[106]

Human cloning

28. Human cloning may be accomplished by either *artificial embryo twinning* or *cell nuclear transfer*. In both cases the goal is the asexual reproduction
of the entire human organism in order to produce a "copy" substantially identical to the original human being. Artificial embryo twinning occurs when cells are
separated from the embryo in the earliest stage of development and transferred
into the uterus so as to obtain identical (twin) embryos. Cloning is more properly
understood as *cell nuclear transfer* and "consists in introducing a nucleus taken
from an embryonic or somatic cell into a denucleated oocyte. This is followed
by stimulation of the oocyte so that it begins to develop as an embryo."[107]

There are two purposes for cloning: reproduction and medical therapy or
research. Reproductive cloning seeks to achieve the birth of a baby for various
reasons such as "control over human evolution, selection of human beings with
superior qualities, pre-selection of the sex of a child to be born, production of a
child who is the 'copy' of another, or production of a child for a couple whose
infertility cannot be treated in another way." Therapeutic cloning is proposed to
produce embryonic stem cells with a predetermined genetic patrimony so as to
overcome immune system rejection and is linked with stem cell production.[108]

There has been an international outcry against human cloning and it is prohibited in a great majority of nations.

> Human cloning is intrinsically illicit in that, by taking the ethical negativity of
> techniques of artificial fertilization to their extreme, it seeks to give rise to a
> new human being without a connection to the act of reciprocal self-giving be
> tween the spouses and, more radically, without any link to sexuality. This leads
> to manipulation and abuses gravely injurious to human dignity.[109]

29. Reproductive cloning is "a form of biological slavery" whereby someone would "arrogate to himself the right to determine arbitrarily the genetic characteristics of another person." This would violate the fundamental equality of
all people: "The originality of every person is a consequence of the particular
relationship that exists between God and a human being from the first moment
of his existence and carries with it the obligation to respect the singularity and
integrity of each person . . . and only the love of husband and wife constitutes a
mediation of that love in conformity with the plan of the Creator and heavenly
Father."[110]

30. Therapeutic cloning is an even more serious affront on human dignity.
Regardless of one's good intention to cure the sick, for example, to create human embryos with the intention of destroying them reduces human beings to
means to be used. "It is gravely immoral to sacrifice a human life for therapeutic

ends."[111]

New techniques have been developed that attempt to avoid using human embryos as a disposable means for research. *Human parthenogenesis, altered nuclear transfer* (ANT) and *oocyte assisted reprogramming* (OAR) posit that what is used is not a true human embryo.[112] However because these techniques raise both scientific and ethical questions regarding the humanity or "ontological status of the 'product' obtained in this way," until such doubts are clarified one must even refrain from destroying what *may* be a human being: "the mere probability that a human person is involved would suffice to justify an absolutely clear prohibition of any intervention aimed at killing a human embryo."[113]

The therapeutic use of stem cells

31. Stem cells are undifferentiated cells with a prolonged ability to multiply while maintaining the undifferentiated state and the ability to produce transitory progenitor cells from which fully differentiated cells, such as nerve cells, blood cells, etc., descend. When transplanted into damaged tissue, stem cells tend to regenerate the tissue. Stem cells have been identified in the human embryo, the fetus, blood from the umbilical cord, and adult bone marrow, brain, mesenchyme and amniotic fluid. *Embryonic stem cells* have the ability to multiply and differentiate but so do *adult stem cells* and the latter give more positive results and are favored for therapeutic protocol.

32. An ethical evaluation must consider the methods of obtaining stem cells as well as the risks connected with their clinical and experimental use. "Methods which do not cause serious harm to the subject from whom the stem cells are taken are to be considered licit." Examples of licitly obtained stem cells include those taken from a) an adult organism, b) umbilical cord blood, and c) fetuses that died a natural death. Examples of stem cells obtained illicitly include those taken from living human embryos: "History itself has condemned such a science in the past and will condemn it in the future, not only because it lacks the light of God but also because it lacks humanity."[114]

Embryonic stem cells provided by other researchers through the destruction of embryos present an occasion for cooperation in evil and scandal. Stem cells that have been obtained licitly may be used in research provided the "common criteria of medical ethics is respected such as reducing to the bare minimum any risks to the patient and the exchange of information among clinicians and full disclosure to the public. Research using adult stem cells should be encouraged since they do not present ethical problems."

Attempts at hybridization

33. Hybrid cloning uses animal oocytes to reprogram the nuclei of human somatic cells in order to extract embryonic stem cells from the resulting embryos. These procedures are an offense against the human dignity "on account of the admixture of human and animal genetic elements capable of disrupting the

specific identity of man." In addition there may be health risks due to the presence of animal genetic material in their cytoplasm. To knowingly expose human beings to such risks is unethical.[115]

The use of human "biological material" of illicit origin

34. In the production of vaccines cell lines are often used that were obtained from the abortion of a pre-natal child or other "illicit interventions against the life or physical integrity of a human being." Cooperation in these unjust acts may be either mediate or immediate. The material is sometimes sold or distributed freely to research centers by government agencies. All of this raises issues of cooperation in evil and scandal. It is important to recall that any intervention on human embryos which results in their destruction is the moral equivalent of an abortion.[116]

35. However, if researchers use "biological material" of illicit origin produced at another research center some, applying "the criterion of independence" claim their use is ethically permissible because there is a clear separation between those who kill the embryos and the researchers who use them in their research. "The criterion of independence is not sufficient to avoid a contradiction in the attitude of the person who says that he does not approve of the injustice perpetrated by others, but at the same time accepts for his own work the 'biological material' which the others have obtained by means of that injustice."[117]

> Therefore, it needs to be stated that there is a duty to refuse to use such "biological material" even when there is no close connection between the researcher and the actions of those who performed the artificial fertilization or the abortion, or when there was no prior agreement with the centers in which the artificial fertilization took place. This duty springs from the necessity to remove oneself, within the area of one's own research, from a gravely unjust legal situation and to affirm with clarity the value of human life. Therefore the above-mentioned criterion of independence is necessary, but may be ethically insufficient.[118]

However, there are degrees of responsibility. Grave reasons that may be morally proportionate to justify the use of such "biological material" such as danger to a child's health "could permit parents to use a vaccine which was developed using cell lines of illicit origin" provided one fulfills their duty to make known their disagreement and ask that other vaccines be derived from sources of licit origin. The responsibility of those who make the decision to use cell lines of illicit origin is not the same as those who have no voice in the decision. People in the field of health care need to be reminded they must be committed to "absolute respect for human life and its sacredness."[119]

Conclusion

36. Human history shows that man is capable of unjust discrimination and oppression of the weak and defenseless. At the same time history also shows real progress in understanding the dignity of every person as the foundation of human rights. Various forms of behavior harmful to human dignity have been prohibited such as slavery, and the marginalization of women, the disabled and children. Such prohibitions are a sign of genuine human progress. The legitimacy of every prohibition is based on the need to protect an authentic moral good.

37. Today human progress is no longer marked by industrial development but by informational technologies, research in genetics and biotechnologies. These areas of development are susceptible to abuse. Just as the Church spoke up for the oppressed worker one hundred years ago, so today she speaks up for those who have no voice, "who are threatened and despised and whose human rights are violated,"[120] especially those in the first stages of existence. The Christian faithful must give this Instruction "religious assent" knowing "God always gives the grace necessary to observe his commandments and that, in every human being, above all in the least among us, one meets Christ himself.[121]

Moral and Legal Reflection on
Artificial Reproductive Techniques

Donum Vitae and *Dignitas Personae* condemned artificial insemination, in-vitro fertilization and cloning. What do these techniques share in common? The key moral principle in the area of reproductive technology is that for a medical intervention to be morally upright it may only *assist* a husband and wife perform a conjugal act or help their conjugal act to achieve its objective once naturally performed. On the other hand any reproductive technique that *replaces* or *substitutes* for the conjugal act of spouses, to achieve the conception of a human embryo, a child, is intrinsically evil. To make this distinction clear Donald DeMarco employs the analogy of an injured ball player who is assisted off the field by someone who slings his arm under his shoulder to steady him as he walks to the sidelines versus the act of paramedics who carry a severely injured ball player from the field in a stretcher thereby replacing his mobility completely. In like manner, a reproductive technique that replaces the natural mobility and route of sperm to achieve union with an ovum would seem to be illicit.[122] The conjugal act of spouses must be the immediate instrumental cause of their child's conception.

A child conceived through IVF is treated in his or her conception as a product, not an equal to his or her parents, and certainly not as an unrepeatable gift from God. As we have seen *Donum Vitae* declared every child has the *"inalienable right"* to be conceived, carried, delivered and brought up by his or her natural parents, united for life in marriage. Surrogate motherhood, IVF and artificial insemination separate genetic and gestational motherhood from parental rearing and thereby violate innate relational bonds, which hinders a child's maturation and sense of identity and self-worth.

The essential relationship of the conjugal act to marriage is underscored in the canonical requirements of the Catholic Church for the validity of sacramental marriage. The inability to conceive a child, sterility, is *not* an impediment to a valid sacramental marriage; but impotence, the inability to perform the conjugal act due to permanent physiological or psychological conditions in one or both spouses, is a diriment impediment.[123] Impotence that occurs after a valid marriage has been consummated (subsequent impotence) does not affect the validity of marriage. But, if one or both persons who intend to marry is impotent with respect to all members of the opposite sex or just their intended spouse (absolute or relative impotence) before marriage (antecedent impotence), and the condition is not remediable without grave risks to that person's life (perpetual impotence), that person is prevented from validly entering into the sacrament of marriage:

> 1) Antecedent and perpetual impotence to have sexual intercourse, whether on the part of the man or that of the woman, whether absolute or relative, by its very nature invalidates marriage.[124]

For women impotence may occur due to psychological causes, "vaginismus," where sudden muscle spasms of the vagina make penetration difficult or impossible. But this is remediable with treatment within a short time and should not pose an impediment to marriage.[125]

Surgery to remedy a physical deformity in a woman's vagina in order to facilitate marital intercourse would be licit and necessary for her to contract a valid sacramental marriage:

> A vagina that is so short or so narrow as to make penetration even of the corona of the penis impossible constitutes impotence, unless the condition is remediable by surgery.[126]

The construction of an artificial vagina by plastic surgery may be licit. If a person is identifiably female, chromosomally and possess internal female genital organs, the reconstruction of a rudimentary vagina, or construction of one where none existed before "in its normal anatomical position is at least probably sufficient for potency," whether or not connected with her internal genital organs. However, in charity a woman would have a grave obligation to inform her intended spouse of her abnormality.[127]

The requirements for canonical potency in a man are that he be capable of an erection, penetration and ejaculation. A vasectomized man is *sterile*, as nothing produced in his testicles ("true semen," including sperm) is ejaculated; his ejaculate includes only secretions from his prostate and seminal vesicles. But a vasectomized man may marry because he is not *impotent*—not only can he sustain an erection sufficient to penetrate his spouse, but he can also ejaculate. He must repent of his sin if he willfully chose to sterilize himself, and has a grave obligation to inform his intended bride of his operation.[128] A man suffering from "paraplegia" (the complete loss of sensation in the legs and lower back including loss of venereal sensation and the inability to have an erection) or "priapism" (a persistent erection, due to neurological conditions or trauma producing a loss of sensation in the penis and an inability to ejaculate) is also impotent, and if this occurs before marriage, these conditions prevent him from entering into a valid marriage. Obviously, medical discoveries that would cure these maladies would be praiseworthy.[129]

From the foregoing analysis we can see that the use of surgical implants to simulate an erect penis in a man suffering from impotency would not cure his condition (would not assist the conjugal act in its performance) since he would still be unable to ejaculate. Hence, such an implant would be illicit since it would not cure antecedent and perpetual impotence in anticipation of marriage. Even in the case of a man suffering from subsequent impotence, such an implant in order to simulate intercourse with his wife would amount to little more than sexual stimulation (foreplay) incapable of culmination and release in an act of genuine sexual intercourse, therefore such surgery would remain illicit.

So what reproductive interventions are moral? Reproductive interventions aimed at remedying impotence, including drug therapy, corrective surgery, and/or counseling, may be licit insofar as they assist but do not replace the conjugal act.[130] Drug therapies that assist the conjugal act to be performed may be licit, depending on the motive and circumstance of the person acting. Estrogen or progestin hormone supplements which aid women to ovulate or to sustain a pregnancy are morally neutral acts that may become good acts with the proper motive and circumstances. Although not intrinsically evil, the health risks associated with hyperovulatory drugs to a woman and the children she is likely to carry (i.e., conceiving quadruplets and more are common side effects of the drugs), tip the scales against their licit use, since the risks generally outweigh the benefits.[131] The list of counter-indications for the hyperovulatory drug Clomid include death, ovarian cancer, increased rate of multiple pregnancy, increased incidence of ectopic pregnancy and breast cancer, pelvic pain and ovarian enlargement (ovarian hyper stimulation syndrome), rupture of ovarian cysts, bloating and stomach pain, blurred vision, jaundice, shortness of breath, nausea, uterine bleeding, nervousness and insomnia, and breast tenderness.[132] Moreover, babies carried in multiple pregnancies are more likely to suffer prenatal development problems affecting lung development and cranial hemorrhaging. After birth, multiple pregnancy children are more likely to develop chronic medical problems, including cerebral palsy, lung disorders, blindness, deafness and learning disabilities. Mothers who have labored with multiple pregnancies are more prone to gestational diabetes, increased incidence of pre-term birth and the need of bed-rest and drug therapy to prevent premature labor, low-birth-weight babies, high blood pressure, uterine bleeding and blood clots.[133]

A testosterone patch to remedy male hypogonadism (low testosterone production), which is one cause of male impotence (inability to sustain a penal erection) may be licit. Commercial products that enable men suffering from impotence to achieve and sustain an erection are morally neutral acts that acquire moral specificity through motive and circumstance. Either of these products taken to facilitate marital intercourse would be licit provided the benefits were proportional to any negative side effects produced.

The congenital genital defect of hypospadias (where the urethra in a man's penis opens at the underside of the penis) may be corrected by wearing a perforated condom to enable his sperm to be deposited within her vagina instead of being ejaculated outside of her vagina.[134]

A cervical spoon, or syringe, or dilator to facilitate may be used to increase the amount of sperm introduced into the cervical canal after intercourse. A physician may use these instruments after conjugal intercourse by spouses to help the husband's sperm travel through the cervical os (which delayed and diminished the quantity of sperm available to meet and fuse with the ovum of his wife) to help their act of intercourse achieve conception.[135]

Developed in 1983 at St. Elizabeth Hospital Medical Center in Dayton, Ohio, Low Tubal Ovum Transfer (LTOT) has also met with the approval of sound Catholic ethicists. In this minor surgery a ripened ovum is transported *in vivo* (not exteriorizing it) around a woman's blocked fallopian tube and allowed to continue to travel down the remainder of the tube. Immediately preceding and/or following this surgery the spouses engage in marital intercourse. Hopefully her ovum will then unite with her husband's sperm in the lower reaches of her fallopian tube and the embryo, their child, will successfully implant in her uterus.[136] This surgical intervention does not replace, but rather assists, the conjugal act, helping it to achieve its end after it has been morally performed. Unfortunately, human conception usually does not occur in the lower reaches of the fallopian tube, and the success rate has been very low.[137]

The following biotechnological interventions affecting human procreation are controversial, with ethicists faithful to the Magisterium of the Church arguing for and against their legitimacy. Tubal Ovum Transfer (TOT) was also developed at St. Elizabeth Hospital Medical Center in Dayton, Ohio, after LTOT failed to achieve the successful live birth of a child. TOT attempts to meet some of the objectionable features raised by Catholic moral theologians to IVF and embryo transfer, such as, masturbation to obtain the husband's sperm and *in-vitro* conception (outside the womb). This is accomplished by harvesting and exteriorizing ova through laparoscopy, and exteriorizing sperm obtained from a "silasitic" (non-interactive material) perforated condom after intercourse between husband and wife has occurred. The perforation in the condom allows a minimal amount of sperm to enter the vagina, providing for a completed conjugal act while preserving most of the sperm for retrieval. An ovum from the wife and sperm from the husband are then placed into a catheter tube with an air bubble separating them until they are transferred into the high reaches of the fallopian tube of the wife and injected where, hopefully, two gametes unite and conception occurs *in vivo*.[138] Gamete Intrafallopian Transfer (GIFT) was developed in 1984 at the University of San Antonio and is identical to TOT, except that sperm is obtained through masturbation.[139]

There has been some degree of confusion among Church authorities over the technical characteristics of TOT. It was wrongly assumed to be similar to LTOT. Significantly, Archbishop of Cincinnati, Daniel E. Pilarczyk approved LTOT but not TOT as meeting the moral requirements outlined in *Donum Vitae*.[140] Once again, the test in evaluating reproductive technology is whether a procedure *assists* the marital act of intercourse naturally performed to achieve pregnancy/conception versus *replaces* it as the efficient instrumental cause of conception/fertilization.[141]

This principle is analogous to "proximate causality" in the legal analysis of negligence. If the causal trajectory of a negligent act is interrupted by a "superseding intervening cause," the harm that results cannot be attributed to the original act of negligence of X, but is the result of exigencies brought into play by the supervening intervening activity of Y.

> If the intervening act is extraordinary under the circumstances, not foreseeable in the normal course of events, or independent of or far removed from the defendant's conduct, it may well be a superseding act which breaks the causal nexus.[142]

In the case of LTOT the trajectory of the ovum may be compared to a salmon helped around a waterfall too high for it to jump up and swim over by the construction of a bypass aqueduct which allows the salmon to swim around the waterfall and continue up river. In LTOT the ovum is helped around a blockage in the fallopian tube to travel on its own the remainder of its natural journey down the fallopian tube to meet and fuse with a sperm cell or not. In LTOT the natural process unleashed in marital intercourse is not stopped and restarted by the supervening intervening technological acts of third parties. A medical intervention does not replace the act of ovulation or intercourse as the proximate cause of fertilization/conception.

In TOT, however, the routing and locomotion of the trajectory of intercourse are replaced. Third parties provide the operative instrumental causes that bring ovum and sperm together. Third parties first exteriorize the gametes, ovum and sperm from the bodies of husband and wife, then they carry them into a laboratory where they place the gametes in close proximity inside a catheter, and then they transport ovum and sperm inside the catheter and place it into the high reaches of the woman's fallopian tube, and finally a technician ejects them and leaves them to unite. Returning to our analogy of the salmon, it is as if salmon were caught and placed in a tank, put on a truck and driven a hundred miles to a quiet pond up river and then released.

Marital intercourse is irrelevant in TOT; it is superseded by intervening technological instrumental causes. The effect of pregnancy/conception cannot be attributed to the personal act and mutual self-giving of husband and wife. In

TOT the child is brought into being by the acts of technicians, with gametes supplied by a man and a woman. It would seem that TOT looks down at the principles of good animal husbandry for guidance, not up to the procession and total self-giving of Persons in the Trinity as its exemplar.[143]

Nonetheless, TOT and GIFT are defended as licit by some Catholic ethicists, including Donald McCarthy, Orville Grise, Peter Cataldo, and John W. Carlson; whereas May, DeMarco, Grisez, Seifert, Tonti-Filippini, Ashley and O'Rourke believe TOT replaces the marital act and so it is an objectively evil act. William May would not give the benefit of a probabilistic doubt to TOT:

> Someone might say that with respect to procedures where reputable Catholic theologians disagree, and since there is no specific magisterial teaching on them, Catholics are at liberty to follow whatever view they prefer as a "probable opinion." This way of looking at the issue is quite legalistic in my opinion. What one ought to do is examine the arguments and reasons given by theologians to support their claims to see which is true and takes into account the realities involved.[144]

Since Rome has not spoken, it would appear a Catholic couple may, after serious study and reflection, use LTOT or GIFT/TOT. Still it would seem better to not use such procedures for the reasons given above. Fr. Bartholomew Kiely, who helped prepare *Donum Vitae*, said both GIFT and LTOT were still open for consideration: "the instruction does not pronounce a judgment on GIFT [or LTOT]. It leaves it open to research by biologists and to further discussion by theologians." Then Joseph Cardinal Ratzinger (Pope Benedict XVI) whose Congregation (SCDF) produced *Donum Vitae*, was asked about the licitness of procedures for fertility enhancement other than those directly discussed in the document. He replied that *as yet,* a doctor *might* in good conscience perform such operations:

> When the discussion is still open and there is not yet a decision by the magisterium, the doctor is required to stay informed, according to classic theological principles and concrete circumstances [and] make a decision based on his informed conscience.[145]

The following reproductive techniques all require the exteriorization of gametes and involve either *in-vitro* fertilization or artificial insemination, and because of one of the later reasons are morally objectionable: Pronuclear Stage Tubal Transfer (PROST), which transfers new human embryos conceived *in-vitro* into the fallopian tube; Sperm Intrafallopian Transfer (SIFT), Zygote Intrafallopian Transfer (ZIFT); Peritoneal Oocyte and Sperm Transfer (POST); and Vaginal Intra-peritoneal Sperm Transfer (VIPST).[146]

Intracytoplasmic sperm injection (ICSI), "the injection into the oocyte of a single sperm, selected earlier, or by the injection of immature germ cells taken from the man,"[147] is specifically condemned in *Dignitas Personae* because "it causes a complete separation between procreation and the conjugal act." Fertilization occurs outside the body of the couple through intervention of third parties and is not an expression or the fruit of conjugal union.[148]

As a general rule procedures which only exteriorize gametes and conception occurs in vivo, and not in-vitro, and do not rely on artificial insemination or masturbation may, *as yet, be licit.* A more cautious approach would be to have recourse to only those procedures that do not exteriorize and reroute the gametes from the causality unleashed in the conjugal act of husband and wife.

The licitness of several techniques aimed at increasing the likelihood of conception in the case of a husband with low sperm count (oligospermia) is disputed by some moralists, and serves to further illustrate the general rule given above. They disagree over whether sperm or ova may be washed and treated to enhance their capacity for achieving fertilization, and whether sperm may be saved in a perforated condom and accumulated from prior acts of marital intercourse and released just prior or following, a final act of intercourse. Some ethicists believe this removal and reintroduction replaces the causality of intercourse to achieve pregnancy/conception.[149] On the other hand, Fr. O'Donnell argues that to reintroduced sperm collected as described above so that there will be sufficient spermatozoa in the husband's ejaculate merely fortifies the husband's ejaculate in the act of final intercourse with "supplemental sperm previously collected in legitimate marital acts" and is a morally licit intervention.[150]

Sperm exteriorized through a perforated condom and then returned to the vaginal canal just prior to or after a final act of intercourse are not rerouted, as in the case of GIFT, but are re-placed in the vaginal canal to travel their normal course. The accumulation of these sperm has not so much replaced the marital act from achieving its end as delayed it. Certainly a wife may simply push back into her vagina her husband's sperm that may have spilled out immediately after intercourse. This would not be an illicit act even though a distinct human act other than intercourse would be the instrumental cause for the re-introduction of some of her husband's sperm into her vagina. It would seem, therefore, that the reintroduction of sperm back into the vaginal canal after it has been collected in a perforated condom would assist and not replace the final act of marital intercourse to achieve its end by increasing the husband's sperm count and, therefore, should be considered morally licit.

The IVF process, intrinsically evil in itself, leads to a host of other immoral practices. Both *Donum Vitae* and *Dignitas Personae* condemn the cryopreservation of human embryos, part and parcel of the IVF process, as another objective evil. In addition, deep freezing human embryos is also evil because of the evil consequences that follow which entail further attacks on their human dignity and exposes them to being treated as a means to an end for the reproductive treatment of infertile couples or as genetic material for scientific research. The regulation of the IVF industry exhibits a plethora of rules and regulations that vary from country to country or states and provinces within countries exposing human embryos to the whim and caprice of their genetic parents, IVF clinics and arbitrary legislative and court decisions. The only consistency in the area of the legal treatment of pre-natal human life is that human embryos and fetuses *in vivo*, inside a woman's body, are treated as expendable ("abortable," if you will) "potential human life" whereas *in vitro* human embryos outside the womb are regarded as expendable genetic material. Human embryos are property not persons or a hybrid that affords them even less protection than if they were simply regarded as bailed goods which both parties, the male and female bailors, have an equal right to possess.[151]

After the first IVF baby was born in the United Kingdom in July of 1978 the British Parliament enacted various protocols regulating the IVF process. More recently disputes arising under British law are subject to an appeal to the European Court of Human Rights Union. One such case, *Evans v. United Kingdom*, illustrates the problems attendant upon attempts to regulate what is essentially an immoral and exploitive enterprise. A more thorough review of this case will follow the moral analysis of frozen embryo adoption provided below.

Suffice to say that since the human embryo is not recognized as a rights bearer with human dignity equal to all other members of the human species, as they should be, the only interests the law regards are those of the embryo's genetic parents and the IVF storage facility. Most often if there is a dispute between the genetic parents of a human embryo the parent wishing to not assume a parental role will prevail over the parent wishing to have the embryo implanted in a womb and brought to term. It is the reverse of Solomon's decision when he had to decide between two mothers both claiming the same child was hers. Whereas Solomon gave the child to the woman who was willing to relinquish her claim rather than see the child die, courts today allows the parent who wishes to kill the embryonic child to prevail. The right of a genetic parent to not become the parent of a child in the full sense, outside the womb, is consistent with the policy considerations that provide justification for abortion on demand. The irony is that in the context of frozen embryos most often it is the woman's right to privacy understood as her right to become a mother that is denied in favor of a man's privacy interests not to become a father.[152]

Rescuing Frozen Embryos—Adoption or Adultery?

Embryo adoption is a commercial enterprise that seeks to match and impregnate married or single women with a "spare" frozen embryo from a donor person or couple. Childless couples are spared the burdens of live child adoptive agency scrutiny, background checks, etc., or the burdens and risks of the IVF procedure. For considerably less than the costs associated with most foreign adoptions, childless couples have a very good chance of taking home a baby in nine months.[153] Some concerned Christians, motivated principally by the desire to save surplus frozen embryos from certain destruction, wonder whether it is licit for them to rescue and adopt these cryo-preserved children. While some pro-life organizations continue to promote embryo transfer and third party impregnation in order to rescue and adopt these children,[154] the licitness of this deed has been hotly disputed among moralists faithful to the Magisterium of the

Church. Some of the protagonists in this debate, such as Msgr. William B. Smith, Edmund Pellegrino, M.D., Rev. Tadeusz Pacholczyk and Nicholas Tonti-Filippini, argue against embryo transfer of abandoned frozen embryos whereas William E. May, Helen Watt, E. Christian Brugger, Robert George and Germain Grisez uphold embryo transfer under these circumstances.[155] The stakes are high: life or death for the human embryo, versus possible complicity in surrogate motherhood and marital infidelity.

Donum Vitae did not specifically address this question. Moralists have, therefore, taken the principles articulated in *Donum Vitae* in regards to IVF and surrogacy, cryopreservation and the right of every human being to life and applied them to the facts presented in "embryo adoption/rescue" according to their gut reactions, i.e., their "moral intuitions."[156] Then vice-president of the Pontifical Academy for Life, Bishop Eilo Sgreccia, indicated that this was an important disputed question in bioethics, worthy of their studied reflection: "In order to investigate this subject the Academy for Life has set up a multidisciplinary task force which will study all the aspects of the whole question and then publish a work on the subject."[157]

All the ethicists mentioned above agree on the following three points: First, even if, for the sake of argument embryo transfer of rescue frozen embryos is licit it is certainly not mandatory—no one is obligated to perform acts of charity that threaten their own health or are otherwise "seriously inconvenient." For example, a stranger is not morally obliged to give blood even if it will improve someone's health or even save their life. Second, all agree that if embryo transfer to save frozen embryos is intrinsically evil it may not be done even to save the lives of innocent persons otherwise doomed to die. For instance, there is no exception to the sixth Commandment—no one is permitted to commit adultery in order to save someone's life. Finally, all ethicists faithful to the Magisterium agree that surrogate motherhood is intrinsically evil. However, they differ, as to which of the two sentences provided in *Donum Vitae* define the essence of surrogate motherhood, to wit:

> *   By *surrogate mother* the instruction means:
> a) [First Sentence] The woman who carries in pregnancy an embryo implanted in her uterus and who is genetically a stranger to the embryo because it has been obtained through the union of the gametes of "donors." [Second Sentence] She carries the pregnancy with a pledge to surrender the baby once it is born to the party who commissioned or made the agreement of the pregnancy.
>
> b) [First Sentence] The woman who carries in pregnancy an embryo to whose procreation she has contributed the donation of her own ovum, fertilized through insemination with the sperm of a man other than her husband. [Second Sentence] She carries the pregnancy with a pledge to surrender the baby once it is born to the party who commissioned or made the agreement of the pregnancy.[158]

Those who condemn embryo rescue emphasize the first sentence and treat it as a form of illicit surrogacy which occurs whenever a woman carries in pregnancy an embryo either implanted in her uterus or conceived within her through artificial insemination to which she and/or her husband are "genetic strangers." Those who support embryo rescue emphasize the second sentence and argue that illicit surrogacy occurs only if a woman "carries the pregnancy *with a pledge to surrender the baby* once it is born," but not if she directs her action to saving its life and/or adopting it.

Those who condemn embryo adoption/rescue argue that their colleagues ascribe to the moral deed what rightly belongs to motive: that is, those who seek to legitimize embryo transfer collapse the distinction between "what" the woman does with "why" she does it. The first sentence describes the moral object— "what" a surrogate mother does, i.e., she becomes pregnant through embryo transfer or artificial insemination with a child to whom she and/or her husband are genetic strangers. The second sentence explains the motive: "why" a surrogate mother becomes pregnant with a child to whom she and/or her husband are genetic strangers, i.e., because she "pledged" (usually for profit) to surrender the child after birth to another.

Tonti-Filippini argues *Donum Vitae* should be read to include "pregnancy" when it speaks of "conception" brought about by IVF and embryo transfer or artificial insemination.[159] So when the instruction condemns "*the generation of the human person*" when "*objectively deprived of its perfection: namely, that of being the result and fruit of a conjugal act,*" we should also understand it to condemn pregnancy objectively deprived of its perfection, namely, that of being the result and fruit of a conjugal act. He believes those who defend embryo adoption/rescue have instrumentalized human pregnancy and reduced its significance to mere incubation, analogous to breast feeding; comparing it only to something a mother does, providing nourishment. On the contrary, he argues being pregnant affects the psychosomatic being of a woman: it alters her identity. Maternity is not something a wife *does,* like breast feeding; rather, she *is* pregnant.[160]

It would not have changed the identity of the Blessed Ever-Virgin Mary if she had nursed her Cousin Elizabeth's child; but to say she carried another child in her womb would. Maternity is a special moment in the lives of spouses; it transforms them both and unites them physically, emotionally and spiritually. Maternity deeply affects a woman's self conception and relationship with her husband. In holding her swelling womb she cannot help but think of the man she loves. That is why we are instinctively repulsed at the thought that a woman should have to bear the child of the man who raped her. But for the humanity of her innocent child we would spare her this constant reminder of the rapist who victimized her.

What man hasn't felt a shudder of awe mixed with fear and joy when he is told by his beloved, "I'm pregnant"? The maternity of his wife changes a husband interiorly; her love has made him a father. Her changing figure reminds him of her vulnerability to his loving touch. To bear his child—and no other's— is an essential good of marriage which a wife pledges to her husband, just as he pledges that no other woman shall bear his children but her. This mutual pledge is part of the Christian faith: "*The fidelity of the spouses in the unity of marriage involves reciprocal respect of their right to become a father and a mother only through each other.*"[161]

Unlike adoption in the usual sense of the term, so called embryo adoption changes the psychosomatic being of a woman in her union with her child in a way that leaves her husband untouched. She says to her husband, "I am wonderfully changed with child." But he is not wonderfully changed since they both know this child is not his; he has not been the cause (efficient or instrumental) of her joy. Even a saint like Joseph, fully capable of heroic love, was disturbed by news of this kind. We read in scripture that it would have divided them if God hadn't revealed the truth of the Incarnation to Joseph and touched his heart with grace.[162] In the ordinary case of an adoption of a child already born, both spouses come to the child on equal terms as strangers, who then unite to form a family of persons through affection and their will to further the true good of each other. But in embryo adoption, the wife becomes the real mother of her child, while her husband is but a step-father. She becomes pregnant with someone else's child. She gives birth to her child, but not to her husband's child. Thus, pregnancy in the case of heterologous embryo transfer, instead of uniting husband and wife as procreators, becomes an occasion of division. Tonti-Filippini expresses this well:

> The matter of impregnation so that a woman becomes a mother and enters into that new union with a child, *from outside her marriage*, thus raises questions about the nature of the communion of persons that is marriage. . . .
>
> It is my conclusion that having given herself, her psychosomatic unity, faithfully, exclusively, totally, and in a fully human way *in marriage*, a woman is not free to give herself to being impregnated with a child from outside of marriage in this way, however altruistic the purpose and however desperate the plight of those to whom she wishes to give herself. This is so because her generative capacity, which, I will argue, includes or is at least so linked to her capacity to become pregnant and to bear a child in her womb, and is not merely her capacity to produce ova and to express her love in the conjugal act, *belongs to the marital union*, and hence may not be given outside marriage. In these ways, but not with all its viciousness, heterologous embryo transfer may be akin to adultery. Heterologous embryo transfer may be at best a mistaken, misguided charity though an extraordinarily generous charity, but the mistake may be a very grave mistake, striking as it would seem to at the very dignity of the woman and of her marriage.[163]

Before the advent of IVF every conception resulted automatically in a pregnancy. It would seem, therefore, axiomatic that if all IVF conceptions are an objective wrong, then all IVF related pregnancies are also wrong. Those who defend embryo adoption point out that if every pregnancy as well as every conception must be the fruit of a conjugal act between spouses, then a couple having repented of their sin of *in-vitro* fertilization would be forbidden to attempt to save their children left frozen in suspended animation because this could only be achieved through impregnation by third parties. Tonti-Filippini, in fact, believes homologous as well as heterologous embryo transfer violates marital chastity:

> In my view there would be a problem with asserting that she [the wife who together with her husband's seed had artificially procreated embryos] must receive those embryos. Such a course would have the clinician impregnating her and, though it would be with the couple's own embryos, it would still be from outside the marriage in the sense that pregnancy would not result from the conjugal act, but from a medical procedure. The clinician is impregnator and the new union would come from that act which is external to the conjugal union . . . . Some think that the woman has an obligation to receive the embryos, but that addresses the wrong question. The question is whether anyone, other than her husband, through the expression of their loving union in the conjugal act, may impregnate a woman.[164]

Father Tadeusz Pacholczyk argues that a couple who attempt to rescue their own frozen embryos commits a "second evil"—"namely, the act of becoming a surrogate mother to the couple's own embryos generated earlier at the clinic. Overall it appears that there is a discernable double violation of the meaning of motherhood whenever one engages in IVF."[165]

However seeing homologous embryo transfer as a second evil, disturbs the "moral intuition" of many people of good will and it seems unnecessary. Certainly, genetic parents are not obligated to attempt the embryo transfer of their cryo-preserved children, as Tonti-Filippini says, since this procedure poses serious risks and burdens. However, what of those praiseworthy accomplishments by physicians who have succeeded in transferring living embryos trapped in non-viable ectopic tubal pregnancy into the wombs of their mothers? Are these physicians to be condemned because they impregnated a woman with her living child?[166] Were these operations immoral just because the new uterine pregnancy was achieved by third parties in an act other than one of conjugal love between husband and wife?

The principle presented in *Donum Vitae* that every child must be conceived in an act of conjugal love is clearly meant to preclude IVF and artificial insemination. Likewise its prohibition against rupturing the genetic, gestational and rearing dimensions of parenthood establishes an absolute prohibition against heterologous embryo transfer. But homologous embryo transfer re-unites these three dimensions of parenthood which is an essential good for the child, the parents and society, not a second evil.

There are three distinct objective evils associated with the reproductive technologies under discussion: separating the conception of a child from the conjugal act of spouses; impregnating a woman with a child to whom she is a genetic stranger; and making a pledge to surrender a child before it is conceived, or as a condition for pregnancy. The following norms light a way out of the dark path tread by cryopreservation of human embryos while respecting the dignity of the embryo, spouses and the marital act:

1) IVF is an objective evil because it separates the unitive and procreative dimensions of marital love so that the conception of a human embryo is not the fruit of an act of conjugal love between spouses;[167]

2) Embryo transfer is an objective evil if it divides the genetic and gestational dimensions of parenthood so that the woman comes to the embryo as a genetic stranger, i.e., a surrogate mother;[168]

3) Artificial Insemination is an objective evil and is also identified as surrogate motherhood if it is accompanied by a pledge to surrender the child upon birth.[169]

The *Charter for Health Care Workers* interpreting *Donum Vitae* defines surrogate motherhood in terms of the second and third objective evils: 1) implanting an embryo into a woman who is a genetic stranger to the child whether or not there is a pledge to surrender the child upon birth; *or* 2) artificially inseminating her with a pledge she surrender her genetically related child upon birth. In either case the embryo is treated as a non-relational being and maternity is seen as a transferable function—mere gestation—rather than as a state of being perfecting spouses and their genetically related child:

> To implant in a woman's womb an embryo which is genetically foreign to her *or* just to fertilize her with the condition that she hand over the newly born child to a client means separating gestation from maternity, reducing it to an incubation which does not respect the dignity and right of the child to be "conceived, borne in the womb, brought to birth and educated by its own parents."[170]

Significantly, *Donum Vitae* discusses surrogate mothers in the section on heterologous artificial procreation, but not when the instruction considers homologous artificial procreation. The introduction of an embryo into its genetic mother's womb does not violate the dignity of her child by dividing genetic and gestational parenthood as in the case of heterologous embryo transfer. On the contrary, by re-uniting the genetic, gestational and rearing dimensions of parenthood, it protects the fundamental human rights of a child.

The instruction decries the "absurd fate" of "spare" embryos—those "not transferred into the body of the mother," but frozen in limbo "with no possibility of their being offered a safe means of survival which can be licitly pursued."[171] The only safe place for the gestation of a human embryo is beneath his or her mother's heart. But she has abandoned her children conceived *in-vitro*, "depriving them, at least temporarily, of maternal shelter and gestation."[172] Hence, these human embryos are indeed left to an absurd fate; abandoned by the one person who might provide them "safe means of survival which can be licitly pursued," they can only be rescued by surrogate mothers who would further violate the embryo's dignity, dividing its genetic and gestational parentage while at the same time violating the unitive good of marriage.

On the other hand, when third parties impregnate a woman through homologous embryo transfer with a couple's own child in order to save their child's life, the unity of their marriage suffers no offense. It does not destroy the pledge given by spouses to become biological parents only through a pregnancy that bears a child who in his or her flesh unites them as procreators. Although they are not the instrumental cause of her pregnancy, the spouses remain the efficient material cause of the conception and birth of their child. At times the instrumental cause of birth or pregnancy may be transferred to third parties without offense to the dignity of marriage as in the cases of caesarean birth, or the impregnation of a woman with her embryo transferred from the site of an ectopic tubal pregnancy.[173]

Allowing the genetic mother to re-unite the genetic, gestational and rearing dimensions of parenthood by homologous embryo transfer makes sense. On the other hand allowing a surrogate mother to save embryos about to be aborted and by analogy frozen embryos about to be destroyed does not make sense and invites scorn. DeMarco ridicules those who would justify heterologous embryo transfer to save a child from a direct abortion through a hypothetical reproductive protocol he dubbed THEFT:

> For the sake of illustration this penchant for attempting to validate a procedure by affirming its good points while ignoring its shortcomings, consider THEFT (The Hijacking of the Embryo from the Fallopian Tube). This technique would be permitted only under certain highly restricted conditions: (1) the embryo is removed only from women who have decided to have an abortion (it is then transferred to the fallopian tube of the infertile wife); (2) only a childless, infertile couple can benefit from THEFT; (3) the procedure does not subject either the embryo or the women to any dangers; (4) the infertile couple cannot have a child in any other way.[174]

It would appear Rome has finally clarified this issue. To say the least, *Dignitas Personae* did not encourage embryo adoption or rescue. It warns women who become pregnant via heterologous embryo transfer that they are acting in ways analogous to those who combine the gametes of persons not married to each other in heterologous IVF. Moreover, despite their "praiseworthy" motive, women who transfer embryos into their womb to whom they are genetic strangers, engage in a form of surrogate motherhood:

> The proposal that these embryos could be put at the disposal of infertile couples as a treatment for infertility is not ethically acceptable for the same reasons which make artificial heterologous procreation illicit as well as any form of surrogate motherhood; this practice would also lead to other problems of a medical, psychological and legal nature.
>
> It has also been proposed, solely in order to allow human beings to be born who are otherwise condemned to destruction, that there could be a form of "prenatal adoption." This proposal, praiseworthy with regard to the intention of

respecting and defending human life, presents however various problems not dissimilar to those mentioned above [heterologous procreation and surrogate motherhood].[175]

In conclusion, a genetic stranger may not attempt heterologous embryo transfer even to save an embryo's life because this would further violate the embryo's dignity, intentionally dividing its genetic and gestational parentage and it would dishonor the unity of her marriage: her pledge to conceive children only in a conjugal act with her husband and to become pregnant only with a child who, in its flesh, unites them as procreators. On the other hand, it seems to this author that repentant spouses may attempt to rescue their embryos conceived *in-vitro* through embryo transfer. In attempting homologous embryo transfer spouses seek to save the life of the child they put in jeopardy while, at the same time, safeguarding their child's dignity by reuniting the genetic, gestational and rearing dimensions of its parentage. Embryo transfer that works no separation of genetic and gestational parenthood does no further dishonor to the embryo or the spouses than has already occurred through *in-vitro* fertilization. The child who enters the womb through homologous embryo transfer commits no trespass, a child who in its flesh unites its parents as fallen, but repentant, procreators.

And what is to become of the thousands of children conceived *in-vitro* and left frozen in suspended animation? They have an absurd fate: having been abandoned by their genetic mother they cannot be rescued by any other woman unless she commits an intrinsically evil act and becomes an illicit surrogate mother as *Donum Vitae* intimated:

> In consequence of the fact that they have been produced in-vitro, *those embryos which are not transferred into the body of the mother and are called "spare" are exposed to an absurd fate, with no possibility of their being offered safe means of survival which can be licitly pursued.*[176]

Like their brothers and sisters murdered in direct surgical abortions, the frozen embryos allowed to die will live in Christ baptized in their blood as martyrs for Christ and the Christian virtue of respect for human life.[177] If, contrary to the condemnation given in *Donum Vitae*,[178] an artificial womb were developed for eugenic purposes it would seem licit to use it for therapeutic purposes attempting to save the lives of abandoned frozen embryos as well as embryos trapped in non-viable ectopic pregnancies.

However the answer to the biotech-terrorists who stir the seeds of human life in a Petri dish for money, and then hold countless the smallest of cryo-preserved children captive for ransom, is not to play into their hands and legitimize their kidnapped conceptions by heterologous embryo transfer: "Furthermore, in the absence of a willingness and an agreement to cease the practice of the production and freezing of embryos, the systematic recourse to adoptive pregnancy can have the effect of legitimizing and motivating that practice."[179] Therefore the Church in *Dignitas Personae* appealed to the world's scientific community to halt the production of human embryos who are abandoned to an absurd fate without a moral licit solution:

> All things considered, it needs to be recognized that the thousands of abandoned embryos represent a situation of injustice which in fact cannot be resolved. Therefore John Paul II made an "appeal to the consciences of the world's scientific authorities and in particular to doctors, that the production of human embryos be halted, taking into account that there seems to be no morally licit solution regarding the human destiny of the thousands and thousands of 'frozen' embryos which are and remain the subjects of essential rights and should therefore be protected by law as human persons."[180]

Human embryos are human beings and worthy of the dignity and respect enjoyed by adult members of the species from the first moment of their existence. This includes the right to be free from injury and not to have their lives placed in jeopardy through IVF and cryopreservation where, "because of the concentration of glycerine in the cryo-conserving agent . . . the embryo shrivel 'like a raisin.'"[181] Cryopreservation serves the needs of adults who commodify nescient human life and "is incompatible with the respect owed to human embryos."[182]

The human drama of the genetic parents who procreate through IVF and then divorce or separate leaving their embryos up for grabs in a legal free-for-all is a matter of public record in *Davis v. Davis* and *Evans v. United Kingdom*.[183] Both cases would have had a moral resolution in keeping with what this author believes to be the teaching of the Catholic Church if, until such time as a total ban on IVF and the cryopreservation of human embryos is possible, heterologous embryo transfer was proscribed but homologous embryo transfer was permitted and encouraged at law.

In *Davis v. Davis* the Supreme Court of Tennessee heard the appeal of a couple who while they were married sought the help of an IVF clinic to procreate seven frozen embryos with their own gametes but shortly afterwards divorced and then disagreed on the disposition of their frozen embryos. Prior to the IVF treatment Mrs. Davis had both her fallopian tubes ligated for contraceptive purposes, so as to prevent a sixth tubal pregnancy (she had already had five tubal pregnancies). In addition, Mr. and Mrs. Davis failed to sign a contract between specifying what should be done with their frozen embryos should either of them die or should they divorce. There was no legislative provision for the disposition of frozen human embryos in case they were abandoned or their procreators disagreed over whether to implant them. This was a case of first impression for the court and it undertook an extensive review of policy considerations regarding who should prevail—the genetic parent who wishes to implant frozen embryos in a woman's uterus or the parent who objects to implantation.

The trial court heard remarkable scientific testimony from Dr. Jerome Lejeune, the French geneticist who discovered the Trisomy-21, an extra chromosome in the twenty-first pair responsible for Down Syndrome.[184] No ordinary expert witness, Dr. Lejeune was the first president of the Pontifical Academy of Life for the Holy See until his death. His cause for beatification was opened in

2007.[185] Dr. Lejeune testified that the eight human embryos at issue "were early human beings" and "tiny persons" and that their mother "wants to rescue babies from the concentration can" and that Mr. Davis also has a duty to try to bring them to term.[186]

The trial court who actually heard the testimony of this world class saintly genius, who stood alone against a bevy of run-of-the-mill experts, knew that one must weigh, not count, experts. The trial judge concluded that the best scientific opinion proved that the importance the bevy of run-of-the-mill experts made between pre-embryos and embryos was a distinction without a difference. Therefore, Dr. Lejeune was "correct when he said 'human life begins at the moment of conception.' From this proposition, the trial judge concluded that the eight-cell entitles at issue were not preembryos but were 'children in vitro.' He then invoked the doctrine of parens patriae and held that it was 'in the best interest of the children' to be born rather than destroyed. Finding that Mary Sue Davis was willing to provide such an opportunity, but that Junior Davis was not, the trial judge awarded her 'custody' of the 'children in vitro.'"[187]

By the time this case came up for hearing before the Supreme Court of Tennessee Mrs. Davis had abandoned the argument that human life begins at conception. But because of the hew and cry of the bevy of run-of-the-mill experts, which had grown to include amici curiae briefs from twenty national organizations, frantic to prove the distinction between pre-embryos and embryos was based on science, not special interests, the Supreme Court of Tennessee found meritorious their request and sided with them "because of its far-reaching implications in other cases of this kind."[188]

> Left undisturbed, the trial court's ruling would have afforded preembryos the legal status of "persons" and vested them with legally cognizable interests separate from those of their progenitors. Such a decision would doubtless have had the effect of outlawing IVF programs in the state of Tennessee.[189]

The decision of the Supreme Court of Tennessee is unremarkable in its following the party line, so to speak, laid out in *Roe v. Wade*. Roe was premised on the presupposition that science could not say when human life begins. Therefore, the court first had to demolish the credibility of Dr. Lejeune who had the courage to say science knows without a doubt—members of the human species come into being at conception. They characterized his opinion as befuddled by religion—"His testimony revealed a profound confusion between science and religion." Moreover, he should not have been qualified as an expert because "[a]lthough he is an internationally recognized geneticist, Dr. Lejeune's background fails to reflect any degree of expertise in obstetrics or gynecology (specifically in the field of infertility) or in medical ethics." In short, because Dr. Lejeune took his Catholic faith seriously, had never worked at an IVF clinic and didn't have a certificate in bioethics he was a "quack" for purposes of offering testimony as to when science says human life begins.

The Court then turned to what the law had to say about when human life begins and concluded that preembryos were not human beings in the full sense any more than human fetuses were. Both can be destroyed at will by those who have possession of them under *Roe v. Wade* since they are not recognized as human "persons"[190]—by their mother in the case of fetuses and by their genetic parents or IVF clinic in the case of human embryos.

On the other hand, human embryos should not be considered simply property because that would lead to the wrong result. If frozen embryos were merely property as the Appellate Court ruled then Mr. and Mrs. Davis would "share an interest in the seven fertilized ova" under a "bailment relationship." Hence the Appellate Court awarded Mr. and Mrs. Davis "joint custody" of their frozen fertilized ova[191] with "equal voice over their disposition."[192] An implication of this theory is that one bailor of joint bailed goods, cannot unilaterally destroy those goods. A court could order the jointly bailed goods divided between the two bailors if they could not decide on what to do between themselves. This would have left Mrs. Davis free to implant at least three of her embryos into her womb and Mr. Davis would be left with the remaining embryos to destroy, a result the court characterized as "the worst of both worlds" since not all the embryos would be saved, upsetting Mrs. Davis, and Mr. Davis might still become a father, which would upset him.[193]

The Tennessee Supreme Court took what it referred to as middle ground approach between recognizing human embryos as persons or property. As it turned out the status of the human embryo, being neither person nor property, was the worst of all worlds for them. As persons all of them would be saved. As property at least half of them would have been saved by their mother. Instead, as person-property hybrids, each embryo "deserves respect greater than that accorded to human tissue but not the respect accorded to actual persons." The court then created a legislative scheme for the disposition of frozen embryos that decided the matter according to the following criteria: 1) the agreed preferences of the progenitors, 2) any prior agreement between them, finally 3) weighing the relative interests in using or not using their embryos so that (a) the party wishing to implant the embryos should be given preference, unless (b) the party wishing to implant the embryos "intends merely to donate them to another couple, [then] the objecting party obviously has the greater interest and should prevail."[194]

The fate of the human embryos hinged on the fact that Mrs. Davis had remarried and changed her mind since the trial court decision and no longer wanted to implant her frozen embryos into her own womb but, rather, intended to donate them to another childless couple if she was awarded custody of them.[195] Hence Mr. Davis had the right to destroy all of their frozen embryos.

The European Court of Human Rights considered a similar case in *Evans v. United Kingdom* and came to a similar conclusion as the *Davis* court. In 2000 Ms. Evans and her unmarried partner, both of them knowing she had ovarian cancer, had a number of her eggs removed prior to the surgical removal of both her ovaries. She and her male partner both signed an IVF agreement in accord with the UK Human Fertilization and Embryology Act of 1990 that prior to implantation either of them could withdraw their consent for any reason and the embryos created from their gametes would be destroyed. Six embryos were created. In 2002 Ms. Evans and her male partner broke up and he withdrew his consent for further use of the frozen embryos. The IVF clinic under an obligation to destroy those six frozen embryos was enjoined from doing so when Ms. Evans sought an injunction in the High Court in the United Kingdom requiring her male partner to restore his consent. Her claim was dismissed; and that decision upheld on appeal. She eventually appealed to the European Court of Human Rights that the provisions of the 1990 Act, to the extent it permitted her former male partner to withdraw his consent after her eggs had been fertilized with his sperm, violated the European Convention for the Protection of Human Rights and Fundamental Freedoms, art 8. The European Court of Human Rights held the UK's 1990 Act did not violate the European Convention because both parties had, with informed consent, signed an agreement that allowed either party to withdraw consent for any reason prior to implantation. The European Court of Human Rights held that this "bright line" test (rather than a case by case test reviewing of the relative interests of the parties) fell within the "margin of appreciation" or discretion afforded member states under the European Convention.[196]

In reaching its decision the European Court of Human Rights reviewed the legal position of frozen embryos in member states of the Council of Europe, the United States, the State of Israel, and relevant international texts. It concluded there is no "international consensus" regarding the regulation of IVF treatment or to the use of embryos by such treatment but there were three basic approaches, namely, no withdrawal of consent to use frozen embryos after fertilization, or no withdrawal after implantation or withdrawal of consent on a case by case basis *as per* contract or as the court so determines after weighing of the relative interests of the parties:

> [W]hile certain states have adopted specific legislation in this area, others have either not legislated, or have only partially legislated, relying instead on general principles and professional ethical guidelines. Again, there is no consensus as to the point at which consent to the use of genetic material provided as part of IVF treatment may be withdrawn by one of the parties; [1] in certain states, it appears that consent may be withdrawn only up to the point of fertilization, [2] whereas in other states such withdrawal may occur at any time prior to the implantation of the embryo in the woman; in still other states [3] the point at which consent may be withdrawn is left to the courts to determine on the basis of contract or according to the balanced of interests of the two parties.[197]

Ms. Evans complained that women who conceive *in vivo* are not subject to abortion at the whim of their male partner so why should women who conceive *in vitro* be subject to their partner's veto in going forward to implantation. The UK Government argued there was no discrimination under the 1990 Act because "the transfer to the woman of the embryo created in vitro was the equivalent of the fertilization of the egg inside a woman following sexual intercourse."[198]

The European Court of Human Rights did not address the heavy cost and grave risk to their health and future fertility egg extraction exacts on women versus the relative ease, lack of health risks and immoral enjoyment masturbation affords men in order to produce their gametes for the IVF process: "The court is not persuaded by the applicant's argument that the situation of the male and female parties to IVF treatment cannot be equated and that a fair balance could in general be preserved only by holding the male donor to his consent."[199] The Court admitted, however, the balance of interest could have reasonably been assessed differently and that "making the consent of the male donor irrevocable or by drawing the 'bright line' at the point of creation of the embryo" might "arguably have struck a fairer balance." The UK is not alone in drawing the bright line at implantation and therefore its discretion must be respected under the European Convention.[200]

The Dissenting Opinion of two justices of the European Court of Human Rights stated the Majority gave too much weight to public policy considerations and the discretion of the states' members of the European Union to the detriment of the individual rights in conflict in this admittedly hard case:

> Denying the implantation of the embryos amounts in this case not to a mere restriction, but to a total destruction of her right to have her own child. In such a case the Convention case law is clear and does not allow a state to impair the very essence of such an important right, either through an interference or by non-compliance with its positive obligations. We do not think that a legislative scheme which negates the very core of the applicant's right is acceptable under the Convention.[201]

The Dissent boldly denied that fundamental human rights should be made to depend on consensus—"We believe that the duty to protect everyone's right to respect for private life [analogous to a right to privacy under US Constitutional law] should not be made to depend on any European consensus, however sensitive the matter may be." It is the duty of the European Court of Human Rights to determine "what" the substance of human rights are and then to strike a balance, and not merely outline the procedural "way" one reconciles contradictory human rights in different state members of the European Union:

> So, the United Kingdom chose to strike a balance by allowing for the possibility to withdraw consent up to the point of implantation of the embryo. Other countries, such as Austria and Italy, have decided that the revocation of consent can be effective only up to the point of fertilization. This is within their margin of appreciation, but the duty to strike a fair balance between individual rights in conflict remains nevertheless the same invariable and imperative requirement under the Convention for all member states.[202]

Distinguishing the facts in *Evans* from those in some American cases, i.e., *Davis*, the Dissent pointed out that Ms. Evan's male partner had no fear she would donate their embryos to another third party for implantation: "The involvement of a surrogate has been one of the reasons why the American courts have declined to enforce contracts on public policy grounds; but we have to underline, such issues of public policy do not apply here." They conclude their dissenting opinion by proposing a legislative scheme very similar to the one imposed in *Davis v. Davis* that upholds the right of the genetic mother to go back and implant her frozen embryos in her womb but denies her the right to assign her right to implantation to a genetic stranger:

> In conclusion, if we apply these principles to the case in hand, the correct approach in our view would be as follows: the interests of the party who withdraws consent and wants to have the embryos destroyed should prevail (if domestic law so provides), unless the other party (a) has no other means to have a genetically-related child; and (b) has no children at all; and (c) does not intend to have recourse to a surrogate mother in the process of implantation. We think this approach would strike a fair balance between public and private interests, as well as between conflicting individual rights themselves. This test is neutral, because it can equally apply to female and male parties.[203]

The conclusion reached by the Dissent in *Evans v. United Kingdom*, in the opinion of this author, seems to conform to the principles laid out in *Donum Vitae* and *Dignitas Personae* and to the criteria laid out in *Evangelium Vitae* concerning material cooperation in evil under circumstances when a complete ban on an immoral practice is infeasible but a partial restriction would tend to mitigate the extent of the harm.[204]

A better law would provide that the male procreator through IVF treatment cannot withdraw his consent after fertilization of an embryo has occurred so as to prevent the female procreator from going forward and implanting their embryonic child into her womb and prohibit her from assigning her right of implantation to a surrogate mother. As discussed previously in this chapter, a genetic mother who implants in her womb her own frozen embryos reunites gestational and genetic parenthood. However, in heterologous embryo transfer the woman who implants an embryo not her own, violates its dignity by separating genetic from gestational parenthood in an act of surrogate motherhood, something forbidden under the principles laid out in *Donum Vitae*[205] as further specified in *Dignitas Personae*.[206]

In March of 2006 in private conversation with a Minister of the European Parliament in Strasbourg, France this author suggested that permitting Ms. Evans to implant her frozen embryos while at the same time denying any other woman a right to implant Ms. Evans' frozen embryos would seem to be a moral solution to the dilemma posed in *Evans v. United Kingdom*.[207] Such a resolution and precedent would save the lives of at least some embryos. It would calm the fears of a genetic father. He could not be heard to complain that he did not get what he bargained for, i.e., a child from the woman he agreed to conceive his child. It would grant to a genetic mother the right to reunite in her womb the dimensions of parenthood sundered by IVF with no further affront to the dignity of the child. Even in the case of the divorce of the genetic parents after an IVF conception (*Davis v. Davis*) or an IVF embryo conceived out of wedlock (*Evans v. United Kingdom*) the mother who reunites gestational and genetic parenthood in her own womb is not committing the objective evil of heterologous embryo transfer or surrogate motherhood. She is no differently situated than a woman who carries to term a child conceived prior to a divorce or a woman who is pregnant without benefit of marriage. In both of these cases the Church encourages such women to not resort to abortion but to give birth to their child. Finally a law which would prevent a genetic mother from saving her own child by giving it maternal shelter in her womb should be considered a form of torture, cruel and unusual punishment. She alone can offer to her child a way out that may be licitly pursued.[208] Civil law should not frustrate what the moral law seems to require.

Human Cloning

When *Donum Vitae* was released in 1987, the cloning of human beings did not seem immediately feasible and one italicized sentence sufficed to treat the subject:

> Also, attempts or hypotheses for obtaining a human being without any connection with sexuality through "twin fission," cloning or parthenogenesis are to be considered contrary to the moral law, since they are in opposition to the dignity both of human procreation and of the conjugal union.[209]

However, within a decade the political pressure to clone human beings was looming just over the horizon as within the technological prowess of embryo science. National and international protocols were debated and decisions made concerning reproductive and so called therapeutic cloning. The Holy See advised the international community at the United Nations that all attempts at human cloning remained morally flawed and must never be pursued no matter the noble goals researchers were tempted to pursue by means of destructive embryo research. Classifying human cloning as reproductive or therapeutic is a distinction without a moral difference, they warned, and unless all forms of human cloning are banned reproductive cloning will remain a distinct possibility:

> The difference between "reproductive" cloning and "research" cloning (so called "therapeutic" cloning) consists only in the objective of the procedure: in "reproductive" cloning one intends to develop a child by implanting the cloned embryo in a womb. In "research" cloning, one intends to use the cloned embryo in such a way that it is ultimately destroyed. To ban "reproductive" cloning only, without prohibiting "research" cloning, would be to allow the production of individual human lives with the intention of destroying these lives as part of the process of using them for scientific research. The early human embryo, not yet implanted into a womb, is nonetheless a human individual. . . . Destroying this embryo is therefore a grave moral disorder.[210]

[A]ny possible attempt to limit a ban on human cloning to that undertaken for reproductive purposes would be nearly impossible to enforce since human embryos cloned for research purposes would be widely available and would have the potential to be brought to birth simply be transfer to a womb using procedures employed for artificial assisted reproduction. Since human reproductive cloning is universally condemned, only a complete ban on all forms of human embryonic cloning would achieve the goal of prohibiting human reproductive cloning.[211]

On March 8, 2005 by a vote of 84 in favor, 34 against and 37 abstaining, the UN General Assembly adopted the *Declaration on Human Cloning*[212] which prohibits "all forms of human cloning [reproductive and therapeutic] *inasmuch* as they are incompatible with human dignity and the protection of human life" (emphasis added).[213] Pro-cloning advocates immediately tried to spin the UN's ban on all forms of cloning as merely a ban on reproductive cloning but not therapeutic cloning. They argued the word "inasmuch" meant "to the degree that" it violates human dignity and, since for pro-cloners therapeutic cloning does not violate human dignity (because the cloned is destroyed rather than being allowed to live a life not worth living), it does not violate human dignity and is not banned by the UN Declaration. This contorted reasoning is simply "baloney," said Wesley Smith.[214] The normal usage of "inasmuch" is "seeing that" which interpretation is what set the delegations opposed to the ban in motion to denounce it. China, the United Kingdon and Belgium said they will not honor the Declaration and will continue to support therapeutic cloning: "'The United Kingdom is a strong supporter of therapeutic cloning research because it has the potential to revolutionize medicine in this century in the way that antibiotics did in the last,' said Emyr Jones Parry, Britain's U.N. ambassador."[215]

On the other hand the United States ambassador under the Bush administration voted for the ban precisely because human cloning takes "advantage of some, vulnerable lives for the benefit of others."[216] It is not insignificant that the debate over human cloning at the United Nations pitted the interests of the Developed World against the Least Developed Nations, the "haves" versus the "have nots" with respect to cloning intellectual property, the exploiters versus those likely to be exploited,[217] as the Holy See warned:

> [T]he massive demand for human oocytes would disproportionately affect the poor and marginalized of the world bringing a new type of injustice and discrimination into existence.
>
> Human cloning would encourage the development of a trade in cloned human embryos and their derivatives for scientific research or for industrial research and development purposes. Therefore, there should be enacted an explicit prohibition of such exchanges regardless of whether they are commercial or not. No intellectual property rights should be granted to information or technologies specific to human cloning.[218]

Having briefly considered the political consensus of the international community to completely ban all forms of human cloning let us now consider the scientific and moral foundation behind such a ban from the perspective of the Catholic

Church. On June 25, 1997, the Pontifical Academy for Life issued *Reflections on Cloning*. This document provides many of the scientific facts and ethical problems connected with human cloning.

Reflection on Cloning begins by pointing out that it is perfectly licit to produce identical twins in animals (called "varieties") by way of "twin splitting," also called "embryo splitting." This has been going on in "experimental barns" since the 1930s:

> The idea of cloning entire organisms can be traced back to a 1938 book by Hans Spemann, an embryologist. In 1952 Thomas King and Robert Briggs were the first to clone frog embryos. In 1962 entire adult frogs were first cloned.[219]

Twin splitting begins with the fertilization of embryos in a Petri dish. After technicians fertilize an oocyte/ovum/egg cell with sperm, the resulting zygote divides in two. Then the normal process of cell division is halted and the coating around the zygote, the zona pellucida, is removed and the two cells are separated. Scientists then re-coat the two zygotes with an artificial zona pellucida which enables cell division to continue as both halves of the original zygote develop into two identical twins. This procedure was first applied to human zygotes in 1993 by Jerry Hall and Robert Stillman of George Washington University who, without prior approval of the proper Ethics Committee, altered the process, allowing two sperm to fuse with the ova they selected, so that the zygote would die within a week.[220]

Reflections on Cloning recalls that the cloning of Dolly the sheep in 1997 by scientists Jan Vilmut and K.H.S. Campell of the Roslin Institute in Edinburgh, Scotland, occurred through a procedure called somatic cell nuclear transfer (SCNT). First the nucleus of a cell from a non-human body (somatic cell) is extracted. The nucleus of any body cell has the complete DNA structure of the whole organism contained within it. Then that somatic cell nucleus is fused with a de-nucleated oocyte, one which has had its nucleus removed. This fused entity is then electrically stimulated so cell division can proceed. Fertilization, properly so-called [between two gametes, male and female], is replaced by the "fusion" of a nucleus taken from a somatic cell of the individual one wishes to clone, or of the somatic cell itself, with an oocyte from which the nucleus has been removed, that is, an oocyte lacking the maternal genome. Since the nucleus of the somatic cell contains the whole genetic inheritance, the individual obtained possesses, except for possible alterations, the genetic identity of the nucleus' donor. It is this essential genetic correspondence with the donor that produces in the new individual the somatic replica or copy of the donor itself.[221]

In the case of Dolly, out of 277 cell fusions only 29 began to grow after electrical stimulation *in-vitro*. Of the 29 zygotes transferred into receptive ewes only 13 ewes became pregnant and only one lamb was born.[222] Before it was thought impossible to return the differentiated somatic cells of the higher forms of animal life (those that already developed into specialized body cells, i.e., brain, muscle, blood cells, etc.) to their original totipotentiality and, consequently, to develop into a new individual. The advent of Dolly opened the door to the cloning of human beings.[223]

Reflections on Cloning warns that the popular image of human clones as identical with their donor and science as "omnipotent" conflicts with the true spiritual origin of human individuality and the personal effort and virtue, as well as the cultural and nurturing environment that shape each distinct human personality. No human clone will ever be identical to his or her donor, no more than identical twins are truly identical given the profound personal and relational differences:

> [T]his duplication of body structure does not necessarily imply a perfectly identical person, understood in his ontological and psychological reality. The spiritual soul, which is the essential constituent of every subject belonging to the human species and is created directly by God, cannot be generated by the parents, produced by artificial fertilization or cloned. Furthermore, psychological development, culture and environment always lead to different personalities; this is a well-known fact even among twins, whose resemblance does not mean identity. The popular image or aura of omnipotence that accompanies cloning should at least be put into perspective.[224]

But the popular fantasy of replicating identical human beings may be expected to feed the "desire for omnipotence" and may lead to cloning for sentimental or eugenic reasons: such as cloning a dying loved one, or cloning a child for an infertile couple, or cloning exceptionally talented, beautiful or disease resistant individuals, or cloning a fetus for spare body parts. There is nothing genuinely compassionate in the despotic "eugenics project" that will enlist human cloning as its most potent weapon. The project for the production of perfect and fungible persons will attempt to replace the family with the "logic of industrial production":

> In the cloning process the basic relationships of the human person are perverted: filiation, consanguinity, kinship, parenthood. A woman can be the twin sister of her mother, lack a biological father and be the daughter of her grandfather. In-vitro fertilization has already led to the confusion of parentage, but cloning will mean the radical rupture of these bonds.[225]

Human reproductive cloning will produce tremendous and negative cultural fallout and exacerbate the "growing conviction that the value of man and woman does not depend on their personal identity but only on those biological qualities that can be appraised and therefore selected." Furthermore, the "clone's radical suffering" must be kept in mind: his inability to think of himself as unique, and his understanding of himself as nothing more than a copy of another being. Being a copy jeopardizes a clone's psychic identity and makes him the object of "fateful expectations and attention, which will constitute a true and proper attack on his personal subjectivity."[226]

Reflection on Cloning points out that human reproductive cloning violates two fundamental principles underlying all human rights, namely, "the principle of equality among human beings and the principle of non-discrimination." These principles are overturned by the discrimination inherent in the "logic of cloning," and its "selective-eugenic dimension." The European Parliament on March 12, 1997 stated these two principles are violated by human cloning and asked for a ban outlawing this practice. The Church explicitly condemned the possibility of human cloning in *Donum Vitae*.[227]

Harmony must be re-established between the "demands of scientific research and indispensable human values." The moral rejection of human cloning must not be viewed as a humiliation of science, for the dignity of the natural sciences lies in its ability to provide for "humanity's welfare." Besides, there is a place for cloning research in the vegetable and animal kingdoms, "provided that the rules for protecting the animal itself and the obligations to respect the biodiversity of species are observed."[228]

In a document published by the Pontifical Council for the Family, *Cloning: the Disappearance of Direct Parenthood and Denial of the Family* (2003), the radical suffering of a cloned human being was shown in clear relief. Commenting on what philosopher Hans Jonas has referred to as a "right of ignorance" they ask what life would be like if one were a clone and were always haunted by the blueprint of the original's life. Who wouldn't fear the approach of an inevitable doom, "if the one who cloned me died at such an age of such a malady, will I also die at that age?" Wouldn't this quasi-precognitive knowledge trap a human clone into either fleeing or surrendering to their fate?

> As Jonas says, this "ignorance" is in a certain sense a "condition for the possibility" of human freedom, and to encroach upon it would mean placing an enormous burden on the individual's autonomy. . . . [T]he clone would foresee his every move, his own illnesses, and correct his future psychological attitudes in an unremitting, hopeless effort to separate himself from his "original," who would always be an omnipresent shadow and model, and the track he would be forced to follow or to avoid. . . . Thus, a wound would be inflicted on the human right to live one's life as an original and unique discovery, basically, a discovery of themselves. As a result, the clone's way through life would become the burdensome implementation of an inhuman and alienating "programme of control."[229]

The human cloning project, ushered in by a value free science, the Pontifical Counsel for the Family warned, is driven by a "profound malaise of our civilization" that looks to technology instead of God for the meaning of human life. The "death of God" has led to the denial of any moral limits on human freedom. The death of God, which at first seemed to exalt human freedom, ends up lifting all restraint on the strong, who find new ways to oppress the weak. Such "supermen," they fear, will then create "new forms of slavery, discrimination and profound suffering." We have a moral duty to halt the human cloning project that must be translated into cultural and legal terms. Human cloning undermines a democratic society based on "respecting human dignity at every phase of life, regardless of the intellectual or physical abilities one possesses or lacks."[230]

Dignitas Personae warns that a cloned human being "with a predetermined genetic identity" would be trapped into a kind of "biological slavery."[231] The "originality" of each person is based on their relational nature, "a consequence of the particular relationship that exists between God and the human being from the first moment of his existence and carries with it the obligation to respect the singularity and integrity of each person, even on the biological and genetic levels."[232]

Even if eugenic science stops short and destroys clones before their birth (reproductive cloning) such scientific manipulation (therapeutic cloning) involves the cruel and immoral experimentation and destruction of human beings: "such experimentation is immoral because it involves the arbitrary use of the human body (by now decidedly regarded as a machine composed of parts) as a mere research tool. The human body is an integral part of every individual's dignity and personal identity. . . ." Moreover, women will be radically exploited and used simply for their biological functions—a source of ova for cloning experiments and a womb, until an artificial womb is designed.[233]

Dignitas Personae makes clear that reproductive cloning is more objectionable ethically than reproductive cloning because it creates human embryos with the explicit intention of destroying them—"a means to be used and destroyed"—and it is always *"gravely immoral to sacrifice a human life for therapeutic ends."*[234] Therapeutic cloning is promoted in order to produce embryonic stem cells so as to overcome immune system rejection in tissue and organ transplantation and regenerative therapies and is linked, therefore, to the issue of stem cells.[235]

Stem Cell Research

The United States' vote to adopt the UN's *Declaration on Human Cloning* in March of 2005 was consistent with President Bush's Executive Order prohibiting the use of federal funds for embryo destructive research by limiting funding to the 60 embryonic stem cell (ESC) lines created before August 9, 2001.[236] President Bush in an Executive Order dated June 20, 2007 supplemented his order of August 9, 2001with language that stated the obvious findings of biology, namely, that human embryos are, after all, human: "[H]uman embryos and fetuses, as living members of the human species, are not raw material to be exploited or commodities to be bought and sold." However, on March 9, 2009 newly elected President Obama, touting ESC's hoped for curative properties, rescinded Bush's Executive Orders limiting funding to 60 ESC lines in existence prior to August 9, 2001. Obama's Executive Order did not limit federal funding to embryo destructive research on embryos destined to be discarded at infertility clinics but instead, gave the biotech industry leave to create new stem cell lines from the destruction of embryos procreated specifically for research or by means of cloning.[237]

What then is the basic science involved in stem cell research? A stem cell may be defined as a cell possessing ability for unlimited self-maintenance and a capacity to produce transitory progenitor cells that develop into highly differentiated cells:

> [A] commonly accepted *definition* of "stem cell" describes it as a cell with two characteristics: 1) the *property of an unlimited self-maintenance*—that is, the ability to reproduce itself over a long period of time without becoming differentiated; and 2) the *capability to produce non-permanent progenitor cells,* with limited capacity for proliferation, from which derive a *variety of lineages of highly differentiated cells* (neural cells, muscle cells, blood cells).[238]

> Stem cells are undifferentiated multipotent precursor cells that are capable both of perpetuating themselves as stem cells and of undergoing differentiation into one or more specialized types of cells (for example, kidney, muscle).[239]

Stem cells are found in various adult tissues and in the embryo blast, or inner cell mass, of human embryos. The difference between adult stem cells and embryo stem cells was believed to lie in the degree of their plasticity or ability to develop into various lineages of highly differentiated cells. Embryo stem cells remain "totipotent" for a few days after fertilization and are able to develop into a complete individual, as happens naturally in the case of homozygous germination, i.e., the development of identical twins. Embryo stem cells after implantation are "pluripotent," that is, capable of developing into any of the more than two hundred cells that make up the human body.

Adult stem cells were at first thought to be only "multipotent," that is, capable of generating the differentiated "cells and tissue of parts of the organism, but not of all or each of them, nor a complete individual. In the human being, in particular, multipotentiality concerns the capacity to generate cell lines and differentiated tissue derived from each one of the embryonic layers, that is, the ectoderm, mesoderm and endoderm."[240] However, more recently, adult stem cells found in bone marrow, brain cells, in the mesenchyme of various organs, and in umbilical cord blood have been proven capable of re-programming so that they regain a pluripotency and have been used to produce blood cells, muscle cells and neural cells.[241]

It must never be forgotten that embryonic stem cells can only be procured through the destruction and death of the human embryo from which they are gathered. The usual process involves five steps. First, human embryos are produced through in-vitro fertilization; or spare embryos are procured from IVF clinics. Second, these embryos are developed into blastocysts. Third, the inner cell mass or embryo blast (stem cells) is removed from the human embryo, which kills it. Fourth, these stem cells are cultured to form colonies. Fifth, these colonies are repeatedly subcultured to form cell lines "capable of multiplying indefinitely while preserving the characteristics of ES [embryo stem] cells for months and years."[242] Other processes under study for the production of human stem cells include transferring the nucleus of a human embryo into an oocyte of an animal, or fusing the embryonic stem cell cytoplast of a patient with one of his somatic cell karyoplast. Both of these proposed techniques would still require the destruction of a human embryo.[243]

One tragic experiment involved the injection of embryonic stem cells into the brains of several patients suffering from Alzheimer's Disease. The ES cells proved to be unstable, and instead of developing into neural tissue some of the patients developed uncontrollable violent spastic shaking. The researchers have no way of removing the stem cells they injected into these patients' brains.[244]

Due to the likelihood of the immunological rejection of foreign stem cells or tissues developed there from, many researchers believe that stem cells derived from a patient's cloned embryos would be more suitable. There is a direct link between human cloning for therapeutic reasons and stem cell research and marketable breakthroughs in regenerative medicine: "Producing cloned stem cell preparations for possible use in individual patients suffering from diseases like Parkinson's disease and Type I diabetes is one reason to pursue cloning-for-biomedical-research."[245] Moreover, "[t]he use of embryonic stem cells necessarily involves the technique of therapeutic cloning to prevent tissue rejections."[246]

Pharmacological businesses are greatly interested in the products and procedures they hope to market from human stem cell research. Their business concerns clash with widespread ethical concerns regarding the status of human embryos destroyed in developing new stem cell lines. On August 9, 2001, U.S. President George W. Bush banned federal funding for the development of new stem cell lines, but allowed federal funds for research conducted on the sixty existing stem cell lines. This meant that the research organizations that developed those stem cell lines would continue to profit from those patented bio-pharmacological products created through the destruction of human beings.

Joseph A. Fiorenza, president of the U.S. Catholic Conference of Bishops, condemned the Bush administration for the scandal caused by its cooperation in using and benefiting from the abortion of human embryos destroyed to create the sixty stem cell lines: "The federal government, for the first time in history, will support research that relies on the destruction of some defenseless human beings for the possible benefit to others. . . . [I]t allows our nation's research enterprise to cultivate a disrespect for human life."[247] The Pontifical Academy for Life also condemned the use of embryonic stem cells, and the differentiated cells obtained from them, which are supplied by other researchers or are commercially obtained because it "entails a proximate material cooperation in the production and manipulation of human embryos on the part of those producing or supplying them."

Unfortunately, tax payers' money spent on illicit embryo stem cell research is diverted from legitimate adult stem cell research, where real breakthroughs are occurring which confirm that adult stem cells can be reprogrammed to be as pluripotent as embryonic stem cells:

It is sufficient to mention, on the basis of the reported references, that in human beings the stem cells of bone marrow, from which the different lines of blood cells are formed, have as their maker the molecule CD34; and that, when purified, these cells are able to restore entirely the normal blood count in patients who receive ablative doses of radiation and chemotherapy, and this with a speed which is in proportion to the quantity of cells used. Furthermore, there are already indications on how to guide the development of neural stem cells (NSC's) through the use of various proteins—amongst them neuroregulin and bone morphogenetic protein 2 (BMP2)—which can direct NSC's to become neurons or glia (myelin-producing neural support cells) or even smooth muscle tissue.[248]

The Use of Human "Biological Material" of Illicit Origin and Vaccines

May one ever use a potentially beneficial therapeutic product derived from embryonic stem cells? The answer to this question involves moral reflection on problems involving cooperation in evil[249] as *Dignitas Personae* points out:

> For scientific research and for the production of vaccines or other products, cell lines are at times used which are the result of an illicit intervention against the life or physical integrity of a human being. The connection to the unjust act may be either mediate or immediate, since it is generally a question of cells which reproduce easily and abundantly. This "material" is sometimes made available commercially or distributed freely to research centers by government agencies having this function under law. All of this gives rise to various ethical problems with regard to cooperation in evil and with regard to scandal.[250]

The Instruction reminds us that scientific experiments that destroy human embryos remain, nonetheless, abortions and "always constitute a grave moral disorder."[251] It is a different matter when researchers use "biological material" obtained from the illicit activities of others, produced apart from their research center or obtained commercially. However, the "criterion of independence" as formulated by certain ethicists is insufficient insofar as it would permit researchers to use biological material of illicit origin so long as there is a clear separation between them and those who "produce, freeze and cause the death of embryos." To do otherwise would express an inner contradiction in the attitude of the person who says he is personally opposed to the evil deeds of others yet "accepts for his own work" their illicitly procured biological material. One must give the appearance of condoning such illicit acts especially when they are endorsed by laws which regulate health care and scientific research lest this contribute to an "appearance of acceptance" and actually contribute to indifference or approval of such actions in medical and political circles.[252]

Because there is a professional duty to avoid material cooperation in evil and the scandal associated with cooperating with unjust laws, they have duty and right of conscientious objection "to refuse to use such 'biological material' even when there is no close connection between the researcher and the actions of those who performed the artificial fertilization or the abortion, or when there was no prior agreement with the centers in which the artificial fertilization took place."[253]

However the "degrees of responsibility" differ with respect to those with profession standing and interest in the use of biological materials of an illicit origin (mediate material cooperators) and those with no such interest or influence (remote material cooperators) who have health needs and have less influence over public policy such as parents who need to vaccinate their children but realize the vaccine in question was derived from biological material of an illicit origin.

For instance, vaccines developed in the 1960s to treat chicken pox, hepatitis-A, rabies, polio and rubella, were cultured from cell lines derived from aborted fetuses. Today, in many cases no alternative vaccines have been developed that are not derived from an elective abortion. On June 9, 2005 the Pontifical Academy for Life released its opinion (approved by the Sacred Congregation for the Doctrine of the Faith) on the lawfulness of using vaccines derived from aborted fetuses. The Vatican reiterated its condemnation of tainted vaccines and those who profit from their sales and encouraged pressure on public and private officials to manufacture untainted vaccines. However they assured those who wish to immunize their children that, when no alternative exists, they may use tainted vaccines because their material cooperation would be remote and passive.[254]

In 2008 *Dignitas Personae* confirmed this teaching—those who had no influence over the production of vaccines of an illicit origin may use them for proportionate reasons if no alternative exists provided they express their objection and call for new morally untainted vaccines:

> Of course, within this general picture there exist differing degrees of responsibility. Grave reasons may be morally proportionate to justify the use of such 'biological material.' Thus, for example, danger to the health of children could permit parents to use a vaccine which was developed using cell lines of illicit origin, while keeping in mind that everyone has the duty to make known their disagreement and to ask that their healthcare system make other types of vaccines available. Moreover, in organizations where cell lines of illicit origin are being utilized, the responsibility of those who make the decision to use them is not the same as that of those who have no voice in such a decision.[255]

Gene Therapy

Gene therapy attempts to treat genes so as to prevent an inheritable disorder or to make them more amenable to treatment. More recently gene therapy "has been attempted for diseases which are not inherited, for cancer in particular."[256] If it affects only the person receiving the treatment it is called "somatic gene therapy." If it affects future generations by altering the sperm or ova of a patient it is referred to as "germ line therapy."[257] Gene modification may occur outside the patient's body (*ex vivo*) by first inserting a normal gene into the removed cells and then returning the modified cells into his body or it may occur within the patient's body (*in situ*) by introducing a virus containing the corrected gene or simply corrected DNA into the site of the disease.[258] Certain types of somatic or germ line gene therapy are applicable to the human fetus before birth, *in utero*.[259]

Somatic cell therapy has proved helpful in treating cystic fibrosis and adenosine deaminase deficiency (ADA) and would be licit provided the patient gave informed consent and the benefits of treatment were greater than the burdens to the patient. *Dignitas Personae* provides the following moral criteria for the licit use of somatic gene therapy:

> *Procedures used on somatic cells for strictly therapeutic purposes are in principle morally licit.* Such actions seek to restore the normal genetic configuration of the patient or to counter damage caused by genetic anomalies or those related to other pathologies. . . . [Also] it is necessary to establish beforehand that the person being treated will not be exposed to risks to his health or physical integrity which are excessive or disproportionate to the gravity of the pathology for which a cure is sought. The informed consent of the patient or his legitimate representative is also required.[260]

In the case of germ line therapy, because of its potential for eugenic alterations and unforeseen consequences in future generations, the risks seem to exceed the benefits, at least until such risks and variables could be eliminated.[261] Given the present state of embryo science and technology all germ line cell therapy must be considered immoral:

> Whatever genetic modifications are effected on the germ cells of a person will be transmitted to any potential offspring. Because the risks connected to any genetic manipulation are considerable and as yet not fully controllable, in the present state of research, it is not morally permissible to act in a way that may case possible harm to the resulting progeny. In the hypothesis of gene therapy on the embryo, it needs to be added that this only takes place in the context of in vitro fertilization and thus runs up against all the ethical objections to such procedures. For these reasons therefore it must be stated that, in its current state, germ line cell therapy in all its forms is morally illicit.[262]

Some bioethicists argue that certain kinds of treatments falling under what is referred to as "genetic enhancement therapy," designed to enhance genetic characteristics such as size, skin color, even intelligence, may be licit. They say, to the extent such interventions corrected genetic defects falling below the normal range of genetic variation in a population they should be attempted. However, if such treatment sought to alter traits falling within the range of normal genetic variation, they should not be attempted.[263] William May is not in favor of genetic enhancement therapy: "At present, there are no good ethical reasons for attempting such engineering and many good moral reasons for not doing so."[264] Genetic enhancement therapy, to the extent it justifies genetic engineering for purposes other than medical treatment, must be read in light of *Dignitas Personae* as exhibiting an arbitrary "eugenic mentality," and "ideological element" wherein man tries to usurp the place of God:

> Some have imagined the possibility of using techniques of genetic engineering to introduce alterations with the presumed aim of improving and strengthening the gene pool. . . . [S]uch manipulation would promote a eugenic mentality and would lead to indirect social stigma with regard to people who lack certain qualities, while privileging qualities that happen to be appreciated by a certain culture or society; such qualities do not constitute what is specifically human. . . . Furthermore, one wonders who would be able to establish which modifications were to be held as positive and which not. . . . Any conceivable response to these questions would, however, derive from arbitrary and questionable criteria. . . . Finally it must be noted that in the attempt to create a new type of human being one can recognize an ideological element in which man tries to take the place of his Creator.[265]

Altered Nuclear Transfer—Oocyte Assisted Reprogramming (ANT-OAR)

Many bioethicists faithful to the Magesterium of the Catholic Church recommend an embryo technology that promises, in their estimation, to provide the benefits of embryo stem cell lines without the destruction of human embryos. Thirty-five bioethicists on June 20, 2005 signed a Joint Statement on *The Production of Pluripotent Stem Cells by Oocyte Assisted Reprogramming* (hereinafter refered to as *Joint Statement*).[266] As described by several of the signers of the Joint Statement, ANT-OAR employs somatic cell nuclear transfer but alters it: "In ANT, the adult body cell nucleus or the egg cytoplasm (or both) are altered before the nucleus is transferred into the enucleated egg so that the newly constituted cell will, from the outset, lack the integrated unity and developmental potential of an embryo, yet will nevertheless possess the capacity for a certain limited subset of growth sufficient to produce pluripotent stem cells."[267]

Experiments using OAR in animals have shown that the enucleated oocyte has the power to reprogram a somatic nucleus to a totipotent state. What is more, by silencing or hyper-activating genes within the somatic nucleus and/or oocyte cytoplasm before electricity is applied, researchers have manipulated OAR cells in animals to bypass the totipotent stage characteristic of an organism and turn directly into a pluripotent cell after electricity is applied. They describe the ANT-OAR cell as a "failure of fertilization" comparable to a teratoma[268] or hydatidiform moles,[269] tumors not organisms, "yet they generate cells with the functional characteristics of embryonic stem cells."[270] Because the ANT-OAR cell is not an organism/embryo, researchers may destroy them to create embryo-like stem cell lines without being culpable for the death of a human being.

However, some bioethicists believe that an ANT-OAR produced cell may well be a severely disabled human embryo. This possibility would need to be ruled out before a bioethicist faithful to the Christian moral principles could endorse this embryo technology:

> It is essential, if this procedure is to provide a genuine and morally upright alternative to embryo-destructive research, that scientists know for sure that the resulting entity is not an embryo. Some fear that rather than creating a nonembryonic entity, scientists would succeed only in creating a defective or radically damaged human embryo.[271]

It would seem an equally plausible explanation of the ANT-OAR process is that what is produced is a "one-cell human embryo made to look like a stem cell" because "the mere act of modifying the epigenetic profile of the OAR product cannot be sufficient to prevent that product from being, or having been, an incipient human organism."[272] David Schindler argues that proponents of ANT-OAR have made assumptions that predetermine the conclusion they desire. Since an ANT-OAR cell behaves like a tumor it was always a tumor. But those opposed to this procedure argue that just because all tumors fail to exhibit totipotency when they implant does not prove that a cell that has been made to not exhibit totipotency was never an organism:

> [A]lthough the OAR-generated entity might behave like a tumor when implanted, it was more likely—with reasonable certitude—to have been an embryo in its original coming into being, albeit an embryo engineered in advance to begin virtually instantaneously to act in a non-embryonic manner (exhibiting pluripotency rather than totipotency).[273]

Philosopher Peter J. Colosi draws out the theological significance of human conception to show that OAR is a form of embryo destructive research: "God is present in human procreation in a way in which He is not present in animal reproduction. . . . When the procreative power of matter is about to work, God becomes immediately present to create a unique and unrepeatable person with a rational soul who is destined for eternal life. . . . Since God respects biology in ways that might surprise us (e.g., in IVF and cloning), it is highly likely that he would have created a soul in OAR, regardless of how many genes were hyperactivated to make it behave, virtually instantaneously, with pluripotent characteristics."[274]

God is not subject to the technician's magic, if you will, he is not like a genie in a bottle that must react when a person performs a ritual. Rather, God is faithful to the natural laws of his universe even if we are not faithful to his moral laws.[275] And just as he does not withhold a human soul should a man rape a woman who is ovulating and prevent the conception of a child, so he may not withhold a human soul from an OAR conception even though we have preprogrammed it to wither away into a tumor. To tamper with human conception in the way those in favor of OAR suggest may amount to stifling the voice of human life crying out for its soul at its first moment of existence which *Declaration on Procured Abortion* expressly forbids:

> This declaration expressly leaves aside the question of the moment when the spiritual soul is infused. There is not a unanimous tradition on this point and authors are as yet in disagreement. For some it dates from the first instant; for others it could not at least precede nidation. It is not within the competence of science to decide between these views, because the existence of an immortal soul is not a question in its field. It is a philosophical problem from which our moral affirmation remains independent for two reasons: (1) supposing a belated animation, there is still nothing less than *human* life, preparing for and calling for a soul in which the nature received from parents is completed; (2) on the other hand, it suffices that this presence of the soul be probable (and one can never prove the contrary) in order that the taking of life involve accepting the risk of killing a man, not only waiting for, but already in possession of his soul.[276]

The signers of the Joint Statement argue that human life is not present in the OAR cell because they have induced it to not exhibit pluripotent characteristics. But what if one defined as human life only those products of conception that exhibit a primitive brain streak and then programmed certain embryos to not develop a primitive brain streak? Are those products of conception not human life just because they fail to exhibit signs of further integration and eventually wither away and die? In the third century Tertullian wrote: "To prevent birth is anticipated murder; it makes little difference whether one destroys a life already born or does away with it in its nascent stage. The one who will be a man, is already one."[277]

Finally, even if one were to grant that OAR does not destroy a human life, would it not prevent conception from occurring in an act meant to be open to life? In this respect does it not bear resemblance to the sin of contraception? To bring together the seeds of human life, to place a somatic nucleus into an oocyte cytoplasm, while chemically sterilizing, if you will, one or both in such a way that they will not conceive human life but produce a tumor like growth, is this not a double contraception? Typically the moral object of contraception entails a decoupling—the pursuit of conjugal pleasure while taking steps to render a possible fertile act positively infertile. But in the case of OAR steps are taken to ensure that neither the unitive nor the procreative ends of an artificial act of human conception occur and that a possibly fertile act is made absolutely infertile. Even if one had moral certainty that an OAR cell was not human life,[278] it would appear that the OAR procedure itself is an artificial contraception of an artificial reproductive conception.

To base bioethics on embryo science and moral philosophy alone may bring too little to bear on the sometimes absurd and dark conundrums opened up by modern biotechnology. Christians must not hesitate to ask and answer (at least amongst themselves) arguments of fittingness: "What is fitting for God to do, that he does." If therefore, we know God "knits them [human embryos] together with his own hands"[279] and "that every human life—from the very beginning—is definitively blessed and welcomed by the look of God's mercy,"[280] then is it fitting that he divert his look of mercy from the first instant of human conception? "He is present in both normal and IVF human conception events and, if reproductive cloning should ever succeed, He may very well be present there as well. In the case of OAR, what happens? Does God notice that human procreative power is about to occur, and then look again and notice that some genes have been hyper-activated and then hold Himself back?"[281]

The instruction of the Congregation for the Doctrine of the Faith, *Dignitas Personae*, reminds us that a good motive and the pressing circumstance of finding new techniques "capable of producing stem cells of an embryonic type without implying the destruction of true human embryos" (i.e., ANT and OAR[282]) cannot, as *Evangelium vitae* warns, justify acting with positive practical doubt when human life may be in jeopardy. *Dignitas Personae* makes clear that the Church does not have moral certainty regarding the ontological status of the product of OAR and that, perhaps, a human life is artificially procreated but programmed to instantly become severely disabled and die. Until this doubt of conscience is resolved, all persons of good will are morally obligated to refrain from promoting ANT and OAR as a source of embryonic stem cells:

> The ethical objections raised in many quarters to therapeutic cloning and to the use of human embryos formed *in vitro* have led some researchers to propose new techniques which are presented as capable of producing stem cells of an embryonic type without implying the destruction of true human embryos. These proposals have met with questions of both a scientific and an ethical nature regarding above all the ontological status of the "product" obtained in this way. Until these doubts have been clarified, the statement of the Encyclical *Evangelium vitae* needs to be kept in mind: "what is at stake is so important that, from the standpoint of moral obligation, the mere probability that a human person is involved would suffice to justify an absolute clear prohibition of any intervention aimed at killing a human embryo."[283]

Human Egg Extraction

Those who see nothing intrinsically wrong with ANT-OAR admit it may be immoral due to the circumstance of "subjecting women to the painful and possibly dangerous process of hormonal stimulation known as superovulation."[284] Dr. Hurlbut, a signer of the Joint Statement, is opposed to superovulation to obtain eggs from women because it is medically risky and its long term effects are largely unknown. But he is hopeful that immature eggs left over from IVF or the laboratory stimulation of surgically removed ovarian tissue surgically removed for therapeutic reasons may provide the requisite number of eggs to overcome this difficulty.[285]

Researchers using Somatic Cell Nuclear Transfer (SCNT) to create a human embryo from which stem cells are extracted require hundreds of human eggs to create one human embryo. Often times they hide this fact or deliberately misrepresent the truth to present their research as low risk and efficient. For instance Dr. Hwang Woo-suk claimed to have made "11 patient-specific stem cell lines with a success rate of 1 line for approximately every 20 oocytes." In fact, he used over 2200 oocytes and failed to produce even one cloned embryo. Moreover "it became clear that payment, coercion, and lying were used to acquire the eggs that we were told many women were eager to donate."[286] A coalition of 35 women's groups is suing the South Korean government on behalf of women exploited through the egg extraction process that involved Dr. Hwang.[287]

The exploitive measures of the human egg hunters begins with a "bait and switch" tactic when an advertisement is run in a college newspaper, saying $50,000 or $100,000 will be paid to young college women who submit to multiple egg extraction. After a woman responds to the ad and provides her medical history a reply is generated indicating that she did not have the right profile for the person willing to pay $100,000 or $50,000 but there is a person willing to pay $15,000 for whom she did fit the profile.[288]

The egg merchants fail to inform the young women adequately about the serious health risks involved in egg extraction, nor do they tell them that their eggs are going to be used for therapeutic cloning research but that no cures, no therapies, have resulted from embryonic stem cells.[289]

First, women are sent in the mail powerful drugs to suppress their ovaries. They are given instructions how to self-inject these drugs. The most often used drug to suppress a woman's ovaries is Lupron (leuprolide acetate), a GnRh agonist. The medical complications associated with Lupron are legion.[290] Lupron has not been approved by the FDA for this indication. It is "off-label." Afterwards different drugs are mailed to these young women to hyperstimulate their ovaries to produce many ripened eggs ready for extraction. There are other complications associated with those drugs, most notably Ovarian Hyperstimulation Syndrome (OHSS) where the ovaries continue to enlarge even after the eggs have been collected. In serious cases many cysts develop and the ovaries remain enlarged along with massive fluid build-up in the body and in rare cases it can lead to stroke, the loss of a limb due to arterial occlusion and death.[291] Moreover, infants may also suffer adverse consequences including low birth weight and "high incidence of congenital anomalies, including delayed formation of bones and an eight-fold increase over background levels of cervical ribs, a condition which, when present in human infants, is associated with stillbirth and cancer."[292]

The recommendations of those most active in the United States to eliminate the abuses or "eggsploitation"[293] of the human egg harvesters include the following:

1. Eggs should be obtained without any hormonal stimulation.
2. No relatives or co-workers of those doing research on eggs should be allowed to provide eggs for research.
3. All medical expenses resulting from egg extraction for research should be covered. In cases where cycles would be hormonally manipulated, longer-

term health care coverage may be necessary to provide medical care for certain delayed health problems.

4. Those performing egg extraction for research purposes should function totally separate from IVF services (an effective firewall is needed to avoid both
   financial and professional conflicts of interest).
5. No research should be allowed on eggs or stem cell lines developed from
   eggs procured by means other than those described in #1-4 [above]. This
   would avoid the use of stem cell lines created in other countries or regions,
   where safeguards to women's health might not be in place.
6. No patents should be allowed for products that might result from research on
   these eggs. Without such a policy, many therapies will likely never be ac-
   cessible to the wider public. In addition, it would be extraordinarily difficult
   to avoid a problematic commercial market in women's eggs.
7. No payment to egg providers beyond direct expenses (e.g., no payment for
   lost wages) should be allowed.[294]

Many feminists are simply calling for a moratorium on egg extraction "until
such time as global discourse and scientific research yields information sufficient to establish adequate informed consent." To better assess the risks associated with egg extraction, Hands Off Our Ovaries, an organization dedicated to
bringing pro-life and pro-choice feminists together to oppose the exploitation of
women in the interests of biotechnology, asks the Federal Food and Drug Administration to examine "the 25 deaths and over 6,000 complaints of medical
complications associated with the drug, Lupron," the long and short term risks
of Ovarian Hyper-Stimulation Syndrome and the possible link between egg extraction procedures and uterine, ovarian and other reproductive cancers, infertility and adverse birth outcomes.[295]

With the pressure mounting in the United States over the coercive practices
of the egg merchants and complaints of serious medical complications to young
women resulting from the egg extraction process it won't be long until the egg
merchants refocus their recruitment from the college campuses of the Developed
World to the farming villages and big city slums of the Developing World. The
World Egg Bank (TWEB) already features reproductive tourism that includes
the cost of a vacation for rich older women seeking to become pregnant with
poor younger women's embryos:

> "This provides not just an economic alternative for American patients," said
> Diana Thomas, president and CEO of TWEB, "but is also well suited to in-
> tended patents who enjoy foreign travel." Now a common solution for infertile
> women who wish to bear children, egg donation can be accomplished with
> fresh donated eggs, which requires both donor and recipient to coordinate care-
> fully timed procedures in the same city. Frozen eggs, however, can be shipped
> nationally or internationally and thawed for transfer.[296]

Even pro-abortion feminists are beginning to wonder why our civilization is
making "women the servants of biotechnology, rather than insisting on a biotechnology that promotes the well-being of all people."[297] This question is ans-

wered by the Church's request that "all persons of good will, in particular physicians and researchers open to dialogue and desirous of knowing what is true . . . seek to safeguard the vulnerable condition of human beings in the first stages of life and to promote a more human civilization."[298]

Conclusion

It seems appropriate that this chapter conclude with a topic that asks the most basic question in the field of artificial reproductive technology—when does human life begin such that it is accorded full human dignity? When we considered abortion we saw that according the prevailing canons of Western civil jurisprudence the answer was over a continuum stretching from fertilization to implantation to viability to delivery and finally to birth, that is, when the baby's head emerges from the birth canal. The Catholic Church, on the other hand, recognizes a human embryo must be accorded full respect and dignity from the first moment of its existence. So, when does the first moment of an embryo's existence begin?

The issue of pre-implantation diagnosis presents us with two possible moments for when an embryo's life begins: 1) When, after the penetration of the ovum by the sperm, a second polar body develops and two pro-nuclei emerge, the "two pro-nuclei-stage," or 2) eighteen to twenty-four hours later when the maternal and paternal genetic material, the female pro-nucleus and the male pro-nucleus, fuse together in what is from then on referred to as a "zygote." German bioethicist, Mareike Klekamp, notes that for a long time the formation of the zygote, when the female and male pro-nuclei fuse, was considered the beginning of a new human existence. "But latest embryonic research results presented by Magadalena Zernicka-Goetz, Maureen Condic and Gunter Rager suggest fixing the beginning of human life already earlier, to the moment where the sperm penetrates the egg membrane of the egg cell."[299] Klekamp notes Robert George and Christopher Tollefsen also hold that it is the union of sperm and egg and not the fusion of their genetic material that marks the first moment of the embryo's existence:

> [W]e are inclined to think that the definitive moment occurs…once the sperm has entered and united with the Oocyte. Once this has happened, both sperm and Oocyte undergo such significant changes that neither seems to exist in its own right anymore. The sperm breaks up on entering the Oocyte, and, other than its nucleus, is largely dissolved. The oocyte also undergoes fundamental changes, as its zona hardens, to prevent polyspermy, and it completes its second meiotic division. We no longer, in consequence, have two distinct organic parts, sperm and egg, each with a distinct identity.
>
> At the same time, when sperm and oocyte cease to be, there now appears to be a distinct organism directing its own processes of growth and development, processes that include the lining up of the maternal and paternal chromosomes at syngamy, as well as the processes just described of hardening the zona and completing the second meitic division. The first process especially seems characteris-

tic of a new organism, whose existence depends upon a structural barrier to outside forces, rather than of a gametic cell, whose existence is fundamentally
oriented toward uniting with another gamete, and thus does not have an imper-
meable external barrier. For these reasons, we think it most likely that the definitive moment marking the existence of a new human organism is fertilization, defined as the union of sperm with oocyte.[300]

The moral and legal significance of which moment signifies the beginning of
human existence, the pro-nuclei stage or the zygote stage, has important moral
and legal repercussions. For instance, the German Embryo Protection Law
(GEPL) stipulates that embryos, defined as "zygotes," are protected whereas
"pro-nuclei" are excluded from the scope of that law. Blastomere biopsy, the
removal of one or two cells from a four to ten cell blastomere, conflicts with
GEPL whereas polar biopsy, the removal of the first and second polar bodies,
does not. Hence, "[i]n Germany thousands of human pro-nuclei are biopsied,
cryo-conserved or killed."[301] Pre-implantation diagnosis is routinely used at IVF
fertility clinics in Germany to screen pro-nuclei for chromosome abnormalities
for older women, i.e., "high risk couples," to improve their rate of success, for
sex selection, i.e., "family balancing or social sexing" and for "designer babies,"
or "children selected from among 80 to 100 embryos and designated to serve
after delivery as immunologically suitable providers of healthy cell material for
siblings who suffer from disease."[302]

   Dignitas Personae deals at length with pre-implantation diagnosis wherein
we read it "is a form of prenatal diagnosis connected with techniques of artificial
fertilization in which embryos formed in vitro undergo genetic diagnosis before
being transferred into a woman's womb. Such diagnosis is done in order to ensure that only free from defects or having the desired sex or other particular
qualities are transferred." Pre-implantation diagnosis is connected with IVF,
which is "always intrinsically illicit" and is directed toward "an act of abortion"
of those embryos deemed defective or undesirable. Hence it is an "expression of
a eugenic mentality" that is "'shameful and utterly reprehensible, since it presumes to measure the value of a human life only within the parameters of "normality" and physical well-being, thus opening the way to legitimizing infanticide and euthanasia as well.'"[303] Pre-implantation diagnosis is an instrument in
the furtherance of invidious discrimination, the Instruction tells us. Just as in the
past the Church defended those unjustly discriminated against on the bases of
race, religion or social condition, so today she defends the new class of social
undesirables, persons, embryonic human beings, with disabilities or diseases:

> Such discrimination is immoral and must therefore be considered legally unac-
> ceptable, just as there is a duty to eliminate cultural, economic and social bar-
> riers which undermine the full recognition and protection of disabled or ill
> people.[304]

In contrast to PID, pre-natal diagnosis is not necessarily directed towards an
act of abortion but may serve therapeutic interventions at the service of the per-

natal child. Prenatal diagnosis and the therapeutic interventions that follow may be licit "if they represent no disproportionate danger to the child and mother, and aim at early therapy or enhance a well-tempered acceptance of the unborn."[305]

Of course, prenatal diagnosis like pre-implantation diagnosis can be used to search and destroy prenatal human life deemed defective or undesirable. The use of these diagnostic techniques has changed the experience of pregnancy in Germany, Klekamp notes, from one being "in good hope" into "a pregnancy on probation" with a "latent reproach of culpability" should a pregnant woman refuse prenatal diagnosis and bring to term a handicapped child. She also decries the "scaremongering" done under the euphemism of "prevention." Will parents who succumb to the scaremongering and abort their embryos after a negative pre-implantation diagnosis experience post-selection-syndrome, she speculates.[306]

For all these reason Klekamp suggests in her paper before the Pontifical Counsel of Justice and Peace that *Dignitas Personae* did not go far enough in its treatment of pre-implantation diagnosis. The first moment of human existence needs and is capable of more precise definition. In light of the recent studies she cites in her paper is seems clear that a distinct human organism (a human being) is present from the moment the sperm unites with the egg, not merely when the new organism unites the two pro-nuclei to form a zygote. Therefore she urges that "[t]his important teaching of the Church [*Dignitas Personae*] should be amended in order to forestall the impression that pro-nuclei are free to be used in PID procedures or selection and deep-freeze conservation."[307]

Notes

1. Rom. 1: 20–26.
2. Ps. 8:4–6.
3. "John Haas at Christendom College Outlines Bioethical Threats to Humanity," *The Wanderer*, 20 November 2003, 8.
4. Germain Kopaczynski, "Reproductive Technologies," in ECST.
5. Leon R. Kass, *The Ethics of Human Cloning* (Washington, DC: AEI Press, 1998), 12.
6. Pontifical Council for Justice and Peace, *Compendium of the Social Doctrine of the Church* (Washington, DC: USCCB, 2005), no. 283.
7. CCC, no. 2418.
8. CCC, no. 2417.
9. Hanna Klaus, "Sexuality (Human)," and Adrian Teo, "Human Life (Dignity and Sanctity of)," in ECST.
10. Donald DeMarco, *Biotechnology and the Assault on Parenthood* (San Francisco: Ignatius Press, 1991), 25.
11. William E. May, "Marriage," in ECST.
12. Russell Hittinger, *Christopher Dawson on Technology and the Demise of Liberalism*, vol. 7 of *Christianity and Western Civilization*, The Proceedings of the

Wethersfield Institute (San Francisco: Ignatius Press, 1995), 80–82; citing Christopher Dawson, *The Judgment of Nations* (New York, NY: Sheen and Ward, 1942), 113.

13. DeMarco, *Biotechnology and the Assault on Parenthood*, 91.

14. John F. Harvey, "Homosexuality," in ECST.

15. DeMarco, *Biotechnology and the Assault on Parenthood*, 91.

16. DeMarco, *Biotechnology and the Assault on Parenthood*, 88–89.

17. C.S. Lewis, *The Abolition of Man* (New York, NY: Macmillan, 1947), 69.

18. Kass, *Ethics of Human Cloning*, 39–40.

19. *Davis v. Davis*, 842 S.W.2d 588, 590–91 (1992).

20. Kass, *Ethics of Human Cloning*, 47–48.

21. J.L.A. Garcia, "Human Cloning: Never and Why Not," in *Life and Learning IX, Proceedings of the Ninth University Faculty for Life Conference*, ed. Joseph W. Koterski (Washington D.C.: University Faculty for Life, 1999), 4; citing Gregory Pence, *Who's Afraid of Human Cloning?* (Lanham, MD: Rowman and Littlefield, 1998), 94.

22. Nicholas Lund–Molfese, "Biotechnology and Human Dignity in The Thought of Germain Grisez," *Catholic Social Science Review* 7 (2002): 112.

23. Gilbert I. Sheldon, "Test Tube Babies," *Steubenville Register*, 5 December 2003, 6.

24. Lund–Molfese, "Biotechnology and Human Dignity in the Thought of Germain Grisez," 113; citing Germain Grisez, "Bioethics and Christian Anthropology," *The National Catholic Bioethics Quarterly* 1, no. 1 (Spring 2001): 34.

25. Donald P. Asci, "*Donum Vitae*," in ECST.

26. DV, intro., no. 1.

27. DV, intro., no. 1.

28. DV, intro., no. 1.

29. Gen. 1:28.

30. DV, intro., no. 2.

31. DV, intro., no. 3. See also Mary Shivanandan, "Theology of the Body," in ECST.

32. DV, intro., no. 3.

33. MM, no. 193.

34. DV, intro., no. 4.

35. DV, intro., no. 5.

36. DV, no. I.1.

37. DV, no. I.1.

38. DV, no. I.1.

39. DV, no. I.2.

40. DV, no. I.2.

41. DV, no. I.2.

42. DV, no. I.3.

43. DV, no. I.3.

44. DV, no. I.4.

45. DV, no. I.4. See also Adrian Teo, "Human Experimentation," in ECST.

46. DV, no. I.4.

47. DV, no. I.5.

48. DV, no. I.5 (emphasis added).

49. DV, no. I.5 (emphasis added).

50. DV, no. I.6.

51. DV, no. II.

52. Philip M. Sutton, "Family," and William E. May, "Marriage," in ECST.
53. DV, no. II.1.
54. DV, no. II.1 (emphasis added).
55. DV, no. II.2.
56. DV, no. II.2 (emphasis added).
57. DV, no. II.2.
58. DV, no. II.2.
59. DV, no. II.3.
60. DV, no. II.3. See also Philip M. Sutton, "Family," in ECST.
61. DV, no. II.3.
62. DV, no. II.4.
63. DV, no. II.4.
64. DV, no. II.4.
65. DV, no. II.4.
66. DV, no. II.5.
67. DV, no. II.5.
68. DV, no. II.6.
69. Pius XII, *Address to Italian Midwives* (27 October 1951), no. 27.
70. DV, no. II.6.
71. DV, no. II.7.
72. DV, no. II.7.
73. DV, no. II.8.
74. DV, no. II-8.
75. DV, no. III.
76. DV, no. III.
77. DV, no. III.
78. Luke 10:29–37.
79. Matt. 25:40.
80. DP, intro.
81. DP, intro., no. 1.
82. DP, intro., no. 3.
83. DV, no. I.4.
84. DV, no. I.4. See also DV, no. 79.
85. Pope Benedict XVI, "Address to the UN General Assembly," *New York Times*, 19 April 2008, http://www.nytimes.com/2008/04/19/nyregion/18popeatun.html (10 Aug. 2009).
86. Pope Benedict XVI, "Address to the Participants in the International Congress organized by the Pontifical Lateran University on the 40th anniversary of the Encyclical *Humanae Vitae*," *L'Osservatore Romano*, 11 May 2008, 1.
87. GS, no. 22.
88. 2 Pet. 1:4.
89. DP, no. 7.
90. DP, no. 10.
91. DV, intro., no. 3.
92. DV, no. II.6.
93. DP, no. 14.
94. DP, no. 15.
95. Gen. 1:26.
96. DP, no. 17 n.32.

97. DV, no. II.5.

98. DV, no. I.6.

99. Pope John Paul II, "Address to the participants in the Symposium on 'Evangelium Vitae and Law' and the Eleventh International Colloquium on Roman and Canon Law," 24 May 1996, 6: *Acta Apostolicae Sedis* 88 (1996): 943–44 (emphasis added).

100. DP, no. 20.

101. DP, no. 21.

102. EV, no. 63.

103. DP, no. 22.

104. CIC, no. 1398.

105. DP, no. 26.

106. DP, no. 27.

107. DP, no. 28 n.47. See also Lawrence F. Roberge, "Cloning," in ECST.

108. DP, no. 28.

109. DV, no. I.6.

110. DP, no. 29.

111. DP, no. 30.

112. DP, no. 30, n.49.

113. EV, no. 60.

114. Benedict XVI, "Address to the participants in the Symposium on the topic: 'Stem Cells: what is the future for therapy?' Organized by the Pontifical Academy for Life," 16 September 2006: *Acta Apostolicae Sedis* 98 (2006): 694 n.51.

115. DP, no. 33.

116. DP, no. 34.

117. DP, no. 35.

118. DP, no. 35.

119. DP, no. 35.

120. EV, no. 84.

121. Matt. 25:40.

122. DeMarco, *Biotechnology and the Assault on Parenthood*, 209.

123. CIC, no. 1084.3.

124. CIC, no. 1084.

125. Thomas J. O'Donnell, *Medicine and Christian Morality*, rev. 3d ed. (New York, NY: Alba House, 1997), 213.

126. O'Donnell, *Medicine and Christian Morality*, 212.

127. O'Donnell, *Medicine and Christian Morality*, 213.

128. O'Donnell, *Medicine and Christian Morality*, 215–23.

129. O'Donnell, *Medicine and Christian Morality*, 214–15.

130. DP, no. 13.

131. William E. May, *Catholic Bioethics and the Gift of Human Life*, 2d ed. (Huntington, IN: Our Sunday Visitor, 2008), 93–94.

132. Debra Evans, *Without Moral Limits: Women, Reproduction, and Medical Technology* (Wheaton, IL: Crossway Books, 2000), 96; citing *Physician's Desk Reference*, 43d ed. (Montvale, NJ: Medical Economics, Co., 1989).

133. Evans, *Without Moral Limits*, 117; citing B.J. Blotting, I.M. Davies, and A.J. Macfarlane, "Recent Trends in the Incidence of Multiple Births and Associated Mortality," *Archives of Diseases in Childhood* 62 (1987): 941–50.

134. O'Donnell, *Medicine and Christian Morality*, 262; May, *Catholic Bioethics*,

89.

135. DeMarco, *Biotechnology and the Assault on Parenthood*, 208–9; citing Edwin Kelly, *Medical Ethics* (Chicago: Loyola Univ. Press, 1956), 154; Gerald Kelly, *Medico–Moral Problems* (St. Louis: The Catholic Hospital Assoc., 1957), 239–40.

136. DeMarco, *Biotechnology and the Assault on Parenthood*, 211–14; May, *Catholic Bioethics*, 89.

137. DeMarco, *Biotechnology and the Assault on Parenthood*, 214.

138. DeMarco, *Biotechnology and the Assault on Parenthood*, 214.

139. DeMarco, *Biotechnology and the Assault on Parenthood*, 218.

140. DV, no. II.6.

141. DeMarco, *Biotechnology and the Assault on Parenthood*, 216.

142. *Derdiarian v. Felix Contracting Corp.*, 51 N.Y.2d 308, 414 N.E.2d 166, 434 N.Y.S.2d 166 (1980).

143. See the section in Chapter 5 entitled, "The Difference Between Animals and Persons."

144. May, *Catholic Bioethics*, 92–93.

145. See marginal notes in *Origins*, March 19, 1987, Vol. 16: No. 40, 699.

146. DeMarco, *Biotechnology and the Assault on Parenthood*, 219, 235.

147. DP, no. 17 n.32.

148. DP, no. 17; citing DV, no. II.5.

149. May, *Catholic Bioethics*, 90–92.

150. O'Donnell, *Medicine and Christian Morality*, 238.

151. *Davis*, 842 S.W.2d at 595–96; citing *York v. Jones*, 717 F.Supp. 421, 424–25 (E.D. Va. 1989).

152. For a good summary of US and international perspective on who prevails in a dispute over the control of frozen human embryos, see *Davis*, 842 S.W.2d at 588, and *Evans v. United Kingdom*, European Court of Human Rights, App. No. 6339/05 [2006] 1 FCR 585m [2006] 2 FLR 172 (7 March 2006).

153. Growing Generations: *Premier Surrogacy Agency Offers Surrogacy Services Worldwide*, http://www.growinggenerations.com/ (1 August 2009).

154. Dave Andrusko, "Parents of Adopted Frozen Embryos Speak Out," *National Right to Life News* 28, no. 7 (July 2001): 1, 6.

155. Grace MacKinnon, "Theologians Argue Frozen Embryos' Fate," *Human Life Report*, August 2001, 10, 11, 19. See also Thomas V. Berg and Edward J. Furton, eds., *Human Embryo Adoption: Biotechnology, Marriage, and the Right to Life* (Philadelphia: The National Catholic Bioethics Center, 2006); May, *Catholic Bioethics*, 94–95.

156. Nicholas Tonti–Filippini, "The Embryo Rescue Debate: Impregnating Women, Ectogenesis, and Restoration from Suspended Animation," *National Catholic Bioethics Quarterly* (Spring 2003): 111.

157. MacKinnon, "Parents of Adopted Frozen Embryos Speak Out," 19. Prior to the release of *Dignitas Personae* (December, 2008) when anyone asked whether they may become pregnant with abandoned embryos in order to adopt them or save them from death I referred them to the following literature on this issue, and told them this was an area of developing doctrine and told them that since bioethicistis faithful to the Magisterium were on both sides of the issue they had a duty to form their conscience and then decide. I referred them some of the literature on the issue, to wit: William B. Smith, "Questions Answered: Rescue the Frozen?" in *Homiletic and Pastoral Review* (October 1995): 72–74; Geoffrey Surtees, "Adoption of a Frozen Embryo," *Homiletic and Pastoral Review* (August–September, 1996): 7–16; William B. Smith, "Response [to

Geoffrey Surtees]," *Homiletic and Pastoral Review* (August–September 1996): 16–17; Maurizio Faggioni, "The Question of Frozen Embryos," *L'Osservatore Romano* [English], 21 August 1996, 4–5; Germain Grisez, *The Way of the Lord Jesus*, vol. 3 of *Difficult Moral Questions* (Quincy, IL: Franciscan Press, 1997), 239–44; Mary Geach, "Are There Any Circumstances in Which It Would Be Morally Admirable for a Woman to Seek to Have an Orphan Embryo Implanted in her Womb?" in *Issues for a Catholic Bioethics: Proceedings of the International Conference to Celebrate the Twentieth Anniversary of the Foundation of the Linacre Center,* ed. L. Gormally (London: Linacre Center, 1999), 341–46; Helen Watt, "Are There Any Circumstances in Which It Would Be Morally Admirable for a Woman to Seek to Have an Orphan Embryo Implanted in her Womb?" in *Issues for a Catholic Bioethics: Proceedings of the International Conference to Celebrate the Twentieth Anniversary of the Foundation of the Linacre Center,* ed. L. Gormally (London: Linacre Center, 1999), 349–50; Mauro Cozzoli, "The Human Embryo: Ethical and Normative Aspects," in *The Identity and Status of the Human Embryo: Proceedings of Third Assembly of the Pontifical Academy for Life,* ed., Juan de Dios Vial Correa and Elio Sgreccia (Vatican: Libreria Editrice Vaticana, 1999), 295–96; May, *Catholic Bioethics,* 94–107; Tonti-Filippini, "The Embryo Rescue Debate," 111–37; Berg and Furton, ed., *Human Embryo Adoption*; Robert P. George and Christopher Tollefsen, *Embryo: A Defense of Human Life* (New York, NY: Doubleday, 2008).

Since the release of *Dignitas Personae* (December 2008) I no longer believe frozen embryo adoption may in good faith be considered licit or an option a Catholic can in good faith pursue. DP paragraph 19 states embryo adoption by infertile couples is "*not ethically acceptable for the same reasons which make artificial heterologous procreation illicit as well as any form of surrogate motherhood.*" First, it seems to this author misleading to claim DP offers merely "caution" and "no definitive statement" on this practice. DP is not so ambiguous – the plain and ordinary meaning of the language used says that the practice of heterologous embryo transfer is "not ethically acceptable" for reasons analogous to the illicit and condemned practices of IVF and surrogate motherhood. It seems clear to this author that the CDF expects the practice of heterologous embryo adoption to cease. Certainly *Dignitas Personae* discouraged couples from adopting or rescuing frozen embryos and so should those expected to represent the mind of the Church whether or not this is a "definitive statement" as taught in *Ad Tuedam Fidem,* Third Proposition, and *Lumen Gentium,* paragraph 25 and noted in the preceding chapter, Chapter 8. See "Interview with Law Professor Brian Scarnecchia," Rome, February 25, 2010 (Zenit.org) and E. Christian Brugger, "Rescuing Frozen Embryos: Is Adoption a Valid Moral Option?" March 17, 2010 (Zenit.org). Second, if those opposed to heterologous embryo transfer are correct and it is an intrinsically evil act that violates the unitive good of marriage, then, even though a couple might be invincibly ignorant and subjectively not culpable of sin, it may still harm their marital relationship. Physical and psychological harm would come to them as a consequence of heterologous embryo adoption similar to that experienced by couples who use contraception and are invincibly ignorant of its sinfulness and its negative effects on marital unity. At the least, pastoral solicitude ought to impel us to warn couples of this dire possibility. See Ruth D. Lasseter, "Sensible Sex," *Why Humanae Vitae Was Right: A Reader,* ed. Janet E. Smith (San Francisco: Ignatius Press, 1993), 473–95.

158. DV, no. II.3.
159. Tonti–Filippini, "The Embryo Rescue Debate," 120–24.
160. CCC, no. 499.

161. DV, no. II.1 (emphasis in original).

162. Matt. 1:18–25.

163. Tonti–Filippini, "The Embryo Rescue Debate," 124.

164. Tonti–Filippini, "The Embryo Rescue Debate," 126 n.37.

164. Tadeusz Pacholczyk, "Some Moral Contraindications to Embryo Adoption," *Human Embryo Adoption: Biotechnology, Marriage, and the Right to Life*, Thomas V. Berg and Edward J. Furton eds., (Philadelphia: The National Catholic Bioethics Center, 2006), 52.

166. For a detailed discussion of this matter, see chapter 2 above. See also James Hostetler and Michael Coulter, "Abortion," in ECST.

167. DV, no. II.4.

168. DV, no. II.2–3.

169. DV, no. II.2–3.

170. CHCW, no. 29; citing DV, no. II.A.3.

171. DV, no. I.5.

172. DV, no. I.6.

173. O'Donnell, *Medicine and Christian Morality*, 180; citing C.J. Wallace, "Transplantations of Ectopic Pregnancy from Fallopian Tube to Cavity of Uterus," *Surgery, Gynecology and Obstetrics* 36 (5 May 1917): 578–79.

174. DeMarco, *Biotechnology and the Assault on Parenthood*, 234–35.

175. DP, no. 19.

176. DV, no. I.5 (emphasis added).

177. EV, no. 99.

178. DV, no. I.6.

179. Cozzoli, "The Human Embryo: Ethical and Normative Aspects," 295.

180. Pope John Paul II, "Address to the participants in the Symposium on '*Evangelium vitae* and Law,'" 943–44 (emphasis added).

181. Mareike Klekamp, "Woman and Actual Challenges of Bioethics: The Perspective of Christian Social Doctrine Shown at the Example of Pre-implantation Diagnosis (PID)," paper presented at the Pontifical Council for Justice and Peace First International Conference on "Life, Family, Development: The Role of Women in the Promotion of Human Rights," Rome, 20–21 March 2009, 3.

182. DP, no. 18.

183. See note 152.

184. Leticia Velasquez, "Down, Not Out: The Legacy of Jerome Lejeune and the Resurgence of Down Syndrome Research," *NCRegister.com*, 1 July 2008, http://www.ncregister.com/site/article/15354/ (19 Nov. 2009).

185. Red River Valley Down Syndrome Society, Newsletter, May 2007, http://redwooddss.camp7.org/content/documenthandlers.ashk?docId=5171 (19 Nov. 2009). For a good biography of Jerome Lejeune, see Clara Lejeune, *Life is a Blessing: A Biography of Jerome Lejeune - Geneticist, Doctor, Father* (San Francisco: Ignatius Press, 2001).

186. *Davis*, 842 S.W.2d at 593. For uncomplimentary commentary on Dr. Lejeune's testimony see George J. Annas, "A French Homunculus in a Tennessee Court," *Hastings Center Report* 19, no. 6 (1989): 20–22, for his own testimony and commentary see Jerome Lejeune, *The Concentration Can: When Does Human Life Begin?* (San Francisco: Ignatius Press, 1992).

187. *Davis*, 842 S.W.2d at 594.

188. *Davis*, 842 S.W.2d at 594.

189. *Davis*, 842 S.W.2d at 595.

190. *Davis*, 842 S.W.2d at 595; citing *Roe v. Wade*, 410 U.S. 113, 162 (1973) for the proposition that "the United States Supreme Court concluded that 'the unborn have never been recognized in the law as persons in the whole sense.'"

191. *Davis*, 842 S.W.2d at 596. The Appellate Court of Tennessee relied on *York*, 717 F.Supp. 421, for the proposition that the parties share an interest in the seven fertilized ova.

192. *Davis*, 842 S.W.2d at 589.

193. *Davis*, 842 S.W.2d at 591, n.6.

194. *Davis*, 842 S.W.2d at 596–97.

195. *Davis*, 842 S.W.2d at 590.

196. *Evans*, App. No. 6339/05, syllabus of the Court.

197. *Evans*, App. No. 6339/05, 16.

198. *Evans*, App. No. 6339/05, 19.

199. *Evans*, App. No. 6339/05, 18.

200. *Evans*, App. No. 6339/05, 18.

201. *Evans*, App. No. 6339/05, 21.

202. *Evans*, App. No. 6339/05, 23.

203. *Evans*, App. No. 6339/05, 24.

204. EV, no. 73.

205. DV, no. II.2–3.

206. DP, no. 19.

207. In March 16, 2006 this author spoke with European Minister of Parliament, Kathy Sinnott, after she provided him an opportunity to address the Bioethics Committee of the European Parliament on American law relevant to their consideration of *Evans v. United Kingdom*. He said to her that in his opinion the Church's ban against surrogacy did not apply in the case of homologous embryo transfer, and a Catholic could support it in the case of Ms. Evans while at the same time opposing heterologous embryo transfer.

208. See DV, no. I.5.

209. DV, no. I.6.

210. Holy See, "The Views of the Holy See on Human Embryonic Cloning," no. 2, 17 July 2003, http://www.holyseemission.org/cloning2003eng.html (20 Nov. 2009); Celestino Migliori, *Statement by Archbishop Celestino Migliori on Agenda Item 158: International Convention against Reproductive Cloning of Human Beings*, 30 September 2003 http://www.holyseemission.org/30sep2003.html (20 Nov. 2009).

211. Holy See, "The Views of the Holy See on Human Embryonic Cloning," no. 4; Migliori, *Statement on Agenda Item 158*.

212. United Nations, Fifty-ninth General Assembly, Plenary, 82nd Meeting (AM), Press Release GA/10333, 8 March 2005, http://www.un.org/News/Press/docs/2005/ga10333.doc.htm (19 Nov. 2009).

213. Wesley J. Smith, "The U.N. on Cloning: Ban It," *The Weekly Standard*, 15 March 2005, http://www.weeklystandard.com/Content/Public/Articles/000/000/005/360mveat.asp?pg=2?ZoomFont=YES (23 Nov. 2009).

214. Smith, "The U.N. on Cloning: Ban It."

215. Colum Lynch, "U.N. Backs Human Cloning Ban," *The Washington Post*, 9 March 2005, A15.

216. Lynch, "U.N. Backs Human Cloning Ban," A15.

217. See United Nations, Fifty-ninth General Assembly, Sixth Committee, Agenda Item 150, *Report of the Sixth Committee: International Convention Against the Repro-

ductive Cloning of Human Beings, 23 February 2005, http://daccess-dds-ny.un.org/doc/ UNDOC/LTD/N05/247/70/PDF/N0524770.pdf (20 Nov. 2009). See also Lori B. Andrews, "Genes and Patent Policy: Rethinking intellectual property rights," Nature Reviews Genetics (October 2002): 803; *World Egg Bank Launches Medical Tourism Program with World's Largest Egg-Donation Fertility Clinic*, 2 November 2009, http://www.prnewswire.com/news-releases/world-egg-bank-launches-medical-tourism-program-with-worlds-largest-egg-donation-fertility-clinic-68641442.html (20 Nov. 2009); David Kravets, "Judge OKs Challenge to Human-Gene Patents," *Wired.com*, 2 November 2009, http://www.wired.com/threatlevel/2009/11/genes (20 Nov. 2009).

218. Holy See, "The Views of the Holy See on Human Embryonic Cloning," nos. 5–6; Migliori, *Statement on Agenda Item 158*.

219. Pontifical Academy for Life, *Reflections on Cloning*, 30 September 2007, http://www.vatican.va/roman_curia/pontifical_academies/acdlife/documents/ rc_pa_acdlife_doc_30091997_clon_en.html (20 Nov. 2009). See also Francis J. Beckwith, "Cloning and Reproductive Liberty," *Life and Learning XII: Proceedings of the Twelfth University Faculty for Life Conference*, Joseph W. Koterski, ed., (Washington, DC: University Faculty for Life, 2003), 24. See also Leon R. Kass, *Human Cloning and Human Dignity: The Report of the President's Council on Bioethics* (Jackson, TN: Public Affairs, 2002), 20–21.

220. Pontifical Academy for Life, *Reflections*, no. 1; Beckwith, "Cloning and Reproductive Liberty," 25.

221. Pontifical Academy for Life, *Reflections*, no. 2.

222. Beckwith, "Cloning and Reproductive Liberty" 26; cf. Kass, *Report of the President's Council*, xxiv.

223. Pontifical Academy for Life, *Reflections*, no. 1.

224. Pontifical Academy for Life, *Reflections*, no. 2.

225. Pontifical Academy for Life, *Reflections*, no. 3.

226. Pontifical Academy for Life, *Reflections*, no. 3.

227. Pontifical Academy for Life, *Reflections*, no. 4.

228. Pontifical Academy for Life, *Reflections*, no. 4.

229. Pontifical Council for the Family, *Cloning: the Disappearance of Direct Parenthood and Denial of the Family* (2003), no. 6 http://www.vatican.va/roman_curia/ pontifical_councils/family/documents/rc_pc_family_doc_20030808_cloning-trujillo_en.html (20 Nov. 2009).

230. Pontifical Council for the Family, *Cloning, 6*.

231. DP, no. 29.

232. DP, no. 29.

233. Pontifical Council for the Family, *Cloning*, 6.

234. DP, no. 30 (emphasis in original).

235. DP, no. 28.

236. William B. Hurlbut, "ANT presentation," A presentation to The President's Council on Bioethics, December 2004, http://www.alterednucleartransfer.com/html/ ANTpresentation.html (4 Nov. 2009).

237. Ron Stein, "Obama's Order on Stem Cells Leaves Key Questions to NIH," *The Washington Post*, 10 March 2009, http://www.washingtonpost.com/wp-yn/content/article /2009/03/09/AR2009030903156.html?sid=ST2009030901296 (20 Nov. 2009) (with video).

238. Pontifical Academy for Life, *Declaration on the Production and the Scientific and Therapeutic Use of Human Embryonic Stem Cells*, 24 August 2000, no. 1,

http://www.vatican.va/roman_curia/pontifical_academies/acdlife/documents/
rc_pa_acdlife_doc_20000824_cellule-staminali_en.html (20 Nov. 2009).

239. Kass, *Report of the President's Council*, 65.

240. Pontifical Council for the Family, *Cloning*, 6. See also note 9; May, *Catholic Bioethics*, 214.

241. Pontifical Academy for Life, *Declaration*, no. 3.

242. Pontifical Academy for Life, *Declaration*, no. 1.

243. Pontifical Academy for Life, *Declaration*, no. 2.

244. Eamonn Keane, *The Brave New World of Therapeutic Cloning* (Front Royal, VA: Human Life International, 2001), 21.

245. Kass, *Report of the President's Council*, 69.

246. Pontifical Council for the Family, *Cloning*, 7.

247. Keane, *Brave New World of Therapeutic Cloning*, 23.

248. Pontifical Academy for Life, *Declaration*, no. 3.

249. For further discussion of this topic, see Chapter Five on Cooperation and Scandal.

250. DP, no. 34.

251. DP, no. 34.

252. DP, no. 35.

253. DP, no. 35.

254. Pontifical Academy for Life, *Moral Reflections on Vaccines Prepared from Cells Derived from Aborted Human Foetuses*, 5 June 2005, http://www.academiavita.org/template.jsp?sez=Documenti&pag=testo/vacc/vacc&lang=english (20 Nov. 2009). See also Children of God for Life, "Vaccines from Abortion: The Hidden Truth," http://www.cogforlife.org/vaxbrochsample.htm (4 Aug. 2009).

255. DP, no. 35.

256. DP, no. 25.

257. May, *Catholic Bioethics*, 215–16; citing *Genetic Intervention on Human Subjects: The Report of a Working Party of the Catholic Bishops' Joint Committee on Bioethical Issues* (London: The Catholic Bishops' Joint Committee on Bioethical Issues, 1996), 6. See also DP, no. 32.

258. May, *Catholic Bioethics*, 217; citing W. French Anderson, "Strategies for Gene Therapy," in *Encyclopedia of Bioethics*, 2d rev. ed., ed. Warren Reich (New York, NY: McGraw-Hill, 1995), 908, 911.

259. DP, no. 25.

260. DP, no. 26 (emphasis in the original).

261. May, *Catholic Bioethics*, 218–20.

262. DP, no. 26.

263. May, *Catholic Bioethics*, 216; citing Anderson, "Strategies for Gene Therapy."

264. May, *Catholic Bioethics*, 216

265. PD, no. 27.

266. Joint Statement, *Production of Pluripotent Stem Cells by Oocyte Assisted Reprogramming*, 20 June 2005, http://www.alterednucleartransfer.com/index.php?page=4a&view=3 (4 Nov. 2009).

267. William B. Hurlbut, Robert P. George, and Markus Grompe, "Seeking Consensus: A Clarification and Defense of Altered Nuclear Transfer," *Hastings Center Report* 36, no. 5 (2006): 45–50, http://www.alterednucleartransfer.com/?page=4a&view=7 (4 Nov. 2009).

268. "Teratomas are germ cell tumors that generate all three primary embryonic

germ layers as well as more advanced cells and tissues, including partial limb and organ primordial. Yet these chaotic, disorganized, and nonfunctional masses lack entirely the structural and dynamic character of organisms." William Hurlbut, "Altered Nuclear Transfer as a Morally Acceptable Means for the Procurement of Human Embryonic Stem Cells," working paper discussed at the President's Council of Bioethics, December 2004, http://alterednucleartransfer.com/index.php?page=4a&view=5 (4 November 2009).

269. "[A] complete hydatidiform mole may result when an egg without a nucleus is 'fertilized' by two sperm. This pathological failure of fertilization, will divide and form a blastocyst-like structure, but produces only an overgrowth of placental tissue with little or no fetal parts at all." William B. Hurlbut, Robert George, and Markus Grompe, "Seeking Consensus: A Clarification and Defense of Altered Nuclear Transfer," *Hastings Center Report* 36, no. 5 (2006): 45–50 n.21, http://www.alterednucleartransfer.com/?page=4a&view=7 (4 Nov. 2009).

270. Hurlbut, George, and Grompe, "Seeking Consensus," 45–50.

271. George and Tollefsen, *Embryo*, 212–13; referring to E. Christian Brugger, "Moral Stem Cells," *First Things* 163 (May 2006), 15–17 n.6, as one such bioethicist who believes ANT-OAR produces severely crippled human embryos.

272. Peter J. Colosi, "Personhood, the Soul, and Non-Conscious Human Beings: Some Critical Reflections on Recent Forms of Argumentation within the Pro-Life Movement," *Proceedings of the 17th Life and Learning Conference*, ed. Joseph Koterski, (Washington D.C., University Faculty for Life, 2007), 281; citing David L. Schindler, "A Response to the Joint Statement 'Production of Pluripotent Stem Cells by Oocyte Assisted Reprogramming,'" *Communio: International Catholic Review* 32 (2005): 369–80.

273. Colosi, "Personhood, the Soul, and Non-Conscious Human Beings," 282; citing Schindler, "A Response to the Joint Statement," 369–80.

274. Colosi, "Personhood, the Soul, and Non-Conscious Human Beings," 283–85.

275. God sustains creation in existence and the laws of nature, but he is not strictly bound to follow the laws of the material universe. He may make an exception and suspend the laws of nature and perform a miracle. God is bound to follow the moral laws know by right reason since they participate in his own Eternal Law founded upon his own divine nature. See also CCC, no. 271.

276. DPA, no. 19. See also EV, no. 60.

277. DPA, no. 6.

278. E. Christian Brugger, "ANT-OAR: A Morally Acceptable Means for Deriving Pluripotent Stem Cells: A Reply to Criticisms," *Communio: International Catholic Review* 32, no. 4 (2005): 753–69; citing Hurlbut, George, and Grompe, "Seeking Consensus," 45–50, notes the distinction between absolute and moral certainty and concludes "the the entity created through ANT-OAR is not an embryo."

279. EV, no. 61.

280. Joseph Ratzinger, *Christianity and the Crisis of Cultures*, trans. Brian McNeil (San Francisco: Ignatius Press, 2006), 71.

281. Colosi, "Personhood, the Soul, and Non-Conscious Human Beings," 286–87.

282. DP, no. 30, n.49, "The new techniques of this kind are, for example, the use of human parthenogenesis, altered nuclear transfer (ANT) and Oocyte assisted reprogramming (OAR)."

283. DP, no. 30.

284. George and Tollefsen, *Embryo*, 213.

285. William Hurlbut, "Altered Nuclear Transfer: Is it the Answer for the Embryonic Stem Cell Research Debate?" interview by Jennifer Lahl, *Center for Bioethics and*

Culture Network (11 November 2006), http://www.cbc-network.org/2006/11/ant-an-answer-to-the-embryonic-stem-cell-debate/ (4 Nov. 2009).

286. Diane Beeson, Testimony before Congressional Hearings, House Government Reform Subcommittee on Criminal Justice, Drug Policy and Human Resources – Hearing on Stem Cell Research, 7 March 2006, 1–2, http://handsoffourovaries.com/images/beesontestimony.pdf (20 Nov. 2009).

287. Beeson, Testimony before Congressional Hearing on Stem Cell Research, 3.

288. The author's personal notes taken from a lecture by Jennifer Lahl, National Director of the Center for Bioethics and Culture Network, at the Florida Respect Life Conference in Orlando, FL, 17 October 2009. More than one woman complained to Ms. Lahl that they were subject to "bait and switch."

289. Judy Norsigian, in a paper presented to the Subcommittee on Criminal Justice, Drug Policy and Human Resources, Government Reform Committee, U.S. House of Representatives – Hearing on Human Cloning and Embryonic Stem Cell Research after Seoul: Examination Exploitation, Fraud, and Ethical Problems in Research, 7 March 2006, http://frwebgate.access.gpo.gov/cgi-bin/getdoc.cgi?dbname=109_house_hearings& docid=f:29580.wais (20 Nov. 2009); citing David Magnus, Mildred K. Cho, "A Commentary on Oocyte Donation for Stem Cell Research in South Korea," *The American Journal of Bioethics* 6, no. 1 (January 2006): W23–W24.

290. "Adverse reaction to this [Lupron] and similar drugs include the following: anemia; high blood pressure; formation of blood clots that could potentially cause damage to vital organs; fluid accumulation in the limbs; thyroid enlargement; liver function abnormality; joint, muscle and bone pain; chest pain; difficulty in swallowing; intestinal bleeding; headaches and migraines; dizziness and blackouts; memory disturbances; depression; anxiety; numbness; swelling of hands; constipation; nausea; vomiting; diarrhea; and vision abnormalities." See Norsigian, Hearing on Human Cloning.

291. Norsigian, Hearing on Human Cloning.

292. Norsigian, Hearing on Human Cloning; citing Marc J. Steigenga, et al., "Evolutionary conserved structures as indicators of medical risks: increased incidence of cervical ribs after ovarian hyperstimulation in mice," *Animal Biology* 56, no. 1 (2006): 63–68.

293. "Eggsplotation" is a term coined by Jennifer Lahl, National Director of The Center for Bioethics and Culture Network, to describe the bait and switch and other unethical practices employed by human egg hunters to meet the needs of biotechnological research for cloning research. For more information see www.cbc-network.org.

294. Norsigian, Hearing on Human Cloning.

295. Hands Off Our Ovaries, *Mission Statement*, http://www.handsoffourovaries.com/mission.htm (20 Nov. 2009).

296. *World Egg Bank Launches Medical Tourism Program*, 2 November 2009.

297. Beeson, Testimony before Congressional Hearing on Stem Cell Research, 5.

298. DP, no. 37.

299. Magdalena Zernica-Goetz, "Patterning the Embryo: The First Spatial Decisions in the Life of a Mouse," *Development*, vol. 129 (2002): 815–29; Maureen L. Condic, "White Paper: When Does Human Life Begin? A Scientific Perspective," *Westchester Institute* 1 (2008), http://www.westchesterinstitute.net/images/wi_whitepaper_life_print.pdf (20 Nov. 2009); Klekamp, "Woman and Actual Challenges of Bioethics," 2; citing Gunter Rager, "Der Beginn des individuellen Menschseins aus embryologischer Sicht," *Zeitschrift für Lebensrecht*, 13. Jg. (2004): 66–74.

300. George and Tollefsen, *Embryo*, 38–39.

301. Klekamp, "Woman and Actual Challenges of Bioethics," 2.

302. Klekamp, "Woman and Actual Challenges of Bioethics," 2.
303. DP, no. 22; quoting EV, no. 63.
304. DP, no.22.
305. EV, no. 63. See also DV, no. I.2.
306. Klekamp, "Woman and Actual Challenges of Bioethics," 4.
307. Klekamp, "Woman and Actual Challenges of Bioethics," 6.

Chapter 10
Homosexuality and Same-Sex Marriage

Introduction

In a post-modern culture it is a virtue to define nothing: "Postmodernity runs away from the 'clear and distinct ideas' of Cartesian civilization and delights in semantic fog. . . . Clear definitions, so the experts say, limit the choice of interpretations, in effect 'impose' a single interpretation of language and thus contradict the central norm of the new culture: the right to choose." [1]

Today the only offense lies in holding moral absolutes; the only sin is the unpardonable fault of imposing your beliefs on someone. In this climate the Catholic Church's condemnation of same-sex marriage and description of the homosexual tendency as an "objective disorder" is not so much controversial, it is simply incomprehensible. As society becomes more and more accepting of the homosexual lifestyle, those who oppose same sex marriage are perceived as bigoted, unsympathetic and potential perpetrators of hate-crimes. We need only recall the 2009 debacle concerning the former Miss California USA, Carrie Prejean, who came under national criticism for stating her views on marriage, to be reminded of the social repercussion of publically declaring that the conferral of a marriage license should be limited to a man and a woman.

In the face of this storm of social upheaval, Catholics are called to stay the course. To better distinguish good from bad discrimination let us recall a book that many of us read in high school: *To Kill a Mockingbird*. Therein, we witness true discrimination and social castigation at its worse. Atticus Finch, a Southern lawyer in the early twentieth century is faced with the moral option of defending a black man, Tom Robinson, accused of rape. What made his case so difficult was the cultural acceptance of segregation of blacks and whites, and of the ban on interracial marriage and laws against miscegenation. Tom Robinson's real crime, according to the society in which he lived, was *not* attempted rape; rather, his offense lay in his supposed rape of a white woman. Throughout the tale, we witness the persecution of Tom Robinson and his family, of the black community, of Atticus Finch and his children who defied their culture's prejudice in defense of the equal human dignity of a black man.[2]

Many today would liken Tom Robinson's unfair discriminatory treatment to the situation of homosexual couples, claiming that both Atticus Finch and gay rights activists fight for intrinsic human rights in the face of irrational bigotry. In the minds of gay rights activists there is no difference between laws banning interracial marriage and same-sex marriage. However, the situation is otherwise. What Atticus Finch opposed were laws and cultural notions that contravene the nature of the human person. Laws against miscegenation were originally based on the false notion that non-Caucasian cultures were sub-human. One only needs to read Thomas Jefferson's *Notes on the State of Virginia* to be reminded that the primary argument for black slavery was that blacks were not fully human and, therefore, not eligible for the rights and privileges afforded whites.[3]

The Catholic Church has always condemned slavery as inconsistent with human dignity, criticizing the "perversity" of mankind whose "absolute forgetfulness of our common nature, and of human dignity, and the likeness of God stamped upon us all" caused the "calamity of slavery."[4] As the Church taught, and as society later came to accept, all human beings share a common humanity, origin and destiny and by virtue of this fact, have equal human dignity.[5] In this light, human beings, regardless of race, have a natural right to marry.

However, human freedom is oriented to seeking that which is good and true. God created marriage "with its own nature, essential properties and purpose"[6] and, so, it is limited to a union of a man and woman open to the procreation of children. It is on this ground that the so-called similarity between interracial and same-sex marriage breaks down. A man and a woman of two different ethnic backgrounds can marry because of the complementarity of their sexes shown in their inherent potential to conceive children. This can never be the case between a man and a man, or a woman and a woman. *In vitro* fertilization cannot cure the lack of complementarity and inherent sterility of the feigned conjugal acts of homosexual partners. Their recourse to artificial reproductive technology compounds the problem by denying the fundamental right of every child to be conceived beneath his or her mother's heart.[7]

Giving legal sanction to homosexual co-habitation and calling it "marriage" can never transform it into "that intimate union of life in complementarity between a man and a woman which is constituted in the freely contracted and publically expressed indissoluble bond of matrimony, and is open to the transmission of life."[8]

There is no objective comparison between interracial marriage and same-sex unions. Laws in defense of marriage protect society from post-modern deconstruction of human nature. Atticus Finch fought against the injustice imposed by society on persons of complementary sexuality able to procreate and found a family but because the pigment of their skin didn't match they ran afoul of a eugenic social policy against miscegenation. Today the Mockingbirds are those who defend society against persons without sexual complementarity who are inherently in-fecund and who seek to bankrupt marriage, inflating it with counterfeit currency. Post-modernist cultural revolutionaries through gender mainstreaming are attempting the "deconstruction of man-woman anthropological complementarity":

> De facto, however, gender training is most often at the service of postmodern ideology: motherhood, fatherhood, male and female identity, the spousal relationship between married man and woman, the male/female anthropological complementarity are treated as basic stereotypes to deconstruct.[9]

Against all those who would attempt to deconstruct reality the Catholic Church upholds creation as a given; all creatures, great and small, have a nature given to them by their Creator[10] which they must not contradict by their behavior. Therefore, the Church has always recognized the validity of sacramental interracial marriages while at the same time condemning acts of sodomy as contrary to the personalist laws inscribed in human nature. It has reiterated its teaching on homosexuality in four major documents: *Declaration on Certain Question Concerning Sexual Ethics (Persona Humana)* (1975); *Letter to the Bishops On the Pastoral Care of Homosexual Persons* (1986); *Some Consideration Concerning the Response to Legislative Proposals on the Non-Discrimination of Homosexual Persons* (1992); *Some Considerations Regarding Proposals to give Recognition to Unions between Homosexual Persons* (2003).

In each of these documents, the Church's teaching is clear and concise: The homosexual inclination does not fulfill human nature. It is anything but a mutual and complementary gift of self open to the procreation of children. Although the genesis of homosexual inclinations remains a mystery,[11] nonetheless, it is not natural to the human condition but, instead, it is "an objective disorder."[12] In the following pages these teachings of the Catholic Church will be explored with the hope of lifting some of the post-modern miasma that shrouds the cultural war over the legal recognition of so called same sex marriage and gender mainstreaming.

The Key Magisterial Document:
On the Pastoral Care of Homosexual Persons (1986)

The Letter to the Bishops of the Catholic Church On the Pastoral Care of Homosexual Persons, published by the Congregation for the Doctrine of the Faith in 1986 clarified and reaffirmed the distinction it made earlier in *Declaration on Certain Questions Concerning Sexual Ethics (Persona Humana)* (1975) between "the homosexual condition or tendency and individual homosexual actions" and stated that while the inclination itself is not sinful, it is a "strong tendency ordered towards an intrinsic moral evil; and thus the inclination itself must be seen as *an objective disorder.*"[13]

This document makes clear that any scriptural exegesis that condones homosexual acts is erroneous and points to the numerous instances in which Scripture clearly and unequivocally condemns homosexual behavior.[14] Scripture reveals God's plan for man and woman that from the beginning included his design that they be fruitful and multiply; therefore to use one's sexual capacity to deliberately frustrate this plan contradicts human nature and is immoral.

> To choose someone of the same sex for one's sexual activity is to annul the rich symbolism and meaning, not to mention the goals, of the Creator's sexual design. Homosexual activity is not a complementary union, able to transmit life; and so it thwarts the call to a life of that form of self-giving which the Gospel says is the essence of Christian living. . . . [W]hen they engage in homosexual activity they confirm within themselves a disordered sexual inclination which is essentially self-indulgent.[15]

Throughout the Letter, Catholics are reminded that homosexual sex acts are sinful and, while bishops and pastors must reach out to homosexual persons, they are to do so in the spirit of truth and refuse to be pressured from groups that seek to condone homosexuality as good or at least neutral. Because of the threat to society and the harm caused to the family by the acceptance of homosexuality, the Church has a duty to the truth:

> It is true that her clear position cannot be revised by pressure from civil legislation or the trend of the moment. . . . She is also aware that the view that homosexual activity is equivalent to, or as acceptable as, the sexual expression of conjugal love, has a direct impact on society's understanding of the nature and rights of the family and puts them in jeopardy.[16]

The Catholic Church condemns violence against homosexuals in speech or action as "deplorable" and calls for respect for the "intrinsic dignity of each person"[17] and "deserves condemnation from the Church's pastors wherever it occurs."[18] The response to such violent behavior, however, must not be used to legitimize legal recognition of the homosexual lifestyle. When society degenerates to the point at which homosexuality is condoned, defended or legalized, one should not be shocked if it causes a backlash of further acts of violence against persons with a homosexual inclination:

> [W]hen civil legislation is introduced to protect behavior to which no one has any conceivable right, neither the Church nor society at large should be surprised when other distorted notions and practices gain ground, and irrational and violent reactions increase.[19]

Certain groups claim that for many persons the homosexual tendency was not chosen and so it must be in some sense innate and, therefore, for them to act in accord with their tendency or orientation is natural. The Church responds that homosexual sex acts are not natural, they are not intended by God and they do not fulfill human nature. Moreover, homosexual person are able to control themselves and are called to live chastely with the help of God's grace:

> What is at all costs to be avoided is the unfounded and demeaning assumption that the sexual behavior of homosexual persons is always and totally compulsive and therefore inculpable. What is essential is that the fundamental liberty which characterizes the human person and gives him his dignity be recognized as belonging to the homosexual person as well.[20]

Homosexual persons are called to choose to abstain from homosexual behavior and unite their sufferings to Christ "by joining whatever sufferings and difficulties they experience in virtue of their condition to the sacrifice of the Lord's cross."[21] Through frequent reception of the sacrament of Penance, they will be able to "convert their lives more fully to His Way."[22]

Bishops are charged to speak truthfully to homosexual persons in their care: "Only what is true can ultimately be pastoral."[23] Bishops and pastors are directed to separate themselves from groups who do not uphold the Church's teaching on homosexuality:

> No authentic pastoral program will include organizations in which homosexual persons associate with each other without clearly stating that homosexual activity is immoral. A truly pastoral approach will appreciate the need for homosexual persons to avoid the near occasions of sin.[24]

> All support should be withdrawn from any organizations which seek to undermine the teaching of the Church, which are ambiguous about it, or which neglect it entirely.[25]

In the face of the cultural promotion and legal toleration of the homosexual lifestyle Church leaders must stay the course and remain true to her teachings and "keep as their uppermost concern the responsibility to defend and promote family life."[26]

Magisterial Teaching and Theological Reflection

On the Pastoral Care of the Homosexual Person addressed the "overly benign interpretation" given to homosexuality following its publication of *Declaration on Certain Question Concerning Sexual Ethics* (1975) that some erroneously claimed taught that the homosexual tendency was itself "neutral, or even good."[27] As Father John Harvey discusses, it is far from a mere restatement of *Declaration on Certain Questions of Sexual Ethics*. It resists the contemporary trend to change "the traditional teaching of the Church on sexuality and the family . . . based on empirical data: for example, that the Church should allow remarriage after divorce because the practice of sexual abstinence is practically impossible for most of the faithful." [28] Instead, it encourages the recognition of the basic dignity of each human person and their ability to freely choose and take responsibility for their actions. The "fundamental liberty" that the Church calls all to exercise is not the self-destructive "sexual liberation" of this generation, but a true freedom, the freedom to do what is right and good.[29]

Declaration on Certain Questions of Sexual Ethics was the Church's first response to the sexual revolution of the 1960's: "In the present period, the corruption of morals has increased, and one of the most serious indications of this corruption is the unbridled exaltation of sex."[30] The Church saw the confusion generated among the faithful by those who taught and favored "a licentious hedonism" and sought to reaffirm her teachings.[31] In response to the growing influence of postmodern ideology and the assumption that human nature can be redefined by personal choice, the Church states that "[i]n moral matters man cannot make value judgments according to his personal whim: 'In the depths of his conscience, man detects a law which he does not impose on himself, but which holds him to obedience. . . . For man has in his heart a law written by God. To obey it is the very dignity of man; according to it he will be judged.'"[32] The law written by God into human nature is unchangeable and only through respect for this law can the dignity of the human person be respected. Cultural conditions and customs may change, but man's essential nature remains the same.[33]

The earmark of postmodern moral relativity that permeates the sexual liberation is its insistence upon a lack of moral absolutes, that "anything goes," that is there is no right and wrong, and the only sin one can commit is to insist that there is an objective reality.

> Hence, those many people are in error who today assert that one can find neither in human nature nor in the revealed law any absolute and immutable norm to serve for particular action other than the one which expresses itself in the general law of charity and respect for human dignity.[34]

> These principles and norms in no way owe their origin to a certain type of culture, but rather to knowledge of the divine law and of human nature. They therefore cannot be considered as having become out of date or doubtful under the pretext that a new culture situation has arisen.[35]

Issues of marriage and family are not a social construct, but rather, part of God's plan for humankind. The Church condemns sexual relations outside of marriage because they "cannot ensure, in sincerity and fidelity, the interpersonal relationship between a man and a woman, nor can they project this relationship from whims and caprices."[36] Thus, sexual union "is only legitimate if a definitive community of life has been established between the man and the woman."[37] Premarital relations deny both the exclusivity of the marital unity and present a detriment to the procreative aspect.[38]

In the same vein, the Church observed the growing trend to "judge indulgently, and even to excuse completely, homosexual relations between certain people."[39] It noted two possible causes of homosexuality:

A distinction is drawn, and it seems with some reason, between homosexuals whose tendency comes from a false education, from a lack of normal sexual development, from habit, from bad example, or from other similar causes, and is transitory or at least not incurable; and homosexuals who are definitively such because of some kind of innate instinct or a pathological constitution judged to be incurable.[40]

The Church observes that many view homosexuality as in some way innate in some persons and so condone "homosexual relations within a sincere communion of life and love analogous to marriage, insofar as such homosexuals feel incapable of enduring a solitary life."[41]

To this claim the Church responds that persons with homosexual tendencies must be treated "with understanding and sustained in the hope of overcoming their personal difficulties and their inability to fit into society."[42] Furthermore, their personal "culpability will be judged with prudence" and that although Scripture condemns homosexuality as a "serious depravity," it "does not of course permit us to conclude that all those who suffer from this anomaly are personally responsible for it."[43]

Declaration on Certain Questions of Sexual Ethics explains that the homosexual inclination is not sinful *per se* but those who act upon those inclinations commit serious sin if they do so knowingly and willingly:

But no pastoral method can be employed which would give moral justification to these acts on the grounds that they would be consonant with the conditions of such people. For, according to the objective moral order, homosexual relations are acts which lack an essential and indispensable finality. In Sacred Scripture they are condemned as a serious depravity and even presented as the sad consequence of rejecting God. This judgment of Scripture does not of course permit us to conclude that all who suffer from this anomaly are personally responsible for it, but it does attest to the fact that homosexual acts are intrinsically disordered and can in no case be approved of.[44]

Some have criticized (or praised, as the case may be) this document for appearing to be more tolerant of homosexuality than later documents by the Congregation for the Doctrine of the Faith. For instance, Paul Hasall, who maintains the website, "People with a History: An Online Guide to Lesbian, Gay, Bisexual and Transsexual History," provides a list of all Catholic Church documents dating from early Church history that address the issue of homosexuality. He describes *Declaration on Certain Questions of Sexual Ethics* as the first official Church document to "comprehend the notion of 'sexual orientation'." He concludes that the Church held therein that "homosexual acts are wrong but the homosexual 'condition' is morally neutral, a position later attacked in the 1986 'Letter to the Bishops of the Catholic Church on the Pastoral Care of Homosexual Persons,' which discussed homosexuality as 'objectively disordered.'"[45]

The Catholic Church takes a pastoral approach with those who suffer from homosexual inclinations and notes that such people are not necessarily "personally responsible" for that inclination. However, it does not follow that their "condition" is morally neutral. Furthermore, when *On the Pastoral Care of Homosexual Persons* was written in 1986, homosexual political activists had made significant gains in law and culture and more needed to be said. The Church's position on the issues is consistent, and becomes increasingly more specific in later documents in response to new errors and pernicious cultural norms and legal precedents.

Legal Developments

The same year *On the Pastoral Care of the Human Person* was released homosexual activists in the United States had championed their cause before the highest court in the land. In *Bowers v. Hardwick* (1986) the United States Supreme Court upheld Georgia's criminal sodomy law stating that there was no fundamental right under the United States' Constitution to engage in homosexual sodomy. Such conduct, they said, was not "deeply rooted in the nation's history or tradition" nor was it "implicit in the concept of ordered liberty"[46] nor was such conduct protected from criminal sanction just because it occurred in the privacy of the home.[47] However, *Bowers v. Hardwick* was not a unanimous opinion, four of the nine Supreme Court Justices dissented, and within a decade the position of the Supreme Court would change significantly.

By 1996 homosexual political activists had made significant gains forcing their view upon many localities in the United States that homosexual proclivities were similar to race, creed and color and that not only must criminal sodomy laws be repealed but that homosexuals needed societal compensation for past discrimination in the way of affirmative action plans such as quota job hires and education placements, etc. In the state of Colorado a referendum was placed on the ballot to repeal any and all county or municipal affirmative action plans and special rights for the homosexual minority. In 1992 Colorado's electorate passed Amendment 2 which read:

> Neither the State of Colorado, through any of its branches or departments, nor any of its agencies, political subdivisions, municipalities or school districts, shall enact, adopt or enforce any statute, regulation, ordinance or policy whereby homosexual, lesbian or bisexual orientation, conduct, practices or relationships shall constitute or otherwise be the basis of or entitle any person or class of persons to have or claim any minority status, quota preferences, protected status or claim of discrimination. This Section of the Constitution shall be in all respects self-executing.[48]

The Supreme Court of Colorado ruled the Amendment 2 infringed upon the fundamental right of homosexuals to participate in the political process and was in violation of the Colorado and United States Constitutions.[49] The United States

Supreme Court affirmed the decision of Colorado's high court in its decision, *Romer v. Evans*, stating that Amendment 2 "nullifies specific legal protection for this targeted class in all transactions in housing, sale of real estate, insurance, health and welfare services, private education, and employment."[50] Amendment 2, the United States Supreme Court said, would impose a "broad and undifferentiated disability on a single named group" and that the rationale for the law is "inexplicable by anything but animus toward the class it affects; it lacks a rational relationship to legitimate state interests."[51]

Three Justices dissented and in their joint opinion stated that the Majority mistakes a cultural struggle for a fit of spite and that Amendment 2 was but "a modest attempt by seemingly tolerant Coloradans to preserve traditional sexual mores against the efforts of a political powerful minority to revise those mores through use of the laws." [52] These Justices argued the only denial of equal treatment homosexuals in Colorado have suffered is "[t]hey many not obtain preferential treatment without amending the State Constitution. That is to say, the principle underlying the Court's opinion is that one who is accorded equal treatment under the laws, but cannot as readily as others obtain preferential treatment under the laws, has been denied equal protection of the laws."[53] Justice Scalia, writing for the Dissent, characterized the Majority's opinion as political grandstanding, not sound jurisprudence:

> Today's opinion has no foundation in American constitutional law, and barely pretends to. The people of Colorado have adopted an entirely reasonable provision which does not even disfavor homosexuals in any substantive sense, but merely denies them preferential treatment. Amendment 2 is designed to prevent piecemeal deterioration of the sexual morality favored by a majority of Coloradans, and is not only an appropriate means to that legitimate end, but a means that Americans have employed before. Striking it down is an act, not of judicial judgment, but of political will.[54]

The Response of the Church to These Legal Developments

Published in 1992, the Congregation for the Doctrine of the Faith (CDF) penned *Some Consideration Concerning the Response to Legislative Proposals on the Non-Discrimination of Homosexual Persons* in response to the growing pressure to grant affirmative action and prefatory legal recognition based on a homosexual sexual orientation. Homosexual activists argued that just as in the past the benign characteristics of race, religion and skin color gave occasion for invidious discrimination so today homosexual orientation provides occasion for similarly bigoted discrimination. The Church countered, saying engaging in homosexual sex acts is not comparable to simply being a member of a particular race or religion.

The CDF reiterated its teaching that homosexual affective inclinations are an "objective disorder," and homosexual sex acts are "'intrinsically disordered' and 'in no case to be approved of.'"[55] It pointed out that not all discrimination is bigoted and rejected the claim "that any and all criticism of or reservations about homosexual people, their activity and lifestyle, are simply diverse forms of unjust discrimination."[56] On the contrary, putting homosexual sex acts on a par with the conjugal intimacy of married men and women puts in jeopardy the fundamental rights of the family.

Homosexuality is not a benign characteristic like religion, race or skin color, rather it is an "objective disorder" that "evokes moral concern."[57] As such, it cannot and should not be granted special protection by civil law. The purpose of civil law is to protect and foster the common good. Certain laws prohibiting homosexuals from involvement in certain aspects of society—"the placement of children for adoption or foster care, in employment of teachers or athletic coaches, and in military recruitment"[58]—stem from society's interest in promoting the common good. Such discrimination is therefore not unjust or unwarranted.

Like all other human beings, homosexual persons are owed respect by virtue of their human dignity. Thus, they have the same right to housing and employment common to all other persons. However, these rights are not inalienable and can be abrogated as "in the case of contagious or mentally ill persons, in order to protect the common good." [59]

Creating a non-discrimination policy based on homosexual orientation essentially creates a right to homosexuality that does not exist. No one has a right to live out an objective disorder.[60] As an aside, in little less than twenty years after *Some Consideration Concerning the Response to Legislative Proposals on the Non-Discrimination of Homosexual Persons* was published the right to live out a gay lifestyle received fulsome support nationally and internationally from the President of the United States in his address of June 2009 to the LGBT community.

> At the international level, I have joined efforts at the United Nations to decriminalize homosexuality around the world. Here at home, I continue to support measures to bring the full spectrum of equal rights to LGBT Americans. These measures include enhancing hate crimes laws, supporting civil unions and Federal rights for LGBT couples, outlawing discrimination in the workplace, ensuring adoption rights, and ending the existing "Don't Ask, Don't Tell" policy in a way that strengthens our Armed Forces and our national security.[61]

The second reason why homosexuality is not comparable to race, sex or age is because, unlike these traits, it is not evident unless made obvious by the practicing homosexual. One cannot be discriminated against unless one makes obvious a reason for the discrimination. The woman who cannot get a job because she is a woman can claim discrimination because she is obviously, a woman. However, unless a practicing homosexual tells the potential employer about his or her sexual life no one will be the wiser and no basis for discrimination can exist on the ground of sexual orientation. Cases of discrimination rarely arise among homosexuals who seek to live chaste lives, while those who publicize their sexual orientation are typically those who believe homosexuality to be a neutral, if not good trait. Giving special protection to homosexuals or requiring affirmative hiring practices could also encourage heterosexual persons to claim or practice homosexuality so as to "exploit the provisions of the law," warned the CDF.[62]

When issues of law and public policy arise, Church authorities are required to assess each provision to determine how it would affect the rights of the family with regard to the adoption of children and the provision of foster care, the conferral of an equivalent status on homosexual unions with respect to public housing "or by entitling the homosexual partner to the privileges of employment which could include such things as 'family' participation in the health benefits given to employees."[63]

Even when proposed legislation offers Church institutions exemptions from affirmative action proposals and laws favoring the homosexual agenda, Church authorities cannot remain neutral or support such measures. The Church's duty to society prohibits it from remaining uninvolved in issues of public morality, especially where the family is concerned.[64]

More Legal Developments

In 2003 homosexual activists again marshaled their political and legal resources and brought before the United States Supreme Court an appeal from a criminal sodomy conviction in the state of Texas. There were three issues presented in *Lawrence v. Texas*: Whether a law which criminalizes homosexual sodomy but not heterosexual sodomy violates the Fourteenth Amendment guarantee of equal protection of the laws? Whether a criminal conviction for homosexual sodomy in one's home violates one's interests in liberty and privacy under the Due Process clause of the Fourteenth Amendment? Whether *Bowers v. Hardwick* should be overturned?[65]

Justice Kennedy, who wrote the opinion for the Majority, addressed the first issue, stating that "the State is not omnipresent in the home," and that there are other spheres of our lives it should not dominate: "Freedom extends beyond spatial bounds. Liberty presumes an autonomy of self that includes freedom of thought, belief, expression, and certain intimate conduct."[66]

Coming to grips with the long standing legal tradition of anti-sodomy laws in the United States Justice Kennedy situated those laws in a conceptual category more inclusive of mainstream America contraceptive practice and which faced similar prejudice based on religious prudery. Anti-sodomy laws, he opined, were really aimed at all non-procreative sexual activity including but not limited to laws prohibiting contraception: "[E]arly sodomy laws were not directed at homosexuals as such but instead sought to prohibit nonprocreative sexual activity more generally"[67] and such "condemnation has been shaped by religious beliefs, conceptions of right and acceptable behavior, and respect for the traditional family."[68] Therefore, *Bowers v. Hardwick*, was "not correct when it was decided, and it is not correct today" and is overruled.[69]

Just as miscegenation laws were based on a widespread cultural consensus that the Supreme Court struck down, so anti-sodomy laws are based on a similar prejudice and misunderstanding of sexual morality as licit only when limited to marital procreative purpose:

> Our prior cases make two propositions abundantly clear. First, the fact that the governing majority in a State has traditionally viewed a particular practice as immoral is not a sufficient reason for upholding a law prohibiting the practice; neither history nor tradition could save a law prohibiting miscegenation from constitutional attack. Second, individual decisions by married persons, concerning the intimacies of their physical relationship, even when not intended to produce offspring, are a form of liberty protected by the Due Process Clause of the Fourteenth Amendment. Moreover, this protection extends to intimate choices of unmarried as well as married persons.[70]

Writing for the three dissenting Justices, Scalia began by noting that what is good for the goose is good for the gander; the reasoning the Majority used to overturn *Bowers v. Hardwick* will apply equally well to overturn *Roe v. Wade* one day:

> Today's approach to *stare decisis* invites us to overrule an erroneously decided precedent (including an 'intensely divisive' decision) if: (1) its foundations have been 'ero[ded]' by subsequent decisions; (2) it has been subject to substantial and continuing criticism, ibid.; and (3) it has not induced 'individual or societal reliance' that counsels against overturning. The problem is that *Roe* itself—which today's majority surely has no disposition to overrule— satisfies these conditions to at least the same degree as *Bowers*.[71]

The Majority opinion has not ruled that homosexual sodomy is a fundamental right under the Constitution of the United States, Scalia said. All they determined was that Texas's sodomy statute has no rational relationship to any legitimate goal of the police powers of the state.[72] Scalia denounced the Majority's ideological motivation: It is "the product of a court which is the product of a law-profession culture, that has largely signed on to the so-called homosexual agenda, by which I mean the agenda promoted by some homosexual activists directed at eliminating the moral opprobrium that has traditionally attached to homosexual conduct."[73] The Supreme Court of the United States, he said, has "taken sides in the cultural war" and views as discriminatory the attempt of a majority of Americans to protect their children from scoutmasters and teachers who openly engage in homosexual conduct because they believe that gay lifestyle to be "immoral and destructive."[74]

Gender Ideology and Same Sex Marriage

The decriminalization of promiscuous homosexual sodomy and constitutional cover for legislative enactments of affirmative action for homosexuals paved the way for legal recognition of homosexual sodomy as a marital act. The prevalence of divorce and contraception in American society began the deconstruction of the institution of marriage. Shorn of its natural endowments, of its vow of life-long fidelity and openness to procreation, the institution of marriage has been reduced in practice to what seems no more than one expression of orgasmic outlet. Why should one expression of libido be entitled to substantial property interests and other sexual preferences be denied? The *Lawrence* court pointed out, the promiscuous and contracepted/non-procreative marital activity of heterosexual couples seem indistinguishable from the activity of homosexual couples.[75]

The laws of several states have been modified to allow same sex marriage because the sexual and procreative practices of heterosexual and homosexual couples seem largely indistinguishable. Both seem simply affective unions not essentially open to procreation. Both have recourse to artificial reproductive technologies in order to take home a baby. Both are not committed to life-long fidelity. So why assign substantial property rights to one and not the other?

Moreover, whether one is homosexual or heterosexual also seems largely a matter of choice to our post-modern elite. After all, gender has replaced sex as the defining feature of human nature for the emerging global culture and "is a prerequisite to overcoming hunger, poverty and disease."[76] Gender is defined as a social construct; today one is heterosexual, tomorrow one may be gay. It all depends on one's choice, they say. The United Nations Development Program (UNDP) Training Kit defines gender as "the social relations between men and women. It refers to the relationship between men and women, boys and girls, and how this is socially constructed. Gender roles are dynamic and change over time."[77] In reply to this brazen example of post-modern deconstruction the Church affirms the importance of the complementarity of the sexes to individuals and society:

> Faced with theories that consider gender identity as merely the cultural and social product of the interaction between the community and the individual, independent of personal sexual identity without any reference to the true meaning of sexuality, the Church does not tire of repeating her teaching: "Everyone, man and woman, should acknowledge and accept his sexual identity. . . . The harmony of the couple and of society depends in part on the way in which the complementarities, needs and mutual support between the sexes are lived out."[78]

In 1999 the Supreme Court of Vermont in *Baker v. Vermont* posed the following legal issues for resolution: "May the State of Vermont exclude same sex couples from the benefits and protections that its laws provide to opposite-sex married couples." It answered, "no," it may not and approved Civil Unions for same-sex couples.[79] The Court rejected the argument that sanctioning same-sex Civil Unions "would diminish society's perception of the link between procreation and child rearing" or that its ruling would "advance the notion that fathers or mothers are mere surplusage to the functions of procreation and child rearing." Why? Because the Court found many couples marry with no thought of having children. So, "if the purpose of the statutory exclusion of same-sex couples is to 'further the link between procreation and child rearing,' it is significantly under-inclusive."[80] Also, a significant number of same-sex couples have conceived children through artificial reproductive technology:

> Thus with or without the marriage sanction, the reality today is that increasing numbers of same-sex couples are employing increasingly efficient assisted-reproductive techniques to conceive and raise children. . . . The Vermont Legislature has not only recognized this reality, but has acted affirmatively to remove legal barriers so that same-sex couples may legally adopt and rear the children conceived through such efforts.[81]

Five years later in *Goodridge v. Department of Public Health* (2003) the Supreme Court of Massachusetts asked if the State may deny the protections, benefits, and obligations conferred by civil marriage to two individuals of the same sex who wish to marry and answered, "no." The court noted that many people have sincerely held religious convictions that urge them to oppose same-sex marriage while others with equally strong religious beliefs are convinced to support it. Be that as it may, it is the function of the court to not meddle in religion but to "define the liberty of all, not to mandate our own moral code."[82]

Revealing a post-modern anthropological, value choice and moral perspective the *Goodridge* court declared that "individual autonomy" was a key constitutional principle and that the choice of whom to marry, including a member of one's own sex, was a momentous act of "self-definition."[83] The court then listed an extensive array of civil rights that attach to civil marriage "touching nearly every aspect of life and death" including but not limited to the following: joint income tax filing, tenancy by the entirety, automatic rights to inherit the property of the deceased spouse, dower, wages owed to the deceased spouse, the right to share in the medical policy of one's spouse, preferential options under a pension system, equitable division of marital property on divorce, the right to bring claims for wrongful death and loss of consortium, presumptions of legitimacy of children born of the marriage, prohibitions against spouses testifying against one another, preferential election to make decision regarding a spouse's health care if he or she is incompetent, the application of predictable rules of child custody, visitation and support, priority to administer the estate of the deceased spouse who dies without a will.[84]

Because so many benefits attach to the civil right to marry the *Goodridge* court declared that to bar an individual from the protections, benefits, and obligations of civil marriage solely because that person would marry a person of the same sex violates the Massachusetts Constitution.[85]

The Response of the Church to These Legal Developments

The Congregation for the Doctrine of the Faith (CDF) responded in 2003 to the growing trend of civil society to grant legal recognition to same-sex marriages by publishing *Considerations regarding Proposals to give Recognition to Unions between Homosexual Persons* wherein it states: "No ideology can erase from the human spirit the certainty that marriage exists solely between a man and a woman."[86] *Considerations* was written to "give direction to Catholic politicians by indicating the approaches to proposed legislation in this area which would be consistent with Christian conscience."[87] Part I of the document reiterates that there can be no right to "homosexual marriage" where there is no ability to fulfill marital duties, i.e., giving of oneself through conjugal relations open to the transmission of new life so as to fulfill the creation mandate: "Be fruitful and multiply."[88]

The CDF refreshed the memory of civil society reminding courts and legislatures that homosexual unions are not even "remotely analogous to God's plan for marriage and family." Sexual intimacy between a man and woman in marriage is both natural and holy, while homosexual acts are contrary to the natural moral law. Marriage by its very nature remains open to life, while homosexual acts are fundamentally closed and incapable of being open to or bringing forth life. Sexual intimacy between a husband and wife "proceed from a genuine affective and sexual complementarity," while homosexual acts do not.[89]

In Part II of *Considerations* the CDF warns if the government's policy is *de facto* tolerance and there is no explicit legal recognition of homosexual unions, politicians must take "discrete and prudent actions" that give witness to the truth. Such actions include stating clearly the immoral nature of same-sex unions; containing these relationships within certain limits to uphold public morality; unmasking how such tolerance is often exploited; and safeguarding children's exposure to such erroneous ideas about marriage and the complementarity between sexes.[90]

The approval or legalization of evil is something far different from the toleration of evil. Should governments grant legal recognition or rights belonging to marriage to so-called homosexual marriage, "clear and emphatic opposition is a duty."[91] One must refrain from "any kind of formal cooperation in the enactment or application of such laws and, as far as possible, from material cooperation on the level of their application and, if necessary, they should exercise the right to conscientious objection."[92]

Part III of *Considerations* notes that the civil law cannot contradict "right reason" and still bind conscience of citizens to obedience. Human laws must conform to the natural law in order to "respect the inalienable rights of every person."[93] Laws in favor of homosexual unions are contrary to right reason. The State cannot grant legal standing to such unions without failing in its duty to promote and defend marriage as an institution essential to the common good.[94]

Homosexual unions are inherently non-fertile, in-fecund and cannot "contribute in a proper way to the procreation and survival of the human race." Therefore there is no reason to grant them the legal protections given to married couples and families. The use of in-vitro fertilization will not cure or alter the inherent biological and anthropological inadequacy of a homosexual union.[95]

Additionally, the absence of sexual complementarity in these unions prevents the normal development of children who would be deprived of the experience of authentic fatherhood or motherhood. Allowing children to be legally adopted by homosexuals would be "gravely immoral" and would amount to "doing violence to these children" by placing them in an environment that is not conducive to their full human development."[96] Allowing homosexuals to adopt children also contravenes the United Nations' *Convention on the Rights of the Child*, as interpreted by the Holy See, by failing to make paramount the "best interests of the child."[97]

The refusal to legally recognize activities that fail to "represent a significant or positive contribution to the development of the human person" cannot violate a person's right to autonomy.[98] Marriage and the family "ensure the succession of generations." Because homosexual unions do not exercise this function for the common good, they do not require or deserve specific legal recognition.[99]

In Part IV of *Considerations* the role of Catholic politicians to oppose legislation that would legalize same-sex marriage is presented in clear and concise terms, that is, a politician must never vote to expand legal recognition to homosexual unions:

> When Legislation in favor of the recognition of homosexual unions is proposed for the first time in a legislative assembly, the Catholic law-maker has a moral duty to express his opposition clearly and publicly and to vote against it. To vote in favor of a law so harmful to the common good is gravely immoral.

> When legislation in favor of the recognition of homosexual unions is already in force, the Catholic politician must oppose it in the ways that are possible for him and make his opposition known; it is his duty to witness to the truth. If it is not possible to repeal such a law completely, the Catholic politician, recalling the indications contained in the Encyclical Letter *Evangelium Vitae*, "could licitly support proposals aimed at limiting the harm done by such a law and at lessening its negative consequences at the level of general opinion and public morality," on condition that his "absolute personal opposition" to such laws was clear and well known and that the danger of scandal was avoided. This does not mean that a more restrictive law in this area could be considered just or even acceptable; rather, it is a question of the legitimate and dutiful attempt to obtain at least the partial repeal of an unjust law when its total abrogation is not possible at the moment.[100]

The document ends by reminding us that good government has a duty to protect marriage "as the basis of the family, the primary unit of society." Granting legal recognition to homosexual unions or placing them on par with marriage would show "approval of deviant behavior" and also obscure the basic values which belong to the common inheritance of humanity. These values—the very bedrock of society—must be faithfully defended at all costs.[101]

Conclusion

The court in *Goodridge v. Department of Public Health* said history and society must yield to a more developed view of invidious discrimination, and not deprive individuals access to the institution of marriage "because of a single trait: skin color in [the past], sexual orientation here."[102] For the court to gloss over the profound differences between invidious discrimination based on a benign characteristic like skin color, and just discrimination based on behavior driven by a sexual desire, leaves one flummoxed.

As a caveat it should be pointed out that this same line of argument could be used to strike down laws that discriminate against behavior based on any sexual preference or fetish. Why should criminal statutes against incest or bestiality be allowed to stand? Why shouldn't animal rights activists be allowed to marry their companion animals or create chimeras to love and marry as one of their spouses? Postmodernist ideology leaves men and women at the turn of twenty-first century with no inalienable rights based on human nature as a given. To deconstruct human nature, male and female sexual complementarity, and every inalienable right does not expand the boundaries of human freedom so much as signals a tremendous shift of power from individual persons to the State. A black-robed elite redefine human nature and marriage with the stroke of a pen while declaring that their job is not to mandate their own moral code.[103]

Notes

1. Marguerite A. Peeters, *The Globalization of the Western Cultural Revolution: Key Concepts, Operational Mechanisms*, trans. Benedict Kobus (Brussels: Institute for Intercultural Dialogue Dynamics, 2007), 35.

2. See generally Harper Lee, *To Kill a Mockingbird* (New York, NY: Warner Books, 1982).

3. See generally Thomas Jefferson, *Notes on the State of Virginia* (New York, NY: Penguin Classics, 1999).

4. Leo XIII, *On the Abolition of Slavery* (1888), no. 4, http://www.ewtn.com/library/encyc/l13abl.html (26 Aug. 2009).

5. CCC, no. 1934.

6. Sacred Congregation for the Doctrine of the Faith, *Some Considerations Regarding Proposals to Give Recognition to Unions Between Homosexual Persons* (2003), no. 2, http://www.vatican.va/roman_curia/congregations/cfaith/documents/rc_con_cfaith_doc _20030731_homosexual-unions_en.html (21 Nov. 2009) (hereafter CDF, *Recognition to Unions*).

7. DV, no. 2.A.1.

8. Holy See, *Charter of the Rights of the Family*, preamble, B, http://www.vatican.va/roman_curia/pontifical_councils/family/documents/rc_pc_family_ doc_19831022_family-rights_en.html (21 Nov. 2009).

9. Peeters, *Globalization of the Western Cultural Revolution*, 152, 155.

10. Gen. 1:27.

11. CCC, no. 2357.

12. PCHP, no. 3.

13. PCHP, no. 3 (emphasis added).

14. PCHP, no. 5–6.

15. PCHP, no. 7.

16. PCHP, no. 9.

17. PCHP, no. 10.

18. PCHP, no. 10.

19. PCHP, no. 10.

20. PCHP, no. 11.

21. PCHP, no. 12.

22. PCHP, no. 12.

23. PCHP, no. 15.

24. PCHP, no. 15.

25. PCHP, no. 17.

26. PCHP, no. 17.

27. PH, no. 3.

28. John F. Harvey, *The Homosexual Person* (San Francisco: Ignatius Press, 1987), 15.

29. PCHP, no. 11.

30. PH, no. 1.

31. PH, no. 1.

32. PH, no.3; citing GS, no. 16.

33. PH, no. 3.

34. PH, no. 4.

35. PH, no. 5.

36. PH, no. 7.

37. PH, no. 7.

38. PH, no. 7.

39. PH, no. 8.

40. PH, no. 8.

41. PH, no. 8.

42. PH, no. 8.

43. PH, no. 8.

44. PH, no. 8.

45. Paul Hazel, "Homosexuality and Catholicism: A Partially Annotated Bibliography," *People with a History* 2007, http://www.fordham.edu/halsall/pwh/lgbcathbib.html (21 Nov. 2009).

46. *Bowers v. Hardwick*, 478 U.S. 185,190–94 (1986).

47. *Bowers*, 478 U.S. at 195–96.

48. COLO. CONST. art. II, § 30b. See also *Romer v. Evans*, 517 U.S. 620, 116 S.Ct. 1620 (1996).

49. *Romer*, 517 U.S. at 625–26.

50. *Romer*, 517 U.S. at 629.

51. *Romer*, 517 U.S. at 632.

52. *Romer*, 517 U.S. at 636.

53. *Romer*, 517 U.S. at 638–39.

54. *Romer*, 517 U.S. at 653.

55. PCHP, no. 3.

56. PCHP, no. 9.

57. Sacred Congregation for the Doctrine of the Faith, *Some Considerations Concerning the Response to Legislative Proposals On The Non-Discrimination Of Homosexual Persons*, no. 10 (1992), http://www.ewtn.com/library/curia/cdfhomol.htm (21 Nov. 2009) (hereafter CDF, *Non-Discrimination of Homosexual Persons*).

58. CDF, *Non-Discrimination of Homosexual Persons*, no. 11.

59. CDF, *Non-Discrimination of Homosexual Persons*, no. 12.

60. CDF, *Non-Discrimination of Homosexual Persons*, no. 13.

61. Barack Obama, "Lesbian, Gay, Bisexual and Transgender Month, 2009," White House Press Release, 1 June 2009, http://www.whitehouse.gov/the_press_office/Presidential-Proclamation-LGBT-Pride-Month (17 Aug. 2009).

62. CDF, *Non-Discrimination of Homosexual Persons*, no. 14.

63. CDF, *Non-Discrimination of Homosexual Persons*, no. 15.

64. CDF, *Non-Discrimination of Homosexual Persons*, no. 16.

65. *Lawrence v. Texas*, 539 U.S. 558, 564 (2003).

66. *Lawrence*, 539 U.S. at 562.

67. *Lawrence*, 539 U.S. at 571.

68. *Lawrence*, 539 U.S. at 569.

69. *Lawrence*, 539 U.S. at 578.

70. *Lawrence*, 539 U.S. at 577–78.

71. *Lawrence*, 539 U.S. at 602.

72. *Lawrence*, 539 U.S. at 594.

73. *Lawrence*, 539 U.S. at 602.

74. *Lawrence*, 539 U.S. at 602–3.

75. *Lawrence*, 539 U.S. at 568.

76 .Secretariat of the United Nations, *Millennium Development Goals Report 2005*, 14, http://www.un.org/summit2005/MDGBook.pdf (23 Nov. 2009).

77. United Nations Development Programme, *Introductory Gender Analysis & Gender Training Module for UNDP Staff* (2001), 9, http://arabstates.undp.org/contents/file/GenderMainstreamingTraining.pdf (21 Nov. 2009).

78. Pontifical Council for Justice and Peace, *Compendium of the Social Doctrine of the Church* (Rome: Libreria Editrice Vaticana, 2004), no. 224; citing CCC, no. 2333.

78. *Baker v. Vermont*, 744 A.2d 864, 889 (1999).

79. *Baker*, 744 A.2d at 881.

80. *Baker*, 744 A.2d at 881.

82. *Goodridge v. Department of Public Health*, 798 N.E.2d 941, 948 (2003); citing *Lawrence v. Texas*, 123 S.Ct. 2472, 2480 (2003); quoting *Planned Parenthood of Southeastern Pennsylvania v. Casey*, 539 U.S. 558, 850 (1991).

83. *Goodridge*, 798 N.E. 2d at 948.

84. *Goodridge*, 798 N.E.2d at 955–57.

85. *Goodridge*, 798 N.E.2d at 974.

86. CDF, *Recognition to Unions*, no. 2.

87. CDF, *Recognition to Unions*, no.1.

88. CDF, *Recognition to Unions*, no. 3.

89. CDF, *Recognition to Unions*, no. 4.

90. CDF, *Recognition to Unions*, no. 5

91. CDF, *Recognition to Unions*, no. 5.

92. CDF, *Recognition to Unions*, no. 5.

93. CDF, *Recognition to Unions*, no. 6; citing EV, nos. 71, 72.

94. CDF, *Recognition to Unions*, no. 6

95. CDF, *Recognition to Unions*, no. 7

96. CDF, *Recognition to Unions*, no. 7.

97. CDF, *Recognition to Unions*, no. 7.

98. CDF, *Recognition to Unions*, no. 8.

99. CDF, *Recognition to Unions*, no. 9.

100. CDF, *Recognition to Unions*, no. 10. See also EV, no. 73.

101. CDF, *Recognition to Unions*, no. 11.

101. *Goodridge*, 798 N.E.2d at 958.

103. *Goodridge*, 798 N.E.2d at 948 (2003); citing *Lawrence*, 123 S.Ct. at 2480; quoting *Casey*, 539 U.S. at 850.

Chapter 11
Contraception

Introduction

Who doesn't remember falling in love? The emotional impact of being "smitten" as portrayed, for instance, in the Walt Disney animated film *Bambi* is often humorous: being, that is, utterly "twitterpated," and captivated by the attractiveness of the beloved, hardly being able to talk or talking too much, not being able to think long about anything else, wanting to see and be near that special person all the time. No matter how inarticulate the couple, each lover knows they do not want their love to end or be stolen by another. Each lover knows their love is propelling them to union—complete and total. When embraces are exchanged the question soon arises, at least interiorly—"is this going too far?"

It may be debated what objectively constitutes "going too far," but without question subjectively every lover longs to go there. They find themselves rushing down currents of deep feeling, afraid to capsize, yet not really wanting to stop; to be swept along, to give in and go over the emotional waterfalls, to stop fighting the current and give in, heedless of the consequences. This is the nature of romance and those who have not felt its pull and emotional power have not experienced sensual love. The Greeks called it *Eros,* and embodied it in a deity who substantiated this transcendent quality and truth about human nature. The Greeks believed man and woman were incomplete in themselves and the attraction of the two halves drew and bound them together into a whole through a fusion of psychic energy.

The last thing lovers want to do is to stop short of complete union, although stopping short is precisely the test of their ability to harness this tremendous energy for domestic purposes. Not wanting to stop, but desiring to go "all the way," bespeaks a truth about human sexuality—lovers want to give themselves completely to their beloved, to hold nothing of themselves back and to see the beloved delight in receiving them and giving themselves in return.

Imagine two lovers who saved their virginity for marriage and then, on their honeymoon, the husband were to initiate intercourse and then feebly to withdraw at the last moment before the climax (*coitus interruptus*). This would be anticlimactic in the fullest sense: a kind of physical impotency revealing a deeper betrayal; a hanging on to the edge and refusing to go all the way and abandon oneself to fate with one's beloved. Every form of contraception shares this unnatural quality although not all are so obvious as *coitus interruptus*. Contraception, whether by withdrawal or by physical or chemical barriers, demonstrates a withholding of self and a rejection, a "no" to one's beloved, a refusal to "go all the way" and risk having a baby to prove your love. Contraception is evil because it is unnatural to lovers to be so unromantic, so un-daring, so calculating and so cold.

Contraception is comparable to enjoying the taste of a delicious meal and then deliberately vomiting it up before its nutrients can have their effect in building up your body. The two aspects of food go together, pleasurable taste and nutrition. They are inseparably joined and to attempt to experience one without the other is unnatural, unhealthy, sick, and even perverse.

Those who use contraception are out of sync with the deep rhythms of human nature. They refuse the biblical "time for embraces." On the other hand, when a couple honors a "time to refrain from embraces,"[1] through the exercise of the virtue of continence and chastity before and during marriage, they are following the natural seasons of human sexuality. The reason adolescents experience sexual desire years before they will be able to act on them and raise a family is so they will have time to learn to deal with, and channel, those desires into culturally productive paths before they are entrusted with the lives and emotional well-being of a spouse and children. Furthermore, children must learn to refrain from embraces until the day that they wed so that they may embrace and refrain from embraces at the right times during their marriage, avoiding the twin evils of contraception and/or infidelity.

It is not so hard to see why Pope Paul VI wrote in *Humanae Vitae* (1968) that the widespread practice of contraception would work against the virtue of chastity and contribute to the social recognition of fornication, adultery, divorce and the cultural de-legitimization of marriage. The trivialization of marriage by the widespread practice of couples using contraceptives will in turn, he said, encourage unscrupulous political leaders to dictate to couples the number of children they should have by mandating contraceptive use.[2] All these evils have come to pass and worse: truly, many don't even see them as evil any longer. For a restoration of a culture of life to occur we must heed his advice and hear afresh the wisdom of *Human Life*.

The Key Magisterial Document:
Humanæ Vitae (1968)

In the opening paragraph of *Human Vitae* Pope Paul VI describes the relationship of the co-creators of human life: God and spouses. God has entrusted husband and wife with an extremely important "duty," or "mission": it is an obligation which, when fulfilled, is meritorious in the eyes of God. It is a mission filled with joys and difficulties, and a duty which will often raise questions of conscience, especially in recent times, to which the Church must continue to respond.[3]

Part I (par. 2-6) New Aspects of this Question and the Competence of the Magisterium

This section addresses changes in the world, in moral theology, the competence of the Magisterium to deal with this issue and the importance to be attached to the report of the Special Commission established by Pope John XXIII to study contraception.

There has been an increase in the world's population which some fear will lead to mass starvation, especially in developing nations, and this tempts some public authorities to use radical methods to contain their populations.[4] Also, raising a large family is often more difficult due to work, housing and increased costs. The role of women in society has changed alongside our understanding of human sexuality. These changes, which parallel the total quest for the conquest of nature, suggest that his own body, social life, and even the transmission of human life should be subject to his will.[5]

These wide ranging changes in culture lead some to believe that the moral norms relevant to human sexuality are also subject to change. Perhaps, they say, the so called "principle of totality" applies in the case of contraception, so that if the whole of married life is open to having children then each act of intercourse need not be.[6]

The Church teaching concerning marriage is rooted in the natural law and illuminated by Divine Revelation. The Magisterium of the Catholic Church is competent to interpret the natural moral law:

> [W]hen Jesus Christ imparted His divine authority to Peter and the other apostles and sent them to all nations to teach His Commandments, He established those very men as authentic guardians and interpreters of the whole moral law, that is, not only of the law of the Gospel, but also of natural law. For natural law [as well as revealed law] declares the will of God; [thus] faithful compliance with natural law is necessary for eternal salvation.[7]

A Special Commission was established by Pope John XXIII in 1963 to reflect on the legitimate means of controlling family size.[8] We are not bound to follow the findings of this Commission, especially when certain methods and criteria used departed from the firm and constant teaching of the Magisterium on what is moral within marriage.[9]

Part II (pars. 7-18): "Doctrinal Principles"

This, the longest section in the encyclical, contrasts the rationale for contraception with the genuine characteristics of conjugal love and parenthood, describes the inseparable connection between the unitive and procreative aspects of married love, explains the morality of intercourse during infertile periods, and foretells the blessings that will follow upon the use of natural family planning (periodic abstinence), versus the negative fallout that will occur from the use of contraception.

Two rationales are used to support contraceptive use: first, it meets the demands of conjugal love, and second, it makes possible planned or so-called responsible parenthood. But these arguments do not hold up in view of an integral vision of the human person as set forth in Vatican Council II.[10]

Marriage is not the product of chance or the blind forces of nature but is a reflection of God, "from whom all parenthood in heaven and earth receives its name."[11] Through mutual self-giving, spouses seek a "communion of persons" which perfects them and thereby enables them to share with God the mission of procreating and educating their children; while for baptized spouses, it is also a "sacramental sign of grace."[12]

Conjugal love has four characteristic marks: 1) it is fully *human* in the sense that it combines one's bodily affections and one's spiritual free will so that spouses promise each other that their love will persevere and grow daily, carrying them toward their human perfection; 2) it is a "special friendship" that is *total*, whereby the spouses share everything, loving the beloved for his or her own sake and joyfully enriching their beloved with their gift of self; 3) it is *"faithful* and exclusive until death" and meritorious in spite of difficulties, and a source of lasting happiness; and 4) it is *fruitful* in that the communion of spouses is focused on raising up new lives: "Marriage and conjugal love are ordained toward the procreation and education of children . . . a gift that contributes immensely to the good of the parents themselves."[13]

Responsible parenthood also has four characteristics that impose duties on spouses: 1) to honor the moral meaning inherent in the biological process of human fertility; 2) to master instinct and bodily desires by their reason and free will; 3) to consider their physical and psychological resources and social circumstances in prudently and generously raising a large family; or for "serious reasons" and "with due respect for the moral law" postpone having children for an definite or indefinite period of time; and 4) to realize that they must behave with deference to an objective moral order which imposes obligations upon them toward God, themselves, family and society.[14]

Since the conjugal acts of spouses remain inherently oriented toward expressing and consolidating their union, they do not cease to be good and meritorious if performed when the married couple is naturally infertile. Acts of conjugal love performed during the natural infertile time in a woman's cycle are not willfully closed to new life but observe the "rhythms of fecundity" and the norms of the natural law that require "each and every marriage act must remain open to the transmission of life."[15]

The conjugal act of spouses has both a unitive and a procreative meaning inseparably joined by God that may not be broken willfully by spouses.[16] Just as it is sinful to use force against the unitive aspect of marriage and impose on one's partner a conjugal act "without regard to his or her condition or personal and reasonable wishes," [i.e., spousal rape] so it is sinful to use force against the procreative dimension of conjugal love through contraception. Moreover, as we do not enjoy unlimited authority to do with our own bodies in general as we wish (as reflected in obscenity laws and laws against prostitution and suicide), so we do not have unlimited license over the generative faculties of our bodies. This is because all "human life is sacred . . . from its very inception it reveals the creating hand of God."[17]

For this reason abortion, even for therapeutic reasons, "is absolutely excluded as a means of regulating births," and so is direct sterilization, whether perpetual or temporary. The same is true of "every action which, either in anticipation of the conjugal act, or in its accomplishment, or in the development of its natural consequences, proposes, whether as an end or as a means, to render procreation impossible."[18] One may not invoke the so-called principle of totality with respect to contraception, claiming it is a lesser evil then an untimely birth, and so long as the whole of marriage remains open to procreation, then single isolated acts of contraception share in that general orientation of openness to new life. Rather, one may not do evil (choose contraception) that good may come of it even for "the gravest of reasons" and "make into the object of a positive act of the will something which is intrinsically disordered."[19] However, to use a medication to treat a disease which also has the unintended effect of inhibiting fertility is not to choose contraception, provided the contraceptive effect is not also directly sought.[20]

It is morally permissible for spouses to calculate their fertility and engage in marital intercourse only during infertile times for "serious reasons" based on the physical or psychological conditions of the spouses or on external factors. There is no inconsistency in the Church's teaching in this matter. Periodic abstinence and contraception are essentially different in the following respects: in the former, spouses respect the order of nature; while in the latter they impede generation, even though both married couples may have similar motives for desiring to space their children.[21]

The widespread practice of contraception will have serious consequences for morals, marriage, women and society. First, it will make it easier, especially for the young, to give in to temptations to adultery and fornication—"to justify behavior leading to marital infidelity or to a gradual weakening in the discipline of morals." Second, husbands who use or expect contraceptives to be used will lose respect for their wives, "no longer caring for her physical and psychological equilibrium" and come to consider her "as a mere instrument of selfish enjoyment, and no longer as his respected and beloved companion." Third, it will place a "dangerous weapon" into the hands of unscrupulous political authorities:

> Who could blame a government for applying to the solution of the problems of the community those means acknowledged as licit for married couples in the solutions of a family problem? Who will stop rulers from favoring, from even imposing upon their peoples, if they were to consider it necessary, the method of contraception which they judge to be most efficacious? . . .
> Consequently, if the mission of generating life is not to be exposed to the arbitrary will of men, one must necessarily recognize insurmountable limits to the possibility of man's domination over his own body and its functions; limits which no man, whether a private individual or one invested with authority, may licitly surpass.[22]

The Church anticipates this teaching will be a "sign of contradiction"[23] yet with humble firmness she is bound to proclaim the whole moral law, both natural and evangelical, of which she is not the author, nor consequently its arbiter, only its interpreter. In upholding this moral teaching on conjugal chastity the Church contributes to the establishment of a "truly human civilization, to ensuring man does not abdicate moral responsibility by over reliance on technology, and to the protection of the dignity of spouses."[24]

Part III (pars. 19-31) Pastoral Directives

The Church is "the Mother and Teacher of all nations" and so must help all peoples to accept this teaching and strengthen them to live it out. In imitation of the Redeemer she does not lessen the truth, but forgives sins and encourages all.[25] Even if it appears difficult, the Church's teaching on the spacing of children is a promulgation of the divine law. Indeed, it requires both strong motivation and God's grace in order to follow this law, but its observance will ennoble men and confer many benefits upon society.[26] Some of these benefits accrued from the practice of periodic absence within marriage include achieving conjugal chastity and the development of character and spiritual values, along with tenderness, attentiveness, selflessness and responsibility towards one's spouse, fostering peace in the home, and being a credible witness to one's children.[27]

Educators and all those with responsibility for maintaining the common good must work to create conditions favorable to an education in chastity and condemn all forms of entertainment and fashions which arouse man's base passions. No appeal to art, learning or so-called "freedom of expression" can legitimize depravity [obscenity] of this kind.[28] Public authorities must not allow the morals of their people to be corrupted by laws allowing practices contrary to the natural and divine law to be introduced into the family in order to resolve problems aggravated by an increasing population, especially in developing nations.

The only worthy solution to demographic problems is one which respects the social and economic progress of individuals and the whole of human society and the promotion of truly human values. Demographic problems must not be blamed on divine providence but rather on misguided governmental policies, a weak sense of social justice, a hoarding of goods and an unwillingness to sacrifice so all peoples may achieve a better standard of living.[29]

Scientists should pool their efforts in studying human fertility so as to assist spouses to better understand the human reproductive cycle and to achieve the "moral regulation of offspring."[30] Doctors must pursue only those solutions in accord with faith and right reason and consider it their special mission to acquire all the learning necessary in this area to direct spouses along the right path. [31]

Strengthened by the sacrament of marriage and "consecrated so that they might faithfully fulfill their duties" let Christian spouses humbly obey the voice of the Church and give witness to the moral law which unites the love of husband and wife with the love of God, the author of human life. Let spouses seek God's help in following this teaching through prayer, the Eucharist, and frequent confession, so as to achieve the perfection in married life described by St. Paul in Ephesians: "husbands, love your wives, as Christ loved the Church."[32] Word will spread from couple to couple of the benefits flowing from periodic abstinence within marriage and so one couple will be a guide to others.[33]

The first task of priests, especially in the case of those who teach moral theology, "is to expound the Church's teaching on marriage without ambiguity" by being an example of obedience "both inwardly and outwardly" to the Magisterium of the Church. Let there be no dissent, please![34] A priest's refusal to compromise the truth with respect to this teaching is an outstanding act of charity to souls when accompanied by patience and goodness. A priest should have confidence that the same Holy Spirit who assists the Magisterium in proposing doctrine also illumines the hearts of the faithful to assent to this teaching. Priests must teach married couples to pray and have recourse to the sacraments of Eucharist and Penance and to not be discouraged.[35] Bishops must lead their priests and consider the safeguarding and holiness of marriage to be their greatest and most urgent responsibility committed to them at this time, a responsibility which requires a coordination of pastoral effort in all areas of human activity— economic, social, and cultural.[36]

Finally, the Magisterium faithfully guards and interprets the deposit of faith which affects the good of the world and the Church. For one to achieve true happiness one must prudently and lovingly cultivate the laws written by God into their human nature.[37]

Magisterial Teaching and Theological Reflections on Contraception

Cultural Developments Prior to *Humanae Vitae*

The first wave of sexual revolution, the Roaring 20s, had not yet receded when Anglican Church leaders met on August 15, 1930 in the halls of Lambeth Palace and revoked their prior condemnations of contraceptives for married couples who had just cause for preventing new life.[38]

On the last day of the same year Pope Pius XI issued the encyclical *Casti Connubii* partially in reply to the Lambeth Conference statement.[39] In it he condemned abortion and eugenic limitations on the right to marry and declared contraception intrinsically evil:

> [A]ny use whatsoever of matrimony exercised in such a way that the act is deliberately frustrated in its natural power to generate life is an offense against the law of God and nature, and those who indulge in such are branded with the guilt of a grave sin.[40]

In the following years Pius XII also condemned abortion, sterilization and contraception. He specifically approved of spouses who chose to confine conjugal relations to infertile periods so as to limit new life temporarily or permanently for "serious reasons" which, he said, included medical, economic, social and eugenic reasons; otherwise they would "sin against the very meaning of conjugal life."[41] Pope John XXIII also wrote that human procreation was subject to the laws of God which differentiated it from the reproduction of plants and animals:

> The transmission of human life is entrusted by nature to a personal and conscious act and as such is subject to all the holy laws of God: the immutable and inviolable laws which must be recognized and observed. For this reason, one cannot use means and follow methods which could be licit in the transmission of the life of plants and animals.[42]

The Second Vatican Council (1961-1965)[43] spoke of the "mission" of spouses finding fulfillment in the procreation and education of children which perfects husband and wife:

> Marriage and conjugal love are by their nature ordained toward the begetting and education of children. Children are really the supreme gift of marriage and contribute very substantially to the welfare of their parents. . . . Parents should regard as their proper mission the task of transmitting human life and education

to those to whom it has been transmitted. . . . They are thereby cooperators with the love of God the Creator, and are, so to speak, the interpreters of that love.[44]

The Council Fathers did not directly address contraception, except to point out that the regulation of birth, like all sound morality, is determined by "objective criteria, criteria drawn from the dignity of the human person and human action."[45] The moral evaluation of the various means of fertility regulation does not depend "solely on sincere intentions or on an evaluation of motives" but, rather, must be made in reference to "objective standards" found inherent in the human person and fully expressed only in "mutual self-giving and human procreation in the context of true love."[46]

Their refusal to say more on this subject was due, in large part, out of deference to the Special Commission set up by Pope John XIII, and enlarged by Paul VI, to study this issue. Excerpts from what would become the majority opinion of this Special Commission, however, were leaked to the press. The excerpts recommended the Church change her position on contraception, at least on oral contraceptives since, they said, it did not inhibit the marital act and merely served to regulate otherwise neutral bodily processes for the good of marriage. Thus, in the years immediately prior to the issuance of *Humanae Vitae,* lay Catholics in the developed world were being prepared to expect a change in the Church's teaching on contraception.[47]

Therefore, when Paul VI issued *Humanae Vitae* in 1968, in the West it was generally attacked or ignored by the secular world and by large segments of the Catholic theological community, seminary professors, the Catholic press, certain individual bishops and even the national bishop conferences of several nations.[48] It was never explained to the Catholic faithful: rather many spouses were advised in the confessional to simply follow their conscience on this matter. This issue triggered a crisis of faith for the laity in the Western world: no longer would they "pay, pray and obey" but instructed by dissenting theologians and pastors, they would decide for themselves on matters of faith and morals. This crisis of faith was both a result and a contributing cause of the second wave of the sexual revolution, "the Sixties", that has continued its advance into the new millennium and is rapidly transforming the developing world through sexual and reproductive rights and gender mainstreaming under the guise of international aid and development.[49]

Whether the Church's Teaching on Contraception is Infallible

Humanae Vitae was attacked by dissenting moral theologians as "fallible" teaching, that is, one susceptible to being changed in the future, like the Church's discipline of abstinence from meat on Fridays. These theologians reasoned that since only those dogmas issued *ex cathedra* or by an ecumenical council are infallible; and since *Humanae Vitae* was not so issued, it was not an infallible teaching. The faithful were told that the Pope's teaching on contraception was, therefore, not binding on their individual consciences, and that they were free to choose what they considered best for their marriage. As a result the contraceptive practice of most Catholic couples in the developed world soon resembled that of the population in general.

But the dissenters and critics of *Humanae Vitae* were wrong. As clarified in *To Defend the Faith, Ad Tuendam Fidem* (1998), Pope Paul VI had simply reiterated in *Humanae Vitae* the Church's infallible teaching condemning contraception promulgated in the past by the constant and clear teaching of the Ordinary Magisterium of the Church (the Pope and bishops in union with him). The Commentary by Cardinal Ratzinger issued together with *To Defend the Faith* notes that infallible doctrine may be promulgated in either "defining acts," that is, specific verbal formulas issued by ecumenical counsels or ex cathedra, or in "non-defining acts," found in the past and present constant and clear teaching of the pope and bishops in union with him (but with no precise verbal formula).[50] On occasion a Pope may reiterate in a timely address or encyclical the infallible teaching of the Ordinary Magisterium of the Church found in her constant and clear teaching on various matters of faith, morals or discipline:

> Consequently, when there has not been a judgment on a doctrine in the solemn form of a definition [Ecumenical Council or *ex cathedra* definition], but this doctrine, belonging to the inheritance of the *depositum fidei*, is taught by the ordinary and universal Magisterium, which necessarily includes the pope, such a doctrine is to be understood as having been set forth infallibly. The declaration of confirmation or reaffirmation by the Roman pontiff in this case is not a new dogmatic definition, but a formal attestation of a truth already possessed and infallibly transmitted by the church.[51]

It should be pointed out that not only does *Humanae Vitae* proclaim infallible truth, but it was and remains a prophetic word. The evils it predicted would come to pass if it was rejected—an increase in marital infidelity, a general weakening in morals, increased infidelity and divorce, and forced contraception and sterilization in many nations of the world—have already come to pass. On the positive side, Pope John Paul II, was absolutely devoted to this issue and developed a new personalist mode of discourse, a "theology of the body," that described contraception as a "lie" against the innate "language of the body."[52] Therefore, the rejection of *Humanae Vitae* forced the Church to break new ground and gave impetus to the development of a richer and fuller theology of marriage and human sexuality.

Is Contraception Intrinsically Evil?

Critics seized upon a salient point in *Humanae Vitae* to undermine its central teaching, namely, that because it failed to explicitly condemn contraception as "intrinsically evil," it was not settled and perhaps the explicit condemnation given in *Casti Connubii*, this was not a settled issue:

But no reason, however grave, may be put forward by which anything intrinsically against nature may become conformable to nature and morally good. Since, therefore, the conjugal act is destined primarily by nature for the begetting of children, those who in exercising it deliberately frustrate its natural power and purpose sin against nature and commit a deed which is shameful and intrinsically vicious.[53]

This lacunae (an argument from silence) was clarified when in *Veritatis Splendor* (1993) John Paul II interpreted *Humanae Vitae* as implicitly condemning contraception as intrinsically evil and included contraception as an additional example to the list of inherently evil practices given in the Vatican Council II document, *The Church in the Modern World*:

Reason attests that there are objects of the human act which are by their nature "incapable of being ordered" to God, because they radically contradict the good of the person made in his image. These are the acts which, in the Church's moral tradition, have been termed "intrinsically evil" (*intrinsece malum*): they are such *always and per se*. . . . The second Vatican Council itself, in discussing the respect due to the human person, gives a number of examples of such acts: "Whatever is hostile to life itself, such as any kind of homicide, genocide, abortion, euthanasia and voluntary suicide . . . all these and the like are a disgrace."[54]

With regard to intrinsically evil acts, and in reference to contraceptive practices whereby the conjugal act is intentionally rendered infertile, Pope Paul VI teaches: "Though it is true that sometimes it is lawful to tolerate a lesser moral evil in order to avoid a greater evil or in order to promote a greater good, it is never lawful, even for the gravest reasons, to do evil that good may come of it."[55]

The *Catechism of the Catholic Church* likewise interprets *Humanae Vitae* to have included contraception as an intrinsically evil act:

These methods respect the bodies of the spouses, encourage tenderness between them, and favor the education of an authentic freedom. In contrast, "every action which, whether in anticipation of the conjugal act, or in its accomplishment, or in the development of the natural consequences, proposes, whether as an end or as a means, to render procreation impossible" is intrinsically evil.[56]

Moreover, the fact that contraceptives may not be prescribed or distributed in Catholic health care facilities to further contraceptive practice is further evidence that their use for the regulation and spacing of new life is intrinsically evil:

Catholic health institutions may not promote or condone contraceptive practice but should provide, for married couples and the medical staff who counsel them, instruction both about the Church's teaching on responsible parenthood and in methods of natural family planning.[57]

Given the condemnation of contraception as intrinsically evil in *Casti Conubbii* and the interpretation of *Humanae Vitae* given in *Veritatis Splendor* and in the *Catechism of the Catholic Church,* there can be no doubt that the knowing and willful use of contraceptives directly intended to disassociate the unitive and procreative dimensions of a conjugal act is seriously sinful, and that this is an infallible teaching given in a non-defining act by the Ordinary Magisterium of the Church, which has been repeated by Popes Pius XI, Pius XII, Paul VI, and John Paul II.

Should Natural Family Planning Be Taught to Unmarried Women?

NFP (Natural Family Planning, that is, simple diagnostic techniques that allow a woman to monitor her ovulation cycle so as to achieve or avoid pregnancy), we are told by the Pontifical Council for Pastoral Assistance, should be presented as a credible alternative to contraception to both spouses and to unmarried "young people" by health care workers. Some have questioned the prudence of providing information about NFP to unmarried young women fearing they might use it for contraceptive purposes. We should presume good faith in the hearts of young women: after all, God does no less by entrusting fertility to young people years before they are in a position to act on their sexual desires so that they may master themselves for their vocation to marry or take vows of celibacy or virginity. As a practical matter, the periodic abstinence required by NFP mitigates its effectiveness as a "natural contraceptive" for the unmarried, given the unpredictable nature of unchaste dating behavior. Furthermore, NFP properly presented will greatly enhance the self esteem of married and unmarried women alike and give women a greater respect for their bodies,[58] therefore encouraging them to follow the varying demands of their states in life:

> Health care workers can contribute, when opportunities occur in their field, towards an acceptance of this human and Christian concept of sexuality by making available to married people, and even before that to young people, the required information for responsible behavior, respectful of the special dignity of human sexuality.[59]

The Essential Anthropological Difference between NFP and Contraception

In his first encyclical to deal specifically with life issues, *Familiaris Consortio* (1981),[60] John Paul II characterized conjugal relations as a "lie" if they were not the sign and fruit of total personal self giving in two ways: if fertility was withheld, or if fidelity was not pledged and honored.[61] He also stated that *Humanae Vitae* had reaffirmed and re-proposed the Church's normative teaching on contraception, which is always old and always new regarding the transmission of human life.[62] He asked theologians to cooperate with the Magisterium and explore the biblical foundation, ethical grounds and personalist reasons behind *Humanae Vitae,* since this issue is determinative of a view of the human person.[63] He repeated what Paul VI taught: that the twin meanings of the conjugal act cannot be broken and all acts which do so are inherently evil. Contraception before, during or after sexual relations is immoral.

Contracepting spouses act as personal judges of the moral law and they attempt to devalue conjugal relations, lessening its "total" self-giving quality. The built-in language of the body in conjugal acts speaks of a total reciprocal self-giving which spouses who use contraception cover over with a willful deceit. On the other hand, those spouses who practice periodic abstinence (NFP) respect both the unitive and procreative meaning of human sexuality, and so act as faithful "ministers" of God's plan.[64] This teaching is not merely an ideal for some, but a norm required of everyone.[65]

The essential difference between contraception and NFP is not that one is artificial or technical: "It is not a distinction simply of techniques or methods, where the decisive element would be the artificial or natural character of the procedure."[66] Rather, it is a difference involving "two irreconcilable concepts of the human person and of human sexuality."[67] What is wrong is that contraception falsifies the innate meaning of the conjugal act; "contraception imposes an objectively contradictory meaning, namely that of not giving oneself completely to the other."[68]

The human soul does not inhabit the body as a ghost in a haunted house, or an imprisoned spirit with *two* natures—one spiritual, the other physical. Rather, the soul is dependent upon the body for even the operation of its spiritual faculties of reason and creativity. A blind person cannot imagine color because he has never seen color with his eyes, nor can the deaf imagine the sound of music, nor can anyone imagine a new sight or sound or animal that is not simply a recombination or blending of what was received through the senses. Man is an incarnate spirit with a spiritualized body with *one* composite nature:

> The unity of soul and body is so profound that one has to consider the soul to be the "form" of the body: i.e., it is because of its spiritual soul that the body made of matter becomes a human, living body; spirit and matter, in man, are not two natures united, but rather their union forms a single nature.[69]

In fact it is precisely a widespread acceptance of this dualistic notion of the human body that seems to legitimize the hedonism and utilitarianism characteristic of our times, which John Paul II referred to as a "neo-Manichaeism"; a dualism wherein the body is treated as a mere instrument of man's spirit, his reason and will. The body considered from this false anthropological perspective is "thingified," when in reality it is profoundly personalized. In the area of morals this has grave consequences, for if my body is an instrument of my spirit, then I determine its uses rather than it informing me of the ethical contours of appropriate human behavior. If my body is no more than a boot covering my soul, so to speak, then I may use it for its common purpose of walking, or I may use it for any other purpose I so conceive, such as a hammer or a door-stop; I may polish and preserve it from rot, or I may wallow with it in manure and leave it unclean if I so choose, because *my body is not really me.* On the contrary, Adam, on the morning of creation, knew he and Eve were both different from all other animals because she was "bone of my bones and flesh of my flesh," and both their bodies were transfused by spirit and translucent to the operation of reason and free-will:

> The separation of spirit and body in man has led to a growing tendency to consider the human body, not in accordance with the categories of its specific likeness to God, but rather on the basis of its similarity to all the other bodies present in the world of nature, bodies which man uses as raw material. . . . When the human body, considered apart from spirit and thought, comes to be used as raw material in the same way that bodies of animals are used—and this actually occurs for example in experimentation on embryos and fetuses—we will inevitably arrive at a dreadful ethical defeat.
>
> Within a similar anthropological perspective, the human family is facing the challenge of a new Manichaeism, in which body and spirit are put in radical opposition; the body does not receive life from the spirit, and the spirit does not give life to the body. Man thus ceases to live as a person and a subject. Regardless of all intentions and declarations to the contrary, he becomes merely an object.[70]

Whether the Use of Artificial Contraceptives Is Ever Justified

Some have humorously noted that there is one chemical the Church allows couples to use to regulate fertility: a glass of wine to make one or both spouses sleepy. After all, it seems to many sleep deprived young couples with fussy babies that the big "S-word" is not "sex" but "sleep"!

In all seriousness, we must consider whether it is ever morally permissible to use contraceptive devices. As we have seen, any medication taken for therapeutic reasons may in some way, as a counter-indication, suppress male or female fertility. For example, thyroxin, a prescription hormone supplement for low thyroid production may affect female fertility. Testosterone therapy for men with low testosterone levels may inhibit sperm production and reduce male fertility.[71] Simply drinking water contaminated with high estrogen levels (due to synthetic estrogen leaching into the water table due to artificial fertilizers and women voiding while on the Pill), has produced lower sperm count in men.[72] Medication with an unintended counter-indication of inhibiting fertility is morally permissible.[73] The principle of "double effect" may apply in such cases: that is, where one moral action has two effects, a good effect directly intended, the other an unintended negative consequence that one foresees but tries to avoid or minimize.[74] In this way a contraceptive device used for therapeutic and not contraceptive purposes or to directly inhibit fertility before or after rape may be a morally just act. Some people have difficulty understanding this seeming inconsistency.

Contraceptive devices or periodic abstinence, considered in the abstract, is a neutral act which acquires moral specificity as good or evil according to an analysis of the three moral determinants: motive, circumstance and deed (i.e., the directly intended moral object) not an unintended secondary effect.[75] So what defines the sin of contraception? It is not the use of a contraceptive device, but rather, it is the use of any product or technique directly intending to effect the willful separation of the unitive and procreative aspects of conjugal love: "Every action which, either in anticipation of the conjugal act, or in its accomplishment, or in the development of its natural consequences, proposes, whether as an end or as a means, to render procreation impossible."[76] It is also important to differentiate between genuine contraceptive devices, those that simply inhibit conception (such as a spermicides), from abortifacient, devices which attack the life of a newly conceived embryo.

With these points in mind, in order to further illustrate the essential quality of the sin of contraception, let us consider three different hypothetical scenarios in which a woman might use spermicides, or an over the counter chemical contraceptive that is not an abortifacient: 1) By spouses to space their children; 2) By a married woman for a therapeutic (non-contraceptive) health related reason; and 3) By any woman of child bearing age before an impending rape from which she is unable to defend herself or shortly after she has been raped.

In the first case, the free and informed use of commercial spermicides to immobilize or kill the sperm of one's husband for, perhaps, a good ulterior motive, such as maintaining her physical health has as its direct object the separation of the unitive and procreative dimensions of conjugal love. This married woman seeks pleasure and comfort in her husband's embrace, but has deliberately set out to kill his sperm so as to not procreate a child for the otherwise praiseworthy motive of maintaining her health. This action, choosing union while making one's husband infertile so as to avoid becoming pregnant with his child, constitutes the grave sin of contraception.

However, for the sake of argument, if a particular spermicide had some genuine medicinal or therapeutic effect that no other product possessed, it would be licit for a woman to use it even if she foresaw, *but not directly intended*, that it would kill most of her husband's sperm when they engaged in conjugal relations. The *direct* moral object of her will in the employment of this commercial product was to restore her health, not to render her husband infertile. She could not in this case be accused of willfully attempting to separate the unitive and procreative aspect of her conjugal relations with her husband. That is simply not what she is doing in using this product. Therefore, the grave sin of contraception—choosing union while rejecting procreation—is not committed in this case.

In the third example, that of a woman who uses spermicides to kill a rapist's sperm, she or the medical staff at the hospital emergency room use this product as it is intended—to kill or immobilize sperm in order to prevent pregnancy. This *does not* constitute the sin of contraception for the simple reason that rape is not conjugal love. In using spermicides to kill the sperm of the rapist so as to, hopefully, avoid pregnancy, she is not *rejecting the procreative dimension of conjugal love while choosing its unitive good.* To speak of the "unitive good" of rape is nonsense.

Thus, by killing a rapist's sperm, the victim is not committing the sin of contraception even though she is using spermicides so as to prevent contraception. Morally she is not sinning but performing a good deed, an act of self-defense. Of course, she has no right to threaten the life of a child who may have already been conceived. Therefore, she may not use so called morning-after (abortifacient) drugs like diethylstilbestrol (DES), which are deceptively referred to as contraceptives. For years the medical establishment has expanded the definition of contraception to include all drugs which either prevent fertilization (contraceptives) or disrupt the implantation of the embryo in the uterus (abortifacients):

> For example, Miller and Keane's *Encyclopedia and Dictionary of Medicine, Nursing, and Allied Health* (3rd ed., 1983) defines contraception as "prevention of conception or impregnation," and lists among various methods of "contraception" all birth control pills and intrauterine devices, which are both abortifacients.[77]

Returning to our example, a victim of rape is justified in attempting to defend herself from a rapist's penetration before or during rape, and if she cannot physically prevent him from penetrating her and ejaculating within her vaginal canal, she may attempt to thwart the penetration of his sperm through her cervix into her uterus afterwards. If she could have shoved him off her before he ejaculated within her vagina she would certainly not have been guilty of the sin of *coitus interruptus*, rather, it would have been a good move.[78] Moreover, when escape is impossible, she may use lethal force to avoid being raped, since such force is proportionate to the harm likely to be inflicted upon her: the rapist may kill his victim to conceal his crime, or he may be infected with HIV/AIDS and cause her death through this contagious and fatal disease. It follows then, that if a woman may kill a rapist to prevent him from penetrating her, she may certainly kill his sperm to end the perpetuation of his penetration. The United States Conference of Catholic Bishops has addressed this issue:

> Compassionate and understanding care should be given to a person who is the victim of sexual assault. . . . A female who has been raped should be able to defend herself against a potential conception from the sexual assault. If, after appropriate testing, there is no evidence that conception has occurred already, she may be treated with medications that would prevent ovulation, sperm capacitation, or fertilization. It is not permissible, however, to initiate or to recommend treatments that have as their purpose or direct effect the removal, destruction, or interference with the implantation of a fertilized ovum.[79]

The trouble with applying the U.S. Bishop's teaching is that it is not usually possible to determine by "appropriate testing" in an emergency room within a few hours after a rape whether conception has already occurred. Perhaps some dosage of estrogen might be administered to prevent ovulation which would not at the same time prevent implantation, that is, induce an abortion. However, the popular mini-pill is high in progesterone and low in estrogen, which means that although it impedes ovulation to some extent, and produces a thickening of cervical mucus which retards sperm entrance into the uterus, it acts primarily as an abortifacient by rendering the uterine lining inhospitable to the implantation of the newly conceived embryo. Since the direct effect of the mini pill is "interference with the implantation of a fertilized ovum" it should not be administered as part of a routine rape protocol. The same analysis applies, even more so, to the administration of a morning after abortifacient drug like diethylstilbestrol (DES).

How Serious Are the Consequences of Using NFP without "Serious Reasons"?

Again, what defines the grave sin of contraception is whether the direct object of the will is (1) choosing union (pleasure and comfort) while at the same time (2) rejecting its concomitant procreative end. This is precisely what spouses who use NFP, without good cause, are guilty of doing: willfully effecting the separation of the unitive and procreative aspects of conjugal love. Note that the choice of a commercial contraceptive used for contraceptive purposes is the choice of an intrinsically evil moral object, whether or not it is chosen for selfish or selfless motives. On the other hand, the choice of NFP for selfish reason, or the *why* couples behave this way, is sinful, but *what* they do—engage in unfettered conjugal relations only during the infertile period—remains "intrinsically life-directed."[80] The motive of spouses using NFP without just cause is selfish and, so, is at least venially sinful. If kept up for a long period of time it may harden into a seriously sinful anti-life attitude in that it is closed to the mutual gift of self to each other, and set firmly against God's mission for spouses: "To do this without any serious reason e.g., merely to be able to avoid the inconvenience of having children is wrong, and if kept up for a long time (e.g., several years) might be a mortal sin."[81]

The Link between Contraception and Direct Sterilization

Direct or voluntary non-therapeutic sterilization entails the deliberate removal or impairment of reproductive organs for a contraceptive purpose. The moral analysis of direct sterilization is essentially the same as that of contraception; because it disassociates the unitive and procreative meanings of the conjugal act of spouses, direct sterilization is an intrinsically evil act:[82]

> Any Sterilization which of itself, that is, of its own nature and condition, has the sole immediate effect of rendering the generative faculty incapable of procreation, is to be considered direct sterilization. . . . [S]uch sterilization remains absolutely forbidden according to the doctrine of the Church.[83]

In fact, because direct sterilization is most likely permanent it is objectively a graver evil than contraception:

> And indeed the sterilization of the faculty itself [reproductive organs] is forbidden for an even graver reason than the sterilization of individual acts [i.e., contraception], since it induces a state of sterility in the person which is almost always irreversible.[84]

There is never an excuse for direct sterilization; neither appeals to the common good or the principle of totality (when considered in light of the highest good of the person—his "ethical good") justify direct sterilization.[85] Moreover, no Catholic health care facility, nor any Catholic health care worker, may cooperate in direct sterilization:

> a) Any cooperation institutionally approved or tolerated in action which are in themselves, that is, by their nature and condition, directed to a contraceptive end, namely, that the natural effects of sexual actions deliberately performed by the sterilized subject be impeded, is absolutely forbidden. For the official approbation of direct sterilization and, a fortiori, its management and execution in accord with hospital regulations, is a matter which, in the objective order, is by its very nature (or intrinsically) evil.
> b) The traditional doctrine regarding material cooperation, with the proper distinctions between necessary and free, proximate and remote, remains valid, to be applied with the utmost prudence, if the case warrants.
> c) In the application of the principle of material cooperation, if the case warrants, great care must be taken against scandal and the danger of any misunderstanding by an appropriate explanation of what is really being done.[86]

Direct sterilization removes or impairs reproductive organs to thwart new life either because the person has decided to have no more children or because he or she is afraid a future pregnancy will pose a serious risk to their health or wellbeing. An indirect sterilization removes or impairs reproductive organs to heal a serious present illness. For instance, a woman may choose to have her uterus removed because she has had multiple cesarean sections and her doctors informed her that if she becomes pregnant in the future her uterus will certainly rupture and the complications could be fatal. What should she do? Because the danger to her health is not imminent, she may not seek a hysterectomy and have her uterus removed in order to prevent herself from becoming pregnant. The principle of double effect does not apply because the good effect flows from and follows the bad effect and one may "not do evil that good come of it."[87] Her good motive (to preserve her health) does not change *what* she did. She had her uterus surgically removed so as to not have an unwanted pregnancy. For an action to be good the motive, circumstance and the deed must all be good.[88] In this example her motive and the circumstances impelling her to act are good but what she does is evil, a direct sterilization, that good come of it, in order to prevent a future life threatening pregnancy from occurring.

By contrast, let us consider a woman whose uterus, because of multiple cesarean sections, has failed to heal and is constantly infected and this condition has proven untreatable. May she have her hemorrhaging and infected uterus removed? Yes, because this would *not* be a direct sterilization. The principle of double effect applies in this case because the serious health problem is not merely threatening but is actually present. She will have not done evil to achieve good; rather, she will have done a good action (removed an infected and incurable organ) for good reason (to preserve her health) under the circumstances, even though she foresees the operation will render her infertile.

The United States Conference of Catholic Bishops addresses the distinction between direct and indirect sterilization:

> Direct sterilization of either men or women, whether permanent or temporary, is not permitted in a Catholic health care institution. Procedures that induce sterility are permitted when their direct effect is the cure or alleviation of a present and serious pathology and a simpler treatment is not available.[89]

Magisterial documents following the 1975 letter on direct sterilization by the Congregation for the Doctrine of the Faith have focused on coerced sterilization implemented for eugenic, demographic or terrorist purposes. In *Familiaris Consortio* the Church condemned government programs that limit the freedom of spouses to decide their family size through forced contraception, sterilization and abortion.[90] The *Charter of the Rights of the Family* (1983) issued by the Holy See condemned the use of contraception, sterilization and abortion by spouses as a form of birth control. Moreover, any economic pressure applied to developing nations to secure the reduction of that nation's fertility rate by means of contraception, sterilization or abortion was denounced: "In international relations, economic aid for the advancement of peoples must not be conditioned on acceptance of programs of contraception, sterilization or abortion."[91] Terrorists who kidnap and amputate, mutilate or sterilize their captives perform acts gravely against the moral law.[92] In *The Gospel of Life* John Paul II repeated the Church's condemnation of public authorities who encourage or use coercion to force their citizens to submit to dictates on family size: "It is therefore morally unacceptable to encourage, let alone impose, the use of methods such as contraception, sterilization and abortion in order to regulate births."[93] *Ethical and Pastoral Dimensions of Population Trends* (1994), issued by the Pontifical Counsel for the Family, noted the lack of "honesty and quality of information" given in developing nations to induce male and female sterilization without their informed consent. They note that besides the harm done to the moral order and the dignity of those deceived, sterilization also produces more "serious long-term demographic effects than contraception and abortion."[94]

The Link between Contraception and In-vitro Fertilization

In 1987 the Sacred Congregation of the Doctrine of the Faith issued *Donum Vitae* (*Respect of Human Life in its Origin and on the Dignity of Procreation*) in order to address the artificial reproduction of human life outside the womb through in-vitro fertilization (IVF).[95] Contraception and IVF are analogous: the former is "sex without babies," the latter is "babies without sex" as Fr. Paul Marx, OSB, founder of Human Life International would say.[96] Both contraception and IVF effect the separation of the two ends of married love; hence both are equally wrong:

> Contraception deliberately deprives the conjugal act of its openness to procreation and in this way brings about a voluntary dissociation of the ends of marriage. Homologous artificial fertilization [fertilization occurs from the sex cells of a married couple rather than unmarried individuals], in seeking a procreation which is not the fruit of a specific act of conjugal union, objectively effects an analogous separation between the goods and the meanings of marriage.[97]

John Paul II's theology of the body was used to defend and explain the Church's rejection of IVF:

> Spouses mutually express their personal love in the "language of the body," which clearly involves both "spousal meanings" and parental ones. It is in their bodies and through their bodies that spouses consummate their marriage and are able to become father and mother. In order to respect the language of their bodies and their natural generosity, the conjugal union must take place with respect for its openness to procreation; and the procreation of a person must be the fruit and result of married love.[98]

The Link between Contraception and Abortion

That contraception leads to abortion is taught, not only by the Pope, but also by the Supreme Court of the United States. Reaffirming the central holding of *Roe v. Wade* that legalized abortion, the United States Supreme Court ruled in *Planned Parenthood of Southeastern Pennsylvania v. Casey* that, regardless of whether *Roe* was correctly decided, women now organize their lives by expecting to be able to avoid pregnancy through contraceptive practice. Therefore they must continue to have access to legal abortion should contraception fail:

> [F]or two decades of economic and social developments, people have organized intimate relationships and made choices that define their views of themselves and their places in society, in reliance on the availability of abortion in the event that contraception should fail. The ability of women to participate

equally in the economic and social life of the Nation has been facilitated by their ability to control their reproductive lives.[99]

On the other hand, those who advocate for sexual and reproductive rights and the legalization of contraception and sterilization in the Developing World say it will prevent women from having recourse to abortion. They also blame the Catholic Church for driving women to have abortions by opposing the legal distribution of contraceptives:

> It is frequently asserted that contraception, if made safe and available to all, is the most effective remedy against abortion. The Catholic Church is then accused of actually promoting abortion, because she obstinately continues to teach the moral unlawfulness of contraception. When looked at carefully, this objection is clearly unfounded.[100]

John Paul II confirmed that while it may be true that some people are motivated to use contraceptives in order to avoid abortion, however, the inner logic of contraceptive mentality moves them inexorably to choose abortion. When one's attitude has been to do what it takes to not be pregnant, they logically advance from contraceptives to abortion as the next step necessary to get the job done: "Indeed the pro-abortion culture is especially strong precisely where the Church's teaching on contraception is rejected."[101]

Certainly contraception and abortion are sins against different human values. Contraception contradicts the full truth about conjugal love and is "opposed to the virtue of chastity in marriage" and violates the Sixth Commandment while abortion "destroys the life of a human being" and is "opposed to the virtue of justice" and violates the Fifth Commandment.[102]

However, despite these differences contraception and abortion are "fruits of the same tree." Both are rooted in a selfish, hedonistic mentality that shirks responsibility for sexual activity. Both imply an egotistical concept of freedom that envisions a child as a threat to personal plans, and an enemy "to be avoided at all costs." The common attitude of those who have recourse to contraception and those who turn to abortion is now being matched by alarming similarities in techniques and "chemical products, intrauterine devices and vaccines which, distributed with the same ease as contraceptives, really act as abortifacients in the very early stages of the development of the life of the new human being."[103]

The Link between Contraception and Totalitarianism

In his encyclical *Letter to Families* (1994) John Paul II assigns central significance to the conjugal act as the defining moment for spouses personally and for our understanding of the human person and human civilization: "The person can never be considered a means to an end; above all never a means of 'pleasure.' The person is and must be nothing other than the end of every act."[104] If the conjugal act becomes a means to an end—an occasion of pleasure in the case of contraception, or is replaced in the case of IVF in a heedless quest for a baby—spouses treat each other as objects, and contribute to a civilization "of use," a culture "of things and not of persons, a civilization in which persons are used in the same way as things are used."[105] This is the deep anthropological distortion that gives rise to "a culture of death."[106]

In *The Gospel of Life* (*Evangelium Vitae*), Pope John Paul II surveyed the terrain and named the threats against human life which he found were many and varied.[107] These threats are "powerful:" a "scientifically and systematically programmed," an "alarming spectacle," a "conspiracy against life,"[108] that could make one feel "overwhelmed" and "powerless" to oppose them.[109] We have come to this crisis, he said, due to an "eclipse of the sense of God," and in this darkness man, his creature, is shorn of all innate dignity: "By living 'as if God did not exist,' man not only loses sight of the mystery of God, but also of the mystery of the world and the mystery of his own being."[110] In this darkness the human body is depersonalized and thingified: "Within this same cultural climate, the body is no longer perceived as a properly personal reality, a sign and place of relations with others, with God and with the world. . . . It is simply a complex of organs . . . to be used according to the sole criteria of pleasure and efficiency."[111] In the eclipse of the sense of God, human sexuality is distorted, its two meanings lost and its procreative dimension exploited for what it can produce, rather than as the unique meeting place of two persons in love:

> Thus the original import of human sexuality is distorted and falsified, and the two meanings, unitive and procreative, inherent in the very nature of the conjugal act are artificially separated. . . . Procreation then becomes the enemy. . . . If it is welcomed, this is only because it expresses a desire or indeed the intention to have a child "at all cost," and not because it signifies the complete acceptance of the other and therefore an openness to the richness of life which the child represents.[112]

From the eclipse of the sense of God, to the eclipse of the innate dignity of man as God's creature, to the "thingification" of the human body and the sundering of the two meanings of conjugal love, we descend into a world ruled by the logic of efficiency and the dominion of the "strong over the weak."[113] However, if we enjoy sexual pleasure apart from procreation through contraception, we soon find that those who are strong use those who are weak for their pleasure, as was predicted by Pope Paul VI: "And then also carefully consider that a dangerous power will be put into the hands of rulers who care little about the moral law."[114]

Unless we see ourselves as God's creature and behave accordingly, respecting the innate language of the body, it is meaningless to speak about inalienable human rights. Without God such rights as we may possess are mere concessions from the State. Rights conferred by the State are mere privileges that may be taken back, especially from the weak who have little or no voice, the unborn, the elderly, the disabled and infirm, whose dignity is less and less self-evident in the darkling light of a civilization of use:

The inviolability of the person which is a reflection of the absolute inviolability of God, finds its primary and fundamental expression in the inviolability of human life.[115]

Those who use contraception thingify themselves. Shorn of all transcendence, no longer regarded as a creature of God but a fungible individual among things, the human person stands naked before the Leviathan. In a civilization of use who will dare to say, "Don't tread on me":

Totalitarianism arises out of a denial of truth in the objective sense. If there is no transcendent truth, in obedience to which man achieves his full identity then there is no sure principle for guaranteeing just relations between people. . . . If one does not acknowledge transcendent truth, the force of power takes over, and each person tends to make full use of the means at his disposal in order to impose his own interests or his own opinion, with no regard for the rights of others. . . . Thus, the root of modern totalitarianism is to be found in the denial of the transcendent dignity of the human person, who, as the visible image of the invisible God, is therefore by his very nature the subject of rights which no one may violate—no individual, group, class, nation, or state. Not even the majority of a social body may violate these rights.[116]

Conclusion

The prediction Pope Paul VI made in *Humanae Vitae* in 1968, that the widespread acceptance of contraception would incite unscrupulous leaders to mandate birth control on their populations, has come to pass. In the early 1970's feminist strategists acknowledged birth control was "an international strategy in application throughout the world; in Vietnam, population control of 'uncontrollables' takes the form of outright genocide, but in Latin America, India, here, and in American colonies, birth control is the favored method."[117] At this same time the State Department of the United States identified population growth in the Developing World as a matter of paramount importance and in *National Security Memorandum 200* (NSSM 200), declassified in 1989, recommended massive population control of the populations of nations in the Developing World in order to secure access to their vital mineral ores necessary for the United States industry and military operations. In order to conceal the imperialistic motivation behind these population control programs NSSM 200 recommended the United States promote fertility reduction in the Developing World as a vindication of the right of indigenous people to freely and responsibly control their fertility and have fewer children and, thereby, to overcome poverty.[118]

China's coercive one-child policy is perhaps the most notorious massive population control program and has raised serious human rights concerns since the early 1980's. It has allowed the leaders of the People's Republic of China to blame the poor, the victims of their failed economic policies, for their own misery. It is not the ineptness of China's command economy but the poor themselves, who have too many children, are responsible for China's lack of economic development.[119] Although the enforcement of a massive coercive population control program, such as China's, requires the agencies of a police state, it is feared that a softer approach mediated through a triage of universal health care may work just as effectively in the Developed World.

In 1965 the United States Supreme Court struck down the State of Connecticut's criminal code provisions prohibiting married couples from using contraceptives. Of course, the Constitution says nothing about contraception. Historically it was left to the states to determine whether or not to criminalize what society deemed as immoral conduct under their general police powers. To strike down Connecticut's law criminalizing contraception the Supreme Court in *Griswold v. Connecticut* took on the role of a "Council of Revision," a role specifically denied to it by the Framers of the Constitution: "[T]he Constitutional Convention did on at least two occasions reject proposals which would have given the federal judiciary a part in recommending laws or in vetoing as bad or unwise the legislation passed by the Congress."[120]

At the same time the Court was creating a constitutional right to privacy out of thin air (from "penumbras formed by emanations" from the Bill of Rights")[121] three of the Justices in a concurring opinion opined on the constitutionality of coercive population control policies. They said in passing (dicta) that the states or the Federal Government has the authority to sterilize its citizens for compelling reasons:

> Surely the Government, absent a showing of a compelling subordinate state interest, could not decree that all husbands and wives must be sterilized after two children have been born to them.[122]

United States President Obama's science czar, John Holdren, wrote a textbook in 1977 in which he noted as a matter of fact that coercive abortion and sterilization laws would be constitutional and legitimate public policy options:

> [I]t has been concluded that compulsory population-control laws, even including laws requiring compulsory abortion, could be sustained under the existing Constitution if the population crisis became sufficiently severe to endanger the society. . . . [123] The law could properly say to a mother that, in order to protect the children she already has, she could have no more.[124]

More recently, in 2007, Holdren addressed the annual meeting of the American Association for the Advancement of Science and indicated that he hasn't changed his mind much over the years: "It is clear that the future course of history will be determined by the rates at which people breed and die."[125]

Why should we be surprised that those who have risen to the top of a civilization of use, and have not flinched at sterilizing the masses of the Developing World for the sake of their own hegemony as rulers of the Developed World, would balk at sterilizing their own population for their own special interests under the guise of meeting "compelling state interest." It would appear the link between totalitarianism and contraception hits very close to home, as Pope Paul VI said it would.

Diagram 11.1
The Three Moral Determinants Applied to Contraception v. Natural Family Planning

Contraception—to withhold the complete gift of self; to separate unitive and procreative aspects of the conjugal act.

1 *Motive*—to space children or to have no children for serious or trivial reasons/circumstances. Closed to new life and firmly rule out pregnancy, often with recourse to abortion if a break-through pregnancy occurs;

2 *Circumstance*—serious or trivial circumstances affecting health, finance, other children or family members' needs, or other external conditions or simple self-serving preferences, whims and caprice, etc.;

3 *Deed or Act*—to make oneself sterile. To violate one's bodily integrity. To withhold the complete gift of self (one's fertility) from one's spouse in each conjugal act.

Periodic Abstinence (Natural Family Planning)—to give complete gift of self; to maintain the integrity of the conjugal act.

1 *Motive*—to fulfill the God-given "mission" of spouses to *have* children and space or cease to have children for only serious, just or worthy reasons/conditions "based on the physical or psychological conditions of the spouses or on external factors" (HV #16.) Open to new life even if, despite one's intention, pregnancy occurs;

2 *Circumstances*—only serious circumstances affecting health, finance, other children or family members' needs, noble (selfless) endeavors or other external conditions— not self-seeking preferences, whims or caprice;

3 *Deed or Act*—to remain virile or fertile. To not violate one's bodily integrity but to freely abstain from conjugal love periodically. To give a complete gift of one's self (including fertility) to one's spouse in each conjugal embrace. One need not always act in favor of a basic human good so long as one never acts against it, as in the case of celibacy and NFP which honor openness to life by not acting against it for proportionate reasons.

Diagram 11.2
The Blessings & Curses of *Humanae Vitae*

If *Humanae Vitae* is accepted—*Humanae Vitae*, no. 21

1   *There will be a growth of true civilization;*
2   *Man will not abdicate human duties by over-reliance on technology; and*
3   *The dignity of spouses will be safeguarded.*

"Yet this discipline which is proper to the purity of married couples, far from harming conjugal love, rather confers on it a higher human value. It demands continual effort yet, thanks to its beneficent influence, husband and wife fully develop their personalities, being enriched with spiritual values. Such discipline bestows upon family life fruits of serenity and peace, and facilitates that solution of other problems; it favors attention for one's partner, helps both parties to drive out selfishness, the enemy of true love; and deepens their sense of responsibility. By its means, parents acquire the capacity of having a deeper and more efficacious influence in the education of their offspring; little children and youths grow up with a just appraisal of human values, and in the serene and harmonious development of their spiritual and sensitive faculties." (HV, no. 21)

If *Humanae Vitae* is rejected—*Humanae Vitae*, no. 17

1   *Marital infidelity will increase;*
2   *A general weakening of morals will occur;*
3   *Scandal (temptation to sensual sin) will be given to youth;*
4   *Husbands will lose respect for their wives—"disregard their psychological and physical equilibrium"—treating them as objects of their pleasure and not as "companions who should be treated with attentiveness and love"; and*
5   *Acceptance of contraception sets a dangerous precedent for "Rulers who care little about the moral law." Legitimizing the private use of contraceptives "will hand over to the will of the public authorities the power of interfering in the most exclusive and intimate mission of spouses." For what is licit for an individual to choose for his own good is licit for the state to impose for the common good.*

"Let it be considered also that a dangerous weapon would thus be placed in the hands of those public authorities who take no heed of moral exigencies. Who could blame a government for applying to the solution of the problems of the community those means acknowledged to be licit for married couples in the solution of a family problem? Who will stop rulers from favoring, from even imposing upon their peoples, if they were to consider it necessary, the method of contraception which they judge to be most efficacious? In such a way men, wishing to avoid individual, family, or social difficulties encountered in the observance of the divine law, would reach the point of placing at the mercy of the intervention of public authorities the most personal and most reserved sector of conjugal intimacy." (HV, no. 17)

Notes

1. Eccles. 3:5.
2. HV, no. 17.
3. HV, no. 1. See also William E. May, "Humanae Vitae," in ECST.
4. George E. Frost, "Malthus, Thomas, and the Neo-Malthusians," in ECST.
5. HV, no. 2.
6. HV, no. 3.
7. HV, no. 4.
8. HV, no. 5.
9. HV, no. 6.
10. HV, no. 7. See also Robert F. Gotcher, "Vatican Council, Second," ECST.
11. Eph. 3:15.
12. HV, no. 8.
13. HV, no. 9. See also GS, no. 50.
14. HV, no. 10.
15. HV, no. 11.
16. HV, no. 12.
17. MM, no. 53.
18. HV, no. 14.
19. HV, no. 14.
20. HV, no. 15.
21. HV, no. 16.
22. HV, no. 17.
23. Luke 2:34.
24. HV, no. 18.
25. HV, no. 19.
26. HV, no. 20.
27. HV, no. 21.
28. HV, no. 22.
29. HV, no. 23. See also Douglas A. Sylva, "Population Control," in ECST.
30. HV, no. 24.
31. HV, no. 27.
32. HV, no. 25; citing Eph. 5:25, 28–29, 32–33.
33. HV, no. 26.
34. HV, no. 28.
35. HV, no. 29.
36. HV, no. 30.
37. HV, no. 31.
38. George P. Graham, "Birth Control Controversy," in ECST.
39. Perry J. Cahall, "Casti Connubii," in ECST.
40. CCC, no. 56. See also CCC, no. 19; Mary Shivanandan, *Crossing the Threshold of Love* (Washington D.C.: Catholic University Press, 1999), 196–98.
41. Pius XII, *Address to Italian Midwives*, no. 27 (27 October 1951), 850.
42. Robert F. Gotcher, "Vatican Council, Second," in ECST.
43. MM, no. 193.
44. GS, no. 50.
45. GS, no. 51.

46. GS, no. 49. See also PH, no. 5.

47. Anthony Zimmerman, *Human Life Issues* (Collegeville, MD: Human Life International, 1996), 1–4.

48. William E. May, "Humanae Vitae," in ECST.

49. Brian Scarnecchia and Terrence McKeegan, "Phantom Goal of Access to Sexual and Reproductive Health," *The Millennium Development Goals in Light of Catholic Social Teaching*, International Organization Research Group, White Paper no.10 (New York, NY: Catholic Family and Research Inst., 2009), 73–85; Scarnecchia and McKeegan, "Goal Three: Promote Gender Equality and Empower Women," *Millenium Development Goals*, 43–48.

50. LG, no. 25. See also Russell Shaw, "Contraception, Infallibility and the Ordinary Magisterium" in *Why Humanae Vitae Was Right: A Reader*, ed. Janet Smith (San Francisco: Ignatius Press, 1993).

51. ATF, no. 9.

52. John Paul II, *The Redemption of the Body and the Sacramentality of Marriage*, given as a series of addresses in his *Wednesday Catechesis* (1984).

53. CC, no. 54.

54. GS, no. 27.

55. VS, no. 80.

56. CCC, no. 2370.

57. ERD, no. 52.

58. Hanna Klaus, "Abstinence Education" in ECST.

59. CHCW, no. 20.

60. Hanna Klaus, "Natural Family Planning," in ECST.

61. FC, no. 11.

62. HV, no. 29.

63. HV, no. 31.

64. HV, no. 32.

65. HV, no. 34.

66. Pope John Paul II, "To the Participants at a Course for Teachers of the Natural Methods," *L'Osservatore Romano*, 10 January 1992, 3.

67. CHCW, no. 18; citing FC no. 32.

68. CHCW, no. 20.

69. CCC, no. 365.

70. FC, no. 19; Cf. Adrian Teo, "Human Embryos" and Adrian Teo, "Human Experimentation," in ECST.

71. C. Bonfiglioli, "Men's Contraception Injections Match Pill's Effectiveness," *Australian Associated Press*, 1 August 1995; Brian Clowes, *The Facts of Life: An Authoritative Guide to Life and Family Issues* (Front Royal, VA: Human Life International, 1997), 56; citing Dorothy Bonn, "What Prospects for Hormonal Contraceptives for Men?" *The Lancet* 347 (3 February 1996): 316.

72. Scott P. Richert, "'Be Fruitful and Multiply' Part II: Is This the Way the World Ends? The Mechanization of Fertility, Cultural and Agricultural," *The Family in America* 10, no. 6 (June 1996): 4. See also Richard M. Sharpe and Niels E. Skakkebaek, "Are Estrogens Involved in Falling Sperm Counts and Disorders of the Male Reproductive Tract?" *The Lancet* 341 (29 May 1993): 1392–95.

73. HV, no. 15.

74. Thomas A. Cavanaugh, "Double Effect, Principle of," in ECST.

75. George P. Graham, "Moral Absolutes," in ECST.

76. HV, no. 14.

77. Clowes, *The Facts of Life*, 35. See also Hanna Klaus, "Birth Control," in ECST; John F. Kippley, "Contraceptive Mentality," in ECST.

78. Thomas O'Donnell, *Medicine and Christian Morality*, 3d ed. (New York: Alba House, 1996), 195–98.

79. ERD, no. 36.

80. CHCW, no. 17.

81. Francis J. Connell, *Outlines of Moral Theology* (Milwaukee, WI: Bruce Publishing Co., 1953), 172.

82. HV, no. 15.

83. Congregation for the Doctrine of the Faith, *Reply of the Sacred Congregation for the Doctrine of the Faith on Sterilization in Catholic Hospitals* (*Quaecumque Sterilizatio*), Origins 10 (1976): 33–35, no. 1.

84. HV, no. 15.

85. HV, no. 2.

86. HV, no. 3.

87. CCC, no. 1753. See also Rom. 3:8.

88. CCC, no. 1755.

89. ERD, no. 51.

90. FC, no. 30.

91. Holy See, *The Charter of the Rights of the Family*, art. 3-b, http://www.vatican.va/roman_curia/pontifical_councils/family/documents/rc_pc_family_doc_19831022_family-rights_en.html (21 Nov. 2009).

92. CCC, no. 2297.

93. EV, no. 91. See also Douglas A. Sylva, "Population Control," in ECST.

94. EV, no. 30.

95. Donald P. Asci, "Donum Vitae," in ECST.

96. D. Brian Scarnecchia, "Human Life International," in ECST.

97. DV, no. 2.B.4.

98. DV, no. 2.B.4; quoting Pope John Paul II, General Audience, 16 January 1980: *Insegnamenti di Giovanni Paolo II*, III, 1, (1980), 148–52.

99. *Planned Parenthood of Southeastern Pennsylvania v. Casey*, 505 U.S. 833, 856, 112 S.Ct. 2791, 2809 (1992).

100. EV, no. 13.

101. EV, no. 13.

102. EV, no. 13.

103. EV, no. 13.

104. FC, no. 12.

105. FC, no. 13.

106. FC, no. 21.

107. EV, no. 12. See also E. Christian Brugger, "*Evangelium Vitae*," in ECST.

108. EV, no. 17.

109. EV, no. 29.

110. EV, no. 23.

111. EV, no. 23.

112. EV, no. 23.

113. EV, no. 23.

114. HV, no. 17.

115. CL, no. 38.

116. VS, no. 99; citing *Centesimus Annus* (1991), no. 44.

117. Clowes, *Facts of Life*, 290.

118. Stephen D. Mumford, *The Life and Death of NSSM 200: How the Destruction of Political Will Doomed a U. S. Population Policy* (Bethesda, MD: Center for Population Research, 1994), 45–186; citing *Implications of Worldwide population Growth for the U.S. Security and Overseas Interests*, National Security Memorandum 200, no. 37. See also Michel Schooyans, *The Totalitarian Trend of Liberalism*, trans. John Miller (St. Louis, MO: Central Bureau, 1995), 57–58; Marguerite Peeters, *Globalization of the Western Cultural Revolution: Key Concepts, Operational Mechanisms*, trans. Benedict Kobus (Brussels: Institute for Intercultural Dialogue Dynamics, 2007), 115–16.

119. See Stephen W. Mosher, *A Mother's Ordeal: One Woman's Fight Against China's One-Child Policy* (Orlando, FL: Harcourt Brace & Co. 1993), 334.

120. *Griswold v. Connecticut*, 381 U.S. 513, n.3, 85 S.Ct. 1678, 1698 (1965). See also Raoul Berger, *Government by Judiciary: The Transformation of the Fourteenth Amendment* (Indianapolis: Liberty Found, 1997), 322–27.

121. *Griswold*, 381 U.S. at 484.

122. *Griswold*, 381 U.S. at 497–98.

123. Emily Belz, "Political science: Obama science czar brings a potentially radical agenda," *World Magazine*, 15 August 2009, http://www.worldmag.com/articles/15708 (21 Nov. 2009); citing Anne H. Ehrlich, Paul R. Ehrlich, and John P. Holdren, *Ecoscience: Population, Resources, Environment* (San Francisco: W.H. Freeman & Co. 1977), 837.

124. Jerome R. Corsi, "Holdren says Constitution backs compulsory abortion," *WorldNetDaily*, 23 September 2009, http://www.wnd.com/index.php/index.php?fa=PAGE.view&pageId=110720 (21 Nov. 2009); citing Paul Ehrlich, Anne Ehrlich and John Holdren, *Ecoscience: Population, Resources, Environment* (San Francisco: W.H. Freeman & Co., 1977), 838.

125. Emily Belz, "Political science: Obama science czar," *World Magazine*.

Chapter 12
Abortion

Introduction

A mother's love, even in the animal kingdom, is something to be reckoned with. Visitors to our national parks are warned that hikers make some noise as they amble along; for to stumble upon a grizzly she-bear and her cubs will usually trigger a ferocious attack. Even small animals risk life and limb to protect their young. Once I encountered a wild Canadian goose crossing my farm leading her goslings behind her. She refused to fly to safety when I drove my field tractor within a few feet of her and the half dozen goslings trailing behind her. Instead of flying away to safety, she ran along the ground just a few feet in front of me honking around my house and through my back yard attempting to decoy me away from her goslings.

Human nature is not immune to maternal instinct. To stifle it unleashes a tremendous destructive energy whereas to respect it as a reflection of God's love leads to heroic virtue. When an ancient Greek poet wished to show the vicious fury of a woman scorned, he could image no scene more unnatural, more horrible, than Calypso atop a seaward cliff killing her children before the eyes of their father, Ulysses, as he sped by in his ship—his punishment for deserting her. Isaiah the prophet describes the love of God for Israel in the pattern of maternal love, yet still stronger, more protective than even that of a mother for her child: "Can a mother forget her infant, be without tenderness for the child within her womb? Even should she forget, I will never forget you. See I have carved your name upon the palm of my hand."[1]

The Church honors the heroic charity that crowned a life of the Italian pediatrician, Gianna Beretta Molla, age 39, who in April of 1962 chose not to end her pregnancy by the removal of her cancerous uterus—a morally licit operation—in order to protect and preserve the unborn life within her. She told her doctor: "If it is a question of choosing between me and the child, do not have the least hesitation: I demand that you choose the child. Save it!" Gianna gave birth to a healthy baby girl, but died herself within a few days. At her beatification Pope John Paul II confirmed the heroic call of true motherhood—exemplar of "invincible love:"

> Gianna Beretta Molla . . . knew how to give her life in sacrifice, so that the being which she carried in her womb—and who is with us today [as a professed religious sister]!—could live. Being a physician, she was aware of what awaited her, but she did not flinch before the sacrifice, thus confirming the heroic nature of her virtues. We wish to pay homage to all brave mothers who devote themselves unreservedly to their families and who are then ready to make all sacrifices, so as to transmit the best of themselves to their families. We thank you, heroic mothers, for your invincible love![2]

From these examples, both good and bad, we learn that the relationship between mother and child expresses the most intense bond; a bond which is horrific when desecrated and beatific when perfected. Nothing comes closer to Paradise than the joy of a mother, exhausted after her journey through her private purgatory of labor and delivery, now blissfully content and resting while nursing her newborn child. Nothing takes us closer to the edge of the Abyss, "the Outer Darkness," than abortion.

All sin is the privation of a necessary moral good. The sin of abortion is the privation of many goods. It demonstrates the absence of the virtue of justice because it is murder: the unjust taking of the most innocent of human lives. Abortion is usually the result of the privation of the virtue of chastity: the child being conceived out of wedlock. But most telling of all, the tragedy of abortion is, by all accounts, *ugly*: a privation of beauty and betrayal of "fairest love":

> When we speak about fairest love, we are also speaking about beauty: the beauty of love and the beauty of the human being who, by the power of the Holy Spirit, is capable of such love. We are speaking of the beauty of man and woman: their beauty as brother or sister, as a couple about to be married, as husband and wife. . . . All that a husband and a wife promise to each other—to be "true in good times and in bad, and to love and honor each other all the days of their life"—is possible only when fairest love is present. Man today cannot learn this from what modern mass culture has to say. Fairest love is learned above all in prayer [to] the Holy Spirit, the source of fairest love.[3]

The most striking thing about abortion is that it is ugly. There is blood, gore and pain. But to the red blood and the blush of shame is added the white pall of regret and despair. Abortion accosts all our senses. In the years since abortion has been legal it has never been able to shake off the look, the smell, the sound, the feel of the back alley from which it sprang. Abortion has never, and will never be acceptable in polite society because it is inescapably ugly. It can only be referred to euphemistically, although better yet not at all. It is telling that for so noble a calling, that of defending the fundamental rights of women, no one wishes to be known an "abortionist." There are no "Abortionist of the Year" awards. To call a person or thing "an abortion" is still to call it grotesque, a monstrosity.

In the final scene of the movie *Life is Beautiful* by Roberto Bernini, the hero Guido, is carrying his sleeping son back to their concentration camp bunk to go to sleep. While walking through a heavy mist dreaming about his wife, he almost stumbles into the deep circular pit into which all the naked, emaciated, broken corpses of the victims of the concentration camp have been flung. The paralyzing scene which comes into view through the swirling mist looks like a vision of the seven rungs of Hell in Dante's *Inferno*. Or perhaps it is better likened to the bottom of the collection jar of a suction aspirator, after it has sucked the life out of a mother's womb: a spiral of broken, mangled body parts, in some infernal cauldron. Abortion, the mass grave, and Hell share the same face.

There is an inherent connection between things foul, just as there is between what is lovely. As we consider the subject of abortion we must remember that only what is fair and beautiful can restore what is hideous and ugly. It took fairest love to cover Golgotha; crucifixion and the grave swathed in the beauty of redemption and sacrificial love. It took fairest love, wrapped in white martyr's robes, to purify the Coliseum walls and floor splattered in red blood and gore. It required many martyrs of fairest love to close the ovens at Auschwitz and bring down the Iron Curtain and the Soviet Gulag. Eventually fairest love will close the yawning gates of the abortion clinic archipelago. With the help of Mary, "Mother of Fairest Love," it will be done because it must, for human life is a gift from God, fair and beautiful and stronger than death.

The Key Magisterial Document:
Declaration on Procured Abortion (1974)

It took the eugenic birth control movement over seventy years to overthrow all criminal sanctions for the sale and use of contraception in the United States, culminating in the 1965 Supreme Court decision *Griswold v. Connecticut*. It took a mere eight years for the Supreme Court to apply the so-called "right to privacy" it had fashioned in *Griswold* to abortion.[4] Shortly after the Supreme Court declared abortion a fundamental human right in its infamous decision, *Roe v. Wade* (1973), the Vatican replied with *Declaration on Procured Abortion* (1974). This pronouncement was timely. The Second Vatican Council reiterated the Church's ageless condemnation of abortion in the encyclical *Gaudium et Spes* (1964) that "abortion and infanticide are abominable crimes."[5] With a few praiseworthy exceptions, however, Catholic political leaders were only too willing to "give their soul" for political power, and betrayed the faith or did little to oppose abortion.[6]

Introduction (pars. 1-5)

The Congregation for the Doctrine of the Faith noted ironically it is often the same voices who most loudly decry violations against human rights such as poverty and the death penalty that speak up most fervently in favor of the legalization of abortion. However, the Church's mission is to defend human dignity against everything that threatens it.[7] Some argue to legalize abortion will violate no one's conscience, because all remain free to not have an abortion. This is nonsense. One may not make a pretext of freedom of opinion so as to attack the rights of others, especially the right to life.[8] Despite the propaganda campaign directed against public figures who oppose legalization of abortion, resistance continues especially from many conferences of Bishops.[9] It is the duty of the Congregation of the Church to confirm what these Bishops have begun "transmitting to the faithful a constant teaching of the supreme Magisterium, which teaches moral norms in the light of faith. It is therefore clear that this declaration necessarily entails a grave obligation for Christian consciences."[10]

Part II. (pars. 5-8) "In the Light of Faith"

Death came into the world because of the Devil's envy[11] not because of God's doing.[12] Death came into the world through sin, but there is no final triumph for death, because of Christ's resurrection.[13] Although Scripture does not spell out the exact moment when human life begins, nonetheless, "the period of life which precedes birth [is] the object of God's attention."[14]

The Church has always held that human life must be protected from the moment new human life begins and so opposed the immorality of the Greco-Roman world that approved of abortion and infanticide.[15] In the *Didache*, we read: "You shall not kill by abortion the fruit of the womb and you shall not murder the infant already born." In the third century Tertullian wrote: "To prevent birth is anticipated murder; it makes little difference whether one destroys a life already born or does away with it in its nascent stage. The one who will be a man, is already one."[16]

Regardless of when the soul is infused, the Church has always considered abortion an "objectively grave fault." True, the penal sanctions differed in the Middle Ages depending on whether a penitent confessed to an abortion prior to or after "quickening" (when the baby's movements are first felt within the womb). Nonetheless, St Thomas Aquinas taught all abortion is a "grave sin against natural law."[17] And when lax canonists "sought to excuse an abortion procured before the moment accepted by some as the moment of the spiritual animation of the new being," this opinion was rejected by Pope Innocent XI. Recent Popes have all condemned direct abortion. Vatican Council II emphatically declared: "Life must be safeguarded with extreme care from conception; *abortion and infanticide are abominable crimes*."[18] Pope Paul VI made it clear the Church's teaching on abortion—"has not changed and is unchangeable."[19]

Part III. (pars. 8-14) "In the Additional Light of Reason"

Human reason alone, even without the aid of Revelation, is sufficient to recognize and respect human life in the womb. Each man is "created immediately by God" and therefore all men are radically equal. From this it follows that each man has a right to life and to the goods necessary to sustain his life in strict justice.[20] However, life in this world is not the final end of man;[21] "there are higher values for which it could be legitimate or even necessary to be willing to expose oneself to the risk of losing bodily life." Even though each person must serve the common good of society, the common good is not man's final end. For this reason the human person "can be definitively subordinated only to God" and must never be treated as a means to an end as is the case with abortion.[22]

Those rights which are inherent in human beings are called "human rights." Because these basic human rights precede society, society cannot grant or deny but, rather, "society has the function to preserve and to enforce them."[23] The first and most important human right is a human being's right to life, and this one is fundamental and the condition of all the others and must be protected above all others. All invidious discrimination is evil, whether it is directed toward race, sex, color or religion, or especially towards human life itself. It does not belong to public authorities "to recognize a right to life for some and not for others." After all, it is not recognition by another that constitutes this right to life: "This right is antecedent to its recognition; it demands recognition and it is strictly unjust to refuse it." [24]

> Any discrimination based on the various stages of life is no more justice than any other discrimination. The right to life remains complete in an old person, even one greatly weakened; it is not lost by one who is incurably sick. The right to life is no less to be respected in the small infant just born than in the mature person. In reality, respect for human life is called for from the time that the process of generation begins. From the time that the ovum is fertilized, a life is begun which is neither that of the father nor of the mother; it is rather the life of a new human being with his own growth. It would never be made human if it were not human already.[25]

Genetics corroborates these philosophical conclusions: that is, the unique individual is fully specified physically from the first instant of his or her "existence." The word "conception" was not used in this context because the debate over when a human soul is infused in the embryo is still an open question:

> This declaration expressly leaves aside the question of the moment when the spiritual soul is infused. There is not a unanimous tradition on this point and authors are as yet in disagreement. For some it dates from the first instant; for others it could not at least precede nidation. It is not within the competence of science to decide between these views, because the existence of an immortal

soul is not a question in its field. It is a philosophical problem from which our moral affirmation remains independent for two reason: (1) supposing a belated animation, there is still nothing less than *human* life, preparing for and calling for a soul in which the nature received from parents is completed; (2) on the other hand, it suffices that this presence of the soul be probable (and one can never prove the contrary) in order that the taking of life involve accepting the risk of killing a man, not only waiting for, but already in possession of his soul.[26]

The "adventure of human life" is begun at fertilization and only time is required for each of the capacities of the human person to be fully actualized. Science does not lend support to those who defend abortion. Even if there is some doubt regarding when the human soul is infused, "it is objectively a grave sin to dare to risk murder. 'The one who will be a man, is already one.'"[27]

Part IV. (pars. 14-18) "Reply to Some Objections"

Circumstances that give rise to a temptation to have an abortion include threats to the health or even the life of the mother, the burden of an additional child (especially if the child may have a disability), a question of dishonor or a loss of social standing, etc. However, "none of these reasons can ever objectively confer the right to dispose of another's life, even when that life is only beginning." The parents can no more choose to end their child's life based on a prognosis of an unhappy future, than a child, when it grows up, can choose to commit suicide because of dire circumstances. "Life is too fundamental a value to be weighed against even very serious disadvantages."[28]

The woman's rights movement is on solid ground "insofar as it seeks to free them of all unjust discrimination," but not when it presumes to rid women from what nature demands of them as well as of men, i.e., responsible childbearing.[29] Sexual freedom, too, is authentic when it seeks to attain the mastery of reason and true love "over instinctive impulse, without diminishing pleasure but keeping it in its proper place." But if by sexual freedom one means "seeking sexual pleasure to the point of satiety, without taking into account . . . the essential orientation of sexual life to its fruits of fertility," then it is unworthy of man, let alone a Christian and certainly does not confer a right to have an abortion.[30]

Scientific progress and technology are achievements of the human spirit but technology and the direction provided by sound morality must go together, "since technology exists for man and must respect his finality." Just as nuclear energy may not be put to every purpose, "there is no right to manipulate human life in every possible direction." While advances in technology may have made early abortion easier, it is no less immoral.[31] No one, neither spouses nor political authorities, may resort to abortion as a means of regulating birth: "The damage to moral values is always a greater evil for the common good than any disadvantage in the economic or demographic order."[32]

Part V. (pars. 19-24) "Morality and Law"

The public debate over the morality of abortion is accompanied by judicial discussion and considerable political pressure to legalize abortion in the name of pluralism, majority rule, difficulties enforcing anti-abortion criminal statutes, and health risks to women who procure an illegal and, therefore, unsafe abortion.[33] These arguments are not conclusive. To leave abortion unpunished by criminal sanction will give the impression it is not a serious crime against human life. Even though human laws cannot prohibit all manner of evil, and sometime must tolerate a lesser evil to avoid a greater evil, this threat to the life of a child is an evil that takes precedence over all opinions to the contrary.[34]

Human law is not required to censure every evil, "but it cannot act contrary to a law which is deeper and more majestic than any human law: the natural law engraved in men's hearts by the Creator as a norm which reason clarifies . . . [and] which it is always wrong to contradict. Human law can abstain from punishment, but it cannot declare to be right what would be opposed to the natural law, for this opposition suffices to give the assurance that a law is not a law at all."[35] Laws which declare abortion a human right are immoral and can never be obeyed, much less may one campaign for, or vote for such a law, or collaborate in its application as, for instance, when "doctors or nurses find themselves obliged to cooperate closely in abortions and have to choose between the law of God and their professional situations."[36]

The task of law is to reform society so that "it may be possible to give every child coming into this world a welcome worthy of a person" through a series of positive policy reforms that will provide a realistic alternative to abortion, such as providing assistance to families and to unwed mothers, as well as grants for children, protection for fatherless children, and reasonable adoption policies and procedures.[37]

Part VI. (pars. 24-27) Conclusion

The path of true progress passes through trials that conform a person's conscience to right reason and the requirements of the divine law. Heroism is sometimes called for in order to do the right thing. We exhort those who are able to lighten the burdens that crush the human spirit tempting many to not follow their conscience and have an abortion, to do so and reach out and help.[38] Bringing up a handicapped child, though it may entail sorrow is not, as some believe, an "absolute misfortune" viewed from the perspective of eternity and man's eternal reward, which is what a Christian is called to do: "To measure happiness by the absence of sorrow and misery in this world is to turn one's back on the Gospel."[39]

The sufferings associated with bearing a child under difficult circumstances must be treated as required by the law of Charity "of which the first preoccupation must always be the establishment of justice." One can never approve of abortion. As a practical matter this means one must combat its causes through political action and law, while at the same time influencing morality, helping families, mothers and children, furthering genuine progress in medicine, and providing programs of charitable assistance.[40] There will be no change in morals unless there is a change in the prevailing cultural attitude—"which considers fertility as an evil." It is true that large families "come up against much greater difficulties in an industrial and urban civilization," requiring prudence in marital relations, but generosity from couples is also asked, in "cooperating with the Creator in the transmission of life which gives new members to society and new children to the Church." The sufferings and sacrifices we endure in order to favor life, St. Paul assures us "can never be compared to the glory, as yet unrevealed, which is waiting for us."[41]

Moral and Legal Reflection on Abortion

In 1965 Vatican Council II condemned abortion as an intrinsically evil act[42] and an "abominable crime."[43] Nonetheless, the United States Supreme Court declared abortion on demand to be a fundamental human right and the law of the land in 1973 in its infamous decision, *Roe v. Wade*.[44]

The *Roe* Court groped through two thousand years of the history of Western civilization, picking here and there, for some prop to support its predetermined result—to legalize abortion on demand throughout all nine months of pregnancy. The Hippocratic Oath from ancient Greece, which the medical profession of the West looked to and revered throughout the whole of the Christian era, forbad medical professionals from providing "a woman an abortive remedy." However according to one obscure expert the Court latched onto the Oath was merely a "Phthagorean manifesto" and not an "absolute standard of medical conduct."[45] Next the Court shuffled through an abridgment of Christian theology and tipped the hat to St. Thomas Aquinas only to note he believed like Aristotle before him that God infused a human soul into a human embryo sometime after conception, 40 days later for a boy and 80 days later for a girl, as codified by the Medieval canonists.[46] The Court's perusal of English common law and statutory law revealed that, like the Scholastics, due to inadequate embryology the criminal law of England discriminated between a human child in the process of being formed and a baby "quickened," i.e., kicking and moving in his or her mother's womb and imposed harsher sentences for the abortion of a live and kicking prenatal child than one, they wrongly believed, was still being knitting together *in utero*.[47]

The Court admitted that with advances in medical science and embryology following the Civil War in the United States the American Medical Association urged that "the grave defects of our laws both common and statute, as regards the independent and actual existence of the child before birth, as a living being." State legislatures followed the urging of the AMA and adopted more restrictive anti-abortion laws.[48] However one hundred years later the AMA reversed itself and, joined by the American Bar Association, urged for a repeal of the anti-abortion criminal laws.[49]

The rationale for the anti-abortion laws of the past one hundred years, the court said, may have been "Victorian social concern to discourage illicit sexual conduct" or fear that abortion posed more risk to a mother's health than the live birth of her child or the State's duty of "protecting prenatal life." The court said it must weigh these public policy considerations thoughtfully.[50]

However, the *Roe* Court's results-oriented jurisprudence is most transparent when, after one paragraph of constitutional analysis, it concluded that no matter where a woman's right to privacy is located in the Constitution (in the "Penumbras of the Bill of Rights" as *Griswold* suggests or the "concept of liberty guaranteed by the first section of the Fourteenth Amendment," or somewhere else) the important thing is that it exists (if for no other reason than the Court says it does) and "is broad enough to encompass a woman's decision whether or not to terminate her pregnancy."[51]

The *Roe* Court wasted a lot of time discussing the "potentiality of human life" and "viability"[52] when all it meant to say was it had adopted a postmodern anthropology. The essential feature of post-modernity is the ability of the individual to define their "self" (their nature, their gender) through meaningful choices open to unlimited redefinition. Therefore, since prenatal children cannot express themselves through meaningful choices they are only potential persons.

Perhaps the most unreasonable and disingenuous statement in *Roe v. Wade* appears when the Court resolves its positive practical doubt over a serious moral and legal question, that is, whether to permit what may be state endorsed murder, with culpable indifference.

> We need not resolve the difficult question of when life begins. When those trained in the respective disciplines of medicine, philosophy, and theology are unable to arrive at any *consensus*, the judiciary, at this point in the development of man's knowledge, is not in a position to speculate as to the answer.[53]

At a criminal trial what would be the result if a person charged with manslaughter for shooting into a bush and killing his hunting buddy explained that he wasn't sure when he shot into the bush if it was the deer he was hunting for or his hunting buddy? But because he was in doubt he had a right to shoot! The judge or jury would rule the hunter had a "depraved heart" in caring so little about whether or not he might kill his hunting buddy and find him guilty of manslaughter.

For the same reason the *Roe* Court's reasoning is depraved. Its reliance on consensus is utterly post-modern—no consensus deconstructs truth, consensus constructs truth. However consensus may be understood in two radically different ways: According to Modern thought to arrive at consensus is to affirm the truth of a certain proposition; Postmodernism arrives at consensus through an agreement among persons in view of a proposed action. In the first case we have a general accord of intellects, in the second case there is an accord of individual wills. But the term "consensus" works a sleight of hand inclining one to slide easily from thinking one has assented to a given truth when one has merely decided to not object or to oppose another's will:

> The "new rights of man" [i.e., abortion, gender mainstreaming, etc.] are the fruit of voluntary decisions to which one holds fast. But one falsely imputes to these decisions the same status as the truth that had been recognized in the principles having already been the object of assent. This semantic fraud allows one to make an ideological use of the classical tradition of man's rights [for instance, the political rights in the Bill of Rights] with the aim of legitimizing inadmissible programs of action.[54]

Griswold and *Roe* make ideological use of the classical tradition of human rights to legitimize inadmissible programs of action when the court struck down criminal statutes proscribing contraception in 1965 and abortion in 1973. Declaring that there is a right of privacy found in the penumbras of the Bill of Rights works a sleight of hand whereby the court inclines us to think they have assented to veracities "so rooted in the traditions and conscience of our people as to be ranked as fundamental"[55] but in reality they impose on us the consensus of our ruling elite.

In his dissent Chief Justice Rehnquist makes clear that the long standing consensus of the American people reflected in the anti-abortion laws of thirty-six states gave assent to the truth that to procure an elective abortion manifest criminal malice in taking the life of a child *in utero*. On the other hand, the majority point to a lack of consensus to oppose their will—"when those trained in the respective disciplines of medicine, philosophy, and theology are unable to" agree—as evidence that they are free to impose their value judgments on the nation.[56] That is why it is important to mount national demonstrations to signify a public objection and vote of "no consensus" to the will of our ruling elite such as the annual March for Life in Washington, DC on the anniversary of *Roe v. Wade* every January 23.

As Justice Scalia noted in his dissent in *Planned Parenthood of Southeast Pennsylvania v. Casey* (1993) the consensus, the "Pax Roeanna," imposed on the American people by the Court exhibits star chamber autocracy, that "[t]he Imperial Judiciary lives."

> It is instructive to compare this Nietzschean vision of us unelected, life-tenured judges-leading a Volk who will be "tested by following," and whose very belief in themselves" is mystically bound up in their "understanding" of a Court that "speak[s] before all others for their constitutional ideals.". . .[57] If, indeed, the "liberties" protected by the Constitution are, as the Court says, undefined and unbounded, then the people *should* demonstrate, to protest that we do not implement *their* values instead of *ours*.[58]

The Imperial Judiciary, however, is offended that every year the American people demonstrate and bracket with their feet, if you will, as they march through the nation's capital one-half million strong, the so called "right to privacy" indicating "no consensus" exists for a right to abortion. The autocratic Court has no Cossack horsemen to sweep the streets of the protestors who march to demand that the innate right to life of pre-natal children be respected, but they teach the protestors a lesson by their indifference:

> We are offended by these marchers who descend upon us, every year on the anniversary of Roe, to protest our saying that the Constitution requires what our society has never thought the Constitution requires. These people who refuse to be "tested by following" must be taught a lesson. We have no Cossacks, but at least we can stubbornly refuse to abandon an erroneous opinion that we might otherwise change—to show how little they intimidate us.[59]

Judge Robert Bork has written the Supreme Court now acts as a "band of outlaws" coercing the American people without warrant in law. He believes that as the institutional arrangements between the other branches of government now stand, this tendency will not change and the Court "can never be made a legitimate element of a basically democratic polity." He recommends three possible solutions to the postmodern transformation of American society and culture by judges:

> Decisions of courts might be made subject to modification or reversal by majority vote or the Senate and House of Representatives. Alternatively, courts might be deprived of the power of constitutional review. Either of those solutions would require a constitutional amendment. Perhaps an elected official will one day simply refuse to comply with a Supreme Court decision.[60]

Removing the most contentious issues from the sweep of the democratic process by declaring them to be fundamental rights that only the Supreme Court can decide, the Court has taken on the role of a Council of Revision, a role denied to it at the Constitutional Convention: "The judiciary should not be concerned with policy, the reasonableness or arbitrariness, the wisdom of legislation."[61] In usurping the democratic process the Court has delegitimized its own authority. By imposing their value judgments as a phony consensus on American society under the guise of constitutional adjudication the Court has undermined its legitimacy. Justice Scalia notes generally lawyers values are suspect:

> [T]he American people love democracy and the American people are not fools. As long as this Court thought (and the people thought) that we Justices were doing essentially lawyer's work up here—reading text and discerning our society's traditional understanding of that text—the public pretty much left us alone. Texts and traditions are facts to study, not convictions to demonstrate about. But if in reality our process of constitutional adjudication consists primarily of making *value judgments* . . . if, as I say, our pronouncement of constitutional law rests primarily on value judgments, then a free and intelligent people's attitude towards us can be expected to be (*ought* to be) quite different.

The people know that their value judgments are quite as good as those taught in any law school—maybe better.[62]

Less than one year after *Roe v. Wade*, the Sacred Congregation for the Faith issued *The Declaration on Procured Abortion,* which as we have seen repeated the Church's clear and constant teaching condemning abortion. Then in 1981 Pope John Paul II issued the encyclical *Familiaris Consortio,* which described legalized abortion as a threat to human dignity and the integrity of the family.[63] Noting the "interplay of light and darkness" in the world he denounced the "scourge of abortion" is one such darkness.[64] He reminded us that children do indeed have rights—they have the right to a family wherein "special attention must be devoted to them by developing a profound esteem for their personal dignity and a great respect and generous concern for their rights." Solicitude for children begins "even before birth, from the first moment of conception and then throughout the years of infancy and youth."[65] Therefore, the Church condemns as a grave offense all violence by public authorities which favor contraception or, still worse, of sterilization and procured abortion or conditioning international aid on the recipient nation putting into place programs to curtail their population's growth through the practice of contraception, sterilization and abortion.[66]

The *Charter of the Rights of the Family,* also promulgated in 1983, declared human life is to be "protected absolutely from the moment of conception,"[67] and as such, abortion is a crime against humanity, "a direct violation of the fundamental right to life of the human being." This fundamental right protects human embryos from "all experimental manipulation or exploitation." Spouses have an absolute right to decide upon the number of children to be born to them, but they have no right to limit their family size through the use of contraception, sterilization or abortion.[68] It condemned rich countries that condition economic aid to developing countries on whether developing countries implemented a national population control program utilizing contraception, sterilization and abortion.[69]

The Link between Abortion and In-vitro Fertilization

By 1987, in the name of curing infertility, many human embryos had been conceived *in-vitro*— (in glass) or in a petri dish. The artificial reproduction of human beings was well under way and surrogate mothers could be found willing to rent their wombs for insemination or embryo transfer when the Congregation for the Doctrine of the Faith addressed these human rights abuses and others in *Instruction on Respect for Human Life in its Origin and on the Dignity of Procreation (Donum Vitae).*[70]

Donum Vitae warned that the practice of *in-vitro* fertilization and its associated practices (artificial insemination, surrogate motherhood, pre-natal diagnosis and experimentation for non-therapeutic reasons,[71] the production of human embryos for scientific or commercial purposes,[72] attempts to fertilize human and animal gametes, gestation of human embryos in animal or artificial uteruses, freezing or cloning embryos,[73]) would only accelerate the deterioration of respect for human life begun by abortion: "the possible recognition by positive law and the political authorities of techniques of artificial transmission of life and the experimentation connected with it would widen the breach already opened by the legalization of abortion."[74] Living human embryos may never be produced *in-vitro* for use as "'biological material' or as providers of organs or tissues for transplants in the treatment of certain diseases."[75] In fact, the artificial production of human beings to supposedly cure the infertility of childless couples ironically exhibits an unmistakable "abortion mentality" that favors the eugenic control of a population:

> The connection between *in-vitro* fertilization and the voluntary destruction of human embryos occurs too often. This is significant: Through these procedures, with apparently contrary purposes, life and death are subjected to the decision of man, who thus sets himself up as the giver of life and death by decree. This dynamic of violence and domination may remain unnoticed by those very individuals who, in wishing to utilize this procedure, become subject to it themselves. The facts recorded and the cold logic which links them must be taken into consideration for a moral judgment on *in-vitro* fertilization and embryo transfer: The abortion mentality which has made this procedure possible thus leads, whether one wants it or not, to man's domination over the life and death of his fellow human beings and can lead to a system of radical eugenics.[76]

It is a shameful for a patient to request prenatal diagnosis with the intention of aborting the fetus if it is found to be defective or of the wrong sex, or for a doctor to deliberately contribute to establishing a link between an unfavorable prenatal diagnosis and abortion.[77] John Paul II in *Evangelium Vitae* reaffirmed the cruelty and baseness of the use of prenatal diagnosis for such eugenic purposes: "Such an attitude is shameful and utterly reprehensible, since it presumes to measure the value of a human life only within the parameters of 'normality' and physical well-being, thus opening the way to legitimizing infanticide and euthanasia as well."[78]

It would constitute a violation of fundamental human rights for civil authorities to force women to undergo fetal testing—to "directly induce expectant mothers to submit to prenatal diagnosis planned for the purpose of eliminating fetuses which are affected by malformations or which are carriers of hereditary illness."[79] Because the human embryo is essentially different from plants or animals,[80] and is sacred from its beginning because it involves the creative action of God who remains its sole end, therefore, it is illicit for anyone to lay claim to the right to destroy directly an innocent human being.[81]

The Link between Abortion and a Death Culture

In 1993, within a year of the United States Supreme Court decision reaffirming a right to abortion in *Planned Parenthood of Southeastern Pennsylvania v. Casey*, Pope John Paul II released *The Splendor of Truth* which cited the condemnation of abortion given in Vatican Council II, *The Church in the Modern World*,[82] as one of many examples of intrinsically evil acts.[83] The following year, dedicated by the Church as "The Year of the Family," John Paul II provided an extended analysis of modern culture, *Letter to Families*, wherein legalized abortion was seen as symptomatic of a fundamentally flawed perception of the human person and emblematic of a "culture of death." He warned that the family is at the center of a cultural storm: "placed at the center of the great struggle between good and evil, between life and death, between love and all that is opposed to love."[84] Civilization or culture, he said, is nothing other than the "humanization of the world"[85] by persons made in the image of God revealed as the "Divine We."[86] The family is founded upon this trinitarian pattern, which begins as a community of persons (husband and wife) and blossoms into a community of persons in parenthood.[87]

True civilization is, then, a civilization of love which originates in God, who is love,[88] which is poured into human hearts by the Holy Spirit[89] so that man may fulfill his nature by becoming a gift of self for others.[90] True civilization is opposed in our day, he said, by an "anti-civilization" of use which values things over persons, function over being. This anti-civilization fosters an anti-life mentality where children are seen as a hindrance to parents.[91]

The Fourth Commandment, "Honor your Father and Mother," contains the implicit expectation of mutual respect, writes the Holy Father:

> Indirectly we can speak of the honor owed children by their parents. . . . You parents, the divine precept seems to say, should act in such a way that your life will merit the honor (and the love) of your children. . . . They deserve this because they are alive, because they are who they are, and this is true from the first moment of their conception [fertilization].[92]

Abortion is diametrically opposed to the honor parents owe their children and their duty to uphold fairest love:

> "God became man so that we might become gods." "Christ Jesus, our Lord, the Son of God, became the son of man so that man could become a son of God." This truth of faith is likewise the truth about the human being. It clearly indicates the gravity of all attempts on the life of a child in the womb of its mother. Precisely in this situation we encounter everything which is diametrically opposed to fairest love. If an individual is exclusively concerned with use, he can reach the point of killing love by killing the fruit of love. For the culture of use, the "blessed fruit of your womb" (Lk 1:42) becomes in a certain sense an "accursed fruit."[93]

The lack of honor and contempt for human life in the womb demonstrated by a modern "civilization of death" is analogous to that of King Herod who slaughtered newborn children to secure his crown.[94] Those who do not welcome human life individually, or create structures of sin (customs and laws) hostile to the life of an unborn child, will hear Christ say on judgment day "Depart from me." Whereas those who welcomed life will hear a benediction:

"Come, O blessed of my Father. . . ." (Mt 25:34-36) "I was an unborn child, and you welcomed me by letting me be born.". . . Or again: "You helped mothers filled with uncertainty and exposed to wrongful pressure to welcome their unborn child and let it be born."[95]

Even though the family is situated at the center of a great storm, the sacraments of Christ are incomparably more powerful than the forces of the world which beset it.[96] Therefore, families should take heart and live their vocation with courage.[97]

The following year, in 1995, John Paul II issued *The Gospel of Life*, which continued to develop the theme of a clash of civilizations. He said that the acceptance of abortion in the popular mind and behavior, as well as its legal recognition bespeaks an "extremely dangerous crisis of the moral sense," increasingly incapable of telling right from wrong even failing to recognize the fundamental right to life. Men and women today lack the courage to "look truth in the eye and to *call things by their proper name*," but instead resort to disingenuous and ambiguous terminology calling abortion the "'interruption of pregnancy'" instead of what it is—"murder."[98]

Abortion kills a child and mars the hearts of those responsible: the mother, the father, and the wider circle of family and friends, doctors, nurses, legislators. Those responsible for abortion also include "those who have encouraged the spread of an attitude of sexual permissiveness and a lack of esteem for motherhood," as well as public authorities who did not create societal support for large families. Furthermore, not only does abortion kill and mar individuals, but it goes beyond them and "takes on a distinctly social dimension" inflicting a "serious wound" on culture creating a " *'structure of sin' which opposes human life not yet born*."[99]

Scripture and Tradition confirm the doctrine taught by the Church for two thousand years. The philosophical speculations regarding the infusion of the spiritual soul never caused the Church to hesitate in its "moral condemnation of abortion."[100] In order to warn the faithful that abortion is "a most serious and dangerous crime," the Church automatically excommunicates anyone who, knowing the penalty attached to this sin, commits or formally cooperates in a successful abortion.[101]

John Paul II fashioned a solemn formula to make clear he was repeating the constant and infallible teaching of the ordinary Magisterium condemning abortion:

[B]y the authority which Christ conferred upon Peter and his Successors, in communion with the Bishops—who on various occasions have condemned abortion and who in the aforementioned consultation, albeit dispersed throughout the world, have shown unanimous agreement concerning this doctrine—*I declare that direct abortion, that is, abortion willed as an end or as a means, always constitutes a grave moral disorder,* since it is the deliberate killing of an innocent human being. This doctrine is based upon the natural law and upon the written Word of God, is transmitted by the Church's Tradition and taught by the ordinary and universal Magisterium.[102]

Abortion in the Cases of Rape, Incest, or a Child with a Disability

The patient's right to life "from conception to natural death; and in every condition, either health or sickness, perfection or handicap, wealth or paupery,"[103] means that the health care worker must not think he or she holds the power of life or death over any patients.[104] Therefore, health care workers owe the unborn child the same consideration given to competent adults: "Prenatal life is fully human in every phase of its development. Hence, health care workers owe human embryos and fetuses the same respect, the same protection and the same care as that given to a human person."[105]

In the case of rape, the rights of potentially two persons, the mother and the child that may have been conceived, need to be respected. Therefore, the rape protocol at a Catholic hospital may never "initiate or recommend treatments that have as their purpose or direct effect the removal, destruction, or interference with the implantation of a fertilized ovum."

However, rape victims may be given contraceptives that do not act as abortifacients because the direct effect of a spermicide, to kill or immobilize the rapist's sperm, does not willfully disassociate the two ends of the conjugal act (union and procreation). Rape is not a conjugal act or an act of union, but rather, an act of violence. One is entitled to defend one's self from unjust aggression. Therefore, the direct effect of using a contraceptive device is that of self defense from the ongoing assault of the rapist which is not the moral object of contraception:

> A woman who has been raped should be able to defend herself against a potential conception from the sexual assault. If, after appropriate testing, there is no evidence that conception has occurred already, she may be treated with medications that would prevent ovulation, sperm capacitation, or fertilization. It is not permissible, however, to initiate or to recommend treatments that have as their purpose or direct effect the removal, destruction, or interference with the plantation of a fertilized ovum.[106]

There is some controversy among faithful Catholic as to whether it is licit to administer "emergency contraceptives" to rape victims after the victim has been tested to determine progesterone levels in the blood, and whether or not she has recently or is about to ovulate. Those in favor of the "Peoria Protocol" (named after the diocese in which it was implemented under Bishop Myers) argue oral contraceptives suppress ovulation and hinder sperm capacitation. However, another effect of oral contraceptives is to thin the uterine lining and prevent the implantation of the newly conceived embryo; that is, causing an abortion. Chris Kahlenborn, MD, among others, believes the effects of oral contraceptives persist for days and if ovulation isn't suppressed a child conceived as a result of the rape will be aborted as an effect of the oral contraceptive. Dr. William May argues that such an abortion would not be a licit indirect abortion but an illicit direct abortion: "here you are conditionally intending abortion," he writes.[107]

Incest is a form of rape that is even more unjust because it involves the betrayal of a minor girl by an older (adult) male relative who is morally bound to protect her. However, what has been said about rape applies also in cases of incest—to knowingly and willingly destroy an unborn child conceived in incest is a direct abortion and seriously sinful.[108]

A eugenic abortion performed so as to prevent a child defective in some way from being born is always a direct abortion and gravely sinful. Even diagnostic testing conducted to discover whether or not a child is "defective" so that he or she can be destroyed in an abortion is immoral.[109] Health care facilities and medical personnel are not allowed to participate in these eugenic abortions, nor in pre-natal tests whose purpose is to establish a link between any fetal anomaly discovered and a procured abortion.[110]

The United Nations *Convention on the Rights of Persons with Disabilities* is a multilateral treaty that was drafted to uphold the dignity and rights of persons with disabilities. In its Sixth Session, August 2005, The Holy See and the Philippines introduced language that would have assured disabled children would not be subject to non-therapeutic medical interventions "before as well as after birth."[111] Unfortunately, the final draft of the Convention included language that provided "sexual and reproductive health and population-based public health programmes" to persons with disabilities. The Holy See refused to ratify the treaty because the inclusion of this language, a code word for abortion, diminished the dignity of persons with disabilities guaranteeing that persons with disabilities have the right to abort their children if they present fetal defect.[112]

Whether or not a human soul is infused into the developing human embryo within the first two weeks after conception does not alter the morality of an abortion in these cases because it is still human life developing under the providential care of its Creator, and must not be left prey to human caprice.[113]

> Even the theory of the fourteenth day—the day when the primitive streak appears, in which the cells lose their totipotentiality and twin divisions are no longer possible—[one] cannot ignore and deny the fundamental and decisive biogenetic fact of the human and individual nature of the fruit of the conception.[114]

Those who suffer from the aftermath of an abortion psychologically, physically or spiritually, should be cared for.[115] The corpus of a dead human embryo must be treated with the respect owed to every human person. Therefore, an autopsy may not be performed nor may an embryo be mutilated before its death, nor may there be any trafficking in their corpses afterwards.[116]A dead aborted fetus must be given the same respect as a human corpse. This means that it cannot be disposed of as just another item of rubbish or biological waste. If at all possible it should be appropriately interred.[117]

Catholic health care facilities may not use human tissue obtained by direct abortions for scientific research or therapeutic treatment.[118] Likewise, the human fetus cannot be used for experimentation or transplant if the abortion was caused voluntarily. To do so would be an unworthy instrumentalization of a human life.[119]

Direct versus Indirect Abortion: The Principle of Double Effect Applied to Ectopic Pregnancy

First we must consider whether any of the medical procedures used to manage an ectopic pregnancy constitutes a direct abortion. If so, then no matter the risk to the mother's life, a direct abortion may not be performed: "In the case of extra-uterine pregnancy no intervention is morally licit which constitutes a direct abortion."[120] A direct abortion is defined as "the directly intended termination of pregnancy before viability or the directly intended destruction of a viable fetus."[121] No person has the right to save their own life at the cost of deliberately killing another person: "It may be a serious question of health, sometimes of life or death, for the mother. . . . We proclaim only that none of these reasons can ever objectively confer the right to dispose of another life, even where that life is only beginning."[122]

Normally when a woman conceives, one of her ova is fertilized in the upper reaches of one of her fallopian tubes, and the human child, once conceived (known as the zygote in this early stage), then travels down the fallopian tube and implants in the lining of her uterus. In the case of extra-uterine pregnancy, a woman conceives but instead of the zygote implanting in its mother's uterus, it implants elsewhere: i.e., in her fallopian tube, ovary, cervix, abdominal cavity or on the organs therein. In some cases of an extra-uterine pregnancy the human fetus will develop to the point of viability and may be delivered by caesarian section. Often it will not develop and will spontaneously abort without harm to the mother. This is the case in 64% of tubal pregnancies.[123] However, in the case of tubal pregnancy, the zygote will grow and erode the tubal musculature and eventually cause the fallopian tube to rupture, endangering the mother's life from internal hemorrhaging.

To follow the moral maxims—"do no harm" and "one must not do evil that good come of it"—one must make careful distinctions when a person foresees that their action will have more than one effect by applying the principle of double effect.[124] The four elements of the principle of double effect are the following:

1) The moral deed ("what" one chooses) must be good or indifferent, but never intrinsically evil;
2) The motive ("why" one chooses) must be good;

3) The good effect must precede, not follow, the evil effect (causally); and
4) The good effect must be proportionate (not necessarily equally) to the
evil effect.[125]

The principle of double effect safeguards against "doing evil that good
come of it." This caveat is found in Scripture and the teaching of the Church:

> But if our wrongdoing provides proof of God's justice, what are we to say? Is
> not God unjust when he inflicts punishment? (I speak in a merely human way.)
> Assuredly not! If that were so, how could God judge the world? Another ques-
> tion: If my falsehood brings to light God's truth and thus promotes his glory,
> why must I be condemned as a sinner? Or why may we not do evil that good
> may come of it? This is the very thing some slanderously accuse us of teaching;
> but they will get what they deserve.[126]

> "Can you not see that it is better for you to have one [innocent] man die for the
> people than to have the whole nation destroyed" (Jn. 11:50). Although this
> statement from Caiaphas, the high priest, is prophetic insofar as the death of Je-
> sus Christ is the ransom which has saved the whole world, at least potentially, it
> is at the same time an implicit condemnation of that treacherous logic St. Paul
> condemned explicitly in Rom 3:8—doing evil that good come of it—as the Ca-
> techism of the Catholic Church states: "The end does not justify the means."
> Thus the condemnation of an innocent person cannot be justified as a legitimate
> means of saving the nation.[127]

> I answer that, Nothing hinders one act from having two effects, only one of
> which is intended, while the other is beside the intention. Now moral acts take
> their species according to what is intended, and not according to what is beside
> the intention, since this is accidental. . . . Accordingly that act of self-defense
> may have two effects, one is the saving of one's life, the other is the slaying of
> the aggressor. Therefore this act, since one's intention is to save one's own life,
> is not unlawful, seeing that it is natural to everything to keep itself in being, as
> far as possible. And yet, though proceeding from a good intention, an act may
> be rendered unlawful, if it be out of proportion to the end. Wherefore if a man,
> in self-defense, uses more than necessary violence, it will be unlawful: whereas
> if he repel force with moderation his defense will be lawful.[128]

> An evil action cannot be justified by reference to a good intention.[129]

> The end does not justify the means.[130]

> If the abortion follows as a foreseen but not intended or willed but merely tole-
> rated consequence of a therapeutic act essential for the mother's health, this is
> morally legitimate. The abortion in this case is the indirect result of an act
> which is not in itself abortive.[131]

> Operations, treatments, and medications that have as their direct purpose the
> cure of a proportionately serious pathological condition of a pregnant woman
> are permitted when they cannot be safely postponed until the unborn child is

viable, even if they will result in the death of the unborn child.[132]

> We have on purpose always used the expression "direct attack on the life of the innocent," "*direct* killing" [to describe the sin of abortion]. For if, for instance, the safety of the life of the mother-to-be, independently of her pregnant condition, should urgently require a surgical operation or other therapeutic treatment, which would have as a side effect, in no way willed or intended yet inevitable, the death of the fetus, then such an act could not any longer be called a *direct* attack on innocent life. With these conditions, the operation, like other similar medical interventions, can be allowed, always assuming that a good of great worth, such as life, is at stake, and that it is not possible to delay until after the baby is born or to make use of some other effective remedy.[133]

In the case of extra-uterine pregnancy, a correct application of the principle of double effect is necessary in order to distinguish between direct and indirect abortion. Tubal pregnancy may be treated in the following four ways: 1) expectant therapy which requires one to wait for the extrauterine pregnancy to resolve itself, as most do, in a spontaneous abortion; 2) perform a partial or total salpin*gec*tomy—remove the part or all of the fallopian tube (in the case of a tubal pregnancy) with a live human zygote inside; 3) perform a salpin*gos*tomy—surgically remove the living human zygote itself from its site of implantation; or 4) use drug therapy—administer methotrexate (MIX) which causes the living human zygote to detach from its site of extra-uterine implantation.[134]

Expectant Therapy

The first approach to manage a tubal pregnancy, expectant therapy, is standing-by and being ready for any complications, but otherwise simply waiting for the tubal pregnancy to resolve itself in a spontaneous abortion which occurs 64 % of the time. Expectant therapy is the morally required approach if the ectopic pregnancy is not yet likely to rupture, and so does not pose an imminent threat to the mother. If this were not the case, the element of proportionality[135] would not be observed and the principle of double effect could not be invoked. The second patient, the unborn child, has a right to life which would be unnecessarily jeopardized if the traumatized tissue was not immediately threatening the pregnant woman so as to warrant direct surgical intervention on the damaged fallopian tube or other site of implantation:[136]

> However, it must be remembered that the entire radical procedure in tubal pregnancy, to be morally justified, must be based on the presumption that the [fallopian] tube itself is so pathologically affected here and now that surgical intervention on the tube itself is indicated.[137]

Salpingectomy

A second approach in the management of a tubal pregnancy is a partial or total salpingectomy. Since the turn of the 20th century ethicists and canonists have defended the morality of a salpingectomy because it is not a direct killing of a human embryo as either an end or a means; nor is it a direct removal of a non-viable human embryo from its life support provided by maternal tissue. A salpingectomy is the surgical removal of all or part of the fallopian tube in order to remove maternal tissue on the point of rupturing, due to an ectopic pregnancy containing (possibly) a living human embryo.

The immediate moral object of a salpingectomy is the body of the mother, her fallopian tube. The surgeon removes traumatized maternal tissue, the inflamed fallopian tube, with the human embryo inside but otherwise undisturbed. Of course, the surgical removal of all or part of a woman's fallopian tube will adversely affect her ability to conceive another child. The removal of both fallopian tubes, in the case of a second total salpingectomy, will render a woman unable to conceive a child. However, a woman who has experienced a tubal pregnancy is more prone to another ectopic pregnancy in the future at the site of scarring and trauma to her fallopian tube. Even a partial salpingectomy may predispose that fallopian tube to further life threatening tubal pregnancies.[138]

Only after it has been verified that a woman's fallopian tube is so damaged as to pose a serious threat to the mother's life may the tube be removed as pathological tissue. This finding must be determined on a case by case basis. There have been cases reported in medical literature of tubal pregnancy advancing to the point of viability. In these cases only if "the danger to the mother notably outweighs the chance for fetal survival" should a salpingectomy be considered.[139]

When there is an immediate threat of the fallopian tube rupturing from an ectopic pregnancy, the elements of the principle of double effect are met. First, what is done, the moral object is not intrinsically evil. The immediate moral object of a salpingectomy is the direct removal of pathological maternal tissue. Therefore the moral object is neutral which acquires further moral specificity as good or evil according to motive and circumstance. Second, her motive is good: she seeks to save her life by this operation, not end the life of her child, although she foresees this unintended consequence. Third, the circumstances must be such that her life is immediately threatened; otherwise, there would not be a proportionately grave reason to possibly hasten the death of her child. Fourth, the good sought, that is, saving her life, is initiated causally at the same time as the evil effect, even though it may possibly hasten the death of her child. Therefore, in a salpingectomy, one does not do evil that good come of it. This is similar to the removal of a cancerous uterus or the administration of chemotherapy to a woman pregnant with a non-viable child where the death of the child is foreseen but not the immediate object of the operation or procedure:

This condition [not doing evil that good come of it] would be infringed if the baby's death were the means to the removal of the uterus, so that those carrying out the procedure would inevitably act from a death-dealing intention, but this is not the case: the surgeon does not first kill the baby so that he can remove the uterus from the woman's body, but on the contrary removes the uterus, which happens to have the baby inside it. So the performance of the hysterectomy involves no direct attack on the baby being carried, and is therefore justified if there is sufficiently grave reasons for carrying it out.[140]

If the abortion follows as a foreseen but not intended or willed but merely tolerated consequence of a therapeutic act essential for the mother's health, this is morally legitimate. The abortion in this case is the indirect result of an act which is not in itself abortive.[141]

Operations, treatments, and medications that have as their direct purpose the cure of a proportionately serious pathological condition of a pregnant woman are permitted when they cannot be safely postponed until the unborn child is viable, even if they will result in the death of the unborn child.[142]

Salpingostomy

Some faithful Catholic ethicists, hoping to preserve the woman's fertility, defend the surgical procedure known as salpingostomy. In this proceedure a surgeon makes an incision in the fallopian tube to excise the living human embryo from the site of its extra-uterine implantation and then sutures up the incision. A salpingotomy is the same procedure except the incision is not sutured but is allowed to heal on its own in the hope there will be less scarring and, therefore, less chance of a future ectopic pregnancy at the same site. Fimbrial expression is sometimes used in cases when the ectopic pregnancy is located in the distal fimbrial portion of the fallopian tube (which occurs in about 5% of ectopic pregnancies), "milking" it out of the distal end of the fallopian tube with extirpation of the embryo.[143]

However, many ethicists faithful to the Magisterium of the Church do not distinguish between a surgical abortion that removes a non-viable human fetus developing within its mother's womb, from a surgical operation that removes a non-viable human embryo developing within its mother's fallopian tube or other site of extra-uterine implantation:

> In the first place it must be understood that abortion, or the removal of a non-viable fetus from the site of implantation, has always been recognized in the teaching of the Church as a grave moral evil. Moreover, from this moral viewpoint, aborting a fetus from a fallopian tube is no different from aborting it from the uterus itself.[144]

The circumstances that give rise to a salpingostomy are serious: a woman's life is in danger, and the motives of both the mother and her physician are upright, that is, to save her life. However, because the immediate object of the operation of a salpingostomy is *the body of the non-viable human embryo, and not the body of the mother* as in a salpingectomy, directly removing the embryo from its site of implantation, it *is* a direct abortion.[145]

Granted, in a salpingostomy, lethal force is not applied directly to the body of the human embryo, crushing or dismembering it. But a direct killing can be committed by omission just as surely as by commission. Some argue a salpingostomy is not a direct abortion, but simply the justified removal of a mis-implanted embryo for proportionate reasons.[146] But the question must be asked: how is the immediate object in directly removing a non-viable human embryo from the maternal tissue in which it has implanted any different than directly removing a pre-natal child from his or her mother's uterus?

The 1971 edition of the *Ethical and Religious Directives for Catholic Health Care Facilities* permitted a salpingectomy but forbad a salpingostomy from being performed in Catholic hospitals. This reflected the accepted definition of abortion as the deliberate expulsion of a non-viable human embryo or fetus:

> In extra-uterine pregnancy the affected part of the mother (e.g., cervix, ovary, or fallopian tube) may be removed, even though fetal death is foreseen, provided that (a) the affected part is presumed already to be so damaged and dangerously affected as to warrant its removal, and that (b) the operation is not just a separation of the embryo or fetus from its site with the part (which would be a direct abortion from a uterine appendage) and that (c) the operation cannot be postponed without notably increasing the danger to the mother.[147]

However, the 4th edition of *Ethical and Religious Directives for Catholic Health Care Facilities* (2004) simply says, "In the case of extrauterine pregnancy, no intervention is morally licit which constitutes a direct abortion."[148] It then refers the reader to the definition of direct abortion, "that is, the directly intended termination of pregnancy before viability or the directly intended destruction of a viable fetus."[149] It appears that the Committee on Doctrine of the National Conference of Catholic Bishops wished to allow the full and vigorous exchange of ideas to continue on what constitutes a direct abortion and whether a salpingostomy or drug therapy is licit. Notable Catholic moralists, all faithful to the Magisterium, have lined up on either side of this issue. For instance Albert Moraczewski, Germain Grisez, Joseph Boyle and Patrick Lee believe the principle of double effect applies to a salpingostomy, provided there is not a formal intention to kill the human embryo but simply to remove it. On the other side, William May, Thomas O'Donnell and Msgr. William Smith believe it to be a direct abortion.[150]

Moraczewski seems to view a salpingostomy as a "mini-salpingectomy", if you will. He interprets the immediate object of the operation to be the pathological tissue of the fallopian tube in which the trophoblastic tissue of the embryo has implanted: "[A]long with the removal of the pathological tissue—the tissue damaged by the ingrowing trophoblastic cells of the embryo—the embryo proper is also removed. . . . The specific focus of the surgical action [of a salpingostomy] is the removal of the damaged tubal tissue and damaging trophoblastic tissue."[151] On the other hand, O'Donnell characterizes the immediate object of a salpingostomy as the removal, not of damaged maternal tissue, but of the embryo itself: its goal is to "shell out the fetus" from its site of implantation:

> [O]ne cannot legitimately shell out the fetus and leave the tube, or even shell out the fetus with the hope of possibly being able to repair the tube. This would clearly be an abortive procedure. . . . Moreover, to distinguish between removing a non-viable fetus from the uterus and from the fallopian tube is patently (from a theological viewpoint) to make a distinction without a difference.[152]

> The direct removal of an embryo or fetus from its site of implantation (except under circumstances of its viability which then becomes induced labor or premature delivery) is clearly the direct infliction of a lethal blow which is, in turn, directly destructive of the fetal life.[153]

The medical facts are best described by medical experts. Moraczewski distinguishes between the trophoblastic cells of the embryo and "the embryo proper," seeing in their destruction no direct attack upon the body of the embryonic child. However, Charles E. Cavagnaro III, M.D., holds that the trophoblastic cells of a human embryo are part of its vital organs and that, although hypothetically with advances in medical technology a salpingostomy could be performed without injury to trophoblastic cells, the way it is now performed the trophoblastic cells are destroyed.[154] Moreover, several prominent physicians involved in defending life issues (Thomas W. Hilgers, John Bruchalski, and Bernard Nathanson—the last two are former abortionists), believe a salpingostomy constitutes an attack on the body of the human embryo and is thus a direct abortion.

Drug Therapy

Whether or not the use of the drug Methotrexate (MTX) in the treatment of ectopic pregnancy is licit must be decided by looking at "the proximate end of the deliberate decision of the acting person" (the moral object) to determine whether it is good, hypothetically neutral, or evil.[155] If the immediate effect of this drug is directed towards the body of the embryo and its operation is *not* therapeutic but lethal to the embryo, then the proximate end of the action of a person who chooses to use this drug with informed consent is to actualize the immediate effect of this drug. The immediate effect of MTX is to interfere with the utilization of folic acid which inhibits DNA synthesis, disabling the functioning of the trophoblast, a vital organ of a human embryo, thereby killing the embryo.[156] Therefore, the proximate end of the deliberate decision of the acting person using MTX is to initiate a process that inescapably kills a human embryo: in other words, a direct abortion. A direct abortion is "the deliberate and direct killing, *by whatever means* it is carried out, of a human being in the initial phase of his or her existence"[157] As we have seen, a direct abortion may not be performed for otherwise legitimate medical reasons, or that good may come of it. So long as the moral object is evil, the whole action is evil, even if the motive and circumstances are good.[158]

There are philosophers and theologians faithful to the Magisterium of the Church, however, who defend this drug therapy in the case of ectopic pregnancy. They ask:

> Does it [methotrexate] kill the child or does it arrest a destructive activity? Exactly how does MTX function? If certain medical facts were established, it might lead to an acceptance of MTX in certain types of tubal pregnancies.[159]

In his article Moraczewski writes that the immediate effect of MTX is the inhibition of the trophoblastic cells to synthesize DNA as required to produce "protein-digesting enzymes" necessary for the implantation of the embryo into the tubal tissue.[160] He points out that the key issue is "whether the interference with DNA synthesis by MTX ultimately constitutes a direct killing of the embryo."[161] However, Moraczewski mischaracterizes the moral object when he says that inhibiting the ability of the trophoblastic cells of the human embryo to synthesize DNA is simply an inhibition of the development of cells "*injurious to the mother and ultimately to the embryo itself.*"[162] His choice of words suggests that inhibiting DNA synthesis in trophoblastic cells in cases of ectopic pregnancy is somehow curative of a fatal pathology afflicting the embryo. This is not the case. The embryo is not destroying itself. The embryo suffers from no pathology. Its trophoblastic cells are not reproducing out of control like cancer cells run amuck, that somehow need MTX to bring them under control and return them to normal functioning. In fact, its trophoblastic cells are functioning fine. They are sustaining the life of the embryo by implanting in maternal tissue, which allows the embryo to draw sustenance. It will not be the activity of the trophoblastic cells that will cause injury to the embryo in the future; rather it is the maternal tissue in question that will eventually prove inadequate to supply those cells and rupture. The activity of the embryo is not defective; rather, it is the potentiality of the maternal tissue in question that is inadequate and life threatening to both mother and child under the circumstances.

The trophoblast cells are embryonic tissue. Later in fetal development they cooperate with maternal tissue to form the placenta. But at the point in embryonic development in almost all tubal pregnancies, they are clearly a "vital organ" of the human embryo.[163] Therefore, it makes little difference morally whether one attacks the inner mass of the body of the human embryo directly (the "embryo proper," as Moraczewski says), destroys its outer mass (the trophoblastic cells), or destroys the trophoblast by first inhibiting its essential functions, that is, "DNA synthesis, cell division, and proteolytic action in the trophoblast *prior* to the death of the trophoblast."[164] According to Dr. Charles Cavagnaro, M.D., the death of the embryo from MTX comes *before* the destructive action of the trophoblast becomes serious: "[E]mbryonic death is going to occur before the threat is serious and is exactly the means by which the serious threat has been avoided. Dead embryos do not continue to implant."[165]

Whether the principle of double effect applies in this case is not simply a question of whether a good effect ("stopping the destructive action of the trophoblast") is initiated causally prior to, or at least at the same time as, the hypothetically neutral effect ("stopping DNA synthesis"), as Moraczewski's analysis suggests. Stopping DNA synthesis in the trophoblast of a human embryo is not a neutral act. Therefore, the principle of double effect does not apply because its first and most important element is not met, namely the moral object, and the "proximate end of a deliberate decision of the acting person," is intrinsically evil. Since Moraczewski admits the function of DNA synthesis in trophoblastic cells is to enable the embryo to grow and divide, it is inescapable that the proximate end of the deliberate decision to administer MTX is to eliminate the ability of the embryo to grow and divide, or, in other words, to kill it.

> Killing the human embryo is not simply foreseen, it is the proximate end of a deliberate decision because it is the target of MTX: 1) the trophoblastic cells and their function are those of a human embryo and 2) there is nothing pathological about these cells, *per se*, that those administering MTX attempt to cure. Rather, they seek to harm healthy trophoblastic cells by rendering them dysfunctional. The "curative inhibition of destructive activity of the trophoblast" directed towards saving the mother's life is the *final end*, the motive, which she accomplishes by way of the *proximate end* of her decision, that is, "stopping DNA synthesis" in a vital organ of her child thereby killing her child. Therefore, the moral object in the administration of methotrexate in cases of ectopic pregnancy is intrinsically evil, it is a direct abortion, for the ulterior purpose of saving the life of the mother. . . . Because MTX benefits only the mother and exerts its pertinent actions on the child, it seems fair to conclude that in this case we have chosen to hurt the child with a lethal force *for the sake of the* mother.[166]

> At issue here is that, in practice, the evil effect of directly removing or killing of the embryo is the direct means to the good effect of saving the mother's fertility (and life) and thus not proper grounds for applying the principle of double effect. . . . The direct act of removing the conceptus from the fallopian tube, be it by suction, forceps, or toxin, is the cause of the well intended health of the mother. . . . Therefore, since the immediate effect of methotrexate and salpingotomy (salpingostomy) is the death of the fetus, the principle of double effect is not applicable because the act is evil.[167]

An Argumentative Analogy:
Salpingectomy versus Salpingostomy

Imagine you are in a crowded classroom with no windows and only one door. Suddenly the heating and air conditioning unit explodes into flame, filling the room with smoke. Everyone runs for the door. The first person to get to the door, Tiny, weighs five hundred pounds and, instead of going through sideways as he did upon entering, he attempts to run straight through the door and gets stuck. No amount of shoving, pushing or pulling can budge him one inch. But low and behold, right next to the door is a fire extinguisher and axe! The fire extinguisher doesn't work, but one student grabs the axe and debates within himself whether it is morally licit to open an escape route through the door. The walls are made of cinder block and steel against which the axe is useless. Can he simply use the axe to chop Tiny up, not to deliberately murder him, but to clear the exit that they may escape certain death?

Another person suggests that they use the axe to pry loose the door jam and pivot it inside the room with Tiny still stuck in it, even though they foresee he may expire sooner because there is even less air in the room than in the door-way. Some argue—"What's the difference? Tiny (who has already passed out) is going to die from smoke inhalation anyways no matter what we do."

But we must ask: is there *really* no difference in moral objects between chopping off Tiny's head and arms, and shoving him out the door into a deep shaft, or loosening the door jam he is stuck in and pivoting him out of the way? What is the direct target of their action in each case? In the first two cases, the axe strikes Tiny, killing him by decapitation or blood loss. In the third scenario, they ram Tiny's body and send him hurtling to his death. Only in the last case do they do him no harm. Similarly, to dismember a human embryo or remove a non-viable embryo from its site of implantation in the fallopian tube into a hos-tile environment, as is done in a salpingostomy, is a direct attack on the body of the pre-natal child which kills him or her. Whereas to cut out the damaged por-tion or all the fallopian tube, as in a salpingectomy, is not a direct or even an indirect attack on the pre-natal child. The operation does the child no good, but it does him no harm. It is a hypothetically neutral act which, under the circums-tance, and for an upright motive becomes a good deed.

Obligation to Save the Embryo in Cases of Ectopic Pregnancy

If the embryo implanted in its mother's fallopian tube or other site of extra-uterine pregnancy could be removed and transplanted into its mother's uterus or an artificial womb without disproportionate risk or burden to the mother, all attempts to do so that had a reasonable chance of success would be morally re-quired. There have been at least three successful transplantations of embryos from the fallopian tube to their mother's uterus, in 1915, 1917 and in 1990.[168]

Professor Edwin Bessler, professor of biology at Franciscan University of Steubenville, suggests that the following procedure may enhance the success of an ectopic embryo transplant. First, a salpingostomy could be licitly performed for this therapeutic purpose. Then the embryo would be introduced into the ute-rus. The surgeon would then perfuse the site of implantation with a high nutrient and high oxygen solution to sustain the embryo's life while it implanted. At the same time a nicotine patch would be administered to the mother in order to faci-litate blood vessel growth, helping the embryo to establish itself and implant in the uterus.[169]

One further consideration that recommends salpingectomy over a salpingostomy or drug therapy: the embryo can be baptized in the former because it is usually alive after the tube is removed but it will be dead after either of the later two modalities are performed.[170]

Cooperation in Abortion

One person may cooperate in the good or evil deed of another in two ways: formally and/or materially.[171] One formally cooperates in the good deeds of missionaries by praying for their good or the success of their labors, by contributing directly to their success by donations or by recommending them to others. Similarly, one formally cooperates in the evil deeds of terrorists by willing their success and providing them aid, either directly furthering their evil projects (helping them build or plant a bomb), or by performing otherwise neutral tasks that in fact assist them accomplish their goals (bringing them newspapers or a short-band radio). The essential element in formal cooperation is unanimity of wills between the principal and the cooperator.

The distinguishing feature of material cooperation is the lack of unanimity of will between the principal and the cooperator. Material cooperation occurs when a person performs a good or neutral deed that he foresees will be used by wicked people for evil purposes he himself repudiates. One may materially cooperate *remotely* in the evil deeds of others by performing an action that contributes in a minuscule way to an evil enterprise over which he or she has no direct control, being completely replaceable. For instance, when one buys a product from a large corporation that as part of its charitable gifting donates to abortion providers, or one is a mere sales clerk in a large store that sells condoms, one is a remote, unnecessary cooperator. One may cooperate *proximately* in the evil deeds of others by performing an action that contributes in a major way to an evil enterprise over which he or she has some direct control, being *necessary* for it to achieve its evil purpose. For example, when one holds a significant amount of voting stock in a corporation that donates to abortion providers, or if one is the manager of a store who can influence whether condoms will be sold, one is both a proximate and necessary cooperator in these evil actions.

The basic rule is that the more proximate and necessary one's material cooperation is, the greater the amount of justification or "inconvenience" one must suffer in order to licitly perform a neutral or good deed that nonetheless aids and abets the evil enterprise. Conversely, the more remote and unnecessary one's cooperation is the less amount of justification or "inconvenience" one need suffer in order to licitly perform a neutral or good deed that aids and abets some evil action of another.

Immediate material cooperation is the most proximate association between the principal and the cooperator. This occurs when the cooperator actually performs the evil deed under protest. It is impossible, however, to plead one has not formally consented to an evil deed if one actually performs it and is sane. Fear is a detriment to free will but unless it causes what would amount to legal temporary insanity it does not relieve one of culpability for doing evil. Coercion or duress do not excuse or exonerate one from crimes that compromise the life or bodily integrity of another person. One may not murder an innocent person, even to save their own life. One may not castrate fellow prisoners to avoid one's own castration and death at the hands of sadistic prison camp guards. Such atrocities and war crimes were reported in the Bosnian conflict in war zones subject to "ethnic cleansing."[172]

The example of being forced at gun point to carry stolen money from a bank, however, illustrates an exception to the rule that immediate material cooperation invariably translates into formal cooperation. In this case, one is not guilty of theft because the nature of the action changes from theft, that is, the unjust taking of the private property of another against his will, into the simple taking of private property, but no longer against the will of reasonable bank depositors. No reasonable depositor would will an innocent person be murdered so as to preserve his bank deposits. Therefore, the depositor's consent to the taking of his money by an innocent bystander ordered to do so at gun-point is presumed. However, the bank robber's removal of the money of the bank depositors remains a theft because the depositors certainly do not consent to his unjust taking of their money.[173]

All persons who help another to procure a successful abortion, by recommending, referring, approving, provoking, concealing, partaking, through silence, or through defending it afterwards—all who thus demonstrate a unanimity of will—are all formal cooperators in the sin of abortion and, if they are aware of the canonical penalty, they are all automatically excommunicated from the Catholic Church:

> Formal cooperation in an abortion constitutes a grave offense. The Church attaches the canonical penalty of excommunication to this crime against human life. "A person who procures a completed abortion incurs excommunication latae sententiae,"[174] "by the very commission of the offense."[175]

> The excommunication has an essentially preventative and pedagogical significance. It is a forceful call from the Church, meant to arouse insensitive consciences, to dissuade people from an act which is absolutely incompatible with Gospel demands, and to awaken unreserved fidelity to life. One cannot be in ecclesial communion and at the same time disregard the Gospel of Life through the practice of abortion.[176]

Although the juridical penalty of excommunication is only imposed upon those who help to secure a successful abortion with knowledge of the canonical penalty, even the attempt to commit an abortion makes those who attempt this knowingly and willingly guilty of the grave sin of abortion: "Direct abortion, willed either as an end or a means, is gravely contrary to the moral law."[177] After all, one may commit all manner of sins in one's heart. An evil motive corrupts a human act. An evil decision to obtain an abortion can even make otherwise good actions evil if they are performed to secure that evil end, such as giving alms to poor persons to help them procure an abortion.[178]

When is a Nurse's Material Cooperation in a Direct Abortion Licit?

The question is often raised—is any degree of cooperation in a direct abortion permitted? There is some controversy over the degree of material cooperation permitted a nurse opposed to abortion who must, nonetheless, as a condition of his or her employment, assist in a hospital obstetric ward when abortions are performed. There is consensus among moralists and ethicists loyal to the Magisterium in the following situations.

First, the Church challenges all health care workers to honor their "professional loyalty" in the service of life and health and to "not tolerate any action which suppresses life" even if they face "serious discrimination."[179] Doctors and nurses must be "*conscientious objectors*" when encouraged by law "to carry out abortions or to cooperate proximately in direct abortions."[180] John Paul II said doctors and nurses must not place their skills at the service of death; rather they are called to be "guardians and servants of human life."[181]

Second, all ethicists faithful to the Magisterium agree that a doctor or nurse may never formally cooperate in a direct abortion. Therefore, a nurse may not attempt to console a person who has had an abortion with words that give the appearance of recommending or condoning an abortion, such as, "It was your only choice," or "Who can blame you?" or "It was the best thing to do under the circumstances." A doctor cannot refer his patient to another doctor for an abortion without committing a grave sin. If he is a Catholic and his patient procures a completed abortion and he is aware of the canonical penalty,[182] he will incur automatic excommunication:

> To actually intend the evil purpose is formal co-operation, no matter how small one's share in the actual physical execution. Advising, counseling, promoting, or condoning an evil action, even when sometimes merely by being silent when one has a duty to speak up or express an opinion, is formal co-operation because such actions signify agreement with evil. [183]

Third, reliable ethicists would allow a doctor or nurse to be material cooperators by contributing their services at a hospital where abortions are performed if they had proportionately grave reasons for doing so, such as not being able to secure another comparable position in the same locality and they were not required to cooperate proximately in direct abortions. In practice, this would mean a doctor could obtain privileges at a hospital that permitted abortions to be performed provided he would suffer serious financial loss if he were to not admit his patients there. A regular floor nurse could work there engaging in the routine functions of a floor nurse, a remote material cooperator, provided she could not find equally suitable employment in the same locality.[184]

Fourth, ethicists loyal to the Magisterium generally agree that medical personnel may cooperate with the pre-operative or post-operative care of patients who are about to undergo or already have undergone a direct abortion. The kind of pre-operative nursing care that meets with general agreement is that of a general nature (i.e., taking blood pressure), not that associated with preparing the patient for the abortion per se (i.e., a prostaglandin drip).[185] They would need more serious reasons to justify intermediate material cooperation. Therefore, they must ask to be relieved of these duties and have been denied with a serious threat of loss of promotion, reduction of work hours, heightened job insecurity, etc., before there would exist proportionate reasons for their intermediate material cooperation. Merely fearing ridicule or being ostracized for their conscientious objection would not be a proportionately grave reason to excuse their intermediate material cooperation in a direct abortion.

In the fourth edition of *Ethical and Religious Directives for Catholic Health Care Services* (2001), the United States Conference of Catholic Bishops retracted its 1995 edition's appendix delineating licit and illicit cooperation in abortion and referred the reader to "Reliable theological experts [who] should be consulted in interpreting and applying the principles governing cooperation."[186]

> By "an authentic moral theologian" is meant someone skilled in moral theology and who adheres to the teachings of the Church. It should be evident that the arguments of dissenting theologians, teaching contrary to the teaching authority of the Church, cannot engender a *solid probability* in favor of their dissident opinions.[187]

However, faithful ethicists are sharply divided over whether or not health care personnel may assist in the operating theater those who actually perform a direct abortion. The older school of thought represented by many conservative moralists permitted such proximate material cooperation, provided it was not absolutely necessary for the operation and after conscientious objection and protest over such an assignment had provoked the threat of grave sanctions, such as losing not only one's job but one's career due to dismissal for insubordination.

Thus, a moral text by Fr. Edwin Healy used in seminaries in the 1940s and 1950s, said that a doctor who performs an abortion or a nurse who "participates in the actual operation or the performing of the evil act" are guilty of crimes against the Fifth Commandment. But if a nurse has weighty reasons for lending her material cooperation, she may prepare the patient's body, bring the patient into the operating room, administer the anesthetic and hand the instruments to the operating surgeon.[188]

Fr. Francis Connell, first president of the Catholic Theological Society and Dean of Sacred Theology at Catholic University of America in the 1950s, dis-

tinguished between the formal cooperation of an assistant surgeon and proximate material cooperation of those assisting them in the operating room:

> But only for a most grave reason could a nurse cooperate *proximately*—e.g., by
> giving the anesthetic, by handing the instruments to the doctors, etc. Such a
> most grave reason would be the well-founded fear that she might be dismissed
> from the hospital and be barred from continuing her profession. However, ordi-
> narily Catholic nurses should protest against being appointed to such opera-
> tions, and in many cases their protests will be heeded. It stands to reason that
> the co-operation of a doctor in the actual performance of the operation would
> never be permissible, no matter what inconvenience he might otherwise suffer,
> for that would be formal cooperation—e.g., the young intern commanded by
> the surgeon in charge to perform a direct abortion.[189]

Following in this tradition, Fr. Thomas J. O'Donnell drew a distinction between proximate and necessary material cooperation versus proximate but not
necessary material cooperation in an abortion. He argued that the moral object
of the anesthetist was not the destruction of the unborn child, but the hypothetically neutral act of administering anesthesia to a patient. He is not an immediate
material cooperator like an intern who performs an abortion under protest but
which translates into formal cooperation nonetheless. His cooperation is certainly proximate, but permissible if it was required to escape very serious damage to
himself. However, if his cooperation is also absolutely necessary for the success
of the operation (he's the only person available to administer anesthesia), only a
harm to himself equal to that threatened the unborn child would excuse his cooperation in giving anesthesia:

> Administering the anesthesia is not the same as doing the abortion. Thus his
> cooperation is not formal but mediate material cooperation. The good effect
> will be the protection of his medical career. The evil effect will be all the viola-
> tions of the law of love that are involved in the situation. . . . If the refusal of
> the anesthetist to cooperate would prevent the abortion, it is difficult to see how
> he could agree to do so under any circumstance. . . . Moreover, in a case in
> which there is a question of serious harm to a third party and the cooperation is
> both proximate and truly necessary (so that the harm to the third party would
> not happen if cooperation were withheld), one could offer such cooperation, if
> by refusing his cooperation he would suffer damage commensurable to the
> foreseen harm to the third party.[190]

Many ethicists writing after the legalization of abortion in the 1970s believe
a clearer and more prophetic stance on the part of Catholic doctors and nurses is
required and tend to equate any proximate cooperation (necessary or not) within
the operating room as formal cooperation in a direct abortion.

Peter E. Bristow holds this position and cites the Italian Bishops conference
in support. They stated a "direct abortion is never licit" and proximate cooperation in abortion "such as that required in the operating room, is never licit."[191]
Bristow distinguishes between *direct* and *indirect* proximate material coopera-

tion depending on the timing of the assistance.[192] Thus, a nurse who assists an abortionist to perform an actual abortion engages in direct proximate cooperation. The nurse not only supplies an instrument that will be used to kill an unborn child in the future (like an orderly that regularly supplies sterile surgical instruments to an operating room), but she provides this instrument in the context of the actual operation: "Cooperation is indirect when someone supplies or provides an instrument which the other person will use in order to commit the evil, but which is not necessarily connected with the evil."[193] Therefore, everyone who assists in the operating room during an abortion is a formal cooperator due to their physical and moral proximity:

> Primarily, we must assess the proximity of the cooperator's action to the act of abortion itself. . . . [W]e are speaking here both of physical and moral proximity. This would include, therefore, both the actions performed in the operating room and those others which are uniquely directed to abortion and make it possible, for example, administering anesthetics prior to the operation, issuing a medical certificate authorizing it, encouraging a wife, partner, relation, friend, etc., to have one. [194]

Likewise F. J. Fitzpatrick of the Linacre Center concludes that a nurse in a hospital setting who assists an abortionist necessarily adopts the abortionist's intention to successfully complete the operation, i.e., a direct abortion and is, therefore, a formal cooperator:

> The decisive criterion here is that of *intention*. A nurse who assists a surgeon to carry out an abortion will have to gear whatever she does in the operating theater to the goal of having the abortion carried out efficiently and successfully. She will therefore identify herself with the surgeon's intention of carrying out the operation; she will share that evil intention. And since our intentions in acting go to make up our actions themselves, the nurse here, precisely because she shares the surgeon's evil intention, performs an action which is intrinsically evil, just as his is.[195]

Fitzpatrick counsels nurses required to cooperate more than remotely in intrinsically evil actions injurious to their patients to quit their jobs immediately if need be, rather than assist proximately in a direct abortion:

> Sometimes the fact that co-operation is required of a nurse as a condition of her employment may be sufficient to justify her in cooperating remotely in certain immoral practices. But if the practices themselves are seriously evil, particularly involving grave injustices to patients, one could not regard even the keeping of one's job as sufficiently valuable to justify co-operation.[196]

Co-authors Edward Hayes, Paul Hayes, Dorothy Ellen Kelly and James Drummey recognize that an occasional instance of proximate material cooperation in evil action may be justified for proportionately grave reasons, as when refusal "would probably result in dismissal, combined with the knowledge that a new position would be very difficult to obtain in the near future." Still, they advise against direct assistance in the operating room in cases of procured abortion:

> Since material cooperation consist in performing morally indifferent actions which make the operation possible, a nurse cannot directly assist at an abortion, i.e., hand the doctor the instruments that he will use to take the life of the unborn child. However, she may clean the operating room after the surgery, or care for the woman who had the abortion, if failure to do so would cost her her job and if she could not easily get another job.[197]

In attempting to resolve this split of opinion over cooperation in abortion it is good to note that the Magisterium of Church has not abandoned its "traditional doctrine" nor the various distinctions of material cooperation.[198] This was made perfectly clear in the letter by the Congregation for the Doctrine of the Faith "Reply on Sterilization in Catholic Hospitals" (1975) and by John Paul II in *Gospel of Life* (1995):

> The traditional doctrine regarding material cooperation, with the proper distinctions between *necessary and free, proximate and remote*, remains valid, to be applied with the utmost prudence, if the case warrants.[199]

> In order to shed light on this difficult question [of obeying unjust laws or regulations that require one to participate in evil actions], it is necessary to recall the "*general principles concerning cooperation in evil actions.*"[200]

Some suggest the older approach permitting direct proximate material cooperation in the operating room in a direct abortion has been rejected by Pope John Paul II in favor of a ban on all proximate material cooperation, necessary or not. Germaine Grisez does not agree:

> Someone might argue that recent Church teaching [referring to EV nos. 59, 89 and CHCW, no. 143] provide a clear answer to your question. . . . Plainly, these statements absolutely exclude doing abortions and wrongly cooperating in them. . . . However, I do not think these statements directly address your question. You [a nurse assistant to an abortionist at a general hospital] have conscientiously objected, and relevant laws and regulations apparently give you no protection. Some faithful Catholic moralists—ones who did not dissent from any teaching of the Church—held that in such a case a nurse assisting in abortion could be morally acceptable material cooperation.[201] It seems to me that if recent teachings were meant to exclude that option, they would have done so more clearly.[202]

Although *Gospel of Life* paragraph 74 does not specifically mention doctors and nurses as it does in paragraphs 59 and 89, it does define formal cooperation as inevitably attaching to certain actions which amount to a direct participation in murder:

Christians, like all people of good will, are called upon under grave obligation of conscience not to cooperate formally in practices which, even if permitted by civil legislation, are contrary to God's law. Indeed, from the moral standpoint, it is never licit to cooperate formally in evil. Such cooperation occurs when an action, either by its very nature or by the form it takes in a concrete situation, can be defined as a *direct* participation in an act against innocent human life or a sharing in the immoral intention of the person committing it.[203]

It is clear that if what one does, directly or indirectly, proximately or remotely, one does so as to further an abortion, that is, "sharing in the immoral intention," that person is a formal cooperator and guilty of the sin of abortion. On the other hand, formal cooperation inevitably occurs when what one does is a "direct participation in an act against innocent human life." A direct participation in an abortion certainly includes immediate material cooperation, actually using surgical equipment to kill an unborn child. We have seen some moralists include those who hand the equipment to the abortionist as guilty of direct participation in abortion.[204] Others include those who prep a patient for an abortion as direct participants in the abortion.[205]

But is this what Pope John Paul II meant? As Grisez notes above, it is not very clear. A narrow reading of this passage would suggest that only those who participate in the intrinsically evil act of using the instruments to kill an unborn child (immediate material cooperators) are inevitably formal cooperators.

This ambiguity is seen reflected in the different positions taken by the Italian Episcopal Conference, which forbade all proximate cooperation in the operating room in a direct abortion; and the U.S. Catholic Conference of Bishops, which forbade "immediate cooperation" in a direct abortion: Catholic health care facilities "are not permitted to engage in *immediate material cooperation* in actions that are intrinsically immoral, such as abortion, euthanasia, assisted suicide, and direct sterilization."[206] As we have seen, immediate material cooperation encompasses the action of the surgical assistant who kills an unborn child with surgical instruments but not those who materially assist him by performing hypothetically neutral acts such as administering anesthesia or handing him surgical instruments.[207]

To provide practical guidance to doctors, nurses and other health care personnel, the following conclusions seem in order. Reliable moral theologians and ethicists agree that a nurse required to participate in a direct abortion must: 1) exercise his or her prerogatives under a contractual or statutory conscience clause; and, if this is not available, then; 2) use up vacation time and sick leave; 3) protest the assignment; and, 4) be threatened with severe sanctions including the loss of employment and likely career possibilities for insubordination. Then, if one cannot do without their nursing career, one may invoke the principle of *probabilism* and "act on a solidly probable opinion in favor of liberty, even if the opinions restricting action are more probable:"[208]

[P]robabilism (which is generally accepted by Catholic theologians and, indeed, also by the teaching authority of the Church) maintains that if, in such circumstances of doubt, one has a *solidly probable opinion in favor of liberty* of action, that is sufficient to fulfill the responsibility of not acting rashly or irresponsibly, even if the opposing opinion favoring restriction is the more probable opinion.

"A solidly probable opinion" . . . is had if one trained at least somewhat in moral theology can defend the opinion with good arguments (intrinsic probability) or if a number of authentic moral theologians propose the opinion as probable (intrinsic probability).[209]

There is one last consideration—one may not give scandal to others: Scandal is an attitude or behavior which leads another to do evil. The person who gives scandal becomes his neighbor's tempter. He damages virtue and integrity; he may even draw his brother into spiritual death. Scandal is a grave offense if by deed or omission another is deliberately led into a grave offense.[210]

The passage quoted above refers to the scandal given to others by one's misdeeds. But scandal may also be given to others by the mere appearance of an impropriety.[211] If one fails to take steps to avoid misunderstanding and, though his action is licit, it appears to others as unjust and they are led to imitate him without following those steps which justified his action, he is guilty of leading his companion into sin: "Take care, however, lest in exercising your right [to eat meat sacrificed to idols] you become an occasion of sin to the weak [i.e., those new converts to Christianity who were but recently devoted to idols]."[212]

Therefore, even if one has protested, been threatened with the loss of one's job and career and, having relied upon reliable ethicists who permit mediate material cooperation in this situation, decide to assist in the operating room during a direct abortion, one must take steps to avoid the appearance of an impropriety. In all cases of licit material cooperation or indirect abortion, attempts must be made to avoid misunderstanding and scandal.[213]

In *Gospel of Life* paragraph 73, John Paul II addressed the issue of those who vote in favor of flawed abortion legislation—for instance, legislation that would restrict some abortions but permit it in cases of rape, incest and to save the mother's life or health. He says a legislator may vote for such a bill only if his reason is to at least save some lives *and* his "absolute personal opposition to procured abortion was well known" so as to avoid scandal. It is important to note that paragraph #73 of *Gospel of Life* provides that a legislator may vote for a bill permitting abortion in some cases while restricting it in others *only* in a state or province where a general so called right to abortion on demand is recognized in law and not if abortion is generally outlawed or restricted and the effect of the bill would be to permit greater access to abortion than before.[214]

Grisez concludes that a nurse required to assist an abortionist in the operating room perform an abortion or else lose their career, may licitly lend such cooperation *only* if she takes steps to avoid scandal. However, her explanations and protests are likely to lead to her termination:

> Nurses who, like you, reluctantly assist at an abortion could forestall scandal in such cases only by clearly stating their position to each patient and anyone else involved who seem to assume or desire their approval, encouragement, and/or psychological support. But that might well be judged to violate patient care standards and lead to your dismissal.[215]

> In sum, your involvement when assigned to assist in abortion [three times in the last seven years] might not require you to intend the abortion or choose to do anything wrong in itself. But the steps that would be necessary to prevent scandal and bear witness to the truth about abortion might well lead to your dismissal. . . . Moreover, you can obtain other adequate employment, and so, unless you do everything you can to prevent scandal and bear witness, assisting in abortions might well be unfair to the babies who will be killed.[216]

Charity demands that Catholic nurses placed in such morally compromised situations be heroic witnesses of the sanctity of human life and avoid scandal by continual protest until finding alternative employment, even at a significant reduction in their salary:

> As a result, doctors and nurses are obligated to be *conscientious objectors*. The great, fundamental value of life makes this obligation a grave moral duty for medical personnel who are encouraged by law to carry out abortions or to cooperate proximately in direct abortion.[217]

Not long ago two nurses were discharged for "insubordination" for refusing to assist in surgical abortions at their hospital. Both nurses first wrote letters to their supervisor at Albany Medical Center Hospital stating their sincerely held religious convictions and reasons for refusing to assist in abortions. They were fired shortly thereafter in retaliation on trumped-up charges for failing to respond to a patient emergency. They sued the hospital on the grounds that New York law protects health care personnel from having to assist in abortion. The trial court threw their case out but the appellate court reinstated it and agreed that their objections to assisting with abortion were premised on their sincerely held religious convictions and that they were fired due to those beliefs. This case took over six years to resolve. But they won for the health care workers of New York State the right to sue under the Executive Law, section 79i, seeking civil or criminal remedies of employers who discriminate against pro-life health care workers.[218] Thanks to the heroic efforts of these two nurses, their victory is having a ripple effect throughout New York. Some insurance companies no longer require their employees with pro-life convictions to process insurance claims for third party payment.[219]

Integrity requires a person demonstrate their convictions. For some this has meant breaking the law through trespass—blocking the entrances of freestanding abortion clinics—so as to deter mothers from aborting their children.

All fifty states allow trespass in cases of emergency, and even the destruction of private property if necessary to save human life. The non-violent abortion clinic rescuers based their actions on this well known affirmative defense, blocked abortion clinic doors and/or entered abortion facilities to prevent the unjust slaughter of innocent children. The courts of this land, however, failed them and refused to allow them to argue a "necessity defense" to their acts of criminal trespass and criminal damaging. Later in 1994, on the heels of the shooting of several abortion clinic workers by a stranger to the rescue movement, Congress rushed to enact federal legislation to have a chilling effect on rescues outside abortion clinics. *Federal Access to Clinic Entrance Act* (FACE)[220] imposed draconian penalties (up to ten years in jail and $10,000 fine per offense) on those who peacefully blocked abortion clinic doors to save children from being killed and young mothers from being victimized.

Ironically, this federal statute has been turned on the abortionist industry that fashioned it. In November of 2001, the 11th Federal Circuit Court of Appeals in Atlanta, Georgia ruled that a woman who is forcibly prevented from leaving an abortion clinic has a cause of action under FACE.[221] The trouble is that a woman demanding to leave an abortion clinic, but who is held down and forcibly aborted, is not likely to find many truthful witnesses to testify on her behalf. Absent hard evidence (a tape recording) an informant inside the abortion clinic may prove necessary to provide sufficient evidence for conviction. Such an informant would most likely be required to cooperate proximately with the clinic staff so as not to blow his or her cover. As discussed previously, provided such an informant did not actually perform the abortion or encourage patients to have an abortion, but only provided pre-operative and post-operative care, or assisted the abortionist perform abortions, there would be a solidly probable opinion he or she would be justified in doing so. Of course, if a young mother begged the doctor to stop the abortion and tried to save her child and struggled to leave the operating table (as was alleged in *Roe II*), and the informant could effect her escape, then he or she would be morally required to do so.

Conclusion

Before Pope John Paul II issued *Gospel of Life* in 1995 some people speculated that the aborted unborn children who died without benefit of baptism would not go to heaven or see the face of God directly. Prayer cards were circulated requesting one spiritually adopt an unborn child about to be aborted and make a vicarious baptism of desire for the child so that he or she could be incorporated into the mystical body of Christ and enter heaven. Why the worry?

Christ himself taught that baptism is necessary for salvation, and commanded his apostles to preach the Gospel and baptize all nations.[222] If one has had good opportunity to hear the Gospel proclaimed and had the possibility of asking for baptism, one cannot be saved without it.[223]

There are two truths the Church must affirm in regards to the necessity of baptism. One, the Church has no assurance of any other way a person may be saved than by baptism. Two, there may be another way a person may be saved other than baptism because, although *"God has bound salvation to the sacrament of Baptism. . . . [H]e himself is not bound by his sacraments."*[224]

The Church recognizes the sacrament of baptism by water and the baptism of blood martyrs undergo if they die for Christ before their own baptism, and the baptism of desire a catechumen experiences who desires baptism but dies before the appointed day. All three are sufficient for salvation:

> The Church has always held the firm conviction that those who suffer death for the sake of the faith without having received Baptism are baptized by their death for and with Christ. This *Baptism of blood*, like the *desire for Baptism*, brings about the fruits of Baptism without being a sacrament.[225]

The Church's understanding of baptism of desire includes not only those with an explicit desire for baptism into Jesus Christ but also includes all those who have never heard the Good News preached but (only God knows) would have accepted Christ had they had the opportunity:

> Every man who is ignorant of the Gospel of Christ and of his Church, but seeks the truth and does the will of God in accordance with his understanding of it, can be saved. It may be supposed that such persons would have *desired Baptism explicitly* if they had known its necessity.[226]

When it comes to infants who die before they are baptized in water they are incapable of formulating an explicit or implicit desire for baptism into Jesus Christ. Even though they are innocent and free of any personal sin, they have still contracted the sin of origin and cannot be saved unless they are in some way incorporated into the mystical body of Christ:

> Following St. Paul[227] the Church has always taught that the overwhelming misery which oppresses men and their inclination toward evil and death cannot be understood apart from their connection with Adam's sin and the fact that he has transmitted to us a sin with which we are all born afflicted, a sin which is the "death of the soul." Because of this certainty of faith, the Church baptizes for the remission of sins even tiny infants who have not committed personal sin.[228]

However, even though the Church has no absolute assurance that infants who die without benefit of water baptism will see God face to face, still she holds out *hope* to all who mourn the loss of a little child:

> As regards *children who have died without Baptism*, the Church can only entrust them to the mercy of God, as she does in her funeral rites for them. Indeed, the great mercy of God who desires that all men should be saved, and Jesus' tenderness toward children which caused him to say: "Let the children come to me, do not hinder them," allow us to hope that there is a way of salva-

tion for children who have died without Baptism. All the more urgent is the Church's call not to prevent little children coming to Christ through the gift of holy Baptism.[229]

This hope in the mercy of Christ, supplemented by various theological speculations concerning a vicariously supplied baptism of desire or an instantaneous awakening of reason just prior to death so the infant could choose for or against Christ, bolstered the conviction that aborted children would see God face to face.

In *Gospel of Life*, John Paul II assures us that children killed in abortion "are now living in the Lord."[230] To live in the Lord is to be in his grace and enjoy eternal beatitude. Perhaps the Holy Father has developed doctrine on this point teaching with authority that these children have been baptized in their own blood. A child martyr is not required to die intentionally for Christ as is the case with adult martyrs. All that is necessary for a child is that 1) they suffer physical harm, which 2) results in their death, 3) by those who do so out of contempt for Christ or some Christian virtue.[231] Aborted children are certainly put to death by those who have contempt for Christ's Gospel of life, justice and charity.

The relevant passage comes in John Paul II's words of consolation to mothers who have killed their children in an abortion. He commends them for admitting their guilt and commiserates with them in their regret, grief and loss. He offers them real hope, the Good News that one day "every tear will be wiped away" and they will see their child who lives in Christ and be eternally happy:

> The wound in your heart may not yet have healed. Certainly what happened was and remains terribly wrong. But do not give in to discouragement and do not lose hope. Try rather to understand what happened and face it honestly. If you have not already done so, give yourselves over with humility and trust to repentance. The Father of mercies is ready to give you his forgiveness and his peace in the Sacrament of Reconciliation. You will come to understand that *nothing is definitively lost and you will also be able to ask forgiveness from your child, who is now living in the Lord.* [232]

Diagram 12.1
An Ectopic Pregnancy Enlarged

Salpingostomy—
A Direct Attack on an
Embryonic Child.

Salpingectomy—
Removal of Traumatized
Maternal Tissue.

Large Man—
The Direct Target of an Ax.

Large Man—
Still in "Jam" but not Axed.

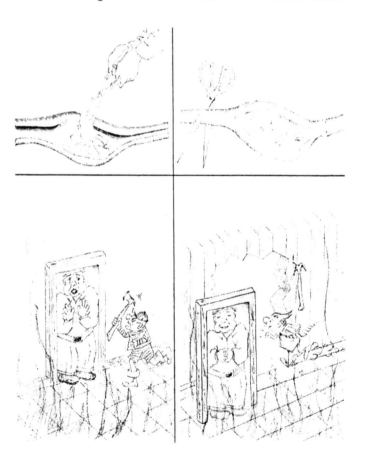

Notes

1. Isa. 49:15–16.
2. Giuliana Pelucchi, *Blessed Gianna Beretta Molla: A Woman's Life* (Boston: Daughters of St. Paul, 2002), 139–40.
3. LF, no. 20.
4. Eileen P. Kelly, "Privacy," in ECST.
5. GS, no 51.
6. Matt. 16:26.
7. DPA, no. 1.
8. DPA, no. 2.
9. DPA, no. 3.
10. DPA, no. 4. See also LG, nos. 12, 25.
11. Wisd. of Sol. 2:24.
12. Wisd. of Sol. 1:13.
13. 1 Cor. 15:20–27.
14. DPA, no. 5. Psalm 118:73 ("Your hands have made and fashioned me"), Jeremiah 1:15 ("Before I formed you in the womb I knew you, before you were born I dedicated you."), and Luke 1:44 (the Visitation of Mary to her cousin Elizabeth) are evidence of God's providential care over the child developing in the womb.
15. See James Hostetler and Michael L. Coulter, "Abortion," in ECST.
16. DPA, no. 6.
17. Thomas Aquinas, *Commentary on the Book of Sentences*, Bk. IV, dist. 31.
18. GS, no. 51 (emphasis in original).
19. DPA, no. 7. See also Peter A. Kwasniewski, "Pope Paul VI," in ECST.
20. DPA, no. 8.
21. See Adrian J. Reimers, "End of Man," in ECST.
22. DPA, no. 9.
23. DPA, no. 10.
24. DPA, no. 11.
25. DPA, no. 12.
26. DPA, no. 19. See also EV, no. 60.
27. DPA, no. 13.
28. DPA, no. 14.
29. DPA, no. 15. See also Richard S. Myers, "Feminism," in ECST.
30. DPA, no. 16.
31. DPA, no. 17.
32. DPA, no. 18.
33. DPA, no. 19.
34. DPA, no. 20.
35. DPA, no. 21.
36. DPA, no. 22. See also Antonia Emma R. Roxas, "Conscientious Objection: Life and Health Care Issues," in ECST.
37. DPA, no. 23.
38. HV, no. 24.
39. DPA, no. 25.
40. DPA, no. 26.
41. DPA, no. 27; citing Rom. 8:18.
42. GS, no. 27. See also D. Q. McInerny, "Evil," in ECST.

43. GS, no. 51.

44. *Roe v. Wade*, 410 U.S. 113, 93 S.Ct. 705 (1973).

45. *Roe*, 410 U.S. at 132.

46. *Roe*, 410 U.S. at 134.

47. *Roe*, 410 U.S. at 132–38.

48. *Roe*, 410 U.S. at 141–42.

49. *Roe*, 410 U.S. at 142–47.

50. *Roe*, 410 U.S. at 148–53.

51. *Roe*, 410 U.S. at 152–53.

52. *Roe*, 410 U.S. at 160–66.

53. *Roe*, 410 U.S. at 159 (emphasis added).

54. Michel Schooyans, *The Hidden Face of the United Nations*, trans. John Miller (St. Louis: Central Bureau, 2001), 15–16.

55. *Roe*, 410 U.S. at 174; citing *Snyder v. Massachusetts*, 291 U.S. 97, 105, 54 S.Ct. 330, 332 (1934).

56. See James R. Kelly, "Roe v. Wade/Doe v. Bolton," in ECST.

57. *Planned Parenthood of Southeastern Pennsylvania v. Casey*, 505 U.S. 833, 996, 112 S.Ct. 2791, 2882 (1992).

58. *Casey*, 505 U.S. at 1001 (emphasis in the original).

59. *Casey*, 505 U.S. 833, 999, 112 S.Ct. 2791, 2884 (1992).

60. Robert H. Bork, "Our Judicial Oligarchy," *First Things*, Dec. 1996, 23.

61. Raoul Berger, *Government by Judiciary: The Transformation of the Fourteenth Amendment* (Indianapolis: Liberty Fund, 1997), 323 n.8; citing Benjamin F. Wright, *The Growth of American Constitutional Law* (New York, NY: Henry Holt, 1942) 18, 244.

62. *Casey*, 505 U.S. at 1000–01 (emphasis in the original).

63. See Perry J. Cahall, "Familiaris Consortio," in ECST.

64. FC, no. 6–7.

65. FC, no. 26.

66. FC, no. 30.

67. Holy See, *Charter of the Rights of the Family* (1983), no. 4, http://www.vatican.va/roman_curia/pontifical_councils/family/documents/rc_pc_family_doc_19831022_family-rights_en.html (27 August 2009). See also Philip M. Sutton, "Charter of the Rights of the Family," in ECST.

68. *Charter of the Rights of the Family*, no. 3.

69. *Charter of the Rights of the Family*, no. 3.

70. See Donald P. Asci, "*Donum Vitae*," in ECST.

71. DV, no. I.2.

72. DV, no. I.4.

73. DV, no. I.6. See also CCC, no. 2275.

74. DV, III.

75. EV, no. 63.

76. DV, no. II.

77. DV, no. I.2.

78. EV, no. 63.

79. DV, no. I.2.

80. DV, int., no. 4.

81. DV, int., no. 5.

76. GS, no. 51.

83. VS, no. 80.

84. LF, no. 23.

85. LF, no. 13.

86. LF, no. 6.

87. LF, no. 7. See also GS, no. 11.

88. See 1 John 4:8.

89. LF, no. 13. See also Rom. 5:5.

90. LF, no. 14.

91. LF, no. 13.

92. LF, no. 15. See also GS, no. 9.

93. LF, no. 21.

94. LF, no. 21.

95. LF, no. 22.

96. LF, no. 18.

97. See Philip M. Sutton, "Family," in ECST.

98. EV, no. 58.

99. EV, no. 59.

100. EV, no. 61.

101. EV, no. 62; citing CIC, no. 1398; cf. Canon Law Society of America, *Code of Canons of the Eastern Churches* (Washington, DC: Canon Law Society of America, 2001), no. 1450.2.

102. EV, no. 62, citing LG, no. 25.

103. John Paul II, *Christifideles Laici*, (1988), no. 38, http://www.vatican.va/holy_father/john_paul_ii/apost_exhortations/documents/hf_jp-ii_exh_30121988_christifideles-laici_en.html (27 Aug. 2009).

104. CHCW, no. 47.

105. CHCW, no. 36. See also CCC, no. 2274.

106. ERD, no. 36.

107. Thomas A. Szyszkiewicz, "A Moral Dilemma," *Catholic World Report*, November 2005, 30.

108. For an extended discussion of why abortion compounds and does not alleviate the negative sequel of rape and incest, see David Reardon, Julie Makimaa, and Amy Sobie, eds., *Victims and Victors: Speaking Out About Their Pregnancies, Abortions, and Children resulting from Sexual Assault* (Springfield, IL: Acorn Books, 2000).

109. DV, no. I.2.

110. DV, no. I.2. See also EV, no. 135; CHCW, no. 60; ERD, nos. 50, 51.

111. See NGO Voice, "Society of Catholic Social Scientists Intervention at UN Disabilities Conference," www.ngovoice.com (20 May 2009). The author had the privilege of making an intervention in support of this language on behalf of the Society of Catholic Social Scientists, an NGO accredited with the United Nations, at the Convention on the Rights of Persons with Disabilities.

112. *Draft Convention on the Rights of Persons with Disabilities*, Article 25, http://www.un.org/esa/socdev/enable/rights/ahc8adart.htm. Permanent Observer of the Holy See to the UN, Archbishop Migliore in a statement to the 61st UN General Assembly final report of the Ad Hoc Committee on a Comprehensive and Integral International convention on the Protection and Promotion of the Rights and dignity of Persons with Disabilities said, "It is surely tragic that, wherever fetal defect is a precondition for offering or employing abortion, the same Convention created to protect persons with disabilities from all discrimination in the exercise of their rights, may be used to deny the very basic right to life of disabled unborn persons." http://www.holyseemission.org/13Dec

2006.html.
    113. CHCW, no. 35.
    114. CHCW, footnote no. 89.
    115. ERD, no. 46.
    116. DV, Part I, no. 4.
    117. CHCW, no. 146.
    118. ERD, no. 66. See also DV, Part I, no. 5 and CCC, no. 2275.
    119. CHCW, no. 146.
    120. ERD, no. 48.
    121. ERD, no. 45.
    122. DPA, no. 14.
    123. See Albert Moraczewski, "Managing Tubal Pregnancies, Part I," *Ethics & Medicine* 21, no. 6 (June 1996): 3; citing J. Rock, "Ectopic Pregnancy" *TeLinde's Operative Gynecology*, 1992, 420.
    124. Rom. 3:5–8. See also Thomas A. Cavanaugh "Double Effect, (Principle of)," in ECST.
    125. See William May, *Catholic Bioethics and the Gift of Human Life* (Huntington, IN: Our Sunday Visitor, 2000), 194–95 n.60.
    126. Rom. 3:5–8.
    127. CCC, no. 1753.
    128. ST II-II, q. 64, a.7. See also CCC, no. 2263.
    129. See Thomas Aquinas, *Dec pracec.* 6.
    130. CCC, no. 1779. See also CCC, no. 1753.
    131. CHCW, no. 142.
    132. ERD, no. 47.
    133. May, *Catholic Bioethics*, 187 n.60; citing Pius XII, "Address to the Biomedical Association of St. Luke," *Discorsi e Radiomessagi di Sua Santita Pio XII*, 12 November 1944 (Vatican City: Libreria Editrice Vaticana, 1945), 191.
    134. See May, *Catholic Bioethics*, 182–83; Thomas J. O'Donnell, *Medicine and Catholic Morality*, 3d ed., (New York, NY: Alba House, 1997), 179.
    135. See Paul F. deLadurantaye, "Proportionalism," in ECST.
    136. See ERD, no. 47.
    137. O'Donnell, *Medicine and Catholic Morality*, 179.
    138. O'Donnell, *Medicine and Christian Morality*, 179–80.
    139. O'Donnell, *Medicine and Christian Morality*, 177.
    140. F.J. Fitzpatrick, *Ethics in Nursing Practice: Basic Principles and their Application* (London: Linacare Center, 1988), 126–27.
    141. CHCW, no. 132.
    142. ERD, no. 47.
    143. See Kelly Bowring, "The Moral Dilemma of Management Procedures for Ectopic Pregnancy," *Life and Learning XII: Proceedings of the Twelfth University Faculty for Life Conference*, ed. Joseph W. Koterski (Washington, DC: University Faculty for Life, 2002), 114.
    144. Bowring, "The Moral Dilemma," 177–78.
    145. See May, *Catholic Bioethics and the Gift of Human Life*, 181, 184–85.
    146. Moraczewski, "Managing Tubal Pregnancies, Part I," 3–4.
    142. ERD, no. 16 (1971).
    148. ERD, no. 48.
    149. ERD, no. 45.

150. See May, *Catholic Bioethics*, 176–86. See also O'Donnell, *Medicine and Christian Morality*, 179.

151. See generally Moraczewski, "Managing Tubal Pregnancies, Part I."

152. Moraczewski, "Managing Tubal Pregnancies, Part I," 179–80.

153. Moraczewski, "Managing Tubal Pregnancies, Part I," 179.

154. See May, *Catholic Bioethics*, 185.

150. VS, no.78.

156. Personal conversation with Edwin Bessler, Professor of Biology, Franciscan University of Steubenville, 24 November 2003.

157. EV, no. 58 (emphasis added).

158. CCC, nos. 1755, 1760.

159. Moraczewski, "Managing Tubal Pregnancies, Part II," 3.

160. Moraczewski, "Managing Tubal Pregnancies, Part II," 3.

161. Moraczewski, "Managing Tubal Pregnancies, Part II," 3.

162. Moraczewski, "Managing Tubal Pregnancies, Part II," 3 (emphasis added).

163. May, *Catholic Bioethics*, 184.

164. Moraczewski, "Managing Tubal Pregnancies, Part II," 4 (emphasis added).

165. May, *Catholic Bioethics*, 185; citing Charles Cavagnaro III, "Treating Ectopic Pregnancy: A Moral Analysis (Part II)," *The NaProEthics Forum* 4, no. 2 (March 1999): 5.

166. May, *Catholic Bioethics*, 185, citing Cavagnaro III, "Treating Ectopic Pregnancy," 5.

167. Bowring, "The Moral Dilemma," 115; citing John E. Foran, *The Linacre Quarterly* (Feb. 1999): 26.

168. Maroczewski, "Managing Tubal Pregnancy: Part I," 3. See also O'Donnell, *Medicine and Christian Morality*, 180; citing C.J. Wallace, "Transplantations of Ectopic Pregnancy from Fallopian Tube to Cavity of Uterus," *Surgery, Gynecology and Obstetrics* 36 (5 May 1917): 578–79.

169. Personal conversation with Edwin Bessler, 24 November 2003.

170. Bowring, "The Moral Dilemma," 117–18; citing Foran, *The Linacre Quarterly*, (Feb. 1999): 27.

171. See Thomas A. Cavanaugh, "Cooperation: Formal and Material," in ECST.

172. See Peter Maass, *Love Thy Neighbor: A Story of War* (New York, NY: Alfred A. Knopf, Inc., 1996), 50–51.

173. See O'Donnell, *Medicine and Christian Morality*, 37.

173. CIC, no. 1398.

174. CCC, no. 2272; citing CIC, no. 1398. See also CHCW, n.277.

176. CHCW, no. 145.

177. CCC, no. 2271.

178. CCC, no. 1753.

179. CHCW, no. 140.

180. CHCW, no. 145. See also Antonia Emma R. Roxas, "Conscientious Objection: Life and Health Care Issues," in ECST.

181. EV, nos. 59, 89. See also James R. Kelly, "Consistent Ethic of Life (Seamless Garment)," in ECST.

182. See CIC, no. 1398.

183. Fitzpatrick, *Ethics in Nursing Practice*, 130; citing Benedict Ashley and Kevin O'Rourke, *Health Care Ethics: A Theological Analysis*, 2d ed. (St. Louis, MO: Catholic Health Association of the United States, 1982), 191.

184. See O'Donnell, *Medicine and Christian Morality*, 38.

185. Fitzpatrick, *Ethics in Nursing Practice*, 235.

186. ERD, no. 66.

187. O'Donnell, *Medicine and Christian Morality*, 17.

188. Edwin Healy, *Moral Guidance: A Textbook in Principles of Conduct for Colleges and Universities* (Chicago: Loyola University Press, 1942), 318–20.

189. Francis J. Connell, *Outlines of Moral Theology* (Milwaukee, WI: Bruce Publishing Co., 1953), 95.

190. O'Donnell, *Medicine and Christian Morality*, 37–39.

191. Peter E. Bristow, *The Moral Dignity of Man* (Dublin, Ireland: Four Courts Press, 1997), 183.

192. See Thomas A. Cavanaugh, "Cooperation: Formal and Material," in ECST.

193. Bristow, *The Moral Dignity of Man*, 182.

194. Bristow, *The Moral Dignity of Man*, 183.

195. Fitzpatrick, *Ethics in Nursing Practice*, 129.

196. Fitzpatrick, *Ethics in Nursing Practice*, 131.

197. Edward Hayes, et al., *Catholicism and Ethics: A Medical/Moral Handbook* (Norwood, MA: C.R. Publications, Inc. 1997), 73.

198. See Thomas A. Cavanaugh, "Cooperation: Formal and Material," in ECST.

199. *Reply on Sterilization in Catholic Hospitals*, no. 3.b (emphasis added).

200. EV, no. 74; emphasis added.

201. See generally Gerald Kelly, S.J., *Medico-Moral Problems* (St. Louis: The Catholic Hospital Association, 1958).

202. Germaine Grisez, *Difficult Moral Questions*, vol 3. of *The Way of the Lord Jesus Christ* (Quincy, IL: Franciscan Press, 1997), 356–57.

203. EV, no. 74.

204. See Bristow, *The Moral Dignity of Man*, 182.

205. See Fitzpatrick, *Ethics in Nursing Practice*, 235.

206. ERD, nos. 45, 70 (emphasis added).

207. See O'Donnell, *Medicine and Christian Morality*, 35–39. See also Bowring, "The Moral Dilemma," 114. N.B.: Thomas J. O'Donnell was a consultant to the U.S. Catholic Conference Committee for Continuing Directives for Catholic Health Facilities.

208. O'Donnell, *Medicine and Christian Morality*, 16.

209. O'Donnell, *Medicine and Christian Morality*, 16–17.

210. CCC, no. 2284. See also Matt. 18:6, 1 Cor. 8:10–13; Matt. 7:15; Eph. 6:4; Col. 3:21; Lk. 17:1.

211. 1 Cor. 8:9.

212. 1 Cor. 8:9.

213. ERD, no. 45; DV, no. I.4.

214. EV, no. 73. See also Damian P. Fedoryka, "Thoughts towards a Clarification of Section #73 of *Evangelium Vitae*," *Life and Learning: Proceedings of the Twelfth University Faculty for Life Conference*, ed. Joseph W. Koterski (Washington, DC: University Faculty for Life, 2002), 315–16.

215. Grisez, *Difficult Moral Questions*, 358.

216. Grisez, *Difficult Moral Questions*, 360.

217. CHCW, no. 143.

218. *Larson v. Albany Medical Center*, 252 A.D. 2d 936 (N.Y. 1998).

219. See *The Wanderer*, 2 Jan. 2003, 7.

219. 18 U.S.C. § 248.

221. See *Roe II v. Aware Women Center for Choice*, 253 F.3d 678 (11th Cir. 2001).

222. John 3:5. See also Matt. 28:19–20.

223. CCC, no. 1257.

224. CCC, no. 1257 (emphasis in original).

225. CCC, no. 1258 (emphasis in original).

226. CCC, no. 1260 (emphasis in original).

227. See Rom 5:12–19.

228. CCC, no. 403.

229. CCC, no. 1260.

230. EV, no. 99.

231. Connell, *Outlines of Moral Theology*, 160.

231. EV, no. 99.

Chapter 13
Marriage and Family

Introduction

A Christmas Carol by Charles Dickens portrays Ebenezer Scrooge as a person cut off from all significant personal relations. The Ghost of Christmas Past reveals to Scrooge some crucial events and decisions that shaped his miserly and miserable character. We learn that it was not so much the hardships he suffered but how he reacted to them that misshaped him. He was rejected by his father and sent off to boarding school at an early age after his mother died giving birth to him. Good people also came into Scrooge's life, yet these he rejected. He failed to follow the good example given him by his mentor, an accountant, who showed kindness and personal concern for the workers in his employ. Even worse, Scrooge refused to marry a girl with no dowry to pursue a marriage that would advance his career, or to remain single so as not to dissipate his earnings by providing for a family. The final misfortune fell when his beloved sister died in childbirth and he rejected her son, the last person who still had affection for him.

In contrast, Dickens shows us an employee of Scrooge, Bob Cratchit. Life had dealt Cratchit and his family many misfortunes, including poverty, inadequate food and housing and poor opportunity for education or advancement. Through no fault of his own, hard working Bob Cratchit was barely able to feed, clothe, and shelter his large family. On top of these deprivations their youngest son, Tiny Tim, was lame, malformed and dying of consumption. But whereas Scrooge was bitter and hateful, Cratchit declared he was "a happy man" surrounded by a loving family, his one and more than sufficient boon in life. Like

Job, whose fortune and family were taken away, Cratchit still blessed God, agreeing with Scrooge's nephew Fred—"though [Christmas] has never put a scrap of gold or silver in my pocket, I believe that it has done me good, and will do me good; and I say, God bless it!"[1] Scrooge, on the other hand, like the wife of Job, was inclined to "curse God and die."[2]

The reformation of Scrooge's character was accomplished by the Spirits of Christmas past, present, and future, who opened his heart to the many persons in his life who really were his "business," even more than his counting house. Dickens shows us in *A Christmas Carol* that the poor, initially described by Scrooge as a drain on the public welfare and as "surplus population," are not lazy nor un-enterprising but, rather, downtrodden by an economic system he and other economic elite exploit to make and hoard great wealth. But those who do so and do nothing to succor the poor are really murderers and like Cain they find themselves cut off from human society, doomed to wander the earth alone.

In the end Scrooge learns that he is his "brother's keeper."[3] The Spirits of Christmas have spared him from the fate of his business partner, Marley, a ghost wandering the world forever restless, dragging a great chain forged of the sins he committed making his fortune in life. Those who hoard and dishonor the "universal designation of all goods," who disparage the social virtues of solidarity and subsidiarity, Dickens assures us, have the mark of Cain upon their forehead. Only God's grace, portrayed as the Spirit of Christmas, has the power to dispel this curse. That school of social virtues, the family, damaged as it was during Scrooge's formative years, left him scared. But with God's grace, Scrooge was made free to choose to repair what was damaged in his past by doing good to all in the future. Scrooge learned to keep Christmas in his heart all year long. He became a second father to Tiny Tim and both he and the little cripple boy lived to walk straight again.

Thomas More, Lord Chancellor of England,[4] was also a man who knew how to keep the spirit of Christmas. Like Bob Cratchit he was blessed with a loving family. There wasn't a day when the young More, even after he was appointed judge, did not kneel to receive his father's blessing. After he was arrested for refusing to swear an oath to the King as the head of the Church in England and imprisoned in the Tower of London, he wrote his family to remind them that regardless of the vicissitudes of life, soon they will all meet again "merrily" in heaven. He said the same to his former friends with whom he worked at the King's court, who, at his trial for treason, had accepted improbable evidence to convict him. More did not lose heart as the following sentence was read condemning him to death by drawing and quartering:

> We command that Sir Thomas More, sometime knight, be carried back to the place from whence he came; and from thence to be drawn through the City to the public place of execution, there to be hanged till he be half dead, then to be cut down, his bowels presently to be taken out and burned, his head to be cut

off, and his body to be quartered into four parts, and the body and head to be set up where the king shall appoint. So [the] Lord have mercy upon you! [5]

After he was sentenced to this gruesome execution, instead of pleading for mercy as was the custom, More forgave his old friends and acquaintances and again said he hoped they would "merrily all meet together" in heaven as brothers in the family of God:

> More have I not to say, my lords, but that like as the blessed Apostle St. Paul, as we read in the Acts of the Apostles, was present, and consented to the death of St. Stephen, and kept their clothes that stoned him to death, and yet be they now both twain holy Saints in heaven, and shall continue there friends forever, so I verily trust, and shall therefore right heartily pray, that though your Lordships have now here in earth been judges to my condemnation, we may yet hereafter in heaven merrily all meet together, to our everlasting salvation.[6]

At his trial More took courage from the fact that he died in defense of what he held most dear—his enemies sought his life primarily because he, like John the Baptist before him, had defended the sanctity of a marriage and family disgraced by an unjust king:

> Yet still free to speak the unspeakable, More had one final salvo for his persecutors, a reminder that in addition to suffering for his fidelity to the primacy of Peter he was also dying in defense of the indissolubility of Christian matrimony: "Howbeit, it is not for this supremacy so much that ye seek my blood, as for that I would not condescend to the marriage."[7]

Unjust rulers have much to fear from the family because the family gives man a home in the wide world; it is his castle. When civilizations shake and collapse the family is a bulwark of sanity as resilient as blades of grass. At home with a loving family a man is not easily led astray, or isolated and paralyzed. If he must, he finds he is capable of resistance to the death in the fight against tyranny.

During the time of the Maccabees, it was strong personalities from strong families who stepped outside the economic and social forces of their times and defeated an empire. Mattathias, a father who knew he could count on the strength of his five sons, began a rebellion that rolled back the mighty Seleucids.[8] Scripture also holds up the death-defying witness of a mother with seven sons who, inspired by filial love and love for the law of God, resisted to the end as, one by one, they were first blinded and then cut to pieces. Her words echo down the ages: "'Do not be afraid of this executioner, but be worthy of your brothers and accept death, so that in the time of mercy I may receive you again with them [in the resurrection of the dead].'"[9]

Today's architects of totalitarianism know it is God and the family that stands in their way, that thwarts their dream of deconstructing and reconstructing each human being in their image, like a modern artist who tears up photographs of persons to reconstruct a collage from the pieces in a shape of their choosing. In the face of the impersonal and dehumanizing forces of modern civilization, marriage and family prevent psychological melt-down and fortify personalities to go against the tide. Totalitarianism is abetted by the cultural disintegration of the family. Cultural and feminist revolutionary Shulamith Firestone is convinced Communism failed in Russia because it did not utterly destroy the family, which was the true source of psychological, economic and political resistance that brought about its collapse. The family, she says, still props up the American dream: "Mom is vital to the American way of life, considerably more than apple pie. She is an institution without which the system really would fall apart."[10]

Pope John Paul II,[11] whom many credit with bringing down the Communist revolution in Russia and Eastern Europe, sees the family at the center of a great storm threatening it, the Church and Western civilization.

> At a moment of history in which the family is the object of numerous forces that seek to destroy it, and aware that the well being of society and her own good are intimately tied to the good of the family, the church perceives in a more urgent and compelling way her mission of proclaiming to all people the plan of God for marriage and the family, ensuring their full vitality and human and Christian development, and thus contributing to the renewal of society and of the people of God.[12]

Today we are subject to social and psychological pressures that take us away from our true home, our place of well being and flourishing. As never before the family is attacked and undermined. Divorce and promiscuity tear spouses apart. Contraception isolates spouses, keeping them a "safe" distance from each other. Abortion tears apart a child's body and a mother's heart. And, while contraception and abortion cut individuals off from their future, euthanasia shuts the door on their past in a farewell that is not a "good-bye." Reproductive technologies sever children from the first draughts of the milk of human kindness and leave most of them frozen in liquid nitrogen for the rest of their earthly lives. So called, homosexual same-sex marriage, brings two injured and isolated individuals together in an arrangement that further wounds them, while trivializing the very meaning of marriage and family.

As we consider the Church's teaching on marriage and family in the following pages, let us not forget that in the cultural war that swirls around us the family is the last defense against a culture of death. Everything depends on what appears to many as a "fool's hope"—men and women giving themselves to each other without reserve, faithful and fruitful, until death. As at Nazareth, so today, God awaits holy families in order to make flesh his plan to renew the face of the earth. It would appear we have an ultimatum: "Be fruitful and multiply"—do or die![13]

The Key Magisterial Document:
Familiaris Consortio (1981)

The following summary of the fourth major encyclical by Pope John Paul II, *Familiaris Consortio (The Apostolic Exhortation on the Family)* (1981) is written with the hope that it may lead others to read the full and complete document while at the same time acknowledging the fact that many will not and so large sections of text are included to better preserve its context and language.

In the *Introduction* John Paul II explains the nature, mission and destiny of the family as a natural and supernatural institution.[14] He addressed it not so much to Bishops or theologians but to families themselves and those preparing for marriage and "to all married couples and parents in the world."[15]

John Paul II addressed his remarks to all the families in the world, Christian and non-Christian alike, especially at this moment in history when so many forces are at work undermining the family, seeking to "destroy it or in some way deform it," the Church is called to defend God's plan for marriage and the family.[16]

Part I. Bright Spots and Shadows for the Family Today

At this point in history families are often presented with a flawed vision of marriage and family by "the powerful and pervasive organization of the means of social communication," i.e., propaganda, "which subtly endangers freedom and the capacity for objective judgment." The family is subject to an interplay of social forces and choices for light or darkness. History is not "a fixed progression toward what is better;" rather, it is "a struggle between freedoms that are in mutual conflict." History is really the struggle of two loves, as St. Augustine said: "the love of God to the point of disregarding self, and the love of self to the point of disregarding God."

The bright spots now at play in history consist of a more lively awareness of personal freedom, in the quality of interpersonal relationships in marriage, in a desire to promote the dignity of women, in a greater desire for responsible procreation and attention to the education of children. However, dark shadows can be seen in the degradation of some fundamental values, and concerning marriage in particular are: a false sense of the independence of spouses in relation to each other; a misshapen notion of authority between parents and children; difficulties in the transmission of values; the "growing number of divorces; the scourge of abortion; the ever more frequent recourse to sterilization; the appearance of a truly contraceptive mentality."[17]

The faithful are not always immune from these negative values so forcefully presented by the mass media, and fail to "set themselves up as the critical conscience of family culture."[18] Rather, all too often they have conformed to their surrounding culture in accepting divorce and remarriage, living in "free unions," or accepting simply a civil marriage, or a sacramental marriage without "living faith;" and rejecting the Church's moral norms for the expression of sexuality within marriage.[19]

Science and technology, which have such great promise, have in many ways been turned against the true good of man "as a consequence of political choices that decide the direction of research and its applications." Our "great task," then, is to recover the primary moral values.[20]

The enculturation of the faith occurs in a special way through marriage and family expressed with living faith.[21] True enculturation holds fast to two principles: 1) the compatibility with the Gospel of the various cultures; and 2) communion with the universal church. So that the goal of the enculturation of the faith may be clear, we must first study God's original design for marriage and family.[22]

Part II. The Plan of God for Marriage and the Family

Man and woman were made in the image and likeness of God who is love.[23] Therefore, love is the "fundamental and innate vocation of every human being." Love, though spiritual, is expressed in men and women, who possess a composite nature of a body and soul, through their whole being:

> As an incarnate spirit, that is, a soul which expresses itself in a body and a body informed by an immortal spirit, man is called to love in his unified totality. Love includes the human body, and the body is made a sharer in spiritual love.[24]

Love is expressed through the whole being of a man or a woman in two ways—through marriage, or through virginity or celibacy.[25] Either vocation actuates the most profound truth of man, of his being created in the image of God who is love. So the love of spouses is not "something purely biological but concerns the innermost being of the human person."[26] Otherwise conjugal union would be a "lie."[27] The requirement of total self-giving, body and soul, also applies to "the demands of responsible fertility." Because the fertility of spouses is directed to the generation of a new human person, it completely "surpasses the purely biological order and involves a whole series of person values." Marriage is the only "place" where the logic of total self-giving makes sense: "A person's freedom, far from being restricted by this fidelity, is secured against every form of subjectivism or relativism and is made a sharer in creative wisdom."[28]

God's love for his chosen people finds expression in the love of spouses: "Their bond of love becomes the image and symbol of the covenant which unites God and his people" which is wounded by Israel's infidelity and idolatry, but powerfully upheld by God ever faithful to an unfaithful people.[29] Jesus Christ is the bridegroom who loves and redeems his bride the Church by laying down his life for her. Christ is the definitive fulfillment of the communion between God and his people and the vocation to be a total self-gift "which God has imprinted on the humanity of man and woman since their creation."[30] In Christ and through the grace the Spirit gives, spouses are finally capable of true Christ-like love.[31]

Marriage is one of the seven sacraments and spouses are bound to each other in "the most profoundly indissoluble manner" which is the "real representation, by means of the sacramental sign, of the very relationship of Christ with the church." Christian marriage expresses all the human values of natural conjugal love: appeal of body, power of feeling, aspiration of the spirit. But the sacrament of matrimony raises these natural values "to the extent of making them the expression of specifically Christian values." Christian marriage "aims at a deeply personal unity, the unity that, beyond union in one flesh, leads to forming one heart and soul; it demands indissolubility and faithfulness in definitive mutual giving, and it is open to fertility."[32]

Marriage and conjugal love are "ordained to the procreation and education of children in whom it finds its crowning." The gift of love which led spouses to the reciprocal knowledge which makes them one flesh does not end there but is capable of "the greatest possible gift, the gift by which they become cooperators with God for giving life to a new human person." Children are a living and inseparable synthesis of the spouse's gift of themselves; what makes them mother and father. With his gift God also lays upon parents a new responsibility of becoming the "visible sign of the very love of God, 'from which every family in heaven and on earth is named.'"[33] However, spouses who suffer from physical sterility must not think that their conjugal love is deprived of its value. Their inability to bear children may be an opportunity for other important services such as adoption, educational work, assistance to other families and to poor or handicapped children.[34] The Christian family is the way the Church enters "human generations and where these in their turn can enter the church."[35]

Virginity and celibacy for the sake of the kingdom of God presuppose and confirm the dignity of Christian marriage. If human sexuality is not regarded as a great value, then its renunciation for the sake of the kingdom of God would mean nothing. The virgin and all celibate persons are awaiting, also in a bodily way, the "eschatological marriage of Christ with the church." They give themselves "completely to the church in the hope that Christ may give himself to the church in the full truth of eternal life. The celibate person thus anticipates in his or her flesh the new world of the future resurrection." Because of this singular link it has with the kingdom of God, the Church has always "defended the superiority of this charism to that of marriage." Celibate persons are called to be fruitful, the spiritual fathers and mothers of many; and Christian couples have the right to expect from them good examples and fidelity to their vocation, which like marriage at times requires "sacrifice, mortification and self-denial." Those who "for reason independent of reasons of their own will have been unable to marry" may, also, benefit from these reflections on celibacy and accept their situation in a spirit of service.[36]

Part III. The Role of the Christian Family

"Family become what you are" is a challenge laid before those called to marriage and family. It requires each family to fulfill its mission to become more and more a community of life and love. With love as its foundation, the 1980 Synod of Bishops identified four general tasks for the family: 1) Forming a community of persons; 2) Serving life; 3) Participating in the development of society; 4) Sharing in the life and mission of the church.[37]

1. Forming a Community of Persons

Without love the human person remains a being that is incomprehensible, whose life is senseless.[38] The same is true for marriage and family: "Without love the family is not a community of persons and, in the same way, without love the family cannot live, grow and perfect itself as a community of persons."[39] Spouses must share their entire life project which fulfills a profoundly human need and is taken up by Christ, who purifies it and elevates it through the sacrament of matrimony. This sacrament unleashes the Holy Spirit who offers the couple the gift of a new communion of love which is a reflection of Christ's love for his church. This profound communion is radically contradicted by polygamy which negates God's plan and "is contrary to the equal dignity of men and women, who in matrimony give themselves with a love that is total and therefore unique and exclusive."[40]

Although today's culture rejects the indissolubility of marriage and mocks the fidelity of spouses, nonetheless, Christian conjugal communion is characterized by these two virtues which are required for the intimate nature of their union and the good of children. The grace of the sacrament of matrimony gives man and woman "a new heart" so that they are able to share in the love of Christ. Bearing witness to the indissolubility of marriage is one of the most precious and most urgent tasks of Christian couples in our time.[41]

Conjugal communion of spouses constitutes the foundation of the family communion of parents and children, brothers and sisters and other members in the household. These interpersonal relationships are rooted in the natural bonds of flesh and blood and mature in the still deeper and richer bonds of the spirit which animates the family communion and community.[42]

All members in the family have the grace and duty to build up the "communion of persons" within the family, thereby making it "a school of deeper humanity" as when there is care for the sick, children, the aged, and mutual service and a sharing of joys and sorrows. The family is a school of deeper humanity in the educational exchange between parents and children. It is also found in the obedience children give their parents and the wise administration of an "unrenounceable authority" exercised by parents, a "service aimed at helping [their children] acquire a truly responsible freedom." When divisions develop in the family the members are called to peace and the joyous and renewing experience of reconciliation through the sacraments of penance and Holy Communion.[43]

The test for judging the authenticity of spousal and family relationships is whether they foster "the dignity and vocation of the individual persons, who achieve their fullness by sincere self-giving." In this light the dignity and rights of women must be considered, as well as those of men, children, and the elderly.[44]

Women are created by God with equal personal dignity, endowing them with the same inalienable rights as men.[45] God has honored women in the highest form possible in the Blessed Virgin Mary, in whom he assumed human nature, making her the "mother of God," and the "new Eve" and the "model of redeemed women." It should be further noted that Jesus first appeared to his faithful women disciples, making them his apostles to the Apostles in announcing his resurrection.[46]

On the one hand, because women enjoy equal dignity and responsibility with men, this fully justifies their equal access to public functions in society. On the other hand, the true advancement of women "requires that clear recognition be given to the value of their maternal and family role, by comparison with all other public roles and all other professions."[47] A better "theology of work" must be articulated showing the "fundamental bond between work and the family, and therefore the original and irreplaceable meaning of work in the home and in rearing children. . . . [So that] the work of women in the home be recognized and respected by all in its irreplaceable value."[48] Society must not be structured in such a way that wives and mothers are "in practice compelled to work outside the home, and that their families can live and prosper in a dignified way even when they themselves devote their full time to their own family."[49] A social prejudice against stay-at-home mothers must be overcome:

> Furthermore, the mentality which honors women more for their work outside the home than for her work within the family must be overcome. This requires that men should truly esteem and love women with total respect for their personal dignity, and that society should create and develop conditions favoring work in the home.[50]

The Church must promote with respect to the different vocations of men and women, the equal rights of women. But under no circumstances do the equal rights of women imply "a renunciation of their femininity or an imitation of the male role, but the fullness of true feminine humanity" with respect for "differences of customs and cultures."[51] A false vision of the human person "as a thing, as an object of trade" makes women its first victims as is seen in pornography and prostitution, especially organized prostitution. Moreover, action must be taken to overcome discrimination shown to certain categories of women such as "childless wives, widows, separated or divorced women, and unmarried mothers."[52]

Men are called to love their wives with a "charity that is both gentle and strong like that Christ has for his church" and, so, love for his wife and children is "for the man the natural way of understanding and fulfilling his own fatherhood." The absence of a father in the home or the "oppressive presence" of a father with a "machismo" attitude causes psychological and moral imbalance and difficulties in family relationships. Therefore, we must work to "restore socially the conviction that the place and task of the father in and for the family is of unique and irreplaceable importance." A father is called to imitate the fatherhood of God and "ensure the harmonious and united development of all the members of the family," which he accomplishes by being responsible for the "life conceived under the heart of the mother" and being concerned about the education of his children, by finding work which is not a cause of division in the family but promotes its unity and stability, and as a witness to his children of a lived Christian faith.[53]

In the family special concern must be taken to ensure the dignity and rights of children who, the smaller and weaker they are, need more attention.[54] Christ himself placed concern for children at the "heart of the kingdom of God" when he said: "let the children come to me, and do not hinder them; for to such belongs the kingdom of heaven."[55] Concern for children "even before birth, from the first moment of conception" is, also, incumbent upon all nations if they have hope in their own future.[56]

The elderly continue to have a role in the civil and ecclesial community, especially within the family. Some cultures honor their elderly member where, although respecting the autonomy of the new family, they serve as a witness to the past and a source of wisdom. The elderly are often able to bridge the gaps in generations. Unfortunately, some cultures do not honor the elderly, but set them aside. Pastoral activity must counter these tendencies and help everyone to see their dignity and continued value even as the elderly find fulfillment is being cherished in the midst of their children and their children's children—"the crown of the aged is their children's children."[57]

2. Serving Life
a) The Transmission of Life

God entrusted man and woman with the responsibility of procreating new human life which is really "transmitting by procreation the divine image from person to person."[58] Today, however, some people ask if it were better they were never born or if they have a right to bring a child into such a cruel world. Others want to hoard all the advantages of technology and "exclude others [especially the poor] by imposing on them contraceptives or even worse means." Still others are imprisoned in a "consumer mentality" and caught up in achieving a continual growth of material goods and amusements, and end up refusing the spiritual riches of a new human life. In these ways "an anti-life mentality" has been born which is fanned into a panic by some ecologists and futurologists who predict an overpopulation crisis, but who "sometimes exaggerate the danger of demographic increase to the quality of life."[59]

Against such pessimism and selfishness "the church stands for life" and, thus, She defends "the human person and the world from all who plot against and harm life." She condemns as grave offenses all efforts of public authorities to "limit in any way the freedom of couples in deciding about children," or coercion by those authorities in favor of contraception, sterilization or abortion. The Church also condemns the conditioning of international aid to developing countries based upon their acceptance and implementation of programs of contraception, sterilization and procured abortion.[60]

The Church is not unaware of the problems associated with population growth. All the more she is convinced of the importance of the authentic teaching on birth regulation. Therefore Pope John Paul II urged theologians to aid the magisterium in the task of "illustrating ever more clearly the biblical foundations, the ethical grounds and the personalistic reasons behind this doctrine." This is a pressing concern because "error in the field of marriage or the family involves obscuring to a serious extent the integral truth about the human person" already contradicted in many ways in contemporary culture.[61]

Just as the human person has an objective nature so does human sexuality. With respect to the responsible transmission of human life "the moral aspect of any procedure does not depend solely on sincere intentions or on an evaluation of motives. It must be determined by objective standards. These, based on the nature of the human person and his or her acts, preserve the full sense of mutual self-giving and human procreation in the context of true love."[62] Pope Paul VI in *Humanae Vitae* taught that it is intrinsically immoral to render a conjugal act impossible of procreation by means taken before, during, or after the act is consummated.[63] This is so because there is "an inseparable connection willed by God and unable to be broken by man on his own initiative between the two meanings of the conjugal act: the unitive meaning and the procreative meaning."[64] When a couple separates these two meanings inscribed by God into their being and into "the dynamism of their sexual communion, they act as 'arbiters' of the divine plan and they 'manipulate' and degrade human sexuality and with it, themselves and their married partner by altering its value of 'total' self-giving." In this way they lie to each other by pretending to make an act of total self-giving, when, in fact, they are "not giving [themselves] totally to the other."[65]

On the other hand natural family planning, which has recourse to the natural periods of fertility in a woman, respects God's plan in that the couple does not act as arbiters but as ministers, and does not deprive the conjugal act of its "original dynamism of 'total' self-giving, without manipulation or alteration." The difference between contraception and natural family planning is not simply technical but "in the final analysis involves two irreconcilable concepts of the human person and of human sexuality." Natural family planning accepts the rhythms of fertility naturally occurring in a woman, hence it involves "dialogue, reciprocal respect, shared responsibility and self-control." Natural family planning enriches a couple; contraception does not.[66]

The Church is a teacher in the area of human sexuality but is also a mother. Although she understands the difficulty of couples struggling with her teaching on human sexuality and the responsible transmission of human life, she believes that charity begins with truth: "to diminish in no way the saving teaching of Christ constitutes an eminent form of charity for souls."[67] She is convinced that only in keeping the conjugal act open to the transmission of new life can it foster authentic married love.[68]

Experts in every field of knowledge must study further the body's rhythms of fertility and render this knowledge available to all married couples and to "young adults before marriage" by serious instruction.[69] This knowledge must lead to self-control and the development of the virtue of chastity: a "spiritual energy capable of defending love from the perils of selfishness and aggressiveness, and able to advance it toward its full realization."[70]

Married people are called to progress unceasingly in their moral life by knowledge of principles and the formation of conscience and, also, by conforming their wills to their conscience, "by an upright and generous willingness to embody these values in their concrete decisions." Spouses must realize that the teaching of *Humanae Vitae* is "the norm for the exercise of their sexuality." Priests must be ready and able to help married couples progress in the moral life.[71]

b) Education

Parents who procreate a child have the vocation to foster the human growth and development of their child and must complete what they have begun by "helping that person effectively to live a fully human life." Therefore, parents must be acknowledged "as the first and foremost educators of their children" who must create a family atmosphere so imbued with love of God and others that their children will experience a well rounded personal and social development.[72] For this reason the family is "the first school of those social virtues which every society needs."[73]

Parents' role as the educators of their children is "original and primary" and "irreplaceable and inalienable" due to parental love—"the uniqueness of the loving relationship between parents and children" which is the "norm inspiring and guiding all concrete educational activity, enriching it with the values of kindness, constancy, goodness, service, disinterestedness and self-sacrifice."[74]

Parents must train their children in social virtues and the virtue of chastity. With regards to the first, they must instill in their children "a correct attitude of freedom with regard to material goods, by adopting a simple and austere life-style. . . ." This same model of spousal self-giving will inspire parents as they "give to their children clear and delicate sex education"[75] which it is their duty to impart:

> Sex education, which is a basic right and duty of parents, must always be car-
> ried out under their attentive guidance, whether at home or in educational cen-
> ters chosen and controlled by them. In this regard the church reaffirms the law
> of subsidiarity, which the school is bound to observe when it cooperates in sex
> education, by entering into the same spirit that animates the parents.[76]

All sex education must aim at an education in chastity "that develops a person's authentic maturity and makes him or her capable of respecting and fostering the 'nuptial meaning' of the body."[77] Parents must not neglect to pass on to their children an understanding of virginity and celibacy "as the supreme form of that self-giving that constitutes the very meaning of human sexuality." Moreover, parents are called to lead their children to respect moral norms which guarantee responsible personal growth in human sexuality. The Church is firmly opposed to the typical sex education programs that merely impart "sex information dissociated from moral principles" which serves as an "experience of pleasure and stimulus" to vice in children, who often are still in the years of innocence.[78]

The sacrament of marriage consecrates parents specifically for the Christian education of their children by enabling them to share in the very authority and love of God and "enriches them with wisdom, counsel, fortitude and all the other gifts of the Holy Spirit" to help their children grow as "human beings and as Christians." The sacrament of marriage raises the educational role of parents to their children to a ministry in the Church which builds up the Church.[79]

Christian parents should present their children with a gradual knowledge of the mystery of salvation, so that they may learn to adore God the Father in liturgical worship, and that they may train and conduct "their personal life in true righteousness and holiness according to their new nature,"[80] and be able to "devote themselves to the up-building of the mystical body"[81] and give witness to the hope that is in them thereby "promoting the Christian transformation of the world."

Parents are to be "the first heralds of the Gospel" to their children. And by praying, reading scripture, introducing them to the body of Christ, i.e., the

Church and the Eucharist, they "become fully parents"—they beget not only bodily life but also life in the Spirit. To facilitate their ministry the synod fathers "expressed the hope that a suitable catechism for families would be prepared."[82]

Christian parents are the primary, but not "the only and exclusive educating community."[83] The social nature of man demands "a broader and more articulated activity," therefore, collaboration between these various educators is necessary. The renewal of Catholic schools will give special attention to their pupils' parents and to forming a perfect "educating community."[84]

On the one hand, parents have an absolute right to "choose an education in conformity with their religious faith." The state and Church owe parents aid to enable them to perform their educational role properly:

> However, those in society who are in charge of schools must never forget that the parents have been appointed by God himself as the first and principal educators of their children and that their right is completely inalienable.[85]

On the other hand, parents have "a serious duty to commit themselves totally to a cordial and active relationship with the teachers and school authorities."[86]

Even though "begetting and educating children are the most immediate, specific and irreplaceable" expressions of fruitful married love in "serving life," all Christian families, including those who experience physical sterility, are called to respond generously to the children of other families. They should be willing to adopt or raise foster children. The Christian family fecundity also reaches out to the needy and suffering of our society who experience cultural exclusion including "the elderly, the sick, the disabled, drug addicts, ex-prisoners, etc."[87]

3. Participating in the Development of Society

The Creator established "the conjugal partnership as the beginning and basis of human society." Therefore, the family is "the first and vital cell of society."[88] The family is the foundation of society and nourishes it continually "in its service to life" by giving birth to children and training them in the "social virtues that are the animating principle of the existence and development of society itself."[89] The communion and sharing that characterizes the relationships in a family are its "first and fundamental contribution to society"—an "irreplaceable school of social life" and "the most effective means for humanizing and personalizing society." Thus, the family releases formidable energies, removing man's "anonymity, keeping him conscious of his personal dignity" and his uniqueness and unrepeatability, within the fabric of society that has become "more and more depersonalized and standardized and therefore inhuman and dehumanizing," tempting many to "forms of escapism—such as alcoholism, drugs and even terrorism."[90]

The family should devote itself to social service activities, especially as the children become older, and they should learn the social virtue of "hospitality in all its forms, from opening the door of one's home and still more of one's heart" especially to the poor. St. Paul said, practice hospitality.[91] Political intervention is also required of the family. They should be proactive in matters pertaining to "'family politics' and assume responsibility for transforming society; otherwise families will be the first victims of the evils that they have done no more than note with indifference."[92]

Society, for its part, must not fail "in its fundamental task of respecting and fostering the family." The family and society are to benefit each other, but the family comes first. However, society—more specifically the state—must recognize that "the family is a society in its own original right"[93] and so it is under a grave obligation in its relations with the family to adhere to the principle of subsidiarity: "By virtue of this principle the state cannot and must not take away from families the functions that they can just as well perform on their own or in free associations."[94] Public authorities must ensure that families have the "economic, social, educational, political and cultural assistance" needed to face their duties in a human way."[95]

But the sad reality is that often today the family is opposed by the state. In various countries the relationship is "highly problematical if not entirely negative" where the "inviolable rights of the family and the human person are unjustly ignored. Too often the family finds itself the victim of society. In this situation God's plan that the family serve as "the basic cell of society and a subject of rights and duties before the state or any other community," is met with "blatant injustice." Therefore, the Church is obliged to defend the following "rights of the family" against the "intolerable usurpations of society and the state:" [96]

1 The right to exist and progress as a family . . . to found a family and to have adequate means to support it;
2 The right to exercise its responsibility regarding the transmission of life and to educate children;
3 The right to intimacy of conjugal life and family life;
4 The right to the stability of the bond and of the institution of marriage;
5 The right to believe in and profess one's faith and to propagate it;
6 The right to bring up children in accordance with the family's own traditions and religious and cultural values, with the necessary instruments, means and institutions;
7 The right, especially of the poor and the sick, to obtain physical, social, political and economic security;
8 The right to housing suitable for living family life in a proper way;
9 The right to expression and to representation, either directly or through associations, before the economic, social and cultural public authorities and lower authorities;

10 The right to form associations with other families and institutions in order to fulfill the family's role suitably and expeditiously;

11 The right to protect minors by adequate institutions and legislation from harmful drugs, pornography, alcoholism, etc.;

12 The right to wholesome recreation of a kind that also fosters family values;

13 The right of the elderly to a worthy life and a worthy death;

14 The right to emigrate as a family in search of a better life.[97]

By virtue of the sacrament of marriage the Christian couple is given a power and a commitment, a "kingly mission" to live their vocation as lay people charged with ordering temporal affairs to the plan of God. The Christian family is called to give witness in a generous and disinterested fashion of dedication to social matters and a "preferential option" for the poor and disadvantaged.[98] Their engagement with social matters now extends to the international order "since it is only in worldwide solidarity that the enormous and dramatic issues of world justice, the freedom of peoples and the peace of humanity can be dealt with and solved." They should support associations devoted to international issues. The spiritual communion between Christian families generates justice and peace among peoples and is a sign of unity for the world and an exercise of its prophetic role.[99]

4. Sharing in the Life and Mission of the Church

The family has an "ecclesial task"—that of "building up the kingdom of God in history by participating in the life and mission of the church." The Church "as mother" gives birth to and educates the Christian family by proclaiming the word of God, by celebrating the sacraments, and by "the continuous proclamation of the new commandment of love," so that it may imitate and relive the "sacrificial love that the Lord Jesus has for the entire human race."[100]

The Christian family's mission in the Church reflects its nature, that is, an intimate community of life and love expressed through a community pattern of the member's shared commitment to works of service to Church and civil community. In this way the Christian family participates in the "prophetic, priestly and kingly mission of Jesus Christ" insofar as it becomes "1) a believing and evangelizing community, 2) a community in dialogue with God, and 3) a community at the service of man."[101]

The Christian family as a believing and evangelizing community

The Christian family both welcomes and announces the Word of God, thus fulfilling its prophetic role which reveals that "their conjugal and family life [is] sanctified and made a source of sanctity by Christ himself." Their preparation for Christian marriage is a faith journey that deepens their faith received at baptism.[102]

The Christian family's ministry of evangelization begins at home where parents' share the faith with their children in word and deed, where children edify their parents in return and they, as a family, edify their neighbors. To be sure, "the future of evangelization depends in great part on the church of the home," especially "in places where antireligious legislation endeavors even to prevent education in the faith" or where there is widespread unbelief.[103]

The evangelization carried out by Christian parents is irreplaceable in the lives of their own children, enabling them to accept the vocation God gives to each child. A Christian family is a "most excellent seedbed of vocations to a life of consecration to the kingdom of God." Even if there are times when a child challenges or even rejects their faith, as often happens, parents must not lose hope, but "face with courage and great interior serenity the difficulties that their ministry of evangelization sometimes encounters in their own children." By facing these challenges Christian parents perform an "ecclesial service."[104]

Christian families' mission to evangelize includes a missionary inspiration as well: "The sacrament of marriage takes up and re-proposes the task of defending and spreading the faith, a task that has its roots in baptism and confirmation." This task may include witnessing to members within one's own family and to other families who are "far away" from belief in Christ or to "those Christian families who no longer live in accordance with the faith that they once received." Some are called to be "missionary couples and families who dedicate at least part of their lives to working in missionary territories." Finally, the missionary inspiration of the Christian family is expressed in "fostering missionary vocations among their sons and daughters and more generally, 'by training their children from childhood to recognize God's love for all people.'"[105]

The Christian family as a community in dialogue with God

Vivified by Jesus Christ, the Christian family is called by him to dialogue with God through sacraments and "the offering of one's life in prayer." This priestly role enables them to be sanctified and to sanctify the Church and world.[106] The sacrament of marriage is the source of the sanctification of Christian couples and families, the grace of which accompanies the married couple throughout their lives and fortifies them by a "kind of consecration in the duties and dignity of their state."[107]

The sanctifying priestly role of the Christian family is intimately connected with the Eucharist—the very source of Christian marriage, its communion and mission. "By partaking in the eucharistic bread the different members of the Christian family become one body" and also one with the whole Church which serves as the "source of [its] missionary and apostolic dynamism."[108] If at times the Christian family is unfaithful to its baptismal grace, its members should seek mutual pardon and the sacrament of penance.

The daily lives of Christian spouses and families are transformed into a "spiritual sacrifice acceptable to God through Jesus Christ"[109] through "celebrating the eucharist and the other sacraments" and through a "life of prayer." The specific characteristics of family prayer include its being offered in "common" amongst members of the family and has as its "object" the varying circumstances of family life "all of these mark God's loving intervention in the family's history."[110]

Christian parents have the responsibility of educating their children in prayer and providing concrete example and living witness of prayerfulness. Christian mothers must teach their children Christian prayers, prepare them to receive the sacraments, and when they are sick "to think of Christ suffering," to teach them to "invoke the aid of the Blessed Virgin and the saints," and to pray the rosary together. Christian fathers must also pray with their children and provide an example of honesty in thought and action which will be "a lesson for life."[111] The Christian family is also encouraged to pray the Divine Office in common and to celebrate the feasts of the liturgical year in the home as well as in Church. The private prayers of the Christian family should include morning and evening prayer, prayer before and after meals, Scripture meditation, devotion to the Sacred Heart of Jesus and veneration of the Blessed Virgin Mary, especially the rosary: "the rosary should be considered as one of the best and most efficacious prayers in common that the Christian family is invited to recite,"[112] so as to imitate better her virtues while it nourishes loving communion in the family.[113] Prayer provides the incentive for the Christian family to fulfill its duties as the "fundamental cell of human society."[114]

The Christian family as a community at the service of man

The whole Church, including the Christian family, has been given the mission of bringing all peoples to Christ and of following the law of Christian life being directed, not so much by a written code, but "in the personal action of the Holy Spirit who inspires and guides the Christian." The Christian family welcomes, respects and serves every human being and the Church, through the family, "can and ought to take on a more homelike or family dimensions, developing a more human and fraternal style of relationships." Therefore, the Christian family is not "closed in on itself, but remains open to the community," moved by a sense of responsibility toward the whole of society.[115]

Part IV: The Pastoral Care of the Family

Pastoral support of the family is a matter of urgency given that "future evangelization depends largely on the domestic church." The Church's pastoral action in support of the family follows the family in the different stages of its formation and development.[116] The stage of preparation for marriage is divided into three phases: remote, proximate and immediate. In early childhood wise family training leads children to know their personality, to discover their strengths and weaknesses; while esteem for "all authentic human values is instilled, both in interpersonal and in social relationships." This remote preparation for marriage also includes "solid spiritual and catechetical formation" revealing marriage and priestly or religious life as a "true vocation and mission."

The proximate preparation for marriage involves young people in a more specific preparation and rediscovery of the sacraments, and presents marriage "as an interpersonal relationship of a man and a woman that has to be continually developed." It will also include a study of conjugal sexuality and responsible parenthood, providing essential medical and biological information, as well as familiarizing them with methods for educating children, providing the "basic requisites for well-ordered family life such as stable work, sufficient financial resources, sensible administration, notions of housekeeping," and finally, a preparation for the family apostolate with like-minded individuals and organizations.

In the final months and weeks before the wedding the immediate preparation for the sacrament of marriage takes place which, in some ways, resembles the catechumenate, especially for those couples "that still manifest shortcomings or difficulties in Christian doctrine and practice." A deeper knowledge of the mystery of Christ and the Church, of grace and Christian marriage and the significance of the marriage liturgy must be stressed.

National bishops' conferences should undertake initiatives for the pastoral care of the family. However, such immediate preparations for marriage "must always be set forth and put into practice in such a way that omitting it is not an impediment to the celebration of marriage."[117]

The next phase of marriage, the celebration of the sacrament of Christian marriage, usually takes place within a liturgy "expressing the conjugal covenant between baptized persons." The celebration of the sacrament of marriage must be "per se valid, worthy and fruitful," there must be free consent, no impediments, proper canonical form and the appropriate liturgy. Moreover, the liturgical celebration must follow the norms of the Church and "should be simple and dignified" although it may incorporate such elements of the culture that express "the profound human and religious significance" of marriage, provided they contain nothing out of harmony with Christian faith and morality.[118]

In the case of non-believing but baptized persons the pastor must exercise some discernment. Since the desire of two baptized persons for Christian marriage is already a movement of grace and "an attitude of profound obedience to the will of God," it should be honored even if it appears their motivation for a church wedding may be for "social as well as personal motives." One mustn't forget these "imperfectly disposed" couples have accepted God's plan for marriage and "therefore at least implicitly consent to what the church intends to do when she celebrates marriage." Pastors should not attempt to judge a couple's "level of faith" as a criterion for admission to the sacrament of marriage. However, if it is clear that a couple "rejects explicitly and formally what the church intends to do when the marriage of baptized persons is celebrated, the pastor of souls cannot admit them to the celebration of marriage."[119]

The pastoral care of Christian couples after marriage is crucial. Young couples and families are especially vulnerable to difficulties occasioned by adaptations to living together and by the birth of their children. Young couples should accept the "discreet, tactful and generous help" of older, more mature couples, who for their part will be enriched by the witness of young couples to live their commitments with joy.[120]

Structures of Family Pastoral Care

Family pastoral care is put into effect by the structures and workers of the Church, especially the particular Church which is more immediate and effective in caring for the family. All those involved in this ministry must be "oriented and trained progressively and thoroughly for the various tasks" in specialized institutes and programs and be open to lay persons, especially those in the medical, legal, psychological, social and educational professions.[121]

God raises up families to be apostles, "sending them as workers into his vineyard and in a very special way into this field of the family:" first by their own witness to a "life lived in conformity with the divine law in all its aspects;" and the formation of their own children in faith and chastity, preparation for life, protecting them from ideological and moral dangers and the gradual inclusion of them in the Church and civil associations, helping them to choose a vocation. Then the family apostolate will reach out to other families in works of spiritual and material charity—especially to the most needy.[122]

Christian families should also become involved at all levels of various worthwhile non-ecclesial associations devoted to ethical or cultural enrichment, to the protection of women and children, to a more just world, or to those who collaborate with schools to improve the education of children.[123]

Agents of the Pastoral Care of the Family

Bishops are principally responsible for the pastoral care of the family and must have a personal interest for this sector of pastoral care and maintain personal support for families and all those who assist him in the pastoral care of the family so that his diocese becomes a true diocesan family. Priests and deacons must teach "in full harmony with the authentic magisterium of the church" so as to avoid troubling the conscience of the faithful. Pastors exercise the prophetic mission of Christ when they distinguish between genuine expressions of faith and what is less in harmony with the light of faith. Theologians and experts can be of great value in explaining the content of the Church's magisterium to the faithful. They must always remain faithful to the obligatory norm which belongs to the hierarchical magisterium.[124]

Those called to religious life and priesthood give witness as to how wonderful God made marriage by waiting to experience it in its fullness in the future age wherein Christ will take the Church, Her members, as His bride. These consecrated individuals are better available to devote themselves to care of families by visiting them, caring for the sick, ministering to single parents, providing marriage preparation, or by "opening their own houses for simple and cordial hospitality so that families can find there a sense of God's presence and a taste for prayer and reconciliation."[125] Lay specialists, doctors, lawyers, psychologists, etc. can help families through their specialties, which is a true mission for the good of society and the Christian community itself.[126]

Those involved in the field of social communication affect the minds of those who use it, for good or ill, profoundly, especially the young. Unfortunately, mass communication is often cleverly manipulated to distort one's way of looking at the family.[127] Parents have a duty "'to protect their young from the forms of aggression they are subjected to by the mass media,' and to ensure that the use of the media in the family is carefully regulated." Parents should seek alternatives to mass media "that are more wholesome, useful and physically, morally and spiritually formative." They must educate their children in calm and objective judgments which will guide them in the selection of entertainment. They will also attempt to influence program selection and remember that "[e]very attack on the fundamental value of the family—meaning eroticism or violence, the defense of divorce, or of anti-social attitudes among young people—is an attack on the true good of man."[128]

Pastoral Care of the Family in Difficult Cases

Often families, independent of their own wishes, must face difficult situations. These categories of persons in more need of pastoral care than others including the following: migrant workers, members of the armed forces, itinerant people, families of those in prison, "families in big cities living practically speaking as outcasts," families with no homes, single parent families, families with handicapped children or drug addicted children, families of alcoholics, families uprooted from their culture, families discriminated against politically, families experiencing religious persecution, teen-age married couples, and the elderly "often obliged to live alone with inadequate means of subsistence. The elderly often feel lonely and abandoned by their children and relatives, or useless and a burden, and left contemplating the onset of death."[129]

Mixed marriages between a Catholic and a non-Catholic Christian, or a Catholic and a non-baptized person present special needs, such as respect for the obligations imposed by faith on the Catholic spouse to practice his or her faith and have the children baptized and raised Catholic. These obligations would be violated by either "undue pressure to make the partner change his or her beliefs, or by placing obstacles in the way of the free manifestation of these beliefs by religious practice."[130]

In preparing a Catholic and non-Catholic Christian for marriage, these duties must be explained and to ensure that the pressures and obstacles mentioned above will not occur and to support and strengthen the Catholic partner in his or her faith so as to give "a credible witness within the family through his or her own life and through the quality of love shown to the other spouse and the children." When a Catholic marries a person of another non-Christian faith "his beliefs are to be treated with respect. If the non-baptized party has no faith, assurances must be given that he will not obstruct with the religious obligations of the Catholic party to practice the faith and raise the children Catholic.[131]

Irregular marriages threaten damage to the very institution of marriage and family and must be given careful consideration.[132]

A) Trial marriages are chosen by a man and woman as an "experiment" for some period of time. But this impermanence contradicts the dignity of human beings which "demands that they should be always and solely the term [the recipient] of a self-giving love without limitations of time or of any other circumstance." If the two persons are both baptized they are a "real symbol of the union of Christ and the church, which is not a temporary or 'trial' union," but must become an "indissoluble marriage." An indissoluble marriage, symbolizing Christ's union with his Church, is not possible "unless the human person from childhood, with the help of grace and without fear, has been trained to dominate concupiscence to establish relationship of genuine love with other people."[133]

B) De facto free unions are those "without any publicly recognized institutional bond, either civil or religious." Some people feel forced into such free unions for various reasons or do so out of ignorance or immaturity, or to scorn the institution of marriage and family and the social order or are seeking simply sexual pleasure. Such unions give scandal and bring about grave social consequences such as "the destruction of the concept of the family; the weakening of the sense of fidelity, also toward society; possible psychological damage to the children; the strengthening of selfishness." Pastors should tactfully attempt to regularize these situations. But, even more, the people of God should campaign to prevent these unions from arising by providing a sound religious training to young persons and by approaching public authorities to resist the pressure to legitimize these irregular situations that lead "public opinion to undervalue the institutional importance of marriage and the family," and to ensure that social and economic structures guarantee a "family wage" and provide "housing fitting for family life and by creating opportunities for work and life" so no one is forced into so called free unions.[134]

C) Catholics in civil marriages at least do not undermine the institution of marriage as do those in so called free unions, since they express "at least a certain commitment to a properly defined and probable stable state of life, even though the possibility of a future divorce is often present in the minds of those entering a civil marriage." Nevertheless, their situation should be regularized and their life brought into harmony with the Catholic faith they profess. Until such time they cannot be admitted to the sacraments.[135]

D) Separated or divorced persons who have not remarried,[136] especially if they were guiltless and have been abandoned, often suffer loneliness and misunderstanding and, so, the Church must show them "respect, solidarity, and practical help, so that they can preserve their fidelity even in their difficult situation" and forgive and, perhaps, "return to their former married life." Both the separated and divorced who are aware of a valid marriage bond and do not remarry give witness before the world and the church of fidelity to Christ and are welcome to receive the sacraments.[137]

E) Divorced persons who have remarried "cannot be abandoned to their own devises" but, as baptized persons, they must share in her life: by listening to the word of God proclaimed while attending Mass, persevering in prayer, doing works of charity and justice, bring up their children in the Catholic faith, by cultivating a spirit of penance and imploring God's grace. However, they may not be admitted to Eucharistic communion since their life "objectively contradicts that union of love between Christ and the Church which is signified and effected by the Eucharist," and it would give scandal by confusing others regarding the indissolubility of marriage. If the divorced and remarried person were to separate from their new partner he or she could then partake in the sacraments of penance and eucharistic communion. Also, if for the sake of their children the divorced and remarried Catholic could not satisfy the obligation to separate but is willing to "take on themselves the duty to life in complete continence, that is abstain from the acts proper to married couples," he or she could be admitted to the sacraments. Finally, a pastor may not attempt to perform a marriage ceremony "of any kind for divorced people who remarry. Such ceremonies would give the impression of the celebration of a new, sacramentally valid marriage and would thus lead people into error concerning the indissolubility of a validly contracted marriage."[138]

Those without a family are a category of people who are "particularly close to the heart of Christ." Regardless of how they came to be in such condition often due to extreme poverty or the breakdown of morality there is good news— no one is without a family: "The Church is a home and family for everyone, especially those who 'labor and are heavy laden.'"[139]

In conclusion it is important to remember that "the future of humanity passes by way of the family." It is a "form of love" to give back to families "reasons for confidence in itself" in light of the "dangers and evils that menace it."

Therefore, "I wish to invoke the protection of the Holy Family of Nazareth over the Christian family" and "assure you all of my constant prayers."[140]

Magisterial Teaching and Theological Reflection on Marriage and Family

Theology of the Body

John Paul II explained that the phrase "Theology of the Body" is really a working term for "the redemption of the body and the sacrament of marriage."[141] He began his four-year long catechesis on love and human sexuality by first reflecting on man and woman made in the image of God in the primordial sacrament of creation.[142] Then he considered the re-creation of matrimonial integrity after The Fall in the new sacrament of salvation through the death and resurrection of Christ.[143] Finally, he brought the weight of his analysis on the theology of the body to bear on the Church's teaching on human procreation in *Humanae Vitae.*[144]

Because man is made in the image and likeness of God, he experiences within himself a completeness, and, at the same time, a task to complete. He is complete in the human nature he receives as a given from his Creator at the moment he first comes into existence. In this sense, he is already a person made in the image of the divine Persons of the Trinity; but this nature and his unique identity are oriented toward loving others so as to know himself in a reciprocal gift of self. This task given to man to unfold himself in "a sincere gift of himself"[145] is not only written into the basic inclination of his mind and soul, but it is signified in masculinity and femininity. Therefore, the only thing "not good" in paradise before the Fall was that man was "alone" and could not evaluate in truth the gift God had given to him:

> When God-Yahweh said, "It is not good that man should be alone," (Gn. 2:18) he affirmed that "alone," man does not completely realize [the essence of the world as gift]. He realizes it only by existing "with someone"—and even more deeply and completely—by existing "for someone.". . . The words ["alone" and "helper"] indicate as fundamental and constitutive for man both the relationship and the communion of persons. The communion of persons means existing in a mutual "for," in a relationship of mutual gift. This relationship is precisely the fulfillment of "man's" original solitude.[146]

Even though Adam, the first man, had named all the animals, he was still alone and unable to discover himself in giving himself sincerely to another. How could he make a gift of himself to creatures fundamentally incapable of self-consciousness, self-possession or self-gift? But when God created Eve and showed her to him, he exclaimed in delight—"bone of my bone, flesh of my flesh."[147] "Exclaiming this way, he seems to say that here is a body that expresses the person."[148] Adam had met another creature with a conscious light in her eyes capable of existing in a mutual "for" him, and receiving "from" him his very self through the medium of their complementary bodies.

They felt no shame naked before each other in their nuptial innocence because God created them free of concupiscence.[149] Therefore, their bodies were translucent; the eyes of their hearts were clear with no cataracts to make opaque the medium of the body and thereby eclipsing the soul and exposing in stark relief the body's substratum of sensuousness:

> Concupiscence entails the loss of the interior freedom of the gift. The nuptial meaning of the human body is connected precisely with this freedom. Man can become a gift—that is, the man and woman can exist in the relationship of mutual self-giving—if each of them controls himself. Manifested as a "coercion sui generis of the body," concupiscence limits interiorly and reduces self-control. For that reason, in a certain sense it makes impossible the interior freedom of giving. Together with that, the beauty that the human body possesses in its male and female aspect as an expression of the spirit is obscured. The body remains as an object of lust and therefore, as a "field of appropriation" of the other human being. In itself, concupiscence is not capable of promoting union as the communion of persons. By itself it does not unite, but appropriates. The relationship of the gift is changed into the relationship of appropriation.[150]

After the sin of our first parents the self-mastery they possessed as part of the gift of the grace of original justice was lost; concupiscence dulled the eyes of their souls so that their bodies became opaque, not a medium of the soul but an end in itself—"a field of appropriation." Since then the union of man and woman has been subject to tensions, and their relations are marked by lust and domination.[151]

Not only did the body in its masculinity and femininity lose its translucence and become "thingified," but its sacramental character was lost. Had Adam not sinned they would have conveyed to their descendants through the act of generation all that he possessed, including the grace of original justice. In a sense conjugal union was intended to convey—to be the material instrumental cause—not just natural life but supernatural life. Man and woman in original justice would have been at the same time procreators and ministers of the grace now conferred in baptism. The womb of Eve was intended to be a baptismal font, if you will, from which sons and daughters of God would have been conceived and born in grace. For this reason John Paul II refers to marriage in the state of original justice as the "primordial sacrament:"

> Christ's words to the Pharisees (cf. Mt. 19) refer to marriage as a sacrament, that is, to the primordial revelation of God's salvific will and deed at the beginning, in the very mystery of creation. In virtue of that salvific will and deed of

God, man and woman, joining together in such a way as to become "one flesh" (Gn. 2:24), were at the same time destined to be united "in truth and love" as children of God (cf. GS no. 24), adopted children in the only begotten Son, beloved from all eternity.[152]

We can say that marriage, as a primordial sacrament, was deprived of that supernatural efficacy which at the moment of its institution belonged to the sacrament of creation in its totality.[153]

[Marriage as instituted by God before the Fall] should serve not only to prolong the work of creation, that is, of procreation. It should also serve to extend to further generations of men the same sacrament of creation, that is, the supernatural fruits of man's eternal election . . . those fruits which man was endowed with by God in the very act of creation.
Ephesians [5:21–23] seems to authorize us to interpret Genesis in this way, and the truth about the "beginning" of man and of marriage contained therein.[154]

The human body in its nuptial capacity was then intended to signify and make present three mysteries: namely, the person of the spouse in their mutual gift of self; the person of their child, a reflection of their distinct selves joined in total donation to the other; and the supernatural presence of God gracing them and divinizing the child conceived in their act of procreation . After the Fall the conjugal act in marriage was shorn of its original power to convey sanctifying grace to the spouses themselves or to their offspring. However, the new economy of grace instituted by Christ is in the figure and form of the original primordial sacrament of creation and God's grace is again bestowed:

This redemptive gift of himself "for" the Church also contains—according to Pauline thought—Christ's gift of himself to the Church, in the image of the nuptial relationship that unites husband and wife in marriage. In this way, the sacrament of redemption again takes on, in a certain sense, the figure and form of the primordial sacrament. To the marriage of the first husband and wife, as a sign of the supernatural gracing of man in the sacrament of creation, there corresponds the marriage, or rather the analogy of marriage, of Christ with the Church, as the fundamental great sign of the supernatural gracing of man in the sacrament of redemption.[155]

John Paul II insists that St. Paul was not speaking metaphorically when he compared the conjugal union of man and woman in Christian marriage to the sacramentality of the union of Christ with the Church in Eph. 5:2–23. Rather, "it is a real renewal (or a "re-creation"; that is, of a new creation) of that which constituted the salvific content (in a certain sense, the "salvific substance") of the primordial sacrament."[156]

In Christ, marriage is renewed so that the spouses are the ministers of a true sacrament—an efficacious sign which creates an enduring bond and a channel for God's gracing:

> From a valid marriage arises a bond between the spouses which by its very nature is perpetual and exclusive; furthermore, in a Christian marriage the spouses are strengthened and, as it were, consecrated for the duties and the dignity of their state by a special sacrament.[157]

In the light of Christ, man and women can again discover the nuptial significance inscribed in the theology of their bodies. Through the grace provided in this sacrament of redemption, the original blessing is renewed and man can be "fruitful and multiply" with purity of heart and the knowledge that their children will again become children of God through a second birth in the sacrament of baptism. Even so, baptism in the new dispensation of grace does not completely remove the fumes of concupiscence which "is left for us to wrestle with" that we may win our crown:[158]

> As much as concupiscence darkens the horizon of the inward vision and deprives the heart of the clarity of the desires and aspirations, so much does "life according to the Spirit" (that is, the grace of the sacrament of marriage) permit man and woman to find again the true liberty of the gift, united to the awareness of the spousal meaning of the body in its masculinity and femininity.[159]

Charter of Rights of the Family

Pope John Paul II agreed to the 1980 Synod of Bishops' request that a Charter of family rights be drawn up. He provided an outline of those rights, fourteen in number, in *Familiaris Consortio* (#46). The *Charter of the Rights of the Family*, promulgated in 1983, is addressed to those responsible for the common good. It is a blueprint, or a constitution, given "principally to governments . . . as a model and a point of reference for the drawing up of legislative and family policy, and guidance for action programs." It provides "fundamental postulates and principles for legislation" and in some cases "binding juridical norms."[160] Of course, the *Charter* is also addressed to families so as to encourage them.

In the Preamble marriage is defined as "that intimate union of life in complementarity between a man and a woman which is constituted in the freely contracted and publicly expressed indissoluble bond of matrimony, and is open to the transmission of life" (B) to which it is "exclusively entrusted" (C). The family based upon marriage, so defined, exists prior to the state and possesses inherent and inalienable rights (D). We are assured the family is much more than a legal entity, it is a "community of love and solidarity, which is uniquely suited to teach and transmit cultural, ethical, social, spiritual and religious values, essential for the development and well being of its own members and of society" (E).

Article 1: "All persons have the right to the free choice of their state of life and thus to marry and establish a family or to remain single."

The only restrictions a state may impose on the right to marry are those required by "grave and objective demands of the institution of marriage itself" (a). Society has the obligation to provide a stable environment so that those who wish to marry may do so responsibly (b). Moreover, public authorities must uphold the institutional value of marriage so that it is not placed on the same level as non-married couples (c).

Article 2: "Marriage cannot be contracted except by free and full consent of the spouses duly expressed."

Families must not pressure or impede their children in "the choice of a specific person as spouse" (a). Spouses have the right of religious liberty which should not compromised by a conversion of faith contrary to conscience as a condition for marriage (b). Both husband and wife enjoy the "same dignity and equal rights regarding marriage" (c).

Article 3: "The spouses have the inalienable right to found a family and to decide on the spacing of births and the number of children to be born, taking into full consideration their duties toward themselves, their children already born, the family and society, in a just hierarchy of values and in accordance with the objective moral order which excludes recourse to contraception, sterilization and abortion."

It is "a grave offense to human dignity and justice" for public authorities to limit in any way couples from deciding about their children (a), such as when foreign governments condition economic aid to developing nations on the "acceptance of programs of contraception, sterilization or abortion" (b). Families have the right to society's assistance in bearing and raising children; especially large families should not be discriminated against (c).

Article 4: "Human life must be respected and protected absolutely from the moment of conception."

Abortion (a), experimentation on human embryos (b), and all non-therapeutic genetic manipulations (c) constitute violation of fundamental human rights. Children and their mothers before and for a reasonable time after birth have the right to special protection and aid (d). All children, legitimate or not, have an equal right to social protection (e) as do orphans (f), who have the right to be adopted; and handicapped children, who have a right to a suitable environment (g).

Article 5: "Since they have conferred life on their children, parents have the original, primary and inalienable right to educate them; hence they must be acknowledged as the first and foremost educators of their children."

"Parents have the right to educate their children in conformity with their moral and religious convictions," in light of their cultural traditions which favor the child's good and should receive necessary aid from society to perform their role properly (a). Parents have the right to choose their children's schools in keeping with their convictions and "public authorities must ensure that public subsidies are so allocated that parents are truly free to exercise this right without incurring unjust burdens. Parents should not have to sustain, directly or indirectly, extra charges which would deny or unjustly limit the exercise of this freedom" (b). Parents have the right to keep their children out of objectionable classes, especially in the case of sex education: "sex education is a basic right of the parents and must always be carried out under their close supervision" (c). "The rights of parents are violated when a compulsory system of education is imposed by the State from which all religious formation is excluded" (d). Parents' right as the primary educators of their children must be upheld in relations with teachers and schools and in the formation of school policy (e). The family has the right to media programming that "reinforces the fundamental values of the family" and to adequate protection, especially of their children, from the negative misuse of the mass media (f).

Article 6: "The family has the right to exist and to progress as a family."

Public authorities must foster the privacy, integrity and stability of every family (a) which is attacked by legal recognition of divorce (b). The extended family should be esteemed and helped to fulfill its role of solidarity, while respecting the rights of the nuclear family (c).

Article 7: "Every family has the right to live freely its own domestic religious life under the guidance of the parents, as well as the right to profess publicly and to propagate the faith, to take part in public worship and in freely chosen programs of religious instruction, without suffering discrimination."

Article 8: "The family has the right to exercise its social and political function in the construction of society."

In order to fulfill its political and social functions families have a right to join with other families to protect their legal rights (a) and to help plan programs touching on family life on the economic, social and cultural level (b).

Article 9: "Families have the right to be able to rely on an adequate family policy on the part of public authorities in the juridical, economic, social and fiscal domains, without any discrimination whatsoever."

Economic conditions must assure families an appropriate standard of living. They must be allowed to own private property which favors stable family life. Inheritance laws must respect the rights of families (a). In the event of the death of one or both spouses, or their abandonment by one spouse, or accidents the family has a right to social assistance (b). The elderly have a right to live their later years in serenity amidst their family or, if this is not possible, then in suitable institutions pursuing suitable activities (c). Prisoners have a right to remain in contact with their families; their families have a right to be adequately maintained (d).

Article 10: "Families have a right to a social and economic order in which the organization of work permits the members to live together, and does not hinder the unity, well-being, health and the stability of the family, while offering also the possibility of wholesome recreation."

"Remuneration for work must be sufficient for establishing and maintaining a family with dignity, either through a suitable salary, called a 'family wage,' or through other social measures, such as family allowances or the remuneration of the work in the home of one of the parents," and mothers should not be forced to work outside the home to the detriment of their children (a). A mother's work in the home must be respected because of its value for the family and society (b).

Article 11: "*The family has the right to decent housing, fitting for family life and commensurate to the number of the members, in a physical environment that provides the basic services for the life of the family and the community.*"

Article 12: "*The families of migrants have the right to the same protection as that accorded other families.*"

Immigrant families have the right to be respected for their culture and to receive the support necessary to integrate into the community (a). Emigrant workers have the right be united as soon as possible with their families. Refugees also have a right to assistance and aid in being reunited with their families (b).

Letter to Families

In the eleven years that elapsed between the publication of *Familiaris Consortium* in 1981 and Pope John Paul II's second encyclical on the family titled *Letter to Families* (Gratissimam Sane) (1994), the social conditions in which the family finds itself had continued to deteriorate. The "irregular" family situations described in first encyclical (marriage alternatives) had continued to gain social acceptability, especially in the economically developed countries of the world; and these countries continued to influence or coerce developing nations into following their example. This would soon be made manifest in the summer of 1994 at the United Nations' Cairo Conference on Population and Development, which attempted to shape world consensus on a *new* human right to abortion and the need for all nations to set target population goals and manage family fertility.[161] This, in part, explains why he preemptively declared the year 1994 the Year of the Family, and wrote a second major address on the subject of the family so soon after the first, in February of 1994:

> Unfortunately various programs backed by very powerful resources nowadays seem to aim at the breakdown of the family. At times it appears that concerted efforts are being made to present as normal and attractive, and even to glamorize, situations which are in fact "irregular." Indeed they contradict "the truth and love" which should inspire and guide relationships between men and women, thus causing tensions and divisions in families, with grave consequences particularly for children. The moral conscience becomes darkened; what is true, good and beautiful is deformed; and freedom is replaced by what is actually enslavement.[162]

The appropriate response to the alarming advance of evil directed toward the family is for a great prayer to rise up from families around the world so that Christ love may triumph "over everything that is not love." The Virgin Mother asks us, as at Cana in Galilee, to do whatever her Son tells us to do. And what is that? John Paul II explains: "What Christ tells us in this particular moment of history constitutes a forceful call to a great prayer with families and for families." In Part I, "The Civilization of Love," Pope John Paul II contrasted a well established term, "*a civilization of love*," with "a civilization of things" and "of use," which in Part II, "The Bridegroom is with You," he further condemns as a "*civilization of death*" (#21). He named the great evil of our times and the name has stuck. These are the concepts he develops throughout the encyclical, contrasting their respective anthropologies, ethics, world-views and social realities. It is between these two poles, these contending civilizations, that the family is drawn and must choose—to live the love that is its identity and makes it the "basic cell" of all genuine human culture or to be paralyzed, de-nucleated and reanimated with an alien logic and cold vital principle, and become a chill depersonalizing force in a frozen waste land.

A civilization of love is founded upon the deepest reality, the triune God that is imaged in each person made in his likeness, and called into being in a family with the vocation to "be fruitful and multiply" in marriage:

> In the light of the New Testament it is possible to discern how the primordial model of the family is to be sought in God himself, in the Trinitarian mystery of his life. The divine *we* is the eternal pattern of the human *we*, especially of that *we* formed by the man and the woman created in the divine image and likeness.[163]

Marriage and family reflect the communion and community, the "*we*," of the three Divine Persons of the Blessed Trinity:

> *Communion* has to do with the personal relationship between *I* and *thou*. *Community* on the other hand transcends this framework and moves toward a *society*, a *we*. . . . The communion of the spouses gives rise to the community of the family. The community of the family is completely pervaded by the very essence of communion.[164]

Therefore human begetting is different from all other begetting on earth because man and woman are called in that moment to be taken into the hand of God and for Him to intervene directly again as on the sixth day of creation fashioning a new Adam, a new Eve:

> In affirming that the spouses, as parents, cooperate with God the Creator in conceiving and giving birth to a new human being, we are not speaking merely with reference to the laws of biology. Instead, we wish to emphasize that God himself is present in human fatherhood and motherhood quite differently than

he is present in all other instances of begetting on earth. Indeed, God alone is the source of that image and likeness which is proper to the human being, as it was received at creation. [Human] Begetting is the continuation of creation.[165]

Every human being is thus an end unto himself, not an object, but a being "meant to express fully his humanity, to 'find himself' as a person," and at the same time called to fully find himself resting in God:

By his very genealogy, the person created in the image and likeness of God exists for his own sake and reaches fulfillment precisely by sharing in God's life. As we read in the book of the prophet Jeremiah: "Before I formed you in the womb I knew you, and before you were born I consecrated you" (Jer. 1:5). The genealogy of the person is thus united with the eternity of God and only then with human fatherhood and motherhood, which are realized in time. At the moment of conception itself, man is already destined to eternity with God.[166]

Having pledged at their wedding to be willing to be taken up in the hand of God as instruments of His creative act in their conjugal acts open to procreation, spouses can never willfully take back their "yes" to begetting by closing an act of conjugal intimacy from potential fecundity. By the same logic, their willful "no" to begetting becomes a "no" to their love and complete union as a couple:

In the conjugal act, husband and wife are called to confirm in a responsible way the mutual gift of self which they have made to each other in the marriage covenant. The logic of the total gift of self to the other involves a potential openness to procreation: In this way the marriage is called to even greater fulfillment as a family.[167]

We read that marriage and family are organically linked to a "civilization of love" as its "center" and its "heart," because marriage and family enable men and women to make and receive a sincere gift of self. But without this civilization of love, this culture of love, "it is impossible to have such a concept of persons and of the communion of persons" who image the divine we. Today we witness the rise of an "anti-civilization" and a "crisis of concepts," where the words "love, freedom, sincere gift and even person and rights of the person" lose their essential meaning: "Only if the truth about freedom and the communion of persons in marriage and in the family can regain its splendor will the building of the civilization of love truly begin and will it then be possible to speak concretely . . . about 'promoting the dignity of marriage and family.'" Utilitarianism has spawned a "civilization of production and of use, a civilization of things and not of persons, a civilization in which persons are used in the same way as things are used." Living in such a culture the family cannot help but feel threatened. For instance, so-called safe sex is really extremely dangerous because it endangers both the person and the family with "the loss of the truth about one's own self and about the family, together with the risk of a loss of freedom and consequently of a loss of love itself."[168]

Chapter thirteen of St. Paul's First Letter to the Corinthians is the "Magna Carta of the civilization of love" because it stresses the understanding of man "as a person who 'finds himself' by making a sincere gift of self. [169] A gift is, obviously, for others: "This is the most important dimension of the civilization of love." The program of utilitarianism rests upon a freedom with responsibilities which, when allied with various forms of human weakness, "proves a systematic and permanent threat to the family."[170]

The emphasis in the Fourth Commandment—to honor your mother and father—falls on the word "honor" which is "essentially an attitude of unselfishness." The *Letter* says, the honor children owe their parents is mirrored by the honor the parents owe their children "from the first moment of their conception." In this way the family built on the foundation of the Fourth Commandment and its requirement of reciprocal honor "is in many ways the first school of how to be human." To obey this Commandment is not a utopian dream but a duty made possible by God's grace.[171]

The "we" of the Trinity found imprinted in the soul of every person, understood in their need to make a gift of themselves to others especially in marriage, develops into the "we" of the family in rearing of children. All education rests on honor: "The principle of giving honor, the recognition and respect due to man precisely because he is a man, is the basic condition for every authentic educational process."[172]

Only the family based on a true conception of marriage can raise children in such a way as to build up the civilization of love. Marriage rightly understood may be described as follows:

> Marriage, which undergirds the institution of the family, is constituted by the covenant whereby "a man and a woman establish between themselves a partnership of their whole life," and which "of its own very nature is ordered to the well-being of the spouses and to the procreation and upbringing of children."[173]

All other interpersonal unions present a "serious threat to the future of the family and of society itself." The self-indulgence and permissiveness they unleash "cannot fail to damage the authentic requirements of peace and communion among people." The family founded upon a correct conception of marriage is "a sovereign society" with certain unalienable rights, as mentioned in the *Charter of the Rights of the Family*.[174] The family is also a part of a nation which to some extent shapes the family's identity. The state is distinct from the nation and is less family-like, more bureaucratic. The family is linked to the state according to the principle of subsidiarity:

> Whenever the family is self-sufficient, it should be left to act on its own; an excessive intrusiveness on the part of the state would prove detrimental, to say

nothing of lacking due respect, and would constitute an open violation of the rights of the family. Only in those situations where the family is not really self sufficient does the state have the authority and duty to intervene.[175]

State assistance ought to be given the family in areas of life, health and employment. Motherhood must be recognized as true work and "because of all the hard work it entails, should be recognized as giving the right to financial benefits at least equal to those other kinds of work undertaken in order to support the family during such a delicate phase of its life" (Ibid.).

In the second part of the *Letter*, "The Bridegroom is with You," John Paul II explains that in using this image of the Bridegroom[176] to describe God's love for humanity, "Jesus shows to what extent the fatherhood and the love of God are reflected in the love of a man and a woman united in marriage." Jesus appears at Cana as a herald of the divine truth about marriage, that as a reflection of the Father's love, "it is a gentle love like that of a mother for her child, a tender love like that of the bridegroom for his bride, but at the same time an equally and intensely jealous love. It is not in the first place a love which chastises but one which forgives." The Bridegroom is also the Good Shepherd who leads families into the pastures of life and is the reason for our hope, who strengthens us in the Sacraments and is the "well-spring of ever new enthusiasm and sign of the triumph of the civilization of love" as we walk through this dark valley.[177]

St. Paul in his Letter to the Ephesians explains that marriage and family life is a "great mystery"[178] because it expresses "the spousal love of Christ for his church" which participates in the grace of divinization. St. Irenaeus said: "Christ Jesus, our Lord, the Son of God, became the son of man so that man could become a son of God." The family as the domestic church is the great mystery of God in its participation in Christ's transforming love expressed in sanctified "conjugal live, paternal and maternal love, fraternal love, the love of a community of persons and of generations."[179]

The modern age, even though it has made progress in its understanding of the material world and human psychology has failed to penetrate to man's deepest metaphysical dimension, and, so, man appears not a mystery but an unknown reality.[180] This has given rise to a "new Manichaeism" in which man is "thingified," "the body does not receive life from the spirit," and is "regarded more as an area for manipulation and exploitation than as the basis of the primordial wonder which led Adam on the morning of creation to exclaim before Eve: 'This at last is bone of my bones and flesh of my flesh.'"[181] In rationalism, from which the new Manichaeism was spawned, it is "unthinkable that God should be a redeemer, much less that he should be the bridegroom, the primordial and unique source of the human love between spouses."[182] Once we lose sight of the wonder of life as an intimate gift from God who loves us as a spouse, elevating us in grace to the level of a divine being, we begin to wonder about the meaningless of life reduced to a grubby struggle to get ahead:

Rationalism provides a radically different way of looking at creation and the meaning of human existence. But once man begins to lose sight of a God who loves him, a God who calls man through Christ to live in him and with him, and once the family no longer has the possibility of sharing in the great mystery, what is left except the mere temporal dimension of life? Earthly life becomes nothing more than the scenario of a battle for existence, of a desperate search for gain, and financial gain before all else.[183]

The wonder that fills the hearts of those redeemed in Christ is also described as "fairest love" which is "a gift of God, grafted by the Holy Spirit onto human hearts and continually nourished in them." Mary is the "mother of fairest love" in the "yes" she said to the Incarnation of God; a yes that St. Joseph takes into his heart and into the Holy Family which has then been "profoundly inscribed in the spousal love of husband and wife and, in an indirect way, in the genealogy of every human family." Fairest love also refers to beauty: "the beauty of love and the beauty of the human being who, by the power of the Holy Spirit, is capable of such love." Fairest love also refers to the world of art "attentive to the deepest dimension of man and his future, [which] originates in the mystery of Christ's incarnation and draws inspiration from the mysteries of his life." However, a culture that makes "films, shows and radio and television programs dominated by pornography and violence" falsifies reality and is "a society which is sick and is creating profound distortions in man."[184]

The modern world is dominated by a spirit of lust, "a way of looking and thinking dominated by concupiscence;" it is a society "marked by consumerism and hedonism," where man "tends to treat as his own possession another human being, one who does not belong to him but to God." Today fairest love cannot be learned from what modern mass media has to say about man and woman, marriage and family, rather, it is learned above all in prayer, which is a "type of interior hiddenness with Christ in God" where "the workings of the Holy Spirit" are revealed.[185]

In abortion we "encounter everything that is diametrically opposed to fairest love." Accustomed to treating human beings as things for pleasure or profit, people reach the point of "killing love by killing the fruit of love." A slaughter of innocent children by King Herod that accompanied the birth of Christ has a certain prophetic eloquence for us today. This attitude of treating persons as things for pleasure or profit has built up a tremendous negative energy so that we now face an immense threat "not only to the life of individuals but also to that of civilization itself. The statement that civilization has become in some areas a *civilization of death* is being confirmed in disturbing ways."[186]

This should be kept in mind as spouses fulfill their responsibilities: "As you beget children on earth, never forget that you are also begetting them for God. God wants their birth in the Holy Spirit. . . . All this is the work of the son of

God, the divine bridegroom." The Bridegroom is the judge of humanity and in passing sentence he will note the love or selfishness that animated our works:

> "I was an unborn child, and you welcomed me by letting me be born"; "I was an abandoned child, and you became my family"; "I was an orphan, and you adopted me and raised me as one of your own children." Or again: "You helped mothers filled with uncertainty and exposed to wrongful pressure to welcome their unborn child and let it be born"; and "You helped large families and families in difficulty to look after and educate the children God gave them. . . ." [Or, we may hear] "Depart from me. . . . For I was hungry and you gave me no food." . . . To this list also we could add other ways of acting, in which Jesus is present in each case as the one who has been rejected. In this way he would identify with the abandoned wife or husband, or with the child conceived and then rejected: "You did not welcome me!". . . Christ's words, "You did not welcome me," also touch social institutions, governments and international organizations.[187]

Conclusion

In his writing on marriage and family John Paul II challenged us to appreciate its grandeur and the "great danger which follows when these realities are not respected or when the supreme values which lie at the foundation of the family and of human dignity are disregarded."[188] As we saw in chapter 10, so-called same-sex marriage is direct assault on marriage and family, an attempt to abolish it by diluting it with forms of cohabitation that give personal expression and societal approval to what in reality is an objective disorder, the homosexual tendency. To discriminate in favor of the marriage of man and woman, the Catholic Church teaches, is not a form of invidious discrimination but accords to that institution which predates civil society the legal and cultural recognition it needs as the basic cell of society. Those who would deny marriage and family its preeminence wittingly or unwittingly play into the hands of those who seek to deconstruct and reconstruct the human person according to ideologies so as to weaken the ego of the human person to fit better as a cell in an organ, an insignificant part of a totalitarian whole.[189]

Notes

1. Charles Dickens, *A Christmas Carol* (New York: Frederick Stokes Co., 1899), 7; see also Job 1:21.
2. Job 2:9.
3. Gen. 4:9.
4. Howard Bromberg, "More, Thomas," in ECST.

5. James Monti, *The King's Good Servant But God's First: The Life and Writings of St. Thomas More* (San Francisco: Ignatius Press, 1997), 442; citing Ro. Ba., *The Lyfe of Syr Thomas More, Sometymes Lord Chancellor of England*; Elsie V. Hitchcock and Msgr. P.E. Hallett, eds., original series, no. 222 (London: Early English Text Society, 1950), 246–47.

6. Monti, *The King's Good Servant*, 442; citing William Roper, *The Lyfe of Sir Thomas More*, ed. Elsie V. Hitchcock (London: Early English Text Society, 1935), 96.

7. Monti, *The King's Good Servant*, 441–42.

8. 1 Macc. 2:28.

9. 2 Macc. 7:29.

10. Allan C. Carlson, *Family Questions: Reflections on the American Social Crises* (New Brunswick, NJ: Transaction Publishers, 1991), 33; citing Shulamith Firestone, *The Dialectic of Sex: The Case for Feminist Revolution* (New York: William Morrow, 1970), 21–22, 30–31.

11. Adrian J. Reimers, "Pope John Paul II," in ECST.

12. FC, no. 3.

13. Philip M. Sutton, "Family" and William E. May "Marriage," in ECST.

14. Perry J. Cahall, "*Familiaris Consortio*," in ECST.

15. FC, no. 3.

16. FC, no. 3.

17. FC, no. 6; John F. Kippley, "Contraceptive Mentality," in ECST.

18. FC, no. 7.

19. FC, no. 7.

20. FC, no. 9.

21. Anthony P. DiPerna, "Inculturation," in ECST.

22. FC, no. 10.

23. Gen. 1:26–27; 1 John 4:8.

24. FC, no. 11.

25. William E. May, "Marriage," in ECST.

26. William E. May, "Marriage," in ECST.

27. FC, no. 11.

28. FC, no. 11.

29. FC, no. 12.

30. FC, no. 13.

31. FC, no. 13.

32. FC, no. 13. See also HV, no. 9.

33. Eph. 3:15; FC, no. 14.

34. FC, no. 14.

35. FC, no. 15.

36. FC, no. 16.

37. Philip M. Sutton, "Charter of the Rights of the Family," in ECST.

38. John Paul II, *On Redemption and the Dignity of Man* (*Redemptor Hominis*) (1979), no. 274.

39. FC, no. 18.

40. FC, no. 19.

41. FC, no. 20.

42. FC, no. 21.

43. FC, no. 21.

44. FC, no. 22.

45. See John F. Quinn, "Women's Suffrage Movement" and Oswald Sobrino, "Feminism in the Church," in ECST.

46. FC, no. 22.

47. FC, no. 23.

48. FC, no. 23.

49. FC, no. 23.

50. FC, no. 23.

51. FC, no. 23.

52. FC, no. 24.

53. FC, no. 25. See also Philip M. Sutton, "Fatherhood," in ECST.

54. Robert A. Rakauskas, "Children's Rights," in ECST.

55. Luke 18:16.

56. FC, no. 26.

57. Prov. 17:6; FC no. 27.

58. HV, no. 11. See also HV, no. 9, 12; FC, no. 29.

59. George E. Frost, "Malthus, Thomas Robert, and the Neo-Malthusians," in ECST.

60. FC, no. 30.

61. FC, no. 31.

62. GS, no. 51.

63. HV, no. 14.

64. HV, no. 12.

65. FC, no. 32.

66. FC, no. 32.

67. HV, no. 29.

68. GS, no. 51.

69. FC, no. 35.

70. FC, no. 33. See also HV, no. 21.

71. FC, no. 34.

72. John J. Conley, "Parental Rights," in ECST.

73. FC, no. 36; quoting GE, no. 3.

74. FC, no. 36.

75. Hanna Klaus, "Sex Education," and John J. Conley, "Parental Rights," in ECST.

76. FC, no. 36; also see John J. Schrems, "Subsidiarity," in ECST.

77. Hanna Klaus, "Abstinence Education," and Basil Cole, "Chastity," in ECST.

78. FC, no. 37.

79. St. Thomas Aquinas, *Summa Contra Gentiles*, vol. 4, 58; FC, no. 38.

80. Eph. 4:22–24.

81. 1 Pet. 3:15.

82. FC, no. 39.

83. FC, no. 40

84. FC, no.40.

85. FC, no. 40. See also John J. Conley, "Parental Rights," in ECST.

86. FC, no. 40.

87. FC, no. 41.

88. AA, no. 11.

89. FC, no. 42.

90. FC, no. 43.

91. Rom. 12:13.

92. FC, no. 44. See also Thomas D. Watts, "Social Welfare," in ECST.

93. DH, no. 5.

94. FC, no. 45.

95. FC, no. 45.

96. Philip M. Sutton, "Family and Human Rights, The," in ECST.

97. FC, no. 46.

98. Thomas D. Watts, "Social Welfare," in ECST.

99. FC, no. 48.

100. FC, no. 49.

101. FC, no. 50.

102. FC, no. 51.

103. FC, no. 51. See also Robert J. Batule, "Evangelization," in ECST.

104. FC, no. 53.

105. AA, no. 30; FC no. 54.

106. FC, no. 55.

107. FC, no. 56.

108. FC, no. 57.

109. 1 Pet. 2:5.

110. FC, no. 59.

111. FC, no. 60. See also Philip M. Sutton, "Motherhood" and Philip M. Sutton, "Fatherhood," in ECST.

112. Pope Paul VI, *Marialis Cultus*, nos. 52, 54.

113. FC, no. 61.

114. FC, no. 62.

115. FC, no. 64.

116. FC, no. 65.

117. FC, no. 66.

118. FC, no. 67.

119. FC, no. 68.

120. FC, no. 69.

121. FC, no. 70.

122. FC, no. 71.

123. FC, no. 72.

124. FC, no. 73.

125. FC, no. 74.

126. FC, no. 75.

127. Francis E. Monaghan, Jr., "Mass Culture," in ECST.

128. FC, no. 76.

129. FC, no. 77.

130. FC, no. 78.

131. FC, no.78.

132. Lisa S. Matthews, "Family Living, Alternatives In," in ECST.

133. FC, no. 80.

134. FC, no. 81.

135. FC, no. 82.

136. Anthony W. Zumpetta, "Family: Single Parent," in ECST.

137. FC, no. 83.

138. FC, no. 84.

139. FC, no. 85.

140. FC, no. 86.

141. Mary Shivanandan, "Theology of the Body," in ECST.

142. See Gen. 1:26. Cf. Matt. 19:8; Mark 10:6–9.

143. Eph. 5:21–33.

144. Pope John Paul II, *The Theology of the Body: Human Love in the Divine Plan* (Boston: Daughters of St. Paul, 1997), 419–20; quoting Pope John Paul II, *General Audience, 28* November, 1984.

145. GS, no. 24.

146. John Paul II, *Theology of the Body*, 60–61.

147. Gen. 2:23.

148. John Paul II, *Theology of the Body*, 61.

149. See D. Brian Scarnecchia, *Illuminating Human Life Issues*, vol. 1, ch. 3.

150. John Paul II, *Theology of the Body*, 127 (emphasis added). See also Kent Wallace, "Concupiscence," in ECST.

151. CCC, no. 400.

152. John Paul II, *Theology of the Body*, 344; quoting John Paul II, *General Audience*, November 24, 1982.

153. John Paul II, *Theology of the Body*, 336; quoting John Paul II, *General Audience*, October 13, 1982.

154. John Paul II, *Theology of the Body*, 335–36; quoting John Paul II, *General Audience*, October 6, 1982.

155. John Paul II, *Theology of the Body*, 337; quoting John Paul II, *General Audience*, October 13, 1982.

156. John Paul II, *Theology of the Body*, 341; quoting John Paul II, *General Audience*, October 20, 1982.

157. CIC, no. 1134.

158. CCC, no. 1264. See also 2 Tim. 2:5.

159. Pope John Paul II, *Theology of the Body*, 349 (quoting *General Audience*, December 1, 1982).

160. Philip M. Sutton, "Charter of the Rights of the Family," in ECST. See also Pontifical Council for the Family, *The Charter of the Rights of the Family*, 22 October 1983, http://www.vatican.va/roman_curia/pontifical_councils/family/documents/rc_pc_family_doc_19831022_family-rights_en.html (1 Aug. 2009).

161. Douglas A. Sylva, "United Nations" and John F. Kippley "Contraceptive Mentality," in ECST.

162. LF, no. 5.

163. LF, no. 6.

164. LF, no. 7.

165. LF, no. 9.

166. LF, no. 9.

167. LF, no. 12.

168. LF, no. 13.

169. GS, no. 24.
170. LF, no. 14.
171. LF, no. 15.
172. LF, no. 16.
173. LF, no. 17.
174. Philip M. Sutton, "Family and Human Rights, The," in ECST.
175. LF, no. 17.
176. Matt. 9:15.
177. LF, no. 18.
178. Eph. 5:32.
174. LF, no. 19
180. Adrian J. Reimers, "End of Man," in ECST.
181. LF, no. 19, Gen. 2:23.
182. LF, no. 19.
183. LF, no. 19.
184. Francis E. Monaghan, Jr., "Mass Culture," in ECST.
185. LF, nos. 19, 20.
186. LF, nos. 19, 21.
187. LF, nos. 19, 22.
188. LF, no. 23.
183. Michel Schooyans, *The Hidden Face of the United Nations*, trans. John Miller (St. Louis, MO: Central Bureau, 2001), 20–21. See also Michel Schooyans, *The Totalitarian Trend of Liberalism*, trans. John Miller (St. Louis, MO: Central Bureau, 1997), 159–65.

Chapter 14
End of Life Issues

Introduction

For many years people who suffered closed brain skull injury, stroke or other pathology and had "lost their thinking abilities and awareness of their surroundings" were diagnosed as in a permanent vegetative state (PVS).[1] For example, in 1994 Louis Vilojen of Johanesburg, South Africa, was hit by a truck while riding his bike. He lived, but his doctors expected him to die and told his mother he would never regain consciousness. Then one day, quite by accident, Louis was prescribed the sedative zolpidem to stop the spasmatic reactions in his left arm. His mother, Sienie, crushed the pill and gave it to him mixed with a soft drink. After twenty-five minutes Louis started to make a noise with his mouth, something he hadn't done in the five years since his accident. When he turned his head in the direction of his mother she said, "Louis, can you hear me?" He said, "Yes." Then she said, "Say hello, Louis." When Louis said, "Hello, mummy," Sienie started to cry, and cry.[2]

Since Louis's remarkable recovery his doctor, Dr. Wally Nel, has treated over one hundred and fifty brain-damaged patients with zolpidem and seen improvements in about sixty percent of them. Dr. Ralf Clauss, a physician of nuclear medicine at the Medical University of Southern Africa has used radioactive isotopes in diagnostic scans on Louis. He said: "We did scans before and after we gave Louis zolpidem. Areas that appeared black and dead beforehand began to light up with activity afterwards. I was dumbfounded—and I still am."[3]

> All of the above [permanent vegetative patients] were roused from their permanent vegetative state on the first application of Zolpidem and repeatedly on a daily base since then. . . . Although the patients return repeatedly to the vegetative state after four hours when drug action subsides, they are repeatedly aroused from this state on a daily base with renewed drug application. . . .

There was no evidence of tolerance to the drug and it remains as effective after years of treatment. . . . It appears that Zolpidem may have a broad application in patients with brain injury. Its mode of action may be due to a GABA [gamma aminobutyric acid] receptor based re-activation of dormant neural tissue of injured brain.[4]

So, where do we go when we fall asleep or end up in a coma for many years until aroused by a wonder drug? Is human consciousness like sight or vision that requires a medium in order to operate? Is a man in a black box blind so much because he has no sight or because the medium, light, by which he is able to see is absent? Similarly is a sleeping person, a PVS brain injured person, or a human embryo, so much unconscious because he is not there or because the medium by which he is able to be self conscious is fatigued, damaged or still under development?

A Canadian novelist and artist of exceptional talent once wrote in reply to my question about the nature of the human "heart" that it was much more, in his opinion, than what I had suggested—that what scripture refers to as the "heart"[5] is our conscience situated in the practical intellect. In his letter he explained that he had once known a child with a severe disability without cognitive ability who still had great heart:

> Dear Brian,
>   To answer your question about the heart, I use the term in the sense of the mysterious core of our being, the seat of one's unique and eternal self. I think Aquinas's concept of natural law residing in the practical intellect is no doubt true, but does it say enough? For example, where does natural law go, where does natural conscience and natural theology go, when Alzheimer's disease wipes out all levels of the intellect? Where are they in a severely mentally handicapped person? Such people often retain the ability to love, to respond to God's presence, to communicate (through the eyes, the spirit, the soul) but not in concepts, only in an essential transfer of meaning that is independent of words and un-definable by words. It is perhaps the 'meaning' embodied in pure love. I have seen it several times in my life. Close friends of ours have raised from childhood a girl (now in her twenties) who is blind, deaf, physically and mentally handicapped, cannot feed or clean herself, in short is totally without any tools of intellect, not even rudimentary sounds. Yet, at the offertory at Mass, she becomes excited and smiles. At communion (which she cannot receive bodily) she becomes peaceful and recollected.
>   So where *is* the heart? Is it the will, the intellect, the instincts, or is it purely the eternal soul? And what, indeed, are each of these? I simply don't know. The *Catechism of the Catholic Church* has a good short section on this. . . . Even so, it only approximates an understanding of what remains a mystery to us.
>   My guess is that the 'heart' referred to by Scripture is the eternal soul. In a completely healthy person, all levels of his being are affected by the graces that flow from God to the 'heart of the soul,' radiating 'outward' from there to the will, intuitions, feelings, thoughts, and also making its effects known in the flesh. Perhaps it also explains the concept of 'infused knowledge' that is given

by the Holy Spirit to the saints and mystics by God. The dynamic is not out-side-to-inside; it's inside-to-outside. Of course, it can be argued that the intel-lect is fed from the outside, thus enriching the heart's ability to receive grace, affecting the will, imagination, feelings, etc. But it has to be remembered in this regard that everything entering us from exterior sources first originate in some-one else's *interior*. Aquinas's heart was disposed to grace, translated into wis-dom, translated into intellectual theological ideas, written down on paper, re-printed, transferred across oceans, into bookstores, into students' hands, through their eyes into their intellects, and eventually penetrating to the heart of the soul, affecting its capacity for truth and its receptivity to grace. Yet it *all* originates in somebody's heart of the soul. And the true Origin behind these human origins is the Great Heart of the Holy Trinity.

I'm not sure if I've answered as clearly as you had hoped, but I can at least say I would never reduce the question of man's knowing capacity to the intellect only. And what on earth *is* the intellect—is it a database, a bio-computer? Surely the mind is more than a mechanism. And what about the im-agination! My guess is that imagination is the incarnating point between spirit and matter, conducted on the field of the mind. But anything I say on these questions is completely an amateur's speculation. In the end we remain myste-ries to ourselves.[6]

The most common medical dilemmas dealt with by hospital ethics commit-tees concern whether or not we value the "heart of the soul" of a person as de-scribed so well above. They set apart Good Samaritans from Pharisees.[7] Ques-tions about "pulling the plug" or being put on "tubes" often splits a family apart pitting them against each other, physicians, ethicists, and hospital administra-tion.

How we care for persons with disabilities and the incurably ill defines who we are as person and a society. Do we shove them aside or do we make a place for them in our lives? Do we see them as enfeebled, or ennobled by their disabil-ity?

William J. Bennett, in his *Book of Virtues*, tells the tale of "Grandmother's Table," a story about a "feeble old woman whose husband died" and who had to move in with her son's family. Her son and his wife "could not help but be an-noyed at the way she spilled her meal all over the table." Finally they could stand it no longer and got her a little table set off in the corner where she could take her own meals alone without disturbing the rest of the family. One day their little girl was seen playing with building blocks. Her father asked her what she was making and she said, "'I'm building a little table for you and mother,' she smiled, 'so you can eat by yourselves in the corner someday when I get big.'"

Her parents sat staring at her for some time and then suddenly both began to cry. That night they led the old woman back to her place at the big table. From then on she ate with the rest of the family, and her son and his wife never seemed to mind a bit when she spilled something every now and then.[8]

In the following pages we will look at end of life issues through the lens of the principles set forth in *Declaration on Euthanasia* to better determine what activities embody a Good Samaritan's attention to "the heart of the soul."

The Key Magisterial Document:
Declaration on Euthanasia (1980)

The Congregation for the Doctrine of the Faith issued its *Declaration on Euthanasia* at a time when the right to die movement was gaining cultural and legal recognition. The document reiterates the Church's perennial teaching that no matter how good one's motives may be, i.e., to end a patient's suffering, if the means used deliberately kills the suffering patient, the action is intrinsically evil.

Vatican Council II condemned "crimes against life such as any type of murder, genocide, abortion, euthanasia, or willful suicide."[9] However, developments in medical science since Vatican Council II have raised new aspects of the question of euthanasia. Medicine has wrought many cures in modern times and prolonged the average life span. People now "wonder whether they have the right to obtain for themselves or their fellowmen an 'easy death,' which would shorten suffering and which seems to them more in harmony with human dignity." Therefore this Congregation must respond to the Catholic bishops who have asked for clarification so they can give correct teaching to the faithful and also offer elements of this reflection to civil authorities to better defeat false appeals to arguments from political pluralism or religious freedom which tend to deny the universal value of the human rights presented in this instruction.[10]

Human life is the basis of all goods, a gift of God's love, which we are called upon to preserve and make fruitful. From this it follows that no one can attempt to take the life of an innocent person, including their own. Rational suicide is a form of murder:

> Intentionally causing one's own death, or suicide, is therefore equally as wrong as murder; such an action on the part of a person is to be considered as a rejection of God's sovereignty and loving plan. Furthermore, suicide is also often a refusal of love for self, the denial of the natural instinct to live, a flight from the duties of justice and charity owed to one's neighbor, to various communities or to the whole of society—although, as is generally recognized, at times there are psychological factors present that can diminish responsibility or even completely remove it.[11]

Suicide is distinguishable from sacrificing one's life for God's glory, the salvation of souls or in the heroic service of one's brethren.

In ancient times *euthanasia* meant an easy death without severe suffering. Today we sometimes think of it as "some intervention of medicine whereby the suffering of sickness or of the final agony are reduced, sometimes also with the danger of suppressing life prematurely." But most by euthanasia is meant "mercy killing" so as to save abnormal babies, the mentally ill, and incurably sick from a painful or miserable life, and from being a burden on their families and society. Euthanasia may be defined as follows:

> By euthanasia is understood an action or an omission which of itself or by intention causes death, in order that all suffering may in this way be eliminated. Euthanasia's terms of reference, therefore, are to be found in the intention of the will and in the methods used.[12]

No one can permit the killing of an innocent human being, whether or not he is an embryo, fetus, infant, adult, elderly person, one suffering from an incurable disease, or even a person who is dying. No one is permitted to ask to be killed either for himself or on behalf of another person entrusted to his care, nor consent to it, either explicitly or implicitly. No authority can legitimately recommend or permit such an action. Euthanasia and assisted suicide are a violation of the divine law and an attack of humanity.[13]

Some people are tempted to ask for death because they must endure barely tolerable pain, or for other deeply personal reasons. This may reduce or completely eliminate the culpability of these individuals, but these errors of conscience in no way change the objective nature of this act of killing.

> The pleas of gravely ill people who sometimes ask for death are not to be understood as implying a true desire for euthanasia; in fact, it is almost always a case of an anguished plea for help and love. What a sick person needs, besides medical care, is love, the human and supernatural warmth with which the sick person can and ought to be surrounded by all those close to him or her, parents and children, doctors and nurses.[14]

Nature itself has made the moment of death more bearable by creating a psychological condition that facilitates the acceptance of death through prolonged illness, advanced old age, or a state of loneliness or neglect. Nonetheless, death still causes people anguish. Physical suffering has a biological usefulness but it can, at times, exceed this usefulness and become so severe as to cause the desire to remove it at any cost.

But suffering, especially one's last suffering, has a special place in God's plan of salvation. For a Christian, one's final suffering and death is a sharing in Christ's passion and a union with his redeeming sacrifice. Therefore, "some Christians prefer to moderate their use of painkillers, in order to accept voluntarily at least a part of their sufferings and thus associate themselves in a conscious way with the sufferings of Christ crucified."[15] But prudence suggests that the majority of sick persons should use medications that alleviate their pain, "even though these may cause as a secondary effect semi-consciousness and reduced lucidity."[16]

The use of painkillers and narcotics leads to habituation and increased dosages, yet they are still morally permissible to those in severe pain, said Pope Pius XII, provided that "no other means exist, and if, in the given circumstances, this does not prevent the carrying out of other religious and moral duties."[17]

Even though painkillers may shorten one's life, if one uses them to alleviate severe pain, one is not choosing suicide because death is not intended or sought, rather, "the intention is simply to relieve pain effectively."[18] However, without serious reasons, it is not right to deprive the dying person of consciousness, said Pius XII, because he has to satisfy his moral duties and family obligations, and prepare to meet Christ.

The "right to die" should be understood to mean the right to die peacefully with human and Christian dignity, but not by "one's own hand." The complexity of the situation surrounding a person's final suffering and death may "cause doubts about the way ethical principles should be applied." These doubts are to be resolved according to person's well formed conscience "in the light of moral obligations and the various aspects of the case."[19]

A primary moral duty requires everyone to "care for his or her own health or to seek such care from others" and requires those who provide such care to "do so conscientiously and administer the remedies that seem necessary or useful." However, this does not mean one is required to use all possible remedies.[20]

One is obligated to use all "ordinary care" or "proportionate means" to preserve one's health. One is, conversely, not obligated to use "extraordinary care" or "disproportionate means." These can be distinguished "by studying the type of treatment to be used, its degree of complexity or risk, its cost and the possibilities of using it, and comparing these elements with the result that can be expected, taking into account the state of the sick person and his or her physical and moral resources."[21]

Experimental medical procedures may be used with the patient's informed consent, provided there are no other sufficient remedies, even if these contain a certain risk. In fact, a patient may perform an act of generosity in the service of humanity in doing so. Also, medical techniques may be discontinued with the patient's consent if the results fall short of expectation:

> But for such a decision to be made, account will have to be taken of the reasonable wishes of the patient and the patient's family, as also of the advice of the doctors who are especially competent in the matter. The latter may in particular judge that the investment in instruments and personnel is disproportionate to the results foreseen; they may also judge that the techniques applied impose on the patient strain or suffering out of proportion with the benefits which he or she may gain from such techniques.[22]

One may make do with only ordinary medical care and forgo extraordinary medical care "which is already in use but which carries a risk or is burdensome:"

> Such a refusal is not the equivalent of suicide; on the contrary, it should be considered as an acceptance of the human condition, or a wish to avoid the application of a medical procedure disproportionate to the results that can be expected, or a desire not to impose excessive expense on the family or the community.[23]

When a person is dying he may refuse medical treatment "that would only secure a precarious and burdensome prolongation of life, so long as the normal care due to the sick person in similar cases is not interrupted."[24]

When death is inevitable we should accept it, without hastening the hour. Death opens the door to immortal life. Therefore, we must prepare ourselves for this event in the light of human values, and Christians must do so in the light of faith. Medical professionals should make all their skills available to the sick but even more, they should provide them with the comfort of boundless kindness and heartfelt charity, since their service is "also service to Christ the Lord, who said: 'As you did it to one of the least of these my brethren, you did it to me.'"[25]

Moral and Legal Reflection on End of Life Issues

Euthanasia comes in two varieties—passive and active. In *Declaration on Euthanasia* a succinct definition of both passive and active euthanasia is provided:

> By euthanasia is understood an action or an omission which of itself or by intention causes death, in order that all suffering may in this way be eliminated. Euthanasia's terms of reference, therefore, are to be found in the intention of the will and in the methods used.[26]

One can kill oneself by either doing something like poisoning oneself or refraining from doing something like going on a hunger strike until one dies. Both the intention of the will and the methods used must be considered. So, if one does what any rational person understands will cause immediate death, such as shooting oneself in the head with a gun, one cannot superimpose upon the built in intentionality of what one does (self murder) an ulterior motive such as ending one's suffering or executing justice on oneself. Likewise one can use relatively harmless or benign methods with a murderous intent such as administering pain killing medications in large doses intending to suppress respiration and circulation so as to cause death.

Basically, there are two systems of bioethics today—an objective, teleological, natural law, "sanctity of life" ethic versus a relative, utilitarian, positivist, "quality of life" ethic. Relativist utilitarian bioethicists promote both passive and active euthanasia: "Thousands of ethicists and bioethicists, as they are called, professionally guide the unthinkable on its passage through the debatable on its way to becoming the justifiable, until it is finally established as the unexceptional."[27] In a relativist ethical system one believes that they themselves are the measure of morality. Too often all this really means is that the powerful impose their health care choices on the weak:

> At its founding [in the 1970s,] bioethics involved a fair number of people who came at it from a religious perspective, but the field since then has been taken

over by a secular form of doing ethics that is very little informed by any kind of metaphysical or transcendent view. Thus, bioethicists proclaim answers to our most pressing moral questions based on attitudes, sensibilities, and mores that are not shared by the very people who are supposed to benefit from their "moral expertise." There is the very real danger that what constitutes a "meaningful life" among the intellectual elite will be imposed on the people as the only standard by which the value of human life is measured.[28]

The United State Supreme Court case *Vacco v. Quill* illustrates the advance of the unthinkable becoming the justified and finally the unexceptional. Respondents sued the State's Attorney General in US District Court because they argued New York's ban on assisted suicide violated the Equal Protection Clause because it treated similarly situated individuals dissimilarly—allowing competent persons to refuse life-sustaining medical treatment but not permitting physician-assisted suicide of competent persons which, they said, is essentially the same thing.[29] They said "that the distinction between refusing life-saving treatment and assisted suicide is 'arbitrary' and 'irrational.'"[30] If the law allows a competent person to refuse life saving treatment, i.e., tube supplied food and water (euthanasia by omission), why can't a competent person ask for a lethal injection (euthanasia by commission)?

Chief Justice Rehnquist in reversing the decision of the Court of Appeals for the Second Circuit made the distinction between refusing medical treatment and asking for assisted suicide. He said this distinction "comports with fundamental legal principles of causation and intent. First, when a patient refuses life-sustaining medical treatment, he dies from an underlying fatal disease or pathology; but if a patient ingests lethal medication prescribed by a physician, he is killed by that medication."[31] Second, if a physician withdraws life-sustaining medical treatment he merely intends to honor a patient's wishes and to "'cease doing useless and futile or degrading things to the patient when [the patient] no longer stands to benefit from them.'"[32] Rehnquist did not address the distinction between active and passive euthanasia. Rather, he said the reason why competent persons could discontinue life saving treatment was not based on a "right to hasten death" but "on well-established, traditional rights to bodily integrity and freedom from unwanted touching." He cited as authority for his position *Cruzan v. Director, Mo. Dept. of Health* wherein Nancy Cruzan's guardians were permitted to discontinue her tube-supplied nutrition and hydration so she could be free from an unwanted touching and die.[33] In *Cruzan* passive euthanasia became normative in the United States as a protected liberty interest—a right to be free from unwanted touching. Having allowed for passive euthanasia how can we deny the logic of active euthanasia?

Pressure to legalize active euthanasia continues to mount internaitonally. Luxembourg, a country with generous pensions and social security, voted on December 4, 2008 to legalize euthanasia. This caused Kathy Sinnott, MEP for Ireland South to express her concern to Luxembourg's Prime Minister, Jean-Claude Juncker. She wrote: "It is very worrying to think that a wealthy and developed country like Luxembourg with an ageing population would decide to solve its demographic problems by legalizing euthanasia, rather than by encouraging a sustainable birth rate through support of women and families." However the Grand Duke of Luxembourg refused to sign the bill into law because his conscience would not permit him to have anything to do with legalizing euthanasia.[34]

The right-to-die movement has two wings. The low-profile wing hopes to produce cultural transformation from below, if you will, through educating individuals to choose suicide, whereas the high-profile wing seeks to impose societal change from the top down through bold legislative enactments legalizing euthanasia and assisted suicide. The low-profile wing, besides promoting palliative care (see discussion below), is actively involved in developing advanced directives (especially Livings Wills) to include withholding nutrition and hydration, even when the patient is able to assimilate food and/or liquids; promoting non-reversible/terminal sedation; producing a cultural acceptance for the more casual use of opioids; redefining chronic disease as terminal disease; redefining "imminent death" to mean within a year. These initiatives are supported by the National Hospice and Palliative Care Organization (NHPCO), the American Academy of Hospice and Palliative Medicine (AAHPM), and the American Board of Hospice and Palliative Medicine (ABHPM).[35]

Futility Care Guidelines

There is a growing trend to curtail patient autonomy in favor of the autonomy of doctors and health care providers to not be forced by their patients to provide to them medical care the doctors and health care providers consider futile. Futility care protocol provides a loop-hole, a green light, for attending physicians and hospital administration to discontinue any medical treatment they deem inappropriate or "futile," given their prognosis of a patient's quality of life. Even if the modality or treatment at issue is life saving and requested by the family or the conscious patient, futility care protocol allows the health care facility, its personnel and the attending physician to deny the patient the health care requested.

> Their theory goes something like this: when a patient reaches a certain stage of age, illness, or injury, any further treatment other than comfort care is "futile" and should be withheld or withdrawn. That the patient may want the treatment because of deeply held values or a desire to live longer or take a chance on medical improvement is not decisive; the doctors and hospitals involved have the right to refuse treatment as an exercise of their autonomy."[36]

Needless to say such protocol presents a conflict of interests between a physician and their patients: "HMO's already induce physicians to keep costs low, using a combination of financial rewards or punishments, which create at least an implicit conflict of interest between doctors and some patients. Futility Care

Theory takes this disturbing trend a step further."[37]

The American Thoracic Society (chest doctors) issued a policy statement endorsing futility care: "if reasoning and experience indicate that the intervention would be highly unlikely to result in a *meaningful* survival for the patient a health care institution has the right to limit a life-sustaining intervention without consent."[38]

Under futility care guidelines patients who merit medical treatment means someone who is in some way productive; be that economically or socially. If a patient cannot be returned to the workforce or has diminished ability for social interaction their life has no "quality" under a quality of life ethic—even if the patient's own family still cherishes him and is willing to care for him.

Futility care guidelines may be implemented informally by hospital administrators who write protocols that permit a doctor's professional integrity and that of the hospital to counterbalance patient autonomy in making medical care decisions.[39] This creates an adversarial relationship between doctors and patients, and severely limits a patient's informed consent and autonomy. Should an actual conflict arise, an attempt will be made by the hospital ethics committee to resolve it. Under the futility care protocol, the ethics committee has the final say and may unilaterally discontinue what they deem to be inappropriate care over the objections of the patient and their family.

Sometimes futility care guidelines are implemented up-front and a patient signs them as part of the hospital admissions contract. These admissions contracts typically stipulate in advance the specific medical conditions for which treatment will be deemed futile including CPR for persons diagnosed as PVS, anencephalic children or those with a terminal illness due to neurological, renal, or oncological disease, those with a lethal congenital abnormality, or those with severe, irreversible dementia. Thus, the only, so called, non-futile treatment for patients in a coma, with renal failure or incurable cancer or Alzheimer's, is comfort measures only.[40]

An even more ubiquitous way to impose the will of the powerful on the health care choices of the weak may present itself in flawed universal health care bills. For instance, the Kansas City bishops joint statement on health care reform referenced the Statement of the National Association of Pro-life Nurses on Health Care Legislation that urged national legislators in the United States to oppose "mandating end of life consultation for anyone regardless of age or condition because of the message it sends that they are no longer of value to society. Such consults place pressure on the individual or guardian to opt for requests for measures to end their lives."[41] The bishops joint statement notes a de facto triage of health care benefits are likely when bureaucrats attempt to keep the cost of health care expenditures down by denying "helpful or necessary treatment for their clients" and their clients have no place else to go in a "health care monopoly."[42]

Ordinary versus Extraordinary Medical Care

The *Declaration on Euthanasia* drew a distinction between ordinary versus extraordinary medical care, also known as proportionate versus disproportionate medical care.[43] Monopolistic health care programs and futility care guidelines must not force citizens to forgo ordinary health care options. Even though there is no bright line that distinguishes ordinary from extraordinary medical modalities or treatments, there is always a moral obligation to choose what is *ordinary care* or *ordinary medical care*. Health care protocol or discretionary policies that would force the weak to submit to the will of the powerful through policies that would deny access to ordinary care or ordinary medical care is a serious breach of public trust and violates the common good of society.

The basic health care obligations one must in charity fulfill exhibit an interplay between personal autonomy and an obligation to maintain one's life and health. The general rule is—"Everyone has a duty to care for his own health or to seek such care from others."[44] But when death is imminent one may refuse medical treatments that only "secure a precarious and burdensome prolongation of life, so long as the normal care due to the sick person in similar cases is not interrupted."[45]

Whether a medical treatment is the normal care due to the sick person must be made on the basis of whether there are more benefits to be gained than burdens to be endured by a particular patient. Such determinations can only be made on a case by case basis. For instance, the battlefield amputation of a limb without anesthesia or antiseptics may be extraordinary medical treatment, for many patients. The pain and horror of enduring a limb being sawed off, coupled with the good chance one would not survive, may tip the scales for some patients in assessing that there were more risks and burdens than benefits to be gained in their case. However, the amputation of a gangrenous limb in a sterile hospital setting would be considered ordinary medical treatment and would be a morally obligatory medical surgery for an otherwise healthy patient.

Ordinary Care (also referred to as comfort care, palliative care or nursing care)[46] is different than ordinary medical care. It would be possible to draw up a list of certain kinds of humane action that is owed to every human being including but not limited to simply health and hygiene measures, food and water, bathing, assistance with the elimination of bodily waste, turning a patient in bed, keeping a patient warm and dry (or cool as need be), being kind and considerate to the sick and suffering patient. *Ordinary Care is always morally obligatory.* JPII has said we are obliged to sustain human life and assist "with the normal task of sustaining life or from assistance with the normal means of sustaining life. Science, even when it is unable to heal, can and should care for and assist the sick."[47] "Even when the sick are incurable, they are never untreatable; whatever their condition, appropriate care should be provided for them."[48] Almost everyone agrees that oral feeding, when it can be accepted and assimilated by the patient, is a form of care owed to all helpless people.[49]

There should be a presumption in favor of providing nutrition and hydration to all patients, including patients who require medically assisted nutrition and hydration, as long as this is of sufficient benefit to outweigh the burdens involved to the patient.[50]

Ordinary Medical Treatment (also known as proportionate medical treatment) includes all medically or technologically developed or administered treatment when the benefits of the treatment outweigh or are proportionate to the risks or burdens of the treatment to the patient and his family, and community. This includes every form of medical treatment from antibiotics to CPR, chemotherapy, brain shunts, kidney dialysis and tube-supplied nutrition and hydration depending primarily upon the condition of the patient, his physical and psychological constitution. *Ordinary Medical Treatment is always morally obligatory.*

Even medical "treatments" are morally obligatory when they are "ordinary" means—that is, if they provide a reasonable hope of benefit and do not involve excessive burdens. . . . *Out of respect for the dignity of the human person, we are obliged to preserve our own lives, and help others preserve theirs, by use of means that have a reasonable hope of sustaining life without imposing unreasonable burdens on those we seek to help, that is, on the patient and his or her family and community.*[51]

[I]t is our considered judgment that while legitimate Catholic moral debate continues, decisions about these patients [PVS patients] should be guided by a presumption in favor of medically assisted nutrition and hydration.[52]

Extraordinary Medical Treatment (also known as disproportionate medical treatment) includes all medically or technologically developed or administered treatment wherein the risks or burdens of the treatment outweigh or are disproportionate to the benefits of the treatment to the patient and his family and community. This includes every form of medical treatment from antibiotics to CPR, chemotherapy, brain shunts, and kidney dialysis, depending primarily upon the condition of the patient, his physical and psychological constitution. *Extraordinary Medical Treatment is not morally obligatory but may be sought and provided.*

One is not obliged to use either "extraordinary" means or "disproportionate" means of preserving life—that is, means which are understood as offering no reasonable hope of benefit or as involving excessive burdens. Decisions regarding such means are complex and should ordinarily be made by the patient in consultation with his or her family, chaplain or pastor, and physician when that is possible.[53]

Even food and fluids may become non-obligatory when they are no longer effective in sustaining the bodily life of a patient who has entered the final or active stage of dying. In such cases we should make the dying person as comfortable as possible. Such a person may lose all desire for food and drink and be unable to digest them. Initiating medical assisted feeding or intravenous fluids in this case may increase the patient's discomfort while providing no real benefit.

Those who believe there is an objective moral order, believe that sustaining human life, even in an incurable and terminal patient, is always a benefit and may be omitted only when it would "secure but a precarious and burdensome prolongation of life."[54] Pope John Paul II taught that the human body is not just an instrument or item of property, but shares in the individual's value as a human being. Therefore, "the body cannot under any circumstances be treated as something to be disposed of at will."[55] Diminished ability to express personality does not indicate the absence of a human person, nor curtail the respect due to the human person still present as an incarnate spirit so long as there is bodily life. Because the human soul communicates existence to the human body, a living human body is always an epiphany of a living human person, says Bishop Sgreccia:

> Compared to other forms, the human soul has specific to it the fact of being subsistent in its being and of communicating to the body the being that is specific to the body. This "poverty" of the body, which receives existence ("esse") from the spiritual soul, ends up by being wealth because human corporeity is thus realized as an epiphany and language of the spirit. And in every one of its acts it becomes the bearer of a higher meaning, it reveals the dignity that comes to it from a spiritual and immortal soul.[56]

Our discussion of the three levels of care would not be complete, however, if the transmutation of palliative care was not discussed. Palliative care has been used in the past as a synonym for ordinary care or basic nursing care. Many pro-life advocates had hoped that a palliative care movement would become the answer to the assisted suicide. Instead it has been co-opted by right to die advocates. Marketed by them as excellent pain control and disassociated with end of life care, it is a means of "masking symptoms" and "letting nature take its course" to end the person's life, a great cost-saving tool for hospitals, nursing homes and insurance companies.[57] The growing acceptance of terminal sedation must not be confused with the correct use of pain-killing analgesic medication. The former expresses a formal intention to suppress the life of another so as to end his pain, the moral object of euthanasia. The latter is directed to the alleviation of pain, while foreseeing that indirectly it may also shorten the patient's life which under the circumstances is an acceptable/proportionate trade off.[58] "TS [Terminal sedation] is controversial, and has been called a legal alternative to assisted suicide. Too often TS is used when a patient is not actively dying, and is combined with removal of food and fluids."[59]

Brain Death

A patient is placed on a ventilator when he is unable to spontaneously contract his diaphragm to inhale and exhale air. Ventilators are often erroneously called respirators. A ventilator cannot make anyone respire: exchange oxygen and carbon dioxide, resulting from a complex series of bio-chemical changes in every cell of the entire body. If a ventilator is attached to a cadaver, it can make the lungs fill with air, but it cannot cause respiration to occur. Often patients placed on a ventilator have suffered a trauma to their brain or central nervous system, or are unconscious from a stroke, head injury, suffocation, drowning, drug overdose or hypothermia. Often the effects of their injury pass relatively quickly, within days, and they may regain consciousness. Other times, however, they continue to remain unconscious for months or years, or indefinitely. At some point a diagnosis may be made that the patient is "brain dead," meaning there is "the definitive death of the nervous system," even though breathing and heartbeat are being maintained technologically.

Both the 1981 President's Commission for the Study of Ethical Problems in Medicine and Biomedical and Behavioral Research and the Working Group of the Pontifical Academy of Sciences in 1985 and 1989 agree that a person is dead if either of the following occur: 1) irreversible cessation of the circulatory and respiratory functions; or 2) irreversible cessation of all functions of the entire brain, including the brain stem which controls automatic nervous reactions, such as breathing.

John Paul II taught that brain death properly understood and rigorously applied could be used as a valid indicator for ascertaining the death of a human person:

> Here it can be said that the criterion adopted in more recent times for ascertaining the fact of death, namely the complete and irreversible cessation of all brain activity, if rigorously applied, does not seem to conflict with the essential elements of a sound anthropology.
>
> Therefore a health-worker professionally responsible for ascertaining death can use these criteria in each individual case as the basis for arriving at the degree of assurance in ethical judgment which moral teaching describes as "moral certainty."[60]

There are two problems, however, with the notion of brain death, one theoretical; the other practical. The theoretical problem concerns the presumption that the brain is the integrative organ of the human body, and when it is dead the person can no longer exercise his functions in and upon his body. There is evidence, however, to the contrary.

Dr. Shewman, a pediatric neurologist, cites the example of a boy he refers to as "TK," who was diagnosed as brain dead at four years of age. Doctors recommended that all life support be removed. His mother, however, insisted that he be put on a ventilator and fed. He was eventually transferred home where he remained for over eleven years. He grew up, developed sexual organs, overcome infections, and healed wounds. Certainly TK was a living human body and his case study would seem to belie the presumption that the brain is the sole integrative organ of the human body. Hence the irreversible cessation of his brain did not lead to his body disintegrating or dying.[61] Therefore, according to the definition provided by John Paul II, he was a living person. Everyone agrees, however, that in the case of TK the use of a ventilator for over eleven years was a form of extraordinary medical treatment and not morally obligatory on his caregivers.

Bishop Elio Sgreccia acknowledged the merit of this argument but still favors the use of a brain death criteria when vigorously applied. Many object and say if brain death is a valid test for determining who is alive, then no human embryo could be considered alive because it has no brain. Bishop Sgreccia argues ultimately it is the human soul that vivifies a human being:

> From the point of view of the personalist approach, the discriminating criterion between the life and no-life of the human individual is not in itself the function of the encephalon [whole brain] but the unifying principle that vivifies the organism (the soul). The principle of life unity in the adult is ultimately linked to the function of the encephalic trunk and can be controlled with appropriate neurological methods, the control of the evoked potentials or the cerebral flow; whereas in the embryo during the first stages of its development the unity of the organism is activated and maintained by the genome which governs the construction itself of the brain.
>
> For this reason, the ill-founded objection that argues that when one holds the criterion of "encephalic death" to be valid, embryos that do not yet have even a rudimentary form of the cerebral system should be seen as lacking life, has no basis. In the embryo the principle of life (the soul) that defines it as an individualized organism is observable in the unity and the biological function of the genome that governs the progressive development of the individual and the formation of the central nervous system.[62]

The practical difficulty with brain death is applying a valid test to determine whether the entire brain has ceased functioning. Considering that there are over thirty different tests for "brain death" depending on a person's state or country of residency, a person could be dead in one state and alive in another.

The oldest and the most complete test for brain death is the Harvard Brain Death criteria. However, even this test was devised without any patient data and without reference to basic science reports.[63] The Harvard brain death criterion is a six-part test that considers the following indicators to determine whether death has occurred:

1. Total unawareness to externally applied stimuli;
2. Observations over at least 1 hour by physicians verifying no spontaneous muscular movement, respiration, or response to any stimuli. To test for respiration the ventilator is turned off for 3 minutes. Provided before it is turned off the patient's carbon dioxide tension is within the normal range and the patient has been weaned onto room air for at least 10 minutes prior to the trial;
3. No elicitable reflexes

- pupils don't react to bright lights
- no reaction to ice water in ears
- no tendon reflexes
- no reaction to noxious smells;
4. A flat EEG (electroencephalogram)
5. Repeat same test 24 hours later
6. Be sure no barbiturate drug overdose or hypothermia

Since there are ethicists both in favor and opposed to brain death as a valid indicator of true death who do not dissent from the Magisterium of the Church, a Catholic may adopt a position for or against the use of brain death.[64] So, if one is satisfied that the practical difficulty of testing for brain death is met by use of the Harvard criteria, one may legitimately discontinue the use of a ventilator of a brain dead patient. However, if a patient diagnosed as brain dead is disconnected from a ventilator and starts to spontaneously breathe on his own, that person is not brain dead, but alive, and must be given ordinary comfort care and/or ordinary medical care.

Permanent Vegetative State (PVS)

The so-called "permanent vegetative state" (PVS) patient "appears to be awake but shows no evidence of conscious content, either confused or appropriate. He often has sleep-wake cycles, but cannot demonstrate an awareness either of himself or his environment."[65] PVS is a form of deep unconsciousness:

> The upper part of the brain (the cerebral cortex) gives evidence of impaired or failed operation. Since it is this part of the brain which is neurologically involved in such activities as understanding, willing, and communicating, persons in this condition are not able to engage in these activities. But the brain stem, which controls involuntary functions such as breathing, blinking, circulation of blood, cycles of waking and sleeping, etc., is still functioning. As a result, persons in this condition may open their eyes and sometimes follow movements with them or respond to loud or sudden noises. . . . It is commonly held that persons in this condition have no conscious experience and are incapable of experiencing pain, and that it is unlikely that persons in this condition will recover consciousness.[66]

Dr. Alan Shewman disagrees with some of the key conclusions just mentioned which he argues are simply presumptions. He contends that the medical community simply presumes that those patients with cortical destruction feel no pain or are unconscious: "[P]erhaps what is eliminated by cortical destruction might be the capacity for external manifestation of consciousness rather than consciousness itself; in other words [he says] . . . what is called 'PVS' might in reality be merely a 'super-locked-in' state [a condition in which the person is indeed conscious but is utterly incapable of manifesting this externally]."[67]

Moreover, most of those classified as being in a *permanent* vegetative state turn out to be *only temporarily* in this condition. In one study which followed the recovery rates of 84 patients with a firm diagnosis of PVS 41 percent became conscious by 6 months, 52 percent regained consciousness by 1 year, and 58 percent recovered consciousness within the 3-year follow-up interval. The study was unable to identify "predictors of recovery from the vegetative state" to tell which patients are more likely to recover than others.[68]

In one dramatic case physicians had pronounced 79-year-old grandfather Harold Cybulski of Barry's Bay, Ontario as "brain-dead and comatose." They stood by to disconnect his life support systems as soon as his family said their last goodbyes. But when his two-year-old grandson ran into the room and yelled "Grandpa!" Cybulski woke up, sat up, and picked up the little boy! Cybulski's doctors could offer "no explanation" for his instant recovery.[69] It has already been noted that Zolpidem causes patients to come out of a so-called permanent vegetative state. In another example, a patient who had not spoken throughout the three years he was in a PVS was able to answer simple questions after a single dose of Zolpidem.[70]

Even without the use of Zolpidem patients recent studies confirm that patents in a PVS can learn. Researchers from the University of Cambridge (UK) and the Institute of Cognitive Neurology played a tone just prior to blowing air into a patient's eye and after frequent repetition the patients would blink when the tone was played but prior to the air puff in the eye. This pattern of behavior was not seen in the control group of volunteers under anesthesia and shows PVS patients can learn associations indicating they can form memories and may benefit from rehabilitation.[71] In a previous study in 2006 the Cambridge Impaired Consciousness Group at the Wolfson Brain Imaging Unit used functional imaging and concluded PVS patients can be conscious even though they do not show consistent voluntary movements.[72]

Despite these developments it is routine in the hospital setting today that as soon as a patient is diagnosed as in a vegetative state (VS) it is presumed that patient will certainly be permanently so. The permanence of the vegetative state is often presumed after the patient has been in that state for only a few days. Having diagnosed a patient to be PVS, physicians then urge the family to discontinue tube-supplied food and water so that the patient may die from what they argue is a fatal pathology, i.e., PVS.

In 1991 Mr. Cruzan allowed the feeding tube to his unconscious daughter, Nancy, to be disconnected and watched as she dehydrated and slowly died over the next twelve days.[73] The legal precedent set in *Cruzan* established the right of legal guardians to dehydrate their PVS wards, provided they have clear and convincing evidence that their ward would have wanted such an outcome.

To complicate matters more, in 1990 the Texas Catholic Conference of Bishops stated that PVS was a "lethal pathology which, without artificial nutrition and hydration will lead to death." Thus, they concluded that the provision of tube-supplied food and hydration was futile and non-obligatory.[74] Two years later the Pennsylvania Conference of Catholic Bishops came to a different conclusion. They wrote that "in almost every instance there is an obligation to con-

tinue supplying nutrition and hydration to the unconscious patient," and that
tube-supplied nutrition and hydration to the PVS patient is "clearly beneficial in
terms of preservation of life." They added that this treatment does not add a serious burden in almost every case.[75] That same year the US Conference of Bishops rejected the position of the Texas Conference of Bishops. They said:
"PVS is best seen as an extreme form of mental and physical disability—one
whose causes, nature and prognosis are as yet imperfectly understood—and not
as a terminal illness or fatal pathology from which patients should generally be
allowed to die."[76] The US Bishops Committee for Pro-Life Activities said there
should be a "presumption in favor of medically assisted nutrition and hydration."[77]

John Paul II on Food and Water to Patients in a PVS

After decades of waiting for Rome to speak on the issue of whether tube-
supplied food and water (nutrition and hydration) may be removed from a non-
dying patient in a vegetative state, in the midst of a well publicized legal and
political battle to dehydrate a PVS patient in Florida (Terri Schiavo), the answer
finally came on March 20, 2004. In the address of John Paul II to the participants in the International Congress on "Life-Sustaining Treatments and Vegetative State: Scientific Advances and Ethical Dilemmas,"[78] his Holiness held that
tube-supplied food and water may not be denied non-dying PVS patients. He
said nutrition and hydration, no matter how they are delivered, remain simply
ordinary care always morally obligatory unless they fail to achieve their essential ends, namely, to nourish and to alleviate pain.

He began by noting that "not a few" persons diagnosed in PVS "have been
able to emerge from a vegetative state." The term PVS denotes those vegetative
patients who continue to remain in a vegetative state for over one year. "Actually, there is no different diagnosis that corresponds to such a definition, but only
a conventional prognostic judgment, relative to the fact that the recovery of patients, statistically speaking, is ever more difficult as the condition of vegetative
state is prolonged in time." Even then, there are well-documented cases of recovery from PVS after many years. So, "we can thus state that medical science,
up until now, is still unable to predict with certainty who among patients in this
condition will recover and who will not."[79] He completely opposed the reduc-
tionist view of a handicapped person expressed in the term "vegetable." He said,
"I feel the duty to reaffirm strongly that the intrinsic value and personal dignity
of every human being does not change, no matter what the concrete circumstances of his or her life. *A man, even if seriously ill or disabled in the exercise of
his highest functions, is and always will be a man,* and he will never become a
'vegetable' or an 'animal.' Even our brothers and sisters who find themselves in
the clinical condition of a 'vegetative state' retain their human dignity in all its
fullness. The loving gaze of God the Father continues to fall upon them, acknowledging them as his sons and daughters, especially in need of help."[80]

Persons in a vegetative state still have the right to ordinary care—"to basic health care (nutrition, hydration, cleanliness, warmth, etc.), and to the prevention of complications related to his confinement in bed. He also has the right to appropriate rehabilitative care and to be monitored for clinical signs of eventual recovery." Most importantly persons in a vegetative state have the right to food and water:

> I should like particularly to underline how the administration of water and food, even when provided by artificial means, always represents a *natural means* of preserving life, not a *medical act*. Its use, furthermore, should be considered, in principle, *ordinary and proportionate*, and as such morally obligatory, insofar as and until it is seen to have attained its proper finality, which in the present case consists in providing nourishment to the patient and alleviation of his suffering.
> To do less, to not provide water and food to PVS patients, would amount to euthanasia as I defined it in *Evangelium Vitae* paragraph 65. Moreover, it is a well established moral principle that "even the simple doubt of being in the presence of a living person already imposes the obligation of full respect and of abstaining from any act that aims at anticipating the person's death."[81]

John Paul II characterized the "quality of life" ethic as exhibiting a "discriminatory and eugenic principle."[82] He urged us to take *"positive actions* as a stand against pressures to withdraw hydration and nutrition as a way to put an end to the lives of these patients" by supporting the families of those caring for a PVS relative in the following ways: Through allocating state resources to establish "awakening centers with specialized treatment and rehabilitation"; by financial assistance and home assistance for the home based care of PVS patients; by facilities for PVS patients with no family to care for them at home; through time away programs for the rest and recuperation of home care-givers of PVS patients; by medical teams to "help the family understand that they are there as allies who are in this struggle with them"; through the help of volunteers "to enable the family to break out of its isolation" and realize it is "not a forsaken part of the social fabric;" and by spiritual counseling and pastoral aid.[83]

In 2007 the Congregation for the Doctrine of the Faith answered certain questions submitted to it by Bishop Skylstad, President of the United States Conference of Catholic Bishops two years earlier[84] and confirmed that it was indeed the mind of the church that food and water provided naturally or artificially was morally obligatory to patients in a PVS except when they cannot assimilate it or it cannot be administered without causing the patient significant physical discomfort:

> The administration of food and water even by artificial means is, in principle, an ordinary and proportionate means of preserving life. It is therefore obligatory to the extent to which, and for as long as, it is shown to accomplish its proper finality, which is the hydration and nourishment of the patient. In this way suffering and death by starvation and dehydration are prevented.[85]

Moreover, the provision of food and water to a patient in a PVS is not subject to termination just because competent physicians determine that the patient will never regain consciousness.[86]

When Is a Patient Really Dying?

Nutrition and hydration should be considered obligatory ordinary medical care for the unconscious patient able to assimilate them: "even for patients who are imminently dying and incurable, food and fluids can prevent the suffering that may arise from dehydration, hunger and thirst."[87] What about feeding a conscious patient? In light of John Paul II's comments on patients in a vegetative state it would seem by extension morally obligatory that a conscious person attempt to sustain himself at least until he enters the "active phase" of dying, i.e., when his body can no longer assimilate food and fluids:

> In the active dying process, the body's systems are failing, and eventually lose the ability to process or to utilize food and fluids. In this case, the patient will take in by mouth only what the body needs. Tube feedings and IV fluids strain marginally functioning systems and cause discomfort. This is not to be confused with removing food and fluids from an unconscious patient—whose body is able to utilize the nutrients—in order to cause death.[88]
>
> But sometimes even food and fluids are no longer effective in providing this benefit [sustaining and fostering life], because a patient has entered the final stage of a terminal condition. At such times we should make the dying person as comfortable as possible. . . . Such a person may lose all desire for food and drink and even be unable to ingest them. Initiating medical assisted feeding or intravenous fluids in this case may increase the patient's discomfort while providing no real benefit; ice chips or sips of water may instead be appropriate to provide comfort and counteract the adverse effects of dehydration. Even in the case of the imminently dying patient, of course, any action or omission that of itself or by intention causes death is to be absolutely rejected.[89]

Some of the physical signs of the active dying process include the following which may appear one by one over a period of days or weeks, or all at once in a few hours: increased weakness, voice becomes weaker, sleeps more, difficulty swallowing, appearance changes—knees, legs, arms start to "mottle" (red-purple splotches), the body can't regulate temperature, a period of restlessness—a few hours to a few days, kidneys shut down, lungs become congested, pharyngeal rails—death rattle, loss of all appetite, loss of ability to swallow and blood pressure drops and heart and respiratory rate increases[90]

Especially as the kidneys shut down, a patient's body cannot assimilate food as quickly as it once could and, as it progresses more and more, even water. The speed at which this happens varies from person to person, so no hard and fast rule can be laid down. All the same, food and water, orally or through a tube to the stomach or intestine, are morally obligatory until they can no longer be assimilated and death is truly imminent, that is to say within a few hours or a couple of days at most, so that the attempt to sustain life is truly futile.

> When people are truly [actively] dying and the body's organs begin to shut down, we often see people lose their appetite and desire to drink much. This is a process that can protect a person from suffering from fluid overload at the end and the dying person remains comfortable. But this is very different from a deliberate decision to "fast" to death.[91]

However, many chronically or acutely ill persons who have not yet entered the active phase of dying may experience depression and a corresponding loss of appetite and the will to live. Should they be required to eat? At times even the ordinary duties of life may become heroic. Certain routine medical procedures take courage to endure. Nonetheless, we are obligated to take care of our health even when we are tempted to avoid these responsibilities. In light of the principles already set forth it would seem that a person who is dying, but has not yet entered the active phase of dying, is required to sustain their life and health by eating and drinking when water and food serve to sustain their life and can be digested without pain or medical complications. They may not simply give up and stop eating or decide to fast themselves to death:

> The implication of . . . making it somehow a work of nature that the dying refrain from food and drink, so it is therefore acceptable for us to withhold from them such sustenance, is disputed by the fact that life is retained by providing sustenance even to those for whom food and drink may have no appeal, or no other salutary effect beyond maintaining life and postponing death. We would not allow a child afflicted with eating disorders such as anorexia or bulimia to starve to death without intervening, even if food and drink were repulsive to that sufferer, who might even have reached the point of the body's rejection of food and drink. Why should we treat an elderly, dying person with less than such care?[92]

UN Convention on the Rights of Persons with Disabilities

Over the course of several years, concluding in August 25, 2006, the UN hammered out a treaty on the Dignity and Rights of Persons with Disabilities.[93] This author brought university students to the Third, Sixth, Seventh and Eighth Sessions of this convention. I asked one of my undergraduate students to address the delegates of the United Nations as an NGO (non-governmental organization) representative of the Society of Catholic Social Scientists (SCSS) on the issue of food and water.

The Pro-Life and Pro-Family coalition at the UN made up of many Catholic, Mormon, Protestant and other family-based NGOs, besides trying to keep abortion under the euphemism of "sexual and reproductive rights" out of the treaty, also tried desperately to get into the treaty a provision stating that food and water is a basic right of persons with disabilities. Their efforts were resisted by the delegations from the European Union (EU), Canada and New Zealand. The Chairman of the Convention was hostile to the inclusion of language from the delegation of Qatar that said that nutrition and hydration was a fundamental right of persons with disabilities, regardless of their quality of life, and especially when their life hangs in the balance. On the other hand, this language was supported by the Holy See, the United States, and many other delegations. The Disabilities Caucus (a group of select disabilities NGOs either sympathetic or co-opted into supporting the EU's overall agenda) did not endorse or make intervention to support Qatar's amendment. The EU dismissed Qatar's language as "NGO language" and "bioethical language" reflecting only "First World concerns" or, more narrowly, the "concerns of the United States": in fact, they stated that it was nothing more than "one American woman's story," i.e., that of Terry Schiavo. After the Sixth Session concluded in August of 2005 the Chairman simply dropped food and water language in his redraft of the treaty for the Seventh Session to begin in January of 2006.

At the very end of negotiations on Section 25 of the treaty dealing with health care, when it appeared that food and water would not be mentioned at all, I asked one of these students if she, as a young woman with a disability (who therefore had credibility with the Disability Caucus), would be willing to address the UN. She asked me how long she would have to prepare. I said in reply, "five, maybe ten minutes." She paused for a couple of seconds and then said "sure."

The previous evening a movie had been shown to the delegates of the UN attending the Disabilities Convention, a documentary on a young man, a Jewish quadriplegic by the name of Ami. It was an inspiring film showing his ability to surmount his disability and lead a happy dignified life that brought joy to others. In the last scene of the film he was shown making one of his dreams come true—riding a Harley Davis motorcycle, albeit in a passenger cab.

Twenty-one year-old Andrea Vrchota, a person with a disability, compared herself to Ami with great effect. She was introduced (simultaneously translated into seven different languages) as the delegate from the Society of Catholic Social Scientists. She began to speak into the microphone from the floor of the Convention hall—at first with just a quiver in her voice—until her twelve years of acting experience kicked-in and she gave the following address, loud, clear, and emphatically:

> Thank you, Mr. Chair, for the opportunity to address this distinguished assembly. On behalf of the Society of Catholic Social Scientists and as a disabled young woman, I would like to commend this convention and yourself for addressing so many pressing needs of disabled persons, especially young disabled women. I hope to one day to have and raise a family and I am supportive of the notion of comprehensive health care for women, but I have reservations concerning the narrow interpretation of women's health care needs, by use of the terms "sexual and reproductive health care services." I believe this term, therefore, is problematic as the delegate of the Holy See has stated.
>
> As a young Catholic woman with a disability, I am also troubled by the

lack of equal health care to persons with disabilities, when their life hangs in
the balance. Therefore, I would urge the delegates to support Qatar's language,
guaranteeing food and water to disabled persons whenever it would help to
keep them alive. As Ami in last night's documentary proved, quality of life
cannot be defined by a person's disability or the medical profession's opinion.
My own doctors stated that I would not live past the first week of my birth.
Therefore, no one should be denied food and water because their life is deemed
to be less valuable to others. On behalf of the Society of Catholic Social Scientists, again thank you, Mr. Chair.[94]

After she finished speaking members of the Disabilities Caucus began to put
their arms around her and embrace her. She later told me that one woman from
the Disabilities Caucus said to her "you have convinced us." Later the Disability
Caucus made an intervention favoring the inclusion of food and water as a basic
right of persons with disabilities. The Chairman reluctantly said, "it appears
there is some consensus in the room about the concept of food and water but the
precise language will need to be worked out." The final draft of the treaty included reference to the right of persons with disabilities to food and water:

> States Parties recognize that persons with disabilities have the right to the
> enjoyment of the highest attainable standard of health without discrimination
> on the basis of disability. States Parties shall take all appropriate measures to
> ensure access for persons with disabilities to health services that are gender-
> sensitive, including health-related rehabilitation. In particular States Parties
> shall . . .
>   (f)   Prevent discriminatory denial of health care or health services or food
> and fluids on the basis of disability.[95]

Legal Documents and Organ Donation

If one must apply a proportionate versus disproportionate test on a case by case
basis to determine whether most health care is required one can immediately see
what is wrong with attempting to predict in advance which treatments will be
appropriate under future contingent circumstances. But this is exactly what living wills attempt to do. Making predictions about future health care needs
should one become incompetent is a guessing game that renders such decisions
suspect for lack of informed consent:

> [A]n advance directive prepared by a healthy person is not a valid indicator of
> the preferences of a similar person when sick. . . . Our experience is that people
> change their minds when they become unwell, but an earlier advance directive
> might still be in force."[96]

Model living wills were first developed as early as 1967 by the Euthanasia
Society of America, by Louis Kunter to help shape public opinion to accept euthanasia. Syndicated columnist Abigail Van Buren, "Dear Abby," embraced the

cause of euthanasia and promoted living wills. Her contributions were acknowledged at the 1988 conference of the World Federation of Societies for the Right to Die.[97]

Living wills were forced upon all fifty states after Congress passed the Patient Self Determination Act of 1990, which required all hospitals, nursing homes, hospice or HMO's which receive Medicare or Medicaid payments to inform patients about, and provide them with, living wills and/or Durable Power of Attorney for Health Care (DPOAHC) or suffer the loss of Medicare/Medicaid payments.

Living wills provide indiscriminately for the termination of extraordinary or ordinary medical treatment. In many states living wills provide for the discontinuation of tube supplied nutrition and hydration upon a diagnosis of PVS by two physicians who also verify that the patient can't feel pain regardless of whether the patient is in the active phase of dying or not. Obviously, to discontinue food and fluids to an otherwise stable PVS patient not in the active phase of dying can hardly be done for reasons other than to end their life—that is by definition euthanasia by omission.

Worse yet, the person who is given *prima facia* authority to interpret a living will is the patient's attending physician, not their next of kin. An attending physician in the hospital setting is not usually a patient's family doctor, but instead whoever is on duty in the emergency room or on call during that shift at the health care facility, who is usually a complete stranger to the patient. Of course, the next of kin may challenge the attending physician's interpretation in court. But most patients would not choose this arrangement if it were properly explained to them.

By all accounts a DPOAHC is better able to secure a patient's best interests by making clear his intentions regarding health care decisions should he become incompetent later. The DPOAHC allows one to name the person one wants to represent them (called the attorney in fact) and express their wishes to doctors and hospital administration should one become incompetent or incapacitated. One should inform this person (who need not be an attorney, but is usually your spouse or child) just what one would like to see happen under various medical and end of life scenarios.

Caveat! If you execute both a living will and a DPOAHC and a conflict should arise between one's attorney in fact under a DPOAHC and the attending physician under one's living will—in many states the prevailing party is the attending physician. This is not an outcome most people would welcome. Therefore it is better to only sign the DPOAHC. To fail to sign a DPOAHC is to leave oneself open to having the court appoint whomever they deem fit. Although this will usually be a family member, it might not be the family member one may have wished. The US Catholic Conference of Bishops recommends signing a DPOAHC:

Each person may identify in advance a representative to make health care decisions as his or her surrogate in the event that the person loses the capacity to make health care decisions.[98]

Young men and women who think themselves invulnerable to death or serious accidents should still sign a DPOAHC. Karen Quinlan and Nancy Cruzan were young women at the time of their trauma. Certain Catholic or Pro-Life organizations have prepared DPOAHC documents with protective language tailored to the laws of your state.[99]

Heart Death and Organ Transplant

A person may only donate a paired organ before his or her death such as a kidney. The "dead donor rule" requires that vital and unpaired organs cannot be donated until the donor has died. John Paul II commends organ donors in his encyclical the Gospel of Life for their heroic gesture which builds up human solidarity and the culture of life.[100]

> The transplantation of organs from living donors is morally permissible when such a donation will not sacrifice or seriously impair any essential bodily function and the anticipated benefit to the recipient is proportionate to the harm done to the donor.[101]

> Such organs [from dead donors] should not be removed until it has been medically determined that the patient has died.[102]

Therefore, it is important to consider when a person is dead for purposes of organ transplant. We have already looked at this issue in the context of brain death. But there are new controversies surrounding heart death as well. For instance, certain aspects of the heart death donor protocol devised by the University of Pittsburgh Medical Center (known nationwide as the "Pittsburgh Protocol") seem to shake public trust in organ transplant by the harvesting of organs from patients whose hearts have stopped for only two minutes.[103] This raises the question of whether a patient whose heart has stopped for only two minutes is really dead. Has there been an "irreversible cessation of circulatory and respiratory function?" Could it start beating again spontaneously?

Another disturbing aspect of the Pittsburgh Protocol is the pool of potential donors they are willing to include. They permit not only the catastrophically brain-damaged patient and terminally ill persons, but also disabled people who are not dying or brain-damaged if they are dependent on ventilator support for survival:

> The Protocol thus unintentionally endangers the lives of disabled patients who may, due to depression, consider their organs of greater value to the world than their own lives.[104]

Robert D. Troug, M.D. and Franklin G. Miller, Ph.D. find donation after cardiac death problematic for organ transplantation because the cardiac definition of death requires the irreversible cessation of cardiac function: "Whereas the common understanding of 'irreversible is impossible to reverse,' in this context irreversibility is interpreted as the result of a choice not to reverse." So, paradoxically, the heart of the donor patient that was declared "heart dead" becomes alive again after its transplantation into the chest of a recipient patient. "[W]e believe the reason it is ethical cannot convincingly be that the donors are dead," they say.[105]

These authors conclude that cardiac death and brain death criteria are both flawed. Cardiac death is skewed because the heart dead patient still has a good heart and the brain dead patient's brain still functions minimally. After all, the brain dead donors still look "very much alive: they are warm and pink; they digest food, excrete waste, undergo sexual maturation, and can even reproduce [give birth]."[106] Arguments about why brain dead patients should be considered dead have never been fully convincing, they say, for the following reasons: brain death requires absence of all functions of the entire brain—yet PVS patients retain essential functions, such as the secretion of hypothalamic hormones; brain death requires permanent unconscious state—but so are those in a PVS who breathe spontaneously. Therefore PVS patients should also be classified as dead; finally, brain death leads to permanent cessation of the functioning of the organism as a whole—but if they are supported beyond the acute phase of their injury, they can survive for many years.[107]

As disturbing as their analysis is, the conclusion these authors come to is even more so. They call for an abandonment of the dead donor rule since it is an embarrassment and passé. The dead donor rule was perhaps necessary a few generations ago to assuage our consciences and lead us to believe that we were not actually killing some people for the betterment of other people. But now it looks as if the medical profession has been "gerrymandering the definition of death" to simply further organ transplantation and provide "ethical cover" that can't withstand careful scrutiny. Most importantly there is a new moral consensus that appears tolerant of killing some people to benefit other people provided there is informed consent and anesthesia. The new protocol should be adopted because it promises to increase the number of organs available for transplant: "[S]urveys suggest that issues related to respect for valid consent and the degree of neurologic injury may be more important to the public than concerns about whether the patient is already dead at the time the organs are removed. . . . [The new protocol] "respects the desires of those who wish to donate organs and has the potential to maximize the number and quality of organs available to those in need."[108]

At the end of World War II Dr. Leo Alexander, a psychiatrist, interviewed many of the Nazi war prisoners held for trial at Nuremberg. He discovered that whatever proportions their crimes finally assumed (massive racial genocide, destructive medical experimentations on children, etc.), it started small—with the incurably ill. "The beginnings at first were merely a subtle shift in emphasis in the basic attitude of the physicians. It started with the acceptance of the attitude, basic in the euthanasia movement, that there is such a thing as life not worthy to be lived. . . . But it is important to realize that the infinitely small wedged-in lever from which this entire trend of mind received its impetus was the attitude toward the nonrehabilitable sick."[109]

Perhaps Troug and Miller are correct when they say that brain death and cardiac death were screens that hid the reality of violating the dead donor rule and to continue with them today is hypocritical. But their proposal is much worse and will legitimize killing on a massive scale. The lessons of Nazi medicine should show us that it was not so much the Himmlers and Hitlers, but medical ethicists who are the greater threat to society because it is they "who can effectively cloak evil in the vestments of scholarly discourse and good intentions."[110] Only a new appreciation for the dignity of the human person and the meaning of human suffering can provide hope for the future.

Conclusion

One hospice nurse compared the process of dying to that of giving birth; and believed it was her role to be "a mid-wife of souls" being born.[111] She noted that as death approaches her patients begin to detach, to lose interest in material things, in all forms of amusements that may have once interested them, such as TV or music. They had little tolerance for conversation and preferred silence. They were less concerned with appearance or modesty. Their final detachment was from relationships. The dying patient may push aside loved ones (family or favorite pets) they once clung to only a short time before. They begin to speak of talking to deceased relatives, whom they see and converse with.[112]

She says there are also psychological complications that affect many persons who are dying, such as fear of punishment for real or imagined misdeeds and needing loved ones permission to die:

> If a patient takes an unusual amount of time to die, there is always a reason. Even if you can't figure it out, there's important work going on. That's why euthanasia is such a tragedy, aside from the fact it's murder. It robs the patient, and the family, of the time they need to resolve vital issues, even if they can't see any purpose to the delay.[113]

In her experience "patients who struggle with suicidal feelings are usually suffering from uncontrolled pain or other distressing symptoms, coupled with a sense of being burdensome or unloved."[114] Therefore, the first goal of hospice is pain management. This conforms to the US Catholic Conference of Bishops' directive:

> Patients should be kept as free of pain as possible so that they may die comfortably and with dignity, and in the place where they wish to die. Since a person has the right to prepare for his or her death while fully conscious, he or she

should not be deprived of consciousness without a compelling reason. Medicines capable of alleviating or suppressing pain may be given to a dying person, even if this therapy may indirectly shorten the person's life so long as the intent is not to hasten death. Patients experiencing suffering that cannot be alleviated should be helped to appreciate the Christian understanding of redemptive suffering.[115]

She explains that those who fail to see the final journey of a soul to God in the dying process would be comparable to those working in labor and delivery who never saw a baby born. It would be very depressing. For they would be tempted to engage in a "kindness without love" (quoting C.S. Lewis): a kindness that leads to indifference; a kindness no different than that which coolly puts animals out of their misery.[116] The pastoral guidance of the Church confirms these insights, that a request for suicide is really a cry for love:

> Dying patients who request euthanasia should receive loving care, psychological and spiritual support, and appropriate remedies for pain and other symptoms so that they can live with dignity until the time of natural death.[117]

In the Christian vision of life suffering and death have significance. Nothing is wasted, not one tear or groan. Rather, each aspiration of the human heart united to Christ, consciously or by a *virtual intention,* is redemptive:

> Some Catholic moralists, using the concept of a "virtual intention," note that a person may give spiritual significance to his or her later suffering during incompetency, by deciding in advance to join these sufferings with those of Christ for the redemption of others.[118]

As Christians we believe Christ joins himself with the sufferer and with those who care for them, the Good Samaritans. St. Paul reveals to us a great mystery that he, Paul, "makes up in his own flesh the sufferings that are lacking in the suffering of Christ for the sake of his body, the Church."[119]

Each of us are invited to "offer up" our crosses daily and follow Christ so that when our final hour comes we will be steady in the faith; to not despair, to not give into that "kindness without love," but rather to look expectantly to the hour we will be born to eternal life. For Christ himself hung on a cross for three hours with no palliation of his suffering: a seemingly meaningless and enervating torture. Why didn't he cut it short after one hour? Yet by his suffering and death he opened heaven for us all. By his suffering and death he redeemed human suffering, making it very meaningful, by opening human suffering to divine action:

> In the cross of Christ not only is the Redemption accomplished through suffering, but *also human suffering itself has been redeemed. . . .* Every man has *his own share in the Redemption.* Each one is also called to share in that suffering through which the Redemption was accomplished. He is *called to share in that*

suffering through which all human suffering has also been redeemed. In bringing about the Redemption through suffering, Christ *has also raised human suffering to the level of the Redemption.* Thus each man, in his suffering, can also become a sharer in the redemptive suffering of Christ.[120]

The sufferer becomes a Christ-bearer, a quasi-sacrament who conveys the grace they symbolize, that is, the redemptive touch of Christ crucified. Christ asks us to "pick up our cross" daily and follow him, thereby making up what is still lacking in his sufferings—the extension of his suffering and redemption in time and space, carrying him like the Eucharist in a monstrance down the corridors of history into every corner of the world.

> The sufferings of Christ created the good of the world's Redemption. This good in itself is inexhaustible and infinite. No man can add anything to it. But at the same time, in the mystery of the Church as His Body, Christ has in a sense opened his own redemptive suffering to all human suffering. Insofar as man becomes a sharer in Christ's sufferings—in any part of the world and at any time in history—to that extent he in his own way completes the suffering through which Christ accomplishes the Redemption of the world.[121]

As the old song goes—and though the river be "deep and wide," there is "milk and honey on the other side" if we cross those chilly waters with faith that human suffering has ultimate meaning, a meaning that will only be revealed on that far shore—a place that gives perspective to this vale of tears, a place where every tear will be wiped away called paradise.

Notes

1. A persistent vegetative state is "a profound or deep state of unconsciousness. . . . Individuals in such a state have lost their thinking abilities, or as a result of injuries, such as head trauma. Individuals in such a state have lost their thinking abilities and awareness of their surroundings, but retain non-cognitive function and normal sleep patterns. Even though those in a persistent vegetative state lose their higher brain functions, other key functions such as breathing and circulation remain relatively intact. Spontaneous movements may occur, and the eyes may open in response to external stimuli. Individuals may even occasionally grimace, cry, or laugh. Although individuals in a persistent vegetative state may appear somewhat normal, they do not speak and they are unable to respond to commands." National Institute of Neurological Disorders and Strokes, *Coma Information Page,* http://www.ninds.nih.gov/disorders/coma/coma.htm (14 Nov. 2009).
2. Steve Boggan, "Reborn," *The Guardian,* 12 September 2006, http://www.guardian.co.uk/science/2006/sep/12/health.healthandwellbeing (14 Nov. 2009).
3. Steve Boggan, "Reborn."
4. Ralf Clauss and Wally Nel, "Drug induced arousal from the permanent vegetative state," *NeuroRehabilitation* 21 (2006): 23, 25, 26–27.

5. Scripture describes conscience as the "heart" of a person. The heart is a place of encounter with God (1 John 3:18–20). Jesus spoke of the heart as the place of inner deliberation and decision: "Wicked designs come from the deep recesses of the heart; acts of fornication, theft, murder." (Mark 7:21).

6. Michael O'Brien to D. Brian Scarnecchia, 30 September 1999, author's private collection, Steubenville, OH.

7. Luke 10:33.

8. William J. Bennett, *The Book of Virtues: A Treasury of Great Moral Stories* (New York, NY: Simon & Schuster, 1993), 143–44.

9. GS no. 27.

10. Sacred Congregation for the Doctrine of the Faith, *Declaration on Euthanasia* (1980), intro., http://www.vatican.va/roman_curia/congregations/cfaith/documents/rc_con_cfaith_doc_19800505_euthanasia_en.html (28 Aug. 2009).

11. *Declaration on Euthanasia*, no. I.3 See also Kevin M. Bryant, "Suicide," in ECST.

12. *Declaration on Euthanasia*, no. II.

13. *Declaration on Euthanasia*, no. II.

14. *Declaration on Euthanasia*, no. II.

15. *Declaration on Euthanasia*, no. III. See also Matt. 27:24.

16. *Declaration on Euthanasia*, no. III.

17. *Declaration on Euthanasia*, no. III; citing Pope Pius XII, Address of February 24, 1957: AAS 49 (1957), 147.

18. *Declaration on Euthanasia*, no. III. See also Michael P. Orsi, "Palliative Care," in ECST.

19. *Declaration on Euthanasia*, no. IV.

20. *Declaration on Euthanasia*, no. IV.

21. *Declaration on Euthanasia*, no. IV.

22. *Declaration on Euthanasia*, no. IV.

23. *Declaration on Euthanasia*, no. IV.

24. *Declaration on Euthanasia*, no. IV.

25. *Declaration on Euthanasia*, concl.; citing Matt. 25:40.

26. *Declaration on Euthanasia*, no. II.

27. Richard John Neuhaus, "The Return of Eugenics," *Commentary* (April 1988): 19.

28. Wesley J. Smith, *Culture of Death: The Assault on Medical Ethics in America* (San Francisco: Encounter Books, 2000), 125. See also Germain Kopaczynski, "Bioethics," in ECST.

29. *Vacco v. Quill*, 521 U.S. 793, 797–98, 117 S.Ct. 2293, 2296 (1997).

30. *Vacco*, 521 U.S. at 807.

31. *Vacco*, 521 U.S. at 801.

32. *Vacco*, 521 U.S. at 801; citing Assisted Suicide in the United States, Hearing before the Subcommittee on the Constitution of the House Committee on the Judiciary, 104th Cong., 2d Sess., 368 (1996) (testimony of Dr. Leon R. Kass).

33. *Vacco*, 521 U.S. at 807; referring to *Cruzan v. Director, Mo. Dept. of Health*, 497 U.S. 261, 278–79, 110 S.Ct., 2841, 2851–52 (1990).

34. ConscienceLaws.org, *Breaking News October – December 2008*, http://www.consciencelaws.org/Conscience-Archive/Breaking-News/Conscience-Breaking-News-2008-04.html#Grand_Duke_of_Luxembourg_to_be_stripped_of_powers_for_opposing_euthanasia (20 Nov. 2009).

35. High profile right-to-die groups include: Hemlock Society, Oregon Right to Die, Death with Dignity, and Compassion in Dying/Compassion & Choices. Low profile right-to-die groups include Choice in Dying/Partnership for Caring funded by both Robert Wood Johnson Foundation and George Soros Project on Death in America, as described in: Elizabeth D. Wickham and Ione Whitlock, "Two Decades to an American Culture of Death," *Life Tree Newsletter*, http://www.lifetree.org/timeline.index.html (5 Oct. 2009).

36. Smith, *Culture of Death*, 125.

37. Smith, *Culture of Death*, 130.

38. Smith, *Culture of Death*, 126, n.6.

39. Smith, *Culture of Death*, 132.

40. Smith, *Culture of Death*, 132–33.

41. Joseph F. Naumann and Robert W. Finn, *Principles of Catholic Social Teaching and Health Care Reform: A Joint Pastoral Statement*, 1 September 2009, http://www.priestforlife.org/magisterium/bishops/09-09-01-naumann-finn-health-care.htm (14 Nov. 2009); citing National Association of Pro-life Nurses on Health Care Legislation, *Position Statement*, 3 August 2009, http://www.nursesforlife.org/napnstatement.pdf (20 Nov. 2009).

42. Naumann and Finn, *Principles of Catholic Social Teaching*; citing Priests for Life, *Kansas City Bishops Issue Joint Health Care Reform Pastoral Statement*, 1 September 2009, http://www.priestsforlife.org/magisterium/bishops/09-09-01-naumann-finn-health-care.htm (20 Nov. 2009).

43. *Declaration on Euthanasia*, no. IV.

44. *Declaration on Euthanasia*, no. IV.

45. *Declaration on Euthanasia*, no. IV.

46. Michael P. Orsi, "Palliative Care," in ECST.

47. Committee for Pro-life Activities, *Nutrition and Hydration: Moral and Pastoral Reflections* (Washington, DC: United States Conference of Catholic Bishops, 1992), 3 (hereafter USCCB, *Nutrition and Hydration*); citing John Paul II, "Address to a Human Pre-Leukemia Conference," 15 November 1985.

48. USCCB, *Nutrition and Hydration*, 3; citing John Paul II, "Address to a Human Pre-Leukemia Conference," 15 Nov. 1985.

49. USCCB, *Nutrition and Hydration*, 4.

50. USCCB, *Nutrition and Hydration*, 7.

51. USCCB, *Nutrition and Hydration*, 2.

52. USCCB, *Nutrition and Hydration*, 7.

53. USCCB, *Nutrition and Hydration*, 5.

54. *Declaration on Euthanasia*, no. IV.

55. John Paul II, "Discourse to the Participants of the Working Group," *Working Group on the Determination of Brain Death and Its Relationship to Human Death*, 10–14 December 1989 (Vatican City: Pontifical Academy of Sciences, 1989).

56. Bishop Elio Sgreccia, "The Subject in Vegetative State: For a Personalistic View," *Address at the International Congress: "Life Sustaining Treatments and Vegetative State: Scientific Advances and Ethical Dilemmas"* 20 March 2004, 3, http://www.zenit.org/article-17474?l=english (27 Apr. 2009).

57. Elizabeth D. Wickham and Ione Whitlock, "Warning: Who's Leading Palliative Care Now?" *Life Tree Newsletter*, 24 September 2007, http://www.lifetree.org/newsletter/09-24-07.html (5 Oct. 2009).

58. *Declaration on Euthanasia*, no. III.

59. Elizabeth D. Wickham, "Medical Decisions at End of Life – Frequently Asked Questions," *Life Tree Newsletter*, http://www.lifetree.org/newsletter/09-24-07.html (5 Oct. 2009).

60. John Paul II, *Address to the 18th International Congress of the Transplantation Society*, 29 August 2000, http://www.healthpastoral.org/text.php?cid=192&sec=5&docid =45&lang=en (20 Nov. 2009).

61. William E. May, *Catholic Bioethics And The Gift of Human Life* (Huntington, IN: Our Sunday Visitor, 2000), 296–97.

62. Sgreccia, "The Subject in a Vegetative State: a Personalistic View," 7.

63. Report of the Ad Hoc Committee of the Harvard Medical School to Examine the Definition of Brain Death, "A Definition of Irreversible Coma," *Journal of the American Medical Association* 205 (5 August 1968): 337–40.

64. "'A solidly probable opinion' . . . is had if one trained at least somewhat in moral theology can defend the opinion with good arguments (intrinsic probability) or if a number of authentic moral theologians propose the opinion as probable (intrinsic probability). By 'authentic moral theologians' is meant someone skilled in moral theology and who adheres to the teachings of the Church. It should be evident that the arguments of dissident theologians, teaching contrary to the teaching authority of the Church, cannot engender *a solid probability* in favor of their dissident opinions." Thomas O'Donnell, *Medicine and Christian Morality*, 3d rev. ed., (New York: Alba House, 1996), 16–17.

65. USCCB, *Nutrition and Hydration*, n.35; citing Ehrlich Levy, "The Comatose Patient," *The Clinical Neurosciences*, vol. 1 (N.Y.: Churchill Livingstone, 1983), 956.

66. May, *Catholic Bioethics*, 264.

67. May, *Catholic Bioethics*, 264.

68. USCCB, *Nutrition and Hydration*, n.39; citing Saydjari Levin, et al., "Vegetative State After Closed-Head Injury: A Traumatic Coma Data Bank Report," *Archives of Neurology*, Vol. 48 (June 1991): 580–85.

69. Brian Clowes, *Facts of Life* (Front Royal, VA: Human Life International, 1997); citing "A Little Child Shall Lead Us," *Presbyterians Pro-Life NEWS* (Summer 1990), 4.

70. Steve Boggan, "Reborn." See also "Pill 'reverses' vegetative state," *BBC News*, 23 May 2006, http://news.bbc.co.uk/2/hi/health/5008744.stm (20 Aug. 2009).

71. Eurek Alert, *Scientists Find that Individuals in Vegetative States Can Learn*, 20 Septembter 2009, http://www.eurekalert.org/pub_releases/2009-09/uoc-sft091809.php (20 Nov. 2009); describing Tristan Bekinschtein, et al., "Classical conditioning in the vegetative and minimally conscious state," Advanced Online Publication of *Nature Neuroscience*, 20 September 2009.

72. Eurek Alert, *Scientists Find that Individuals in Vegetative States Can Learn*.

73. *Cruzan*, 497 U.S. at 265.

74. Texas Conference of Catholic Bishops, "On Withdrawing Artificial Nutrition and Hydration" (7 May 1990), in *Origins: NC News Service* 20 (1990): 53–55.

75. Pennsylvania Conference of Catholic Bishops, "Nutrition and Hydration: Moral Considerations," in *Origins: NC News Service* 21 (1992): 542–53.

76. USCCB, *Nutrition and Hydration*, 6.

77. USCCB, *Nutrition and Hydration*, 7.

78. John Paul II, *Address of John Paul II to the participants in the International Congress on 'Life-Sustaining Treatments and Vegetative State: Scientific Advances and Ethical Dilemmas'*, 20 March 2004, http://www.vatican.va/holy_father/john_paul_ii/ speeches/2004/march/documents/hf_jp-ii_spe_20040320_congress-fiamc_en.html   (10

Aug. 2009) (hereafter John Paul II, *Life Sustaining Treatments*).

79. John Paul II, *Life Sustaining Treatments*, no. 2.

80. John Paul II, *Life Sustaining Treatments*, no. 3.

81. John Paul II, *Life Sustaining Treatments*, no. 4.

82. John Paul II, *Life Sustaining Treatments*, no. 5.

83. John Paul II, *Life Sustaining Treatments*, no. 6.

84. Sacred Congregation for the Doctrine of the Faith, *Responses to Certain Questions of the United States Conference of Catholic Bishops Concerning Artificial Nutrition and Hydration*, 1 August 2007, commentary, http://www.vatican.va/roman_curia/congregations/cfaith/documents/rc_con_cfaith_doc_20070801_risposte-usa_en.html (20 Nov. 2009) (hereafter CDF, *Artificial Nutrition and Hydration*).

85. CDF, *Artificial Nutrition and Hydration*, response to question no. 1.

86. CDF, *Artificial Nutrition and Hydration*, response to question no. 2.

87. USCCB, *Nutrition and Hydration*, 3.

88. Kathy Kalina, *Midwife for Souls: Spiritual Care for the Dying* (Boston: Pauline Books and Media, 1993), 28.

89. USCCB, *Nutrition and Hydration*, 3.

90. Kalina, *Midwife for Souls*, 43–45.

91. Wickham, "Medical Decision at the End of Life."

92. Frank Morris, "When Nutrition and Hydration are a Moral Absolute," *The Wanderer*, 6 May 2004, 4–8.

93. Catherine Vanek, "Disabilities (Persons With)," and Douglas A. Sylva, "United Nations," in ECST.

94. Andrea Vrchota, *Living with Disabilities - Franciscan University Student and Disabilities Activist*, 26 January 2006, http://ngovoice.libsyn.com/index.php?post_id=51724 (10 Aug. 2009) (podcast).

95. United Nations *Convention on the Rights of Persons with Disabilities and Optional Protocol*, Article 25, December 13, 2006, http://www.un.org/esa/socdev/enable/rights/convtexte.htm (20 Nov. 2009).

96. M.C. Tierney et al., "How Reliable are Advanced Directives for Healthcare? A Study of the Attitudes of the Healthy and Unwell to Treatment of the Terminally Ill," *Annals of the Royal College of Physicians and Surgeons of Canada* (1992): 25, 267–70.

97. Mary Senander, *The Living Will: Expansion or Erosion of Patients' Rights?*, 2d ed. (St. Paul, MN: Leaflet Missal Co., 1996), 11–12.

98. ERD, no. 25.

99. For examples of DPOAHCs, contact The International Task Force on Euthanasia and Assisted Suicide, P.O. Box 760 Steubenville, Ohio 43952, or Medical Ethics Project, 419 7th Street NW, Suite 400, Washington, D.C. 20004.

100. EV, no. 86. See also William E. May, "Organ Donation from the Living (Inter Vivos)," in ESCT.

101. ERD, no. 30.

102. ERD, no. 64. See also ERD, no. 63.

103. Smith, *Culture of Death*, 166.

104. Smith, *Culture of Death*, 166.

105. Robert D. Troug and Franklin G. Miller, "The Dead Donor Rule and Organ Transplantation," *The New England Journal of Medicine* 359, no. 7 (14 August 2008): 674.

106. Troug and Miller, "The Dead Donor Rule," 674.

107. Troug and Miller, "The Dead Donor Rule," 674.

108. Troug and Miller, "The Dead Donor Rule," 675.

109. Leo Alexander, "Medical Science under Dictatorship," *New England Journal of Medicine* 241, no. 2 (July 1949): 39–47.

110 Gary E. Crum, "Nazi Bioethics and a Doctor's Defense," *The Human Life Review* 8, no. 3 (Summer 1982), 68.

111. Kalina, *Midwife For Souls*, 43–50. See also Peter W. Riola, "Hospice Movement," in ECST.

112. When my grandfather was dying in the hospital he told my father, a physician, who came to visit him in the morning while making rounds that "Mommy was here last night, and so was your brother, Jerry." Both my grandfather's wife and his youngest son had died years earlier. My father said that Grandpa, not prone to sentimentality, relayed this information in a matter-of-fact, "take it or leave it" manner.

113. Kalina, *Midwife For Souls*, 55.

114. Kalina, *Midwife For Souls*, 57.

115. ERD, no. 61.

116. Kalina, *Midife for Souls*, 85.

117. ERD, no. 60.

118. ERD, n.40.

119. Col. 1:24.

120. SD, no. 19.

121. SD, no. 24.

Appendix A
Summary of The Gospel of Life:
Evangelium Vitae (1995)

Introduction:

"The Gospel of life is at the heart of Jesus' message" to be preached as "good news" to everyone. The birth of the savior is a great joy the "foundation and fulfillment of joy at every child born into the world." The new and eternal life which Jesus gives, "communion with the Father," gives the full significance to all the aspects and stages of human life.[1]

Incomparable Worth of the Human Person:

Man is called to share the very life of God which reveals the "greatness and inestimable value of human life even in its temporal phase." Human life on earth is "not an ultimate but a penultimate reality", still it remains a sacred reality entrusted to us. The Church knows the Gospel of life fulfills and surpasses the expectations of the human heart. Every person can "come to recognize in the natural law written in the human heart the sacred value of human life from its very beginning until its end, and can affirm the right of every human being to have this primary good respected to the highest degree. Upon the recognition of this right, every human community and political community itself are founded."[2] The incarnation of the Son of God reveals the "incomparable value of every human person."

The mystery of the redemption is the source of her invincible hope and joy. "The Gospel of God's love for man, the Gospel of the dignity of the person and the Gospel of life are a single and indivisible Gospel." So, man represents the way for the Church.[3]

New Threats to Human Life

The Word of God entrusted every person to the maternal care of the Church. So, all threats to human life are felt in the heart of the Church. Today the proclamation of the Gospel of Life is especially pressing because of "the extraordinary increase and gravity of threats" to life. In addition to poverty, hunger, disease, violence and war, "new threats are emerging on an alarmingly vast scale." I repeat the condemnation of VCII of crimes against humanity.[4]

Science and technology have opened up new prospects of attacks on the dignity of the human person. A new cultural climate "gives crimes against life a new and—if possible—even more sinister character," whereby "public opinion justify certain crimes against life in the name of the rights of individual freedom, and on this basis they claim not only exemption from punishment but even authorization by the State, so that these things can be done with total freedom and indeed with the free assistance of health-care systems."[5]

The legalization of crimes against life is "both a disturbing symptom and a significant cause of grave moral decline." Even the medical profession is willing to carry out these acts against the person. This distorts the medical profession. In such a cultural and legislative situation false and deceptive solutions are openly considered. Not only are the innocent lives of the young and elderly subject to destruction but the moral conscience itself is darkened by such widespread conditioning.[6]

In Communion with All the Bishops of the World:

The Extraordinary Consistory of Cardinals (1991) asked me to reaffirm the value of human life in light of the new attacks against human life. I asked them for their written suggestions and thank those who replied. Just as the Church spoke out against the oppression of the working class one hundred years ago, so today she raises her voice in defense of another class of persons oppressed in their fundamental right to life. "Today there exists a great multitude of weak and defenseless human beings, unborn children in particular, whose fundamental right to life is being trampled." This injustice is "being presented as elements of progress in view of a new world order."

Justice, development, true freedom, peace and happiness can only be reached if the value of every human life is reaffirmed as inviolable.[7]

> I pray that at every level a general commitment to support the family will reappear so that the "family will always remain . . . the 'sanctuary of life.'" (CA, no. 83) I appeal to the Church that we offer the world our witness of justice and solidarity so that "a new culture of human life will be affirmed, for the building of an authentic civilization of truth and love."[8]

Chapter 1. Present-Day Threats to Human Life
"Cain rose up against his brother . . ."(Gen. 4:8)—The Roots of Violence
against Life

The Gospel of life was proclaimed in the beginning when God created man in his image for a destiny of perfect life. It was contradicted when sin and death entered the world and "casts its shadow of meaninglessness over man's entire existence." Death entered the world when Cain killed Abel. This story is rewritten daily in the book of human history.[9]

God reminds Cain before he murdered his brother "of his freedom in the face of evil: man is in no way predestined to evil." But the temptation to envy and anger has the upper hand over Cain and "brother kills brother." Every murder is a violation of the spiritual kinship uniting mankind in one great family, based on equal personal dignity. The kinship of flesh and blood is violated between parents and children in acts of abortion or euthanasia. We learn Cain's crime was a concession to the "thinking" of the devil who was a murderer from the beginning.[10] Man's revolt against God is followed by man's deadly combat against his fellow man. When questioned by God, Cain, instead of apologizing in remorse, arrogantly eludes the question and cover up his crime with a lie. "This was and still is the case, when all kinds of ideologies try to justify and disguise the most atrocious crimes against human beings. 'Am I my brother's keeper?' . . . Symptoms of this trend include the lack of solidarity towards society's weakest members—such as the elderly, the infirm, immigrants, children— and the indifference frequently found in relations between the world's peoples even when basic values such as survival, freedom and peace are involved."[11]

God will not leave sins which cry from the ground, first of which is willful murder, unpunished. Life belongs to God and he who attacks human life attacks in some way God himself. Cain is cursed by God and the earth. But God is merciful and puts a mark on Cain lest any one seek revenge on him for slaying Abel. Not even a murderer loses his personal dignity, and God himself pledges to guarantee this. St. Augustine says that "God, who preferred the correction rather than the death of a sinner, did not desire that a homicide be punished by the exaction of another act of homicide."[12]

"What have you done. . . ." (Gen. 4:10)—The Eclipse of the Value of Life

The attacks against life, which God's question to Cain—"What have you done?"—come from nature itself made worse by the "culpable indifference and negligence of those who could in some cases remedy them." Other attacks come from situations of violence, hatred and conflicts of interest that lead to murder, war, and in the millions of children forced into poverty because of unjust distribution of resources and in the arms race which spawns armed conflict, and in the reckless tampering with the world's ecological balance, and in the criminal spread of drugs, and in the promotions of sexual activity morally unacceptable and involving grave risks to life.[13]

There is another category of attacks against life in its earliest and final stages which present new characteristics of extraordinary seriousness insofar as they "tend no longer to be considered as 'crimes'; paradoxically they assume the nature of 'rights,'" and the State makes them available through free health care services. Worse yet, these new attacks are carried out in the heart of the family.

These attacks arose out of the crisis of culture and skepticism as to the foundations of knowledge and ethics obscuring the nature of man and his rights and duties. Existential and interpersonal difficulties add to this made even worse by the isolation of individuals and families alone with their problems. The struggle to make ends meet, or unbearable pain, or violence against women especially, make the choice to defend life heroic at times. This helps to explain how the value of life has gone into eclipse today.[14]

On top of it all today we are confronted by a "veritable structure of sin" characterized by a culture that denies solidarity and becomes "culture of death"—a "society excessively concerned with efficiency." It is a "war of the powerful against the weak" where those who require more care are considered the enemy of those well off who must be resisted and eliminated. A "conspiracy against life" is unleashed on the personal, familial and international level, distorting relations between peoples and States.[15]

Enormous amounts of money have been invested in the production of pharmaceutical products making it possible to abort children in their mother's womb without medical assistance and removing abortion from social responsibility and control. The Catholic Church is accused of promoting abortion because it is opposed to contraception. On the contrary, the negative values of a contraceptive mentality strengthen the temptation to abortion when an unwanted life is conceived. Contraception contradicts the full truth of the sexual act and is opposed to chastity while abortion destroys the life of a human being and is opposed to justice. But despite their differences contraception and abortion are "fruits of the same tree." People are tempted to commit these sins under the pressure of real-life difficulties or because of a hedonistic life style "which regards procreation as an obstacle to personal fulfillment." So, an unwanted child "becomes an enemy to be avoided at all cost, and abortion becomes the only possible decisive response to failed contraception." This link is further substantiated in so far as many contraceptives are really abortifacients.[16]

Techniques of artificial reproduction which seem to be at the service of life open the door to new attacks against life. They are morally unacceptable because they separate procreation from the human context of the conjugal act. In addition, they have grave consequences in so far as they show a high failure rate in the healthy development of the human embryo, exposing it to risks of death, producing more embryos than necessary for implantation, i.e., "spare embryos," which are then destroyed or used for research "under the pretext of medical progress" and so human life is reduced to the level of mere "biological material."[17]

Prenatal diagnosis often becomes an opportunity for proposing an abortion if limitation, handicap or illness is detected. The mentality which legitimizes eugenic abortion also denies nourishment to babies born with serious handicaps. A right to infanticide is being advanced with similar arguments to those used to justify abortion.[18]

Given the cultural context which denies any meaning or value in suffering there is a temptation to eliminate it by hastening death at the moment considered most suitable. The sick person undergoes a sense of anguish, severe discomfort and desperation because of prolonged suffering. Even though medical and social assistance is increasingly effective, still the sick person often feels overwhelmed by his frailty and those close to him with a misguided compassion. There is also a Promethean cultural attitude that leads people to think they can control death by taking the decision into their own hands. "What really happens in this case is that the individual is overcome and crushed by a death deprived of any prospect of meaning or hope. Euthanasia is justified by misguided pity and a utilitarian motive of avoiding costs which bring no return or in order to increase the supply of organs for transplant without respect for adequate criteria which verify the death of the donor."[19]

Demographics are used to justify attacks on life. In developed countries there is a collapse of the birth rate. In developing countries with a high birth rate and little means to provide for the poor, instead of serious policies of cultural development and fair production and distribution of resources, anti-birth policies are enacted. Today the powerful of the earth act as did Pharaoh of old. "They too are haunted by the current demographic growth, and fear that the most prolific and poorest peoples represent a threat for the well-being and peace of their own countries." So they promote and impose massive programs of birth control making economic help conditional on the acceptance of anti-birth policies.[20]

Attacks against life today present an alarming spectacle given their "unheard of numerical proportion" and the widespread support they receive from a broad societal consensus, legal approval and the involvement of certain sectors of health care personnel. They are taking on vast proportions being "scientifically and systematically programmed threats." Intentions aside, "we are in fact faced by an objective 'conspiracy against life,' involving even international Institutions, engaged in encouraging and carrying out actual campaigns to make contraception, sterilization and abortion widely available. Nor can it be denied that the mass media are often implicated in this conspiracy, by lending credit to that culture which presents recourse to contraception, sterilization, abortion and even euthanasia as a mark of progress and a victory of freedom, while depicting as enemies of freedom and progress those positions which are unreservedly pro-life."[21]

"Am I my brother's keeper?" (Gen. 4:9)—A Perverse Idea of Freedom

What are the motives, circumstances and consequences of attacks against life? Often they arise from tragic situations of profound suffering, a total lack of economic prospects, depression or anxiety about the future. Such circumstances can mitigate the culpability of those who make evil choices. But today there is a "more sinister" tendency to interpret "crimes against life as legitimate expressions of individual freedom, to be acknowledged and protected as actual rights." This marks an historical turning-point in the history of the development of the idea of "human rights." Ironically, in an age that proclaims the inviolable rights of the person, the right to life is trampled upon at the moment of birth and death.[22]

While people are more sensitive to human rights inherent in every person without distinction of race, nationality, religion, etc. in practice they are repudiated. "This denial is still more distressing, indeed more scandalous, precisely because it is occurring in a society which makes the affirmation and protection of human rights its primary objective and its boast." The present day attacks against life legitimized as expressions of individual freedom "represent a direct threat to the entire culture of human rights" and jeopardize the meaning of "democratic coexistence." Looking at the wider global perspective it appears the affirmation of the rights of peoples made in distinguished international assemblies is mere rhetoric when faced with the "selfishness of rich countries which exclude poorer countries from access to development or make such access dependent on arbitrary prohibitions against procreation."[23]

The root of the contradiction in human rights lies in a mentality that carries subjectivity to an extreme in the totally autonomous individual. But this contradicts the idea of "man as a being who is 'not to be used,'" which is the basis of human rights; that man "unlike animals and things, cannot be subjected to domination by others." This mentality is linked to a view of personal dignity based on the capacity to communicate. Force then becomes the criterion for choice in interpersonal relations. But this contradicts the rule of law in which "the reasons of force" are replaced with the "force of reason." A culture of death "betrays a completely individualistic concept of freedom, which ends up becoming the freedom of 'the strong' against the weak who have no choice but to submit."[24]

Yes, we are our brother's keeper "because God entrusts us to one another. And it is also in view of this entrusting that God gives everyone freedom, a freedom which possesses an inherently relational dimension." Human freedom is to be used to make a gift of self and openness to others. But when it is made absolute in an individualistic way, its dignity is contradicted. The essential link of freedom to truth must also be recognized, otherwise freedom leads to the destruction of others as when a person "shuts out even the most obvious evidence of an objective and universal truth, which is the foundation of personal and social life."[25]

Freedom considered as an absolute value leads to a society of individuals without any mutual bonds, only their own special interests. Still, some compromise must be found for people to live together, no longer with reference to truth, but based on consensus. "At that point, everything is negotiable, everything is open to bargaining: even the first of the fundamental rights, the right to life."[26]

In this way democracy contradicts its own principles and moves towards a form of totalitarianism. It becomes a "tyrant State, which arrogates to itself the right to dispose of the life of the weakest and most defenseless members" while maintaining "the appearance of the strictest respect for legality." In fact, all that remains is "the tragic caricature of legality; the democratic ideal, which is only truly such when it acknowledges and safeguards the dignity of every human person, is betrayed in its very foundations." To recognize at law a right to abortion, infanticide and euthanasia attributes to human freedom a "perverse and evil significance: that of an absolute power over others and against others. This is the death of true freedom."[27]

"And from your face I shall be hidden" (Gen. 4:14)—The Eclipse of the Sense of God and of Man.

At the heart of the tragedy of a culture of death we find "the eclipse of the sense of God and of man, typical of a social and cultural climate dominated by secularism." This leads to a sad vicious circle: "when the sense of God is lost, there is also a tendency to lose the sense of man, of his dignity and his life; in turn, the systematic violation of the moral law."[28]

Cain is capable of confessing his sin only because he stands before God as did King David when he said: "Against you, you alone, have I sinned; what is evil in your sight I have done."[29] Vatican Council tells us "when God is forgotten the creature itself grows unintelligible" meaning we are no longer able to see a difference between ourselves and other creatures. We tend to regard ourselves as an "organism which, at most, has reached a very high stage of perfection." Both he himself and human life are mere "things" which man claims as his exclusive property, completely subject to his control and manipulation. Likewise, birth and death become "things" to be "possessed" or "rejected." Nature is reduced to so much matter and the "idea that there is a truth of creation which must be acknowledged" is lost. At the other extreme certain ideologies divinize nature and hold that it is wrong to interfere with it in any way. "The loss of contact with God's wise design is the deepest root of modern man's confusion" and causes man to lose sight of the mystery of the world and his own being.[30]

In the eclipse of the sense of God a "practical materialism" breeds hedonism, utilitarianism and extreme individualism. This confirms the words of St. Paul: "And since they did not see fit to acknowledge God, God gave them up to an abase mind and to improper conduct."[31] The values of being are replaced by those of having. The so-called "quality of life" is interpreted primarily or exclusively as economic efficiency, inordinate consumerism, physical beauty and pleasure, to the neglect of the more profound dimensions—interpersonal, spiritual and religious—of existence.[32]

Suffering in the eclipse of God is considered evil and always to be avoided. When it can't be avoided people wrongly claim the right to suppress it. The body is no longer seen as "a sign and place of relations with others" but "simply a complex of organs, functions and energies to be used according to the sole criteria of pleasure and efficiency. So too, human sexuality is depersonalized and reduced from a "sign, place and language of love" to an instrument for self-assertion and the selfish satisfaction of personal desires and instincts. The unitive and procreative meanings of human sexuality are artificially separated. Procreation becomes the enemy to be avoided or, if it is sought, it is accepted "only because it expresses the desire, or indeed the intention, to have a child 'at all costs,'" and not as a sign of complete openness to the other and the richness of life represented in the child.[33]

   The eclipse of God is taking place today at the heart of the moral conscience of individuals and "of society." Because of media the moral conscience of society is subjected to an "extremely serious and mortal danger: that of confusion between good and evil, precisely in relation to the fundamental right to life." A large part of our world looks like that described by St. Paul who warned: "claiming to be wise, they became fools,"[34] carrying out works deserving of death and approving of "those who practice them."[35] But the voice of the Lord echoing in the conscience of each person is still heard and from it a new journey of and *openness* to life can begin.[36]

"You have come to the sprinkled blood" (cf. Heb 12:22, 24)—Signs of Hope and Invitation to Commitment

The blood of Christ reveals the Father's love and how precious man is in God's sight and how "priceless the value of his life." Truly, "How precious must man be in the eyes of the Creator, if he 'gained so great a Redeemer.'" It also reveals that man's vocation consists in "the sincere gift of self." The blood of Christ is a sign of communion. Whoever drinks the blood of Christ is drawn into the "dynamism of his love and gift of life." "It is form the blood of Christ that all draw the strength to commit themselves to promoting life" and the hope that in "God's plan life will be victorious." Our present victory over sin is a sign, St. Paul says, of our future definitive victory over death.[37]

   Signs of victory over death are to be found even in cultures of death although it is often hard to see because the media does not pay attention to them. There are many individuals and groups that strive to help the weak. There are many married couples who accept children as "the supreme gift of marriage."[38] There are families ready to accept abandoned children, handicapped persons and the elderly. There are many crisis pregnancy centers. There are people to help persons in distress or who are addicted to various things. Medical science continues to discover cures and treatments that were once inconceivable and many people are mobilizing to bring these discoveries to those afflicted with natural disasters, epidemics and war. This shows a growing sense of solidarity among peoples and a greater respect for life.[39]

   Pro-life, pro-family movements in various parts of the world are a sign of hope. Then there are the countless daily gestures of unselfish care which people lovingly make in families, hospitals, orphanages and homes for the elderly which defend life. The Church, too, is a sign of hope, being in the front line in providing charitable help. All these deeds strengthen "the civilization of love and life." Even if they go unnoticed by the world the heavenly Father sees them and will reward them here and now and make them produce lasting fruit. There is a growing sensitivity that is opposed to war as "an instrument for the resolution of conflicts between peoples" and recourse to "non-violent means to counter the armed aggressor." Opposition to the death penalty is a sign of hope: "Modern society has the means of effectively suppressing crime by rendering criminals harmless without definitively denying them the chance to reform." Concern for the ecology is a sign of hope. Bioethics is promoting more reflection and dialogue on ethical problems.[40]

We are facing "an enormous and dramatic clash between good and evil, death and life, the 'culture of death' and the 'culture of life.'" We must choose to be "unconditionally pro-life." Moses urged us to make a religious and moral choice that gives our lives its basic orientation especially when it is nourished by faith in Christ: "I have set before you life and death, blessing and curse; therefore choose life."[41] In facing the present situation the Church, with faith in the blood of Christ, is more aware of the grace and responsibility to proclaim the Gospel of life.[42]

Chapter II. "I came that they may have life"—The Christian Message Concerning Life
"The life was made manifest, and we saw it." (1 John 1:2) With Our Gaze Fixed on Christ, 'the Word of Life'

One could feel overwhelmed and powerless when faced with the countless grave threats to life. Then it is that we are called to humbly trust in Jesus Christ. The Gospel of life is essentially consists in "the proclamation of the very person of Jesus." In the person of Jesus man is given the possibility of knowing the value of human life and of defending and promoting it. The Gospel of life is "written in the heart of every man and woman and can be known in its essential traits by human reason."[43]

In Jesus God's eternal life is proclaimed and this gives the full value and meaning to our lives "for God's eternal life is in fact the end to which our living in this world is directed and called. Therefore the Gospel of life includes all that human experience tells us about the value of human life, purifying it and bringing it to fulfillment."[44]

"The Lord is my strength and my song, and he has become my salvation."(Exod. 15:2)—Life is Always a Good

The Old Testament reveals the Gospel message about life. In Exodus, when Israel seemed doomed to be exterminated, God revealed himself as a Savior. Israel learned its existence is not at the mercy of Pharaoh but is the object of God's love. Suffering challenges faith and puts it to the test above all else. The Book of Job shows that suffering is a mystery and nothing can thwart the plan of

God. A longing for immortal life is planted by the Creator in man's heart and revelation gradually confirms this with greater clarity.[45]

"The name of Jesus . . . has made this man strong." (Acts 3:16)—In the Uncertainties of Human Life, Jesus Brings Life's Meaning to Fulfillment

Jesus proclaims to all who feel threatened that their lives are a good. This is good news of God concerning them: that their lives are carefully guarded by the Father and that the hope of salvation is well founded.[46] Faith in Jesus gives to lives that seem abandoned self-esteem and full dignity. They have meaning on a moral and spiritual level for every person's life. Those who think they are secure in their material possessions and do not need a savior are "fools."[47]

The life of Jesus is a dialectic between the uncertainty of life and an affirmation of its value from the moment of his birth. "Life's contradictions and risks were fully accepted by Jesus." He became lowly and poor and subjected himself to the "most vulnerable conditions of human life."[48] He continued in the way of poverty until his death on a cross. In his death Jesus reveals "all the splendor and value of life, inasmuch as his self-oblation on the Cross becomes the source of new life for all people."[49] How great is the value of human life that the Son of God took it on and made it the instrument of salvation for all humanity.[50]

"Called . . . to be conformed to the image of his Son" (Rom. 8:28-29)—God's Glory Shines on the Face of Man

Human life is different from the life of all other living creatures. We see in the Book of Genesis that human life is summit of God's creative activity and everything in creation is made subject to man. This shows the "primacy of man over things" and that he cannot "be made subject to other men and almost reduced to the level of a thing." The difference between man and other creatures is shown in the fact that his creation is the result of a deliberate decision by God to establish a unique bond with man—made in his image and likeness.[51] Also, in his spiritual faculties man is like God insofar as reason can discern good and evil and his free will can embrace the former and shun the latter. Moreover human life is more than "mere existence in time." It is a drive towards the fullness of life which transcends time.[52]

Because God breathed his divine breath into man when he created him we experience a "perennial dissatisfaction" so long as our "sole point of reference is the world of plants and animals." Only the appearance of woman satisfied his need for "interpersonal dialogue, so vital for human existence." Only in another human being is to be found the reflection of God, "the definitive goal and fulfillment of every person." God rested after he created man—"He rested then in the depths of man, he rested in man's mind and in his thought."[53]

Unfortunately, through sin man rebelled against God and ends up worshiping creatures; this deforms God's image in him and tempts him to offenses against others as well: "When God is not acknowledged as God, the profound meaning of man is betrayed and communion between people is compromised."[54] God's image is revealed anew in Christ. What the first Adam lost the new Adam, Christ Jesus, restores and "opens wide the gates of the kingdom of life." Only in the image of Christ can we be free from the slavery of idolatry and also find our true identity.[55]

"Whoever lives and believes in me shall never die." (John 11:26)—The Gift of Eternal Life

The Son of God came to give more than "mere existence in time." To give eternal life is the reason for Jesus' mission. Eternal life is more than immortality but signifies a "full participation in the life of the 'Eternal One'" and enter into the loving communion of the Father, Son and Holy Spirit.[56]

Eternal life is both the life of God and the life of the children of God. This fills those who believe it with wonder. "The dignity of this life is linked not only to its beginning, to the fact that it comes from God, but also to its final end, to its destiny of fellowship with God in knowledge and love of him." Human life seen from this perspective has the following consequences: love of life will find further inspiration and strength, new depth and meaning; love of life means more than desire for space for self–expression and entering into relationships with others but, rather, a place where God manifests himself.[57]

"From man in regard to his fellow man I will demand an accounting." (Gen. 9:5)—Reverence and Love for Every Human Life

Our life comes from God, therefore, "man cannot do with it as he wills."[58] The sacredness of human life has its foundation in God. In the loving hands of God human life is protected and his hands are like those of a mother. Therefore the history and destiny of people and nations is not the outcome of mere chance or blind fate.[59]

Because human life is sacred it is inviolable: "You shall not kill" (Ex. 20:13); "Do not slay the innocent and righteous" (Ex. 23:7). It extends to personal injury as well.[60] The sense of the value of human life in the Old Testament will reach perfection in the Beatitudes. This imperfect sense of respect for the sacredness of human life "is apparent in some aspect of the current penal legislation, which provided for severe forms of corporal punishment and even the death penalty." It culminates in the command: "You shall love your neighbor as yourself."[61]

Jesus quotes the Fifth Commandment to the rich young man who asked what he needed to be perfect.[62] But Jesus takes this to a new level, not only must a believer not kill, but he tells us "I say to you that every one who is angry with his brother shall be liable to judgment."[63] Jesus shows that the sacredness of human life extends to caring for the life of a brother, a stranger and even an enemy. The parable of the Good Samaritan shows that with respect for human life everyone is our brother. The height of this love is to pray for one's enemy and imitate God who makes his "sun rise on the evil and on the good and sends rain on the just and on the unjust"[64]: "Thus the deepest element of God's commandment to protect human life is the requirement to show reverence and love for every person and the life of every person." Love is the fulfillment of the law—"Thou shalt not Kill."[65]

"Be fruitful and multiply, and fill the earth and subdue it" (Gen. 1:28)—Man's Responsibility for Life

God gave man dominion over the earth: "Be fruitful and multiply, and fill the earth and subdue it; and have dominion over the fish of the sea and over the birds of the air and over every living thing that moves upon the earth."[66] Man has a specific responsibility over the environment not only for the present but for future generations: It is the ecological question—ranging from the preservation of the natural habitats of the different species of animals and of other forms of life to "human ecology" properly speaking[67] but this is not an absolute dominion, rather, "the prohibition not to 'eat of the fruit of the tree'"[68] shows we are subject not only to biological laws but to moral ones as well.[69]

Man's sharing with God responsibility for human life reaches its highest point in the giving of new life through procreation. Having a child is a deeply human event full of religious significance. Human procreation is a continuation of Creation because God is present in human fatherhood and motherhood differently than in other forms of begetting on earth insofar as he provides an image and likeness of himself in the immortal soul of each child. Man and woman joined in marriage become partners in a divine undertaking through the act of procreation.

Over and above the mission of parents is everyone's task to serve life when it is weakest in the sick, the naked, the imprisoned. Whoever serves the weakest, serves Christ, himself.[70]

"For you formed my inmost being." (Ps. 139:13)—The Dignity of the Unborn Child

Human life is most vulnerable when it enters and leaves the world. Although there is no specific reference in scripture to protecting life at these times in particular, that is because the mere possibility of doing so is "completely foreign to the religious and cultural way of thinking of the People of God." In fact sterility is seen as a curse[71] and conception in the womb bespeaks "the intimate connection between the initial moment of life and the action of God the Creator."[72] The value of the person from the moment of conception is especially celebrated in the meeting of St. Elizabeth and the Virgin Mary. Their children reveal the advent of the Messianic age.[73]

"I kept my faith even when I said, 'I am greatly afflicted.'" (Ps. 116:10)—Life in Old Age and at Times of Suffering

It would be anachronistic to expect the Bible to make explicit reference to end of life issues because the cultural and religious context of the Bible is not touched by temptations to end the lives of the elderly by force. On the contrary old age is accorded reverence in scripture.[74] A believer accepts old age and death as coming from the hands of God[75] and knows he is not the master of life or death. Illness does not drive him to despair.[76]

Jesus' mission shows he was concerned with bodily life and he sends his disciples to heal the sick and raise the dead.[77] But bodily life is not the greatest good. A believer must be willing to lose it for the sake of the gospel[78] as the death of John the Baptist and Stephen the first martyr and most of all the death and resurrection of Jesus, make clear. But it is the Creator's decision, not ours, when we will die.[79]

"All who hold her fast will live." (Bar. 4:1)—From the Law of Sinai to the Gift of the Spirit

"Life is indelibly marked by a truth of its own" and to detach oneself from it is to condemn oneself to meaninglessness and possibly become a threat to the existence of others. All of scripture shows the course life must follow if it is to respect its own truth.

God's covenant with his people is linked to the path of life.[80] It is impossible for life to remain authentic if it is detached from the good which is bound to the commandments of God. Doing good is not a burden but the purpose of life. If we fail to follow the words of life found in scripture then the command "You shall not kill" are hard to keep.[81]

The history of Israel shows it is hard to be faithful to the words of life inscribed on the human heart and in the Covenant. The prophets call God's people back to the Lord as the source of life when they show contempt for life and violate the people's rights. The prophets are most concerned to awaken hope in a new principle of life capable of bringing about a renewed relationship with God and others by fulfilling the demands of the Gospel of life. God's gift will make this possible by creating a new heart and a new spirit within the believer[82] so one is able "achieve the deepest and most authentic meaning of life: namely, that of being a gift which is fully realized in the giving of self." With the coming of Jesus the Holy Spirit is given who renews the hearts of believers. The law of Christ makes possible the gift of self summed up in the golden rule.[83]

"They shall look on him whom they have pierced." (John 19:37)—The Gospel of Life is Brought to Fulfillment on the Tree of the Cross

Looking at the cross we see fulfillment of the whole Gospel of life. Just as scripture depicts a great cosmic disturbance in the heavens when the "sun's light failed"[84] as symbolic of a massive conflict between good and evil, so today "we find ourselves in the midst of a dramatic conflict between the 'culture of death' and the 'culture of life.'" In both instances the cross of Christ is not overcome but shines forth in the darkness as the center of all history and every human life. In his powerlessness on the cross Jesus is revealed as the most powerful, Son of God.[85] His greatest manifestation of power is seen in his forgiveness of sins, that is, "in setting man free from his greatest sickness and in raising him to the very life of God." Like those who looked upon the serpent Moses lifted up, those whose lives are threatened today and who look upon the cross of Christ find sure hope of freedom and redemption.[86]

When Jesus gave up his spirit in his death upon the cross,[87] he died like every other person yet it also alludes to his gift of the Holy Spirit and the new life of grace that comes to us through the Sacraments. Jesus' death proclaims that life finds its meaning when it is given up in obedience to the will of the Father. "Thus we shall learn not only to obey the commandment not to kill human life, but also to revere life, to live it and to foster it."[88]

Chapter III. You Shall Not Kill. God's Holy Law
"If you would enter life, keep the commandments." (Matt. 19:17)—The Gospel and Commandments

To have eternal life one must keep the commandments including "Thou shall not kill."[89] God's commandments are never detached from his love. Man is a king in the image of the King of the universe. Man is king over lesser creatures and himself and the life he is able to transmit through procreation. Man's lordship is not absolute but ministerial.[90]

"From man in regard to his fellow man I will demand an account for human life." (Gen. 9:5)—Human Life is Sacred and Inviolable

Human life is sacred in its origin and its end, both being God. No one can, therefore, "claim for himself the right to destroy directly an innocent human being."[91] God will severely judge those who violate this command. Only Satan delights in the death of the living. Satan leads man to "projects of sin and death, making them appear as goals and fruits of life."[92]

Scripture, Old and New Testaments and the living Tradition of the Church categorically repeat "Thou shall not kill." Murder, apostasy and adultery were listed as the three most serious sins in the first centuries of the Church requiring heavy penance.[93]

There are seeming exceptions to the command not to kill such as legitimate self-defense: "the intrinsic value of life and the duty to love oneself no less than others are the basis of a true right to self-defense." And no one can "renounce the right to self-defense out of lack of love for life or for self" but only out of heroic love and a "radical self-offering, according to the spirit of the Gospel Beatitudes."[94]

"Moreover, 'legitimate defense can be not only a right but a grave duty for someone responsible for another's life, the common good of the family or of the

State.'[95] Unfortunately it happens that the need to render the aggressor incapable of causing harm sometimes involves taking his life. In this case, the fatal outcome is attributable to the aggressor whose action brought it about, even though he many not be morally responsible because of a lack of the use of reason."[96]

The Death Penalty must be seen in the context of penal justice ever more in line with human dignity. "The primary purpose of the punishment which society inflicts is 'to redress the disorder caused by the offence."[97] This defends public order and ensures personal safety and offers the offender a chance to change his or her behavior. So to achieve these goals the punishment "ought not go to the extreme of executing the offender except in cases of absolute necessity: in other words, when it would not be possible otherwise to defend society. Today however, as a result of steady improvements in the organization of the penal system, such cases are very rare, if not practically non-existent."[98]

As the Catechism of the Catholic Church teaches: "If bloodless means are sufficient to defend human lives against an aggressor and to protect public order and the safety of persons, public authority must limit itself to such means, because they better correspond to the concrete conditions of the common good and are more in conformity to the dignity of the human person."[99]

If the command "thou shall not kill" applies to even criminal and unjust aggressors how much more to innocent persons and especially the weak and defenseless. The Magisterium of the Church and the "supernatural sense of the faith" consistently upholds the inviolability of innocent human life. The Bishops of the Church has seconded this teaching. "Therefore, by the authority which Christ conferred upon Peter and his Successors, and in communion with the Bishops of the Catholic Church, I confirm that the direct and voluntary killing of an innocent human being is always gravely immoral." This law is based on that found within the human heart.[100] To kill an innocent human being can never be licit as an end or as a means to a good end. No one is permitted to ask to be killed. Nor can a state authority permit it.[101] "As far as the right to life is concerned, every innocent human being is absolutely equal to all others." The demands of morality apply equally to all.[102]

"Your eyes beheld my unformed substance." (Ps. 139:16)—The Unspeakable Crime of Abortion

Abortion is a particularly serious and deplorable crime against life. Vatican Council II referred to abortion and infanticide as an "unspeakable crime."[103] The moral sense of our times has been slowly corrupted so that people cannot distinguish right from wrong even when the fundamental right to life is at stake. We need the courage to call things by their right name and not indulge in self-deception through ambiguous terminology. But abortion remains a deliberate and direct killing of human life. It has all the elements of murder: The child in its mother's womb is innocent, not an unjust aggressor; he or she is weak and defenseless and totally entrusted to its mother.

Sometimes the decision to abort is not based on pure selfishness but made to protect important values, the mother's health, standard of living of the other members of the family. But no reasons can "justify the deliberate killing of an innocent human being."[104]

The father may be to blame as well as the mother in directly pressuring her to abort or indirectly by simply abandoning her. Also the wider circle of family and friends can encourage or condone an abortion. Doctors and nurses also bear responsibility for an abortion. Legislators "who promoted and approved abortion laws" and administrators of health care centers that allow abortions to be performed are also morally culpable. Those who encourage "sexual permissiveness and lack of esteem for motherhood" and those who could have and did not affect social policies in support of families, especially large families and those with special financial and educational needs bear responsibility too. International institutions, foundations and associations that systematically campaign for the legalization of abortion are morally complicit in abortion. "We are facing what can be called a 'structure of sin' which opposes human life not yet born."[105]

Those who would justify abortion on the claim that the pre-natal child cannot be considered "a personal human life" are mistaken both philosophically and scientifically because genetically all that is lacking from the first moment of conception for all its personal capacities to function completely is time. Even if a spiritual soul can't be detected empirically "how could a human individual not be a human person?" Moreover, from the perspective of moral duty "the mere probability that a human person is involved would suffice to justify an absolute clear prohibition of any intervention aimed at killing a human embryo." Therefore, each "human being is to be respected and treated as a person from the moment of conception."[106]

Scripture never addresses the question of procured abortion directly but because the whole of scripture shows such respect for the human being within its mother's womb, it requires as a logical consequence that the command "thou shall not kill" must be extended to the unborn child as well. God knits together the child in its mother's womb and he knows them and loves them as "personal objects of God's loving and fatherly providence" and so their human life is sacred and inviolable from when they are conceived.

Christian tradition has always declared abortion "a particularly grave moral disorder." The early Church radically opposed abortion and infanticide which were rampant in the Greco-Roman world. The Fathers and Doctors of the Church condemned abortion. "Even scientific and philosophical discussions about the precise moment of the infusion of the spiritual soul have never given rise to any hesitation about the moral condemnation of abortion."[107]

The Papal Magisterium has "vigorously reaffirmed the common doctrine" in *Casti Connubi* by Pius XI, as did Pius XII and John XXIII and Vatican Council II. The canonical discipline of the Church imposed penal sanctions on those guilty of abortion. The 1917 Code of Canon Law punished abortion with excommunication as does the 1983 code of Canon Law: "a person who actually procures an abortion incurs automatic excommunication"[108] and includes all those "who commit this crime with knowledge of the penalty attached, and thus, includes those accomplices without whose help the crime would not have been committed." In doing so the Church encourages those guilty of so serious a crime to repentance. Pope Paul VI declared this condemnation of abortion an infallible and unchanging teaching of the Church. Therefore with the authority of the Peter's Successor "I declare that direct abortion, that is, abortion willed as an end or as a means, always constitutes a grave moral disorder, since it is the deliberate killing of an innocent human being. This doctrine is based upon the natural law and upon the written Word of God, is transmitted by the Church's Tradition and taught by the ordinary and universal Magisterium. No circumstance, no purpose, no law whatsoever can ever make licit an act which is intrinsically illicit, since it is contrary to the Law of God which is written in every human heart, knowable by reason itself, and proclaimed by the Church."[109]

The condemnation of abortion also applies to interventions on the human embryo which ends up killing those embryos as is the case with experimentation on embryos for biomedical research. This condemnation does not apply to "licit procedures carried out on the human embryo which respect the life and integrity of the embryo and do not involve disproportionate risks for it, but rather are directed to its healing, the improvement of tits condition of health, or its individual survival." Experimentation on human embryos "produced" by IVF to be used as "biological material or as providers of organs or tissue for transplants in the treatment of certain diseases" is to be condemned: "The killing of innocent human creatures, even if carried out to help others, constitutes an absolutely unacceptable act."[110]

Diagnostic techniques that do not pose disproportionate risks to the child and mother and which make early therapeutic intervention possible or makes serene acceptance of the unborn child possibly are morally licit. But if such techniques are used with eugenic intention and selective abortion in mind they are "shameful and utterly reprehensible" and tend to legitimize infanticide and euthanasia. The courage and dignity of those persons who suffer from serious disabilities bear eloquent witness to the authentic value of life. The Church is close to those married couples who willingly accept gravely handicapped children or who adopt children with disabilities.[111]

"It is I who bring both death and life." (Dt. 32:39)—The Tragedy of Euthanasia

In a culture that values life only when it gives pleasure, suffering seems unbearable, something one must be rid of at all costs. Death seems senseless when it interrupts a life full of promise, but it becomes a "rightful liberation" when life is no longer full of promise and meaningful because it is filled with suffering. Moreover, when man neglects his relationship with God he thinks he has a right to demand of society the right to complete autonomy in deciding his fate. Modern medicine allows those in developed societies to treat illnesses that were once considered incurable and to prolong their lives or bodily functions for organ transplantation. In this context one may be tempted to euthanasia so as to bring about a gentile end to human life. This is the case in societies marked by an attitude of efficiency and concern with the growing number of elderly considered burdensome because they are no longer productive in the work force.[112]

Euthanasia is "an action or omission which of itself and by intention causes death, with the purpose of eliminating all suffering. 'Euthanasia's terms of reference, therefore, are to be found in the intention of the will and in the methods used.'"[113] To forgo extraordinary medical treatment that is "disproportionate to any expected result" or that "impose an excessive burden on the patient and his family" is not euthanasia.

Palliative care attempts to make "suffering more bearable in the final stages of illness" and to support the patient in his ordeal. It is licit to use painkillers that may shorten a patient's life: "While praise may be due to the person who voluntarily accepts suffering by forgoing treatment with painkillers in order to remain fully lucid and, if a believer, to share consciously in the Lord's Passion, such 'heroic' behavior cannot be considered the duty of everyone."[114] The use of painkillers that may shorten one's life is not the same as euthanasia. All the same it is not right to deprive someone of the use of consciousness without a serious reason because people must prepare for death.

In union with the Magisterium of my Predecessors and the bishops of the Catholic Church I confirm that "euthanasia is a grave violation of the law of God, since it is the deliberate and morally unacceptable killing of a human person. . . . Depending on the circumstances, this practice involves the malice proper to suicide or murder."[115]

Suicide is morally as objectionable as murder even if cultural and psychological factors may lessen one's subjective moral culpability. Suicide is a rejection of love of self, and the obligations of justice and charity towards others and God. Only God has the right to number the days of each person's life.[116] It is never licit for one to answer another's request for assisted suicide.

Euthanasia is at best a false perversion of mercy: "True 'compassion' leads to sharing another's pain; it does not kill the person whose suffering we cannot bear." It takes on the aspect of murder when perpetuated on one who has not even requested it. No legislator has the right to take to themselves the power to decide who ought to live and who ought to die.[117]

The request for euthanasia is above all a "request for companionship, sympathy and support in time of trial." The natural aversion to death and "incipient hope of immortality" find fulfillment in Christian faith. "Dying to the Lord"[118] is experiencing one's death as the supreme act of obedience to the Father.[119] "Living to the Lord" is recognizing that suffering, while an objective evil, can be a source of good when experienced for love by God's grace. In this way a person who suffers becomes more conformed to Christ and is more closely associated with his redemptive work as St. Paul said, "in my flesh, I complete what is lacking in Christ's afflictions for the sake of his Body, that is, the Church."[120]

"We must obey God rather than men." (Acts 5:29)—Civil Law and the Moral Law

Today attacks on human life tend to demand a legal justification as if they were rights which the state must acknowledge and provide the safe and free assistance of medical personnel. It is claimed only the person involved in the personal decision has a right to decide abortion or euthanasia and that the civil law cannot demand all citizens live according to the same moral standards so the will of the majority must govern these matters and to criminalize them would only lead to an increase in their illegal practice.[121]

Some assert that in a democratic culture "an objective truth shared by all is de facto unattainable" so the will of the majority is the only way to establish societal norms and every politician must separate the "realm of private conscience from that of public conduct." This is ironic: In the individual sphere people claim absolute freedom of conscience and demand the State not impose any ethical position; but in the public sphere a politician has no right to express freedom of conscience.[122]

Ethical relativism is the basis of these tendencies in contemporary culture. Some see such relativism as the only guarantee of tolerance necessary for democratic culture and view objective moral norms as expressions of authoritarianism and intolerance. True crimes have been committed in the name of "truth" but crimes have been and still are being committed in the name of "ethical relativism." When a democracy or majority decree it is legal to kill innocent and defenseless human life is this not a tyrannical decision?:

> Everyone's conscience rightly rejects those crimes against humanity of which our century has had such sad experience. But would these crimes cease to be crimes if, instead of being committed by unscrupulous tyrants, they were legitimated by popular consensus?
>
> Democracy cannot be idolized to the point of making it a substitute for morality or a panacea for immorality. Fundamentally, democracy is a "system" and as such is a means and not an end. Its "moral" value is not automatic, but depends on conformity to the moral law to which it, like every other form of human behavior, must be subject. . . .
>
> Democracy stands or falls on the values it embodies which must include the innate dignity of the human person and their inalienable human rights and the common good as the end and criteria for regulating political life. The basis of these values is not shifting majority opinion but the "objective moral law which, as the 'natural law' written in the human heart, is the obligatory point of reference for civil law itself." If skepticism brings into question these fundamental principles of the moral law, the foundation of the democratic system would be destroyed and it would be "reduced to a mere mechanism for regulating different and opposing interests on a purely empirical basis." Without objective grounding the democratic system is not capable of ensuring even a stable society because it often occurs the interests of the powerful are capable of "maneuvering not only the levers of power but also of shaping the formation of consensus. In such a situation, democracy easily becomes an empty word."[123]

Therefore we must recover a vision of the relationship between the moral law and civil law, "which are put forward by the Church, but which are also part of the patrimony of the great juridical traditions of humanity." Civil law must guarantee that everyone enjoys certain innate fundamental rights. "First and fundamental among these is the inviolable right to life of every innocent human being. Legalized abortion and euthanasia can not be legitimized in the name of conscience or the pretext of freedom because society has a right to protect itself from abuses of freedom."[124] The common good is best protected when personal rights and duties are guaranteed. Any government that violates authentic human rights fails in its duty and its decrees lack binding force.[125]

The whole tradition of the Church confirms that civil laws must conform to moral law: "human law is law inasmuch as it is in conformity with right reason and thus derives from the eternal law. But when a law is contrary to reason, it is called an unjust law; but in this case it ceases to be a law and becomes instead an act of violence."[126] Hence laws that legalize abortion and euthanasia deny the equality of everyone before the law, opposed to the good of individuals and the common good and "completely lacking in authentic juridical validity" and cease to be morally binding.[127]

There is no obligation to obey laws legitimizing abortion and euthanasia but, rather, "a clear obligation to oppose them by conscientious objection." The Church has always pointed out Christians have an obligation to generally obey civil law[128] but oppose it when it conflicts with God's law.[129] Hebrew midwives refused to obey the civil law of Pharaoh ordering the murder of all male children born to the Hebrews because they feared God.[130] Fear of God gives strength to resist unjust human laws even to death. This makes possible "the endurance and faith of the saints."[131] So it is never licit to take part in a propaganda campaign in favor of laws legitimizing abortion or euthanasia or to vote for it:

> [W]hen it is not possible to overturn or completely abrogate a pro-abortion law, an elected official, whose absolute personal opposition to procured abortion was well known, could licitly support proposals aimed at limiting the harm done by such a law and at lessening its negative consequences at the level of general opinion and public morality. This does not in fact represent an illicit cooperation with an unjust law, but rather a legitimate and proper attempt to limit its evil aspects.[132]

Sometimes the choice not to cooperate in morally evil actions provided for by unjust laws may require the sacrifice of professional positions or hopes of career advancement. But other times material cooperation with unjust laws may be justified when the actions provided for under unjust legislation are "in themselves indifferent or even positive" and serve to protect human lives under threat. However such material cooperation may not only cause scandal and weaken opposition to attacks on life but lead to "further capitulation to a mentality of permissiveness."

Christians and all persons of good will have a moral obligation not to formally cooperate in evil practices permitted by civil law: "Such cooperation occurs when an action, either by its very nature or by the form it takes in a concrete situation, can be defined as a direct participation in an act against innocent human life or a sharing in the immoral intention of the person committing it."[133] To refuse to take part in injustice is not only a moral duty but a basic human right. So, "the opportunity to refuse to take part in the phases of consultation, preparation and execution of these acts against life should be guaranteed to physicians, health-care personnel, and directors of hospitals, clinics and convalescent facilities. Those who have recourse to conscientious objection must be protected not only from legal penalties but also from any negative effects on the legal , disciplinary, financial and professional plane."[134]

"You shall love your neighbor as yourself" (Lk. 10:27)—"Promote" Life

The negative moral precepts are "valid always and everywhere, without exception"[135] and cannot be redeemed by the goodness of one's motive or any consequences "they are irrevocably opposed to the bond between persons; they contradict the fundamental decision to direct one's life to God."[136] They are a floor beneath which we may not descend. The negative moral precepts of the Commandments are the first necessary stage of the journey towards freedom. St Augustine said, "the beginning of freedom is to be free from crimes . . . like murder, adultery, fornication, theft, fraud, sacrilege and so forth. Only when one stops committing these crimes . . . one begins to lift up one's head towards freedom. But this is only the beginning of freedom, not perfect freedom."[137]

The command to not kill is the departure point of human freedom. But the law of reciprocity reaches it height with the gift of the Spirit of Christ which gives new content to this law of our being entrusted to one another. The Spirit builds up between us a new solidarity, a true reflection of the mystery of mutual self-giving proper to the Holy Trinity, a sharing in the boundless of love of Christ.[138]

The Spirit gives a new shape to the command not to kill. Now we must lay down our lives for the brethren.[139] The positive aspects of the command not to kill are binding on everyone. We are all obligated to respect, love, and promote human life. This is known in the conscience of everyone. Our commitment to serve our neighbor must extend to "make unconditional respect for human life the foundation of a renewed society" and "the establishment of a new culture of life, the fruit of the culture of truth and of love."[140]

Chapter IV: "You did it to Me"—For a New Culture of Human Life
"You are God's own people, that you may declare the wonderful deeds of him
who called you out of darkness into his own marvelous life." (1 Pet. 2:9)—A
People of Life and for Life.

The Church exists to evangelize.[141] This is also the case with the Gospel of life which is integral to Gospel of Christ. "With humility and gratitude we know that we are the people of life and for life."[142]

Being at the service of life is a duty sustained by the law of love founded on Jesus Christ. It is an ecclesial responsibility but it does not lessen the individual commitment and serve it with various programs and structures which promote life.[143]

"That which we have seen and heard we proclaim also to you." (1 John 1:3)—
Proclaiming the Gospel of Life

"To proclaim Jesus is itself to proclaim life" because he is "the Word of life."[144] The Gospel of life is one with Jesus and "makes all things new and conquers the 'oldness' which comes from sin and leads to death." The joy of being one with Christ makes it impossible to not share the Gospel of life with everyone and make it penetrate all of society.[145]

The "core" of the Gospel of life is proclaiming "a living god who is close to us, who calls us to profound communion with himself and awakens in us the certain hope of eternal life. It is the affirmation of the inseparable connection between the person, his life and his bodiliness. It is the presentation of human life as life of relationship, a gift of God, the fruit and sign of his love. It is proclamation that Jesus has a unique relationship with every person, which enables us to see in every human face the face of Christ. It is the call fro a 'sincere gift of self' as the fullest way to realize our personal freedom." We must also make clear the consequences of the core of the Gospel of life: One, human life is sacred and inviolable. Therefore abortion and euthanasia are absolutely unacceptable. Two, human life must be protected with loving concern. Three, the meaning of life is found in giving and receiving love which gives human sexuality and suffering its full significance. Four, society must respect the dignity of every person at each moment of their lives.[146]

We must proclaim these truths of the Gospel of life in catecheses and preaching, in personal dialogue and in all education activity. Teachers have the task of emphasizing the anthropological reasons underlying respect for every human life. Our commitment to a culture of life will establish new points of contact and dialogue with nonbelievers. This duty to preach the Gospel of life is visited first upon bishops. "We need to make sure that in theological faculties, seminaries and Catholic institutions sound doctrine is taught, explained and more fully investigated. May theologians, pastors and teachers "never be so grievously irresponsible as to betray the truth and their own mission by proposing personal ideas contrary to the Gospel of life as faithfully presented and interpreted by the Magisterium." We must not conform to the world's way of thinking.[147]

*"I give you thanks that I am fearfully, wonderfully made." (Ps. 139:14)—
Celebrating the Gospel of Life*

A "people for life" must let the world see through many expressions that we celebrate the Gospel of life. For this to happen we need to foster a contemplative outlook and see each person as a "wonder," a "gift" created by God. This attitude does not despair when confronted by sickness or death but it looks for meaning in these circumstances.[148]

We must celebrate the God of life who gives both earthly life and Eternal life. Human life "is one of the greatest marvels of creation: for God has granted to man a dignity which is near to divine."[149] We are called to celebrate the Gospel of life above all in the sacraments and liturgy.[150]

We need to avail of the gestures and symbols from various traditions and cultures to celebrate the Gospel of life at the key moments of human life—birth, suffering or need, mourning and yearning for immortality. So, I propose a Day for Life be celebrated each year in every country to better form and foster in individual consciences, families and civil society the value of human life at every stage and condition. "Particular attention should be drawn to the seriousness of abortion and euthanasia, without neglecting other aspects of life which from time to time deserve to be given careful consideration."[151]

The Gospel of life is to be celebrated most of all in daily living by acts of self-giving. Heroic actions are the most solemn celebration of the Gospel of life because they proclaim a total gift of self and a sharing in the cross of Christ. The everyday heroism of big and small gestures of self-giving build up an authentic culture of life. "A particular praiseworthy example of such gestures is the donation of organs, performed in an ethically acceptable manner." Part of the daily heroism concerns the witness of brave mothers who not only pass on new life to their children but "who are ready to make any effort, to face any sacrifice, in order to pass on to them the best of themselves." These heroic women often do not find cultural support:

> On the contrary, the cultural models frequently promoted and broadcast by the media do not encourage motherhood. . . . We thank you, heroic mothers, for your invincible love! We thank you for your intrepid trust in God and in his love. We thank you for the sacrifice of your life.[152]

"What does it profit, my brethren, if a man says he has faith but has not works?" (Jas.2:14)—Serving the Gospel of Life

The royal mission of Christ impels us to works of charity on behalf of the Gospel of life, that is, through personal witness, volunteer work, and political commitment. This is very important now when the culture of death seems to have the upper hand. But for our activity to not be "dead" but living works, it must be animated by divine charity.[153] We must care for the other as for one whom God has made us responsible. We must be a neighbor to everyone and especially care for the poor and those most in need.[154] We must not harbor bias or discriminate between those we serve on behalf of the Gospel of life. New pastoral programs in support of life must be implemented offering special help to mothers so that they can bring their children into the world and for those who are dying.[155]

We need a "patient and fearless work of education" that will encourage vocations of service especially among the young as well as long-term projects inspired by the Gospel. We need to have centers for natural methods of regulating fertility, marriage and family counseling agencies and newborn assistance centers where unmarried mothers and couples in difficulty may discover hope and assistance to welcome newly conceived life into the world. Also we need centers for drug addiction, homes for abandoned minors, and the mentally ill, centers for HIV/AIDS victims and associations of solidarity with persons with disabilities. The elderly need care and especially the terminally ill and their families may require palliative care. Hospitals, clinics and convalescent homes must provide more than medical assistance but also provide an atmosphere where suffering, pain and death are understood with regard to their Christian meaning especially when they are associated with the Church.[156]

These centers need to be directed by people who are dedicated and generous in the service of the Gospel of life. Doctors, nurses, pharmacists bear a unique responsibility as their profession calls them to be guardians and servants of human life. The health care profession has an intrinsic and undeniable ethical dimension as recognized in the ancient and still relevant Hippocratic Oath. Medical personnel must exercise conscientious objection when asked to cooperate with abortion or euthanasia. Bio-medical research must always reject experimentation, which disregards the inviolable dignity of every human being.[157]

Volunteer workers who combine professional skills and generous service make a valuable contribution to serve the Gospel of life. A realistic implementation of the Gospel of life requires that it be implemented in forms of social activity and politics. Individuals, families, groups and associations all must be involved in developing cultural, economic, political and legislative projects that build up the dignity of all persons. Civil leaders are called to serve the common good. In democracies where decisions are based on consensus the sense of personal responsibility in civic leaders may be lessened. But they may not relinquish their moral responsibility and act contrary to the common good. "Although laws are not the only means of protecting human life, nevertheless they do play a very important and sometimes decisive role in influencing patterns of thought and behavior." Legislators must not pass laws contrary to the natural law. Political leaders must make choices that are realistically attainable that will lead to the reestablishment of a just social order that promotes the value of human life. More than merely removing unjust laws we must ensure proper support for the family and motherhood. "A family policy must be the basis and driving force of all social policies. Social policies must be enacted that "guarantee conditions of true freedom of choice in matters of parenthood." Labor policies must be redesigned to harmonize work so that time will be available to spend with family and care of children and the elderly.[158]

The issue of population growth prompts public authorities to "intervene to orient the demography of the population."[159] But such intervention must respect married couples and cannot employ methods which fail to respect the right to life of innocent human beings. It is immoral to encourage or impose contraception, sterilization and abortion in order to regulate births. "Government and the various international agencies must above all strive to create economic, social, public health and cultural conditions which will enable married couples to make their choices about procreation in full freedom and with genuine responsibility." They must ensure a fairer distribution of wealth so everyone can share equitably in the goods of creation. Global solutions must be sought to establish a "true economy of communion and sharing of goods."

We should seek to serve the Gospel of life in cooperation with members of other Churches an effort in practical ecumenism. It may be a providential area for dialogue with members of other religions. No one has a monopoly on the defense and promotion of life. Only the efforts of all those who believe in the value of life can prevent "a setback of unforeseeable consequences for civilization."[160]

"Your children will be like olive shoots around your table." (Ps. 128:3)—The Family as the "sanctuary of life"

The family has a decisive role to play as the natural community of life and love, founded upon marriage, and from its mission to "guard, reveal and communicate love" to spreading the Gospel of life. Within the family each member experiences a share of God's own love where each are accepted and respected just because he or she is a person.

As the sanctuary of life the family is the place where life can be properly welcomed and protected from attacks. As the domestic church it is call to proclaim, celebrate and serve the Gospel of life. In raising children the family fulfills its mission to proclaim the Gospel of life. Parents lead their children to "authentic freedom, actualized in the sincere gift of self, and they cultivate in them respect for others." Christian parents must be concerned about their children's vocation and give them an example of the true meaning of suffering and death which they can do if they are sensitive to those who suffer around them.[161]

The family celebrates the Gospel of life through daily prayer in good times and times of difficulty. But that which gives effect to every family prayer is found in "the family's actual daily life together if it is a life of love and self-giving."[162] Solidarity is an expression of the Gospel of life and families do so well in the ordinary events of every day and in a willingness to adopt or take in children abandoned or in situations of serious hardships. Adoption-at-a-distance should be given special consideration for children in poverty when the gift of monetary support allows children to remain with their parents. Working in solidarity with other families various associations of families must influence politics so that laws are passed protecting human life from conception to natural death.[163]

The elderly must not be left alone and regarded as a useless burden. "Their presence in the family, or at least their closeness to the family . . . is of fundamental importance in creating a climate of mutual interaction and enriching communications between the different age-groups." We must rediscover a "covenant" between generations where it has been lost. This way parents receive in return what they first gave to their children when they brought them into the world—acceptance and solidarity. The Fourth Commandment requires this. What is more, the elderly have a positive contribution to make to the Gospel of life as "sources of wisdom and witnesses of hope and love." To fulfill its task as the sanctuary of life the family needs support, including economic help, from the state.[164]

"Walk as children of light" (Eph. 5:8): Bring about a Transformation of Culture

Today we need to develop a "deep critical sense" to discern true values and authentic needs. A "general mobilization of consciences" is need to unite ethical efforts in support of a campaign in support of life and together build a "new" culture of life: new in the sense that it must confront and solve "unprecedented problems affecting human life", new because it will unite Christians with deeper convictions, and because it will foster a serious cultural dialogue. The renewal of the culture of life must begin in Christian communities so they resist the temptation to separate their "Christian faith from its ethical requirements."[165]

For a cultural transformation to occur a formation of conscience must take place reestablishing the "connection between life and freedom. These are inseparable goods: where one is violated, the other also ends up being violated. . . . Love is a sincere gift of self; it is what gives the life and freedom of the person their truest meaning." Also the connection between freedom and truth needs to be reestablished because "when freedom is detached from objective truth it becomes impossible to establish personal rights on a firm rational basis and the ground is laid for society to be at the mercy of the unrestrained will of individuals or the oppressive totalitarianism of public authority." Man must admit he is a creature given existence by God:

> Only by admitting his innate dependence can man live and use his freedom to the full, and at the same time respect the life and freedom of every other person. Here especially one sees that "at the heart of every culture lies the attitude man takes to the greatest mystery: the mystery of God" (Pope John Paul II *Centesimus Annus* (1991), no.17). Where God is denied and people live as though he did not exist, or his commandments are not taken into account, the dignity of the human person and the inviolability of human life also end up being rejected or compromised.[166]

Education is also closely connected with the formation of conscience. There is need for education on the value of human life from its origin. We must help the young to experience sexuality and love as a manifestation of a gift of self in love. The trivialization of human sexuality is a principal reason for holding human life in contempt today. The young must be educated in chastity as "a virtue which fosters *personal* maturity and makes one capable of respecting the 'spousal' meaning of the body."

The work of education in the service of life also includes training married couples in responsible procreation and obedience to God's call and faithful interpreter of his plan by being generously open to new life. Of course each married couple may choose to avoid a new birth "for a time or indefinitely" for "serious reasons" if, in doing so they "respect the moral law" which requires that they "control the impulse of instinct and passion" and also "respect the biological laws inscribed in their person" through the "use of natural methods of regulating fertility." The Church is grateful to those who researched and developed to a precise science these methods at the service of responsible procreation.

The work of education also encompasses suffering and death which have meaning when considered in connection with the love given and received. Suffering is salvific when offered up in union with Christ. Even death expresses hope—"it is a door which opens wide on eternity and, for those who live in Christ, an experience of participation in the mystery of his death and resurrection."[167]

The cultural transformation we are calling for requires courage to adopt a new life-style based on "a correct scale of values: the primacy of being over having, of the person over things." Other people are brothers and sisters, not rivals. Everyone has a role to play, the family, educators, intellectuals, and those involved with the mass media. Intellectuals "ought to place themselves at the service of a new culture of life by offering serious and well documented contributions, capable of commanding general respect and interest by reason of their merit." Mass media professionals need to "present noble models of life and make room for instances of people's positive and sometimes heroic live for others."[168]

Women occupy a key role in the transformation of culture. They are called to develop a "new feminism" one not tempted to imitate models of "male domination" but, rather, seeks to express the genius of women to "reconcile people with life." Motherhood makes women acutely aware of the other person. "This unique contact with the new human being developing within her gives rise to an attitude towards human beings not only towards her own child, but every human being, which profoundly marks the woman's personality."[169] Women understand the worth of a person rests in who they are, not their "usefulness, strength, intelligence, beauty or health." Authentic cultural change cannot occur without these expressions of the genius of women.

Regarding abortion I have this "special word":

The church is aware of the many factors which may have influenced your decision, and she does not doubt that in many cases it was a painful and even shat-
tering decision. The wound in your heart may not yet have healed. Certainly
what happened was and remains terribly wrong. But do not give in to
discouragement and do not lose hope. Try rather to understand what happened
and face it honestly. If you have not already done so, give yourselves over with
humility and trust to repentance. The father of mercies is ready to give you his
forgiveness and his peace in the Sacrament of reconciliation. You will come to
understand that nothing is definitively lost and you will also be able to ask forgiveness from your child, who is now living in the Lord.[170]

There is a tremendous disparity between the material resources of those
promoting the culture of death and those who seek to advance the culture of life
but with God's help, nothing is impossible.[171] Therefore we must pray to God—
"a great prayer for life is urgently needed, a prayer which will rise up throughout
the world."

Let us pray and fast that "power from on high" will break down the walls of
lies and deceit: the walls which conceal from the sight of so many of our brothers and sisters the evil of practices and laws which are hostile to life. May this
same power turn their hearts to resolutions and goals inspired by the civilization of life and love.[172]

*"We are writing this that our joy may be complete" (1 Jn. 1:4)—The Gospel of
Life is for the Whole of Human Society*

The Gospel of life is for believers and everyone alike: "The issue of life and its
defense and promotion is not a concern of Christians alone. . . . Life certainly
has a sacred and religious value, but in no way is that value a concern only of
believers. The value at stake is one which every human being can grasp by the
light of reason; thus it necessarily concerns everyone." The Church simply
wants to promote a "human state" when she proclaims the Gospel of life. There
can be no true democracy or peace without respect for human life: "'Every
crime against life is an attack on peace, especially if it strikes at the moral conduct of people. . . . But where human rights are truly professed and publically
recognized and defended, peace becomes the joyful and operative climate of life
in society.'"[173]

Conclusion

The mystery of the birth of Jesus Christ, "the Life,"[174] throws light on every
human life. The one who accepted "Life" for us all was Mary who is thus "most
closely and personally associated with the Gospel of life." Mary, like the Church
is "a mother of all who are reborn to life." She is the "incomparable model of
how life should be welcomed and cared for."[175]

"A great sign appeared in heaven, a woman clothed with the sun" (Rev. 12:1)—
The Motherhood of Mary and of the Church

The sign of a woman clothed with the sun describes both Mary and the Church. Both are "with child." Both carry the Savior of the world "giving men and women new birth into God's own life." In Mary, Theotokos, God Bearer, the vocation to motherhood bestowed on every woman is raised to its highest level. The Church knows that its motherhood is only achieved through labor with the evil forces that still roam the world. Like the Church Mary lived her life amid suffering: "The yes spoken on the day of the Annunciation reaches full maturity on the day of the Cross, when the time comes for Mary to receive and beget as her children all those who become disciples, pouring out on them the saving love of her Son."[176]

"And the dragon stood before the woman . . . that he might devour her child
when she brought it forth: (Rev. 12:4)—Life Menaced by the Forces of Evil

The dragon "represents Satan, the personal power of evil, as well as all the powers of evil at work in history and opposing the Church's mission." Mary and Joseph's flight into Egypt with the child Jesus helps the Church realize it is at the center of a great struggle between good and evil. The child in the Great Sing is also every person whose life is threatened. The rejection of human life, in whatever form, is a rejection of Christ.[177]

"Death shall be no more" (Rev. 21:4)—The Splendor of the Resurrection

The Angel of the Annunciation said to Mary "Do not be afraid" because "with God nothing will be impossible."[178] The Lamb who was slain lives in the splendor of resurrection and proclaims the power of life over death in the new Jerusalem where "death shall be no more, neither shall there be mourning nor crying nor pain any more, for the former things have passed away."[179] We, the pilgrim people of life look to Mary as a sign of sure hope—"O Mary, bright dawn of the new world, Mother of the living, to you do we entrust the cause of life."[180]

Notes

1. EV, no. 1.
2. Rom. 2:14–15.
3. EV, no. 2.
4. GS, no. 27; EV, no. 3.
5. EV, no. 4.
6. EV, no. 4.
7. EV, no. 5.

8. EV, no. 6.
9. EV, no. 6.
10. John 8:44.
11. EV, no. 8.
12. EV, no. 9.
13. EV, no. 10
14. EV, no. 11.
15. EV, no. 12
16. EV, no. 13.
17. EV, no. 14.
18. EV, no. 14.
19. EV, no. 15.
20. EV, no. 16.
21. EV, no. 17.
22. EV, no. 17.
23. EV, no. 18.
24. EV, no. 19.
25. EV, no. 19.
26. EV, no. 20.
27. EV, no. 20.
28. EV, no. 21.
29. Ps. 51:6.
30. EV, no. 22.
31. Rom. 1:28.
32. EV, no. 23.
33. EV, no. 23.
34. Rom. 1:22.
35. Rom. 1:32.
36. EV, no. 24.
37. 1 Cor. 15:54-55; EV, no. 25.
38. GS, no. 50.
39. EV, no. 26.
40. EV, no. 27.
41. Deut. 30:15, 19.
42. EV, no. 28.
43. EV, no. 29.
44. EV, no. 30.
45. EV, no. 31.
46. Matt. 6:25–34.
47. Luke 12:20; EV, no. 32.
48. Phil. 2:6–7.
49. John 12:32.
50. EV, no. 33.
51. Gen. 1:26.
52. EV, no. 34.
53. EV, no. 35.
54. Rom. 1:25.

55. EV, no. 36.
56. EV, no. 37.
57. EV, no. 38.
58. Gen. 9:5.
59. EV, no. 39.
60. Exod. 21: 12–27.
61. Lev. 19:18; EV, no. 40.
62. Matt. 19:18.
63. Matt. 5:21–22.
64. Matt. 5:44–45.
65. Rom. 13:9–10; EV, no. 41.
66. Gen. 1:28.
67. EV, no. 41 citing CA, no. 28
68. Gen. 2:16–17.
69. EV, no. 42.
70. EV, no. 43.
71. Ps. 127:3.
72. EV, no. 44.
73. EV, no. 45.
74. 2 Mac. 6:32.
75. Sir. 41:3–4.
76. Ps. 116:10; EV, no. 46.
77. Matt. 10:7–8.
78. Matt. 8:35.
79. EV, no. 47.
80. Deut. 30:15–16.
81. EV, no. 48.
82. Ezek. 36:25–26.
83. Matt. 7:12; EV, no. 49.
84. Luke 23:44.
85. Mark 15:39.
86. EV, no. 50.
87 John 19:30
88. EV, no. 51.
89. Matt. 19:6.
90. EV, no. 52
91. DV no. 5.
92. EV, no. 53.
93. EV, no. 54.
94. Matt. 5:38–40.
95. CCC, no. 2265.
96. EV, no. 55.
97. CCC, no. 2265.
98. EV, no 56.
99. CCC, no. 2267; EV, no. 56.
100. Rom. 2:14–15.
101. *Declaration on Euthanasia*, no. 72.

102. EV, no. 57.
103. GS, no. 51.
104. EV, no. 58.
105. EV, no. 59.
106. EV, no. 60.
107. EV, no. 61.
108. CIC, canon1450 sec. 2.
109. EV, no. 62.
110. EV, no. 63.
111. EV, no. 63.
112. EV, no. 64.
113. *Declaration on Euthanasia*, no. 72.
114. EV, no. 65.
115. EV, no. 65.
116. Wisd. 16:13.
117. EV, no. 66.
118. Rom. 14:7–8.
119. Phil. 2:8.
120. Cor. 1:24; EV, no. 67.
121. EV, no. 68.
122. EV, no. 69.
123. EV, no. 70.
124. *Declaration on Religious Freedom*, no. 7.
125. EV, no. 71 citing Pope John XXIII, *Pacem in Terris*, no. 55.
126. Aquinas, *Summa Theologiae*, I-II, q. 93, a. 3, ad 2.
127. EV, no. 72.
128. Rom. 13:1–7; 1 Pet. 2:13–14.
129. Acts 5:29.
130. Exod. 1:17.
131. Rev. 13:10.
132. EV, no. 73.
133. Rom. 2:6; 14:12.
134. EV, no. 74.
135. EV, no. 75.
136. CCC, 1753–1755, VS, no. 81–82.
137. EV, no. 75.
138. EV, no. 76.
139. 1 John 3:16.
140. EV, no. 77.
141. 1 Cor. 9:16.
142. EV, no. 78.
143. EV, no. 79.
144. 1 John 1:1.
145. EV, no. 80.
146. EV, no. 81.
147. EV, no. 82.
148. EV, no. 83.

149. Ps. 8:5–6.
150. EV, no. 84.
151. EV, no. 85.
152. EV, no. 86.
153. Jas. 2:14–17.
154. Luke 10:29–37.
155. EV, no. 87.
156. EV, no. 88.
157. EV, no. 89.
158. EV, no. 90.
159. CCC, no. 2372.
160. EV, no. 91.
161. EV, no. 92.
162. EV, no. 93.
163. EV, no. 93.
164. EV, no. 94.
165. EV, no. 95.
166. EV, no. 96.
167. EV, no. 97.
168. EV, no. 98.
169. Pope John Paul II, *Mulieris Dignitatem* (1988) no. 18, http://www.vatican.va/holy_father/john_paul_ii/apost_letters/documents/hf_jpii_apl_150 81988_mulieris-dignitatem_en.html (accessed 29 Aug. 2009).
170. EV, no. 99.
171. Matt. 19:26.
172. EV, no. 100.
173. EV, no. 101 citing Pope Paul VI, *Message for the 1977 World Day of Peace*: AAS 68 1976, 711-712.
174. 1 John 1:2.
175. EV, no. 102.
176. EV, no. 103.
177. Matt. 25:40; EV, no. 104.
178. Luke 1:30, 37.
179. Rev. 21:4.
180. EV, no. 105.

Appendix B
On the Christian Meaning of Human Suffering: *Salvifici Doloris* (1984)

I. Introduction

1. St. Paul declares the power of salvific suffering: "In my flesh I complete what is lacking in Christ's afflictions for the sake of his body, that is, the Church."[1] These words mark the end of man's long search for the meaning of human suffering; a final discovery, valid for everyone.

2. The salvific meaning of human suffering demands to be constantly reconsidered. Man, even though he knows and is close to the sufferings of the animal world, when he uses the word "suffering" expresses what "seems to be particularly essential to the nature of man" and "seems to belong to man's transcendence." In a mysterious way, he is "in a certain sense 'destined' to go beyond himself."

3. In a special way "every man becomes the way for the Church" when suffering enters his life.[2] It is on the path of suffering that the Church has to try to meet man in this special way.

4. Human suffering evokes compassion, respect, and it intimidates because it contains the "greatness of a specific mystery." Respect for suffering touches the deepest need of the heart and the deep imperative of faith, which become one: "the need of the heart commands us to overcome fear," the imperative of faith provides the meaning by which we dare to touch what remains in each person who suffers an intangible mystery.

II. The World of Human Suffering

5. Even though subjectively human suffering "seems inexpressible and not transferable," it must be dealt with in its objective reality as an explicit problem with questions asked and answered. Medicine discovers the best known area of

human suffering, one counterbalanced by therapy. But human suffering is wider, more varied and complex than this, more deeply rooted in humanity itself. The distinction between physical and moral suffering deals with this complexity in human suffering based on "the double dimension of the human being," that is man's bodily and spiritual elements "as the direct subject of suffering." The word "pain" expresses physical suffering when the body is hurting, whereas moral suffering is uniquely a "pain of the soul" or "pain of a spiritual nature." This spiritual suffering is not merely the psychological dimension which also accompanies both moral and physical suffering.

6. Scripture is a great book about human suffering, such as that experienced in facing death, the death of one's children, infertility, exile, persecution, the hostility of nature, the mockery of one who suffers, loneliness and abandonment, remorse of conscience, failing to understand why the wicked prosper and the just suffer, disloyalty and ingratitude, and the misfortunes of one's nation. In treating the human person as a whole, the Old Testament often links moral suffering with specific parts of the body, such as bones, or viscera, or the heart. None would deny that moral sufferings have a certain somatic element.

7. Human persons suffer whenever they experience any kind of evil. The Old Testament identifies suffering and evil with each other. There was no specific Hebrew word to indicate suffering—"it defined as 'evil' everything that was suffering." On the other hand, the Greek language allowed "suffering to be no longer directly identified with (objective) evil, but expresses a situation in which man experiences evil and in doing so becomes the subject of suffering."

Suffering has a passive character and a specific psychological activity of pain, sadness, disappointment, discouragement and despair and an experience of evil that causes the person to suffer.

Thus suffering prompts questions about the nature of evil. Certain cultural and religious traditions hold human existence is itself an evil from which man needs to be liberated. On the contrary, Christianity proclaims that creation and its Creator are good. Evil "is a certain lack, limitation, or distortion of good. We could say that man suffers because of a good in which he does not share, from which in a certain sense he is cut off, or of which he has deprived himself." He suffers when he "ought" to share in a good but does not. Christianity explains that man suffers through evil which always refers to a good.

8. Human suffering constitutes a specific "world" which appears in man. Sometimes it passes, and other times it does not, but consolidates and becomes rooted in him. Everyone who suffers is a part of the world of suffering, "but at the same time 'that world' is present in him as a finite and unrepeatable entity." It also has its own solidarity:

> People who suffer become similar to one another through the analogy of their situation, the trial of their destiny, or through their need for understanding and care, and perhaps above all through the persistent question of the meaning of suffering.[3]

The world of suffering becomes particularly concentrated at particular points in history, in cases of natural disaster, epidemics, social upheavals and catastrophes. World War II, for example, brought a "much greater harvest of death and a much heavier burden of human suffering." Our contemporary world, with the threat of nuclear war and the self-destruction of humanity, has transformed our "world," more than any other moment of time, into a special world never before so at danger because of man's offenses.

III. The Quest for an Answer to the Question of the Meaning of Suffering

9. Within each form of suffering endured by man, and simultaneously at the basis of the whole world of suffering, the inevitable question of *why does man suffer?* arises. Distinct from the physical pain suffered by animals, only the suffering human being *knows* that he is suffering and questions the cause, the reason, and the purpose of his suffering. A person suffers more acutely when he fails to find a satisfactory answer to why he is suffering.

The human person questions the existence of evil in a way similar to his confrontation with human suffering. Man often comes to see the existence of God through the world; however, evil and suffering often obscure this image, especially undeserved suffering. Often, in wrestling with these difficult questions, man denies God. Properly addressing the *meaning of suffering* is thus pivotal.

10. The Book of Job exemplifies how man struggles with suffering in his own life and how God guides man to a better understanding of the purpose of suffering. Job particularly embodies the struggle with suffering because Job is a just man and through no fault of his own encounters innumerable sufferings. He struggles with whether he is suffering as punishment for his past actions. Many attempt to convince themselves of the moral justice of the evil, or even to justify the moral meaning of suffering. They see suffering as having meaning only as a punishment for sin—as God's justice who repays good with good and evil with evil.

The God of Revelation in the Old Testament is the Lawgiver and Judge who gave man existence and made the good of creation. When man violates this good, he not only transgresses the law, and sins, but also offends his Creator. Punishment for sin guarantees the moral order according to the will of the Creator, who justly rewards good and punishes evil. "For thou art just in all that thou hast done to us, and all thy works are true and thy ways right and all thy judgments are truth."[4]

11. Job challenges the validity of the principle that identifies suffering solely as a punishment for sin because he knows of his own fidelity to God. In the end, God himself reproves Job's friends for their accusations and recognizes that Job is not guilty. Job's suffering as an innocent man must be accepted as a *mystery*. While the Book of Job does not deny that suffering can have a meaning as punishment in connection to a fault, the Book of Job firmly points out that not all suffering is a consequence of a fault nor has the nature of a punishment.

The Book of Job presents a paradigm of God allowing Job to be tested as a result of Satan's provocation. For Satan challenged before the Lord the righteousness of Job: "Does Job fear God for naught? . . . Thou hast blessed the work of his hands, and his possessions have increased in the land. But put forth thy hand now, and touch all that he has, and he will curse thee to thy face."[5] In other words, the Lord consents to *test* Job with suffering to prove Job's righteousness and faithfulness to God.

The Book of Job broadens man's understanding of suffering and also foretells the Passion of Christ. Nevertheless, this Old Testament book in and of itself reaffirms that the meaning of suffering is not solely linked to the moral order, based on justice alone, but has a transcendent value.

12. The Old Testament reveals that suffering has a meaning that surpasses merely a punishment for sin, although it still recognizes as beneficial the value of suffering as punishment. Thus in the sufferings inflicted by God upon the Chosen People there is included an invitation of his mercy, which corrects in order to lead to conversion: "these punishments were designed not to destroy but to discipline our people."[6]

Thus, the personal dimension of punishment is affirmed in that punishment does not merely repay objective evil, but primarily creates the possibility of deepening goodness in the person who suffers. This important truth regarding suffering is profoundly rooted in the entire Revelation of the Old, and above all the New, Covenants. Suffering must serve for conversion, that is, for the rebuilding of goodness in the person as he repents and asks for mercy. Penance assists man overcome evil, as well as strengthen goodness both in man himself and in his relationships with others and God.

13. To adequately comprehend the true answer to "why" man suffers, he must look to the revelation of Divine Love, the ultimate source of meaning that belongs to all creation. Divine love provides the fullest answer to the question of suffering because God gave man the perfect embodiment of human suffering with perfect love through the Cross of Jesus Christ. Man therefore must above all accept the light of Revelation not only as it expresses justice, but also as it illuminates Love as the source of everything that exists.

IV. Jesus Christ, Suffering Conquered by Love

14. "For God so loved the world that he gave his only Son, that whoever believes in him should not perish but have eternal life."[7] These words, spoken by Christ in his conversation with Nicodemus, reveal the very heart of God's salvific work and express the very essence of the theology of salvation.

Salvation means liberation from evil, and thus it is closely connected to the problem of suffering. According to the words spoken to Nicodemus, God gave his Son to "the world" to free man from evil, which bears within itself the definitive and absolute perspective on suffering. Additionally, the very word *"gives"* (*"gave"*) indicates that this liberation must be achieved by the only-begotten Son through his own suffering. In Christ's act of self-sacrifice on the cross, perfect love was manifested as God liberated man from eternal suffering by allowing his only son to suffer.

In this idea of salvific love, a new dimension of suffering emerges from the idea of suffering within the limit of justice previously explored. This new dimension relates to Redemption, to which the Old Testament seems to refer: "For I know that my Redeemer lives, and at last. . . . I shall see God."[8] The words taken from Jesus' conversation with Nicodemus refer to *suffering in its fundamental and definitive meaning* and surpass an understanding of suffering in its multiple temporal dimensions.

God gives his only-begotten Son so that man "should not perish" and be condemned to eternal suffering. Man "perishes" when he loses "eternal life." The opposite of salvation is not, therefore, only temporal suffering, but definitive suffering: rejection by God in eternal damnation. Christ's mission thus consists in conquering sin and death at its very transcendental root and he conquers sin by his suffering unto death, and overcomes death by his Resurrection.

15. Although Christ struck evil at its very root and conquered definitive, eschatological suffering, evil still remains bound to sin and death. Thus, while man cannot view his suffering solely as a pure consequence of concrete sins, suffering cannot be divorced from the sin of Adam and Eve. In other words, at the basis of all human suffering is a complex involvement with sin.

The same truth applies to death. Although death is often awaited even as liberation from the suffering of this life and can be seen as beyond all forms of suffering, the evil which the human being experiences in death has a definitive and total character. Only through the salvific work of Christ is man liberated from sin and death. Christ blots out from human history the "dominion of sin" and gives man the possibility of living in Sanctifying Grace. In the wake of his victory over sin, he also takes away the dominion of death by his Resurrection.

As a result of Christ's salvific work, therefore, man exists on earth with the hope of eternal life and holiness. Even though Christ's victory over sin and death does not abolish temporal suffering from human life, it nevertheless gives temporal suffering a new purpose in light of man's journey toward salvation. This truth radically changes the picture of man's history and his earthly situation: in spite of the sin that took root, God the Father in his everlasting love for man sent His only son to demolish the very root of human evil, while taking part in man's suffering in a salvific way.

16. Throughout history, Christ has drawn increasingly closer to the world of human suffering. At the very heart of his teaching there are the eight beatitudes, which are addressed to people tried by various sufferings in their temporal life. These include "the poor in spirit" and "the afflicted" and "those who hunger and thirst for justice" and those who are "persecuted for justice's sake."[9]

Christ drew close above all to the world of human suffering through his having taken this suffering upon his very self. During his public activity, he experienced not only fatigue, homelessness, misunderstanding even on the part of those closest to him, but, more than anything, he became progressively more and more isolated and encircled by hostility and the preparations for putting him to death. Precisely by means of this suffering Christ accomplished the work of salvation. In the plan of eternal Love, his suffering had a redemptive character.

Christ thus severely reproved Peter when he suggested Christ abandon the thoughts of suffering and death on the Cross.[10] "Shall I not drink the *cup which the Father has given* me?"[11] Christ thus went toward his own suffering, aware of its saving power, united in love with the Father for all men.

17. The Scriptures had to be fulfilled. There were many messianic texts in the Old Testament which foreshadowed the sufferings of the future Anointed One of God. Particularly touching is the one which is commonly called the *Fourth Song of the Suffering Servant,* in the Book of Isaiah, which presents an image of the sufferings of the Servant.

> He had no form or comeliness that we should look
> at him, and no beauty that we should desire him.
> He was despised and rejected by men;
> *a man of sorrows,* and acquainted with grief;
> and as one from whom men hide their faces
> he was despised, and we esteemed him not.
> Surely he has borne our griefs and carried our sorrows;
> yet we esteemed him stricken, smitten by God, and afflicted.
> But he was wounded for our transgressions,
> he was bruised for our iniquities;
> upon him was the chastisement that made us whole,
> and with his stripes we are healed.
> All we like sheep have gone astray
> we have turned every one to his own way;
> and *the Lord has laid on him the iniquity of us all.* [12]

The depth of Christ's sacrifice particularly stands out. "Behold, He, though innocent, takes upon himself the sufferings of all people, because he takes upon himself the sins of all."[13] In Christ's suffering, sin was wiped away precisely because he alone as the only-begotten Son could take them upon himself and accept them with that love for the Father which overcomes the evil of every sin.

Here we touch upon the duality of nature of a single personal subject of redemptive suffering. Christ in his divine nature brings about man's redemption through his suffering on the Cross, while at the same time Christ suffers with man in his human nature.

18. The next verses of the Song prophetically anticipate the Passion at Gethsemane and Golgotha. The Suffering Servant, essential for an analysis of Christ's Passion, takes on himself those sufferings which were spoken of, in a totally voluntary way:

> He was oppressed, and he was afflicted,
> yet he opened not his mouth;
> like a lamb that is led to the slaughter,
> and like a sheep that before its shearers is dumb,
> so he opened not his mouth.

By oppression and judgment he was taken away;
and as for his generation, who considered that
he was cut off out of the land of the living,
stricken for the transgression of my people?
And they made his grave with the wicked
and with a rich man in his death,
although he had done no violence,
and there was no deceit in his mouth.[14]

Christ suffers voluntarily and innocently, which emphasizes, and at the same time answers, why innocent people suffer. The "word of the Cross" completes with a definitive reality the image of the ancient prophecy of how Christ would accept suffering for the salvation of the world. In particular, the prayer in Gethsemane, "My Father, if it be possible, let this cup pass from me; nevertheless, not as I will, but as thou wilt" have a manifold eloquence.[15] They prove the truth of that love which the only-begotten Son gives to the Father in his obedience and at the same time attest to the truth that suffering is the undergoing of evil before which man shudders.

After the words in Gethsemane come the words uttered on Golgotha: "My God, My God, why have you abandoned me?"[16] Christ's words express that abandonment that he suffered on man's behalf in taking on himself man's rejection of God. Thus, in the words of Saint Paul: "For our sake he made him to be sin who knew no sin."[17] Christ suffered in a human way complete estrangement from God in his perfect sacrifice on the cross for man's sin. Precisely through this suffering, however, he accomplished the Redemption.

Human suffering thus reaches its culmination in the Passion of Christ. At the same time, human suffering enters into a completely new dimension and a new order as it links itself to love. In the Cross of Christ, therefore, people will find a deeper understanding of suffering and its inseverable union with love.

V. Sharers in the Suffering of Christ

19. The same Song of the Suffering Servant in the Book of Isaiah sheds light on this deeper understanding of suffering:

When he makes himself an offering for sin,
he shall see his offspring,
he shall prolong his days;
the will of the Lord shall prosper in his hand;
he shall see the fruit of the travail of his soul
and be satisfied;
by his knowledge shall the righteous one, my servant.
make many to be accounted righteous;
and he shall bear their iniquities.
Therefore I will divide him a portion with the great,
and he shall divide the spoil with the strong;
because he poured out his soul to death,

and was numbered with the transgressors;
yet he bore the sin of many,
and made intercession for the transgressors.[18]

The Passion of Christ gives all human suffering a fuller meaning. In the Cross of Christ not only is man's redemption accomplished through suffering, but *also human suffering itself was redeemed*. Christ, without any fault of his own, took on himself "the total evil of sin," which became the price of man's redemption. St. Peter speaks to this: "You know that you were ransomed from the futile ways inherited from your fathers, not with the perishable things such as silver or gold, but with the precious blood of Christ."[19]

Christ suffered in place of man and for man. In bringing about the Redemption through suffering, Christ raised human suffering to the level of the Redemption. Therefore, each person now shares in the redemptive suffering of Christ through uniting individual suffering to Christ's salvific suffering on the Cross.

20. The texts of the New Testament express this concept in many places. In the Second Letter to the Corinthians the Apostle writes:

We are afflicted in every way, but not crushed; perplexed, but not driven to despair; persecuted, but not forsaken; struck down, but not destroyed; always carrying in the body the death of Jesus, so that the life of Jesus may also be manifested in our bodies. For while we live we are always being given up to death for Jesus' sake, so that the life of Jesus may be manifested in our mortal flesh knowing that he who raised the Lord Jesus will raise us also with Jesus.[20]

The eloquence of the Cross and death is, however, completed by the eloquence of the Resurrection. The Resurrection provides man a completely new light, enabling him to go forward through the thick darkness of humiliations, doubts, hopelessness and persecution.

Man's very participation in Christ's suffering finds a twofold dimension. Because Christ has opened his suffering to man, man can become a sharer in the sufferings of Christ. God allows man to see through faith the redemptive aspects of man's own personal sufferings, giving them new meaning. Faith thus enables man to know that the love which led Christ to the Cross lives on in those people who unite their sufferings with Christ's perfect sacrifice on the Cross.

21. The Cross of Christ casts salvific light, in a most penetrating way, on man's life and in particular on his suffering. Through faith, the Cross joins man together with the Resurrection: the mystery of the Passion is contained in the Paschal Mystery. St. Paul writes: "That I may know him (Christ) and the power of his Resurrection, and may share his sufferings, becoming like him in his death, that if possible I may attain the resurrection from the dead."[21]

The witnesses of the Cross and Resurrection were convinced that "through many tribulations we must enter the Kingdom of God."[22] St. Paul states: "We ourselves boast of you . . . for your steadfastness and faith in all your persecutions and in the afflictions which you are enduring. This is evidence of the righteous judgment of God, that you may be made worthy of the Kingdom of God, for which you are suffering."[23] Thus, to share in the sufferings of Christ is, at the same time, to suffer for and become worthy of the Kingdom of God.

22. The Kingdom of God encompasses that glory which has its beginning in the Cross of Christ. Those who share in the sufferings of Christ are also called, through their own sufferings, to share in glory. St. Paul notes: "We are . . . fellow heirs with Christ, provided we suffer with him in order that we may also be glorified with him. I consider that the sufferings of this present time are not worth comparing with the glory that is to be revealed in us."[24]

Christ's Cross and Resurrection unite suffering and glory. On the Cross, Christ fully gave of himself in obedience to the Father. The Father lifted him up through the Cross in the Resurrection, the manifestation of glory. In weakness Christ manifested his power, and in humiliation he manifested all his messianic greatness. Suffering is thus an invitation to manifest the moral greatness of man, his spiritual maturity.

Christ's Resurrection has revealed "the glory of the future age" and, at the same time, has confirmed "the boast of the Cross": the glory hidden in Christ's suffering, which is often mirrored in human suffering as an expression of man's spiritual greatness. In the sufferings of all people, the great dignity of man is strikingly confirmed.

23. Suffering is always a trial—at times a very hard one—to which humanity is subjected. St. Paul writes often of this paradox of weakness and strength.[25] Those who share in Christ's sufferings can relate to the Paschal Mystery of the Cross and Resurrection, in which Christ descends first to the ultimate limits of human weakness as he is nailed on the cross, but then rises in glory. To suffer, therefore, means to become particularly susceptible, particularly open to the working of the salvific powers of God, offered to humanity in Christ. In Christ, God has confirmed his desire to act especially through suffering, through man's weakness and emptying of self.

St. Paul focuses on the theme of this "birth of power in weakness," this spiritual tempering of man in the midst of trials and tribulations, which is the particular vocation of those who share in Christ's sufferings.[26] Suffering contains a special call to the virtue of perseverance which man must exercise. Perseverance unleashes hope, which assists man in maintaining the conviction that suffering will not prevail, nor will it deprive him of his dignity as a human being, so long as he unites his sufferings to the love of Christ.

24. St. Paul takes the understanding of suffering a step further in man's spiritual journey by uniting all men together in the Church: "Now I rejoice in my sufferings for your sake, and in my flesh I complete what is lacking in Christ's afflictions for the sake of his body, that is, the Church."[27]

The mystery of the Church is expressed in the act of Baptism, which brings about a configuration of the human person with Christ, and then through his Sacrifice—sacramentally through the Eucharist—the Church is continually being built up spiritually as the Body of Christ. In this Body, Christ wishes to be united with every individual, and in a special way he is united with those who suffer. Whoever suffers in union with Christ not only receives from Christ immeasurable strength, but also "completes" what is lacking in Christ's afflictions.

Although the sufferings of Christ are inexhaustible and no man can add anything to it, in the mystery of the Church as his Body, Christ has opened his own redemptive suffering to all human suffering. Thus, insofar as man becomes a sharer in Christ's sufferings, man in his own way completes the suffering through which Christ accomplished the Redemption of the world. In other words, the Redemption of Christ remains continually open to all love expressed in human suffering. Christ's redemption lives and develops as the body of Christ, the Church, and in this dimension, human suffering completes that suffering just as the Church completes the redemptive work of Christ.

It is precisely the Church, then, which ceaselessly draws on the infinite resources of the Redemption, which is the dimension in which the redemptive suffering of Christ can be constantly completed by the suffering of man. Suffering therefore is particularly reverenced by the Church who sees those who suffer as special members of the living Body of Christ.

VI. The Gospel of Suffering

25. The witnesses of the Cross and Resurrection of Christ have handed on to the Church and to mankind a specific Gospel of suffering. Christ's suffering became a particular source of grace to all those who suffered for Christ through the centuries.

Mary's entire life bore great testimony to the Gospel of suffering. She walked alongside her son Jesus throughout his life and shared in his suffering along with her own. Mary's suffering reached an intensity on Calvary that can hardly be imagined from a human point of view, yet it was supernaturally fruitful for the redemption of the world. Because Mary witnessed her Son's Passion and shared in it by her compassion, she offers insight to man in understanding the Gospel of suffering.

In the light of the unmatchable example of Christ, reflected with singular clarity in the life of his Mother, the Gospel of suffering becomes an inexhaustible source for new generations. The Gospel of suffering signifies not only the presence of suffering in the Gospel, as one of the themes of the Good News, but also the revelation of the salvific power and salvific significance of suffering in Christ's messianic mission and in the mission and vocation of the Church. Christ did not conceal from his listeners the need for suffering. He said very clearly: "If any man would come after me . . . let him take up his cross daily."[28]

The Gospel of suffering contains in itself a special call to courage and fortitude, sustained by the eloquence of the Resurrection. Christ has overcome the world definitively by his Resurrection. Yet, because of the relationship between the Resurrection and his death, Christ has simultaneously overcome the world by his suffering.

26. While the beginnings of the Gospel of suffering are written down in Scripture, this Gospel message is continually lived out through the course of

history by those who suffer together with Christ. Through the centuries, man has come to see that in suffering there is concealed a particular power—a special grace—that draws a person interiorly close to Christ. To this grace many saints, such as Saint Francis of Assisi and Saint Ignatius of Loyola, owe their conversion.

A result of such a conversion is not only that the individual discovers the salvific meaning of suffering, but above all that he discovers a new dimension of his life and vocation. This discovery confirms that man's spiritual greatness surpasses his body in a way that is completely beyond compare. Thus, even when man's body is gravely ill or totally incapacitated, man's interior maturity and spiritual greatness shines forth, stressing his dignity.

Man's interior maturity and spiritual greatness in suffering result from man's cooperation with Christ's grace. Although suffering in itself is an experience of evil, Christ has made suffering the firmest basis of the definitive good, namely the good of eternal salvation. Christ thus reveals to the suffering man a world free from sin and built on the saving power of God's love. In this way, Christ leads the suffering man to the very heart of Christ's suffering. For suffering cannot be transformed and changed by a grace from outside, but only from within. Christ, through his own salvific suffering, is therefore intensely present in every human suffering, and can act within man's suffering.

Man often initially reacts to suffering on a human level and asks why he is suffering. As he wrestles with his suffering, however, he realizes he is asking the Man who epitomizes suffering—Christ who experienced the most intense suffering on the Cross. Nevertheless, it often takes a long time for man to interiorly perceive Christ's abstract answer for man hears Christ's answer as he himself gradually becomes a sharer in the sufferings of Christ.

The answer which man eventually discovers is far greater than a mere abstract answer to the question of the meaning of suffering. It is above all a call and a vocation to unite his suffering with Christ's work of salvation. Man does not discover this meaning at his own human level, but at the level of the suffering Christ. It is then that man finds in his suffering interior peace and even spiritual joy.

27. Saint Paul speaks of such joy in the Letter to the Colossians: "I rejoice in my sufferings for your sake."[29] Man finds joy in overcoming his sense of the uselessness of suffering, a feeling often strongly rooted in human suffering. This feeling not only consumes the person interiorly, but seems to make him a burden to others. The suffering person feels condemned to receive help and assistance from others, and at the same time seems useless to himself. The discovery of the salvific meaning of suffering in union with Christ, however, transforms this depressing feeling, and leads the suffering person to realize he carries out an irreplaceable service.

It is suffering, more than anything else, which clears the way for the grace which transforms human souls. Thus, the Church sees in all Christ's suffering brothers and sisters "a multiple subject of his supernatural power." How often is it precisely to them that the pastors of the Church appeal and precisely from them that they seek help and support!

VII. The Good Samaritan

28. The parable of the Good Samaritan belongs to the Gospel of suffering and exemplifies the relationship man must have toward his suffering neighbor. Man must not "pass by on the other side" indifferently, but must "stop" beside him. This stopping does not mean curiosity but availability. The name "Good Samaritan" fits every individual who is sensitive to the sufferings of others. Therefore, man must cultivate this sensitivity of heart, which bears witness to compassion towards a suffering person and allows man to have solidarity with the sufferer.

Nevertheless, the Good Samaritan of Christ's parable does not stop at sympathy and compassion alone. Christ calls man to action to help the injured. Man cannot "fully find himself except through a sincere gift of himself."[30] A Good Samaritan is the person capable of exactly such a gift of self.

29. Following the parable of the Gospel, suffering is also present in this world to unleash love in the human person, that unselfish gift of one's "I" on behalf of other people, especially those who suffer. The world of human suffering unceasingly calls for others to respond in love and action.

Over the centuries, Christ's call for man to respond to those who suffer as Good Samaritans has resulted in a variety of organized professions, such as health care providers, that exist solely to serve those who suffer. The parable of the Gospel's Good Samaritan has thus become one of the essential elements of moral culture and universally human civilization. In Christ's call to serve those who suffer, man finds the value of human solidarity and the value of Christian love of neighbor in the framework of social life and inter-human relationships. This gift of self also combats hatred, violence, cruelty, contempt for others, and insensitivity.

It is particularly critical to foster proper attitudes towards those who suffer in the family, the school, and other education institutions. The Gospel calls every individual to bear witness to love in suffering. The institutions are very important and indispensable; nevertheless, no institution can by itself replace the human heart, human compassion, human love or human initiative when assisting the physical or moral sufferings of another.

30. The parable of the Good Samaritan, which belongs to the Gospel of suffering, witnesses through the history of the Church and Christianity to the fact that the salvific meaning of suffering is in no way identified with an attitude of passivity.

Christ tells man in the Beatitudes that suffering is present in the world in order to release love, in order to give birth to works of love towards neighbor, and in order to transform the whole of human civilization into a "civilization of love." In this love, the salvific meaning of suffering is completely accomplished and reaches its definitive dimension. Man more clearly sees that at the basis of all human sufferings lies the redemptive suffering of Christ. Christ exists in the person who is suffering and thus when man loves and helps his suffering neighbor, he in reality loves and helps Christ.

VIII. Conclusion

31. This is the meaning of suffering, which is truly supernatural and at the same time human. It is supernatural because it is rooted in the divine mystery of the Redemption of the world, and it is likewise deeply human, because in it man discovers himself, his own humanity, his own dignity, his own mission.

Suffering is certainly part of the mystery of man. Perhaps suffering is not wrapped up as much as man is by this mystery, which is an especially impenetrable one. The Second Vatican Council expressed this truth that "only in the mystery of the Incarnate Word does the mystery of man take on light. In fact, Christ, the final Adam, by the revelation of the mystery of the Father and his love, fully reveals man to himself and makes his supreme calling clear."[31] If these words refer to everything that concerns the mystery of man, then they certainly refer in a very special way to human suffering.

The mystery of the Redemption of the world is inextricably rooted in suffering, and this suffering in turn finds in the mystery of the Redemption its supreme and surest point of reference. It is the weak who become a source of strength for the Church and humanity. In the terrible battle between the forces of good and evil that exists in the world today, the suffering of the weak in union with the Cross of Christ will arise victorious.

Notes

1. Col. 1:24.

2. John Paul II, *Redemptor Hominis* (1979), nos. 14, 18, 21, 22, http://www.vatican.va/holy_father/john_paul_ii/encyclicals/documents/hf_jpii_enc_04031979_redemptor-hominis_en.html (accessed 29 Aug. 2009).

3. John Paul II, *Salvifici Doloris* (1984), no. 8, http://www.vatican.va/holy_father/john_paul_ii/apost_letters/documents/hf_jp-ii_apl_11021984_salvifici-doloris_en.html (accessed 29 Aug. 2009).

4. Dan. 3:27.

5. Job 1:9–11.

6. 2 Macc. 6:12.

7. John 3:16.

8. Job 19:25-26

9. Math. 4:3-11.

10. See Matt. 16:23.

11. John 18:11.

12. Isa. 53:2–6.

13. John 1:29.

14. Isa. 53:7–9.

15. Matt. 26:39.
16. Psalm 22:2.
17. 2 Cor. 5:21.
18. Isa. 53:10.
19. 1 Pet. 1:18–19.
20. 2 Cor. 4:8–11, 14.
21. Phil. 3:10–11.
22. Acts 14:22.
23. 2 Thes. 1:4-5.
24. Rom. 8:17-18.
25. See 2 Tim. 1:12, Phil. 4:13, 2 Cor. 12:9.
26. See Rom. 5:3-5.
27. Col. 1:24.
28. Luke 9:23.
29. Col. 1:24.
30. GS, no. 24.
http://www.vatican.va/archive/hist_councils/ii_vatican_council/documents/vatii_cons_19
651207_gaudium-et-spes_en.html (accessed 29 Aug. 2009).
31. GS, no. 24.

Bibliography

"A Definition of Irreversible Coma" Report of the Ad Hoc Committee of the Harvard Medical School to Examine the Definition of Brain Death. *Journal of the American Medical Association* 205 (5 August 1968): 337–40.

Alexander, Leo. "Medical Science under Dictatorship." *New England Journal of Medicine* 241, no. 2 (July 1949): 39–47.

Anderson, W. French. "Strategies for Gene Therapy." 908 in *Encyclopedia of Bioethics*, edited by Warren Thomas Reich. New York: Macmillan, 1995.

Andrews, Lori B. "Genes and Patent Policy: Rethinking Intellectual Property Rights." *Nature Reviews Genetics* (October 2002): 803.

Andrusko, Dave. "Parents of Adopted Frozen Embryos Speak Out." *National Right to Life News* 28, no. 7 (July 2001): 1–6.

Annas, George J. "A French Homunculus in a Tennessee Court." *Hastings Center Report* 19, no. 6 (1989): 20–22.

Aquinas, Saint Thomas. *Commentary on the Book of Sentences, Book IV: The Perfection of God's Works.* http://www.op-stjoseph.org/Students/study/thomas/Sentences.htm#1 (28 Nov. 2009).

———. *Summa Contra Gentiles, Book IV: Of God in His Revelation.* London: Burns and Oates, 1905.

———. *Summa Theologica.* New York: Benzinger Bros., reprinted by Christian Classics, 1981.

Ashley, Benedict and Kevin O'Rourke. *Health Care Ethics: A Theological Analysis.* Washington, D.C.: Georgetown University Press, 1981.

Augustine, Saint. *Confessions.* Translated by John K. Ryan. Garden City, NY: Image Books, 1960.

Ba., Ro. *The Lyfe of Syr Thomas More, Sometymes Lord Chancellor of England* Original series, no. 222. Edited by Elsie V. Hitchcock and Msgr. P.E. Hallett. London: Early English Text Society, 1950.

Baker v. Vermont. 744 A.2d 864, 889 (1999).

BBC News. "Pill 'reverses' vegetative state." 23 May 2006. http://news.bbc.co.uk/2/hi/health/5008744.stm (20 Aug. 2009).

Beckwith, Francis J. "Cloning and Reproductive Liberty" in *Life and Learning*

XII: Proceedings of the Twelfth University Faculty for Life Conference, edited by Joseph W. Koterski. Washington, D.C.: University Faculty for Life, 2002.

Beeson, Diane. Testimony before Congressional Hearings, House Government Reform Subcommittee on Criminal Justice, Drug Policy and Human Resources—Hearing on Stem Cell Research, 7 March 2006, 1–2, http://handsoffourovaries.com/images/beesontestimony.pdf (20 Nov. 2009).

Benedict XVI. "Address to the Participants in the International Congress organized by the Pontifical Lateran University on the 40th anniversary of the Encyclical Humanae Vitae." *L'Osservatore Romano*, 11 May 2008.

———. "Address to the participants in the Symposium on the topic: 'Stem Cells: what is the future for therapy?' Organized by the Pontifical Academy for Life," 16 September 2006. *Acta Apostolicae Sedis* 98 (2006): 694 n.51.

———. "Address to the UN General Assembly." *New York Times*. 19 April 2008, http://www.nytimes.com/2008/04/19/nyregion/ 18popeatun.html; (10 Aug. 2009).

Bennett, William J. *The Book of Virtues: A Treasury of Great Moral Stories*. New York: Simon and Schuster, 1993.

Belz, Emily. "Political science: Obama science czar brings a potentially radical agenda." *World Magazine*, 15 August 2009.http://www.worldmag.com/ articles/15708 (21 Nov. 2009).

Berg, Thomas V. and Edward J. Furton, eds., *Human Embryo Adoption: Biotechnology, Marriage, and the Right to Life*. Philadelphia, PA.: The National Catholic Bioethics Center, 2006.

Berger, Raoul. *Government by Judiciary: The Transformation of the Fourteenth Amendment*. Indianapolis, IN.: Liberty Foundation, 1997.

Blotting, B.J., I.M. Davies, and A.J. Macfarlane. "Recent Trends in the Incidence of Multiple Births and Associated Mortality." *Archives of Diseases in Childhood* 62 (1987): 941–50.

Boggan, Steve. "Reborn." *The Guardian*, 12 September 2006. http://www.guardian.co.uk/science/2006/sep/12/health.healthandwellbeing (14 Nov. 2009).

Bonfiglioli, C., "Men's Contraception Injections Match Pill's Effectiveness." *Australian Associated Press*, 1 August 1995.

Bork, Robert H. "Neutral Principles and Some First Amendment Problems." *Indiana Law Journal* 47, no. 1 (Fall 1971): 30.

———. "Our Judicial Oligarchy." *First Things*. (Dec. 1996): 23.

Bowers v. Hardwick. 478 U.S. 185, 190–94 (1986).

Bowring, Kelly. "The Moral Dilemma of Management Procedures for Ectopic Pregnancy." 114 in *Life and Learning XII: Proceedings of the Twelfth University Faculty for Life Conference*, edited by Joseph W. Koterski. Washington, D.C.: University Faculty for Life, 2002.

Bristow, Peter. *The Moral Dignity of Man*. Dublin, Ireland: Four Courts Press, 1997.

Brugger, E. Christian. "ANT-OAR: A Morally Acceptable Means for Deriving

Pluripotent Stem Cells, A Reply to Criticisms." *Communio: International Catholic Review* 32, no. 4 (2005): 753–69.

Burleigh, Michael. "Return to the Planet of the Apes? *History Today*. Oct. 1994, Vol. 44, Issue 10, 6.

Cameron, Peter J. "The Lord's Prayer." *Magnificat*. Vol. 11, No. 8 (Oct. 2009): 2.

Canon Law Society of America. *Code of Canon Law (Codex Iuris Canonici)*. 1983.

———. *Code of Canons of the Eastern Churches*. Washington, DC: Canon Law Society of America, 2001.

Carlson, Allan C. *Family Questions: Reflections on the American Social Crises*. New Brunswick, N.J.: Transaction Publishers, 1991.

Carroll, Warren H. *The Founding of Christendom*, vol. 1 of *A History of Christendom*. Front Royal, VA.: Christendom College Press, 1985.

———. *The Building of Christendom*, vol. 2 of *A History of Christendom*. Front Royal, VA.: Christendom College Press, 1987.

———. *The Rise and Fall of the Communist Revolution*. Front Royal, VA: Christendom Press, 1995.

Catechism of the Catholic Church, 2d ed. United States Catholic Conference, Inc., 1994.

Cessario, Romanus. *Introduction to Moral Theology*. Washington, DC: Catholic University of America Press, 2001.

Chesterton, G. K. *The Everlasting Man*. Garden City, N.Y.: Image Books, 1925.

Clauss, Ralf and Wally Nel. "Drug induced arousal from the permanent vegetative state." *NeuroRehabilitation* 21 (2006): 23, 25, 26–27.

Children of God for Life. "Vaccines from Abortion: The Hidden Truth." http://www.cogforlife.org/vaxbrochsample.htm (4 Aug. 2009).

Clowes, Brian. *The Facts of Life: An Authoritative Guide to Life and Family Issues*, Front Royal, VA: Human Life International, 1997.

COLO. CONST. art. II, § 30b.

Colosi, Peter J. "Are Zygotes People? The Personhood of Embryos: Framing the Question." Eighteenth Annual University Faculty for Life Conference, Marquette University. May 30–June 1, 2008. http://www.vatican.va/holy_father/ benedict_xvi/speeches/2008/january/ documents/hf_ben-xvi_spe_20080128_convegno-individuo_en.html (accessed November 14, 2008).

———. "Personhood, the Soul, and Non-Conscious Human Beings: Some Critical Reflections on Recent Forms of Argumentation within the Pro-life Movement." *Life and Learning XVII*. Joseph Koterski, ed. Bronx, NY: University Faculty for Life, 2007.

Committee for Pro-life Activities. *Nutrition and Hydration: Moral and Pastoral Reflections*. Washington, DC: United States Conference of Catholic Bishops, 1992.

Condic, Maureen L. "White Paper: When Does Human Life Begin? A Scientific Perspective." *Westchester Institute* 1

(2008).http://www.westchesterinstitute.net/images/wi_whitepaper_life_
print.pdf (20 Nov. 2009).

Connell, Francis. *Outlines of Moral Theology*. Milwaukee: Bruce Pub. Co.,
1953.

ConscienceLaws.org. *Breaking News October—December 2008*.
http://www.consciencelaws.org/Conscience-Archive/Breaking-News/
Conscience-Breaking-News-2008-04.html#Grand_Duke_of_
Luxembourg_to_be_stripped_of_powers_for_opposing_euthanasia   (20
Nov. 2009).

Copleston, Fredrick. *A History of Philosophy, Vol. 1, Modern Philosophy Part
II*. Garden City, NY: Doubleday, 1962.

———. *A History of Philosophy, Vol. 6, Modern Philosophy Part II*. Garden
City, N.Y.: Doubleday, 1964.

Corsi, Jerome R. "Holdren says Constitution backs compulsory abortion."
WorldNetDaily, 23 September 2009.
http://www.wnd.com/index.php/index.php?fa=PAGE.view&pageId=11070
(21 Nov. 2009).

Cozzoli, Mauro. "The Human Embryo: Ethical and Normative Aspects." 260–
300 in *The Identity and Status of the Human Embryo: Proceedings of Third
Assembly of the Pontifical Academy for Life*, edited by Juan De Dios Vial
Correa and Elio Sgreccia. Vatican City: Libreria Editrice Vaticano, 1999.

Crum, Gary E. "Nazi Bioethics and a Doctor's Defense." *The Human Life
Review* 8, no. 3 (Summer 1982), 68.

Cruzan v. Director. Mo. Dept. of Health, 497 U.S. 261, 278–79, 110 S.Ct.,
2841, 2851–52 (1990).

Danielski, Deborah. "Paradise by way of 'Animal Farm.'" *Our Sunday Visitor*,
29 November 1998, 8.

Davis v. Davis. 842 S.W.2d 588, 590–91 (1992).

Derdiarian v. Felix Contracting Corp. 51 N.Y.2d 308, 414 N.E.2d 166, 434
N.Y.S.2d 166 (1980).

DeMarco, Donald. *Biotechnology and the Assault on Parenthood*. San
Francisco: Ignatius Press, 1991.

Dickens, Charles. *A Christmas Carol*. New York: Frederick Stokes Co., 1899.

Dulles, Avery. "The Truth About Freedom: A Theme from John Paul II." In
*Veritatis Splendor and the Renewal of Moral Theology: Studies by Ten Out-
standing Scholars*, edited by J. A. DiNoia, O.P. Chicago: Midwest Theological Forum, 1999.

Eurek Alert. *Scientists Find that Individuals in Vegetative States Can Learn*. 20
September   2009.   http://www.eurekalert.org/pub_releases/2009-09/uoc-
sft091809.php (20 Nov. 2009).

Evans, Debra. *Without Moral Limits: Women, Reproduction, and Medical
Technology*. Wheaton, IL.: Crossway Books, 2000.

Evans v. United Kingdom. European Court of Human Rights, App. No. 6339/05
[2006] 1 FCR 585m [2006] 2 FLR 172 (7 March 2006).

Faggioni, Maurizio P. "The Question of Frozen Embryos," *L'Osservatore*

Romano (English) (21 August 1996): 4–5.

Fedoryka, Damian P. "Thoughts towards a Clarification of Section #73 of Evangelium Vitae." 315–16 in *Life and Learning: Proceedings of the Twelfth University Faculty For Life Conference*, edited by Joseph W. Koterski. Washington, D.C.: University Faculty for Life, 2002.

Firestone, Shulamith. *The Dialectic of Sex: The Case for Feminist Revolution.* New York: William Morrow, 1970.

Fitzpatrick, F.J. *Ethics in Nursing Practice: Basic Principles and Their Application.* London, England: Linacre Center, 1988.

Freedom of Access to Clinic Entrances Act. 18 U.S.C. § 248 (1994).

Garcia, J.L.A. "Human Cloning: Never and Why Not." 1–24 in *Life and Learning IX: Proceedings of the Ninth University for Life Conference*, edited by Jospeh W. Koterski. Washington, D.C.: University Faculty for Life, 1999.

Geach, Mary. "Are There Any Circumstances in Which It Would Be Morally Admirable for a Woman to Seek to Have an Orphan Embryo Implanted in her Womb?" 341–46 in *Issues for a Catholic Bioethics: Proceedings of the International Conference to Celebrate the Twentieth Anniversary of the Foundation of the Linacre Center*, edited by L. Gormally. London: Linacre Center, 1999.

George, Robert P. and Christopher Tollefsen. *Embryo: A Defense of Human Life.* New York, NY: Doubleday, 2008.

Glenn, Paul J. *A Tour of the Summa.* Rockford, IL: Tan Books, 1960.

Goodridge v. Department of Public Health. 798 N.E.2d 941, 948 (2003).

Grisez, Germaine. *The Way of the Lord Jesus Christ.* Vol. 3, *Difficult Moral Questions.* Quincy, IL.: Franciscan Press, 1997.

———. "Bioethics and Christian Anthropology." *The National Catholic Bioethics Quarterly* 1, no. 1, (Spring 2001): 34.

Griswold v. Connecticut. 381 U.S. 513, n.3, 85 S.Ct. 1678, 1698 (1965).

Growing Generations. *Premier Surrogacy Agency Offers Surrogacy Services Worldwide*, http://www.growinggenerations.com/ (1 August 2009).

Hahn, Scott and Kimberly. *Rome Sweet Home: Our Journey to Catholicism.* San Francisco: Ignatius Press, 1993.

Hands Off Our Ovaries. *Mission Statement.* http://www.handsoffourovaries.com/mission.htm (20 Nov. 2009).

Harvey, John F. *The Homosexual Person: New Thinking in Pastoral Care.* San Francisco: Ignatius Press, 1987.

Hayes, Edward, et. al. *Catholicism and Ethics: A Medical/Moral Handbook.* Norwood, Mass.: C.R. Publications, 1997.

Hazel, Paul. "Homosexuality and Catholicism: A Partially Annotated Bibliography." *People with a History 2007.* http://www.fordham.edu/halsall/pwh/lgbcathbib.html (21 Nov. 2009).

Healy, Edwin. *Moral Guidance: A Textbook in Principles of Conduct for Colleges and Universities.* Chicago, Ill: Loyola University Press, 1942.

Hittinger, Russell. "Christopher Dawson on Technology and the Demise of

Liberalism," in *Christianity and Western Civilization: The Proceedings of the Wethersfield Institute,* vol. 7. San Francisco: Ignatius Press, 1995.

Holy See, The. *Charter of the Rights of the Family.* 1983. http://www.vatican.va/roman_curia/pontifical_councils/family/documents/r c_pc_family_doc_19831022_family-rights_en.html (31 Aug. 2009).

———. "The Views of the Holy See on Human Embryonic Cloning." 17 July 2003, http://www.holyseemission.org/cloning2003eng.html (23 Nov. 2009).

Hurlbut, William. "Altered Nuclear Transfer as a Morally Acceptable Means for the Procurement of Human Embryonic Stem Cells." Working paper discussed at the President's Council of Bioethics, December 2004. http://alterednucleartransfer.com/index.php?page=4a&view=5 (4 November 2009).

———. "Altered Nuclear Transfer: Is it the Answer for the Embryonic Stem Cell Research Debate?" Interview by Jennifer Lahl. *Center for Bioethics and Culture Network* .11 November 2006. http://www.cbc-network.org/2006/11/ant-an-answer-to-the-embryonic-stem-cell-debate/ (4 Nov. 2009).

———. "ANT presentation." A presentation to The President's Council on Bioethics. December 2004. http://www.alterednucleartransfer.com/html/ ANTpresentation.html (4 Nov. 2009).

Hurlbut, William, Robert P. George, and Markus Grompe. "Seeking Consensus: A Clarification and Defense of Altered Nuclear Transfer." *Hastings Center Report* 36, no. 5 (2006): 45–50. http://www.alterednucleartransfer.com/?page=4a&view=7 (4 Nov. 2009).

Jefferson, Thomas. *Notes on the State of Virginia.* New York, NY: Penguin Classics, 1999.

John XXII. *Mater et Magistra.* 1961. http://www.vatican.va/holy_father/john_xxiii/encyclicals/documents/hf_j-xxiii_enc_15051961_mater_en.html (31 Aug. 2009).

John Paul II, 'Address to the 18th International Congress of the Transplantation Society," 29 Aug 2000, http://www.healthpastoral.org/text.php?cid=192&sec=5&docid=45&lang=e n (20 Nov. 2009).

———. "Address to the Participants in the International Congress on "Life-Sustaining Treatments and Vegetative State: Scientific Advances and Ethical Dilemmas." 2004. http://www.ewtn.com/library/papaldoc/jp2lifss.htm (31 Aug. 2009).

———. "Address to a Human Pre-Leukemia Conference" 15 Nov. 1985. *Acta Apostolicae Sedis* 78 (1986): 361.

———. "Address to the participants in the Symposium on 'Evangelium Vitae and Law' and the Eleventh International Colloquium on Roman and Canon Law" 24 May 1996, *Acta Apostolicae Sedis* 6, no. 88 (1996): 943–44.

———. *Christifideles Laici,* 1988. http://www.vatican.va/holy_father/john_paul_ii/apost_exhortations/docume

nts/hf_jp-ii_exh_30121988_christifideles-laici_en.html (31 Aug. 2009).
———. *Centesimus Annus*. 1991.
http://www.vatican.va/holy_father/john_paul_ii/encyclicals/documents/hf_j
p-ii_enc_01051991_centesimus-annus_en.html.
———. "Discourse to the Participants of the Working Group" in *Working Group on the Determination of Brain Death and Its Relationship to Human Death*, 10–14 Dec. 1989. Vatican City: Pontifical Academy of Sciences, 1989.
———. *Evangelium Vitae*, 1995.
http://www.vatican.va/holy_father/john_paul_ii/encyclicals/documents/hf_j
p-ii_enc_25031995_evangelium-vitae_en.html (31 Aug. 2009).
———. *Familiaris Consortio*, 1981.
http://www.vatican.va/holy_father/john_paul_ii/apost_exhortations/docume
nts/hf_jp-ii_exh_19811122_familiaris-consortio_en.html (31 Aug. 2009).
———. *Letter to Families*, 1994.
http://www.vatican.va/holy_father/john_paul_ii/letters/documents/hf_jp-
ii_let_02021994_families_en.html (31 Aug. 2009).
———. *Love and Responsibility*. Trans. H.T. Willetts. San Francisco: Ignatius Press, 1993.
———. *Redemptor Hominis*, 1979.
http://www.vatican.va/holy_father/john_paul_ii/encyclicals/documents/hf_j
p-ii_enc_04031979_redemptor-hominis_en.html (31 Aug. 2009).
———. *Salvifici Doloris*, 1984.
http://www.vatican.va/holy_father/john_paul_ii/apost_letters/documents/hf
_jp-ii_apl_11021984_salvifici-doloris_en.html (31 Aug. 2009).
———. *The Theology of the Body: Human Love in the Divine Plan*. Boston: Daughters of St. Paul, 1997.
———. "The Redemption of the Body and the Sacramentality of Marriage." General Audience of 28 Nov. 1984.
———. "To the Participants at a course for teachers of natural methods," 10 Jan. 1992, in *L'Osservatore Romano*, 11 Jan. 1992, n.3.
———. *Veritatis Splendor*, 1993.
http://www.vatican.va/holy_father/john_paul_ii/encyclicals/documents/hf_j
p-ii_enc_06081993_veritatis-splendor_en.html (31 Aug. 2009).
Johnson, Brian P. *Death as a Salesman: What's Wrong with Assisted Suicide*. Sacramento, CA: New Regency Pub., 1998.
Jones, E. Michael. *Degenerate Moderns: Modernity As Rationalized Sexual Misbehavior*. San Francisco: Ignatius Press, 1993.
Kalina, Kathy. *Midwife for Souls: Spiritual Care for the Dying*. Boston: Pauline Books & Media., 1993.
Kass, Leon R. and James Wilson. *The Ethics of Human Cloning*. Washington, D.C.: AEI Press, 1998.
———. *Human Cloning and Human Dignity: The Report of the President's Council on Bioethics*. Jackson, TN: Public Affairs, 2002.
———. *Life, Liberty and the Defense of Dignity*. San Francisco: Encounter

Books, 2002.

———. "John Hass at Christendom College Outlines Bioethical Threats to Humanity." *The Wanderer* (November 20, 2003): 8.

Keane, Eamonn. *The Brave New World of Therapeutic Cloning.* Front Royal, Va.: Human Life International, 2001.

Kelly, Edwin. *Medical Ethics.* Chicago: Loyola Univ. Press, 1956.

Kelly, Gerald. *Medico-Moral Problems.* St. Louis: The Catholic Hospital Association, 1958.

Klekamp, Mareike. "Woman and Actual Challenges of Bioethics: The Perspective of Christian Social Doctrine Shown at the Example of Pre-implantation Diagnosis (PID)." Paper presented at the Pontifical Council for Justice and Peace First International Conference on "Life, Family, Development: The Role of Women in the Promotion of Human Rights." Rome, 20–21 March 2009, 3.

Kravets, David. "Judge OKs Challenge to Human-Gene Patents." *Wired.com.* 2 November 2009. http://www.wired.com/threatlevel/2009/11/genes (20 Nov. 2009).

Larson v. Albany Medical Center. 252 A.D. 2d 936 (N.Y. 1998).

Lasseter, Ruth D. "Sensible Sex." 473–95 in *Why Humanae Vitae Was Right: A Reader,* edited by Janet Smith. San Francisco: Ignatius Press, 1993.

Lawrence v. Texas. 539 U.S. 558, 564 (2003).

Lee, Harper. *To Kill a Mockingbird.* New York, NY: Warner Books, 1982.

Lejeune, Clara. *Life is a Blessing: A Biography of Jerome Lejeune—Geneticist, Doctor, Father.* San Francisco: Ignatius Press, 2001.

Lejeune, Jerome. *The Concentration Can: When Does Human Life Begin?* San Francisco: Ignatius Press, 1992.

Leo XIII. *On the Abolition of Slavery.* 1888. http://www.ewtn.com/library/encyc/l13abl.html (26 Aug. 2009).

Levy, Ehrlich. "The Comatose Patient." 956 in *The Clinical Neurosciences* vol. 1. New York: Churchill Livingstone, 1983.

Lewis, C.S. *The Abolition of Man: How Education Develops Man's Sense of Morality.* New York: Macmillan Pub. Co., 1947.

Lucal, John and Robert Araujo. *Papal Diplomacy and the Quest for Peace: The Vatican and International Organizations from the Early Years to the League of Nations.* Fort Collins, CO: Sapienta Press, 2004.

Lund-Molfese, Nicholas. "Biotechnology and Human Dignity in The Thought of Germain Grisez." In *The Catholic Social Science Review, Vol. VII,* edited by Stephen M. Krason and Ryan J. Barilleaux. Steubenville, Ohio: Society of Catholic Social Scientists, 2002.

Lynch, Colum. "U.N. Backs Human Cloning Ban." *The Washington Post,* 9 March 2005, A15.

Maas, Peter. *Love Thy Neighbor: A Story of War.* New York: Alfred A. Knopf, Inc., 1996.

MacIntyre, Alasdair. "How Can We Learn What *Veritatis Splendor* Has to Teach?" In *Veritatis Splendor and the Renewal of Moral Theology,* edited by J. A. DiNoia and Romanus Cessario. Princeton: Scepter Pub., 1999.

MacKinnon, Grace. "Theologians Argue Frozen Embryos' Fate." *Human Life Reports* (August 2001): 10–11, 19.

May, William. *Catholic Bioethics and the Gift of Human Life.* Huntington, ID: Our Sunday Visitor Pub., 2000.

Migliori, Celestino. "Statement by Archbishop Celestino Migliori on Agenda Item 158." At the International Convention against Reproductive Cloning of Human Beings, 30 September 2003. http://www.holyseemission.org/30sep2003.html (20 Nov. 2009).

Monti, James. *The King's Good Servant But God's First: The Life and Writings of St. Thomas More.* San Francisco: Ignatius Press, 1997.

Moraczewski, Albert. "Managing Tubal Pregnancies, Part I." *Ethics & Medicine* 21, no. 6 (June 1996): 3-4.

———. "Managing Tubal Pregnancies, Part II." *Ethics & Medicine* 21, no. 8 (August, 1996): 3.

Morris, Frank. "When Nutrition and Hydration are a Moral Absolute." *The Wanderer*, 6 May 2004, 4–8.

Mosher, Stephen W. *A Mother's Ordeal.* Front Royal, VA: Population Research Institute, 1993.

Mumford, Stephen D. *The Life and Death of NSSM 200: How the Destruction of Political Will Doomed a U. S. Population Policy.* Bethesda, MD: Center for Population Research, 1994.

National Conference of Catholic Bishops. *Ethical and Religious Directives for Catholic Health Care Services.* Washington, D.C.: NCCB, 1971.

National Institute of Neurological Disorders and Strokes. *Coma Information Page.* http://www.ninds.nih.gov/disorders/coma/coma.htm (14 Nov. 2009).

Naumann, Archbishop Joseph F. and Bishop Robert W. Finn. *Principles of Catholic Social Teaching and Health Care Reform: A Joint Pastoral Statement.* 1 September 2009. http://www.priestforlife.org/magisterium/bishops/09-09-01-naumann-finn-health-care.htm (14 Nov. 2009).

Neuhaus, Richard John. "The Return of Eugenics." *Commentary* (April 1988): 19.

NGO Voice. "Society of Catholic Social Scientists Intervention at UN Disabilities Conference." www.ngovoice.com. (20 May 2009).

Norsigian, Judy. Paper presented to the Subcommittee on Criminal Justice, Drug Policy and Human Resources, Government Reform Committee, U.S. House of Representatives—Hearing on Human Cloning and Embryonic Stem Cell Research after Seoul: Examination Exploitation, Fraud, and Ethical Problems in Research. 7 March 2006. http://frwebgate.access.gpo.gov/cgi-bin/getdoc.cgi?dbname=109_house_ hearings& docid=f:29580.wais (20 Nov. 2009).

Obama, Barack. "Lesbian, Gay, Bisexual and Transgender Month, 2009." White House Press Release, 1 June 2009. http://www.whitehouse.gov/the_press_office/Presidential-Proclamation-

LGBT-Pride-Month (17 Aug. 2009).

O'Donnell, Thomas. *Medicine and Christian Morality*, 3d rev. ed. NY: Alba House, 1996.

Oocyte Assisted Reprogramming. "Joint Statement, Production of Pluripotent Stem Cells." 20 June 2005. http://www.alterednucleartransfer.com/index.php?page= 4a&view=3 (4 Nov. 2009).

Pacholczyk, Tadeusz. "Some Moral Contraindications to Embryo Adoption." In *Human Embryo Adoption: Biotechnology, Marriage, and the Right to Life*, edited by Thomas V. Berg and Edward J. Furton. Philadelphia: The National Catholic Bioethics Center, 2006.

Paul VI. *Humanae Vitae*, 1968. http://www.vatican.va/holy_father/paul_vi/encyclicals/documents/hf_p-vi_enc_25071968_humanae-vitae_en.html (31 Aug. 2009).

———. *Marialis Cultus*, 1974. http://www.vatican.va/holy_father/paul_vi/apost_exhortations/documents/h f_p-vi_exh_19740202_marialis-cultus_en.html (31 Aug. 2009).

Peeters, Marguerite A. *The Globalization of the Western Cultural Revolution: Key Concepts, Operational Mechanisms*. Translated by Benedict Kobus. Brussels: Institute for Intercultural Dialogue Dynamics, 2007.

Pelucchi, Giuliana. *Blessed Gianna Beretta Molla: A Woman's Life*. Boston: Daughters of St. Paul, 2002.

Pence, Gregory. *Who's Afraid of Human Cloning?* Lanham, MD: Rowman and Littlefield, 1998.

Pennsylvania Conference of Catholic Bishops. "Nutrition and Hydration: Moral Considerations." *Origins*. NC News Service 21 (1992): 542–53.

Physician's Desk Reference, 43d Ed. Montvale, N.J: Medical Economics, Co., 1989.

Pinckaers, Servais-Théodore. "An Encyclical for the Future: Veritatis Splendor." In *Veritatis Splendor and the Renewal of Moral Theology*, edited by J. A. DiNoia and Romanus Cessario. Princeton: Scepter Pub., 1999.

Pius XI. *Casti Connubii*, 1930. http://212.77.1.247/holy_father/pius_xi/encyclicals/documents/hf_p-xi_enc_31121930_casti-connubii_en.html (31 Aug. 2009).

Pius XII. "Address to Italian Midwives" October 27, 1951. http://www.fisheaters.com/addresstomidwives.html (31 Aug. 2009).

———. "Address to the Biomedical Association of St. Luke" 12 November 1944. 191 in *Discorsi e Radiomessagi di Sua Santita Pio XII*. Vatican City: Libreria Editrice Vaticana, 1945.

———. *Humani Generis*, 1950. http://www.vatican.va/holy_father/pius_xii/encyclicals/documents/hf_p-xii_enc_12081950_humani-generis_en.html (24 Nov. 2009).

Planned Parenthood of Southeastern Pennsylvania v. Casey. 539 U.S. 558, 850 (1991).

Pontifical Academy for Life. *Reflections on Cloning*, 1997.

http://www.vatican.va/roman_curia/pontifical_academies/acdlife/document
s/rc_pa_acdlife_doc_30091997_clon_en.html (31 Aug. 2009).
———. *Declaration on the Production and the Scientific and Therapeutic Use
of Human Embryonic Stem Cells*, 2000.
http://www.vatican.va/roman_curia/pontifical_academies/acdlife/document
s/rc_pa_acdlife_doc_20000824_cellule-staminali_en.html (31 Aug. 2009).
———. *Moral Reflections on Vaccines Prepared from Cells Derived from Aborted Human Foetuses.*
http://www.academiavita.org/template.jsp?sez=Documenti
&pag=testo/vacc/vacc&lang=english (4 Aug. 2009).
Pontifical Council for Pastoral Assistance. *Charter for Health Care Workers*,
1995.
http://www.vatican.va/roman_curia/pontifical_councils/hlthwork/document
s/rc_pc_hlthwork_doc_19950101_charter_en.html (31 Aug. 2009).
Pontifical Council for Justice and Peace. *The Compendium of the Social Doctrine of the Church*. Vatican City: Libreria Editrice Vaticana, 2004.
Pontifical Council for the Family. *Ethical and Pastoral Dimensions of
Population Trends*, 1994. http://www.ewtn.com/library/curia/pctrend.htm
(31 Aug. 2009).
———. *Cloning: the Disappearance of Direct Parenthood and Denial of the
Family*, 2003.
http://www.vatican.va/roman_curia/pontifical_councils/family/documents/r
c_pc_family_doc_20030808_cloning-trujillo_en.html (31 Aug. 2009).
President's Council on Bioethics. *Human Cloning and Human Dignity: An
Ethical Inquiry.* http://www.bioethics.gov/reports/cloningreport/index.html
(31 Aug. 2009).
Ratzinger, Joseph. *Christianity and the Crisis of Cultures.* Translated by Brian
McNeil. San Francisco: Ignatius Press, 2006.
Reardon, David; Makimaa, Julie; and Sobie, Amy, eds. *Victims and Victors:
Speaking Out About Their Pregnancies, Abortions, and Children Resulting
from Sexual Assault.* Springfield, IL: Acorn Books, 2000.
Red River Valley Down Syndrome Society. *Newsletter*, May 2007.
http://redwooddss.camp7.org/content/documenthandlers.ashx?docld=5171
(19 Nov. 2009).
Rhonheimer, Martin. "Intentional Actions and the Meaning of Object: A Reply
to Richard McCormick." In *Veritatis Splendor and the Renewal of Moral
Theology,* edited by J. A. DiNoia and Romanus Cessario. Princeton: Scepter
Pub., 1999.
Rice, Charles. *50 Questions on the Natural Law*, rev. ed. San Francisco, Ignatius
Press 1999.
Richert, Scott P. "'Be Fruitful and Multiply' Part II: Is This The Way the World
Ends? The Mechanization of Fertility, Cultural and Agricultural." *The
Family in America* 10, no. 6, (June 1996): 4.
Roe v. Wade. 410 U.S. 159, 93 S.Ct. 705, 730 (1973).
Roe II v. Aware Women Center for Choice. 253 F.3d 678 (11th Cir. 2001).

Romer v. Evans. 517 U.S. 620, 116 S.Ct. 1620 (1996).

Sacred Congregation for the Doctrine of the Faith. *Considerations Regarding Proposals to Give Recognition to Unions Between Homosexual Persons,* 2003. http://www.vatican.va/roman_curia/congregations/cfaith/documents/rc_con _cfaith_doc_20030731_homosexual-unions_en.html (31 Aug. 2009).

———. *Declaration on Certain Question Concerning Sexual Ethics (Persona Humana),* 1975. http://www.vatican.va/roman_curia/congregations/cfaith/documents/rc_con _cfaith_doc_19751229_persona-humana_en.html (31 Aug. 2009).

———. *Declaration on Euthanasia,* 1980. http://www.vatican.va/roman_curia/congregations/cfaith/documents/rc_con _cfaith_doc_19800505_euthanasia_en.html (31 Aug. 2009).

———. *Declaration on Procured Abortion,* 1974. http://www.vatican.va/roman_curia/congregations/cfaith/documents/rc_con _cfaith_doc_19741118_declaration-abortion_en.html (31 Aug. 2009).

———. *Reply of the Sacred Congregation for the Doctrine of the Faith on Sterilization in Catholic Hospitals (Quaecumque Sterilizatio),* 1975. *Origins* 10 (1976).

———. *Responses to Certain Questions of the United States Conference of Catholic Bishops Concerning Artificial Nutrition and Hydration.* 2007. http://www.vatican.va/roman_curia/congregations/cfaith/documents/rc_con _cfaith_doc_20070801_risposte-usa_en.html (20 Nov. 2009).

———. *Instruction in Respect of Human Life in its Origin and on the Dignity of Procreation (Donum Vitae),* 1987. http://www.vatican.va/roman_curia/congregations/cfaith/documents/rc_con _cfaith_doc_19870222_respect-for-human-life_en.html (31 Aug. 2009).

———. *Some Considerations Concerning the Response to Legislative Proposals on the Non-Discrimination Against Homosexual Persons,* 1992. http://www.ewtn.com/library/curia/cdfhomol.htm (31 Aug. 2009).

———. *To Defend the Faith (Ad Tuendam Fidem),* 1998. http://www.vatican.va/holy_father/john_paul_ii/motu_proprio/documents/h f_jp-ii_motu-proprio_30061998_ad-tuendam-fidem_en.html (31 Aug. 2009).

Scarnecchia, Brian and Terrence McKeegan. *The Millennium Development Goals in Light of Catholic Social Teaching.* International Organization Research Group, White Paper no.10. New York, NY: Catholic Family and Research Inst., 2009: 73–85.

Scarnecchia, D. Brian. *With Faith and Reason.* Self-published, 2002.

———. *The Light to Choose.* Self-published, 2003.

Schooyans, Michel. *The Hidden Face of the United Nations.* Translated by John Miller. St. Louis: Central Bureau, 2001.

Schooyans, Michel. *The Totalitarian Trend of Liberalism.* Translated by John Miller. St. Louis, MO: Central Bureau, 1995.

Secretariat of the United Nations. Millennium Development Goals Report, 2005.

Senander, Mary. *The Living Will: Expansion or Erosion of Patients' Rights?* St. Paul, MN: Leaflet Missal Co., 1996.

Sgreccia, Bishop Elio. "The Subject in a Vegetative State: A Personalist View" Life-Sustaining Treatments and Vegetative State: Scientific Advances and Ethical Dilemmas (March 20, 2004). www.zenit.org. (24 April 2004).

Shakespeare, William. *Macbeth*. 1.4.40-46 in *The Complete Signet Classic Shakespeare*. Edited by Sylvan Barnet. New York, NY: Harcourt Brace Jovanovich, 1972.

Sharpe, Richard M. and Niels E. Skakkebaek. "Are Estrogens Involved in Falling Sperm Counts and Disorders of the Male Reproductive Tract?" *The Lancet* 341 (29 May 1993): 1392–95.

Shaw, Russell. "Contraception, Infallibility and the Ordinary Magisterium." 343–362 in *Why Humanae Vitae Was Right: A Reader*, edited by Janet Smith. San Francisco: Ignatius Press, 1993.

Sheldon, Bishop Gilbert I. "Test Tube Babies." *The Steubenville Register*. 5 December 2003.

Shivanandan, Mary. *Crossing the Threshold of Love: A New Vision of Marriage*. Washington, D.C.: Catholic University Press, 1999.

Singer, Peter. *Applied Ethics*. Bethesda, MD: Oxford University Press, 1986.

Smith, Msgr. William B. "Questions Answered: Rescue the Frozen?" *Homiletic and Pastoral Review*. (October 1995): 72–74.

———. "Response [to Geoffrey Surtees]," *Homiletic and Pastoral Review*. (August–September 1996): 16–17.

Smith, Wesley J. *Culture of Death: The Assault on Medical Ethics in America*. San Francisco, CA: Encounter Books, 2000.

———. "The U.N. on Cloning: Ban It." *The Weekly Standard*, 15 March 2005. http://www.weeklystandard.com/Content/Public/Articles/000 /000/005/360mveat.asp?pg=2?ZoomFont=YES (23 Nov. 2009).

Snyder v. Massachusetts. 291 U.S. 97, 105, 54 S.Ct. 330, 332 (1934).

Stein, Ron. "Obama's Order on Stem Cells Leaves Key Questions to NIH." *The Washington Post*, 10 March 2009. http://www.washingtonpost.com/wp-yn/content/article/2009/03/09/AR2009030903156.html?sid=ST2009030901 296 (20 Nov. 2009) (with video).

Surtees, Geoffrey. "Adoption of a Frozen Embryo." *Homiletic and Pastoral Review*. (August–September 1996): 7–16.

Szyszkiewicz, Thomas A. "A Moral Dilemma." *Catholic World Report*, November 2005.

Thiselton, Anthony C. *The Two Horizons: New Testament Hermeneutics and Philosophical Description with Special Reference to Heidegger, Bultman, Gadamer and Wittgenstein*. Grand Rapids, MI: W.B. Eerdmans Pub. Co., 1979.

Tierney, M.C. et al. "How Reliable are Advanced Directives for Healthcare? A Study of the Attitudes of the Healthy and Unwell to Treatment of the Terminally Ill." *Annals of the Royal College of Physicians and Surgeons of Canada* (1992): 25, 267–70.

Texas Conference of Catholic Bishops, "On Withdrawing Artificial Nutrition and Hydration" 7 May 1990. *Origins* 20 (1990): 53–55.

Tonti-Filippini, Nicholas. "The Embryo Rescue Debate: Impregnating Women, Ectogenesis, and Restoration from Suspended Animation." 111–37 in *National Catholic Bioethics Quarterly*, Denville, NJ: The National Catholic Bioethics Quarterly, 2003.

Troug, Robert D. and Franklin G. Miller. "The Dead Donor Rule and Organ Transplantation." *The New England Journal of Medicine* 359, no. 7 (14 August 2008): 674.

United Nations. *Convention on the Rights of Persons with Disabilities and Optional Protocol.* 13 December 2006.
    http://www.un.org/esa/socdev/enable/rights/convtexte.htm (20 Nov. 2009).

United Nations Fifty-ninth General Assembly Plenary 82nd Meeting (AM). *Press Release* GA/10333, 8 March 2005.
    http://www.un.org/News/Press/docs/2005/ ga10333.doc.htm (19 Nov. 2009).

United Nations Fifty-ninth General Assembly, Sixth Committee, Agenda Item 150. *Report of the Sixth Committee: International Convention Against the Reproductive Cloning of Human Beings.* 23 February 2005. http://daccess-dds-ny.un.org/doc/UNDOC/LTD/N05/247/70/PDF/N0524770.pdf (20 Nov. 2009).

United Nations Development Programme. *Introductory Gender Analysis & Gender Training Module for UNDP Staff* (2001).
    http://arabstates.undp.org/contents/ file/GenderMainstreamingTraining.pdf (21 Nov. 2009).

United States Conference of Catholic Bishops. *Ethical and Religious Directives for Catholic Health Care Services*, 4th ed., 2001.

United States Conference of Catholic Bishops, Committee for Pro-life Activities. *Nutrition and Hydration: Moral and Pastoral Reflections*, 1992.
    http://www.usccb.org/prolife/issues/euthanas/nutindex.shtml (31 Aug. 2009).

Vacco v. Quill. 521 U.S. 793, 797–98, 117 S.Ct. 2293, 2296 (1997).

Vatican Council II. *Pastoral Constitution on the Church in the Modern World* (*Gaudium et Spes*) 1964 in *Vatican Council II: The Conciliar and Post Conciliar Documents* edited by Austin Flannery, et al. New York: Costello Publishing Co., Inc., 1975.

———. *Lumen Gentium.* 1964.

———. *Apostolicam Actuositatem.* 1965.

Velasquez, Leticia. "Down, Not Out: The Legacy of Jerome Lejeune and the Resurgence of Down Syndrome Research." *NCRegister.com*, 1 July 2008.
    http://www.ncregister.com/site/article/15354/ (19 Nov. 2009).

Vrchota, Andrea, *Living with Disabilities—Franciscan University Student and Disabilities Activist.* 26 Jan. 2006.
    http://ngovoice.libsyn.com/index.php?post_id=51724 (10 Aug. 2009) (podcast).

The Wanderer. 2 Jan. 2003, 7.

Watt, Helen. "Are There Any Circumstances in Which It Would Be Morally Admirable for a Woman to Seek to Have an Orphan Embryo Implanted in her Womb?" 349–50 in *Issues for a Catholic Bioethics: Proceedings of the International Conference to Celebrate the Twentieth Anniversary of the Foundation of the Linacre Center,* edited by L. Gormally, London: Linacre Center, 1999.

Wickham, Elizabeth D. "Medical Decisions at End of Life—Frequently Asked Questions." *Life Tree Newsletter.* http://www.lifetree.org/newsletter/09-24-07.html (5 Oct. 2009).

Wickham, Elizabeth D. and Ione Whitlock. "Two Decades to an American Culture of Death." *Life Tree Newsletter.*
http://www.lifetree.org/timeline.index.html (5 Oct. 2009).

———. "Warning: Who's Leading Palliative Care Now?" *Life Tree Newsletter,* 24 September 2007. http://www.lifetree.org/newsletter/09-24-07.html (5 Oct. 2009).

Willke, John C. *Assisted Suicide and Euthanasia Past and Present.* Cincinnati, Oh.: Hayes Pub. Co., 1998.

Wilson, Mercedes. *Love and Family: Raising a Traditional Family in a Secular World.* Ignatius Press, 1996.

"World Egg Bank Launches Medical Tourism Program with World's Largest Egg-Donation Fertility Clinic." *PR Newswire,* 2 November 2009. http://www.prnewswire.com/news-releases/world-egg-bank-launches-medical-tourism-program-with-worlds-largest-egg-donation-fertility-clinic-68641442.html (20 Nov. 2009).

York v. Jones. 717 F.Supp. 421, 424–25 (E.D. Va. 1989).

Zernica-Goetz, Magdalena. "Patterning the Embryo: The First Spatial Decisions in the Life of a Mouse." *Development,* vol. 129 (2002): 815–29.

Zimmerman, Anthony. *Human Life Issues.* Collegeville, Md.: Human Life International, 1996.

Index

About the Author

D. Brian Scarnecchia, M. Div., J.D., is an associate professor of law at Ave Maria School of Law in Naples, Florida and an associate professor of human life studies and legal studies at Franciscan University in Steubenville, Ohio. He is a member of the expert committee of the Rome Forum for Catholic Non-Governmental Organizations (which works in close association with the Holy See). He serves on the Board of Directors of the Society of Catholic Social Scientists (SCSS) and is their primary representative to the United Nations. He is the founding President of the International Solidarity & Human Rights Institute (ISHRI). Attorney Scarnecchia lectures nationally and internationally and has authored articles and books on law, human rights, integral human development and bioethics. He is a practicing attorney in the State of Ohio and has served as an assistant county prosecutor for Jefferson County, Ohio. He and his wife, Victoria, have six children and one grandchild.

CPSIA information can be obtained at www.ICGtesting.com
Printed in the USA
BVOW022106260412

288678BV00003BC/1/P